I0124321

The Burial Locations of Free Will Baptist Ministers

Volume I

Compiled
by

Dr. Alton E. Loveless

ISBN 978-1-940609-09-6 Softcover
Updated 2018

Volume I

This book was printed in the United States of America.

To order additional copies of this book, contact:

FWB Publications
1006 Rayme Drive
Columbus,   Ohio 43207
740--777-1944

Published by
FWB Publications

Table of Contents

This is Volume I

of a

Two volume set.

This Volume I contains 2015
Ministers and leaders.

Volume II can be ordered using

ISBN 978-1-940609-10-2

Acknowledgments

I am grateful to many who made this book possible. It has been an inexhaustible task and without their help it would not have been possible.

I wish to thank Winnie Yandell, Oklahoma, who furnished me hundreds of names and information from her research. She was a generous helper and worked tirelessly; Geraldine Waid, Archivist Georgia; Karen Hollback, Ohio; Robert Picirilli, Tennessee; Gary Barefoot, North Carolina; Greg McCarty, Indiana; Deborah St. Lawrence, Tennessee; a descendant of David Marks; Jack Copet, Wisconsin; Thurmon Murphy who allowed me to print his research of Texas ministers; and various state promotional directors, who in their publications encouraged others to contribute information toward this project. And to many individuals whose names are lost to me and too numerous to itemize.

I do want to thank Eric Thomsen, editor of One Magazine, Free Will Baptist Historical Collection, National Assn. of Free Will Baptists and The Free Will Baptist Historical Collection, Mount Olive College for providing many photos for this book.

I sincerely thank everyone.

This will be a continuing project and if any of you have a father, brother, son or a friend that was a minister or missionary that you would like added in future editions, please forward to the address on the previous page.

I am grateful to many who made this book possible. It has been an inexhaustible task and without their help it would not have been possible.

Editors Remarks

This volume has 2015 burial locations covering 46 states and 4 foreign countries from one of the oldest denominations in the United States and covers a vast range of ministers who set the pace for growth and change where they were. In the north this movement were abolitionist and active in the Underground Railroad and began training schools to teach the freeman as they came from the south after the Civil War. They were stronger than the southern group in establishing colleges and active in government. But every territory had its own story to tell. This book will share these messages.

This Volume I includes an additional women ministers or missionaries from every area of the country and abroad.

I have found the history of every minister fascinating. I know you will also.

Pioneer Minister's and their burial cemeteries' are listed below:

Georgia	211
Maine	209
Ohio	206
North Carolina	197
Oklahoma	175
New Hampshire	130
Tennessee	124
New York	125
Arkansas	106
Missouri	95
West Virginia	83
Michigan	75
Texas	68
Illinois	55
Vermont	54
Rhode Island	48
Alabama	40
Virginia	40
Iowa	38
Wisconsin	38
California	35
Pennsylvania	34
South Carolina	32
Kentucky	26
Kansas	21
Nebraska	19
Mississippi	13
Florida	12
Minnesota	12
Massachusetts	11
Indiana	11
Connecticut	9
Canada	8
Washington	4
South Dakota	3
Louisiana	2
North Dakota	2
Colorado	2
Idaho	2
New Mexico	1
Arizona	1
District of Columbia	1
New Jersey	1
Oregon	1
Utah	1
Brazil	1
India	1
Africa	1
New Mexico	1

This book represents the National Association, Randall Movement that united with the Northern Baptists in 1911, the Stone, John-Thomas, John

Wheeler Assn's, North Carolina Original Free Will Baptists and unidentifiable.

Many of the photos are poor quality, but it was all I had. Likewise, I do not have photos or tombstones for many of them. The information about these ministers were all that was available to me or found in archives. I made every effort to include those from which they would be remembered. Some I had no information, but research had shown they were of our denomination. Others were with the National Association but left and I included their contribution to the movement.

There were some that somewhere, sometime, someone within these movements contributed to what we are today. It was not my purpose to promote any single group, but to let history present its own case. Likewise, the length of the column of the person does not denote the lesser or greater value of the person.

There are many words not spelled correctly, but were taken from the text of the history or book written about the person. E.g. Freewill, Free Baptist, Free Communion Baptists, Free Will Baptists, etc.. In different periods clergy were addressed as Elder, Rev., Dr. etc. I have made every effort to make it reliable, grammatically correct, but errors still reflect the time.

The sources used for accumulating these hundreds of men and women; were found in graveyard records, county histories, church records, genealogies, biographies, Google research, valuable denomination resource materials such as: Cyclopedia of Free Baptists, pub. 1889 by Burgess and Ward. The Native Ministry of New Hampshire, published by Rev. N. F. Carter, 1906 and reprinted by FWB Publications, 2014. There is no way I could remember all of the resources used. But it is the product of hundreds of hours and the help of others to put these two volumes together.

Please advise me at alton.loveless@prodigy.net to help me make the corrections for future editions.

Every time I update these volumes, I think of the countless ministers that I personally knew that have gone on to their reward. I remain sadden due to my acquaintance with each for their families, friends and influence to our denomination.

Dr. Alton E. Loveless

Africa

**Missionary Glennda
Leatherbury**
Birth:
Kansas
Death:
October 15, 1994
Free Will Baptist Hospital
Doropo, Cote d'Ivoire, Africa
Buried:
Doropo, Cote d'Ivoire, Africa

Missionary Leatherbury had a heart failure in Africa, departing this life at 43 years of age. She was converted to Christ in 1973 and graduated from Hillsdale FWB College and Hutchinson Community Junior College. The Kansas native was appointed to the mission field in 1985.

**My Peace
I Leave With you**

Alabama

Rev Byrd Thomas Alexander
Birth:
Dec. 10, 1913
Marion County, Alabama
Death:
Aug. 5, 1979
Pleasant Grove
Jefferson County, Alabama
Burial:
Piney Grove Free Will Baptist
Cemetery
Beaverton
Lamar County, Alabama

An ordained Free Will Baptist minister who organized Deaverton FWD church.

Brian Atwood
Birth:
June 7, 1956
Death:
March 9,, 2010
Huntsville,
Madison County, Alabama
Burial:
Maple Hill Cemetery, Huntsville,
Madison County, Alabama

For many years he was pastor of the Emmanuel FWB church in Wabash, Indiana. At the time of his passing he was pastor of the Pathway Church In Huntsville, Alabama at his untimely death.

J A Brown
Birth:
Sep. 23, 1841
Death:
Jul. 20, 1916
Burial:
Old Corinth Cemetery
Lamar County, Alabama

Early Alabama Minister in the Vernon Association. He was married to Lydia C Barnes Brown (1841 - 1905) and secondly to Francis Brown (1882 - 1906).

Elder Walter Pool Bond
Birth:
May 10, 1874
Death:
Jun. 26, 1943
Burial:
Nebo Church,
Limestone County, Alabama
He Was A FWB Preacher In The 30's In Jefferson Co., Alabama.

Tommy Lynn Burch
Birth:
Aug. 1, 1924
Death:
Dec. 13, 1996
Burial:
Weavers Cemetery,
Brewton, Escambia County,
Alabama

He was an educator, minister and builder. He was the Social Studies professor at Free Will Baptist Bible College. Nashville, Tn. For 20 years. He also built houses, churches and commercial buildings in several states.

Jackson Malone Cobb
Birth:
May 7, 1922
Alabama
Death:
Mar. 1, 1995
Fayette Co., Alabama
Burial:
Fayette Memorial Gardens
Fayette
Fayette County, Alabama

He pastored for 48 years, having been licensed in 1947, and ordained a Free Will Baptist minister in 1949. He attended FWB Bible College, Nashville, TN, from 1949-1951. His first full-time congregation was at the New Mission Church (now First FWB Church) in Fayette. His

funeral was conducted at that same church 43 years later. He was a WW II Veteran, entering in 1942, fought in invasion of France and was wounded June 16, 1944. He met and married Clara Smith in 1946. He was an evangelist and had a missionary's heart, from which pastorates resulted from his own soul-winning efforts. He participated in a wide range of FWB activities, including being elected to district Home Mission boards, in both Alabama and Georgia.In the 1950's, he served as Superintendent at the FWB Childrens Home in Al. He was pastor of Union Chapel FWB Church in Crossville at the time of this death.

Charles B Craddock
Birth:
Feb. 17, 1922
Death:
May 24, 2000
Burial:
York Municipal Cemetery
York, Sumter County,
Alabama

Craddock, a native of Roper, N.C.

was a pastor and minister in the Free Will Baptist Church for 26 years, serving at various churches. He served in Belk, Ala., Fulton, Miss., Ayden, N.C., Dothan, Marianna, Fla., Cottondale, Fla., and Wicksburg, Ala. He served as a Chief Petty Officer in the U.S. Coast Guard during World War II. A graduate of Free Will Baptist Bible College in Nashville, Tn., and attended Troy State University in Dothan, Alabama and Candler School of Theology in Atlanta, Georgia.

Tunis Michael Creech
Birth:
Unknown
Alabama
Feb. 22, 2002
South Carolina
Burial:
Oak Hill Cemetery,
Jasper, Walker County,
Alabama

He attended the Free Will Baptist Bible College in Nashville, Tennessee. After ordination he served as an Associate Pastor of the Fellowship Free Will Baptist Church in Flat River, Missouri, then the following Free Will Baptist churches in Thomaston, Georgia; Smithville, Mississippi; and First Free Will Baptist Church of Florence, South Carolina beginning in 1994.

Capt Benjamin F. Eddins
Birth:
Mar. 12, 1813
South Carolina, USA
Death:
Apr. 10, 1865
Tuscaloosa County
Alabama
Burial:
Greenwood Cemetery
Tuscaloosa
Tuscaloosa County
Alabama, USA

The 41st AL Infantry, under which Capt. B.F. Eddins served. He was the only Tuscaloosa native to die in Tuscaloosa County during the Civil War (1861–1865),. (Flag in AL Hist. Archives, courtesy of).

11

He is listed in some old church records after the war, and so is remembered here for all his service to his country and fellowman.

George Columbus Elliott
Birth:
Dec. 20, 1855
Alabama
Death:

Feb. 16, 1914
Burial:
Mount Pleasant Cemetery
Brilliant
Marion County, Alabama

Early minister in Vernon Assn. He was married to Lucinda A Elliott (1853 - 1927).

O. L. Fields
Birth:
Jan. 16, 1911
Death:
Mar. 31, 1989
Burial:
Millport City Cemetery, Millport.
Lamar County. Alabama

Joe Sephus Frederick
Birth:
1893
Death:
1973
Burial:
Union Hill Cemetery,
Hackleburg,
Marion County, Alabama

An ordained Free Will Baptist minister, well-loved and esteemed.

Milton R. Gann

Birth:
unknown
Death:
Apr. 22, 1992
Hamilton,
Marion County, Alabama,
Burial:
Poplar Log Freewill
Baptist Church Cemetery,
Hamilton,
Marion County, Alabama

A Free Will Baptist minister for 37 years, serving four churches in Alabama and Florida. He served as a denominational leader in both states being the state association moderator in Florida and moderator of the Pastors and Deacons Meeting in Alabama. A navy veteran. He did studies at Free Will Baptist Bible College.

Ellis Gore

Birth:
Oct. 3, 1800
South Carolina
Death:
Oct. 5, 1883
Pickens County, Alabama

Burial:
Gore Cemetery
Pickens County, Alabama

Ellis Gore was pastor of Mount Moriah Free Will Baptist Church from spring 1846 until September 1883, a month before his death. See Tuscaloosa News, "Church's missionary spirit still alive after 150 years", June 5, 1996 his parents were :
Thomas Tindall Gore (1776 - 1855) and Nancy Sanders Gore (1778 - 1831) and he had two spouses: Dorcas B Gore (1804 - 1866) Annie Mae Burdine Gore (1833 - 1896)

Whitaker W. Guyton

Birth:
1807
South Carolina
Death:
Feb. 4, 1860
McShan
Pickens County, Alabama
Burial:
Guyton Family
McShan
Pickens County, Alabama

Rev. Whitaker W. GUYTON, moved to AL by 1834, (date of his marriage) where he was associated with Rev. Ellis GORE, and J. Eddins, which records show when they petitioned for membership in the Baptist Union Association, Pickens Co. The Union Ass'n met in 1849, at the Mt. Moriah church which Gore had organized. By 1853 Minutes, (earliest after 1849) Mt. Moriah was no longer a part of the Association. It is reported to be the oldest Free Will Baptist church in Alabama. Rev. W. W. GUYTON, and the GORE family had kinship connections from genealogy of the families. Rev. Guyton married Luvina N (Bankhead) Nov. 29, 1834, Lamar Co. AL. Family Tree shows his parents as Abraham Guyton (1765-1816) and Martha Ellis, (1769-1838) Union Co. SC. U.S. Land records show he received 80 acres in 1839, Pickens Co, and the Alabama Homestead and Cash Entry Patents, show he received 40.015, issued May 1, 1849, from the Tuscaloosa Land Office.When the census was taken in 1860, Levina, age 48, was a widow, with Sophrona A.J. Bird, age 21, and John J. Funderburk, age 28, in HH. In the 1850 census, there was also a Mariam Bird, male, b. AL, who d. in battle in the Civil War, son of James and Mary Guyton Bird, bur. in AR, with #70799738. (Mariam and Saphrona Bird, were possibly a nephew and niece, from the m/n name given as Marion's mother.)Not much is known about the ministry of Whitaker Guyton; there is old minutes of Macedonia Primitive Bapt. church, Lamar Co. AL, which states: "Macedonia Church convened on Saturday before the 3rd Sun in July 1832. Received by letter Bro. Whitaker Guyton." Then in conference Saturday before the 3rd Sun in November 1833, "Brother Whitaker Guyton applied for a letter and obtained." This ended his membership from that church.The number of churches increased in the confines of Pickens county with Rev. Gore, and we can probably surmise, that Rev. Whitaker was involved in some of those churches after he left the Lamar Co (formerly Marion Co) AL County. His name is linked with Rev. Ellis Gore..........This burial info was posted on Pickens Co. Message Forum by "redjugwadi, on Apr. 7, 2004, showing Whitaker and Luvina's graves here, and 2 or 3 small, unmarked ones. his spouse was Luvina N Bankhead Guyton (1812 - 1887)

Daniel George Washington Hollis
Birth:
Feb. 24, 1855
Marion County, Alabama
Death:
Feb. 4, 1930
Lamar County, Alabama
Burial:
Wofford Cemetery
Vernon
Lamar County, Alabama

Early Alabama minister. Daniel was the son of Jonathan Shelton Hollis and Barbara Milender Webb. He married Josephine Millicent "Princess Millie" Pennington, 19 Nov 1874 in Sanford Co., AL. his parents were Jonathan Shelton Hollis (1815 - 1872) and Barbara Webb Hollis (1824 - 1904). And he was married to Josephine Millicent Pennington Hollis (1851 - 1910).

Eugene Howard
Birth:
Unknown
Death:
May 9, 2011
Alabama
Burial:
Lawleys Chapel Cemetery,
Shelby County
, Alabama

Mr. Howard was saved at the age of 21. He was ordained a deacon in 1953 and to be a minister in 1957 by the Cahaba River Free Will Baptist Association. He pastored many churches all over the area. He attended school at High Point which is now Davis Chapel church in Sterrett. He pastored Davis Chapel Church for 24 years, was assistant pastor for 3 years. Mr. Howard worked at the Stockhom Valve Fitting in Birmingham 38 years where he retired. Over the years he conducted 340 funerals, performed 213 weddings, and numerous revivals. He was a member of Ben M. Jacobs

Masonic Lodge in Pell City. He served as Chaplain for many years.

William Bonnie Hughes
Birth:
Nov. 15, 1919
Death:
Nov. 16, 2004
Burial:
Fulton Bridge Cemetery
Marion County, Alabama

William Bonnie Hughes died unexpectedly on November 16, 2004, one day after his 85th birthday. Mr. Hughes answered the call to preach shortly after returning from a tour of duty in World War II and spent the next 47 years pastoring churches in Florida, Tennessee, North Carolina and Alabama. A 1953 graduate of Free Will Baptist Bible College, he served on the Colleges' Board of Trustees for more than 10 years. Mr. Hughes was instrumental in establishing youth camp programs in Tennessee and Alabama. Although retired, Hughes remained an active member of Mt.

Olive Free Will Baptist Church in Twin, Alabama.

Thomas Russell Hulsey
Birth:
Feb. 8, 1850
Death:
May 7, 1921
Burial:
Fairview Cemetery
Fairview
Cullman County, Alabama

Thomas married Mary Jane Mote on 16 Feb 1873 in Jefferson Co, AL. .Thomas was ordained as a Minister on 5 Jun 1884 and pastored a number of churches between 1901 and 1916 in Jackson Co AL. Churches he pastored were Pleasant Hill, Mt Tabor, Bethany, Friendship, Sulpher Springs and Center Point.

Death is the fundamental human problem.

Rev Dallas Jack Jones
Birth:
Mar. 21, 1941
Death:
Aug. 17, 2014
Burial:
Mount Olive Cemetery Waterloo
Waterloo
Lauderdale County, Alabama

Jones Chapel Free Will Baptist Church with Bro. Danny Williams, Bro. Jack Allen Jones and Bro. Barry Kelly officiating. Mr. Jones was retired from Local #48 as a Sheet Metal worker after 20 plus years and a Minister for 52 years. He pastured 49 years in MS. and AL. and is presently pastor of Corinth Free Will Baptist Church, Waynesboro, MS.

W R Latham
Birth:
Nov. 10, 1830
Death:
Mar. 23, 1909
Burial:
Shiloh Cemetery
Gordo
Pickens County, Alabama
Plot: 123A

Early Alabama minister.

Woodrow Matthews
Birth:
Mar. 4, 1919
Death:
Mar. 2, 2012
Burial:
Guin City Cemetery, Guin,
Marion County, Alabama

Woodrow Matthews, age 92, of Guin, Alabama passed away at the Northwest Regional Medical Center in Winfield, Alabama. Born in Mine LaMotte, Missouri. He was united in marriage to Blanche Huffman on October 28, 1939. Matthews answered the call to preach in 1939 and was ordained in 1940. He pastored churches in Missouri and Oklahoma. In 1973, he moved to Guin, Alabama and pastored the Mt. Olive FWB Church until 1985. He then accepted the pastorate of Barnesville FWB Church in Hamilton, Alabama. In 1998 after 58 years of faithful service.

Bro. Matthews was actively involved in the Missouri FWB State Association, serving on the state youth camp board for many years, the state general board, and moderator of the Missouri State FWB Association.

As pastor of the Mt. Olive FWB Church, he was involved in the development of the Trinity Youth Camp, and served on the camp board for a number of years. He also served as moderator of the State Pastor and Workers Conference. Bro. Matthews was an active supporter of state and national programs, and especially missions. Numerous pastors, pastors' wives, home and foreign missionaries have come from his churches throughout his years of ministry. His philosophy of ministry was: "If you genuinely love your people, your people will love you."

Trellis L Mayhall

Birth:
Aug. 13, 1933
Death:
Jan. 29, 1998
Burial:
Winston
Memorial Cemetery,
Haleyville,
Winston County, Alabama

He was ordained to preach in 1964 as a Free Will Baptist minister. He served churches in Florida, Georgia, Indiana and Alabama. Three men answered the call to preach during his pastorate at the Free Water Free Will Baptist Church in Alabama. He was active in denominational work serving as moderator of Alabama's Jasper Association, Executive Board Member, General Board Member, and Ordaining Council Member. He graduated from the Alabama Bible Institute.

Elihue Roy Mayo

Birth:
Sep. 13, 1923
Boyd County,
Kentucky
Death:
Sep. 17, 2011
Alabama
Burial:
New Home Cemetery,
Coffee County, Alabama

He was one of our WW II heroes, serving in the Army Aircorp. He received a purple heart, three bronze stars and many medals during his service and tour over Normandy during D-day. He was an ordained minister and had pastored churches in Gadsden, Wattsville, Pell City, Adamsville, Enterprise, Alabama and Houston, Texas. He served as a Home Missionary from 1973 to 1992.

Rev Peter McGee, Jr

Birth:
1825
Tuscaloosa
Tuscaloosa County, Alabama
Death:
Apr. 7, 1887
Vernon
Lamar County, Alabama
Burial:
Walnut Grove Cemetery
Vernon
Lamar County, Alabama

An early Free Will Baptist ordained minister, who was well loved and esteemed.

W H McGee
Birth:
1843
Death:
unknown
Burial:
Hargrove Cemetery
Gordo
Pickens County, Alabama

A member of the Mt Moriah Association.

Luther D Nance
Birth:
Jul. 19, 1920
Death:
Dec. 9, 1993
Burial:
Cullman City Cemetery,
Cullman,
Cullman, County, Alabama

He was an ordained Free Will Baptist minister, pastor, and was in the early minutes of the Nat'l Ass'n of FWB, serving on the FWB League Board in 1945 to?

He was living and pastoring in Detroit, MI at the time.

Herman A. O'Donnell
Birth:
May 20, 1896
Death:
Nov. 12, 1985
Burial:
Mount Zion Methodist Church
Cemetery,
Ragland,
St. Clair County,
Alabama

Ottis Ray Parmer
Birth:
unknown
Death:
Jan. 24, 2015
Burial:
West Alabama Memorial ardens
Gu-Win, Marion County,Alabama

Ottis Parmer died. Published in The Birmingham News from Jan. 24 to Jan. 25, 2015

Rev John T Quick
Birth:
Mar. 14, 1901
Death:
Apr. 3, 1964
Burial:
Laodicea Freewill Baptist
Church Cemetery
Hanceville
Cullman County, Alabama

An ordained Free Will Baptist minister/leader whose name appeared with others in 1930 Minutes, as 'making a great impact' in the church, state and nation, in 1929-30.

J R Robertson
Birth:
Apr. 22, 1839
Death:
Nov. 29, 1912
Burial:

Shiloh Methodist Episcopal
Church Cemetery
Hightogy
Lamar County, Alabama

Minister in the Mt. Moriah Association.

Thomas M. Scott
Birth:
May 10, 1931
Pike County
Alabama
Death:
May 18, 2014
Red Bay
Franklin County
Alabama
Burial:
Kimbro Cemetery
Dozier
Crenshaw County
Alabama

He was a member of Red Bay Free Will Baptist Church where he was a former pastor for 15 years. He was a veteran of the U.S. Air Force serving 20 years. Services were held at the Red Bay Free Will Baptist Church with Bro. Steve Lindsay, Bro. Barry Raper, David Corum and Ron Scott officiating. Services was held at First Baptist Church, Dozier, Al.

Rev Thomas Alden Springfield
Birth:
May 1, 1881
Death:
Jan. 16, 1972
Burial:
Shiloh Cemetery,Gordo
Pickens County,Alabama
Plot: 30A

Minister.

Thomas Woods Springfield
Birth:
Mar. 11, 1854
Lamar County, Alabama
Death:
Aug. 25, 1922
Ethelsville, Pickens County,
Alabama.
Burial:

Ethelsville Cemetery
Ethelsville
Pickens County, Alabama

He was an early minister that joined with Ellis Gore in the work in Alabama after which the churches multiplied in the countries throughout the region making it necessary to divide the Mt. Moriah Association. . He served 46 years. Springfield was the son of Thomas Springfield and Emily Woods. He married Amanda Catherine Guin on 10/10/1875 in Sanford County, Alabama.

William James Springfield
Birth:
Sep. 15, 1852
Death:
Jul. 6, 1883
Burial:
Vernon Cemetery
Vernon
Lamar County, Alabama

Early minister in Alabama. He was the son of Emily Calloway Woods and Thomas Walker Springfield, and was married to Tessie M Haley (1858 - 1891).

J. J. Staab
Birth:
Apr. 14, 1906
Alabama
Death:
Apr. 22, 1983
Alabama
Burial:
Forest Crest Cemetery,
Birmingham,
Jefferson Co., Alabama

He was an officer in the Alabama State Assn. serving as Assistant Moderator

J. D. Stephens
Birth:
Feb. 21, 1826
Death:
Apr. 24, 1896
Burial:
Deerman Chapel Cemetery
Steele
St. Clair County, Alabama

Early FWB minister in Alabama.

Rev Michael E. Vail
Birth:
Nov. 5, 1822
Lancaster County
South Carolina
Death:
Jul. 24, 1900
Lamar County, Alabama
Burial:
Mount Pleasant Cemetery
Lamar County, Alabama

Michael E. (Mikel) Vail was the son of Jeremiah Vail and Mary Funderburk. He was a nephew of Jeremiah Vail b. 1817, who came to Bienville Parish, Louisiana, in 1859 from Pickens Co., Alabama. Found his name in early FWBapt church records, as ministers serving the Mt. Moriah Association in 1851. Alabama CSA veteran.

Leon D. Vance
Birth:
1937
Death:
1994
Burial:
New Horizon Memorial Gardens,
Dora, Jefferson County,
Alabama

Somewhere,
up in the
measureless
dome,

Beyond the
power of the
eye to see

Arizona

Paul Timothy Thompson
Birth:
1951
Death:
2002
Burial:
City of Mesa Cemetery,
Mesa,
Maricopa County, Arizona

Before moving to Arizona, he served with his father at the Heritage Temple church in Columbus, Ohio. He was an able associate to his father and very capable speaker. He was on the pastoral staff of the Heritage Free Will Baptist Church in Gilbert, Arizona, before his untimely death. A great preacher, teacher and servant to the church.

Arkansas

John O Adrian
Birth:
1850
Death:
1895
Burial:
Duty Cemetery
Lesterville
Randolph County, Arkansas

Early FWB preacher in the General Free Will Baptist Assn.

Rev Ozro A. Ashcraft
Birth:
Feb. 16, 1871
Arkansas
Death:
Feb. 18, 1946
Cleveland County
Arkansas
Burial:
Prosperity Cemetery
Pansy
Cleveland County
Arkansas, USA

Wed Sarah Elizabeth Patrick on 25 Jan 1894 in Cleveland, Arkansas and had 4 known children.

He was an early Free Will Baptist minister, in Arkansas, as shown in old church records and minutes, and in 1932 was living at Herbine, Arkansas.

Rev Johnny Atwell
Birth:
Dec. 21, 1895
Rudy
Crawford County, Arkansas
Death:
Apr. 13, 1986
Van Buren
Crawford County, Arkansas
Burial:
Mount McCurry Cemetery
Rudy
Crawford County, Arkansas,

A lifelong Crawford County resident, he was a minister and member of the 88 Freewill Baptist Church. Funeral services were held at Ocker Memorial Chapel, with Reverends Earl Gentry.

Rev E Baldwin
Birth:
1860
Death:
1943
Burial:
Sandlin Cemetery
Ola
Yell County
Arkansas

Rev. E. Baldwin's name is in a roll of ministers for the AR State Association 1902, locally, The Western Arkansas Ass'n of the Free Will Baptists. He is probably the "L.E. Baldwin," who mar. Mrs. M.L. Sanford, on March 2, 1898, Deisha Co. AR as shown in state marriages.

Rev Herman Dean Benson
Birth:
Jul. 22, 1930
Springdale
Washington County
Arkansas
Death:
Dec. 23, 1996
Washington County
Arkansas
Burial:
Shady Grove Cemetery

Springdale
Washington County
Arkansas

Lifetime resident of Northwest Ar. Freewill Baptist Minister. Husband Of. Ruby Benson
His name is listed as "Dean Benson" in AR State Association of Free Will Baptist ministers who had died from 1990-98. He was a member of the District Old Mt. Zion Association at time of his death, per report.

J.W.Blanks
Birth:
Oct. 22, 1927
Flint, Genesee County,
Michigan
Death:
Jan. 11, 2001,
Batesville,
Independence County,
Arkansas
Burial:
Egner Cemetery, Salado,
Independence County,
Arkansas

He was a Free Will Baptist Minister for 54 years, of which he was pastor of the Allen Chapel Free Will Baptist Church for 28 years, where he was a member at his death. He was elected multiple terms on the State Executive Board which became the State Youth Board and was a strong instrument in moving the state of Arkansas into a state youth camp program. He has a son, Ron Blanks who is also a Free Will Baptist Minister in Missouri. He served as a medic in the United States Army.

Rev Sterling E. Bowlin
Birth:
1938
Death:
1997
Burial:
Burkshed Cemetery
Washington County,
Arkansas

Shown in a List of deceased ministers in the AR Free Will Baptist State Association minutes, as being a member at time of death of the Old Mt. Zion Association.

Joe Burney Braddy
Birth:
Dec. 8, 1940,
Green Forest,
Carroll County, Arkansas
Death:
Jan. 20, 1993,
Fredericktown,
Madison County, Missouri
Burial:
Pickens Cemetery,
Green Forest,
Carroll County, Arkansas

He was killed in an auto accident and was pastor at First FWB Church in Fredericktown, Missouri at his passing.

Rev Thomas Brashear
Birth:
May 1, 1919
Pottsville
Pope County, Arkansas
Death:
Jun. 30, 1985
Dardanelle
Yell County, Arkansas,
Burial:
Saint Joe Cemetery
Atkins
Pope County, Arkansas

Son of Thomas L and Amanda Suzanne (Braham) Brashear.
Ordained a Free Will Bapt minister and served last in the Antioch Dist. Association of FWB, AR. His name is documented in roll of ministers in the Minutes of the 1989 AR State Meeting.

Rev A Braughton
Birth:
Mar. 27, 1865
Death:
Jul. 22, 1938
Burial:
Union Cemetery
Johnson County
Arkansas

Rev Andrew Newton Best
Birth:
Nov. 13, 1867
Nevada County, Arkansas

Death:
Apr. 11, 1942
Logan County, Arkansas
Burial:
Landmark Cemetery
Chismville, Logan County
Arkansas

Rev. Andrew "A,N." Newton Best was the son of John Dolphin Best and Susan Catherine Tennessee (Benge) Best. He married Sarah "Sallie" Florence Woods on May 21, 1891 in Logan County, Arkansas.
He was an ordained Free Will Baptist minister in the Arkansas State Ass'n of Free Will Baptists in the early part of the 1900's, as his name is shown in old church records there.

The Statistics On Death Have Not Changed. One Out Of One Person Dies.

Henry P. Brown
Birth:
Oct. 16, 1926
Arkansas
Death:
Jun. 12, 2012
Springdale,
Washington County, Arkansas
Burial:
Mount Hope Cemetery,
Vesta,
Franklin County, Arkansas

Rev. Brown was a school teacher and a deacon before he became a preacher. Although a pastor himself, he did much to preserve history of ministers in making records and taping sermons and songs of other ministers. He was a denominational leader and a World War II Army veteran

James F. Brown
Birth:
Aug. 17, 1854
Henderson County
Tennessee
Death:
Mar. 17, 1922
Cleveland County
Arkansas
Burial:
Friendship Cemetery
Friendship,
Cleveland County,Arkansas

James Franklin Brown was born near Lexington in Henderson Co., Tennessee. His parents were Abner S. Brown and Emma Amie Reed. James F. was the last of the children to be born in TN. His Father moved the family to Arkansas around 1858 and homesteaded land in what is today NE Cleveland County Arkansas. At one time, James F. was a "circuit preacher" and traveled to various churches in the area to serve as Pastor for those churches.There are still a number of FWB preachers in the area who are of his descent.
Inscribed on stone
"I have fought a good fight, I have finished my course,I have kept the faith"

Harvey Benjamin Bugg
Birth:
Nov. 24, 1853
Johnson County
Arkansas
Death:
Jan. 13, 1937
Sebastian County
Arkansas
Burial:
Steep Hill Cemetery
Fort Smith
Sebastian County
Arkansas, USA
Plot: Southeast Section, Row 3

Harvey Benjamin Bugg was born to Benjamin Nicholas Bugg and Annis Tucker Bugg. His parents migrated from Tennessee to Arkansas in the 1840s.

March 1, 1860, Harvey's father was awarded a land grant for 40 acres in Johnson County. The document was issued from the Clarksville land office and signed by U.S. President James Buchannan.

According to the 1860 census, Benjamin, his wife, and children removed from Johnson County, to Sebastian County, Arkansas. According to a contributor, old church records indicate H. B. Bugg, was an early Free Will Baptist minister as listed in the minutes of the Western Arkansas Association when it met in 1902. This Association included counties of Franklin, Logan, Scott and Sebastian.

J. H. Bullard
Birth:
Oct. 22, 1848
Tishomingo County,
Mississippi
Death:
Apr. 16, 1912
Burial:
Old Union Cemetery
Magazine
Logan County, Arkansas

He moved with his parents when he was four years old to Upshur Co., Texas remaining there till 1865 then moved to Hunt Co., Texas and in 1869 moved to Crittenden County, Arkansas where he married Louisa Manning. He was converted in September, 1878 at Gilmore Station and joined the Methodists. In 1882 he united with the Missionary Baptist church at New Hope, in Mississippi County and was licensed to Preach. He was ordained August, 1886 and continued preaching till 1890 baptizing about fourty into the church. In 1890 he received a letter stating he was a consistent member and an ordained minister. With this letter he attended the Flat Creek Assn. of Free Will Baptists in Tennessee, which convened with the Union Church in Hardeman County in 1890 and was received as an ordained minister. He formed three churches—one at Wardell, one at Tyronza and another at Dead Timber, in Mississippi County, Ark.; and in 1892 formed the Tyronza Assn. He formed and assisted in forming thirteen churches and attended every session of the association being elect moderator in 1899. He baptized more than 300 persons.

Rev. W.R. Burnett was an early pioneer Free Will Baptist minister in Arkansas. He was elected moderator of the 1918 session of the New Mt. Zion Association when it met at the Mountain View Church in Sept. 1918. Boone, Madison and Newton County churches were represented. When and where he was ordained, churches he pastored and other info of his ministry are unavailable.

Preacher William "Buck" Burnett; wife Sarah; sons: Alf, Jim and John. Hilltop about 1907.

Rev William Robert Burnett
Birth:
Mar. 3, 1857
Meade County, Kentucky
Death:
May 23, 1938
Hill Top
Boone County, Arkansas
Burial:
Hilltop Cemetery
Hill Top
Boone County, Arkansas

George Washington Burris, Sr
Birth:
Jan. 18, 1856,
Atkins,
Pope County,
Arkansas
Death:
Mar. 9, 1929,
Atkins,
Pope County,
Arkansas
Burial:
Saint Joe Cemetery
Atkins,
Pope County,
Arkansas

From a October 4, 2007 newspaper article, noting the 120th anniversary of the establishment of St. Joe Freewill Baptist Church on October 7, 2007: *"In the year of 1885, George W. Burris organized a Sunday school under a bunchy top Gum Tree at St. Joe on Pea Ridge 10 miles north of Atkins. They had logs for seats and took School Readers to Sunday school. The Freewill Baptist Church was organized there in 1886."*.

George W. Burris was the principal leader there during his entire life.

Ordained Free Will Baptist minister, recorded in the Antioch Dist. Association of the AR State Association

Clarence Elijah Campbell
Birth:
Aug. 9, 1920,
Lost Corner,
Pope County, Arkansas
Death:
Aug. 10, 2011,
Hanford, Kings County,
California
Burial:
Rock Springs Cemetery, Hector,
Pope County, Arkansas

He was raised and educated in Scotland and Greeley graduating from Dover High School in 1942. Clarence entered the U.S. Army and served in Europe until his discharge in 1945, earning the Good Conduct Medal, EAME Service Ribbon and Three Bronze Service Stars. Following his discharge, he obtained his AA degree in business. Clarence was ordained into the ministry in Russellville and served as pastor for Free Will Baptist Churches in Arkansas, Oklahoma and North Carolina for more than 30 years.

Rev Clyde Cleston Campbell
Birth:
Mar. 17, 1918
Hagarville
Johnson County, Arkansas
Death:
Mar. 14, 1985
Lamar
Johnson County, Arkansas
Burial:
Minnow Creek Cemetery
Hagarville
Johnson County, Arkansas

Third of seven children of parents Grover Lee and Etta Sara Jones Campbell. Married Vivian Mae Smith. He was a Free Will Baptist minister.

Glynn Campbell
Birth:
1925
Death:
Nov. 24, 2001,
Walnut Ridge,
Lawrence County,
Arkansas
Burial:
Lawrence Memorial Park,
Walnut Ridge,
Lawrence County,
Arkansas

Free Will Baptist minister who celebrated 50 years in the ministry. He pastored six churches in Arkansas and Missouri. He was an amateur ventriloquist. His son, Tim, became the Arkansas State Executive-Secretary.

Rev Willie R. Capps
Birth:
Sep. 18, 1906
Death:
Nov. 30, 1988
Burial:
Bland Cemetery
Rogers
Benton County
Arkansas

Rev. Willie R. Capps is listed in AR State Free Will Bapt. minutes roll of deceased ministers from 1980-89, from Old Mt. Zion Association. He was also in the previous list of ministers in 1958. When and where he was ordained and his pastorates, etc are not known. He was married to Clara O. Capps (1906 - 1978).

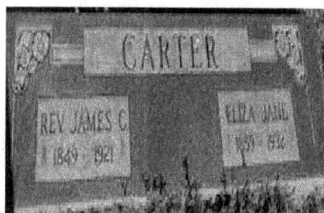

Rev James C. Carter
Birth:
1849
Death:
1921
Burial:
Lawrence Memorial Park
Walnut Ridge
Lawrence County, Arkansas
Plot: Section 8, Old Lane Block 6-7, Between Wren & Lark

He came from the Presbyterian Church and joined the General Free Will Baptists and ordained the year he joined. He was a quiet speaker and his favorite theme was the operation of the spirit. He did a great deal of good in this conference.

William Pleas Carter
Birth:
Apr. 14, 1854
Tennessee
Death:
Feb. 16, 1926
Warm Springs
Randolph County, Arkansas
Burial:
Carter Cemetery
Warm Springs
Randolph County, Arkansas

Early FWB preacher in the General Free Will Baptist Assn. who married Emily Jane Burrow Carter (1855 - 1938).

Enoch Thomas Chew
Birth:
Dec. 10, 1842
Indiana
Death:
Aug. 10, 1914
Burial:
Halbrook Cemetery
Conway County,
Arkansas

Enoch T. Chew married Sarah C. Upton 3 March 1870 in Perry County, Missouri.
E.T. Chew married Margaret S. Morris 27 June 1896 in Randolph County, Arkansas. Thomas Chew married Mary E. McKuin 10 February 1905 in Van Buren County, Arkansas. Son: James Zachariah Chew (1870 - 1940). Enoch died at 71 years of age.

Rev Earl L. Christian
Birth:
Nov. 2, 1916
Death:
Dec. 3, 1978
Burial:
Woody Memorial Cemetery
Rudy
Crawford County
Arkansas

Listed as an ordained Free Will Baptist minister in 1957 Minutes of the Zion Hope Association in western AR, when it met with Walnut Street
FWB Church in Ft. Smith.
--from "History of Arkansas Free Will Baptists," by Rev. David A. Joslin, Editor, pub. 1998, pg. 14.

Inscription:
TEG5 US Army- World War II

Jimmy Lee Chronister
Birth:
Mar. 3, 1939
Russellville
Pope County, Arkansas
Death:
Jul. 22, 2014
Buttermilk
Pope County, Arkansas
Burial:
Walnut Grove Cemetery
Hector
Pope County, Arkansas

He was son of the late William and Syble Duvall Chronister.
He was a Free Will Baptist Minister and retired farmer, and member of the Sweet Home Free Will Baptist Church.
Jim started preaching January 1, 1965. He preached in the Antioch Association for one year before he was ordained as a Free Will Baptist Minister. He and his wife, Mary, pastored several churches in Arkansas, including St. Joe-Atkins, Union Grove-Atkins, Woodlawn-Russellville, First Free Will Baptist-Glenwood, Slaty Crossing-Dardanelle, Center Valley-Russellville (now Baker's Creek), Johnson-Scranton, Salem-Glenwood, Smith Springs-Morrilton, New Life-Morrilton, and finally Sweet Home Free Will Baptist Church of Atkins, where they have been since February 2004.

Arthur Edward Coffman
Birth:
Jul. 20, 1932,
Jerusalem,
Conway County,
Arkansas
Death:
Dec. 11, 2009,
Russellville,
Pope County, Arkansas
Burial:
Cedar Creek Cemetery,
Jerusalem,
Conway County, Arkansas

He was a member of the Dover Free Will Baptist Church. Bo was a Free Will Baptist Minister for 55 years (pastoring numerous churches over forty-nine years). He had numerous occupations over his lifetime: a farmer, a Dow Chemical employee, a MacDonald-Douglas Aircraft employee, owner and operator of the Coffman Tile Company.

Joseph Dempsey Coffman
Birth:
Jan. 11, 1892,
Hector,
Pope County, Arkansas
Death:
May 24, 1975,
Russellville,
Pope County, Arkansas
Burial:
Walnut Grove Cemetery, Hector,
Pope County, Arkansas

Lawnie Coffman
Birth:
Feb. 22, 1922,
Arkansas
Death:
Jun. 3, 2008,
Arkansas
Burial:
White County Memorial
Gardens,
Searcy,
White County, Arkansas

Coffman received numerous awards and honors for his action with the 35th infantry during the World War II, including two bronze stars, two silver stars, four battle stars, and two Purple Hearts for being wounded in action. When asked about his heroic service, Lawnie once replied, "I did not mean to be a hero, I just did what had to be done. In 2004, Coffman was invited by public officials in France to return for a hero's welcome. During the trip, three different French towns honored him for his role in their liberation. After being struck in the shoulder by a large caliber 37mm shell intended for a tank during a battle in the Rual Valley of Germany, Coffman promised God that if He would spare His life, He would spend the rest of it doing the Lord's work. Lawnie kept his promise, pastoring for more than 45 years, and serving the Free Will Baptist denomination on the local, state, and national level. He is especially remembered for his role in establishing Camp Beaverfork, the state youth camp in Arkansas. In his book, *My Leg of the Race*, Coffman said, *"This I believe to be the greatest achievement of my church work."* He was one of Arkansas' most decorated soldiers.

John Francis Crafton
Birth:
1836
Death:
Apr. 19, 1914
Burial:
Mount Carmel Cemetery
Sidney
Sharp County, Arkansas

Early minister in the Polk Bayou Assn. Married to Malissa McKee Crafton.

Emery J. Crossland
Birth:
Aug. 31, 1938
Tuckerman
Jackson County
Arkansas
Death:
Dec. 5, 2014
Hensley
Pulaski County
Arkansas
Burial:
Cheshier Cemetery
Elgin
Jackson County
Arkansas

He was born to the late John Emery Crossland and Lola Hunter Crossland.
He was a pastor for 28 years for the Faith Free Will Baptist Church. He was a wonderful husband, dad, Papa, Papa Jr. and friend.

John M Crouch
Birth:
Jan. 5, 1890
Death:
Apr. 30, 1987
Burial:
Forks of the Creek Cemetery,
Hector,
Pope County, Arkansas

He was a Free Will Baptist Minister and pastored the Kenwood church from 1952. He was 93 in this photo.

William Calvin Curnutt
Birth:
Dec. 16, 1847
Tennessee

Death:
Mar. 28, 1920
Compton
Newton County
Arkansas
Burial:
Plumlee Cemetery
Compton
Newton County
Arkansas

William was the son of James Calvin and Nancy Johnson Curnutt. He married Sabra Ann Reynolds on March 19, 1868. William Calvin was a Baptist minister.

He was an ordained Free Will Baptist minister, shown in old minutes in the 1918 State Association meeting at Mountain View Church. He listed his address as Compton, AR.

Thomas Sewell "Tommy" Day
Birth:
Sep. 16, 1910
Henryetta
Okmulgee County,
Oklahoma
Death:
May 7, 1997
Springdale
Washington County,
Arkansas
Burial:
Friendship Cemetery,
Springdale
Washington County,
Arkansas

DAY spent 51 years in the ministry. He was the son of James Atlee Day (1888-1964) and Lula Lenorah (Nation) Day, (1889-1972). He was married to Mary Pearl (Shepherd) DAY for 61 years. She preceded him in death in 1993. Rev. Day was ordained as a Free Will Baptist preacher in January 1948. He was the founder of Phillips Chapel FWB Church in Springdale and pastored the church four years. He held membership there at the time of his death. Bro. Day pastored 12 FWB churches in Arkansas, Oklahoma and Missouri during his half-century long ministry. He also did extensive evangelistic work in those states as well as in Kansas. Rev. Day served on the state executive boards in Arkansas and Missouri. He was active in the ministry even after he retired in 1975. He taught Sunday School until he was 84 years old.

Rev Carl Davis
Birth:
Dec. 2, 1885
Death:
May 25, 1976
Burial:
Mountain Home Cemetery
Mountain Home
Baxter County
Arkansas

Rev. Carl Davis was an ordained Free Will Baptist minister, whose name appears in the 1960 minutes of the Big Springs Association, AR in a list of ministers, which Ass'n was organized in 1907, in north-central part of AR. He was listed as pastor of four churches. [i.e. one each Sun, which was a common practice in former years when there were not enough ministers for the churches].

Willard C. Day
Birth:
Aug. 25, 1913
Death:
Aug. 29, 1984
Burial:
Grace lawn Cemetery,
Van Buren,
Crawford County, Arkansas

He was the son of Francis Marion DAY (b. MO.) and Katherine (Catherine?) Mahalia (Hayes) DAY (b. AR.). He married Helen I. Chambers, May 1, 1934, in OK.

He was an ordained Free Will Baptist minister, who pastored in Oklahoma, Arkansas and Missouri. He was elected moderator and served the Oklahoma State Ass'n of Free Will Baptists in the 1950's. He was recognized as a teacher and taught from printed lessons on Biblical subjects he sent out to his radio listeners, and from which he taught in church schools. He was awarded a D.D. degree and was known among his brethren as Dr. Willard C. Day. He died of cancer problems in Ft. Smith, Arkansas.

He became the first Promotional Secretary in the state of Arkansas. He was also a member of the Foreign Missions Board in the early 50s.

Preston Clark "Press" Denton
Birth:
Jul. 9, 1883
Dublin
Logan County
Arkansas

Death:
Mar. 19, 1983
Clarksville
Johnson County, Arkansas
Burial:
Ware Chapel Cemetery
Cane Creek Township
Logan County, Arkansas

He was a member of Dublin Freewill Baptist Church and a retired blacksmith. His name is in a list of Free Will Baptist ministers in a book by Rev. David Joslin, "Hist of AR Free Will Baptists," showing ministers who had d. between 1980-89. He was shown as in the Antioch Association of Free Will Baptists. Date of his ordination is unknown.

Glenn G. Dipboye
Birth:
Jan. 9, 1903
Death:
Mar. 15, 1976

Burial:
Woody Memorial Cemetery,
Rudy, Crawford County,
Arkansas

Oris Doggett
Birth:
Nov. 27, 1918
Arkansas
Death:
Nov. 7, 1999
Burial:
Pleasant Valley Cemetery,
Warren,
Bradley County,
Arkansas

He married Ollie Sweeney, 18 aug. 1945, Bradley Co. AR. His parents: George W. and Sarah Margaret (Elder) Doggett.
He was a very active leader in the Arkansas Free Will Baptist movement serving Rev. Dogett served as pastor in various churches, and on the Ark. Exec. Board, in 1973, as well as other offices.

Rev Ralph E Doggett
Birth:
Oct. 22, 1916
Death:
Jul. 30, 1980
Burial:
Pleasant Valley Cemetery
Warren
Bradley County
Arkansas

Minister in Saline Assn.

Rev Henry Doyle
Birth:
Jul. 20, 1897
Death:
Jun. 11, 1984
Burial:
Ballews Chapel Cemetery
Grubbs
Jackson County
Arkansas

Husband of Gertie McCall Doyle. Father of Ealem, Martha

Elizabeth, William Harold, and Chester T. Doyle.

Henry Doyle's name was in the minister's 1958 Minutes of the AR State Association, and again in a list of deceased ministers from 1980-89, from David Joslin's book, Hist of AR Free Will Baptists. He reportedly d. as a member of the Polk Bayou Association.

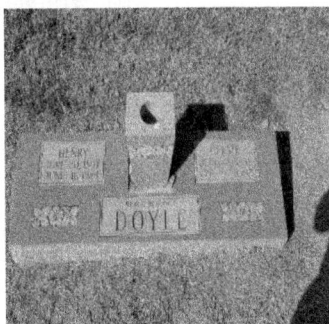

He was a early Arkansas FWB preacher and leader.

Jefferson Davis "Judge" Doyle
Birth:
Sep. 21, 1861
Strawberry
Lawrence County,
Arkansas
Death:
Feb. 13, 1945
Walnut Ridge
Lawrence County,
Arkansas
Burial:
Lawrence Memorial Park
Walnut Ridge
Lawrence County,
Arkansas
Plot: Section 10 -
Old Lane Block 4-9

Adrian E Duvall
Birth:
1881
Death:
Sep. 9, 1937
Russellville
Pope County, Arkansas
Burial:
Hudson Cemetery
Moreland
Pope County, Arkansas

Funeral services were held this morning for Adrian E. Duvall, 56,

Moreland, who died at his home Wednesday. The services were conducted by Rev. Dempsey Coffman. FWB Baptist pastor at Hector. Note: posted in Arkansas Democrat Sept 10, 1937.

Rev Ernest Hayden Elms
Birth:
Apr. 20, 1915
Independence County
Arkansas
Death:
Oct. 16, 1983
Burial:
Egner Cemetery
Salado
Independence County
Arkansas

A Free Will Baptist minister, shown in Rev. David Joslin's Hist. of AR FWB, in list of ministers having d. from 1980-89. He had served in the Polk Bayou Association of FWB at time of this report.

Rev Everett G Farnam
Birth:
Aug. 6, 1907
Death:
Dec. 31, 1989
Burial:
Hicks Cemetery
Lonoke
Lonoke County
Arkansas

Ordained Free Will Baptist minister in the Antioch Association in AR, shown in the 1958 State Minutes.

Rev Bennie Fisher
Birth:
Oct. 29, 1912
Death:
Oct. 30, 1994
Burial:
Mollie Gann Cemetery
Hatfield
Polk County
Arkansas

A ordained Free Will Baptist minister.

Rev Richard E. Ford, Sr
Birth:
Oct. 10, 1806
Warren County
Tennessee
Death:
Aug. 10, 1871
Benton County
Arkansas
Burial:
Blaylock Cemetery
Avoca
Benton County
Arkansas

Richard E. Ford was a Free-Will Baptist minister, who traveled from Tennessee to Arkansas and Missouri in a cart pulled by oxen. He had three sons, Josephus Wesley Ford, James Alexander Ford, and William Henry Ford

who also became Free-Will Baptist ministers. Josephus and James went on to Texas and were active there and where buried. William is buried in Missouri. Each are in this book under those states. The 1850 census listed Richard E. as a wagon maker.

His Father Henry Ford, was b. 23 Dec 1767, Asheville, Buncombe, North Carolina; d. 11 Nov 1845, Cannon County, Tennessee (Age 77 years); Mother Mary Magdalene Moore, b. 8 Aug 1776, Asheville, Buncombe, North Carolina 28 Jun 1858, Maury County, Tennessee (Age 81 years)

He Married Martha Barham "Patsy" Middleton, b. 26 Oct 1810, Tennessee d. 5 Dec 1893, South Garfield, Benton, Arkansas (Age 83 years) Married 1826 Tennessee

Rev Charlie Glee Forrest
Birth:
Sep. 10, 1910
Death:
Apr. 30, 1995
Scott County, AR
Burial:
New Bethel Cemetery
Kingston
Yell County
Arkansas

Charlie Forrest, age 84, a resident of Plainview, AR died at Chambers Memorial Hospital hi Danville, AR. He was son to Foster and Floy E. Peeler Forrest. He was a cabinet maker and retired Free Will Baptist minister. He was a member of the Free Will Baptist Church.
Funeral services officiated by Rev. Scott Miller and assisted by Rev. Monroe Hunt.

Ralph J Fowler
Birth:
Jul. 27, 1922
Death:
Mar. 31, 1982
Burial:
Fowler Cemetery
Damascus
Van Buren County
Arkansas

His name is in a list of dec'd ministers of the New Hope Association of Free Will Bapt. in AR, from 1980-89. He was a veteran of
WW II Army

Cecil Oliver Garrison
Birth:
Oct. 2, 1909,
Pryor, Okla.
Death:
Nov. 6, 2003
Burial:
Bland Cemetery,
Rogers,
Benton County,
Arkansas

He began preaching in 1932. During his life, he helped organize 15 churches, preached more than 6,200 sermons, witnessed more than 2,000 professions of faith, baptized over 1,000 worshippers, conducted more than 1,200 weddings and about 2,600 funerals. His career included pastoring 12 churches, a radio ministry for 18 years with a broadcast every Sunday morning in his early years. Rev. Garrison was an evangelist with the Old Mount Zion Free Will Baptist Association for 19 years.

Rev Harold Hunter Garner
Birth:
Dec. 11, 1921
Death:
Jan. 14, 2002
Burial:
Rankin Cemetery
Lone Elm
Franklin County
Arkansas

Funeral services for Rev. Harold Hunter GARNER, 80, of Alma,

Ark., were held at Mulberry First Free Will Baptist Church with Phillip Davis, Revs. Chester B. Smith and Cliff Ahart officiating. Pastor of Freedom FWB Church in 1997 Minutes

The Lord Is Coming

Jesse Franklin Gates
Birth:
May 1, 1877
Arkansas
Death:
1962
Arkansas
Burial:
Masonic Cemetery
Pocahontas
Randolph County, Arkansas
He was first a member of the Social Band Assn. but helped form the Union Band but later returns. He was one of the best students of the Bible and took a

great interest in points of doctrine held by the FWB. He was clerk of the association and quarterly meeting a number of times. He married Minnie Lee Wright Gates (1882 - 1961).

Rev John Garvin
Birth: 1849
Arkansas
Death:
May 22, 1924
Washington County
Arkansas
Burial:
Burkshed Cemetery
Washington County
Arkansas

Rev. John Garvin, was the son of Samuel and Jane GARVIN. He became a minister, ordination unknown. He was listed as an ordained minister in the Old Mt. Zion Association of Free Will Baptists, in northwest AR, in its

1919 Minutes, the earliest available, being age 70 yrs, from Spring Valley (Washington Co). He was married to Martha Lyall, 12 Oct. 1873, AR. His parents were in 1850 Washington Co. census, and later, he and Martha lived in the Brush Creek township, Washington, Co., in 1900,

A Light That Still Shines

Rev Earl W Gentry
Birth:
Mar. 24, 1914, USA
Death:
Nov. 21, 1994
Evansville
Washington County, Arkansas
Burial:
Mount McCurry Cemetery
Rudy
Crawford County, Arkansas

He was a retired drill press operator for Kay Chair Co. and a retired minister. He was a member and former pastor of 88 Freewill Baptist Church as well

as several other area churches. He also was a member of Fine Springs Masonic Lodge.

John David Glover
Birth:
Jan. 28, 1951
Star City, Arkansas
Death:
Jul. 10, 2014
Little Rock, Arkansas
Burial:
Kyler Cemetery
Batesville
Independence County, Arkansas

He was a retired meat market manager and a Free Will Baptist minister. He was a member of the Oakland Free Will Baptist Church at Bradford.

Kyle Elliot Goss
Birth:
Feb. 19, 1935
Pencil Bluff,
Montgomery County,
Arkansas
Death:
May 28, 2012
Arkansas
Burial:
Woody Memorial Cemetery,
Rudy, Crawford County,
Arkansas,

He was a retired ordained minister, having served at the 88 Freewill Baptist and Catcher Freewill Baptist Churches.

Herman A. Greenwood
Birth:
Dec. 2, 1917
Death:
Mar. 22, 1999
Burial:
Pleasant Valley Cemetery,
Warren,
Bradley County, Arkansas

Popular minister in the Saline Assn. in southern Arkansas.

William M. Guinn
Birth:
Aug. 8, 1885
Death:
Sep., 1977
Burial:
Oak Hill Memorial Cemetery,
Booneville,
Logan County, Arkansas
Plot: Section 3-3; Block 25;
Row Ac.

Guinn married Mary Elizabeth Fritz in 1906 in Branch, Franklin County, Arkansas. Rev. Guinn was a Free Will Baptist minister and records reveal he was in OKlahoma in 1946 at the State Conference in Tulsa.

Don P. Guthrie
Birth:
Sep. 21, 1953,
Gassville,
Baxter County, Arkansas
Death:
Jan. 27, 1998,
Hot Springs,
Garland County,Arkansas
Burial:
Memorial Gardens Cemetery,
Hot Springs,
Garland County,Arkansas

A Free Will Baptist, church planter, and denominational officer. He was listed in *"Outstanding Young Men of America."* Pastored in Oklahoma, Texas and Arkansas. Chairman of the Christian Education Board of the Oklahoma State Association. Board of Trustees for Hillsdale College, Member of the Texas Home Missions Board and the National Home Missions Board. Chairman of the State Youth Board in Arkansas. He was a member of the Optimist Club and the U. S. Army National Guard. He graduated from Hillsdale Free Will Baptist College, Moore, Okla. and had a Master's degree from Southern Nazarene University in Bethany, Oklahoma.

Charles Wesley Hager
Birth:
Sep. 8, 1871
Arkansas
Death:
1944
Burial:
Whittaker Cemetery
Minturn
Lawrence County, Arkansas

He served in WWI. He was minister in the New Hope Association in Central Arkansas.

Records conflict regarding the birthdate for Charles and his twin brother, Alfred. Some indicate they were born in 1871, others suggest 1872. Charles headstone lists the date as 1871 (Alfred's headstone says 1872). Minister in the Eureka church who attended the third annual meeting of the Union Band Assn. Spouse: Betty Vines Hager (1887 - 1937).

Rev Ed Hall
Birth:
Apr. 6, 1893
Death:
Apr. 20, 1964
Burial:
Thorn Cemetery
Greenbrier
Faulkner County
Arkansas

Rev Faber Henry Hall

Birth:
Jun. 12, 1930
Death:
Aug. 18, 1996
Burial:
Thorn Cemetery
Greenbrier
Faulkner County
Arkansas

An ordained Free Will Baptist minister who ministered in AR. His name is listed in roll of ministers in the AR State Association roll of ministers, in 1959.
DS w/ Dwade E. Doyal Hall; married April 13, 1950; US Army-Korea; Back of Monument: children: Larry, Ronda, Eddie, Peggy, Faber, Jr.; Grandchildren: Hope, Charity, Elisha, Angel Rygel.

Rev Opie C Hargrave

Birth:
Aug. 1, 1920
Gassville
Baxter County
Arkansas
Death:
Jul. 31, 2010
North Little Rock
Pulaski County
Arkansas
Burial:
Conley Cemetery
Mountain Home
Baxter County
Arkansas

Reverend Opie C. Hargrave, the day before his 90th birthday. He was born Gassville, Arkansas, the son of Grover Cleveland "Buck" and Myrtle Brewer Hargrave.
He served in the Air Force in World War II, and was married to Patricia Knight on June 5, 1948 in Tampa, Florida. He was a graduate of Columbia Bible College in Columbia, South Carolina, and served as pastor of a number of churches in North Central Arkansas.
Funeral services was held at Roller Funeral Home, with Bro. John Black and Reverend Mark Spripling officiating.
He served as Moderator of the Big Springs Association of Free Will Baptists in the 1960 session. His address was Mountain Home, AR. Unknown when and were he was ordained, as that is the oldest available minute for that association, which was organized in 1907.

Rev Velon Eugene Harmon
Birth:
Feb. 11, 1925
Boldman
Pike County, Kentucky
Death:
Jun. 11, 2014
Taylor
Wayne County, Michigan
Burial:
Cleburne County Memorial
Gardens
Heber Springs
Cleburne County, Arkansas

He was born in Boldman, Kentucky to the late John C. and Gracie Keathley Harmon. He was a US Army Veteran of WWII and a Free Will Baptist minister.
Funeral service was at the Olmstead Chapel with Rev. David Copeland officiating. Interment was with Military Honors.

**Is the city of Gold
-Eternal Home-
Where he is waiting for you
and me.**

Mark Metcher Harris
Birth:
Aug. 8, 1861,
England
Death:
Oct. 12, 1935,
Coaldale,
Scott County, Arkansas
Burial:
Coaldale Cemetery, Coaldale,
Scott County,
Arkansas

Harris was born in England and came to this country. He was found in the Chickasaw Nation, I.T. before statehood, and was affiliated with the Free Will Baptist. In 1901, the Center Ass'n approved him for license, and in 1902 he was ordained. He served as clerk of that conference for about two years, when he was elected to be moderator. He pastored churches in the association until about 1906 when he and some of his family moved to Scott Co. AR., where he lived until his death, remaining faithful.

Rev Hosea G Harrelson
Birth:
Feb. 1, 1909
Death:
Nov. 30, 1989
Burial:
Bluff Cemetery
Springdale
Washington County
Arkansas

Ordained minister in the Free Will Baptist church, and a member of the Old Mt. Zion Association at the time of his death

Inscription:
DAD
THE LORD IS MY SHEPHERD
Plot: Addition:1979;
Section:12 A;Plot:3

Rev James Harrington
Birth:
Oct. 6, 1864
Missouri
Death:
Jun. 4, 1923
Carroll County, Arkansas
Burial:
Shady Grove Cemetery
Osage
Carroll County, Arkansas

Rev. John Harrington, was an ordained Free Will Baptist minister and a member of the AR FWB State Association of churches in 1918, when it met with the Mountain View church. His name was in the roll of ministers, and his address was Osage, AR. When and where he was ordained is unavailable at this time. The 1920 census shows that he said he was born in Missouri.

--taken from *"History of Arkansas Free Will Baptists,"* Rev. David A. Joslin, Editor, pub. 199 [pg. 34].

Shady Grove Church and Cemetery Osage, Ark.

Rev Henry W Hart
Birth:
Aug. 30, 1924
Death:
Jun. 19, 1991
Burial:
Greene County Memorial
Gardens Cemetery
Paragould
Greene County
Arkansas

Born in Knobel, AR. He was an ordained minister in the Free Will Baptist church, listed in a roll of deceased ministers in the Arkansas State FWB Association in 1998 as being in the Social Band (District Ass'n) at the time of his death.

John R. Hartley
Birth:
1863
Death:
1942
Burial:
Shady Grove Cemetery,
Glendale, Lincoln County,
Arkansas

He was Jim Puckett's great grandfather. He married Barbara Ellen Anderson, who was born in 1867 and died in 1931. He pastored in Arkansas all his life.. His daughter – Lillian Geneva Hartley –married James H. McClellan. She was a devout Christian woman who died following the birth of her eighth child. Her eldest was just a teenage boy, and Jim's mother Anna, was the oldest daughter. At age 11, Anna remembers her father gathering the children around her mother's bedside just before she died. She told them all that she loved them and wanted them to live for the Lord and meet her in Heaven. From that day forward, Anna cooked, cleaned, sewed and raised her siblings. The entire family lived for the Lord, and their family heritage of godliness continued. Anna's brother Elbert McClellan, was also a pastor. Hartley pastored Macedonia Free Will Baptist Church from 1912-1914, and again from 1919 – 1925. Anna was born in 1919, during the time of his tenure. Rev. Hartley also had a son named Johnny who was a preacher. He never married. He did not pastor, but did preach. He adopted and raised a mentally retarded boy name Nonnie, and took care of him his entire life.

Rev George W. Hassell
Birth:
1851
Death:
1921
Burial:
Barren Fork Cemetery
Mount Pleasant
Izard County, Arkansas

Rev. George W. Hassell was an ordained minister in the Polk Bayou Association of Free Will Baptists, when it met with the AR State Ass'n of FWB in 1902. When or where he was ordained is unknown at this time.
--taken from "History of Arkansas Free Will Baptists," by Rev. David A Joslin, Editor, pub. 1998, pg. 58

Claude Joseph Hendrix
Birth:
1921
Death:
1996
Burial:
Benton County Memorial Park
Rogers
Benton County
Arkansas

His name is included in a list of deceased ministers in the Arkansas State Association of Free Will Baptists, his affiliation at the time was the Old Mt. Zion District Ass'n

Carl Leo High
Birth:
Jul. 10, 1913
Death:
May 6, 1983,
Arkansas
Burial:
Pirtle Cemetery,
Peach Orchard,
Clay County, Arkansas

He served many years as a leader and pastor in the Social Band Association in Northeast Arkansas.

Rev Edward Washington Hill
Birth:
Jan. 19, 1880
Newhope
Pike County
Arkansas
Death:
Apr. 20, 1946
Newhope
Pike County, Arkansas
Burial:
Langley Hall Cemetery
Langley
Pike County, Arkansas

Ed was the son of George Washington and Eliza Jane Pate Hill. He married Lucinda Jane Barentine August 17, 1902 in Howard County Arkansas. Ed was a Free Will Baptist Preacher. His name was in the Aug. 31, 1923, Minutes as pastor of Rock Springs Church

Elmer Holiman
Birth:
Sep. 3, 1926
Death:
Nov. 14, 2014
Pine Bluff,
Arkansas
Burial:
Mount Pleasant Cemetery
Plumerville
Conway County
Arkansas

Elmer Lee Holiman, 88, was a retired farmer, pastor and army veteran. He dedicated his life to sharing the gospel of Jesus Christ and leaves behind a legacy of being a man who lived what he taught. He was a member of Oak Grove Freewill Baptist Church in Lake Village.

He was a Free Will Baptist minister in the New Hope Assn.

Terrell Holland
Birth:
Apr. 21, 1929
Duncan,
Greenlee County, Arizona
Death:
Jun. 8, 2012
Burial:
Glenwood Cemetery, Glenwood,
Pike County, Arkansas

Rev. Terrell pastored Free Will Baptist churches in Oklahoma and Arkansas for 48 years and served at the Glenwood Free Will Baptist Church for 13 years. He was always able to bring a smile through a story, joke or encouraging word as he was concerned and loved everyone.

James Monroe Holleman
Birth:
Aug. 25, 1895,
Rose Bud,hite County, Arkansas
Death:
May 31, 1973,
Rose Bud,White County,
Arkansas
Burial:
Mount Bethel Cemetery,
Rose Bud,White County,
Arkansas

David Monroe Holder
Birth:
Mar. 9, 1863
Union Point
Union County, Illinois
Death:
Mar. 1, 1934
Pocahontas
Randolph County, Arkansas
Burial:
Masonic Cemetery
Pocahontas
Randolph County, Arkansas

He came from Missouri to Arkansas about 1901-2. Living about 5 miles east of Pocahontas. He held several revivals each year and pastoring about five churches. He came from the Union Band Assn. to the Social Band.

John Robert Holt
Birth:
Nov. 27, 1868
Death:
1950
Burial:
Warm Springs Cemetery
Warm Springs
Randolph County, Arkansas

Early FWB preacher in the General Free Will Baptist Assn. His parents were William Littleton Holt (1842 - 1926) and Nancy G. Phillips Holt (1837 - 1907). He married Carrie M. Boas Holt (1871 - 1918).

Gaylord Huckaba
Birth:
Unknown
Death:
Jan. 4, 2013
Rosie Independence County
Arkansas
Burial:
Maple Springs Cemetery,
Batesville,
Independence County, Arkansas

He was veteran and long-time Free Will Baptist pastor. His funeral message was preached by Rev. Shane King, pastor of the Blackland Chapel FWB church.

Francis Marion Hudson, Sr
Birth:
Mar. 20, 1829
Alabama
Death:
Oct. 29, 1920
Moreland
Pope County, Arkansas
Burial:
Hudson Cemetery
Moreland
Pope County, Arkansas

Francis married Mary Mary Magdelaine Yates on Jan 16, 1848 in Pope County, Arkansas, He helped organize Free Will Baptist (FWB) churches, and a J.M. Hudson's name appears in a list of moderators of the AR State Association of FWB. He also served in the Civil War, per this family history note:"F.M. Hudson Sr. enlisted as a private in the Arkansas Infantry of the Confederate Army in the War Between the States on Dec. 21, 1861 at Dardanelle, Arkansas, and served for about a year. He was in a Union Prison for war prisoners for a time."
Served as a Sergeant in Company E of the 17th Arkansas Infantry, CSA (LeMoyne's). Later served as a private in Company I of the 21st Arkansas Infantry

Earcel Huggins
Birth:
Sep. 15, 1905
Franklin County, Arkansas
Death:
Jun. 8, 1975
Crawford County, Arkansas
Burial:
Rankin Cemetery
Lone Elm
Franklin County, Arkansas,

He was a Free Will Baptist minister, listed with others in the 1957 Minutes of Zion Hope Ass'n, when it met at Walnut Street FWB Church, Ft. Smith, AR.
--from "History of Arkansas Free Will Baptists," by Rev. David A. Joslin, Editor, pub. 1998 (p.14).

Rev Oscar Clayton Hunt
Birth:
Sep. 11, 1866
Missouri
Death:
May 7, 1938
Waldron
Scott County, Arkansas
Burial:
Lamb Cemetery
Waldron
Scott County, Arkansas

An ordained Free Will Baptist minister in AR.

Dr John Campbell Gilliland
Birth
:   Oct. 6, 1932
Death:
Mar. 12, 1988
Burial:

Rose Lawn Park Cemetery
Fort Smith
Sebastian County
Arkansas

Also, a minister, listed in roll from Old Mt. Zion Association of AR Free Will Baptists, showing he had died between 1980-89

William Sherman Isbell
Birth:
May 4, 1891
Death:
Sep. 13, 1987,
Russellville,
Pope County, Arkansas
Burial:
Saint Joe Cemetery,
Atkins,
Pope County, Arkansas

He was a strong leader for Arkansas Free Will Baptist in the central part of the state. Most followed his leadership due to his wisdom and firm commitment to the FWB denomination.

William Rufus Jobe
Birth:
Aug. 11, 1865
Death:
Jul. 24, 1938
Burial:
Shiloh Cemetery
Atkins
Pope County, Arkansas

Son of James Robert and Lizzie (Choat) Jobe. Married first to Viola Jane Norris on 17 Jul 1887, and second to Alva Duvall on 20 Oct 1895, both in Pope Co., AR.

His death notice in the Northwest Arkansas Times, 25 Jul 1938: "Pea Ridge Minister Dies at Russellville: Russellville, Ark. July 25 - AP - Stricken while preaching at a revival, the Rev. W. R. Jobe, 73, Free Will Baptist minister of the Pea Ridge Community near here, died yesterday."

Rev Clyde Franklin Johnson
Birth:
Mar. 6, 1906
Kingston
Madison County
Arkansas
Death:
Jan. 9, 1989
Fayetteville
Washington County
Arkansas
Burial:
Kingston Cemetery
Kingston
Madison County
Arkansas

Rev. Clyde Franklin Johnson, 82, of Fayetteville, Ark., at the City Hospital in Fayetteville. He was a member and former pastor of the First Free Will Baptist Church in Fayetteville. He had taught for 13 years in public schools in Madison County and had been an ordained Free Will Baptist minister for 32 years and had pastored churches in Madison and Washington counties. He was preceded in death by his wife, Mrs. Allie Virginia Lane Johnson on April 11, 1980. Services were held at the First Free Will Baptist Church in Fayetteville, with the Rev. Dennis Artman and the Rev. Tommy Day officiating.

Joseph H. Johnson
Birth:
Apr. 1, 1854
Lawrence Co., Tennessee
Death:
Jan. 21, 1934
Washington Co., Arkansas
Burial:
Lincoln Cemetery
Lincoln
Washington County, Arkansas
Plot: row 28

He joined the Methodist Episcopal church in 1871 and received license to exhort in 1872 and to preach in 1879. He became dissatisfied with sprinkling in 1881 and joined the Free Will Baptist church at Mt. Cabo, Henderson County, Tennessee and was ordained the same year. He served as moderator of the Flat Creek Association from 1889 to 1891. He moved to Tyronza, Arkansas in 1896 and took charge of four churches—Tyronza Chapel, Dead Timber, Bullard's Chapel and Holly Grove. He was moderator in the Tyronza association in 1892-93. He was Secretary of the association in

1896 and served six years and also served as Secretary of the State Association as well as the State Evangelist two years. He pastored churches up till 1908 when he resigned pastoral work moving to Wynne in 1902 but continuing to preach.

Keith Johnson
Birth:
Jun. 4, 1934,
Alton, Oregon County,
Missouri
Death:
Jan. 11, 2010,
Conway, Faulkner County,
Arkansas
Burial:
Crestlawn Memorial Park,
Conway, Faulkner County,
Arkansas

Bro. Johnson was the pastor of First Free Will Baptist Church in Conway until just months before his death and pastored churches in Missouri and Arkansas. He managed the Christian Supply Store in Conway for 23 years.

Rev M. P. Johnson
Birth:
Oct. 21, 1855
Death:
Nov. 30, 1912
Burial:
Sharum Cemetery
Pocahontas
Randolph County, Arkansas

Early FWB preacher in the General Free Will Baptist Conference.

Rev Paul Jones
Birth
Dec. 2, 1890
Death:
Nov. 2, 1981
Burial:
Maplewood Cemetery
Harrison
Boone County
Arkansas, Plot: 2, 1A, 5

In list of Free Will Baptist ministers in the 1989 Minutes of the AR State Association of FWB. He was shown as being from the Antioch Association. Unk when he was ordained or his ministry.

David A. Joslin
Birth:
Mar. 10, 1937,
Arkansas
Death:
Sep. 10, 2011,
Conway,
Faulkner County, Arkansas
Burial:
Mount Bethel Cemetery,
Rose Bud,
White County, Arkansas

Rev. Joslin is a son of the late Rev.
Joel Arthur and Clara Flossie

Jones Joslin. Rev. Joslin was licensed to preach at age 19 while working as a telegrapher for the Santa Fe Railroad on an Indian reservation near Albuquerque, New Mexico. He was ordained to preach in 1957. Joslin graduated from Free Will Baptist College in Nashville, Tenn. in 1960, then attended Arkansas College in Batesville. He was Executive Director of the Arkansas Free Will Baptist State Association for 30 years after pastoring 13 years in Arkansas and Tennessee. Rev. Joslin spent 43 years of his 49-year ministry in Arkansas, pastoring six churches and helping establish two others. He served on numerous Free Will Baptist Boards including the Christian Education Board, and the General Board, the Historical Commission, and 18 years on the Executive Committee of the National Association of Free Will Baptists. Rev. Joslin founded the Ministers' Benevolent Association for Arkansas Free Will Baptists, worked to create the guidelines for the Acts 1:8 Plan for missionary support and other denominational programs. He oversaw the publications of *"The Fifty-year Record,"* a brief historical book of the national association, and he collaborated with a group of writers in 1976 to publish *"History of Free Will Baptist State Association."* He also wrote adult Sunday School curriculum and prepared manuscripts for publication in *Contact,* the Free Will Baptist national magazine. He also edited *The Vision,* a monthly publication focusing on events and people among the 220 Arkansas Free Will Baptist churches for 30 years.

Joel Arthur Joslin
Birth:
Apr. 5, 1902,
Van Buren,
Crawford County,Arkansas
Death:
Nov. 10, 1993,
Fort Smith,
Sebastian County, Arkansas
Burial:
Gracelawn Cemetery,
Van Buren,
Crawford County, Arkansas

He was a Freewill Baptist minister, a farmer and retired employee of Missouri Pacific Railroad. He was a member of Catcher Freewill Baptist Church and had been an ordained Freewill Baptist minister since 1921. He organized the Catcher Free Will Baptist Church near Van Buren in 1930 and re-organized it in 1943. He was the father of Rev. David Joslin. He

assisted in the Organization Of Several Other Free Will Baptist Churches in eastern Oklahoma and western Arkansas.

Charles Rice Kellam
Birth:
May 11, 1809
Vermont
Death:
Apr. 4, 1854
Burial:
Parks Cemetery
Charleston
Franklin County, Arkansas

He was founder of Charleston, Arkansas. Rev. Charles R. Kellam appeared in the southern part of Franklin Co. AR, via way of North Carolina, at least by 1846. In that year, he served as post-master for the area and opened the Post Office for Charleston on Aug. 10, 1846 (David Joslin, author of *"The Arkansas State Association,",* Randall House Pub, 1976).Rev. Kellam married his wife, Susan, in N.C. and they had two children, Charles and Edward P., both bn AR, in 1850 census (by 1860, they had added Mary B.) Rev. Kellam exerted a significant influence and the commuity was named Charles Towne--later, Charleston. Rev. Kellam organized a FreeWill Baptist church in 1846, the same year he opened the post office. He remained its pastor until 1850. His work may have been brief but it was here the Arkansas District Association was organized in 1869. The church he organized was later referred to by "Goodspeed's Hist of NW AR", as a Missionary Baptist Church, but the church changed hands a number of times, and probably was a M.B. Church by the time Goodspeed's was published in 1889. After Kellam's ministry ended there in 1850, the church remained w/o a pastor until 1857. It was later reorganized and numerous churches worshipped in the same 'meeting house,' and so confusion was not uncommon. Nevertheless, Rev. Charles Kellam did a good work and his name is found in old records and is noted here for it.He died at 45 years of age...unknown as to cause of death.

Darwin Eugene Kelton
Birth:
Mar. 13, 1937,
Roswell, Chaves County,
New Mexico
Death:
Dec. 12, 1999,
Atkins,Pope County, Arkansas
Burial:
Oakland Cemetery,
Atkins, Pope County, Arkansas

He was ordained to preach in 1974 in Fresno, California, where he chaired the Ministry Department at California Christian College. After teaching two years in Florida (1976-78), Rev. Kelton began pastoring the First Free Will Baptist Church in Berryville, Arkansas. He served the First Free Will Baptist Church in Athens, Hatfield and Pine Hill Free Will Baptist churches until declining health required him to cease full-time pastoral duties. He served as a Minister of Music at the Union Grove church at Athens until his death. He was a gifted musician, vocally, instrumentally, and began his first radio program at age 16. He later sang with gospel quartets, directed choral groups, teach guitar lessons and guide music programs on collegiate and local church levels. He had only one eye, but his ability far exceeded the handicap as he served the Lord in many areas of the United States.

Rev James Alexander Kesner
Birth:
Mar. 19, 1853
Madison County, Arkansas
Death:
Feb. 2, 1925
Madison County, Arkansas
Burial:
Kingston Cemetery
Kingston
Madison County, Arkansas

He was a preacher and his full name was James Alexander" "James mother was Martha Hill Kesner and father was John Gatley Kesner"

Inscription:
I have fought a good fight. I have finished my course. I have kept the faith.

Ernest McKinley Kennedy
Birth:
Jan. 11, 1905
Death:
Jun. 24, 1977
Burial:
Sutton Cemetery,
Pocahontas,
Randolph County, Arkansas

He was the first State Executive Secretary in Oklahoma, begining in 1955. The office had been a part time office until the State

Convention elected him. The office was in Oklahoma City.

Rev Chester U. Kinder

Birth:
Feb. 18, 1899
Death:
Sep. 16, 1964
Atkins
Pope County
Arkansas
Burial:
Saint Joe Cemetery
Atkins
Pope County
Arkansas

Rev. Kinder was an ordained minister with the Free will Baptist Church and was affiliated with the Arkansas Antioch District Association Church, at least in 1959, which records show, and probably before. Married Cassie B. Brown Aug 26 1917 in Pope County

Dilmus Newton King

Birth:
Jan. 13, 1852
Georgia
Death:
Dec. 10, 1932
Randolph County, Arkansas

Burial:
Warm Springs Cemetery
Warm Springs
Randolph County, Arkansas

He was the son of Carter & Louisa Jane Flanigan King. He married Mary Samantha Wooldridge on 25 Jan 1872 in Warm Springs, Randolph Co, AR.

The following was taken from 1889 *Goodspeed of NE Arkansas*: Rev D.N. King, minister and farmer, Warm Springs, Ark. Although young in years, Mr King has already done much good in the world by administering to the spiritual wants of his fellowmen and by living a life of such consistency and purity as cannot fail to have its effect on the rising generation. His birth occurred in Georgia on the 13th of January 1852, and he is the son of Carter and Louisa (Flannigan) King, natives of Georgia and of Irish parentage. Carter King was a farmer and a tanner by occupation, which he followed in Georgia until 1866, when he moved to Tennessee and settled in Roan County. He there farmed on rented land until 1869, when he came to Randolph County, Ark, and settled in Warm Springs Twp, where, in 1869, he purchased eighty acres. This he proceeded to improve but one year later moved into a different neighborhood, where he died shortly afterward, in March 1871. He was a member of the Masonic fraternity, a member of the Baptist Church, and was well respected by all who knew him. He served one year during the latter part of the war in the Confederate service, and surrendered in 1865. Mr & Mrs King were the parents of eleven children, six now living: D.N., Rebecca F. (wife of F. M. Thornsberry), James M., Sarah E. (wife of H.C. Croger), Joseph J., and Mary L. (wife of James Hovis). Mrs King then married in 1873 to Rev. G. A. Barrett and by him became the mother of two children. At the age of twenty years, D.N. King was married to Miss Mary S. Wooldridge of Arkansas, and immediately afterward engaged in tilling the soil. He had very little property at the time of his marriage (1872) but he is now the owner of 160 acres, of which seventy-five acres are under a good state of cultivation and with good buildings, etc. He is one of the enterprising citizens of this section, and lays a great deal of his success in life to the exertions of his companion. He was ordained a minister in the General Free Will Baptist Church, and began preaching Gospel on the 8th of October, 1882. Since then he has performed the marriage ceremony for about nine couples and has baptized a large number of converts. Mr & Mrs King became the parents of seven children: Louisa J. born on 15th of Apriol 1873 and died on the 14th of September 1874; W.L. born on the 22d of September 1876and died on the 6th of April 1880; John C. born on the 25th of January 1879; E.E. born on the 8th of November 1881; Jasper N. born on the 10th of February 1884; Dora L. born on the 23d of August 1886 and one who died young.

Zane T. Kirkland
Birth:
unknown,
Arkansas
Death:
Feb. 2, 1992,
Little Rock,
Pulaski County, Arkansas
Burial:
Strangers Home Cemetery,
Alicia,
Lawrence County, Arkansas

Pastored Free Will Baptist churches in Arkansas. He was a state leader serving on the Arkansas State Mission Board for eight years and the state Executive Board for five.

67

He was pastor of the Conway church at his death.

Rev Charles Cleveland Kitchens
Birth
14 Mar 1885
Death
3 Dec 1972
Burial Parks Cemetery
Nola,
Scott County, Arkansas

Rev. Charles C. Kitchens, age 87, of Gravelly, at the St Marys Hospital in Russellville. Rev. Kitchens was a Minister, a native of the Waltreak Community, a son of the late Mr. and Mrs. Charles Kitchens. Rev. Kitchens was a member of the Mulberry Freewill Baptist Church.
Survivors include his wife, Mrs. Minnie Blagg Kitchens; two sons, Jesse Kitchens of Gravelly and Ariel Kitchens of Tampa, Fla.; four daughters, Mrs. Velma Jones of Dumas, Mrs. Syble CopelandRead More of Waldron, and Mrs. Verta Seay of Georgia and

Miss Etoyl Kitchens of the home; two sisters, Mrs. Decie Davison of Oklahoma and Mrs. Addie Dennis of Danville; and 21 grandchildren.
Funeral services were held at the Mulberry Freewill Baptist Church with the Rev. Pat Millard officiating. Published in Yell County Record, Danville, Arkansas: 12-7-1971). He was the author of the book, *How Firm A Foundation.*
He was the grandfather of the well-known piano player Floyd Kamer.

Samuel Edward Lane
Birth:
Jul. 4, 1908
Madison County
Arkansas
Death:
Mar. 21, 1986
Rogers
Benton County
Arkansas
Burial:
Colbaugh Cemetery
Madison County
Arkansas

Listed in roll of ministers of the AR State Association of Free Will Baptists, who had died between 1980-89. He was reported from the Old Mt. Zion Dist. Unk when and where he ministered. He was Son of Joseph L and Lucy Ann Woolsey Lane and Husband of Lela Kirk Lane

Miles R. Langley

Birth:
Dec. 4, 1851
Gwinett County
Georgia
Death:
March 2, 1894
Arkansas
Burial:
Warm Springs Cemetery
Warm Springs
Randolph County, Arkansas

At the age of 17 went from Georgia to Tennessee. When twenty years old he married and moved to Randolph County, Arkansas, in 1872. Here he joined a General Free Will Baptist church and began preaching. He was ordained Oct. 7, 1876,m by Elders D. L. Poyner, L.J. Thornbury and G. A. Barrett. He pastored four churches till a year before his death. He was one of the best pastoral preachers the denomination afforded. Among his last words were: "I am going home."

Robert Lee, Jr

Birth:
1814,
Tennessee
Death:
Apr. 22, 1887,
Madison County,Arkansas
Burial:
Lee Family Cemetery,
Aurora,Madison
County,Arkansas

An Arkansas pioneer Free Will Bapt. preacher in the late 1830's,

Herman A. Lewis

Birth:
Mar. 8, 1898,
Lebanon,
Laclede County, Missouri
Death:
Sep. 20, 1996,
Batesville,
Independence County,
Arkansas,
Burial:
Reeves Cemetery,
Melbourne,
Izard County, Arkansas

Pioneer   Free   Will   Baptist

preacher, pastor, and church planter. During his 73 years he pastored churches in Arkansas, California, & Washington. He had little education but memorized hundreds of Bible verses and quoted them extensively in his sermons. In his early ministry he pastored as many as seven churches at a time and was a widely-used revivalist he baptized hundreds of converts. He was a moderator of the Arkansas State Association during his ministry. A biography was written about him in 1974. To a grandson he wrote: "Observe with care of whom you speak, to whom you speak, and how and when and where you speak."

Rev James Silas Lovett
Birth:
Nov. 23, 1865
Death:
Mar. 30, 1957
Burial:
Cedar Grove Cemetery
Paris
Logan County, Arkansas

An ordained Free Will Baptist minister whose name appears in a list of moderators for the Arkansas State Association.

Curtis L. Lybarger
Birth:
Feb. 9, 1917
Death:
Jun. 29, 1993
Burial:
East Shady Grove Cemetery,
Greenbrier,
Faulkner County,
Arkansas

A Free Will Baptist minister, listed in 1959 minutes AR State Association, a minister serving in the New Hope District Association. Again his name was in the 1998 Minutes with those who had died.

Rev George E. Lynch
Birth:
Feb. 10, 1910
Death:
Sep. 17, 1990
Burial:
Hickory Grove Cemetery
Madison County
Arkansas

Listed in Minutes of AR Free Will Baptist State Association in 1959, as an ordained minister. He was also listed as a minister again in the 1991 Minutes, from the Old Mt. Zion Association, as having died,

Walter B. Maddox
Birth:
Jun. 6, 1887,
Arkansas
Death:
Sep. 12, 1982,
White County,
Arkansas
Burial:
Honey Hill Cemetery,

Searcy,
White County,
Arkansas

Most of his ministry was spent in the New Hope Association in central Arkansas.

Bennie P. Maness
Birth:
Aug. 18, 1898
Death:
Oct. 29, 1983
Burial:
Edgewood Memorial Park
North Little Rock
Pulaski County
Arkansas

**Rev Thomas Jefferson
Mantooth**
Birth:
Sep. 23, 1853
Polk County
Tennessee,
Death:
Feb. 18, 1907
Burial:
Lowes Creek Cemetery
Peter Pender
Franklin County
Arkansas

Rev. T.J. Mantooth, was the son of John (b.ca 1812) and Sophia (Hall) Mantooth, of Tennessee.
He married Julia Elizabeth Rector 28 Nov. 1873, Franklin Co. AR.
He was an ordained Free Will Baptist minister serving in the Western Arkansas Ass'n, when the ARK State Ass'n of Free Will Baptists convened in 1902 in Logan Co. AR. When and where he was ordained, nor churches he pastored or assisted, is not available in the old Minutes.

--from "History of Arkansas Free Will Baptists," by Rev. David A. Joslin, Editor, pub. 1998 (pg. 58).

Dock Edgar Marchant
Birth:
Jul. 18, 1910
Death:
Jun. 13, 2000
Union Parish
Louisiana
Burial:
Woodlawn Memorial Park
Fort Smith
Sebastian County
Arkansas

Dock Marchant was a Free Will Baptist minister in Arkansas. His name is listed with other ministers in the Minutes of the Zion Hope Ass'n of FWB, in 1957, when it convened with the Walnut Street FWB Church, Ft. Smith, AR. Unknown at this date when and where he was ordained nor the churches he may have pastored.
--taken from "History of Free Will Baptists," by Rev. David A. Joslin, Editor, pub. 1998, p.14.
24 Oct 1996 Dock married Judy Alice Black Foster in Union Parish, Louisiana. His Death Certificate states that he was cremated by Kilpatrick Funeral Home in Farmerville, LA 71241.

Franklin Ray Matchett
Birth:
May 28, 1948
Athens
Pope County
Arkansas
Death:
Dec. 20, 2014
Star City, Arkansas
Burial:
Oakland Cemetery
Atkins
Pope County
Arkansas,

Franklin Ray Matchett, 66 of Star City died Saturday at his home in Star City. He was born May 28, 1948 in Atkins to the late, Delmer and Naomi Pettit Matchett. He was a retired Free Will Baptist Minister after serving the following church's over 34 years, Maple Springs, Smith Springs, Woodlawn and Yorktown. He was currently a member of Smith Springs Free Will Baptist Church in Morrilton. Frank served in the Army during the Vietnam War from 1968-1970, had Previously worked as the Parts Manager at Price Chevrolet in Morrilton, loved to garden, ride horses, write songs and poetry and sing with his family.

He was also preceded in death by his first wife of 42 years, Bonnie Sue Hubbard Matchett.

Elbert McClellan
Birth:
Jun. 11, 1914,
Cleveland County,
Arkansas
Death:
Apr. 6, 2010,
Pine Bluff,
Jefferson County,
Arkansas
Burial:
Shady Grove Cemetery,
New Edinburg,
Cleveland County, Arkansas

McClellan pastored Macedonia Free Will Baptist Church from 1958-60, and 1964-1966. His daughter Geraldine is married to a preacher/Bible scholar, Rev. Dr. Cecil Sanders of New Edinburg, AR, and they have a son who is a pastor, Rev. Marvin Ray Sanders of Oklahoma City, OK.

He served many congregations in southern Arkansas and member of Macedonia Free Will Baptist Church. He was a farmer and carpenter.

James Samuel McClellan
Birth:
Nov. 13, 1834
Annibelle, Abbeville County,
South Carolina
Death:
Mar. 30, 1930
Ain, Grant County, Arkansas
Burial:
Camp Creek Cemetery,
Grant County, Arkansas

Born in South Carolina, Migrating with his parents first to Georgia then to Holmes County, Mississippi by 1846. Came to Arkansas from Mississippi after July 1860 - Holmes County, Mississippi Census to Hurricane Township in what was 'old' Bradley County Arkansas, which became Dorsey in 1873 and then Cleveland County in 1885. Served in the 2nd Ark Cavalry Co. D during the Civil War attaining the rank of Corporal. Was present at the Fall of Vicksburg in 1863 by his own statement and verified in the records at Vicksburg National Battlefield Park. After he was captured at the Fall of Vicksburg with his brother David and brother in Laws, Ben Tyler and Gus Muirhead with the Vaiden Mississippi Light Artillery, he was interred for a time at the Union POW Camp, Rock Island, Illinois eventually being 'paroled' returning to Arkansas debarking at what was known as 'Red River Landing'. His enlistment papers, pension application and war records held at the Old State Capital Archives; Little Rock, Arkansas. He did receive a war pension from the State of Arkansas for his service during the Civil War Pension Record from Arkansas State Archives. He was married in 1854 to Miss Huldah Scott Mathis of Attala County, Mississippi. Patriarch of the McClellan Clan of Arkansas and the progenitor of over 1300 descendants - one Grandson was Sen. John L. McClellan, also listed on this site, elected as one of Arkansas' United States Senators for thirty-five years.

He had a long list of Free Will Baptists in southern Arkansas and FWB preachers, namely; Elbert McClellan, James Puckett, Ray Sanders, Marvin Ray Sanders, Ron Puckett, etc.

Robert Henry McCuin
Birth:
Nov. 23, 1940
Lake Village
Chicot County, Arkansas
Death:
Oct., 2013
Bastrop
Morehouse Parish, Louisiana
Burial:
Tate Cemetery
Hector
Pope County, Arkansas

He was the son of the late James S. and Bertha Sammons McCuin. Rev. McCuin was currently serving the Hill View Free Will Baptist Church in Bastrop, La., and pastored numerous churches across Arkansas, Tennessee, Louisiana, Alabama, Oklahoma and Mississippi.

William Franklin "Will" McGee
Birth:
Aug. 19, 1878
Death:
Jan. 2, 1959
Russellville
Pope County,
Arkansas
Burial:
Saint Joe Cemetery
Atkins
Pope County,
Arkansas

He was an early Free Will Baptist minister and leader in the state of Arkansas. His parents were George Washington McGee and Nancy Melvina Burris. He married Alice Clemons Oct 22 1899 in Pope County.

Elder Spartan M. McMillan
Birth:
Feb. 8, 1845
Arkansas
Death:
Jun. 30, 1925
Carroll County
Arkansas
Burial:
Shady Grove Cemetery
Osage
Carroll County, Arkansas,
Rev. Spartan M. McMillan's name is in a list of ministers in the 1918 Minutes of the AR State Association of Free Will Baptist, when it met at Mountain View Church.
He stated his address as Delmar, AR.
--Hist. of AR FWB, by Rev. David A. Joslin, Ed., pub. 1998.

Marriage: 1 James Henderson STRANGE b: 1829 in Spartanburg Co, SC •Married: 26 Jun 1851 in Chattooga Co, GA

Marriage: 2 Spartan M MCMILLAN b: 8 Feb 1845 in AR •Married: Bef Aug 1870 in Carroll Co, AR

George W Million
Birth:
Sep. 25, 1877,
Randolph ,Arkansas
Death:
Jan. 8, 1969,
Pocahontas,
Randolph County, Arkansas
Burial:
Masonic Cemetery,
Pocahontas,
Randolph County, Arkansas

He was a well-known preacher and author of two books on the history of Free Will Baptists. He was remembered for the use of charts while he preached. He influenced many ministers in the Social Band Association and tutored many of the early preachers that helped to form the National Association of Free Will Baptists in 1935.

R. F. Million
Birth:
Unknown
Death:
Unknown
Burial:
Sutton Cemetery
Pocahontas
Randolph County, Arkansas

Rev Daniel J Molloy
Birth:
Oct., 1843
Mississippi
Death:
Jul. 22, 1915
Ashley County
Arkansas
Burial:
Zion Cemetery
Hamburg
Ashley County
Arkansas

Daniel J. Molloy, became a Free Will Baptist minister as shown in old Hamburg Association of 1887 minutes, when he was elected its moderator; he gave a report of his work: which was quite active, and the monies he received that year for all his services: $30.10! When and where he was ordained is unavailable. He appeared to be active in the church until his death. Veteran: U. S. Navy

Steve P Montgomery
Birth:
Madison County, Arkansas
Feb. 15, 1906
Death:
Madison County, Arkansas
Feb. 7, 1983
Burial:
Alabam Cemetery
Alabam
Madison County
Arkansas

Father: William Jones MONTGOMERY b: 17 July 1883 in Alabam, Madison Co., Arkansas-Mother: Esteller Belle HATFIELD b: 29 March 1886 Marriage 1 Jewel OWENS b: 10 July 1907 in Arkansas Married: 1 Oct 1927 in Madison County, Arkansas. Marriage 2 Maxine Frances DOTSON b: 20 JAN 1921

Married: 9 OCT 1942
Listed in roll of Free Will Bapt. ministers, having d. from 1980-89. He was a member of the Old Mt. Zion Association when his death was reported. He was also in the 1958 roll of ministers from the same district.

Roy M. Moore
Birth:
Nov. 21, 1901
Death:
May 9, 1978
Burial:
Oak Grove Cemetery,
Yorktown,
Lincoln County, Arkansas

He was a popular preacher in Arkansas. It was common for him the pastored churches many miles away all the weekend should drive back to his job for Monday morning.

Rev Jewel Franklin Morrison Jr
Birth:
Mar. 18, 1906
Crawford County, Arkansas
Death:
May 4, 1992
Van Buren
Crawford County, Arkansas
Burial:
Gracelawn Cemetery
Van Buren
Crawford County, Arkansas

He was a retired Free Will Baptist Minister and a member of the First Free Will Baptist Church of Fort Smith. He also founded and built the Oliver Springs Free Will Baptist church in 1959. He was a lifelong resident of Crawford County.
Funeral services at First Assembly of God Church Reverend Jimmy Morrison and Reverend Gilbert Pixley officiated.

Rev A A Noggle
Birth:
Jan. 21, 1902
Georgia
Death:
Apr. 21, 1975
Arkansas
Burial:
Saint Mary's Cemetery
Rose Bud
White County
Arkansas

Rev. A. A. "Dolph" Noggle was a Free Will Baptist minister as shown in 1922 Arkansas FWB State Association Minutes, from the New Hope Ass'n #2. He was married to Nora and they had two children, Cletus D. and Flecia A. Noggle.

Rev E J O'Neal
Birth:
Dec. 9, 1864
Center Point
Howard County
Arkansas
Death:
Dec. 14, 1944
Burial:
Mount Joy Cemetery
Daisy
Pike County, Arkansas

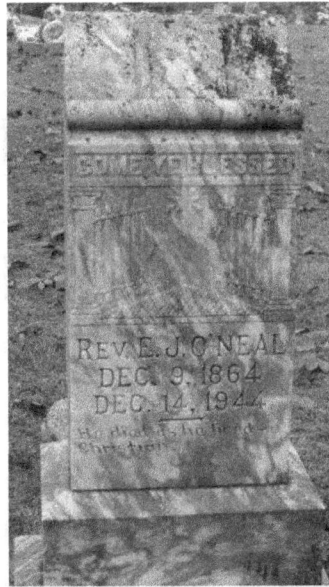

Son of Jim & Jane O'Neal. He married Alice Golden. He was of the Baptist faith.

Rev. E.J. O'Neal (name shown Elias/Elijah in census) was an ordained Free Will Baptist minister in the early years of their work in AR. He was affiliated with the Little Missouri Association in 1902. Where and when he was ordained is unknown. He also pastored the Piney Grove Church, Pike ,Co. He was elected moderator in 1923 of the Little Missouri Association, when it met at the Mt. Joy Church, near Daisy, AR. In the 1926 Session of the AR State Ass'n of Free Will Baptists, he was one of those chosen to preach. It convened with the Glenwood FWB Church of Glenwood, in Pike Co. Sep. 30 to Oct 3, 1926.
He preached a double funeral in 1927, for Charlie and Sarah

Coplin, husband and wife, bur. in this cemetery.

Rev Lonnie Palmer, Jr
Birth:
Mar. 9, 1932
Pfeiffer
Independence County,
Arkansas
Death:
Aug. 23, 2015
Ada
Pontotoc County, Oklahoma
Burial:
Oaklawn Cemetery
Batesville
Independence County, Arkansas

Born to Lonnie and Minnie Williams Palmer. He came to the Allen, Oklahoma area in 2000. He married Lillian Bernice Crow on September 12, 1951. She preceded him in death in 2012. He received his degree from Free Will Bible College in Nashville, Tennessee. Rev. Palmer served as a Free Will Baptist Missionary to the Koulango, of Ivory Coast, Africa for 43 years. He formed The Association of Free Will Baptist Churches of Ivory Coast, translated The Old Testament into the Koulango language, and founded the Free Will Baptist Bible Institute of Ivory Coast.

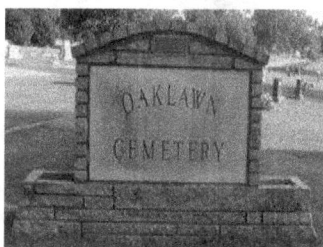

Missionary Bernice Crow Palmer
Birth:
Jan. 4, 1935
Cave City
Sharp County, Arkansas
Death:
Jan. 19, 2012
Batesville
Independence County, Arkansas
Burial:
Oaklawn Cemetery,
Batesville, Independence County
Arkansas

She served as a missionary to the Ivory Coast in Africa for 43 years.

She retired from the White River Medical Center in Batesville where she worked as a registered nurse. She was a member of the Bethel Free Will Baptist Church in Allen, Oklahoma.

Rev John J Partain
Birth:
Jun. 29, 1871
Arkansas, USA
Death:
Sep. 25, 1941
Arkansas
Burial:
Harmony Cemetery
Harmony
Johnson County
Arkansas

Rev. John J. Partain, was an ordained Free Will Baptist minister in the early beginnings of the Free Will Baptist Church in AR, being named in a roll of ministers in the 1902 session convened at Paint Rock Church in Logan County. He was on a committee to help organize Sunday Schools along with two other ministers, who reported they had organized five S.S. in Mt. Zion Ass'n, (Johnson Co.) the previous year. When and where Rev. Partain was ordained is unavailable to me, but he was active in the work.
--taken from *"History of Free Will Baptists,"* by Rev. David A. Joslin, Editor, pub. 1998. [pg 57].
Rev. Partain was married to Susan A. Jacobs/Susanna Jacobs, per AR Mar records, on 27 Dec. 1891.

James Monroe Patrick
Birth:
Mar. 12, 1854
Bradley County, Arkansas
Death:
Sep. 16, 1933
Herbine
Cleveland County, Arkansas
Burial:
Prosperity Cemetery, Pansy
Cleveland County, Arkansas

Rev. Patrick, was a pioneer Free Will Baptist Minister, spent a large portion of his life in this county and was the founder of the Free Will Macedonia church in Lee Township. He was a candidate for representative from this county several times, losing twice by narrow margins. He had many friends wherever he was known. Funeral services were conducted by Rev. J. R. Hartley, lifelong friend. His spouse was Celia Jane Johnson Patrick (1859 - 1918).

retirement years, he was a member of the Center Point Free Will Baptist Church. He was a veteran of the Navy serving during WWII.

Raymond Armster Patrick
Birth:
Sep. 12, 1919,
Vilonia, Faulkner County,
Arkansas
Death:
Jun. 30, 2001,
Vilonia,
Faulkner County,
Arkansas
Burial:
Cypress Valley Cemetery,
Faulkner County, Arkansas

He was a minister and pastor in central Arkansas. During his

Rev Henry Clay Pauley
Birth:
May 14, 1914
Death
Dec. 11, 1990
Piggott
Clay County
Arkansas
Burial:
Mount Zion Cemetery
Walcott
Greene County
Arkansas,

Henry Clay Pauley, 76, of Piggott, formerly of Greene County, retired minister, died Tuesday at his home. Services at Pruett's

Chapel Free Will Baptist Church in Light, where he was a member.

Inscription:
CPL US Army Air Corps
World War II
May 5, 1914 - December 11, 1990

L D Payne
Birth:
Aug. 29, 1936
Death:
Oct. 27, 1997
Burial:
Oak Grove Cemetery,
Chicot County,
Arkansas

He was a popular Free Will Baptist minister serving in Arkansas pastorates. He served as Private First Class in the US Army in Korea.

Rev John Mason Perren
Birth:
Unknown
Death:
Apr., 1903
Burial:
Richwoods Cemetery
Corning Clay County. Arkansas

Obituary stated he was a minister of Free Will Church.

Bruce Erwin Phillips
Birth:
Oct. 29,1902,
Washington,
Hempstead County, Arkansas
Death:
Mar. 13, 1995,
Springdale,
Washington County, Arkansas
Burial:
Burkshed Cemetery,
Washington County, Arkansas

During the time of his ministry, he was one of the strongest leaders in northwest Arkansas among some of the oldest churches in the state.

C A Pickney
Birth:
Oct. 14, 1876
Death:
Feb. 25, 1919
Burial:
Oak Forest Cemetery
Black Rock
Lawrence County, Arkansas

Early FWB minister of the Union Band Assn. pastoring the Mt. Vernon church.

Inscription:
HUSBAND OF IDA PICKNEY

Edward Louis Pickney
Birth:
Feb., 1872
Tennessee
Death:
Nov. 24, 1958
Gentry
Benton, Arkansas
Burial:
Gentry Cemetery
Gentry
Benton County. Arkansas
Plot: Blk 11 lot 31

His home in 1900 was at Dent, Lawrence, Arkansas [Imboden, Lawrence, Arkansas] Age: 28. His father, Charles Jules Pickney (1849 - 1887) was born in France. His father married Mary Louise Yarbrough Pickney (1848 - 1924), who was born in Tennessee. Edward was married twice: Jessie Edaline McConnell Pickney (1885 - 1968) and Lucy Songer Pickney (1881 - 1919).
Early FWB Minister and member of the Union Band Assn.

James H. Pierce
Birth:
Aug. 19, 1844
Death:
Jan. 24, 1922
Burial:
Thompson Cemetery
Randolph County, Arkansas
Early FWB minister pastoring the Stoney Point church and attending the Third Annual Meeting of the General Free Will Baptist at the Stoney Point church near Lima, Arkansas in 1895. Note: Civil War Veteran

Rev David W Pinkston
Birth:
Dec. 11, 1902
Arkansas
Death:
Nov. 7, 1985
Cave City
Sharp County
Arkansas
Burial:

Fairview Cemetery
Cave City
Sharp County, Arkansas

A Free Will Baptist minister, whose name is in roll of AR State Association minutes, who died between 1980-89, listing by the Districts with which they were affiliated. He was in the Social Band.

Benjamin Perry "Ben" Pixley
Birth:
Feb. 17, 1890
Death:
Nov., 1981
Fort Smith,
Sebastian County, Arkansas
Burial:
Gracelawn Cemetery,
Van Buren, Crawford County
Arkansas

The Rev. Benjamin Perry Pixley was a member of 88 Freewill Baptist Church. He was a minister for 65 years at several area Freewill Baptist churches. He was a former Mountainburg and Chester, Arkansas School board member and civic leader. He had twin sons, the Rev. Rupert Pixley and the Rev. Gilbert Pixley of Fort Smith, Arkansas who were greatly known as Free Will Baptist ministers throughout the United States.

Gilbert J. Pixley
Birth:
Jan. 25, 1920,
Rudy,
Crawford County, Arkansas
Death:
Sep. 17, 2006,
Van Buren, Crawford County,
Arkansas
Burial:
Gracelawn Cemetery,
Van Buren,
Crawford County, Arkansas

He was a minister, pastor, and evangelist for over 60 years in Arkansas, Oklahoma, California, Texas and other states. He pastored nine churches during his career. He sang, taught music schools, and wrote songs, including a popular one, *"My Child, You're Home at Last,"* which became his epitaph. He was a Navy veteran of WW II. He and his twin brother, Rupert, were an evangelistic team for years.

He baptized the author of this book.

Rupert E. Pixley
Birth:
Jan. 25, 1920,
Arkansas
Death:
Oct. 31, 2000,
Fort Smith,
Sebastian County, Arkansas
Burial:
Gracelawn Cemetery,
Van Buren,
Crawford County, Arkansas

He was a Freewill Baptist minister for 63 years, serving the

First Freewill Baptist Church in Fort Smith for 44 years before his retirement. He led this church through seven major building programs including the 700 seat auditorium that was built in 1957. In 1984 the church built a 16 thousand square-foot multipurpose building and named it the R. E. Pixley Family Center.

He was widely known as an evangelist and baptized more than 3000 converts during his ministry and the preformed over 2000 marriages. For years he had an ongoing radio ministry with a wide following. He and his twin brother, Gilbert, were known throughout the Free Will Baptists denomination as able evangelists. Many people and ministers owe their conversion to these brothers. In addition to his pastoral work, served 23 years on the Arkansas State CTS Board, a member of the State Executive Committee and served as the State Moderator. He moderated Zion Hope and Unity associations and served five years on the National Home Mission Board. At the time of his death, he was pastor of Bethlehem Free Will Baptist in Van Buren. He also was involved in the ownership of three local nursing homes.

> **The compiler of this book owes his conversion to him.**

Rev W R Porter
Birth:
Oct. 25, 1911
Death:
Oct. 3, 1982
Burial:
Manila Cemetery
Manila
Mississippi County
Arkansas

Jesse E Pratt
Birth:
Jan. 13, 1898
Death:
Nov. 4, 1983
Burial:
Rose Bud Cemetery,
Rose Bud,
White County, Arkansas

Most of his ministry and pastorates were all within the New Hope Quarterly Meeting.

Reuben E Pruitt, Jr
Birth:
Sep. 8, 1929
Death:
Dec. 10, 2000
Burial:
White County Memorial Gardens,
Searcy, White County, Arkansas

He was a popular pastor and minister in the New Hope Association in central Arkansas.

Willis L Queen
Birth:
Jan. 20, 1843
Iuka
Tishomingo County
Mississippi
Death:
Aug. 30, 1928
Logan County
Arkansas
Burial:
Carolan Cemetery
Carolan
Logan County
Arkansas

Willis L. Queen was the son of John Queen and Elizabeth Carolina "Susan" Hovis. He was first married to Vinnie Catherine Willis on September 12, 1868 in Tishomingo, Mississippi. He married his second wife, Susan Unknown, about 1885.

His name is listed in a roll of ministers in 1902 minutes of the Western Arkansas Ass'n. of Free Will Baptists, which included counties of Franklin, Logan, Scott and Sebastian.

Rev Thomas Houston Rail
Birth:
Nov. 16, 1842
Tennessee
Death
Sep. 23, 1904
Conway County
Arkansas
Burial:
Campground Cemetery
Overcup
Conway County
Arkansas

Rev. Richard Jackson Rail was married to Mary Catherine Bostian

Civil War Veteran, 117 IL Inf. Co. E; He was awarded a disability pension in 1890 for his service.

Rev. T. H. Rail, was an ordained Free Will Baptist minister in the Antioch Association of FWB, whose name appeared with those in the Arkansas State Ass'n of FWB when it met in Sept. 1902, at Paint Rock Church in Logan Co. AR. This was the fifth session of the state meeting, and the list of ministers was one of the earliest available. When and where Rev. Thomas Rail was ordained is not known at this time. He had a part in spreading the gospel in the early years of the work in Arkansas.

---taken from *"History of Arkansas Free Will Baptists"* by Rev. David A. Joslin, Editor, pub. 1998.

J. C. Rauls
Birth:
Mar. 11, 1924,
New Edinburg,
Cleveland County, Arkansas
Death:
Mar. 5, 2010,
Monticello,
Drew County, Arkansas
Burial:
Union Cemetery,
Rye, Cleveland County,Arkansas

Bi-vocational pastor, retired from Burlington Industries and served as a Free Will Baptist minister in southeast Arkansas.

John Lafayette Reding
Birth:
Dec. 18, 1839
McNairy County
Tennessee
Death:
Jan. 9, 1923
Burnville
Sebastian County
Arkansas
Burial:
Mount Harmony Cemetery
Greenwood
Sebastian County
Arkansas
Plot: M-47

He was a Free Will Baptist Minister, also a farmer. His name is listed in the 1902 minutes of the Western Arkansas Association of churches. These churches were located in Franklin, Logan, Scott and Sebastian Counties. Enlisted Union Army 10 Sep 1863 at Ft Smith, AR, age 23.into CO. F 1 AR. INF. Son of John Thomas & Sarah E. "Brown" Reding

Rev James M Richardson
Birth:
May 8, 1840
Tennessee
Death:
Feb. 14, 1923
Arkansas
Burial:
Plumlee Cemetery
Compton
Newton County
Arkansas

James M. Richardson, was listed in the ministers of the 1916 session of the AR State Ass'n of Free Will Baptists, when it convened at at Mountain Home, AR. He gave his age as '78', which is consistent with the DOB on his stone.
Also, noted that churches in Newton Co. (where he lived) were represented.
James Michael RICHARDSON "Enlisted:" on April 27, 1861 at

Murfreesboro, Tenn. by Capt. S. N. WHITE for 12 months & "Joined for duty and enrolled:" on May 1, 1861 as a Pvt. in Capt. Stephen N. WHITE's Company, 2nd Regiment Tennessee Volunteers. & finally when the Company was "Organized and Mustered into Service of the Confederate States" on May 6, 1861 he was since listed as a Pvt., Co. A, 2nd (ROBISON's) Reg't. TN. Inf.

Rev Dewitt Columbus Ring

Birth:
Jun. 11, 1851
North Carolina
Death:
Oct. 25, 1921
Arkansas
Burial:
Macey Cemetery
Monette
Craighead County
Arkansas

In honor of the pioneer work as a minister in Arkansas.
Son of, James Ring & Parmella Quillan Ring.

Rev Andrew Jackson Rowlett

Birth:
Dec. 15, 1854
Missouri
Death:
Mar. 17, 1929
Lawrence County, Arkansas
Burial:
Broom Cemetery
Lawrence County, Arkansas

A.J. Rowlett, was an ordained Free Will Baptist minister, his name appearing in Minutes of the 1902 AR State Ass'n of FWB, serving in the Polk Bayou Association. Where and when he was ordained is not available.
--from "History of Arkansas Free Will Baptists," by Rev. David A. Joslin, Editor, pub. 1998 [pg 58]. He was 8 when the Civil War took his father. General Order No. 11, forced the family to move down to Arkansas. He became a circuit preacher, riding all over to preach the gospel. He married Lucy in 1876 & when she died in 1918, he remarried. His second wife died in the horrible 1929 tornado that ravaged that portion of Arkansas.

Rev Albert Rozell
Birth:
Feb. 5, 1905
Death:
Jul. 16, 1988
Burial:
Gracelawn Cemetery
Van Buren
Crawford County, Arkansas,

A Free Will Baptist minister from Zion Hope #2 Association listed in names of ministers having d. from 1980-89, in David Joslin's "Hist. of AR Free Will Baptists. "His name was also in the 1950 list of ministers. Unknown when he was ordained.

Rev Othaniel Safirt
Birth
:   Apr. 8, 1910
Death:
Dec. 30, 1989
Burial:
Ballews Chapel Cemetery

Grubbs
Jackson County
Arkansas

Othaniel Safirt is listed in 1959 in AR state minutes, as a Free Will Baptist minister from Polk Bayou District Association in AR, and then later, in 1998, in a list of deceased ministers.

Rev Robert Satterfield
Birth:
May 15, 1915
Arkansas
Death:
Jul. 9, 1993
Fort Smith
Sebastian County
Arkansas
Burial:
Mount McCurry Cemetery
Rudy
Crawford County
Arkansas

Rev. Robert Satterfield, 78, of Alma, Arkansas died Friday, July

9, 1993, at a Fort Smith, Arkansas hospital. He was a retired minister for Freedom Freewill Baptist Church in Alma where he had pastored 20 years. He also pastored at Oliver Springs Community Church, 81 Freewill Baptist Church, Locke Freewill Baptist Church and Pigeon Creek Freewill Baptist Church.

Funeral services were at Freedom Freewill Baptist Church in Alma, Arkansas.

Rev Arch E Sebastion
Birth:
Aug. 19, 1902
Death:
Jul. 3, 1989
Burial:
Forest Park Cemetery
Fort Smith
Sebastian County
Arkansas

Arch E. Sabastion's name is listed in a roll of Free Will Baptist deceased ministers in the minutes of the Arkansas FWB State Association, his affiliation being with the Unity District Ass'n at the time of his death.

Rev Floyd W Scogin
Birth:
Apr. 30, 1919
Death:
Jun. 10, 2002
Burial:
Memorial Park Cemetery
Camden
Ouachita County
Arkansas

He was a Free Will Baptist minister in 1959, listed in roll of ministers in the Little Missouri River Association in Arkansas. When and where he was ordained is unavailable to me.

Benjamin Randle "Ben" Scott
Birth:
Feb. 23, 1924,
Mountain Grove,
Wright County, Missouri
Death:
May 20, 2010,
Pocahontas,
Randolph County, Arkansas
Burial:
Sutton Cemetery,
Pocahontas,
Randolph County, Arkansas

He was a Free Will Baptist minister serving as full time pastor for more than 50 years. His early pastorates were in the states of Oklahoma Missouri, and in Arkansas. He pastored First Free Will Baptist Church in Pocahontas, First Free Will Baptist Church in Jonesboro, and for twenty-four years, the First Free Will Baptist Church in North Little Rock.

In semi-retirement Bro. Scott served as interim pastor for First Free Will Baptist Church in Myrtle, Missouri; United Free Will Baptist Church in Walnut Ridge and First Free Will Baptist Church in Jonesboro. He served on numerous boards within the denomination on all levels; District Assn's, State Convention and the National Association. Bro. Scott was a member of Sutton Free Will Baptist Church in Pocahontas.

He was natural church builder and had good success at all the places where he pastored. All three of his sons are Free Will Baptist pastors. His wife Genelle was very active with and in the Woman's Auxiliary.

James Leroy Scudder
Birth:
Sep. 18, 1931
Coffman
Lawrence County
Arkansas
Death:
Jan. 22, 2014
Jonesboro
Craighead County
Arkansas
Burial:
Crossroads Cemetery
Portia
Lawrence County, Arkansas

Leroy Scudder was the son of the late Murrell and Fay Oldham Scudder. He was an ordained preacher and minister of music for many years and served at the First Freewill Baptist Church, Walnut Ridge, Arkansas, for over twenty-five years. He was employed by Scripture Press Publications for many years, a Piano Tuner and Manager of the Walnut Ridge Shepherd's Care. He was a member of the Lawrence County Ministerial Alliance. He had a brother who was a Southern Baptist minister. Leroy was a graduate of Free Will Baptist Bible College in Nashville.

He was united in marriage December 16, 1950 to Luella Bearry. Bro. David Harper and Rev. Steve Trail officiated.

Charles Freeman Seals
Birth:
Aug. 10, 1918
Kingston
Madison County, Arkansas
Death:
Oct. 25, 1990
Springdale
Washington County, Arkansas,
Burial:
Upper Campground Cemetery
Kingston, Madison County
Arkansas

Charles F. Seals, 72, died at Springdale Memorial Hospital. He was in Kingston, the son of Charlie Columbus and Ada Edna Cline Seals. He was a retired truck driver for Duncan Produce in Springdale and was a member of the Colbaugh Free Will Baptist Church. He was ordained as a Free Will Baptist minister in 1970. His name was listed in roll of "Ministers Deceased" in 1997 Minutes of the Arkansas State Association of Free Will Baptists. Services were at Sisco Chapel of Springdale with the Rev. Earl Dean Morris and the Rev. Dave Casteel officiating.

Melvin Lee Shelton
Birth:
Mar. 13, 1922
O'Kean Randolph County
Arkansas
Death:
May 26, 2012
Jonesboro
Craighead County Arkansas
Burial:
Randolph Memorial Gardens
Pocahontas
Randolph County Arkansas

Melvin was a pastor for 64 years and had been the pastor of Northside Freewill Baptist Church in Pocahontas for the last 35 years.

Robert S Shelton
Birth:
Aug. 3, 1888,
Mountain View,
Howell County, Missouri
Death:
Oct. 31, 1954,
Old Reyno,
Randolph County, Arkansas
Burial:
Sharum Cemetery,
Pocahontas,
Randolph County, Arkansas

He was a preacher along with running his merchandise store in Okean. He was very active in the Social Band Association and a leader in the state Association.

H. D. "Dick" Shipley
Birth:
Jul. 3, 1917,
Arkansas
Death:
Jan. 3, 1996,
Barling, Sebastian County,
Arkansas
Burial:
Gill Cemetery,
Van Buren,
Crawford County, Arkansas

He pastored a number of churches in Arkansas and Oklahoma and founded the First Free Will Baptist Church of Greenwood and the Cavanaugh First Free Will Baptist of Fort Smith. He also was employed by Harding Glass Co. for 31 years. He was a member of First Free Will Baptist Church for 46 years.

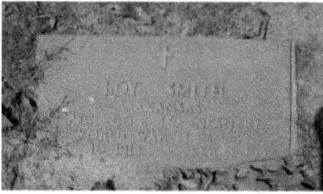

Rev Loy Smith
Birth:
Dec. 10, 1915
Death:
Feb. 4, 1967
Burial:
Mount Zion Cemetery
Jerusalem
Conway County
Arkansas,

He was a WW II U.S. Army
veteran and a   FWB minister..

Berne Ora Stahl
Birth:
Dec. 8, 1913
Arkansas
Death:
Mar. 4, 1971
Dardanelle, Yell County,
Arkansas
Burial:
Bethel Cemetery,
Kingston,Yell County, Arkansas

He had been an active minister
for his last 14 years. Rev. Stahl
was a native of Plainview, pastor
of the Danville Free Will Baptist
Church. He left many of his family
active in the Lord's service. His
legacy remains in them.

Rev Jeremiah Arnold Stark
Birth:
1848
Death:
1942
Arkansas
Burial:
Pollard Cemetery
Dover
Pope County
Arkansas

Rev. J. A. Stark was in a roll of
minister's names in the 1900
Pope Co. Association meeting of
the Free Will Baptists, where he
stated he had been in the
ministry thirteen (13) years at
that time. His address was at
Moreland.
--from *"History of Arkansas Free
Will Baptists,"* by Rev. David A.
Joslin, Editor, pub. 1998, pg. 11.

Fred B. Starnes
Birth:
Dec. 6, 1875
Death:
Oct. 20, 1909
Burial:
Jenkins Cemetery
Lawrence County, Arkansas

He was first licensed as an exhorter in the Methodist denomination but becoming dissatisfied united with the Free Will Baptists spending time in Portia and old Walnut Ridge. He was a co-worker with Elder Dave Bandy during his life-time.

Charles R Staten
Birth:
unknown
Death:
Nov. 7, 1986
Burial:
Browns Chapel Cemetery,
Paragould,
Greene County, Arkansa,
Plot: 11, row 32

His ministry was mainly in the north eastern part of the state.

Ralph Lee Staten
Birth:
Jul. 11, 1911,
O'Kean,
Randolph County,Arkansas
Death:
Oct. 6, 1997,
Knoxville,
Knox County, Tennessee
Burial:
Masonic Cemetery,
Pocahontas,
Randolph County, Arkansas

He was a combination itinerant pastor and public school teacher in Northeast Arkansas in his early ministry. He later pastored in Arkansas, Alabama, Oklahoma, North Carolina and Virginia. In the early days of his ministry he was known for his debates with ministers of other denominations debating the doctrines of Free Will Baptists. He was also a writer beginning in his early ministry. He attended the 1935 organizational meeting in Nashville, Tenn. which formed the National Association of Free Will Baptists.

Samuel Thomas Sutton
Birth:
Jul. 29, 1872
Death:
Jun. 5, 1932
Burial:
Sutton Cemetery
Pocahontas
Randolph County, Arkansas

He was the son of James F. Sutton and Ann Noblin. He married Dora B. Cannon in 1891 at Randolph Co., Arkansas and they had Ira Tom Sutton (1892 - 1974), Clarence Sutton (1899 - ___), Nellie Sutton (1907 - 1914).

Rev Lowell Lonnie Tanner
Birth:
1914
Death:
Jun. 21, 1985
Burial:
Pisgah Cemetery
Pottsville
Pope County
Arkansas

An ordained Free Will Baptist minister,who is listed in roll of deceased ministers names from 1980-89, as recorded in the annual Minutes of the AR State Association of FWB. His name was also in a 1958 list of ministers, but unk where and when he was ordained.

Rev Andrew Franklin Taylor
Birth:
1876
Murray County, Georgia
Death:
Mar. 25, 1941
Greene County, Arkansas
Burial:
North New Hope Cemetery
Dover
Pope County, Arkansas

He was an early minister in the Free Will Baptist church,and church records show he preached in the 1913 Arkansas State Association, and he served on the temperance committee in 1918.

Elder John W. Tharp
Birth: 1882
Death: 1960
Burial:
Lawrence Memorial Park
Walnut Ridge
Lawrence County, Arkansas
Plot: Section 12,
Old Lane Block 2-11,
Between Bluejay & Bluebird

"John W. Tharp was the son of a Pennsylvanian from German descent, small of stature with a keen eye and mind.

He was ordained a Free Will Baptist minister at the Yearly Meeting of Union Band Ass'n, AR, in 1907. After his ordination he was engaged some in pastoral supply and revival work. He united with the Social Band Association in 1910. He was pretty well posted in the scriptures, a fairly good speaker and an energetic worker."

Rev Rayburn Arnold Teague
Birth:
Oct. 23, 1918
Death:
Jan. 22, 1988
Russellville
Pope County, Arkansas
Burial:
Saint Joe Cemetery
Atkins
Pope County, Arkansas

He was an ordained Free Will Baptist minister from the Antioch District Association of FWB, in 1959 church records.

Roy Lathan Thompson
Birth:
Jan. 16, 1938
New Edinburg,
Cleveland County, Arkansas
Death:
Dec. 7, 2002
Heber Springs,
Cleburne County, Arkansas
Burial:
Hickory Springs Cemetery,
Hermitage,
Bradley County, Arkansas

Rev Lewis J Thronesberry
Birth:
Jan. 29, 1835
Bedford County, Tennessee.
Death:
Jan. 28, 1896
Burial:
Sutton Cemetery
Pocahontas
Randolph County, Arkansas

He moved with his father's family, while yet a youth, to Randolph County, Arkansas. He was one of the pioneer preachers and one of the charter members of an Independent church organized by Elder Poyner, and was ordained and did a great work. The association, as a remembrance of his labors, erected a monument at his grave. At the age of fourty was ordained to preach by the Free Will Baptist. He had a son Lewis Carlson Thronesbery (1888 - 1930).

Clarence H Tice
Birth:
Feb. 13, 1907
Marble
Madison County, Arkansas
Death:
May 1, 1985
Spring Valley
Washington County, Arkansas
Burial:
Big Sandy Church Cemetery
Purdy
Madison County, Arkansas

An ordained Free Will Bapt. minister listed in AR FWB State Association Minutes of dec'd ministers from 1980-1989. He was affiliated with the Old Mt. Zion District Association. Unk when and where he was ordained or pastorates he held. He served during World War II. Hia Parents: John Samuel Tice (1876 - 1948) & Mary Alice Garrison Tice (1886 - 1941

Rev James Henry Treadwell
Birth: 1851
Death: 1914
Burial:
Walnut Grove Cemetery
Hector
Pope County
Arkansas

Rev Morris Lee Tucker
Birth:
Aug. 8, 1909
Rosie
Independence County
Arkansas
Death:
Mar. 14, 1989
Steelville
Crawford County
Missouri
Burial:
Maple Springs Cemetery
Batesville
Independence County
Arkansas

The Rev. Morris Lee Tucker, 79, of Steeleville, Missouri, died, at his home. He was the son of the late Robert & Bessie Young Tucker.. He married Raye Prater at Batesville on June 30, 1934. She preceded him in death on December 7, 1965. He married Hester Glenn at St. Louis, Missouri, on April 8, 1966. He was also preceded in death by his parents; a son, Don Tucker. Tucker had been a minister with the Freewill Baptist denomination since 1955. He was retired from McDonnell-Douglas Aircraft of St. Louis. At the time of his sickness & death he was attending & involved in the ministry of the 1st Baptist Church of Steeleville. Funeral services were at the Britton Brothers Funeral Home Chapel with the Rev. Dale Skiles officiating.
Remembered here as a Free Will Baptist minister, shown in list of ministers having d. from 1980-89 in "David Joslin's Hist. of AR FWB" pg 139. He was reported in the Polk Bayou FWB Dist. Association.

Wayne Tucker, Jr
Birth:
Jul. 22, 1921
Death:
Jan. 31, 1996
Burial:
Pirtle Cemetery,
Peach Orchard,
Clay County, Arkansas
His ministry was mainly in the Social Band Association in north eastern Arkansas. He served with the US Army During WWII.

Rev Elmer Turner
Birth:
Sep. 5, 1895
Branch
Franklin County, Arkansas
Death:
Apr. 10, 1987
Fort Worth
Tarrant County, Texas
Burial:
Garden of Memories Cemetery
Charleston
Franklin County, Arkansas

A Free Will Baptist minister, whose name is listed in AR State Association of FWB minutes, 1989, who had died between 1980-1989. In 1959, he was listed in same Arkansas Dist. Association on their ministers' roll.

Rev George Robert Turney
Birth:
Mar. 10, 1879
Death: 1957
Burial:
Low Gap Cemetery
Low Gap
Newton County
Arkansas

He was born at St. Joe, AR to John and Zula Eoff Turney. He was a retired minister and life resident of Boone and Searcy counties. He was 78 when he passed away at his home in Harrison, AR.

Elder John Scott Turney
Birth:
Jul. 14, 1854
Arkansas
Death:
Aug. 14, 1919
Arkansas
Burial:
Union Chapel Cemetery
Garfield
Benton County
Arkansas

Eld. John S. Turney was a pioneer Free Will Baptist minister in the old Mt. Zion Ass'n, in northeastern AR. He was listed in a roll of ordained ministers in the 1919 association minutes, stating he was 65 yrs of age. When and where he was ordained is not available.
He married Zuba Ann Eoff, and in 1900 Benton Co. AR census, stated they were m. abt 1874.

Rev James Buchanan Vaughan
Birth:
1857
Pope County
Arkansas
Death:
1929
Moreland
Pope County
Arkansas
Burial:
Hudson Cemetery
Moreland
Pope County
Arkansas

s/o Archibald Dodson Napier and Melissa Elizabeth (Vaughan) Napier Pinnell Brown. NOTE: They had 5 children but only 1

child was given the surname Napier for reasons unknown at this time.

James's siblings were: George Washington Vaughan b.1855; Joannah J. Napier b.1859; Telitha K. Vaughan b.1860; and Lucinda Parleen Amanda Jane Lincoln Vaughan b.1863. James B. Vaughan married Eliza M. Jones 11 March 1877 in Pope County, Arkansas. They had 4 children of whom only two lived to adulthood.

- Beckie (Carter) Williams

Joanna J. Napier was a daughter of Archibald and his wife Mary H. Vaughan, Melissa Elizabeth Vaughan's sister. The stone visible in the Napier family cemetery clearly reads M.H. as the mother. Melissa's children were all named Vaughan.

Rev Joe A Venable
Birth:
Dec. 1, 1872
Death:
Jan., 1966
Arkansas
Burial:
Saint Joe Cemetery
Atkins
Pope County, Arkansas

His name is Joseph Albert

Venable, the son of Joseph Ezekiel Venable. He pastored St. Joe Free Will Baptist Church, in Adkins, AR from 1906-1908.

Ruben Bunyan Venable
Birth:
Jul. 12, 1877
Arkansas
Death:
Jul. 19, 1954
Atkins
Pope County, Arkansas
Burial:
Saint Joe Cemetery
Atkins
Pope County, Arkansas

A Free Will Baptist minister and pastor from Pope Co. AR. Listed in a 1953 photo as a minister at the Ark. State Association of FWB. His spouse: Mary Ann Atkins Venable (1876 - 1959).

Christians have no fear of death.

Robert Newton Vinson
Birth:
Mar. 3, 1845
Arkansas
Death:
Dec. 27, 1904
Pocahontas
Randolph County
Arkansas
Burial:
Thompson Cemetery
Randolph County, Arkansas

He married Mrs. Frances Poe, 6 October 1901 in Clay Co, AR. Other spouses: Sarah F. Adair Vinson (1826 - ___), Elizabeth Ann Tyler Vinson (1857 - 1901) Minister of the Beautiful Home church and represented it at the 1895 Third Annual Meeting of the Union Band Assn. at the Stony Point Church near Lima, Arkansas.

Ray Watkins
Birth:
Jun. 22, 1905
Death:
Aug. 25, 1985
Burial:
Ballews Chapel Cemetery
Grubbs
Jackson County
Arkansas

A Free Will Bapt. minister, shown in list of dec'd ministers from 1980-89, in David Joslin's Hist. of AR FWB, pg. 139. He was reported as being from the Polk Bayou Association.

Elder Hugh Warren
Birth:
Jan. 29, 1837
Indiana
Death:
Apr. 3, 1936
Johnson County
Arkansas
Burial:
Union Cemetery
Johnson County
Arkansas,

Eld. Hugh Warren, was listed in the roll of ministers of Mt. Zion Association, located principally in Johnson Co., 1904 being the earliest available minutes. When and where he was ordained is unavailable. Another, minister, William Warren, was also listed in Johnson Co. Whether related is unknown. [This info taken from *"History of Arkansas Free Will Baptists,"* by Rev. David A. Joslin, Editor, pub. 1998.]

Reece G. Webb
Birth:
Jul. 10, 1900
Death:
Feb. 7, 1981
Burial:
Atkins City Cemetery
Atkins
Pope County, Arkansas

An ordained FreeWill Baptist minister in early Arkansas records. His name is listed in the roll of ministers in 1953 State Association Minutes. (see David Joslin's *"History of Arkansas FWB."* Spouse: Ada M. Littleton Webb (1900 - 1993)*

Rev Chester F Weir
Birth:
Oct. 7, 1921
White County
Arkansas
Death:
Jul. 31, 1980
Pulaski County
Arkansas
Burial:
Weir Cemetery
Searcy
White County
Arkansas
Tec 4 US Army WWII
DS w/ Virginia

He is listed in AR Association of Free Will Baptists in a list of deceased ministers from 1980-1989. He was from the New Hope District.

Rev Bill Wheeler
Birth:
Apr. 26, 1926
Warren
Bradley County, Arkansas
Death:
Aug. 19, 2004
Little Rock
Pulaski County, Arkansas
Burial:

Willoughby Cemetery
Warren
Bradley County, Arkansas

Rev. Bill Wheeler, age 78, of Little Rock, (formerly of Warren), died at John McClellan V.A. Medical Center in Little Rock.
He was a retired Freewill Baptist minister, a mechanic and maintenance director at Camp Beaverfork, member Faith Freewill Baptist Church and a World War II Army veteran.
Funeral services was at Frazer's Chapel by Rev. Johnny Jones and Rev. Rudell Smith. Janice Sullivan was the organist and Bernadette Jones sang. Burial was in Willoughby Cemetery by Frazer's Funeral Home of Warren.

James E White
Birth:
Feb. 4, 1905
Arkansas
Death:
Jan. 10, 2000
Arkansas
Burial:
Willoughby Cemetery,
Warren,
Bradley County, Arkansas

Rev. White was the son of an ordained Free Will Baptist minister, as was his brother Stanton White. He had a long ministry in Arkansas completing over 70 years as a pastor, evangelist and church organizer. He was 94 years of age at the time of his death which was just short of his 95th birthday. He was saved at age 12 and ordained to the ministry at age 25 in 1929. His ministry was basically a bi-vocational one serving during the great depression. He labored in both south Arkansas and north Louisiana, pastoring 14 churches and organizing three.

He officiated at more than 700 funerals and finally lost the count of the number of his converts that he baptized. Rev. Ben Scott, who preached the funeral of, Rev. White, said of him, "He was a typical old-fashioned, Bible-toting, hard-hitting preacher. And was always where the action was. He was very forthright, but that the same time very tender and loving. His influence in the Saline Association was without equal. He was a moderator, served on the executive committee, examining board, and many other positions during his time as a pastor. He was well known for his doctrinal sermons and his compassion for the lost.

Jack Williams, Former *Contact* editor was saved under Brother Whites ministry, as well as many others. Brother Williams, said that the sermons of Brother White still echo in his life after more than 50 years of service.

Stanton B. White
Birth:
Mar. 14, 1913
Death:
Oct. 31, 1997
Burial:
Willoughby Cemetery,
Warren, Bradley County,
Arkansas

He was a retired machine operator for Potlatch Corp., a Freewill Baptist minister and a member of Willoughby Freewill Baptist Church at Warren. He was the son of W.P. White and a brother of J.E. White, both FWB preachers. His daughter Sue White married Bobby Aycock and they served as missionaries in Brazil.

Founders and strong leaders in building Saline Assn. in South Arkansas.

William Pleasant White
Birth:
Nov. 5, 1873
Death:
May 26, 1952
Arkansas
Burial:
Willoughby Cemetery,Warren,
Bradley County, Arkansas

He was an early ordained Free Will Baptist minister, who had two sons, James E. and Stanton, who were also FWB ministers and whose influence still exists in the Saline Assn. in Southern Arkansas.

Will S. White
Birth:
Aug. 29, 1890,
Death:
Mar. 27, 1973,
Randolph County,
Arkansas Burial:
Masonic Cemetery,

Pocahontas,
Randolph County,
Arkansas

He was a faithful servant coming to Christ later in life. Organizing at least four churches and ministered them until a pastor came. He was also an active school teacher leaving many Christian roots in his students and churches. He published a book on his life in the mid 50's that has been reprinted by FWB Publications.

Rev Isaac Jasper Whiteley
Birth:
Apr. 4, 1802
Russell County, Virginia
Death:
1889
Carroll County, Arkansas
Burial:
Liberty Cemetery
Dinsmore
Newton County, Arkansas

Son of Joseph & Sarah Ann (Stapleton) Whiteley. Married Priscilla Seehorn, March 24, 1867 Newton County, Arkansas, they later divorced. Isaac was a

Tanner and a United Baptist Church Missionary.

Rev. Isaac Whiteley's name is associated with the earliest United/Free Will Baptist ministers in Arkansas. Goodspeed credits with early Arkansas church in 1837, and Isaac's bro, Samuel Whitely, also a minister, and Charles B. Whitely, were in NW AR by 1832, per family history. Isaac was in the Madison Co. 1840 census, and a land record is found for him there, in Aug. 1844.

Rev. Whiteley had 3 known wives and 10 children.

Susannah Johnston (1803-1842) married Ike in 1823 and bore him 9 children: Cynthia, Mary Elizabeth, Samuel, Joseph, Louisa, William, Nancy Adeline, Sarah Ann and Lewis W. Whiteley.

Elizabeth McCamish (1811-1867) married Ike in 1850 and bore him 1 child: James Knox Polk Whiteley.

He married Priscilla Seahorn (1805-1903) in 1867 and they divorced in 1883. They had no children.

Rev Jerrell Willingham
Birth:
Apr. 6, 1936
Beaumont
Jefferson County, Texas
Death:
Mar. 26, 2011
Little Rock
Pulaski County, Arkansas
Burial:
Shady Grove Cemetery
Atkins
Pope County, Arkansas

Rev. Jerrell Willingham, 74, of Russellville died at the Arkansas Heart Hospital.

He was born to the late William "Bill" and Versa Hamilton Willingham. He was retired from Tyson Foods and was a minister at the Egypt Free Will Paptist Church in Blue Ball. He was married to his wife, Lilla Duvall Willingham, on Sept. 24, 1955, in Russellville.Funeral services were held at Lemley Chapel with the Rev. Hank Duvall and Rev. Jackie Allen officiating.

Chester Emmit Wilson
Birth:
Jan. 9, 1897
Arkansas
Death:
Dec. 4, 1949

Pulaski Co.
Little Rock, Arkansas
Burial:
East Shady Grove Cemetery
Greenbrier
Faulkner County, Arkansas

He was an early FWB minister in Central Arkansas and pastored a number of churches in the New Hope Assn., He married a Ethel Smith in 1918 and at his passing she continued his ministry. He served in WWI Ark Pvt 158 Inf 40th Div.

Ethel E Wilson
Birth:
Dec. 14, 1901
Death:
Nov. 23, 2001
Burial:
East Shady Grove Cemetery
Greenbrier
Faulkner County
Arkansas

She was a lady minister in New Hope Assn. after assuming the ministry of her husband.

Rev Issac Jefferson Wilson
Birth:
Jun. 15, 1876
Gravelly
Yell County
Arkansas
Death:
Jun. 25, 1968
Booneville
Logan County
Arkansas
Burial:
Parks Cemetery
Charleston
Franklin County
Arkansas

Son of John Anderson Wilson and Nancy Ann Holiman. He was an ordained minister of the Freewill Baptist Church.

He obtained his nickname "one eye"due to being struck in the eye by a thorn bush limb while riding in an open wagon. The thorn pierced his eye causing him to lose vision in that eye.

**IF GOD CALLED YOU TO
PREACH-PREACH!!**

Rev Dewel Lee Wright
Birth:
Aug. 22, 1920
Death:
Jul. 24, 1981
Burial:
Oakland Cemetery
Atkins
Pope County
Arkansas

An ordained Free Will Bapt. minister, shown in list of dec'd ministers from 1980-89, in David Joslin's Hist. of AR FWB, pg. 139. He was from Little Missouri River Association when he died.

I bless the Christ of God,
I rest on love divine,
And with unfaltering lip and heart,
I call the Saviour mine.
His cross dispels each doubt;
I bury in his tomb
Each thought of unbelief and fear,
Each lingering shade of gloom.

Brazil

Missionary Geneva Poole
Birth:
unknown
South Carolina
Death:
Nov. 20, 2013, Brazil
Burial:
Buried in Brazil

Geneva Poole, veteran missionary to Brazil entered her heavenly home November 20, 2013. Diagnosed with lung cancer in April 2012, Mrs. Poole's trust in the Lord and His plan for her remained firm as did her determination to continue to serve Him as He provided strength.

Bobby and Geneva were appointed to missionary service in Brazil in April 1960. They were married in September and entered Brazil as newlyweds in December 1960. The couple has served faithfully through the tenures of all six of the Mission's general directors.

When the Pooles entered Brazil, less than 2% of the people claimed to be Protestant Christians. Today, that number has risen to approximately 23%. Ribeirão Preto, an educational center in the state of São Paulo, has been the Pooles' place of service since February 1962. They started four churches in the area. Geneva continued to plan, develop, and prepare vacation Bible school materials and teach in the seminary over the last year.

Geneva accepted Christ when she was 13 years old at Lebanon FWB Church in Effingham, S.C. At a young age she developed a conviction that God wanted her on the mission field. That conviction was confirmed while at Welch College.

Bobby and Geneva have garnered 53 years of faithful missionary service and have spent the last few months in transition in preparation to retire on December 31, 2013. Over the years, they engaged in prison ministry, prepared Bible studies, established a long-running radio ministry and telephone answering service that shared Scripture 24/7, sponsored vacation Bible schools, began and promoted camps and retreats to foster spiritual growth and encourage community, and founded a Bible institute/seminary that has trained men and women for more than 40 years.

Geneva Poole leaves behind her husband Bobby and sons Robert and John, both born in Brazil, and their families. Brazil's laws require interment within 24 hours. The funeral service was held at 9:00 a.m. November 21st at the Marincek FWB Church, which is the most current church started by the Pooles.

I bless the Christ of God,
I rest on love divine,
And with unfaltering lip and heart,
I call the Saviour mine.
His cross dispels each doubt;
I bury in his tomb
Each thought of unbelief and fear,
Each lingering shade of gloom.

California

Rev Blaine David Bishop
Birth:
Aug. 21, 1912
Scircleville
Clinton County, Indiana
Death:
Feb. 23, 2002
Turlock
Stanislaus County, California
Burial:
Turlock Memorial Park
Turlock
Stanislaus County
California

His name was included in the New Mexico Association as being moderator of fourth session in 1972.

Rev Francis W. Boyle
Birth:
unknown
Death:
Sep. 24, 2015
Santa Paula
Ventura County, California
Burial
Pierce Brothers Santa Paula
Cemetery
Santa Paula
Ventura County,California

Boyle served in the 526th Armored Infantry Battalion, Company B. He landed at Utah Beach in June of 1944, and fought in the Battle of the Bulge. He served two years in the Europe campaign after being deployed from Santa Paula, where he had lived on and off since he was 11 years old. Boyle was drafted in February 1943.

After stateside training Boyle's unit was sent overseas in January 1944.Boyle's unit landed on Utah Beach and then his unit worked their way through France and Belgium where they fought in the Battle of Bulge. His unit got four Battle Stars. . .they were in combat for 208 days, loss over half of our unit. He was discharged in March 1946. Post war Boyle became a Free Will Baptist minister and a Realtor/Broker. He has led 10 churches, including in Santa Paula, Boyle became a Charter Member of the WWII Memorial effort and helped in fundraising. Francis Boyle served as Business Manager for Hillsdale FWB College in the 80's.Memorial Services was at the Santa Paula Free Will Baptist Church.

Bobby Lee Brown
Birth:
Jun. 1, 1945
Turlock,
Stanislaus County, California
Death:
Jun. 18, 1967
Modesto,
Stanislaus County, California
Burial:
Turlock Memorial Park. Turlock
Stanislaus County; California,
Plot: Lot 64 Block 27

Had not long been a minister
when he was stricken with a
deadly disease.

Rev Chester S. Burgess
Birth:
May 8, 1926
Death:
Feb. 21, 2001
Burial:
College City Cemetery
College City
Colusa County
California

An ordained Free Will Baptist
minister, and active in its Calif.
state work. He served on
Program Committee in 1973, and
was residing in College City then.

Inscription:
POPPIE PVT US Army Air Forces
World War II

Rev William Halsey Callison
Birth:
Dec. 7, 1899
Missouri
Death:

Nov. 12, 1972
Yolo County, California
Burial:
Winters Cemetery
Winters
Yolo County, California
Plot: Sec 5 Lot 182 NWQ
Callison Plot

In list of Calif. State Association
of Free Will Bapt. minister's
deaths, in June, 1973 Minutes. He
was pastor of Winters church.
Note: died in Davis, Ca 72 yrs old
-Smith Chapel.

Rev Charles R. Cantrell
Birth:
1932
Death:
2005
Burial:
Oak View Memorial Park
Antioch
Contra Costa County, California

Minister/pastor for several years
of Exeter, CA Free Will Bapt.
church. He was active in the state
and local work of his church.

Rev Daniel Clay
Birth:
Aug. 25, 1816
Buxton
York County,
Maine
Death:
Mar. 18, 1907
Los Angeles
Los Angeles County,
California
Burial:
Angelus Rosedale Cemetery
Los Angeles
Los Angeles County
California
Plot: Section N

Rev Daniel Clay
Birth:
Aug. 25, 1816
Buxton
York County, Maine
Death:
Mar. 18, 1907
Los Angeles
Los Angeles County,California
Burial:
Angelus Rosedale Cemetery
Los Angeles

Los Angeles County
California
Plot: Section N

Affiliated with the Free Baptists in the Northeastern U.S. A bio sketch states he ministered mostly in San Pedro, CA.

William E. B. Condit
Birth:
May 1, 1924
Locust Grove
Mayes County, Oklahoma
Death:
Jun. 24, 2013
Pryor
Mayes County, Oklahoma
Burial:
Cherokee Memorial Park
Lodi
San Joaquin County, California

Dr. William E. B. Condit was born to W. C. Pigeon (Ross) Condit. E. B. graduated from Locust Grove High School in 1943. He furthered his education at Northeastern State College where he graduated in 1953 with a degree in Industrial Arts. He finished his education by obtaining his Doctorate of Theology while living in Sacramento, CA. E. B. served his country proudly in the United States Navy from October 1, 1943 until January 11, 1946. On July 5, 1946, Mary Louise Littlefield and William E.B. Condit were united in marriage. This began a marriage of 67 years that coupled raising a family in the ministry, pastoring churches from North Carolina to California, ministering for over 64 years. On Aug. 1, 1949 Condit was ordained to preach as a Free Will Baptist Minister. In 1949 he organized the Little Rock Free Will Baptist Church east of Locust Grove where he was their first pastor. He then spent 1 year at Lowry Free Will Baptist Church before organizing Trinity Free Will Baptist Church in Muskogee. After 3 years there, E.B. was the pastor at Free Will Baptist Churches in Wewoka, OK, Bakersfield, CA, Ponca City, OK, Modesto, CA, Campbell, CA, Concord, CA, Ontario, CA, Farmville, NC, back to Campbell, CA, and Lompoc, CA. He also served as interim pastor for home missions at many churches in between. E.B. served on the California State Mission Board as well as the California Christian College Board for 17 years. Many pastors and Christian leaders were born from E.B.s ministry throughout the years. Before moving back to OK, they lived in Lodi, CA. Their ministry in California spanned over 38 years. He and his wife moved back to Mayes County, OK in

1998 where they lived west of Pryor. He remained an honorary member of Capital Free Will Baptist Church in Sacramento, CA. He always put God first. He also treasured the time he spent with his family provided a great fatherly image for his children grandchildren to follow. Every two months, his family would receive a hand written encouraging message from him. E.B. loved to watch football. He was a avid Oklahoma Sooner Football fan! He was also a fan of the San Francisco 49ers. E.B. was very patriotic was known to write governmental dignitaries to share what he believed to be right. For 5 years, E.B. played guitar sang in a family quartet that shared in song preaching by broadcasting at KOLS radio in Pryor. He was also a founding member of the original Cherokee Ramblers Band. E.B.'s life serves as an example to follow his ministry will flourish for many generations to come. Reverend Adrian Condit and Reverend Larry Condit officiated.

Osmondo Corrales
Birth:
Dec. 4, 1921
Pinar del Rio, Cuba
Death:
Mar. 7, 2013
Culver City
Los Angeles County, California
Burial:
Inglewood Park Cemetery
Inglewood

Los Angeles County, California Osmundo Corrales was born in the small community of El Sábalo located in the Pinar del Rio province of Cuba.

His parents, Cerbellon Corrales Yut and Rosa Blanco Menéndez, were excellent examples and guided him well in his life especially in the areas of respect, honor and interpersonal relations. He was the next to the last among eight siblings: Antonio, Eusebia, Luz Maria, Josefina, Andrea, Cándido, Osmundo and Magdalena.

He embraced the Gospel of Jesus Christ during the decade of the 40's when he was 19 years old. In October 1941 he was baptized by immersion in a strong flowing river by Rev. Luis Díaz. In October 1944 he enrolled in the Free Will Baptist Seminary, "Cedros del Libano". During the summer of 1947 he was called as interim pastor of the church in the small town of Arcos de Canasí, in the Province of Matanzas. He later returned to the Seminary in the fall of 1948 to continue his Seminary studies. He received his graduation degree from the

Seminary in 1950. One year later, May 16, 1951, he was ordained as a minister of the Gospel with the laying on of hands of the presbytery of the Seminary where he graduated and where they were celebrating the National Convention. In the fall of 1945, Osmundo met a young lady that had come to enroll as a student in the Seminary. For 62 years Celia was his faithful companion in the ministry which he had chosen in obedience to God's calling. From Osmundo and Celia's marriage were born two children, a daughter, Omayda and a son, Omar. Corrales was pastor of several churches: Free Will Baptist, Viñales, provincial de Pinar del Rio, Cuba, Free Will Baptist, La Lisa – Marianao, Cuba. Free Will Baptist Church, Bryan, Texas; Resurrection Free Will Baptist Church, Culver City, California. Brother Corrales was a living example of love for God. He has left a void in the pews of his church and in the hearts of all of his brothers and sisters in Christ, which will only be filled when we too are in the presence of our glorious Savior.

Luther R Crumb
Birth:
1891
Death:
1973
Burial:
North Kern Cemetery,
Delano,
Kern County, California

He began preaching in the many rural churches found in eastern OK. Where he was ordained is unknown, but was enumerated in old minutes of the Free Will Baptist Association of churches and was an active minister. Sometime after 1940, removed to central California, where he again, preached and carried on with church work, while working to provide for his family. During a time when he stopped to help a motorist, a fire ensued, burned his arm so badly, it was amputated from the elbow down. For sure, this was a great loss, but after some recovery, he went on working with one hand. He preached, attended meetings, until health prevented it.

William H. Dalton
Birth:
16 Jan 1870
Arkansas
Death:
9 Dec 1947
Solano County,
California
Buria:
Sunrise Memorial Cemetery
Vallejo, Solano County,
California

Spouse:Effie Leona Thomas Dalton 1875–1944
He and his wife were both Free Will Baptist ministers in Arkansas and Oklahoma. They were the parents of the wellknown song writer Marvin P. Dalton.

Rev. Effie Leona Thomas Dalton
Birth:
12 Jun 1875 Texas
Death:
6 Jul 1944
Solano County, California
Burial:
Sunrise Memorial Cemetery
Vallejo, Solano County,
California

Orbin Hurst Doss
Birth:
Feb. 28, 1912,
Arkansas
Death:
Dec. 28, 1985,
Stanislaus County,
California
Burial:
Turlock Memorial Park,

Turlock,
Stanislaus County,
California,
Plot: Lot 233 Block 28

Native of Arkansas, he had lived in Turlock since 1979. He was a pastor in Arizona, Oklahoma, Arkansas, and in California at Hughson and Modesto. He served on various boards and committees during his successful ministry.

Israel Bunyan Dunaway
Birth:
Apr. 7, 1884,
Hartselle,
Morgan County,Alabama
Death:
Mar. 30, 1960,
Fresno County,California
Burial:
Mountain View Cemetery,
Fresno,Fresno County,
California.

He was an ordained minister of the Free Will Baptist Church, and was elected moderator of the Eastern Association of Oklahoma in March of 1940. He was one of the founders. It is believed he came from the Texas West Fork Association to Oklahoma, probably from Eastland, where his family is shown in the census. His name was in records and old news items in the Ada Weekly of

Pontotoc, Oklahoma. At what point he moved to California is not known. He was probably a bi-vocational minister as many were in his time.

Dr Aristide T Ferguson
Birth:
1851
Death:
1935
Burial:
Forest Lawn Memorial Park
Glendale
Los Angeles County
California
Plot: Gardenia Terrace, Great Mausoleum, Columbarium of Protection, Niche 12211

Rev. Aristide T., son of William J. and Caroline (Heitgeberg), was born on the Island of Guernsey, England, Oct. 1, 1859. He studied at his native place and at

Moody's School, Northfield, Mass. He was converted in 1870. In 1885 he did the work of an evangelist in Chicago. After two years he became pastor at Bulver, P.Q., where he was ordained June 19, 1887. In 1888 he moved to La Grange, ME, and has also under his care the churches at Milo and Medford Centre. He has been commission agent in France two years, mineralogist in California and Arizona, and cashier in Chicago. In 1888 he married Miss Nellie Turville.

Rev Horace Graves
Birth:
Sep. 27, 1834
Guilford
Piscataquis County, Maine
Death:
May 5, 1912
California,
Burial:
Woodlawn Memorial Park
Compton
Los Angeles County, California
Plot: Section S, Lot 34, Grave 1S

He became a Christian at the

age of nineteen and was a student in Bangor Theological Seminary one term. His license to preach was granted in March, 1859, and in June 1863, he ws ordained at South Dover, ME., by a council of the Sebec Quarterly Meeting (Q.M.)

His pastorates have been at South Dover, Atkinson, Bradford, East Bangor, Dover, and Springfield (1887).

In the last two places he has had revivals, and also in Bradford, where he organized the church. He married Miss Sarah A. Magoon, of Dover, ME, and has five children living.

Claudie Hames
Birth:
Nov. 22, 1925,
Kellyville,
Creek County, Oklahoma
Death:
Mar. 9, 2011,
Bakersfield,
Kern County, California
Burial:
Hillcrest Memorial Park,
Bakersfield,

Kern County, California He attended schools in Sapulpa and started working at an early age at Liberty Glass Co. He joined the 503rd Regimental Combat Paratroop Division of the Army on February 10, 1944, to serve his country during World War II. He served on Lyte, Corregidor and Negros, in the Philippine Islands. While on the Island of Corregidor, he was wounded by shrapnel with injuries to the spine. He was temporarily paralyzed and spent 59 days in the hospital before returning to battle. He was a recipient of the Purple Heart. He returned to Oklahoma and relocated to Taft to work in the oilfields after the war. He worked for Rocky Mountain Drilling Co. On May 13, 1953, he accepted the Lord as his Savior. Mr. Hames accepted the call to preach the Gospel of Christ, and within a few months accepted the pastorate of the Lamont Free Will Baptist Church. He moved to Oxnard, California to pastor the Oxnard Free Will Baptist Church, a position he held for eight years before his move to Bakersfield in July 1964 to pastor the First Free Will Baptist Church. He pastored this church until his retirement in 2001. He also served on the National Home Mission Board of Free Will Baptists during this pastorate. His greatest joy in life was door-knocking, asking people to come and visit the church, and leading someone to the Lord.

Alfred C Hogbin
Birth:
May 9, 1846
Buckland
Kent, England
Death:
Sep. 20, 1920
Los Angeles County
California
Burial:
Forest Lawn Memorial Park
Glendale
Los Angeles County, California
Plot: Azalia Terrace
Great Mausoleum
Azalia Columbarium, Niche 28

Alfred C. Hogbin was born in Buckland, Kent, England and came to American when his family immigrated to Wisconsin about 1855. He was the oldest of John and Mary's sons who survived into adulthood. On Feb 21, 1865, he enlisted as a Corporal in Company D, Wisconsin 49th Inf. Reg. and mustered out on November 1 1865. Later in his life, he was active in the GAR.

He graduated from Hillsdale College in 1872 and Harvard Divinity in 1875. He had two other brothers that were graduates of Hillsdale College who were FWB ministers. George and Richard Lawrence who had changed their name for an unknown reason. In 1876, he married Flora Preston (Hillsdale class of 1876). He and his wife traveled extensively. In addition to his ministerial work, he was a published author.

He served as a pastor in New York City prior to going to Sabatha, Kansas where he served for twenty-one years. He then served as pastor for eight years in Laramie,Wyoming.

He and his wife went to Europe in 1916 where he studied modern language and history. They were at the University of Grenoble in France when World War I broke out. He remained in France until 1919, when they returned to Hollywood, California.

Truman Niece Huddleston
Birth:
Jan. 19, 1910
Hartshorne, Pittsburg County,
Oklahoma

Death:
Sep. 8, 2004
Olympia, Thurston County,
Washington
Burial:
Chowchilla Cemetery
Chowchilla,
Madera County, California

Rev. Huddleston's parents were William Adam Huddleston and Nancy Belle (Allen) Huddleston. She died in 1918, when Truman was a child. His father remarried to Beulah Alice (unk) Huddleston, and both died in California. Truman N. Huddleston was ordained a Free Will Baptist minister when he was 35 years of age at the FWB Church at Non, OK. He was active in the church's ministry, and in the Center Ass'n meetings. He married Isadele and they removed to California in the 1940's. He lived at Chowchilla for years and held pastorates in the area.

Rev Ansel H Huling
Birth:
Jun. 7, 1838
New Berlin
Chenango County, New York

Death:
Sep. 4, 1917
Los Angeles County,
California
Burial:
Forest Lawn Memorial Park
Glendale
Los Angeles County, California
Plot: Section H, Map 1,
Lot 120, Space 8

An ordained Free Baptist minister/pastor, editor and writer. From NY, where his father, Rev. Daniel Huling, was a Freewill Bapt. for 35 yrs. After Daniel's dth, the family moved west, to OH, Mich, Wis, Neb, and to Calif. Rev. Ansel H. Huling, son of the Rev. Daniel and Lydia (Burlingame) Huling. He was educated at Mendota Seminary and Hillsdale College.[Mich]. His ordination took place in 1863. He has held pastorates at Sugar Grove, Ill, Raymond and Evansville, Wis. He was one of the founders of the Christian Freeman and was one of its editors and corporators. In 1874 he was chosen editor and manager of the Western Department of the *Morning Star.* He was instrumental, as agent of the Wisconsin Yearly Meeting, in the founding of the Cairo, Ill. Mission. He has been several times elected delegate to General Conference, and has been a member of the Home Mission Board. He was married in April, 1860, to Emily L. Stewart. His home is in Cincinnati, where he is engaged in literary work."

John Jay Hull
Birth:
May 31, 1847
Death:
Aug. 8, 1933
Burial:
Chrome Cemetery
Chrome
Glenn County,
California

An ordained FWB minister who labored in Wisconsin churches and with his father in South Dakota.

Rev Jesse L. Jeffrey
Birth:
Jun. 23, 1913
Ellis County,
Texas
Death:
Feb. 27, 1984

Colusa County,
California
Burial:
Oak View Memorial Park
Antioch
Contra Costa County
California

First moderator of the Arkansas State Association of FW Baptists. His name is listed in "Hist. of Free Will Baptist State Associations," Edited by Dr. Robt. E. Picirilli, in 1976. Parents: John Jesse Welch Jeffrey and Lena Wilma (Anderson) Jeffrey.

Edward "Butch" Johns
Birth:
May 7, 1924
Death:
Oct. 20, 2010
Burial:
Shafter Memorial Park
Shafter, Kern County, California

Edward "Butch" Johns, U.S. Veteran, who was faithful to the Free Will Baptist denomination serving as preacher and church planter for 60 years.

Paul Kennedy
Birth:
Apr. 4, 1921
Quinton, Oklahoma
Death:
Aug. 6, 2009
Tulsa, Tulsa County, Oklahoma
Burial:
Sunset View,
Amador County, California

Paul Kennedy was an active layman in California serving as a state leader and Pomotional Director. Paul was a generous man and shared his rare book denominational collection to the Historical Archives at Hillsdale College, Moore, OK,

124

Rev Benjamin Franklin Kelley
Birth:
Nov. 11, 1832
Middlebury
Wyoming County, New York
Death:
Jan. 29, 1914
Santa Cruz
Santa Cruz County, California
Burial:
Santa Cruz Memorial Park
Santa Cruz
Santa Cruz County, California
Plot: Block D, Lot 33

Ordained Freewill Baptist minister in 1859 from NY; went West, and ministered in Minn/Wis. and organized churches there. He also occupied the office of town treasurer. On Jan. 1, 1887, he resigned the pastorate of the Delavan (Wis.) He organized the Free Baptist Church in Madelia, MN, on 27 Mar 1875. Later he held a state-wide position with the Baptist Church.
Married: Charlotte Adelia Douglas about 1852 in Plainfield, Wisconsin. They had at least 6 children: Laura, Lucetta, Angelena "Annie", Mary, Emeline "Emma", and Viola. Charlotte died on 11 May 1886.
Married: Missouri A. Connor on 18 Nov 1886 in Watonwan County, MN. She was born in 1840 in Indiana. Her parents were Alexander and Louisa (Reavis) Connor. With Benjamin, she appears on the 1895 Minnesota census, living in Rockford, MN. No further information (death/burial) has been found for her.

Married: Frances A. "Fannie" Blood on 18 Oct 1898 in Madelia, MN. She had previously been married to Manilius Snow and had 5 sons with him; he died in 1898. She died in 1918.

Winston Benton Lawless
Birth:
Feb. 1, 1913
Death:
May 30, 1986
Burial:
Clovis Cemetery,
Clovis,
Fresno County, California

Free Will Baptist ordained minister, pastor and leader. He was the California State Executive-Secretary of California FWB's and editor of *"Voice"*. He was manager of the state bookstore.

Raymond Earl Letsinger
Birth:
Aug. 17, 1902
Death:
Sep. 12, 1983
Burial:
Hillcrest Cemetery
Porterville
Tulare County, California,
Plot: M-1770-2

A Free Will Bapt. minister, whose name is in list of 1961 State roll of ministers. His address was Porterville at that time.

The Rev. Mayhew lived in Modesto for 32 years and for his past six years served the Free Will congregation. Previously, he spent more than 17 years as a missionary in Ivory Coast, West Africa. According to his wife, "The Lord called him to go to Ivory Coast and that's where he was happiest. Most of the work was village work. We would go and teach in the villages." Rev. Mayhew lived in Modesto from the time he was 12. He served in the Navy during World War II.

Archie J. Mayhew
Birth:
May 10, 1926,
Saint Cloud,
Stearns County, Minnesota
Death:
Oct. 26, 1997,
Modesto,
Stanislaus County, California
Burial:
Lakewood Memorial Park,
Hughson,
Stanislaus County, California

Doice Lee McAlister
Birth:
Oct. 23, 1929
Pottawatomie County
Oklahoma
Death:
Apr. 27, 2010
Turlock,
Stanislaus County, California
Burial:
San Joaquin Valley National
Cemetery,
Santa Nella Village,
Merced County, California

He was the pastor of Tulock Free Will Baptist church for about 35 yrs. He preached for about 60 yrs. He was great brother and and good pastor and many people loved him. He had over 400 people at his funeral service in the church.

Inscription:
US ARMY Note: KOREA

Rev J. L. McAlister
Birth:
Sep. 29, 1924
Hector
Pope County, Arkansas
Death:
Oct. 23, 2013
Farmersville
Tulare County, California
Burial:
Exeter District Cemetery

Exeter
Tulare County, California

He was the youngest of five brothers and five sisters. J.L. was educated in Hector, Arkansas and later earned his Associate of Arts degree at California Christian College. On August 19, 1950, he married Wilma Juanita Rodgers and they enjoyed 63 happy years of marriage. After becoming a Christian at the age of 40, J.L. spent the rest of his life telling people about Jesus. He pastored Free Will Baptist churches in Lindsay, Farmersville, Earlimart, Visalia and Exeter for 35 years. He served as a mentor to many young preachers. He lived his life to the fullest. His favorite place to be was church. He enjoyed spending time with his family, gardening, shelling and selling walnuts and, most of all, visiting people.
Rev. J. L. McAlister was 89.
Published in Visalia Times-Delta and Tulare Adv-Register on Oct. 25, 2013

George W McLain
Birth:
Jun. 6, 1894,
Oklahoma
Death:
Jan., 1965,
Fresno County, California
Burial:
Odd Fellows Cemetery, Fresno, Fresno County, California

Rev. McLain was a pioneer minister in the state of Oklahoma and known for his successful evangelism and as a church planter. Rev. McLain was of Choctaw Indian descent, of which he was proud. He as a young man, worked closely with Rev. Elzie Yandell, an older minister, in eastern Oklahoma, who mentored him and held revival services with him. He was a motivator wherever he pastored. He often went to a church that was in a low state, and brought it to vitality and on successful financial footing. A son, Joy McLain, was elected delegate to the General Cooperative Ass'n. meeting in Denison, TX in 1934. When the State Ass'n met in Ada, OK; he was elected as Okla. State Evangelist in 1936, along with Dr. I.W. Yandell and Rev. Paul Purcell. In 1941, as state evangelist, he reported having eight revivals, 249 conversions, and organized three churches the past year. He was active in the state work, and often called upon to preach in their meetings. Rev. McLain pastored Ada First FWB in Oklahoma before moving to California, and then the Richmond First and Selma, churches.

Rev Joe L Mooneyham
Birth:
1916
Mississippi
Death:
Feb. 24, 2001
Ceres
Stanislaus County
California
Burial:
Cremated,
Specifically: unknown

Rev. Mooneyham, 85, died in a fire that consumed his home at las Casitas mobile home.

An ordained Free Will Baptist minister/pastor for 55 years in California's San Joaquin Valley.

The Rev. Brown, state director of ministries of the Free Will Baptist Church, will led funeral service.

Rev Mooneyham Founded Village Chapel in 1957 and served 10 years before resigning because of health from related to muscular dystrophy. A church building, Mooneyham Hall, was named after him.

Rev. Mooneyham next worked briefly as a cook at the California Bible Institute in Fresno before returning to Modesto in 1969 to serve as visitation Minister at Prescott Bible Church in Modesto (now Prescott Evangelical Free Church.). He led a Spanish-language congregation at one point and did missionary work in Central America.

He led churches in Visalia and Tulare befor moving Stanislaus County. Family members say he served in the ministry 55 years.

Walter Stanley Mooneyham
Birth:
Jan. 14, 1926
Houston,
Chickasaw County, Mississippi
Death:
Jun. 3, 1991
Los Angeles,
Los Angeles County, California
Burial:
Desert Memorial Park,
Cathedral City,
Riverside County,
California,
Plot: b-30,264

Dr. W. Mooneyham joined the U.S. Navy and served in the Pacific Theater (1943-45). He received his Bachelor of Science degree in journalism at Oklahoma Baptist University, Shawnee, Oklahoma (1950) while ministering as pastor at First Free Will Baptist Church, Sulphur, Oklahoma (1949-53). After working with the National Association of Free Will Baptists in Nashville, Tennessee (1954), he became Director of Information (1959) and Interim Executive Director of the National Assn. Of Evangelicals in Wheaton, Illinois (1964).

As a special assistant to Billy Graham, he coordinated the World Congress on Evangelism in Berlin (1966). One year later, he was appointed Vice-President of International Relations for the Billy Graham Evangelistic Association. From 1969 to 1982, he was the President of World Vision Intl., a service agency providing childcare, emergency relief assistance and mission's research to Christian denominations in over 30 countries.

He was the recipient of three honorary doctorates: Houghton College, New York (1964), Taylor University, Indiana (1977) and Seattle Pacific University, Washington (1978). Dr. Mooneyham hosted and appeared in many television documentaries and prime-time specials such as *Come Walk the World*, a weekly documentary about Christian missions, and a weekly program, *Larry Jones Presents*, that he produced and which was aired on 200 stations. In 1980, he was the subject of a prime-time documentary about the refugee Vietnamese "boat people" who he helped rescue at sea.

He was the author of eight books and of innumerable magazine articles. His latest book was *Dancing on the Strait and Narrow* from Harper and Row, 1989.

He holds many honors such as the Polish Orthodox Church's Order of Mary Magdalene for extraordinary service to children and the Republic of Korea's highest award to foreigners, the Distinguished Service Award.

George N. Musgrove
Birth:
December 10, 1855
Kings County,
New Brunswick,
Canada
Death:
1924
Burial:
Evergreen Cemetery
Los Angeles
Los Angeles County, California
Plot: Section I

He was converted when 19 years of age. He would was a student for the ministry ever made theological Seminary, received his licensed to preach on December 1, 1879 and was ordained February 20, 1883 by Rev. Louis mild learned, EM. Eight. Quimby and others he held a few churches in New Hampshire before excepting the call to the Arlington church in Rhode Island.

Roy E. Pembrook
Birth:
Aug. 28, 1917
Death:
Dec. 10, 1993
Burial:
Westwood Hills Memorial Park
Placerville
El Dorado County, California
Plot: Parkcreek 74-A4-181

He was a retired minister at the time of His death at age 76. He was converted at age 12 and began to preach at age 15. He was ordained in Missouri on August 17, 1934 at the Mountain Grove FWB church. A native of Watson, Missouri he preached in various churches and held revivals in the state. After moving to California, he served on the Executive Committee and helped organize new churches. He organized or pastored the Martinez, Brentwoods, Antioch and Pleasant Hill churches.

John Lee Reel
Birth:
Jun. 7, 1905
Appleton
Pope County, Arkansas
Death:
Jul. 10, 1989
Visalia
Tulare County, California
Burial:
Visalia Public Cemetery
Visalia
Tulare County,California
Plot: Sect.A, Blk 16, Lot 15,
C/E Grave

His parents were james c. Reel, and Josephine (Prince) Reel.He married Elsie Violet "Vi" Eakin, Oct. 25, 1924, in Pope Co. AR. They had four children: .It was after 1940 census that John and Violet moved to Oklahoma, around the Tulsa area. He became an ordained Free Will Baptist minister, and later moved to California, where he pastored the Visalia FWB Church, and others. He was active in his district association of churches, serving on boards, and was a good pastor.

Tip Richardson
Birth:
Sep. 16, 1923
Norwood, Wright County, Missouri
Death:
Mar. 3, 2013
Tulare County, California
Burial:
Visalia Public Cemetery
Visalia, Tulare County, California

Tip was born to Arthur and Dora Richardson. He Married the former Nina Kelley in Norwood, Missouri on December 6, 1942. Tip served in the navy during World War II as a dental assistant. In later years, he retired from Tulare County Family Support Division. He served as a minister of the Free Will Baptist Church in various valley locations. He was known for his love of singing and did so until he became ill. He left behind his wife of 70 years, Nina. (Published in Visalia Times-Delta and Tulare Adv-Register on March 6, 2013)

Rev Charles P Roam
Birth:
Apr. 18, 1941
Death:
Dec. 21, 2015
California
Burial:
Floral Memorial Park
Selma
Fresno County, California

He was a Pastor of Grace Free Will Baptist Church, Selma, CA, at the time of his death. He had been pastor in other churches in the state during the previous years. He was active in his church's enterprises.

J L Roler
Birth:
Jan. 23, 1845
Racine, Ohio
Death:
Apr. 5, 1939
Burial:

Lindsay-Strathmore Cemetery
Lindsay
Tulare County, California

He was converted in January, 1866 and received his license to preach 10 years later. He was ordained in November, 1884. He was pastor of the Third Alexander and Lodi churches in South East Ohio. He was clerk of the Athens Quarterly Meeting. On March 11, 1869 he married to Alvira Smith.

Rev Daniel Joshua Rowlett
Birth:
Apr. 21, 1901
Dutton
Madison County, Arkansas
Death:
Oct. 21, 1964
Exeter,Tulare County, California
Burial:
Exeter District Cemetery
Exeter,Tulare County, California

Rev. Daniel Joshua Rowlett son of John Anderson Rowlett (1874-1950) and Polly Weatherby (1883-1927). Married to Maudie Rae Phillips on 30 Oct 1925. Children: Daniel Joshua Rowlett Jr. (1927-1967) and Wesley Eugene Rowlett (1929-1981). In list of Calif. ministers for the State Association of FWB in 1961.

Rev Tom I. Rowlett
Birth: 1904
Death: 1984
Burial:
Visalia Public Cemetery
Visalia
Tulare County
California, USA
Plot: Sec. F, Track 2,
Tier 8, Grave 81

Ministered to churches in Calif. FWBapt.

Sheldon J. Smith
Birth:
Apr. 14, 1836
Elbridge
Onondaga County, New York
Death:
May, 1914
California
Burial:
Woodland Cemetery
Woodland,
Yolo County,California
Plot: Blk-17 Lt-31 Gr-15

Son of Bliss and Priscilla (Rounds) SMITH, was married to Miss Emily Hakes Feb. 14, 1856. In 1882 she died, and he afterwards married Miss Susan Stevens.In September 1873. He was ordained by the Church of God. In 1885 he united with the Free Baptists, and pastored of the church at Corey HIll, Van Buren County, Mich. In 1882 he was elected department chaplain of the G.A.R. of the state of Michigan, having served in the late civil war in a New York Regiment." He moved from Michigan to Yolo Co. CA, where in 1910 census, he was living alone at age 74.

John Alexander Logan Waltman
Birth:
Dec. 13, 1886
Kirbyville,
Taney County, Missouri
Death:
Dec. 11, 1959
Turlock
Stanislaus County, California
Burial:
Turlock Memorial Park
Turlock,
Stanislaus County, California

He was married to Livia Elizabeth (Graham) sometime after he arrived in Oklahoma from Missouri, before 1910. They lived in Oklahoma for some years where their children were born. Shortly after 1940, they moved to central Calif., where Rev. Waltman began the Turlock Free Will Baptist Church March 22, 1942, with nineteen charter members. He was elected its first pastor. In the following months lots were purchased and in 1945, a new church auditorium was built at Landers and "C: streets.

The church worshiped there for almost twenty years. Rev. Waltman was pastor from 1942-1946. He was active in the state work. He was a member of Turlock at the time of his death at 73 years lacking three days being 74 years. ---info from HISTORICAL CORNER, of the *"Voice"*, official organ of the State Assn of Free Will Baptists.

Rev Jerry Dale Watson
Birth:
Jan. 11, 1935
Sulphur
Murray County, Oklahoma
Death:
Dec. 29, 2003
Fresno
Fresno County, California
Burial:
Visalia Public Cemetery
Visalia
Tulare County, California

An ordained Free Will Baptist minister, and pastor. He served on the Calif. FWB State Mission Board in 1973, and later, and

other offices. He was active, and esteemed by all who knew him.
Jerry married Betty Lois Cooley in Visalia, Calif. December 28, 1955. He was born and raised in Sulphur and graduated from Sulphur High School in 1953, where he was active in sports and in the agricultural program. Jerry moved to California in 1955. He attended the College of Sequoias, California Christian College in Fresno and Pacific Bible University in Fresno. He was ordained in 1961 and served as Pastor for the Freewill Baptist Church for 42 years in the Visalia and Fresno areas. He retired from pastorship in August of 1988. He was employed by Miller Memorial Chapel as Funeral Director for over 25 years, continuing his ministry to families and co-workers.
Services for Pastor Jerry was at the Miller Memorial Chapel in Visalia, Calif. with Rev. Tim Rolen officiating.

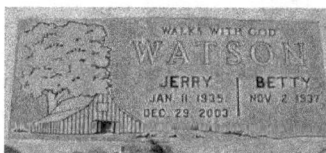

Rev John Jay Weage
Birth:
1831
Cattaraugus County, New York
Death:
1898
California
Burial:
La Vista Memorial Park
National City
San Diego County, California

Rev. John Jay WEAGE, son of Ira and Keziah (Darling) WEAGE, was born in Cattaraugus Co. N.Y., in 1830. He received a license to preach in the Free Will Baptist Church in 1855, and was ordained by the Honey Creek Quarterly Meeting (Wis), in 1863.

He was five years principal of Prairie City Academy, Illinois, and has held pastorates at Raymond, Wis., St. Albans, Paloma, Fairview, Wheatland, Curnes and Kawanee, Illinois, also six years with congregational churches, and later ministered to the church at Smyrna, NY.

He was married to Mary C. Dudley, daughter of Rev. D. Dudley, 19 Nov. 1856, Warren, OH.

James Clinton Wood
Birth:
Oct. 25, 1928
Oklahoma
Death:
Dec. 14, 200
Fresno, Fresno County, California
Burial:
Clovis Cemetery, Clovis, Fresno County, California

James Clinton Wood's parents were Walter F. and Hallie Wood. He was an ordained Free Will Baptist minister and pastor, pastoring at Salinas and Tulare, CA.

James M. Woodman
Birth:
Feb. 12, 1824,
Tamworth, Carroll County, New Hampshire
Death:
Dec. 27, 1903,
San Leandro,
Alameda County, California
Burial:
Chico Cemetery, Chico, Butte County, California

He united with the Free Will Baptist church in Sanbornton

when fifteen years of age, and the following year was in preparatory studies of theology with Rev. J. Woodman at Lowell, Mass. He then studied at the Dracut Biblical School in Dracut, Mass, traveled as an evangelist two years and was ordained in 1844 at Limerick, Maine. He entered the Biblical School at Whitestown, N.Y., in 1845, and graduated two years later. He later attended the Botanico Medical College in Cincinnati, Ohio where he received a medical degree May 15, 1848. After preaching a short time at South Parsonfield and at North Berwick, Maine, he went West for his health and ministered to the Honey Creek, Wisconsin church during 1850-56, and the Mt. Pleasant church 1856-61, when in 1862 he went to California, where he has been principal of the Chico Academy. Sometime prior to 1866, Rev. Woodman erected a building for use as Mrs. Woodman's private school. On Nov. 12, 1874, the building was destroyed by fire, evidently the work of arsonists. The Academy was rebuilt and in 1884-5, the academy listed Rev. James M. Woodman, principal, his wife, Selena, ass't principal; his son, Charles, teacher. In 1897 Rev. Woodman formally retired from active preaching and built a new home in San Leandro, CA. He is author of *"God in Nature and Revelation," "The Song of Cosmology;" "The Neptunian Theory of Creation"* and other articles for newspapers in Boston and Chicago.

Arvel Earl Woolery
Birth:
Feb. 14, 1912
Oklahoma
Death:
Jun. 20, 1982
Lindsay, Tulare County,
California
Burial: Hillcrest Cemetery,
Porterville, Tulare County,
California
Plot: Z-86-4

Woolery was a WW II Army veteran, enlisting 30 Oct. 1943 at Fresno, and mustered out, 09 Jan. 1946. After his service, he became a bi-vocational, ordained Free Will Baptist minister. He worked at different jobs that allowed him to have flexible time. He retired from the Kern Co. School District, in the 1970's. He became pastor of Selma Church, Porterville for several years, then at Earlimart for about a decade. Each place saw progress under his leadership. Rev. Woolery was a kind and generous man, soft spoken, and he usually thought before he spoke. His wisdom was useful to many of his peers and friends.

Joseph Elzie Yandell
Birth:
Feb. 5, 1880
Scott County, Arkansas
Death:
Jan. 23, 1970
Burial:
Clovis Cemetery
Clovis
Fresno County, California

He was ordained at Lodi (Latimer County Oklahoma) to preach for the Free Will Baptist Church in 1904. He farmed as most ministers did during this time, and went far and near to preach. He baptized probably more people in eastern minister of his day. He organized churches, held revivals, funerals and weddings, and was in demand as a speaker wherever he went. In 1929 he took his family to California. He was in the organization of the Oklahoma State Association of Free Will Baptists, at Holdenville, Oklahoma in 1908, where he was elected moderator, and his brother, Dr. I.W. Yandell, clerk. He had a serious demeanor, a good head, and was known for his honesty. He had an active life of faith and preaching for over 67 years. His memorial service was held in the Chapel of California Christian College, Fresno, with Dr. Wade T. Jernigan, officiating.

Their Works
Do Follow Them.

Canada

Andrew Banghart
Birth:
1777
Death:
May 18, 1860
Burial:
Lambeth Community Cemetery
Lambeth
Middlesex County
Ontario, Canada

Rev. A. Banghart that was in Upper Canada, 100 miles west of Buffalo in 1821. He became an ordained Free Bapt. minister. He went to NY for ordination and returned.

*Death is not the end of the story
for those who know the Lord*

Willard Bartlett
Birth:
Sep. 8, 1783
Massachusetts

Death:
Aug. 1, 1856
Burial:
Stone School House Cemetery
Richmond
Estrie Region
Quebec, Canada

Although he had lived in Canada where he was converted, he settled in Wheelock, VT, where he began to preach. He gathered a church at Meltowne in 1818, and pastored it for forty years. He became ill, and was thought better, but died suddenly and was buried on the Sabbath in good hope."He had a good mind, and was brave in the right."

Rev Alder B. Boyer
Birth:
Aug. 28, 1860
Somerville
New Brunswick, Canada
Death:
Jun. 9, 1891
Orissa, India
Burial:
Greenwood Cemetery
Hartland
Carleton County
New Brunswick, Canada

Died at Balasoret, India
31 Years

A Free Baptist minister and missionary to India. His parents were William J. and Ausan (Shaw) Boyer.
He was converted in Feb. 1873; graduated from the Univ. of New Brunswick in June, 1885;

resigned, the Mathematical Mastership of the Union Bapt. Seminary, St. John, N.B., in June 1886, to enter upon the Foreign Mission work in India, to which he was ordained by the New Brunswick Free Baptist Conference, Oct. 11, 1886.
He was married July 20, 1886, to Miss Clara I. Shea, a native of Grafton, Carleton Co. New Brunswick, and daughter of John A. and Aurilla S. H. (Barrows) Shea. She had been a teacher in the Model School in connection with the Normal School of New Brunswick.
Sailing in October 1886, they arrived in India, Jan. 1, 1887.....

William D Crowell
Birth:
Dec. 9, 1804
Barrington, Nova Scotia, Canada
Death:
Mar. 7, 1869
Barrington, Nova Scotia, Canada
Burial:
Old Meeting House Cemetery
Barrington, Nova Scotia, Canada

Rev. William Donaldson Crowell's name is listed in records from Twenty-First Gen. Conference of Freewill Baptist, as having deceased in 1869, Nova Scotia. From the Crowell-Nickerson Family Tree, and their sourses from Barrington, Shelburne, Nova Scotia, he was the son of Heman Crowell, (1779-1858), and Abigail Young, (1786-1866) both listed as bur. in this cemetery also. Not much is known of his ministry, except that he was active in his area. He died of Stomach Cancer. Thomas Crowell, possibly a brother, is also listed as ordained in 182? and served in Barrington, N.S., area Free Baptist churches.

Rev. James E. Gosline
Birth:
Jul. 21, 1860
Farmingdale,
New Brunswick, Canada
Death: 1937
Canada
Burial:
Gosline Cemetery
Studholm
Kings County
New Brunswick, Canada

In 1876 he was converted, and was licensed in July 1883. He studied at the Union Baptist Seminary at St. John in 1884, and at Cobb Divinity School in the class of 1889. He has labored at Campobello, N.B., where, in fourteen months, 138 were converted and joined the church. He served the church at West Poland, ME, and is now [1889] pastor of the Houlton, and First and Second Hodgdon churches."

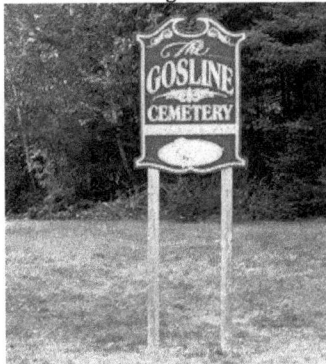

What a day!
What a place!
What a delight!

Rev Jacob Goble
Birth: 1851
Death: Dec. 12, 1925
Burial:
Greenwood Cemetery
Waterford
Haldimand-Norfolk Regional
Municipality
Ontario, Canada

Rev. Jacob Goble was connected with the Free Communion Baptist Conference of Canada.

Chester Heard
Birth:
September 22, 1806
Newport, Canada
Death:
Sep. 3, 1887
Massawippi, Québec
Burial:
Massawippi Cemetery
Massawippi,
Quebec, Canada

He was a son of William Heard, who fought in the battle of Bunker Hill, and of Tirza, daughter of Col. William Williams, who fought in Bennington, Vermont. His father moved from Holton, Massachusetts to Newport, Canada, 30 miles into the wilderness, where in a log cabin, Chester was born. There was no church nor schoolhouse. Marcy Harvey, afterwards the mother of Dr. George H, Ball, taught school for short time in a log cabin on the farm of Mr. Heard. On his 16th birthday, after earnest prayers knelt alone in the woods by the side of a tree stump and began his first prayer. 'Oh Lord', were the only words that he could pray, but he'd read to the Bible for comfort and peace and erected a family altar. This was the beginning of revival that continued for years. Converted in September, 1822 he was licensed in September, 1841. He could not accept the doctrine of the only church, a Calvinistic Baptist, in this vicinity. Finding himself in accord with the teaching of the Free Baptist treaties, he was ordained in September 1842. He was an earnest supporter of all of the Free Baptist missionary interest and a firm friend of his denomination. He took *The Morning Star* for over 50 years. He was present at the General Conference at Weare's, New Hampshire in 1880.

Rev John Ingram
Birth:
1840
Ontario, Canada
Death:
Jan. 21, 1875
Ontario, Canada
Burial:
Iona Cemetery
Iona
Elgin County
Ontario, Canada

Jennie Johnson
Birth:
1868
Death:
1967
Burial:
Dresden Cemetery
Dresden, Ontario,
Canada

"Ingram, Rev. John, began to preach with the Methodists. He joined the Free Baptists in July, 1866, and was ordained the following January. He took charge of the Ionia, Dexter and Loudon churches, which were greatly strengthened under his labors. He then moved to Woodstock, and, while devoting himself to study, preached to the Zorra churches. A Bible class of seventy-five members evinced his success. The studies in school completed, and engaging as home missionary, he organized a church at Napier, enjoyed a revival at Duttan, and was taking up the work at Bloomsburgh, when, after a sudden and brief illness, he died aged 35 years. His death, at Crumment Family Tree gives his parents as Robert and Jane Ingram. That he was married to Rosetta Parker Dec. 10th, 1866, by Thomas Mills, Bapt. minister of Yarmouth.

After her conversion at a Baptist revival at sixteen, Jennie Johnson followed the call to preach. Raised in an African abolitionist community in Ontario, Canada, she immigrated to the United States to attend the African Methodist Episcopal Seminary at Wilberforce University. On an October evening in 1909 she stood before a group of Free Will Baptist preachers in the small town of Goblesville, Michigan, and was received into the ordained ministry. She was the first ordained woman to serve in Canada and spent her life building churches and working for racial justice on both sides of the national border.

Joseph McLeod
Birth:
1844
Death:
1913
Burial:
Forest Hill Cemetery
Fredericton, York County
New Brunswick, Canada

Father: Rev. Ezekiel McLeod, a Freewill Baptist minister, began the denominational paper, "The Religious Intelligencer," which was going well in 1853, and had enlarged several times.

It is stated that Rev. Ezekiel died in Frediction, NB, Canada, but have not located his nor Amelia's graves.

Note: (Rev DD) "As editor, pastor and temperance worker, his life was spent on behalf of his fellow men"

Asa McGray
Birth:
Sep. 18, 1780
Maine
Death:
Dec. 30, 1843
Nova Scotia, Canada
Burial:
Centreville Cemetery,
Centreville,Nova Scotia, Canada
Plot: McGray Burial Plot -
behind the church

From the Shelburne County Genealogical Society: The Free Will Baptist Church Records gives Asa's death date as 30 December, where as his gravestone gives 28 Dec.----. Information provided from a letter written by Arthur N. McGray (1862-1949) In 1871-72 my grandfather, Asa T. McGray, had decided to move all the McGray family who had been buried back of the old, first Meeting House, where the land was low and wet, to new graves on the higher land back of the present Church. He had recently bought that property for a home for his daughter, Almira (McGray) Kenney.The morning of the day when the remains of the old Minister, Rev. Asa McGray, was to be removed, many of the family came to the new cemetery, for grandfather has announced that he would remove the wooden cover, over the glass face-plate to see what change had taken place in the 30 years of burial. Edgar Smith and I, on our way to school, were allowed to come close to the coffin, when grandfather took off the wooden coverage of the glass. Everyone gasped, for under that glass was a face that might have been alive only a day before. Silently, we all looked on, as tears flowed. The state of preservation was perfect. Then, as grandfather worked a small chisel under the glass, the outside air flowed in, and the film of features collapsed to dust forever.

Inscription:
In Memory of REV. ASA MCGRAY
WHO died Dec. 28, 1843
in the 64 year of his age.
A native of the United States and
first founder of the
Freewill Baptist Denomination
in Nova Scotia.

Written in Durham, ME History, that he was a successful evangelist and organizer of churches. Ordained Sept 26, 1814.

Rev Abial Moulton
Birth:
May 31, 1798
Gilmanton
Belknap County
New Hampshire
Death: Nov. 16, 1885
Stanstead
Quebec, Canada
Burial:
Fairfax Cemetery
Fairfax
Estrie Region
Quebec, Canada

His father Avery Moulton (1770 - 1828) and brother Albanus K Moulton (1810 - 1873) were FWB preachers.

Rev George Whitfield Orser
Birth:
Jun. 27, 1813
Hartland
New Brunswick, Canada
Death:
Mar. 20, 1885
Wakefield
New Brunswick, Canada
Burial:
Wakefield Community Cemetery
Wakefield
Carleton County
New Brunswick, Canada

George Whitfield Orser was the famed Reverend George W. Orser, and he devoted his life to the ministry. His extraordinary gift of language in the pulpit made him much revered and admired throughout Carleton County. He was founder of the Primitive Baptist Denomination, and its churches were sometimes referred to as "Osserite Churches." The story of his life may be read in "The Life and Ministry of the Reverend George W. Orser", by the Reverend Charles H. Orser, printed by The Observer, 1914. (Hayward article, Page 4 of 5)
The Primitive Baptist Conference of New Brunswick, Maine and

Nova Scotia, not to be confused with Calvinistic Primitive Baptists, are a group of Free Baptists in Canada and New England.

The roots of the Primitive Baptist Conference are found in the work of Benjamin Randall, whose convert Asa McCray was instrumental in forming churches in Nova Scotia. These churches were generally known as Free Christian Baptists.

George Wightfield Orser (1813–1885) was ordained among the Free Christian Baptists in 1843. As the idea of salaried ministers developed and grew, Orser stood against the practice, proposing belief in "a free gospel and free access to it." Other items of disagreement included Sunday Schools, church discipline, missionary organizations, music, and church offerings. Because of this opposition, Orser was expelled from the Free Christian Baptists in 1874. In July 1875, representatives from seven churches met and formed the Free Baptist Conference of New Brunswick. Due to disagreements over the use of the name "Free Baptist", Orser's group incorporated under the name Primitive Baptist Conference of New Brunswick in 1898. As churches were added from Nova Scotia, Maine and Massachusetts, the conference became the Primitive Baptist Conference of New Brunswick, Maine and Nova Scotia. The Nova Scotia churches incorporated a regional conference -- Primitive Baptist Conference of Nova Scotia -- in 1926.

In July 1981, 16 churches joined the Free Will Baptists and became the regional Atlantic Canada Association of Free Will Baptists in alignment with the National Association of Free Will Baptists. A small group of Christians from these churches have maintained themselves separately as Primitive Baptists.

References:

Biographical Directory of Nova Scotia and New Brunswick Free Baptist Ministers and Preachers, Frederick C. Burnett, 1996

George Whitfield Orser: Another View, Frederick C. Burnett, 1989

The Atlantic Canada Association of Free Will Baptists, by Fred D. Hanson, Contact magazine, January 1982, pp. 2–4 (access 7 Apr 2011)

(Buried In The Primitive Baptist Cemetery At Lower Wakefield.)

Rev Calvin Sawyer
Birth:
Jun. 30, 1809
Eaton
Quebec, Canada
Death:
Feb. 22, 1879
Quebec, Canada
Burial:
Eaton Cemetery
Eaton, Estrie Region
Quebec, Canada

Rev. Calvin R. Sawyer, son of Josiah and Nancy Sawyer, of Eaton, P.Q., was born June 30, 1809. The country was new and means of education limited. His father was the first convert in a revival in 1824. In 1835, after deep conviction, he yielded to Christ. He began to preach in 1840, and was licensed in 1841 by the Stanstead Quarterly Meeting. He labored successfully with the Eaton and Newport church. In 1856 he was ordained and installed pastor of this church. He continued to preach ten years, though in poor health. He worked on a farm for a time, but his health continued to fail. He died Feb. 22, 1879, aged 67 years.

His name was not listed as was his brother, Green's, in the Eaton Cemetery, but they lived close to each other, Green had been bur. here, 1873, and it seems that he would also.

Rev Green Sawyer
Birth:
1812
Canada
Death:
May, 1873
Compton
Quebec, Canada
Burial:
Eaton Cemetery
Eaton
Estrie Region
Quebec, Canada

Rev. Green SAWYER, brother of Rev. Calvin R. Sawyer, and son of Josiah and Nancy Sawyer, of Eaton, P.Q., died in Eaton, P.Q., May 1875. He became an active Christian at the age of fourteen. He began to preach in the same year with his brother, Calvin, in 1840. He was licensed and soon after ordained, and went to the church at Barnston. He labored hard there eight years. For three years he was in the Farmington Quarterly Meeting, Maine. He returned to Canada in failing health and was unable to preach. He gave largely to the Eaton and Newport church and for education and missions.

His name, as well as his wife, Esther Cook Sawyer, are listed in this cemetery list for Eaton Cemetery. It says he was bn 1873, and the book stated 1875. (could be transcription error).

Year of birth is est. from his age at death.

Their Works Do Follow Them.

Colorado

Virgil Florence
Birth:
Dec. 25, 1906
Death:
Feb. 26, 1979
Burial:
Linn Grove Cemetery, Greeley,
Weld County, Colorado,
Plot: Blk 17, lot 58, spc 2

Rev. Florence was licensed to preach in 1930, and in 1931,he was ordained to the gospel ministry by the Free Will Baptists.

He served as Evangelist for the Grand River Ass'n of Oklahoma, and then as moderator for the Grand River Association. He was the first Free Will Baptist minister to go to the Northwest Area of U.S. in 1951. He organized six new Free Will Baptist churches and pastored the following: (In chronological order: Oak Grove, OK; Watonga, OK; Shahan, OK; Coweta, OK; Duck Creek, at Mounds, OK; Bixby, at Bixby, OK; Broken Arrow, OK; In Idaho: he organized Buhl; In Oregon: Klamath Falls; California: Norwalk and Hughson; Shellenberger FWB at Bixby, OK; Guymon, Guymon, OK; and in retirement as pastor, he served as supply pastor, evangelist and mission worker. It was in Greeley, Colorado when he was working in mission work he went to his reward. He was also listed in *Who's Who Among Free Will Baptists.*

Roy L. Thomas
Birth:
Sep. 14, 1930
Greeley, Colorado
Death:
Mar. 23, 2003
Burial:
Linn Grove Cemetery, Greeley, Weld County, Colorado, Plot: Blk 24, lot 44, spc 1

Dr. Roy L. Thomas, former General Director of the Home Missions Dept. of the National Association of Free Will Baptists. He grew up on a farm near Buhl, Idaho. After high school, he attended the University of Idaho in 1948-49. He served in the U. S. Air Force the years of 1951-1955, with foreign service in Korea and Japan. He accepted Christ as his Savior in 1951 at the First FWB Church, Buhl, Idaho, but was immediately sent to Korea. After returning to the states, he was ordained as a FWB minister in 1954, and also was married to his wife, Pat, who is a native of Hobbs, New Mexico. He organized the First FWB Church of Artesia, New Mexico that same year. After serving the Artesia congregation for two years, he moved to Nashville, Tennessee to attend FWB Bible College. He graduated with honors from that institution in 1960 with a Bachelor of Arts Degree. While a student he pastored two different churches in Tennessee; Shady Grove Free Will Baptist Church and First FWB Church, Springfield, Tennessee. Dr. Thomas was sent to Denver, Colorado as a home missionary by the National Home Missions Board in 1961 where he established the First Free Will Baptist Church of that city. He furthered his education by earning a Masters of Divinity Degree from Luther Rice Seminary in 1978, and was granted a Doctor of Divinity Degree from Bethany Seminary in 1989. In December 1970 he was appointed as Associate Director of the National Home Missions Department, Nashville, Tennessee, and became General Director in 1978. He served in that position until his retirement in December 1995, making a total of 25 years on the National Home Missions staff, and a total of 35 years' affiliation with the Department. While he served as General Director of the Home Missions Department, there were over 200 churches established throughout the North American continent and the U.S. owned islands of Puerto

Rico and the Virgin Islands. Under his leadership, the Home Missions Department sponsored countless Evangelism and Church Growth Conferences, and the Old-ime Camp Meeting at the National Convention. He started the Church Extension Loan Fund, the Helping Hands Church Building Team, the Associate Missionary Program, the Aquila and Priscilla Program, the Tentmaker Program, and developed numerous Evangelism and Church Growth publications. He also authored the books, *Planting and Growing a Fundamental Church* and published *The Journal of Benjamin Randall*, and many other historical Free Will Baptist and church growth books and materials. Dr. Thomas has been an evangelist, conducting over 150 revival meetings and conferences in almost every state where Free Will Baptists have churches, and in some foreign countries.

Connecticut

Albert H Chase
Birth:
June 1, 1823
Killingly, Connecticut
Death:
1883
Burial:
Chase Cemetery #2
East Killingly,
Windham County, Connecticut

An early Freewill Baptist minister, editor, and leader. Served in several states. His ancestors were of Puritan stock and Oliver, his father, was a Revolutionary soldier. His thirst for knowledge lead him for a time to Smithville Seminary in Rhode Island. He married in 1844 and nine years later in the ministry. He then attended New Hampton Institution. In 1855 he became the pastor of the church at Cherry Valley, Ohio where he remained for two years and then entered upon a seven-year pastorate in New Lyme, Ohio. During the next three years he was employed in raising money for the Freeman's Mission. In January 1867 he became publishing agent and business manager of the *Christian Freeman,* a position he held for two years. He then labored in Cleveland, Ohio and in Harrisburg, Pennsylvania remaining with the latter church until he was elected corresponding Sec. of the Home Mission Society. During his labors in this position he made Hillsdale, Michigan his home publishing for a time *The Evangelist.* Later he preached in various churches in the vicinity. On account of delicate health he visited Tennessee, yet gained but little. Called back to his home in New Lyme, Ohio to attend a wedding he was attacked with hemorrhage to his lungs where his earthly life ended. He was a man of positive convictions and found no time for neutral ground and disliked compromises. However, he had many warm friends and his influence was widely felt in the denomination. His children Roscoe and Mary graduated from Hillsdale College, Michigan and became successful educators.

Rev William Colegrove
Birth:
Jul. 31, 1824
Lisbon
New London County
Connecticut
Death:
1913
Tallula, Ill.
Burial:
Cedar Grove Cemetery
New London
New London County,Connecticut
Plot: Section 23A

Colegrove, Rev. William, D. D., LL.D., son of Christopher and Eliza (Brewster) Colegrove, was born at Lisbon, Conn., in 1824. In 1846 he was married to Catherine Waterman, and two of their three children now living are teachers. His education was received at Smithville and Whitestown Seminaries. He was ordained in 1848, but has spent the most of the time since then in

teaching in Geauga Seminary [OH]. Middleboro Academy and West Virginia College and other schools. He has been a contributor of the *Morning Star* and other papers, is the author of an English Grammar, and has delivered a number of lectures on different topics. The degrees of D. D. and LL.D. were conferred upon him by West Virginia College.

He is listed as the second president of the West Virginia College, a school for freedmen, following the presidency of Rev. A.D. Williams.

Rev. Colegrove wrote a popular book of his Colegrove family, entitled, "History and Genealogy of the Colegrove Family in America." 804 pages, published before 1923

Inscription:
Prof. William Colegrove, born in Lisbon, CT, died in Tallula, Ill. Co. K, 26th C.V.

William Dick
Birth:
Jan. 31, 1812
Bathgate
West Lothian, Scotland
Death:
Mar. 7, 1853
Danielson
Windham County, Connecticut
Burial:
Westfield Cemetery,Danielson
Windham County, Connecticut

Rev. William Dick was one of eleven children, four of whom became ministers of the gospel.

At about nine years of age, he lost both his parents--his father drowned while bathing in the St. Lawrence River, while traveling to Quebec, Canada, and eight days later, their mother. The family travelled on with the company and settled at Lanark, Canada, their destination. William was licensed to preach in 1836, and his thirst for knowledge led him to prosecute studies while others slept. He entered Hamiliton Academy, now Madison Univ., 1836-37, with with his brother, Robert, but both dismissed for their adhering to an anti-slavery society. He entered Hamiliton College, at Clinton in 1837, graduated in 1841. During this time he was a faithful member of the church of which Rev. Hiram Whitcher was pastor. He preached successively in Norway, Middleville, and Plainfield (NY). While a student of theology at Yale Seminary he preached much at Naugatuck, where he afterward married Maria L. Baldwin. He then spent several years in Canada where he organized churches. In the fall of 1851, he settled at Chepachet, R.I., but because of his views not well supported. He was unanimously chosen by the yearly Meeting to become the pioneer of an interest at Danielson, Conn. Here, in four short months, he drew together a large and permanent congregation, and completely won their affection and confidence. He died after a brief, distressing illness, March 7,

1853, aged 41 years. Martin J. Steere preached his funeral sermon; twenty ministers were in attendance. A stone marks his resting-place in Danielson, erected by his brethren of the Rhode Island Quarterly Meeting.

Louisa Arnold Fenner
Birth:
Jun. 22, 1832
Massachusetts
Death:
Jun. 17, 1909
Connecticut
Burial:
Grove Street Cemetery,Putnam
Windham County, Connecticut

Her parents were Nathaniel and Sarah Cook Buzzell. She was married twice; namely, Alvin Arnold and James Madison Fenner. She was converted in Providence, Rhode Island and was greatly blessed in Christian work. After the death of her second husband she labored as an evangelist in several of the New England states with great success. She was ordained on March 5, 1878 at Foster. She passed at the Union Church in Foster, Rhode Island, the East Putnam, Connecticut church. Afterwards, an evangelist in

Starksboro, Vermont. Her later ministry was spent in the state of Connecticut.

Josiah Graves
Birth:
September 27, 1775
Middletown, Connecticut
Death:
Jul. 24, 1825
Burial:
Old East Cemetery,Middletown
Middlesex County, Connecticut

He was the son of a Congregational clergyman, and was converted in the spring of 1794. In 1800, he united with the Baptist Church at Hartford. June 25, a Baptist Church was organized near his home which he joined and soon began to preach. He was ordained on October 31, 1811 and began an earnest ministry throughout the adjoining counties and met with some opposition but was blessed of God. Becoming convinced that close communion was unscriptural and un-Christian, he plainly told his church his position and began to preach free full salvation. In 1821, 12 persons put their trust in Christ and came out to form the first Free Will Baptist Church in Connecticut. At the close of the following year, Mr. Graves received a visit from David Marks, a nephew of Mrs. Graves. Marks stayed in the native place of his parents, comforting the people and introducing among them The Religious Former. Thus, Mr. Graves heard his own sentiments preach for the first

time. After this, Rev. Eli Towne's saddlebags were stolen while passing through from Maryland to Connecticut. A copy of the Buzzell's magazine, had been left in the woods as worthless by fell into the hands of Graves. On December 28, 1832, he wrote to The Informer, of his becoming known of the denomination. Two brethren from Rhode Island visited him in June, 1824 and the acquaintance was so mutually satisfying that in October the same year Mr. Graves attended the session of that body and with his church and united. The members of this church had greatly increased in opposition had ceased. He was a man of true convictions and with meekness he overcame opposition.He was a Elder for 50 years.

Rev Silas Griffiths
Birth:
Apr. 27, 1837
Coventry
Kent County,Rhode Island
Death:
Feb. 5, 1922
Burial:

Griffiths Cemetery
Sterling
Windham County, Connecticut

He was the son of George and Dorcan GRIFFITHS. At age nineteen he learned a trade and commenced business.

At age twenty-one he married Miss Julia A. Boswell, and settled in Sterling, Conn. He was converted in 1867, and was disturbed for four years over a call to the ministry. In 1871, a revival under Rev. Thomas Jones, former slave, in the Union church, Foster, R.I., he became awakened and joined the church, having decided to preach if God would open the way. Being in Pottersville, South Scituate, in October 1873, a stranger, never seen before or since, invited him to preach. His efforts were followed at once by a revival which resulted in the organization of the South Scituate church June 8, 1874. He was ordained June 19 as its pastor.

The pastorate continued till March, 1882, and thirty were added to its original members.

Clarissa H *Danforth* Richmond
Birth:
1792,
Weathersfield, Vermont
Feb. 15, 1864
Burial:
Westford Village Cemetery,
Westford, Windham County,
Connecticut

She entered John Colby's meetings in 1815 as a thoughtless, vain young lady, but she was awakened to a greater power, and began to follow in a new life.

She was well educated; had extraordinary talent and undoubted piety. Tall in person, dignified in appearance, easy in manners, and she had all the elements of a noble woman. As a speaker her language was ready and simple, her gestures appropriate, and her voice penetrated to the corners of the largest house. She held hundreds with fixed attention for an hour, to listen to the claims of her heavenly Master. Revivals attended her labors wherever she went.

She preached in western Massachusetts, New Hampshire, and Rhode Island. Her many revivals resulted always in the organization of several churches. Many people of other denominations flocked to hear her preach and listened with deep emotion. She preached in 1820 in Vermont to large congregations with much success.

Zalmon Tobey

Birth:
Jul. 27, 1791,
Norfolk, Litchfield County,
Connecticut
Death:
Sep. 17, 1858,
Warren, Bristol County,
Rhode Island
Burial:
Canaan Valley Cemetery,
North Canaan
Litchfield County, Connecticut

A graduate of Brown University in 1817; an early minister of the Freewill Baptist church, uniting from the Calvinism to the Freewill Bapt. in 1826. He resided in Providence, Rhode Island between 1817-1831.

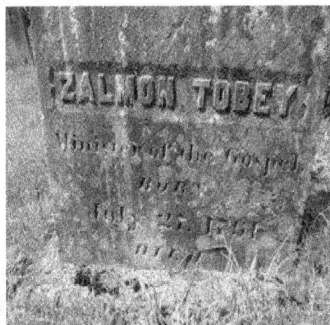

His name is linked in the early Minutes of the General Connection. He was elected moderator of Union Conference, 1824, in Cranston, RI, where a society was formed "for the purpose of furnishing interest in preaching in destitute places in the state." He "rendered efficient service by publishing the *Freewill Baptist Magazine* for about four years. In January, 1828, at the Q.M. held in Pawtucket, Tobey gave a report as he had been a delegate this first General Conference in VT. He was a good scholar and a useful and estimable man.

Daniel Williams

Birth:
Oct. 6, 1790,
Rhode Island
Death:
Jul. 16, 1876,
Connecticut
Burial:
Bartlett Cemetery #1,
Killingly, Windham County,
Connecticut,
Plot: 1st sec R/E

He was baptized by Rev. John Colby in 1813. He organized the Foster church in 1824 and remained the pastor until his death. He was a descendant of Rev. Roger Williams.

*They
served
faithfully*

District of Columbia

Richard M Lawrence
Birth:
Feb. 29, 1848
Dover, Kent, England
Death:
Dec. 25, 1934
Washington
District of Columbia
Burial:
Rock Creek Cemetery
Washington
District of Columbia
Plot: Section M, Lot 140, Site 5

Rev. Lawrence came to America with his parents at seven years of age, and lived on a farm in Wisconsin until twenty-one, when he entered Hillsdale College and graduated from the Classical Course in 1873. He was a loyal member of the Theological Society, and afterward, with his brother, founded the Lawrence Prize, which is still a stimulus to efforts of the noblest kind. He taught school in California the year following his graduation, and in October, 1874. sailed for India, where he labored for the next seven years as a Free Baptist missionary. In December, 1878, he was married to Miss Frankie Millard, who died in September, 1881. Mr. Lawrence then returned to the United States and took a course in the Grand Rapids Business College. After graduation he kept books for the Voight Milling Co., until opportunity opened to enter business for himself. He was a co-founder of the Valley Milling Co. in Grand Rapids, Michigan.He was married a second time, May 1, 1884, at Grand Rapids, to Miss Mary J. Ford. After a successful business career of five years he retired to devote himself more exclusively to Christian work. He took charge of the "Free Baptist" for sixteen months, but left that position after getting it upon a self-supporting basis. After a period of comparative retirement he was, in the fall of 1896, called to the Presidency of Parker College, which post held for 4 years. His 2nd wife died in 1909 and in 1912, he married Charlotte Loukes who was from Fairwater, Wisconsin.

Rev Francis Little Hayes
Birth:
Jan. 5, 1858
New Hampton
Belknap County
New Hampshire
Death:
Apr. 3, 1926
Oak Park
Cook County, Illinois
Burial:
Congressional Cemetery
Washington
District of Columbia
District Of Columbia
Plot: Range: 80; Site: 377b

From WHO'S WHO IN TOPEKA, 1905. Hayes, Francis Little-- Pastor First Congregational Church. He was born in New Hampton, N. H. Jan. 5, 1858; son of Benjamin F. and Allie Cary Hayes; educated at Nichols Latin School 4 years, Gymnasium in Halle, Germany, 1 year, Bates Coll., A.B., '80 a. M., '83, Cobb Divinity School, '85; received D. D. Washburn College, 1902, and Bates Coll., 1902; married June 26, 1884, to Cora May Walker, Wash., D. C.; tutor, 1 year, and 2 years prof. Greek, Hillsdale Coll.; gen. sec. YMCA, Lewiston, Me., 1 year; pastor, Boston First Free Baptist Church, 1885 to 1890; pastor of First Free Baptist, Minneapolis, Minn., 1890-94; pastor, Congregational Church, Manitou, Colo., 1895 to 1902; pastor of First Congregational Church, Topeka, since 1902; regular contributor to Boston Morning Star since 1885; occasionally contributed to religious journals; member of Kan. St. Hist. Soc.

Welcome All You That Are Faithful

Florida

Isaac Joshua Blackwelder
Birth:
Dec. 16, 1896
Death:
May 9, 1980
Burial:
New Zion Cemetery,
Lake Butler,
Union County, Florida

A very active pastor, minister and leader in the early part of the Free Will Baptist denomination. He was one of the committee members selected by the Co-operative General Association in Denison, Texas in 1934 to make farther plans for the merger with the General Conference to form the National Association of Free Will Baptists in 1935. He was a member of the Publication Board and the first Secretary-Treaurer of Foreign Missions in the newly formed association. He was active as a pastor, church planter, and provided leadership in the denomination during his 52 years as a minister. He served 24 churches in his pastoral services. He was the founder the Trinity FWB church in Nashville, Tn. in 1942 and pastored in North Carolina, Georgia and Florida.

Rev John C. Dazey
Birth:
1854
Central America.
Death:
1934
Glades, Florida
Burial:

Ortona Cemetery
Ortona, Glades County
Florida, Plot: J

1900 Census John and Mary are living in Henry Co., IL. He is listed as Rev., birth Mar 1855 'at sea'. His name is in a list of "Nebraska Ministers," who were affiliated with the FreeWill Baptist church, when he org. a church in Nov. 1883, Keenest, Neb. His name and work is in "Four Years of Cooperation, 1883, Neb., by Dr. A.D. Williams.

Rev Aquilla "Quillie" Hansley
Birth:
Jun. 13, 1895
Sneads Ferry
Onslow County
North Carolina
Death:
Apr. 16, 1979
Florida
Burial:
Riverside Memorial Park
Jacksonville
Duval County
Florida

Rev. Aquilla "Quillie" Hansley, was born in a log cabin near the coastal town of Sneads Ferry, North Carolina. He spent most of his childhood and teen years working in the fields to help support the family.

He volunteered for naval service during World War I. There he received a Bible. He read it, especially the Book of Proverbs, which he read again and again, although at the time he had no understanding of what it meant to be a Christian.

With naval service complete, Quillie returned home and began earning a living as a farmer and grocer. In 1922, he married Janie Penelope (Penny) HEATH, and the couple soon moved to Durham where they found jobs in a hosiery mill.

With deep roots in Free Will Baptists, Penny insisted they go to church and they began attending First FWB Church pastored by T.C. Marks. Before long, Quillie accepted Christ and began to study the Scriptures earnestly, sharing what he learned with anyone who would listen.

In 1933, the couple moved to Sherron Acres community just outside Durham, and Quillie, concerned about the lack of a church in the area began to organize prayer meetings in neighborhood homes. When the meetings grew too large, he purchased a small building, a former dance hall, and began holding services. Hansley's Chapel, as it was named, grew quickly, and in 1934, with the help of co-founder and retired carpenter R.L. Hutchins, he purchased and dismantled an old Baptist church building and moved it, piece by piece, more than 30 miles to be reconstructed in Durham. Eighty-five years later, the church, now Sherron Acres FWB Church, continues to thrive.

After studying briefly at Holmes Bible Institute in the early 1940s, Quillie returned to the Durham area, continuing working to support his family while pastoring four struggling churches. He developed a successful fruit and vegetable delivery business, with a weekly route through the city. Everywhere he went, he shared Christ, helping and ministering to those he could help along the way.

Quillie didn't stop when he came to the "segregated streets" of Hayti. Despite the deep racial tension in the 1940's South, he took his unique ministry into Durham's traditionally black community, determined to share the gospel with everyone who would listen.

In 1951, the Hansleys moved to Jacksonville, Florida. He purchased Timiquana Trailer Park, with 10 cottages and spaces for travel trailers or mobile homes. The family began to host Sunday School classes in their home, but soon needed more room.

After purchasing a corner lot nearby, in Nov. 1952, the 110th Street FWB Church (later Wesconnett FWB Church) held its first service. It was the church where Quillie would serve faithfully until his death in 1979, first as pastor and later as quiet leader and encourager.

He continued faithful laboring with his hands and heart to carry the good news to those who did not know. His legacy lives on in the lives of their family, their congregations, the young men who answered the call to preach under their ministry, and in churches they left behind.

Ralph R Kennan
Birth:
Sep. 16, 1866
Minnesota
Death:
Nov. 18, 1948
Nassau County, Florida
Burial:
Oakwood Cemetery
Hilliard
Nassau County,Florida
Plot: Section 2, Grave 54

Rev Harvey Lee Henderson, Sr
Birth:
Dec. 9, 1924
Houston County, Alabama
Death:
Nov. 5, 2008
Donalsonville
Seminole County, Georgia
Burial:
Damascas Freewill Baptist
Cemetery
Marianna
Jackson County, Florida

Rev. Henderson was born to William Dolphus and Ossie Bell Ingram Henderson. He had served his country in the US Navy and was married for 64 years to Edna Mae Henderson Rev. Henderson had pastored Free Will Baptist churches in Florida, Texas, Tennessee, Alabama, and Georgia, the most recent having been Corinth Free Will Baptist Church in Iron City. Funeral services were at Damascus Free Will Baptist Church in Marianna, FL, with Rev. Donnie Hussey, Rev. Charles Powell, and Rev. Gene Gilbert.

His parents moved to Michigan where they were active in church work, and their children could obtain an education. Rev. Ralph R. as well as his brother Rev. Albert L., obtained degrees from Hillsdale College, Hillsdale, Michigan, and Albert L. served in India as a missionary in the Free Baptist mission endeavor there. As seen from censuses, Rev. Ralph R. edited a church paper in Minneapolis, and then pastored until he moved to Florida, where he engaged in business where his brother, Albert, had already located. Ralph married Stella D. Cole, b. NY. Numerous city directories list him as being pastor of the Free Baptist church in Portland ME. His parents were Rev's. George Kennan (1832 - 1905) and Ada Montgomery Kennan (1839 - 1894).

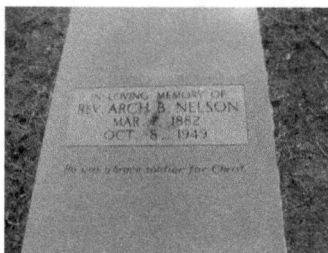

Rev Archibald Bishop Nelson
Birth:
Mar. 7, 1882
Death:
Oct. 8, 1949
Burial:
Saint Johns Free Will Church
Cemetery
Bonifay
Holmes County
Florida

He was listed as a FWB minister from Bonifay, FL in the Eastern Gen. Association in 1936 session convened in Glennville GA.

To Live is Christ

To Die is Gain.

Daniel Frederick Pelt
Birth:
Mar. 25, 1909
Death:
Jun. 22, 1975
Burial:
Comerford-Pelt Cemetery,
Marianna,
Jackson County, Florida

He attended Zion Bible School (1930-32) near Blakely, Georgia. He was ordained in 1930.
He attended Alabama State Teachers College in Troy where he graduated. He did graduate work at Emory University in Atlanta, Ga. He was a teacher and pastor, pastoring churches in Alabama, Georgia and Florida. He was one of the founders of the Florida State Association and served as the moderator for eleven years. He attended some of the National Associational meetings, including the first one in 1935 in Nashville, Tennessee. He was writer for the Advanced Sunday School Quarterly for the Free Will Baptist Press.

Chester H. Pelt, Sr
Birth:
Apr. 3, 1912
Death:
Nov. 7, 1994
Burial:
Comerford-Pelt Cemetery,
Marianna,
Jackson County, Florida

He was licensed to preach at Marvin Chapel FWB church near Marianna, Florida in 1932 at age twenty. He attended Zion Bible School 1932-34 near Blakely, Georgia. In the fall of 1935 entered Bob Jones University in Cleveland, Tennessee. In 1938 he and his wife, Mildred Watson Pelt, moved to pastor churches in Pitt County, North Carolina. There he attended East Carolina Teachers College and then transferred to Atlantic Christian College, Wilson, N.C. and graduated in 1940. In 1941 he became pastor of the Edgemont Church in Durham, NC. He was commissioned on June 29, 1943 as a First Lieutenant in the Chaplains Corps to the Army Air Force and served as chaplain of the 39th Bomb Group, 314 Wing of the 20th Air Force on the Island of Guam until VJ Day in 1945. After returning from overseas in January 1946, he was stationed at Pope AFB at Fort Bragg, NC and was relieved from active duty in June 1948. He remained in active reserve in the Army until he was honorable discharged on April 3, 1972 with the rank of Colonel. He was the first Free Will Baptist Chaplain. After the war he did graduate work at Florida State University and afterwards become the Director of Student Personnel at Chipola Junior College and a instructor in Psychology, while pastoring rural churches in Georgia and Alabama. Afterwards he resumed his education at Alabama State Teachers College, Troy, Alabama.

James Alfred Ray
Birth:
Jul. 20, 1855
Georgia
Death:
Jan. 3, 1929
South Jacksonville
Duval County
Florida
Burial:
Greenlawn Cemetery
Jacksonville
Duval County
Florida

A pioneer Free Will Baptist minister in Georgia, Alabama, and Florida was the father-in-law of Dr. Eugene St. Claire, Georgia, the blind preacher.

1992).

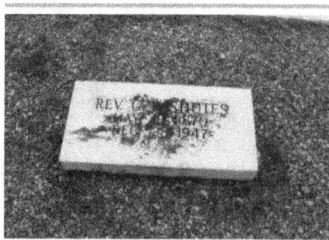

Rev Gordon L. Shutes
Birth:
May 9, 1870
Death:
Dec. 28, 1947
Burial:
Bethlehem Baptist Church
Cemetery
Jackson County
Florida

John M. Rich
Birth:
Apr. 6, 1919
Death:
Jul. 18, 2003
Burial:
Shiloh Baptist Church Cemetery
Chipley
Washington County,
Florida

Family links:
  Spouse:
    Mamie F. Lash Shutes (1876 -
1937)*
    Children:
    Leroy Shutes (1899 - 1976)*

He was a minister serving in
Georgia and Florida. He married
Mary Velma Parker Rich (1915 -

Come Blessed Ones

Missionary
Mabel Alice Bailey Willey
Birth:
Jun. 13, 1905,
Huntsville,
Madison County, Alabama
Death:
Jan. 15, 1998,
Texas
Burial:
Woodlawn Cemetery,
Miami, Dade County, Florida

Mabel Alice Bailey Willey was a pastor's wife, missionary, mother, teacher and missions lecturer. Born in Huntsville, Alabama, she was a graduate of Toccoa Falls College in north Georgia and Nyack College in New York. In 1930. she and her new husband arrived in Miami to pastor the newly organized Alliance Gospel Tabernacle. A year later they had pastorates in North Carolina. In 1938 they went to Panama to work as missionaries among the Choco Indians. They returned to Miami a year later where Mrs. Willey survived a bout with black water malaria. In 1940, they packed the family and moved to Jaruco, Cuba where they assisted in a training program for Cuban pastors. In 1942 they moved to the province of Pinar del Rio and founded the Seminario Los Cedros del Libano, which trained pastors to serve in Iglesia Bautista Libre de Cuba (the Free Will Baptist Church of Cuba). Mabel Willey served as an instructor and the school administrator there for 16 years. Their days as missionaries to Cuba ended in 1960 and they returned to Miami due to Fidel Castro's regime. Undaunted, they opened the Free Will Baptist Refugee Center which responded to the needs of thousands of Cubans fleeing from the oppression of Castro's communism. Mabel, after the death of her husband in 1968, embarked on an extensive ministry speaking to mission conferences, women's seminars and retreats in Japan and Europe. In her mid-60's she started a ministry to professional women in Panama, which included the wives of some of the high ranking government officials. In 1978, she was one of the first former U.S. missionaries allowed to return to Cuba for a visit. She returned six times before her death. In 1988, the government of Cuba allowed the re-opening of the Seminario. Her autobiography, *Through the Gate*, was published by Randall House Publications. She died in Bryan, Texas while living with daughter Barbara Willey Moehlman. In addition to her daughter she is survived by her son Tom Willey, Jr. the director of the Miami Office of World Relief. Her services were at the Iglesia

Bautista Libre Ebenezer in Miami.

Thomas Willey, Sr
Birth:
Jan. 31, 1898,
New Jersey
Death:
Oct. 18, 1968,
Miami, Dade County, Florida
Burial:
Woodlawn Cemetery,
Miami-Dade County,
Florida,

The Rev. Thomas H. Willey, veteran Free Will Baptist missionary to Latin America, died undergoing treatment for cancer. Willey, was one of the denomination's early senior missionaries, serving in Latin America under Free Will Baptist auspices since 1936. The scene was a crude altar in a little Baptist church in the North. The year was 1898. The infant Willey was taken there by his loving, God-honoring, praying mother who gave her most cherished possession, the son of her own

womb, to the Lord with a prayer that he would be used for the Lord's glory. The steps were all steps of faith. He was converted as a small lad and licensed to preach at age 14. He had an unforgettable encounter with a lost world at a missionary meeting in St. George Church, Philadelphia. He became Methodism's oldest enrollment at Asbury College for Christian training with no financial backing -a circuit riding ministry as a Methodist preacher in the rolling hills of Kentucky-a missionary assignment in the jungles of Peru - a home missions ministry then to Panama and, ultimately, Cuba. The Funeral service was held at Ebenezer Free Will Baptist Church (Spanish) in Miami. Foreign mission board Vice-Chairman Raymond Riggs of Detroit and General Director Reford Wilson of Nashville, long associates of the deceased, officiated assisted by other associates of the veteran missionary. They invited those wishing to express respects to do so by memorial contributions to the Thomas H. Willey Memorial Loan Fund, established by the family in cooperation with the foreign board to assist church construction in Panama. Surviving Mr. Willey are his wife, the former Mabel Alice Bailey; one son, Thomas, Jr., a Free Will Baptist missionary to Panama; and one daughter, Mrs. Barbara Willey Moehlman of Miami. Mr. Willey, known throughout the denomination as "Pop," was the first sent by his denomination to Latin America where he pioneered work in Panama in 1936 and in Cuba in 1942. He also made surveys leading to the establishment of Free Will Baptist work in Brazil in 1958. Prior to appointment by Free Will Baptists, Mr. Willey served in Peru under auspices of the Christian and Missionary Alliance.

Charles Cecil Williamson
Birth
Bowling Green,
Florida
February 20, 1940
Death
Lakeland,
Florida
October 25, 2011

Cecil was a Minister and a member of the Freewill Baptist Organization and also a Army veteran. He was a well-known evangelist and pastored the Bartow church for many years.

Maynard Blair Woodlief
Birth:
Aug. 14, 1912
Wake County
North Carolina
Death:
Feb. 15, 1950
Johnston County
North Carolina
Burial:
Marvin Chapel Freewill Baptist
Church Cemetery
Marianna
Jackson County
Florida

Registered as a minister of the Free Will Baptists in N.C. when the Eastern General Association met in sessions in the mid-1930's.

The will of the One who understands.

Nathan Woodworth
Birth:
Mar. 29, 1824
Wayne,
Ohio
Death:
Mar. 16, 1901
Welaka
Putnam County,
Florida
Burial:
Oakwood Cemetery
Putnam County,
Florida

He was a son of John Woodworth. He experienced the new birth in 1841. He was a student at Geauga Seminary and received license to preach in 1847 and ordained four years later. His pastorates were in Warren, Illinois; Rochester, Wheatland, and Wayne, Wisconsin; Crystal Lake and Nashua, Florida. He served as a delegate to the General Conference.

Georgia

Amos Banks Adams
Birth:
Sep. 13, 1897
Death:
Nov. 12, 1953
Burial:
Satilla Freewill Baptist Church Cemetery
Hazlehurst
Jeff Davis County,
Georgia

His name appeared in the South Georgia Minutes in 1936 and during 1938-1953. He married Annie Warnock Adams (1904 - 1982).

William Amos Addison
Birth:
Apr. 14, 1907
Georgia
Death:
Nov. 17, 1977
Seminole County,Georgia
Burial:
Pilgrims Rest Church Cemetery
Colquitt
Miller County,Georgia

He served in the Martin and Little River Conferences according to the minutes of both Q.M's. Son of George M. Addison and Rosa Miller. His wife was Alma Monday (1907 - 1991).

Inscription:
In Heaven There is One Angel More.

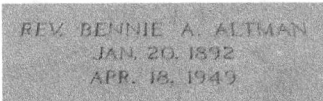

Bennie Allen Altman
Birth:
Jan. 20, 1892
Death:
Apr. 18, 1949
Burial:
Pineview Cemetery
Folkston
Charlton County, Georgia

According to South Georgia

minutes he served there between 1940-48.He was a son of Marion Altman (1866 - 1946) and Maggie Altman (1860 - 1926) he was married to Mattie Lou Mizell Altman (1896 - 1982).

John R Amburgey
Birth:
Apr. 30, 1940
West Virginia
Death:
Aug. 14, 2002
Patmos
Baker County,Georgia
Burial:
Patmos Free Will Baptist Church Cemetery
Patmos,Baker County Georgia

He was licensed to preach in 1979, ordained in 1980, and had served as pastor at Patmos since 1997. Rev. Amburgey, a native of W. VA, and U.S. Army Veteran, was an alumnus of Hillsdale FWB College, and Salem Bible College, Brevard Com. College (FL) and Bethany Theological Seminary in Dothan, AL. He had pastored churches in AL, MS, and FL, before coming to Patmos Church in GA. In addition to his pastoral ministry, Amburgey served on various boards and committees. He was elected Sec'y of Georgia State Board on Camping (1986-'88; 1998-2002). John Amburgey was known as a man with a sense of humor who supported and promoted every phase of denominational work.

W L Amerson
Birth:
Oct. 27, 1911
Death:
Feb. 1, 1996
Burial:
Pine Level Freewill Baptist
Church Cemetery
Chester
Dodge County,Georgia

He was a Georgia minister serving in the Georgia Union.

H A Ammons
Birth:
1845
Death:
1915
Burial:
Memorial Freewill Baptist
Church Cemetery
Surrency
Appling County,Georgia

Early Georgia minister whose record is found in the 1907 South Georgia Minutes. He was a private in the CSA in Company A, 4th Regiment. he was married to Arvenie James Ammons (1848 - 1920).

Leonard Short Anthony
Birth:
May 28, 1881
Death:
Jan. 19, 1944
Burial:
New Life Freewill Baptist
Church Cemetery
Marion County,Georgia
Active minister whose name appears in the Chattahoochee, Little River, Midway, Union and Georgia Union Minutes.

Allen Bruce Ard
Birth:
Jul. 21, 1877
Death:
Mar. 5, 1966
Burial:
Salem Cemetery
Desser
Seminole County,Georgia

Early minister serving in the Martin Assn. according to their minutes from 1919 to 1964. His name also appears in the Midway Minutes in 1919.

John Calvin Arnold
Birth:
Apr. 25, 1886
Death:
May 1, 1943
Burial:
Zion Hill Cemetery
Millwood
Ware County,Georgia
Minister in the Little River Conference.

Missionary Laura Belle Barnard
Birth:
Feb. 13, 1907
Death:
Mar. 10, 1992
Burial:
Ebenezer Cemetery,
Glennville,
Tattnall County,
Georgia,
Plot: E2

Free Will Baptist educator, missionary, humanitarian was born and reared in Glennville, Georgia. After graduation from high school, she attended South Georgia Teachers College in Statesboro, and then transferred to Columbia Bible College in South Carolina. She graduated from Columbia in 1932 and shortly thereafter she sensed a call to evangelical mission work. In 1935 she was commissioned for mission work in India by the General Conference of Free Will Baptists of the South. That year the General Conference merged with the Cooperative General Association of Free Will Baptists, a group in the Midwest and

Southwest, to form the National Association of Free Will Baptists, becoming the first missionary of a newly formed denomination. Barnard began her mission in Kotagiri, South India, in the summer of 1935. She worked among the "untouchables," the lowest class in the Hindu caste system. In the early 1940s she moved back to the United States and served briefly as a teacher at the fledgling Free Will Baptist Bible College in Nashville, Tennessee, but she soon returned to India, where she remained until 1957. Upon completion of her Master's Degree at Columbia Bible College in 1960, she became a Professor of Missions at the Free Will Baptist Bible College, from which she retired in 1972. Barnard wrote a number of books, including *His Name among All Nations* (1946), which is a theology of missions, and *Touching the Untouchables* (1985), her autobiography. Barnard retired to her hometown of Glennville, where she engaged in numerous ministries, including humanitarian aid to Mexican migrant workers.

William J Barksdale
Birth:
Mar. 28, 1932
Worth County, Georgia
Death:
Dec. 26, 2014
Tifton
Tift County,Georgia
Burial:

Poulan Cemetery
Poulan
Worth County,Georgia

Rev. Barksdale was born in Worth County on March 28, 1932 to the late Jutson and Mamie Lois Ellis Barksdale. Rev. Barksdale had lived in Tifton since 1987. He was ordained as a minister in November 1965 and retired after 49 years. He was a veteran of the United States Navy having served during the Korean War. Rev. Barksdale was formerly employed with Lawhorne Tire and liked to hunt and fish. He enjoyed visiting people and seeing to the needs of others. Rev. Barksdale was a member of the Corinth Freewill Baptist Church and was affiliated with the Freewill Baptist Association.

John Nelson Barnes
Birth:
Sep. 18, 1895
Death:
Sep. 18, 1961
Burial:
Sowhatchee Cemetery, Blakely
Early County, Georgia

Their Works Do Follow Them.

Gerald Baxley
Birth:
Sep. 17, 1943
Dothan
Houston County, Alabama
Death:
Oct. 25, 1995
Jesup
Wayne County, Georgia
Burial:
Omega Cemetery
Baxley
Appling County, Georgia

The 52-year-old minister pastored Surrency Free Will Baptist Church for seven years. Rev. Baxley was ordained to preach in Feb. 1968. His first pastorate was at his home church, Corinth FWB in Midland City, Alabama. During his 27-year ministry, he pastored eight churches in three states--AL, KY, and GA. He was within 10 days of relocating to his ninth pastorate (New Lebanon FWB Church in Tishomingo, MS, when he died. In addition to pastoral work, Baxley was active in local associational outreach. He served as clerk of Alabama Cahaba River Ass'n, and Georgia's So. Georgia Assn. The Alabama Home Missions Board

employed him for a time as interim pastor for the mission work in Enterprise.

John Lewis Batchelor
Birth:
Sep. 10, 1925
Death:
May 29, 2004
Burial:
Father's Home Church Cemetery
Camilla
Mitchell County,
Georgia

Minister in the Martin and Midway Assn's. His wife was Margie Horn Batchelor (1931 - 2013).

Johnny Ralph Batchelor
Birth:
Aug. 1, 1893
Miller County,Georgia
Death:
Jul. 6, 1962
Mayhaw
Miller County,Georgia
Burial:
White Plains Freewill Baptist
Church Cemetery
Lucile
Early County,Georgia

Minister. Married to Pauline Inez Cooper Batchelor (1889 - 1963) and a son named Bruce Lawton Batchelor (1911 - 1985).

L R Beach
Birth:
1867
Death:
Jun. 12, 1950
Burial:
Live Oak Freewill Baptist Church
Cemetery
Milford
Baker County, Georgia

He was a minister in the Martin Assn.

Ed. C. Beers
Birth:
Unknown
New York
Death:
Sep. 18, 1872
Muscogee County, Georgia
Burial:
Rock Baptist Church Cemetery
Cataula
Harris County, Georgia

SPECULATIVE that this individual is buried at Rehoboth (a.k.a. Rock) Baptist Cemetery - he was residing near Cataula at the time of his death and his son is buried at this cemetery. Said to have been of Dutch ancestry. Aged 74 years on the 1870 census, so evidently born about 1796. Married Sarah Unknown, who survived him. In 1854, he was preacher at the Providence Free Will Baptist Church on St. Mary's Road in Muscogee County, Georgia. They appear as Edmund BEARS (74, born in New York, retired tailor) and Sarah BEARS (61, born South Carolina), with William (38, grist miller), Victoria (33, farm hand), Emma (11, at home), James (9), Charles (7), Ida (5), and Clinton (3), as well as John McNEIL (30, farm hand), Mary WELLS (40, at home) and William WELLS (8) in the household. Sarah appears as a widow, aged 75 years, in the 1880 census household of her son, E. W. BEERS in Georgia Militia District #672 (Hamilton District) in Harris County, Georgia."E. C. BEERS KILLED.-- We learn that when the workmen engaged in bridging Standing Boy Creek returned from dinner yesterday, they found the body of E. C. BEERS in the creek. His satchel was on the tressel at the end of the bridge. It is supposed from this fact that he was resting on the bridge and had fallen asleep and fell, and in the fall struck his head against one of the timbers. He was aged about 70 years. He left a wife and son (E. W. BEERS) who lives near

Cataula, Harris County. This is in substance that we learned of the sad affair." [Columbus (GA) Sun newspaper, Thursday, 19 SEP 1872, p. 3.]"THE GEORIGA PRESS [news from around the state].

Ralph J. Bell
Birth:
Jul. 25, 1924
Death:
Oct. 19, 1967
Burial:
New Enterprise Freewill Baptist Church Cemetery
Seminole County,Georgia

Member of Midway Conference.

David W Blanton
Birth:
Jun. 2, 1857
Death:
Nov. 12, 1916
Burial:
New Hope Free Will Baptist Church Cemetery
Madray Springs
Wayne County,Georgia

Preacher in the Ogeechee and South Georgia Quarterly Meetings.

Isaac J. Blanton
Birth:
Feb. 14, 1861
Duplin County,North Carolina
Death:
Mar. 16, 1926
Surrency
Appling County,Georgia
Burial:
Memorial Freewill Baptist Church Cemetery
Surrency
Appling County,Georgia

Isaac was born to Joshua Isham BLANTON (b. c1827) and Elizabeth "Bettie" BLAND (marr. 03 Jul 1852 Duplin Co, NC). He was a minister in the Oqeechee and South Georgia Assn's serving from 1903 to 1925 acccording from the minutes of said conferences.

David Louis Boatright
Birth:
Oct. 29, 1868
Death:
Nov. 14, 1950
Burial:
Lake Cemetery
Metter, Candler County,Georgia

Minister in the Ogeechee Assn. He married Lillian Cornelia Rogers Boatright (1870 - 1924) and they had son Reuben Lloyd Boatright (1894 - 1918).

Zachariah Taylor Bone
Birth:
Nov. 26, 1848
Butler
Taylor County,Georgia
Death:
Dec. 24, 1909
Butler
Taylor County,Georgia
Burial:
Mount Pisgah Cemetery
Butler, Taylor County,Georgia

He is recorded in the Chattahoochee minutes from 1891 until 1909. He was married to Sarah L. Decker Bone (1823 - 1912).

Seaborn Bowen
Birth:
May 29, 1882
Death:
Jul. 11, 1960
Burial:
Sunnyside Cemetery
Pearson
Atkinson County,Georgia

He was a minister and member of the South Georgia Conference.

Thomas J. Bowen
Birth:
Jan. 2, 1814
Death:
Nov. 24, 1875
Burial:
Greensboro City Cemetery
Greensboro
Greene County,Georgia

He was an early minister in the Chattahoochee Conference and appears in the minutes of 1842. Lurana H. Bowen (1832 - 1907) was his wife.

Barney B. Bradley
Birth:
Jul. 26, 1907
Death:
Jun. 24, 1949
Burial:
Oak Hill CemeteryGriffin
Spalding County,Georgia
Plot: Section B; Block 2

Records show he was a member of the Chattahoochee Assn.

David Rowan Braswell
Birth:
Jan. 8, 1877
Decatur County,Georgia
Death:
Jul. 1, 1947
Decatur County,Georgia
Burial:
Salem Cemetery,Desser
Seminole County,Georgia

He pastored in the Martin Association. He was married to

Perry Lee Alday Braswell (1874 - 1968).

Benjamin F. Bratcher
Birth:
Apr., 1883
Georgia
Death:
Mar. 11, 1951
Georgia
Burial:
Carters Chapel Cemetery
Bacon County,Georgia

Minutes of the South Georgia record him as a minister from 1907 until 1931, He married twice.(1) Ella "Ellie" Carter, daughter of Jackson and Mary A. Carter. She is supposed to be buried at Fishing Creek in Pierce Co. GA and second to Lula Deen Powell (1915 - 1998).

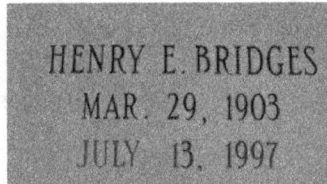

Henry Elmer Bridges
Birth:
Mar. 29, 1903
Death:
Jul. 13, 1997
Burial:
Mount Calvary Baptist Church
Cemetery
Cary
Bleckley County,Georgia

COCHRAN--- Services for the Rev. Henry E. Bridges was held in

Mount Calvary Baptist Church with burial in the church cemetery. Bridges, 94, died in a Cochran nursing home. The son of the late West and Cindy English Bridges, he was born in Laurens County but lived most of his life in Bleckley County. A Coast Guard veteran, he was retired from Paulk Lumber Company and as minister of Freewill Baptist Church. He was a member of Little Bethel Freewill Baptist Church. FROM: The Macon Telegraph 7-14-1997 Page 6B

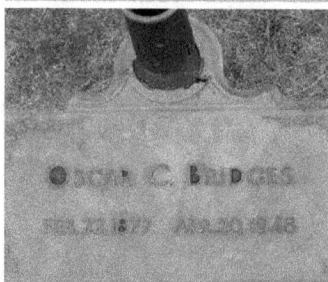

Oscar C. Bridges
Birth:
Feb. 22, 1877
Death:
Apr. 20, 1948
Burial:
Parkhill Cemetery
Columbus
Muscogee County
,Georgia
Plot: Garden 29

Listed in some of the Chattahoochee minutes of 1917-1947. He was married to Bessie Cromer Bridges (1890 - 1959).

James Edward Brodnax
Birth:
Dec. 11, 1822
Hancock Co. Georgia
Death:
Feb. 28, 1885
Muscogee Co. GA
Burial:
New Providence Baptist Church
Cemetery
Muscogee County, Georgia

Rev. James Edward Broadnax, son of John Travis Brodnax and Hettie (Gordy) Brodnax, with his brothers settled near Columbus, GA, and was pastor of the Free Will Baptist Church where the Broadnax/Brodnax family have their burial plot. One of these brothers, John M. Broadnax, died from accidental wounds received during the War Between the States and is buried at Providence with Irvin near him. (Rev.) James Edward Broadnax m. Martha Watkins [19 August 1847], and they had 7 children. John Travis Broadnax, a veteran of War of 1812. was living in Hancock, Co., Ga., in 1827, where he drew in that land lottery. The goodness and faithfulness of Rev. Jas. E. Broadnax was appreciated by the whole neighborhood where he preached for 35 years." --from "History of Chattahoochee Co. GA, by N.K. Rogers, copyright, 1933.

Inscription on slab:
"Pioneer Free Will Baptist Preacher; Gave the Land to Providence Free Will Baptist Church.

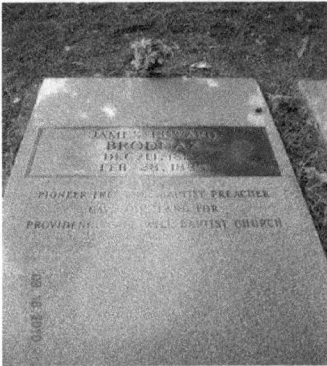

Gerald E. Brown
Birth:
Jan. 9, 1930
Death:
Aug. 14, 2006
Burial:
Cedar Creek Cemetery
Cordele
Crisp County,Georgia

He was a minister in the Georgia Union, Midway, Union, Little River and Chattahoochee conferences from 1895 through 1998. He was a veteran of the Korean War in the United States Army.

James Earl Bryant
Birth:
Jun. 8, 1926
Death:
Oct. 6, 2006
Burial:
Little Bethel Freewill Baptist
Church

Cochran
Bleckley County,Georgia

He was a member of the Georgia Union Association and his ministry is recorded in its minutes from 1981 until 1999.

Robert L Burnett
Birth:
Feb. 26, 1883
Death:
Jun. 15, 1934
Burial:
Mount Nebo Primitive Baptist Church Cemetery
Charing
Taylor County,Georgia

An early Free Will Baptist preacher whose ministry is recorded in the Chattahoochee minutes from 1915 until 1933.

T. P. Carr
Birth:
Jan. 8, 1845
Death:
Oct. 26, 1909
Burial:
Mount Olive Freewill Baptist Church Cemetery
Potterville
Taylor County,Georgia

Early minister in the Chattahoochee Association. His name appears in the Chattahoochee minutes in 1889 and in other editions until 1907.

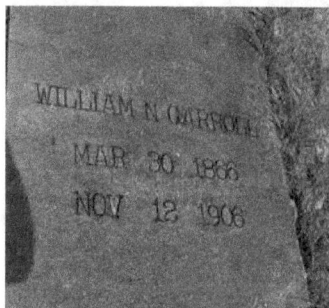

William N. Carroll
Birth:
Mar. 30, 1866
Death:
Nov. 12, 1906
Burial:
New Providence Baptist Church Cemetery
Muscogee County, Georgia
Early minister that served in the Chattahoochee Association. His name appears in the minutes of 1908 and 1909.

J. C. Hubert Carter
Birth:
May 2, 1925
Death:
Oct. 7, 1988
Burial:
Blackshear City Cemetery
Blackshear
Pierce County,Georgia

He ministered in the Little River, Martin, and South Georgia

Association's. His name appears in all three of the minutes of these conferences. he was married to Marjorie J. Carter (1925 - ___).

T M Carter
Birth:
Apr. 25, 1900
Death:
Dec. 31, 1953
Burial:
Memorial Freewill Baptist
Church Cemetery
Surrency
Appling County,Georgia

He was a minister in the South Georgia conference. His World War I Draft Registration Cards, 1917-1918 Name: Theopheilus Marion Carter County: Appling State: Georgia Birth Date: 25 Apr 1900 Race: White FHL Roll Number: 1556940 Draft Board: His parents were Millard W Carter (1875 - 1940) and Dealphia Edenfield Carter (1879 - 1954).

Martin Franklin Cason
Birth:
Jun. 15, 1858
Ware County,
Georgia
Death:
Mar. 31, 1939
Bemiss
Lowndes County,
Georgia
Burial:
Royals Cemetery
Kirkland
Atkinson County,Georgia

Martin was a farmer and a minister serving in the South Georgia conference according to the minutes of 1905 and 1907. He is the son of Hillery William Cason and Pheby Walker Cason. He was married three times to Martha Frances Royal Cason (1868 - 1893),Alice Pafford Cason (1863 - 1910) and Emma Jane Smith Cason (1886 - 1955).

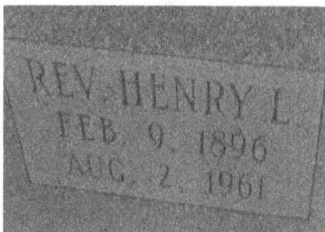

Henry L Catrett
Birth:
Feb. 9, 1896
Death:
Aug. 2, 1961
Burial:
Colquitt City Cemetery
Colquitt
Miller County,Georgia

He served in the Midway, Georgia Union, and Martin Associations during the period of 1940 through the 1960s. his wife was Nettie S Catrett (1895 - 1959).

L J (James) Chambless
Birth:
Feb. 9, 1926
Alabama
Death:
May 30, 1998
Tift County,Georgia
Burial:
Tift Memorial Gardens and Mausoleum
Tifton
Tift County,Georgia

He was a minister in the Little River Association. His parents were Oscar H. Chambless (1898 - 1953) and Lonia Beasley Chambless (1908 - 1968). He was married to Betty Mason Chambless (1934 - 1994) and to this union was born Barbara Franks Chambless (1943 - 2011).

"I See Heaven Open And Jesus On The Right Hand Of God."

Edward S. Cheshire
Birth:
Apr. 20, 1842
Stewart County,Georgia
Death:
Mar. 31, 1926
Burial:
Friendship Cemetery
Hahira
Lowndes County,Georgia

He was an early minister in the Midway Association. He was married to Julia George Cheshire (1844 - 1918).

W C Coleman
Birth:
May 14, 1880
Death:
Jan. 21, 1959
Burial:
Bethel Free Will Baptist Church
Cemetery
Appling County,Georgia

Early minister serving in the Georgia Union and South Georgia Associations during the periods from 1916 until 1957.

George W. Collins
Birth:
Apr. 10, 1880
Death:
Mar. 3, 1960
Burial:
Collins-McCullough Cemetery
Emanuel County,Georgia

He was a minister in the Ogeechee and South Georgia Assn's. His wife was Sarah McCullough Collins (1887 - 1964).

C C Coursey
Birth:
Aug. 2, 1872
Death:
Nov. 3, 1946
Burial:
Lyons City Cemetery
Lyons
Toombs County,Georgia
In the quarterly meeting minutes it revealed that he served as a minister in the South Georgia conference from 1913 until about 1946.

William Robert Crawley
Birth:
Jan. 9, 1912
Ben Hill County,Georgia
Death:
Mar. 28, 1990
Peach County,Georgia
Burial:
Sunset Memorial Gardens
Americus
Sumter County,Georgia
His parents were William Asberry Crawley (1882 - 1960) and Lillie Crawley (1888 - 1915) and he was married to Mary P. Lowell Crawley (1916 - 2007).

R. Paul Creech
Birth:
Oct. 11, 1962,
Durham,
Durham County,
North Carolina
Death:
Sep. 15, 2011,
Macon,
Bibb County,
Georgia
Burial:
Glen Haven Memorial Garden,
Macon,
Bibb County,
Georgia

Free Will Baptist Minister, missionary to Japan from 1987 to 1988, and to the Ivory Coast, West Africa, from 1989 to 1998. He served churches in New Brunswick, Canada and Georgia. He was a member of the Board of International Missions for the National Association of Free Will Baptists.

Madison Lamar Crook
Birth:
Dec. 20, 1867
Macon County,Georgia
Death:
Jan. 14, 1934
Burial:
Mount Olive Freewill Baptist Church Cemetery
Potterville
Taylor County,Georgia

Minister in the Chattahoochee Association according to minutes of 1907-1912.

Gene Autry Cross
Birth:
Mar. 15, 1947
Death:
Dec. 5, 2004

Burial:
Dawn Memorial Park
Decatur
DeKalb County,Georgia

He served in the Oqeechee and Georgia Union conferences.

Joshua Edward Daniel
Birth:
Jun. 19, 1861
Death:
Aug. 6, 1928
Burial:
Forest Park City Cemetery
Forest Park
Clayton County,Georgia

Early minister in the Middle Georgia association. He was the son of Richard Daniel (1813 - 1891) and Sarah Norman Daniel (1831 - 1897). He was married to Mary J. Daniel (1861 - 1942).

Willie Dawson
Birth:
Unknown
Death:
Sep. 12, 2012
Jamieson,Gadsden County,Florida
Burial:
Cool Springs Cemetery

Faceville, Decatur County, Georgia

He served churches in Florida and Georgia living to the age of 76 dying at his home in Jamieson, Florida. He served as a deacon at the First Free Will Baptist church in Quincy, Florida and after his call to the ministry served as a bi-vocational preacher. By trade he was a construction worker. His last church was the First FWB in Bainbridge, Ga. He gave sacrificially to both home and international missions because missionary Sandra Payne was his sister.

G Thomas Dell
Birth:
Aug. 17, 1872
Death:
Mar. 10, 1956
Burial:
Wesley Chapel Methodist Church Cemetery
Berlin
Colquitt County,Georgia

Minister in the Union Assn.

Damon C. Dodd
Birth:
Feb. 14, 1916,
Flat River,
St. Francois County, Missouri
Death:
Apr. 27, 2000,
Colquitt, Miller County,Georgia
Burial:
Donley, Bellview,
Miller County,Georgia

Free Will Baptist leader, pastor, and missionary. Bro. Dodd was converted at the age of 15 during an evangelistic crusade by the McAdams Evangelistic Team. The speaker on that blessed, fateful evening was a woman, Lizzie McAdams. He was ordained into the Gospel Ministry in 1936 at the St. Francois County Quarterly meeting in Missouri. Damon married Sylvia R. Wood in 1938, and God gave them two lovely girls and fifty-eight years of companionship and service together.

Sylvia's roots came from Joshua Wood who was one of three Wood families that came to St.

Francois County Missouri from Ohio near 1866. They started most of the Free Will Baptist churches in the area. Damon attended Flat River Jr. College, but when the Free Will Baptist Bible College began in 1942. He and his wife, Sylvia, joined seven other students. Two years later they made up half of the first graduating class. Brother Dodd went on with his formal education until he received a Doctor of Ministries degree in the 1980s. Study was a joy and writing was a passion for him. He wrote as he spoke, with enthusiasm. He published, *All of Mine For Him,* 1954, *The Free Will Baptist Story,* 1956; *Go Home Tell Thy Friends,* 1957; *Trailways to Adventure, 1963; Study Guide for Revelation, 1967; Handbook for New Church Members,* 1970; *Marching Through Georgia,* 1977.

Damon and Sylvia were foreign missionaries to Cuba, 1945-48. He served as the fourth National Association Executive-Secretary, 1949-53. In 1953 he was the first full-time Promotional Secretary for the National Home Missions Dept. and opened its first national office. Damon was a Foreign Missions Board Member, 1944-46, and a Free Will Baptist Bible College Trustee Board Member, 1962-76.

In Georgia, Brother Dodd served as: the State Moderator; the state's Historical Commission; Chairman of the Committee that wrote the Standard and Doctrinal Examination for Licensing and Ordaining Free Will Baptist Ministers in Georgia, which was adopted by the state association, November 16, 1979. He served as an evangelist, church planter and pastor.

He served churches in Missouri, 1937-42, 1947-50; Tennessee, 1942-46; and in Georgia. His first Georgia pastorate was in Savannah, 1958-62, South Georgia Association. Later he served the congregations at Homerville, 1965-73, Little River Association; Bay, 1974-75, Union Association; New Home, Miller County, 1975-81 and 90, Martin Association; Bellview, 1983 and 1987, Midway Association.

Missionary Sylvia *Wood* Dodd
Birth:
Jan. 25, 1917,
Missouri
Death:
May 5, 1996,
Colquitt, Miller County,Georgia
Burial:
Donley Cemetery,Colquitt,
Miller County,Georgia

She traveled with Texas woman preacher, Lizzie McAdams, playing the piano in her evangelistic ministry. Damon Dodd had been converted in her revival in Missouri. Lizzie was unhappy to lose her to Damon, but concluded that she'd be a blessing to Damon in his ministry. Sylvia's roots came from Joshua Wood who was one of three Wood families that came to St. Francois County Missouri from Ohio near 1866. They started most of the Free Will

Baptist churches in the area. It is the oldest conference in the state of Missouri and contains many churches in the lead belt section of the state.

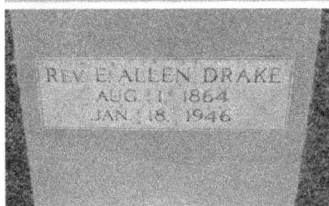

E Allen Drake
Birth:
Aug. 1, 1864
Death:
Jan. 18, 1946
Burial:
Corinth Cemetery
Iron City
Seminole County,Georgia

According to the Martin conference minutes he served from 1902 until about 1943. he was married to Sallie W. Drake (1871 - 1962).

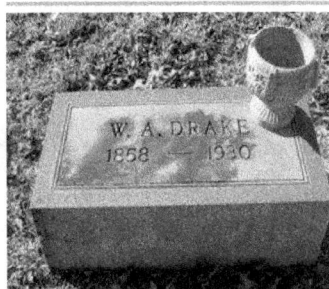

W A Drake
Birth:
1858
Death:
1930

Georgia
Burial:
Finch Cemetery
Philomath
Oglethorpe County,Georgia

He was an early minister serving in the Martin Association according records from1919 and 1921.

William S Driggers
Birth:
Apr. 1, 1910
Death:
May 31, 1987
Burial:
Mount Gilead Freewill Baptist Church Cemetery
Decatur County,Georgia
As a minister he served in the South Georgia, Chattahoochee, Midway and Martin Associations.

Inscription:
TEC 5 US ARMY WWII

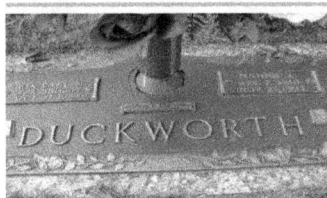

Earl B Duckworth
Birth:
Apr. 18, 1905
Death:
Oct. 11, 1989
Burial:
Glen Haven Memorial Garden
Macon
Bibb County,Georgia
Plot: Everlasting Life 163 D # 3

According to the South Georgia and Georgia Union minutes he served as a minister from about 1935 to 1988 in both of these conferences.

Harold Keith Dunlap
Birth:
Nov. 3, 1926
Death:
Feb. 1, 1999
Burial:
Macon Memorial Park
Macon, Bibb County,Georgia

He was a member of the Georgia Union Conference according to its minutes from 1967 until 1979 his record appears.

James M Dunn
Birth:
Mar. 5, 1856
Georgia
Death:
1929
Georgia
Burial:
Bay Springs Free Will Baptist
Church Cemetery
Plainfield
Dodge County,
Georgia

The Georgia Union of minutes show him serving as a clergyman in their 1925 through 1927 records. He was married to Isabella Jones Dunn (1875 - 1923) to whose union was born Joseph T Dunn (1914 - 1987).

J H Dupree
Birth:
Nov. 29, 1846
Death:
Jun. 12, 1922
Burial:
New Prospect Freewill Baptist
Coverdale
Turner County,Georgia

According to the Chattahoochee minutes he ministered within the Association from 1879 until 1913. He also served in the Confederate States of America Army.
Inscription:
Co C 55 GA INF
Confederate States Army

James Thomas Edwards
Birth:
Jan. 23, 1876
Baker County, Georgia
Death:
May 28, 1964
Baker County, Georgia
Burial:
Travelers Rest Freewill Baptist
Church Cemetery
Newton
Baker County, Georgia

He was a minister in the Martin conference. He was married to Rossie Bailey Edwards (1880 - 1964).

Adolphus Emanuel
Birth:
Oct. 29, 1868
Cumberland County, North Carolina
Death:

Sep. 18, 1948
Emanuel County, Georgia
Burial:
Collins Cemetery
Oak Park
Emanuel County, Georgia

Named as one of the ministers in the promotion and organization of the GA Free Will Bapt. State Association in 1917.

John M Emanuel
Birth:
Sep. 24, 1875
Death:
Aug. 24, 1943
Burial:
Cool Spring Cemetery
Candler County,
Georgia

He served as a minister in the Chattahoochee, Midway and South Georgia conferences from 1906 until about 1942.

George Troup Embry
Birth:
Dec. 4, 1832
Death:
Apr. 11, 1916
Burial:
Morgan Methodist Church
Cemetery
Morgan
Calhoun County,
Georgia

He was the son of Hezekiah Luckie Embry and Martha Slaton Lowe. He was an early minister in the Liberty and Martin Associations 1892 through 1894.

He was married to Sarah Elizabeth Wolfe Embry (1834 - 1906) and they had one child Nancy E Embry (1854 - 1890).

Elder William H. Emerson
Birth:
Mar. 26, 1876
Georgia
Death:
Aug. 16, 1948
Macon County, Georgia
Burial:
Little Bethel Freewill Baptist Cemetery
Ideal
Macon County, Georgia

Minutes show that he appeared as a minister from 1903 until 1948 in the Chattahoochee, Georgia Union and Midway Associations.

Charles B Ethridge
Birth:
May 1, 1886
Death:
Jul. 13, 1929
Burial:
Underwood Memorial Cemetery
Conyers
Rockdale County, Georgia

He served as a minister in the Chattahoochee and Georgia are Union Associations. He was married to Ludie Mae Ethridge (1891 - 1969).

Grady C Etheredge, Sr
Birth:
Apr. 14, 1910
Death:
Dec. 28, 1975
Burial:
Live Oak Freewill Baptist Church Cemetery
Milford
Baker County, Georgia

He was a minister in the Chattahoochee Association.

Alton Everson
Birth:
Sep. 4, 1922
Death:
Feb. 7, 1988
Burial:
Colquitt City Cemetery
Colquitt
Miller County, Georgia

His combined ministry was in the Little River, Georgia Union, South Georgia, Union, and an Martin associations.

Death Is The Fundamental Human Problem.

Howard Dewitt Faircloth
Birth:
Jan. 5, 1924
Dodge County,
Georgia
Death:
Oct. 24, 2014
Dublin
Laurens County,
Georgia
Burial:
Bay Springs
Free Will Baptist Church
Cemetery
Plainfield
Dodge County
Georgia

Rev. Howard Faircloth, age 90, of Eastman died at Carl Vincent Medical Center.

Rev Faircloth was a member of Bay Springs Freewill Baptist Church where he served as pastor for twenty-five years and a total of fifty-six years in various churches. He was also retired from Robins Air Force Base and a veteran of WW II.

Kenneth L. Faison
Birth:
May 23, 1935
Death:
Jul. 19, 1990
Burial:
Glennville City Cemetery
Glennville, Tattnall County,
Georgia
Plot: D5

Rev. Faison died at age 55 in Millen, Georgia after a long illness. He was a native of Moultrie, Georgia and pastor of the Deep Creek Free Will Baptist Church in Millen. He was a pastor and lifelong Free Will Baptist. The Reverends James Ussery, Larry Dale Williams, and Galen Dunbar officiated at his service.

Hoyt Duard Finley
Birth:
Sep. 21, 1920
Death:
Sep. 19, 1989
Hart County, Georgia
Burial:
Poplar Springs Baptist Church
Cemetery
Lavonia
Franklin County, Georgia
He was a minister in the Georgia Union and Chattahoochee Associations during a period of around 1954 through 1992. He was a S SGT US ARMY in WWII where he received a Purple Heart.

Joseph Otis Fort
Birth:
May 2, 1910,
Early County, Georgia

Death:
Mar. 7, 1976,
Early County, Georgia
Burial:
Jakin Freewill Baptist Church
Cemetery,
Jakin, Early County, Georgia

He was a minister in three of the Georgia associations, namely; Midway, South Georgia and Martin. His name appears in nearly all of the minutes beginning as early as 1933 until 1968.

Drew Floyd
Birth:
Sep. 5, 1882
Miller County, Georgia
Death:
Mar., 1971
Miller County, Georgia
Burial:
Rawls Cemetery
Colquitt
Miller County, Georgia

He was a minister in the Martin Association where records show he served from 1943 until about 1969. First wife: Eula Inez Pickren. Second wife: Linda Grimes Powell. Son of Thomas Newton Floyd and Eliza Rawls Floyd.

Herschel Greeley Fowler
Birth:
Nov. 8, 1888
Death:
Jul. 20, 1981
Burial:
Bethlehem Baptist Church
Cemetery
Condor,Laurens County, Georgia

He is listed as a minister in the
Chattahoochee minutes.

Elder Harvey W Giddens
Birth:
Jul. 12, 1909
Death:
Apr. 14, 1981
Burial:
Bridge Creek Cemetery
Colquitt County,Georgia

During his ministry he served in
the Chattahoochee, Little River
and Georgia Union Associations.

Murray Elvin Giddens
Birth:
Nov. 15, 1930
Adel
Cook County, Georgia
Death:
Jan. 3, 2009
Moultrie
Colquitt County, Georgia
Burial:
Suncrest Memorial Gardens
Moultrie, Colquitt County,
Georgia
The course of his ministry was
spent in the Union, Little River,
and Martin Association's from
about 1974 until 1990. A
veteran, he was retired from the
Marines and was a Free Will
Baptist minister. In addition to

his parents, He was preceded in
death by his wife, Myrtice Foster
Giddens.

Teedom M. Giddens
Birth:
Aug. 23, 1891
Coffee County, GA
Death:
Oct. 19, 1961
Burial:
Sunnyside Cemetery
Pearson
Atkinson County,Georgia

His ministry was confined to the
Little River Association. Spouse:
Beadie Mae Burch. Married: Abt.
1914 in Georgia and his parents
were. Kindred Jasper Giddens
(1861 - 1938) and Martha Lewis
Giddens (1871 - 1954) and he
married Beadie Mae Burch
Giddens (1891 - 1972).

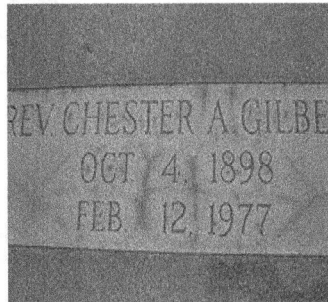

Chester A Gilbert
Birth:
Oct. 4, 1898
Death:
Feb. 12, 1977
Burial:
New Salem Cemetery
Miller County, Georgia

His ministry spanned from 1943 until 1969 in the Martin Association. Spouse: Ida Jane Nobles Gilbert (1902-36).

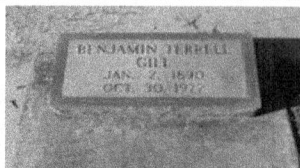

Benjamin Terrell Gill
Birth:
Jan. 2, 1890
Death:
Oct. 30, 1972
Burial:
Trinity Freewill Baptist Cemetery
Taylor County,Georgia
His ministry was held in the Chattahoochee Association and he is recorded in its minutes from about 1934 until 1971.

Walter D Gill
Birth:
Oct. 9, 1866
Death:
Apr. 18, 1934
Burial:
Trinity Freewill Baptist Cemetery
Taylor County,Georgia

His ministry appears in many of the minutes of the Chattahoochee Association ranging from 1903 until 1933.

Richard Harold Goolsby
Birth:
Jul., 1855
Jasper County, Georgia
Death:
Mar. 16, 1935
Monticello
Jasper County, Georgia
Burial:
Hebron Cemetery
Jasper County, Georgia

Records in 1897 show him as a minister in the Middle Georgia minutes.

William Hancil Gray
Birth:
Mar. 9, 1915
Death:
Apr. 16, 1995
Burial:
Chastain Memorial Park Cemetery
Blue Ridge
Fannin County, Georgia

He was a minister in the Georgia Union association.

Benjamin Franklin Green
Birth:
1873
Monroe County,Georgia
Death:
1938
Marion County,Georgia
Burial:
New Life Freewill Baptist
Church Cemetery
Marion County,Georgia

His parents were Thomas C Green (1824-) and Irena M (Helton) (1836-).He married Lucy Bone on Nov 17, 1892 in Taylor Co, GA. He was a minister in the union conference.

Since I Became A Christian Dying Is All I Have Been Living For!

Doctor Evan Green
Birth:
Oct. 5, 1852
Death:
Jul. 6, 1936
Ideal
Macon County, Georgia
Burial:
Ideal City Cemetery
Ideal
Macon County, Georgia

Macon County Citizen-Montezuma Georgian July 9, 1936. Ideal, Ga. - July 8, Funeral services were held in the Free Will Baptist Church in Ideal Tuesday afternoon for Rev. D. E. Greene, 83, prominent minister and former postmaster of Ideal, whose death occurred at his home Monday following a lingering illness. Rev. Greene was the first citizen who moved to the town of Ideal and was postmaster here from the founding of the town until two years ago. For many years he walked and carried the mail from Oglethorpe to Ideal, a distance of 15 miles, until the A. B. C. Railroad was built, connecting these points. For 40 years he was a minister in the Free Will Baptist Church and served many charges. He was married to Miss Frances Dyson who died in 1922.

Benjamin J. Griffin
Birth:
Jul. 26, 1849
Death:
Mar. 25, 1926
Burial:
Leila Cemetery
Colquitt County, Georgia,

The Liberty minutes show him as early as 1895 as a minister in the Association.

Death Is The Fundamental
Human Problem.

E C Grimsley
Birth:
Apr. 29, 1859
Death:
May 3, 1939
Burial:
New Life Freewill Baptist
Church Cemetery
Marion County, Georgia

The Chattahoochee minutes revealed that he appeared in their conference from 1898 until 1938.

William Thomas Grimsley
Birth:
Apr., 1879
Georgia
Death:
Oct. 20, 1942
Marion County, Georgia
Burial:
Parmer Cemetery
Oakland
Marion County, Georgia
He served as a minister in the Chattahoochee Association whose minutes revealed his presence from 1919 until 1942.

Claud H Hadden
Birth:
Jul. 12, 1890
Death:
Oct. 11, 1970
Burial:
Lake Cemetery
Metter
Candler County, Georgia

He served in the Ogeechee and South Georgia Quarterly Meetings from about 1940 untill 1960.

C W Harrell
Birth:
Oct. 13, 1943
Death:
Oct. 18, 1992
Burial:
Mizpah Primitive Baptist Church Cemetery
Cairo
Grady County, Georgia

He was a minister in both the Union and Martin Associations.

The Lord Has Prepared For His Warriors

Kelly C Harrell
Birth:
Jan. 28, 1934
Death:
Apr. 16, 1997
Burial:
Mount Gilead Freewill Baptist Church Cemetery
Decatur County, Georgia

He served as a minister in the Martin Association.

Inscription:
AMN US AIR FORCE KOREA

James G Harris
Birth:
Sep. 7, 1883
Death:
Nov. 3, 1926
Burial:
Christ Methodist Church Cemetery
Baker County, Georgia

Minutes from the Martin and Midway Associations revealed him as a minister from 1916 until 1926 within their associations.

C J Harvey
Birth:
Jan. 6, 1889
Death:
Aug. 2, 1960
Burial:
Oakview Cemetery
Camilla
Mitchell County, Georgia

He was a minister in the Georgia Union, the Midway, and Union conferences during the period of 1929 until 1959.

R Slaten Hayes
Birth:
May 28, 1913
Death:
Nov. 9, 2002
Burial:
Forest Hill Freewill Baptist Church Cemetery
Adel
Cook County, Georgia

From 1952 until 1999 he served as a minister in the Little River and Union Associations.

Bessie *Widener* Hillis
Birth
April 23, 1890
Death
July 9, 1969
Burke County, Georgia
Burial
Corinth Cemetery
Burke County, Georgia

She was an early Free Will Baptist preacher in Georgia.

Joel I Hill
Birth:
Apr. 13, 1851
Early County, Georgia
Death:
May 10, 1914
Early County, Georgia
Burial:
Springfield Baptist Church Cemetery
Early County
Georgia

He was converted in 1872 and two year's later and received license to preach. He was ordained in 1875 by J. B. McCullers and others. He ministered to the Howard's Grove church, Alabama; New Salem church, Georgia, and the Springfield church, Georgia.

Robert W Holmes
Birth:
Jun. 2, 1899
Death:
Oct. 12, 1976
Burial:
Pelham City Cemetery

Pelham
Mitchell County, Georgia

He was a minister in the Martin conference.

W. H. Holmes
Birth:
Jun. 10, 1870
Death:
Jun. 10, 1925
Burial:
Pine Level Church Cemetery
Alma
Bacon County, Georgia

Records in the Chattahoochee, the Georgia Union, and South Georgia minutes revealed his ministry among them from 1902 until 1924.

George Sherrod Holton
Birth:
Oct. 9, 1909
Death:
Unknown
Burial:
Mount Zion Church Cemetery
Lyons
Toombs County
Georgia

He served in the South Georgia and Ogeechee Associations ranging from about 1952 until 1995.

Benjamin Franklin Horne
Birth:
Sep., 1866
Laurens County
Georgia
Death:
Oct. 6, 1944
Dodge County
Georgia
Burial:
Bay Springs
Free Will Baptist Church
Cemetery
Plainfield
Dodge County
Georgia

The Georgia Union minutes record him from 1914 until 1943. He was married to Maryann Francis Jones Horne (1867 - 1934) and they had the following children: Joseph William Horne (1890 - 1967) John Benjamin Jefferson Horne (1896 - 1965) Charlton James Horne (1898 - 1985) Henry H Horne (1904 - 1958) Seaborn Horne (1905 - 1905) Athie Belle

Horne Graham (1906 - 1947) Fannie C Horne Rodgers (1909 - 1999).

Carlton Robert Houston
Birth:
May 7, 1914
Death:
Aug. 10, 1983
Burial:
Roberts Cemetery
Miller County, Georgia

He served as a minister in the Martin and, Midway Associations.

Dennis Oliver Irvin
Birth:
Oct. 25, 1926
Death:
Jun. 13, 1981
Burial:
Travelers Rest Freewill Baptist Church Cemetery
Newton, Baker County, Georgia

His ministry was in the Midway and Union Associations.

Paul H Irvin
Birth:
Nov. 25, 1925
Baker County, Georgia
Death:
Dec. 2, 2008
Albany
Dougherty County, Georgia
Burial:
Travelers Rest Freewill Baptist Church Cemetery
Newton
Baker County, Georgia

He had a broad ministry serving in the Georgia Union, Midway, Union, and Martin Associations. He was a member of Travelers Rest Free Will Baptist Church. Rev. Irvin had pastored 12 churches in the past 47 years. He was preceded in death by four brothers, Herman Irvin, Price Irvin, Dennis Irvin and Lawrence Irvin,

Von Deron Irvin
Birth:
Jul. 14, 1910
Death:
Dec. 9, 1985
Burial:
Travelers Rest Freewill Baptist
Church Cemetery
Newton
Baker County, Georgia

His ministry was in two associations: the Midway and Chattahoochee Quarterly Meetings.

John Pierce James
Birth:
Sep. 2, 1809
Rockingham County,
North Carolina
Death:
Oct. 9, 1847
Burial:
Sardis Baptist Church Cemetery
McDonough
Henry County, Georgia

John professed conversion at the age of twenty-four, and was baptized by Rev. Cyrus White at Teman church, Henry County, Georgia. He was subsequently ordained to the gospel ministry at said church in 1835, by what presbytery the author is not informed. Though his ministry was thus commenced under those who were known as Whiteites, (and who were deemed as rather Arminian in sentiment,). He subsequently connected himself with the Central Association, in which body he was highly esteemed and eminently useful.

He was engaged in the ministry only about twelve years, yet he baptized about sixteen hundred persons. His labors were confined mostly to the counties of Jasper, Butts, Henry, Newton and Campbell. His burning zeal impelled him forward day and night, summer and winter. His first sermon was preached under a bush-arbor in Gwinnett County, and from that day until he ceased from his labors was his voice heard in the highways and hedges, inviting and urging the poor and needy to come to the gospel feast. It was by no means an uncommon thing with him to work hard on his farm all day, and, leaving his horse to rest, to walk from three to four miles and preach to his neighbors at night, after which he would return home, and resume his work in the morning. His last sermon was preached at Enon church, Jasper County, from Acts xx. 32: "And now, brethren, I commend you to God," etc.

In October, 1830, he was married

to Miss Nancy Strickland, daughter of Colonel Solomon Strickland, of Henry county, who proved herself eminently qualified for the position she was called to occupy as a preacher's wife, and as the mother of six orphan children, which were left upon her hands by his death. His father, Martin James, was a soldier in the war of 1812, was taken prisoner, and died at Fort Johnson. His mother's maiden name was Martha Woodall. She died in 1869, in the ninetieth year of her age.

John H Jenkins
Birth:
Aug. 26, 1869
Georgia
Death:
Aug. 10, 1899,
Burial:
Sand Hill Cemetery
Fort Stewart
Tattnall County, Georgia
His name is recorded as a minister in the 1890s minutes of the Chattahoochee Association.

G W Jones
Birth:
Aug. 22, 1877
Death:
Jun. 23, 1938
Burial:
Satilla Freewill Baptist Church Cemetery
Hazlehurst
Jeff Davis County, Georgia

Minutes from the South Georgia conference revealed him serving in their area from their minutes dated 1916 until 1937.

Spurgeon Jones
Birth:
Dec. 22, 1914
Death:
May 29, 1970
Burial:
Mt. Ararat Free Will Baptist Church
Chauncey
Dodge County
Georgia

He preached in the Georgia Union conference.

Dr. Linton C. Johnson

Birth:
Feb. 3, 1914,
Alma, Bacon County,Georgia
Death:
Jun. 26, 2002,
Norfolk, Norfolk City, Virginia
Burial:
Pine Level Church Cemetery,
Alma, Bacon County,Georgia

He was a Free Will Baptist minister, pastor, educator and Bible college president. He attended Middle Georgia College, 1932-33 and earned his degree from Bob Jones College in 1939. He pursued graduate studies at Winona Lake School of Theology in 1943, and Bob Jones Graduate School in 1945.

Bob Jones University bestowed the honorary Doctor of Humanities degree on him in 1952.

He was the founding president of Free Will Baptist Bible College in Nashville, Tennessee in 1942, where he served for 34 years until his retirement in 1979. From 1979 until 1981 he was Chancellor of the college. His pastorates included Free Will Baptist churches in Georgia, Mississippi, Florida and Tennessee.

He considered the Free Will Baptist Bible College his great life work and never allowed anything to distract him from that focus. As the president of the college, Johnson became well known and respected in academic circles.

He was listed in Who's Who in American College and University Administrations, served on Executive Committee of the American Association of Bible Colleges, participated on the program of the 1976 World Congress of Fundamentalists in Edinburg, Scotland and was a member of the over view committee for the New King James Version of the Bible.

Dr. Johnson preached six times in the national convention and was elected as moderator of the National Association of Free Will Baptist twice. His influence marked the denomination for almost 70 years. In a 1999 tribute, Dr. Robert Picirilli wrote of him, "When the history of Free Will Baptists in the last half of the 20th century is written, the role of Dr. L.C. Johnson will be perhaps the most prominent of any,"

No one as touched more lives within the Free Will Baptist denomination.

Hughie J. Kelly

Birth:
Feb. 16, 1907
Death:
Jul. 20, 1957

Burial:
Evergreen Memory Gardens
Cemetery,
Columbus,
Muscogee County,
Georgia,
Plot: Christus Garden

His ministry was in the
Chattahoochee Association..

Hiram Leroy Knighton
Birth:
Jul. 20, 1906
Georgia
Death:
Jul. 31, 1984
Albany
Dougherty County, Georgia
Burial:
Parkhill Cemetery
Columbus
Muscogee County, Georgia
Plot: Section I-30

Hiram Leroy Knighton was first
married to Mary Elizabeth Hearn
and upon her death in 1939

married Sarah (Harrell)
Knighton. His ministry was in the
Chattahoochee and Midway
Associations.

William Berrien Wesley Lane
Birth:
Jan. 24, 1854
Early County, Georgia
Death:
Mar. 5, 1893
Early County,Georgia
Burial:
Sowhatchee Cemetery
Blakely, Early County, Georgia

An early minister in the
Chattahoochee and Martin
Associations and is recorded in
their minutes beginning in 1981
until 1892. He was the husband
of Margaret J. (Anglin) Lane and
son of Joseph William Lane, III
and Chloe Elizabeth (Sheffield)
Lane. He was converted in 1870,
received license to preach in
1879, and was ordained the
following year by Rev. C. C.
Martin and J. E. Hill. His ministry
was spent in the Chattahoochee
Association, Georgia, where he
baptized 125 converts organized
two churches and aided in the
gathering of three others.

Greenville L. Laney
Birth:
Mar. 5, 1941
Death:
Nov. 15, 1983
Burial:
Riverdale Cemetery
Columbus
Muscogee County, Georgia
Plot: 80 Sec. 10

His ministry was in the Chattahoochee Association.

Simeon Roy Lawhorn
Birth:
Feb. 23, 1879

Death:
Aug. 16, 1935
Burial:
New Providence Baptist
Cemetery
Marion County, Georgia

He was a minister in the Chattahoochee Association whose minutes show him from 1921 until 1934.

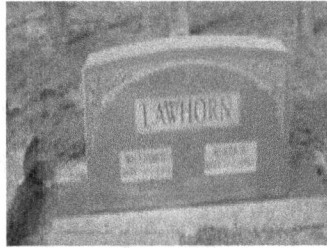

William Randolph Lawhorn
Birth:
Jun. 10, 1883
Death:
Feb. 8, 1971
Burial:
Sand Bethel Cemetery
Rupert
Taylor County, Georgia

He was the son of William H "W H" Lawhorn (1853 - 1897) and the husband of Effie Alberta "Berta" Watson Lawhorn (1884 - 1961). He was a member the Chattahoochee Association where the minutes revealed that he was active from 1918 until 1970.

Bruce V Lisle
Birth:
1901
Death:
1952
Burial:
Parkhill Cemetery
Columbus
Muscogee County, Georgia
Plot: Section F

He was a minister in the Chattahoochee Association.

Ralph Lightsey
Birth:
1918
Appling County, Georgia
Death:
Sep. 2, 2012
Statesboro, Bulloch County, Georgia
Burial:
Eastside Cemetery, Statesboro, Bulloch County,Georgia

Dr. Lightsey received his A.B. degree from Mercer University in 1945, a B.D. degree in Theology from Emory University in 1951, a Master's in Theology from Columbia University in 1955 and a doctorate degree in Education from the University of Georgia in 1965. He was ordained to the gospel ministry in 1940. He served churches in Georgia, Alabama, North Carolina and Mississippi. After serving as an active pastor for more than 52 years, he served as a supply speaker at more than 50 churches in Bulloch and surrounding counties. In addition, he was an educator. He served 16 years as professor of Educational Research at Georgia Southern University and as an assistant to the vice-president. Upon his retirement, the Board of Regents conferred on him the title of Professor Emeritus of Educational Research. In keeping with his concern for his fellow human being, he received the Dean Day Smith Service to Mankind Award. He was also the original owner of Lightsey Construction Company, Inc.

Tom Joseph Lightsey
Birth:
Jun. 24, 1929
Appling County
Georgia
Death:
Jan. 25, 2010
Palm Garden Rehabilitation Center
Jacksonville
Duval Co. Florida
Burial:
Piney Grove Free Will Baptist Church Cemetery
Appling County, Georgia

He was a member of the Piney Grove Free Will Baptist Church and was an ordained Free Will Baptist minister. He served several churches as pastor in

Southeast Georgia including Alabaha Free Will Baptist in Pierce County. After teaching for several years in the public school system, he completed his career at West Georgia University in Carrollton, from which he retired. Rev. Dr. Charles Thigpen and the Rev. Steve Hughes officiated. According to the South Georgia minutes he is recorded from 1956 through 1998 as a minister.

James D. Little
Birth:
Mar. 3, 1875
Death:
Aug. 16, 1958
Burial:
Sunnyside Cemetery Pearson
Atkinson County Georgia

Minutes of the Chattahoochee, Georgia Union and Little River associations from 1910 through 1957 record him as a minister.

S. N. Little
Birth:
Apr. 3, 1848
Death:
Mar. 3, 1932
Burial:

New Prospect Freewill Baptist
Coverdale
Turner County, Georgia

He was an early Free Will Baptist preacher in Georgia.

Theron Wyndell Long
Birth:
Nov. 24, 1935
Death:
Aug. 1, 2011
Coffee Regional Medical Center,
Burial:
Surrency Cemetery
Surrency
Appling County, Georgia

Rev. Long, a former Free Will Baptist minister and a native of Appling County, was a Southern Baptist Minister for many years. He was an Alumnus of the Freewill Baptist College of Nashville, Tennessee.He was the son of the late Doric Quitman Long and the late Ola Evelyn Carter Long. He was also preceded in death by a brother, Wyndell Long. Funeral Services were held at the College Avenue

Baptist Church, with Rev. Don Harper, Rev. Luther Burns, and Rev. J. E. Blanton officiating.

James B Lovering
Birth:
Feb. 7, 1912
Death:
Dec. 4, 1976
Burial:
Colquitt City Cemetery
Colquitt
Miller County, Georgia

He was a minister in the Midway, Martin, Little River, and George Union associations recorded as early as 1940 until 1963 in their minutes. Spouse: Flora Newsom Lovering (1915 - 1997).

L O Lovett
Birth:
Mar. 9, 1882
Death:
May 10, 1965
Burial:
Pine Grove Baptist Church Cemetery
Nashville
Berrien County, Georgia

He was a minister in the Union Association.

J W Loyless
Birth:
Jan. 6, 1907
Death:
Feb. 21, 1976
Burial:
Oak City Cemetery
Bainbridge
Decatur County, Georgia

He was a minister in the Midway Association.

Henry Lewis Lumpkin

Birth:
Mar. 9, 1878
Talbot County, Georgia
Death:
Dec. 26, 1946
Taylor County
Georgia
Burial:
Pine Level Cemetery
Mauk
Taylor County, Georgia

He married Emma Virginia Whitley in Talbot County on July 28, 1897. His parents were William J. and Sarah Lumpkin and he was the grandson of J.L and Jane (Hancock) Lumpkin. He was called to preach at the age of 18. He served in the Free Will Baptists denomination. He was a member of Woodmen of the World. He was the father of seven children. His two sons, William Robert and John Beverly were well known preachers. Henry and his two sons, William Robert and John Beverly all at some time were Pastors at New Life Church. During his ministry he preached in the Chattahoochee, Georgia Union and South Georgia conferences from about 1903 till 1942.

Johnnie Beverly Lumpkin

Birth:
Oct. 29, 1906
Georgia
Death:
Jan. 30, 2002
Georgia,

Burial:
Pine Level Cemetery
Mauk
Taylor County, Georgia

Husband of Blanche Hart Lumpkin. He was the son of Henry L. Lumpkin and Emma Watson Lumpkin. During his ministry he preached in the Chattahoochee, Georgia Union, Little River, Union, and Martin associations.

William Robert Lumpkin, Sr

Birth:
Aug. 19, 1904
Taylor County, Georgia
Death:
Jun. 13, 1991
Blountsville
Blount County, Alabama
Burial:
Pine Level Cemetery
Mauk, Taylor County, Georgia

W.R., attended Mauk and Berry High School. He worked with Goodrich in Silvertown, Thomaston, Georgia. He was raised on a farm. He was a Mason in the late 1920's and early 1930's. He was a member of Woodmen of the World. He was saved in his bedroom in 1938. He was called to preach the Gospel and pastored several churches including; New Life in Talbot County, Spring Hill in Marion County, Trinity in Charing, Eastman in Dodge County, Cloud Springs in Ft. Oglethorpe, Temple in Rossville and Ft. Perry in Taylor County. He was married to Leila Foster on January 2, 1927 by and at the residence of Rev. J.L. Whitley in Mauk, Georgia.

John T Lunsford
Birth:
May 4, 1884
Death:
Oct. 27, 1940
Burial:
Mothers Home Cemetery
Miller County, Georgia

He was an early minister in the Martin Association.

Levi B. Manning
Birth:
Dec., 1879
Death:
1956
Burial:
Manningtown Presbyterian Cemetery
Manningtown
Wayne County, Georgia

Early minister in the South Georgia Association.

Charles Courtney Martin
Birth:
Mar. 9, 1827
Jasper County, Georgia
Death:

Nov. 25, 1910
Randolph County, Georgia
Burial:
Martin Family Cemetery
Randolph County, Georgia

He was one of six brothers, four of whom were preachers of the gospel. He united with the Free Will Baptist when 14 years of age; received license to preach at 21 and was ordained when 22. At this time many of the churches of his vicinity united with the larger Baptist body, but brother Martin remained faithful to the smaller denomination. He went to work seriously and incessantly to propagate a free salvation and his labors were blessed of God to the saving of many. He assisted in the organizing of numerous churches and two associations, one named the Martin Assn., and baptized 1531 converts. For more than 30 years he was a pastor of two churches in the Chattahoochee Association.

Robert M Massey
Birth:
Jun. 6, 1872
Death:
Nov. 26, 1966
Burial:
Oak Ridge Cemetery
Tifton
Tift County, Georgia
Plot: Annex III

He pastored in the Chattahoochee, Little River, and Union associations from about 1925 until 1946.

Newton Elmore Massey
Birth:
Aug. 25, 1850
Muscogee County, Georgia
Death:
Nov. 3, 1914
Worth County, Georgia
Burial:
Hillcrest Cemetery
Sylvester
Worth County, Georgia

He was a minister in the Chattahoochee Association where records show that he was a pastor in 1892 through 1903. He was married to Julia Hill Massey (1850 - 1926) and they had two Children: Newton Elmore Massey (1878 - 1947) and Emma Massey Heath (1882 - 1952).

Jordan B. McCullers
Birth
May 30, 1831
Dooley County, Georgia
Death:
Nov. 22, 1887
Burial:
Hodges Cemetery
Jakin
Early County,
Georgia

He was converted in 1852, licensed in 1868, and ordained in

April, 1874 by Bishop Pierce of the Methodists denomination. Since uniting with the Free Baptists his ministry has been in the Chattahoochee and Martin Associations baptizing over 100 converts and organized four churches, one of them in Thomas County, Georgia while laboring as a missionary.

Inscription:
Confederate Memorials. D32 Ga. Inf. C.S.A.

Solomon Oscar McCorvey
Birth:
Mar. 31, 1879
Death:
Oct. 30, 1955
Burial:
Oak Ridge Cemetery
Tifton
Tift County, Georgia
Plot: Annex III

The Liberty minutes show that he was recorded in the 1926 edition as a minister.

Frank Steely McDanal
Birth:
Aug. 9, 1914
Death:
Jun. 21, 1966
Burial:
Parkhill Cemetery
Columbus
Muscogee County, Georgia

He was a minister in the Chattahoochee Association.

John D McDaniel
Birth:
May 28, 1879
Death:
Jun. 24, 1947
Burial:
Satilla Freewill Baptist Church Cemetery
Hazlehurst
Jeff Davis County, Georgia

He was in the Ogeechee Association.

Walter Ballenger McDaniel
Birth:
Feb. 6, 1875
Death:
Mar. 1, 1931
Burial:
Oak Grove Cemetery
Americus
Sumter County,
Georgia

Walter married Willie Adkins on 10 AUG 1902. He served as a minister in the Chattahoochee and UnionAssociations.

Inscription:
An Honest man is the noblest work of God

Warren Arthur McDonald
Birth:
Dec. 25, 1848
Death:
Jul. 28, 1933
Burial:
Shepard Cemetery ,
Miller County,Georgia

Rev. McDonald started several churches in the area, was quite prominent in his community and was a surveyor in Miller county as well. An old newspaper article concerning him stated there had been some stealing going on in the community; pigs, chickens, and homes entered and pilfered. No one knew who was doing it and could not seem to catch the thieves. One Sunday after church, Warren was going home in the mule and wagon. Suddenly, two unknown men jumped from the ditch bank and tried to hold him up. They apparently believed he would have the Sunday offering money with him. He told them to allow him to get it out of his inside coat pocket. He reached into the pocket, came out with a pistol instead, and shot and killed both men. He then left them lying there while he went to town and got the sheriff. He had no charges filed against him, and the stealing in the area stopped.

Richard B. McFadden, Jr
Birth:
Mar. 17, 1951
Death:
Jul. 12, 2008
Burial:
Macon Memorial Park
Macon, Bibb County, Georgia

He ministered in the Georgia Union Association

Peter McLain

Birth:
Nov. 19, 1843
Death:
Oct. 27, 1939
Burial:
New Hope Free Will Baptist
Church Cemetery
Madray Springs
Wayne County, Georgia

He was a minister in the Ogeechee and South Georgia Associations between 1903 and 1941 being recorded in the minutes of both associations on a regular basis.

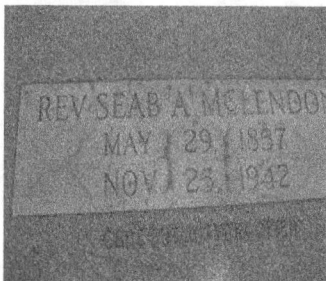

Seab A McLendon

Birth:
May 29, 1857
Death:
Nov. 25, 1942
Burial:
New Salem Cemetery
Miller County, Georgia

The Martin Association minutes from 1892 to 1921 record him as a minister.

Clarence McMillan

Birth:
Jul. 14, 1920
Death:
Dec. 19, 1994
Burial:
Sardis Cemetery
Folkston
Charlton County, Georgia

He was a minister in the South Georgia and Little River associations and whose record is found in the 1955 through 1988 minutes. He was married to the Leona Mock McMillan (1924 - 2011).

Thomas B. Mellette

Birth:
Apr. 25, 1892
Death:
Oct. 31, 1962
Burial:
Sowhatchee Cemetery,
Blakely
Early County, Georgia

He was one of the first educators in the early days of the denomination, who created Zion Bible School near Blakely. Mellette, who held degrees from several schools, including Columbia Bible College in Columbia, South Carolina, Zion served as the training ground for numerous ministers in Georgia,

Florida, and Alabama. Many Zion graduates went on to become leaders in the national association. In 1942, after the national association established the Free Will Baptist Bible College in Nashville, Tennessee, Zion closed its doors and donated all its assets to the new school. He had been on the joint Education Committee that had been working together for the purpose of establishing a Free Will Baptist school. Mellette was from the Eastern General Conference.

Henry Mills
Birth:
Dec. 28, 1908
Death:
Dec. 20, 1988
Burial:
Oakland Cemetery
Waycross
Ware County, Georgia
Plot: Section K Lot 9C
Minister in the South Georgia Association.

Cecil C Mock
Birth:
Oct. 25, 1917
Death:
Feb. 27, 1983
Burial:
Corinth Cemetery
Iron City
Seminole County, Georgia

He was a minister in the Martin Association. He was the son of John Henry Mock (1893 - 1966) and Alma Womble Mock (1898 - 1961).

H. S. "Monty" Montgomery
Birth:
1919
Death:
1973
Burial:
Carroll Memory Gardens
Carrollton
Carroll County, Georgia
Plot: Sec 3, Row 11

He was a member of the Chattahoochee Association.

Donald W. Moore
Birth:
May 24, 1919
Dodge County, Georgia
Death:
Oct. 12, 2002
Bibb County, Georgia
Burial:
Bay Springs Free Will Baptist
Church Cemetery
Plainfield, Dodge County,
Georgia

He was a minister in the Georgia Union Association. His parents were Jim Moore and Mary Hogan. He was married on July 14, 1941 in Dodge County to Ruby Lee Horne Moore (1913 - 2006) Service Info.: S1 US NAVY WORLD WAR II.

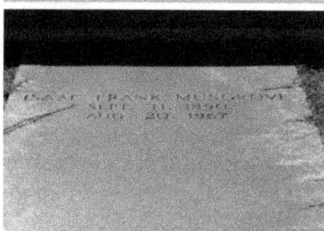

Isaac Frank Musgrove
Birth:
Sep. 11, 1890
Death:
Aug. 20, 1967
Burial:
Liberty Hill Baptist Church
Cemetery
Hartsfield
Colquitt County, Georgia

Was a member of the Martin Association.

Franklin "Scab" Myers
Birth:
Oct. 28, 1846
Gordon
Wilkinson County, Georgia
Death:
Feb. 8, 1911
Douglas
Coffee County, Georgia
Burial:
Carver Baptist Church Cemetery
Douglas
Coffee County, Georgia

He was the son of David and Mary Myers in Gordon, Wilkinson county Ga. On 09, July 1861 He along with Brother William, enlisted in Co. "B" 14th Ga Infantry Regiment CSA. They were joined later by their two brothers, John, and Daniel. William, John, and Daniel were all released before war end from illness, or wounds sustained in battle. But Seab served till surrender at Appomattox Courthouse, Virginia on April 09, 1865. He had been captured a month earlier, on March 25, near Petersburg Va, and was released on May 15th, at Point Lookout Maryland. He returned to Ga, and Married Susanna (Susan) Hersey on March 21, 1872 in Coffee county. His grave is marked with a confederate stone. Susan died at her daughter Ida's home in Perry, Taylor county Florida, and is buried in that county at New Hope cemetery. Her gravestone reads, Susan wife of S.F Myers Dec 22 1849-April-6-1918 having finished life's duty, she now sweetly rest. He was a member of the South Georgia conference.

William T. Park
Birth:
Oct. 30, 1830
Death:
Sep. 6, 1919
Burial:
Boynton Cemetery
Catoosa County,
Georgia
Plot: Row 6

He was an early minister in the Chattahoochee Association and is recorded in the 1848 minutes of that conference.
Inscription:
2nd Co. "D", Ist Ga Inf., C.S.A.

William H. Parkman
Birth:
Jan. 8, 1831
Death:
May 7, 1907
Burial:
Fort Benning Cemetery #02
Fort Benning
Chattahoochee County,
Georgia

In the 1848 minutes of the Chattahoochee Association listed as a minister. Confederate Civil War Veteran. 1850 Census McNorton's, Muscogee Co GA. Film M432_79 pg 403A in household with his parents, John and Susan V. A Parkman and a lot of siblings. U.S. Civil War Soldier Records and Profiles Name: William Parkman Residence: Muscogee County, Georgia Enlistment Date: 5 Dec 1862 Rank at enlistment: Private State Served: Georgia Survived the War: Service Record: Enlisted in

Pemberton's Company G, Georgia 54th Infantry Regiment on 16 May 1862. Mustered out on 25 May 1862 at Savannah, GA. Sources: Roster of Confederate Soldiers of Georgia 1861-1865. C. L. Torbett Funeral Home, Columbus, GA Funeral Services Billed for May 7, 1907 $28.00.

Neal H Parrish
Birth:
Jul. 13, 1880
Death:
Sep. 6, 1962
Burial:
Friendship Cemetery
Hahira,Lowndes County, Georgia

Records revealed in four different associations that he pastored or was a minister there in. Namely; South Georgia, Georgia Union, Little River and Union Associations.

Oliver Hazard John Perry
Birth:
Jan. 7, 1865
Death:
Mar. 14, 1942
Burial:
Cedar Springs Cemetery
Cedar Springs
Early County, Georgia

He was an early minister in the Martin and Midway Association at the turn-of-the-century from 1902 until 1926.

August Jonathan Peters
Birth:
Dec. 5, 1847
Death:
Aug. 31, 1917
Burial:
Jesup City Cemetery
Jesup
Wayne County, Georgia

The minutes of the Martin Association record him in the 1893 edition. Then he is found in 1902 in the Midway Association.

James L Pittman
Birth:
Mar. 27, 1892
Death:
Jan. 22, 1977
Burial:
Smyrna Baptist Church Cemetery
Deepstep, Washington County, Georgia

A record of him is found in 1961 Chattahoochee minutes.

Roscoe Pitts
Birth:
Feb. 23, 1923
Georgia
Death:
Nov. 2, 1994
Columbus
Muscogee County, Georgia
Burial:
Riverdale Cemetery
Columbus
Muscogee County, Georgia

Roscoe was married to Avie Lou Howard. He was a preacher in the Chattahoochee and Georgia Union Association's ranging from about 1955 until 1987. He is recorded numerous times in these record books.

James Monroe Posey
Birth:
Mar. 5, 1852
Taylor County, Georgia
Death:
Aug. 1, 1918
Burial:
New Prospect Free Will Baptist Church Cemetery
Reynolds
Taylor County, Georgia

His name is recorded in the Chattahoochee mintues from

1885 until 1917 in most all editions.

James L Poston
Birth:
Jul. 7, 1881
Death:
Jul. 20, 1952
Burial:
Pine Level Freewill Baptist
Church Cemetery
Chester
Dodge County, Georgia
His ministry was confined to the
Georgia Union Association.
Spouse: Eunice T Poston (1889 -
1982)

James W. Potter
Birth:
Aug. 15, 1931
Death:
Jan. 24, 1991
Burial:
Middle Georgia Memory
Gardens
Jones County, Georgia

He ministered in three Georgia associations. Namely; South Georgia, Chattahoochee and Georgia Union Associations.

William S Powell
Birth:
Jul. 24, 1875, USA
Death:
Mar. 13, 1932
Georgia
Burial:
Satilla Freewill Baptist Church
Cemetery
Hazlehurst
Jeff Davis, Georgia

He was an early minister in the South Georgia conference whose name is recorded in the 1929 and 1931 minutes.

William L Presley
Birth:
Apr. 8, 1820
Death:
Aug. 31, 1887

Burial:
Mount Zion Baptist Church
Cemetery
Towns County, Georgia

He is a minister whose name appears in the Chattahoochee minutes of 1842, 1847 and 1848.

William Lester Purvis
Georgia Birth:
Feb. 20, 1899
Death:
Aug. 8, 1979
Burial:
Purvis Cemetery
Coffee County, Georgia

He preached in a number of conferences in Georgia, namely; South Georgia, Georgia Union, Chattahoochee, Union and Little River Conferences.

Calvin C Quinn
Birth:
Jan. 3, 1870
Death:
Dec. 13, 1942
Burial:
Satilla Freewill Baptist Church
Cemetery
Hazlehurst
Jeff Davis County, Georgia

He preached in the South Georgia conference and his name appears in the 1907 minutes. He was married to Rebecca A Bland Quinn (1893 - 1927) and they had two children: Alvin H and Esther Lee.

Henry Smith Reese
Birth:
Nov. 21, 1827
Jasper County, Georgia
Death:
Nov. 11, 1922
Turin
Coweta County, Georgia
Burial:
Tranquil Cemetery
Coweta County, Georgia

He is in the 1848 minutes of the Chattahooche Assn. He was a twin brother of John Palmer Reese. He was the son of Reverend James Reese and Rebecca (Smith) Reese. He was an ordained Baptist minister despite his lack of a formal education as well as a prominent writer and singer of Sacred Harp music. His ministry covered almost seventy years at churches throughout Georgia. In 1857, he married Amanda Brawner and this union produced one daughter. In 1865, he married a widow, Martha Jane (Leavell) Brooks, and there were seven children born of this union. He was also a teacher of Sacred Harp music according to the Baptist Biography (1920).

C D Rentz
Birth:
May 7, 1916
Death:
Jun. 22, 2001
Burial:
Memorial Freewill
Baptist Church Cemetery
Surrency
Appling County, Georgia

He is recorded many times in the South Georgia and Georgia Union conferences.

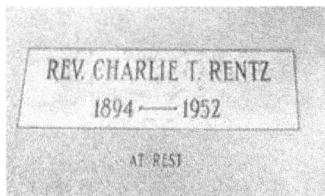

Charlie T Rentz
Birth:
1894
Death:
1952
Burial:
Westview Cemetery
Moultrie
Colquitt County, Georgia
Plot: Lane 10 East; Section 6,
Block C, Lot 45 (6 C 45 10th
East)

He was a minister in the Union Conference.
Inscription:
RENTZ Rev. Charlie T.
Rentz 1894 ----- 1952
At Rest

Wilbur L Rentz
Birth:
Nov. 16, 1923
Death:
Aug. 29, 2007
Burial:
Memorial Freewill Baptist
Church Cemetery
Surrency
Appling County, Georgia

He was a preacher in the Midway and Martin conferences

G W Rhodes
Birth:
Mar. 6, 1870
Death:
Mar. 9, 1941
Burial:
Bethlehem Schley Baptist
Church Cemetery, Moultrie
Colquitt County, Georgia

He was a preacher in the Union Association.

Charles W Rickerson
Birth:
1868
Death:
1930
Burial:
Oak Ridge Cemetery
Tifton
Tift County, Georgia
Plot: old sect. blk 21, lot 4;
C W Rickerson plot
He was a preacher in the Chattahoochee Association.

Bill Robinson
Birth:
Apr. 11, 1927,
Liberty, Tennessee
Death:
May 13, 2005
Bainbridge, Georgia
Burial:
Mount Gilead
Freewill Baptist Church
Cemetery, Brinston,
Decatur County, Georgia

He was a United States Navy veteran of World War II and a 1962 graduate of Free Will Baptist Bible college in Nashville Tennessee. He was very active in denominational affairs and served for 12 years on the Board of Trustees of Free Will Baptist Bible College. He pastored churches in Tennessee, Michigan, Mississippi, North Carolina and Georgia. He retired as a Minister after 45 years of service and his retirement was only because of his health. He had diabetes for 35 years, had an open heart surgery, and only months before his death he lost a leg. He also had a brother of whom he was proud, Paul Robinson, who was a Free Will Baptist missionary to Uruguay.

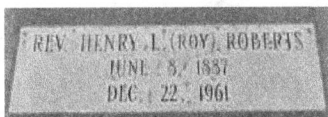

Henry Leroy "Roy" Roberts
Birth:
Jun. 8, 1887
Miller County, Georgia
Death:
Dec. 22, 1961
Miller County, Georgia
Burial:
Primitive Union Cemetery
Colquitt
Miller County, Georgia

He was a minister in the Martin and Midway conferences between the years of 1921 until 1959 according to the minutes of both associations.

Harris Edgar Rogers
Birth:
Aug. 13, 1888
Death:
Feb. 3, 1969
Burial:
Roberta City Cemetery
Roberta
Crawford County, Georgia
Plot: 351B

He is recorded as a minister in the Union minutes in 1952.

Eugene F. Ross
Birth:
Sep. 10, 1933
Dodge County, Georgia
Death:
Nov. 1, 2009
Cochran
Bleckley County, Georgia
Burial:
Bethany Baptist Church Cemetery
Bleckley County, Georgia

His ministry is recorded in the Georgia Union, Union and Chattahoochee minutes.

Vester Sadler
Birth:
Aug. 31, 1934
Death:
Jan. 13, 2007
Burial:
New Hope Cemetery
Cairo
Grady County, Georgia

Minister in Martin Association.

Pete Allen Sangster
Birth:
Jun. 12, 1872
Dooly Co, GA
Death:
Dec. 20, 1944
Burial:
Blackshear City Cemetery
Blackshear
Pierce County,
Georgia

He was a minister in the Georgia Union conference.

Leon L. Sapp, Jr.
Birth:
Jan. 2, 1928
Death:
Oct. 13, 1974
Burial:
Lone Hill Cemetery
Coffee County,
Georgia

He was a preacher in the following four conferences; Chattahoochee, Georgia Union, South Georgia and Union conferences. He was married to Heloyse Turner Sapp.

Joseph Washington Sauls
Birth:
Oct. 18, 1847
Death:
Mar. 7, 1919
Burial:
Bethlehem Freewill
Baptist Church Cemetery
Shellman
Randolph County,
Georgia

Brother Saul's was born and reared in Randolph County, and there he spent his entire life and raised a large and useful family. He became converted, joined the church, was baptized and soon afterwards began to preach and was ordained as a minister of the Gospel, and served a number of churches in the Bethel Association. In his own home church and community he was most useful. The lives of such men as this are jewels and they become the very foundation of the church and community life wherever they live. He and some of his family migrated from NC to Georgia..

Kenneth V. Shutes
Birth:
Jul. 9, 1905
Death:
Dec. 18, 1962
Burial:
Floral Memory Gardens, Albany,
Dougherty County,Georgia

Shutes for many years directed the Superannuation Board, which administered an insurance program for full-time ministers in the denomination.

Dr. Eugene Louis St. Claire
Birth:
Jun. 9, 1865,
Georgia
Death:
Feb. 6, 1916,
Florida
Burial:
Ebenezer Cemetery, Glennville,
Tattnall County,Georgia

Prominent evangelist of the Free Will Baptist denomination. At the time of his death, not yet 50 years old, he was living in Live Oak, FL, trying to regain his health following several paralytic strokes. Dr. St. Claire had been pastoring the church in Glennville, GA, and his body was returned for burial in the Ebenezer F.W.B. cemetery. Reverend O. B. Rustin officiated at his funeral. An account of his death appeared in the *Free Will Baptist* published. in Ayden, North Carolina. on Feb. 16, 1916, with a tribute to his life and ministry. Editor Phillips stated, "Dr. St. Claire, had conducted many revival campaigns there and had won many friends by his kind and genial disposition. Especially was he remembered for the great zeal and energy he had put in building and strengthening the Free Will Baptist Seminary in Ayden, N.C. He was orphaned at age four years, and it is unknown if he had any siblings. Both parents were of English descent. He spent his early life on an old-fashioned plantation. He pursued his higher education at the University of Alabama, with Master of Arts, and in one paper, the editor states he studied and graduated from "several theological colleges."
The Doctor of Divinity designation appears wherever his name appears in print. Upon completing his secular education, he embarked upon a successful business career, but soon felt the call to the ministry. In his relatively short period of twenty-three years of ministry,

his accomplishments were nothing short of phenomenal. In several of our Southern states he has done a great work. Association after association has been organized and put in working order. Thousands of souls have been led to the Lord in his meetings. In his first year of ministry, he helped to organize three associations. In his autobiography, he stated he organized 73 churches and won and baptized 4,879 persons.

FWB church records at Glennville, show that Dr. St. Claire was its founder in the year 1899. He pastored this church off and on up until his death.

Dr. St. Claire was also known as an orator, writer, and public debater. Debating was one of his skills, done in a witty manner, and at least five of these occasions are on record. He is acclaimed as one of the foremost preachers of the land, of scholarly ability, a man of culture and zeal, and service to his denomination.

For Dr. St. Claire's entire life as a Christian and as a minister of the Gospel, he was almost totally blind. This would mean that his Bible and theological education was acquired in spite of his lack of physical vision. How he acquired such vast and thorough knowledge of letters is hard to imagine for that time. However it came to him, he got it. This is a tribute to his indomitable spirit, for such a man cannot be defeated. His wife died shortly before he did. [It is unknown where she is buried]

Tombstone of Dr. St. Claire

Linza D Scott
Birth:
Mar. 29, 1896, USA
Death:
Aug. 22, 1977, USA
Burial:
Brinson Cemetery
Brinson
Decatur County, Georgia

He was a minister in the Martin conference according to its minutes from about 1943 until 1975.

Farest W Sellers
Birth:
May 26, 1912
Death:
Jun. 16, 1984
Burial:
Branchville United Methodist
Church Cemetery
Camilla,Mitchell County, Georgia

He pastored in the Martin, Union and Ogeechee conferences according to the minutes of all three conferences beginning in 1946 until 1983.

Willie A. Sellers
Birth:
Jan. 23, 1881
Death:
Jul. 14, 1975
Burial:
Branchville United Methodist
Church Cemetery
Camilla
Mitchell County, Georgia

He pastored in the Liberty, Union and Martin conferences according to the records of all three beginning in 1926 and continuing until 1969.

Thomas J. Strickland
Birth:
Aug. 1, 1861
Tattnall County, Georgia
Death:
Mar. 18, 1920
Wayne County, Georgia
Burial:
Hopewell Methodist Church
Cemetery
Tattnall County, Georgia

He is found in the Ogeechee minutes in 1903 and later in the South Georgia 1905-1911. He was married to Caroline Surrency.

James R. Stroup
Birth:
Nov. 16, 1914
Death:
Jun. 29, 1987
Burial:
Middle Georgia Memory
Gardens
Jones County, Georgia

He was a minister in the Chattahoochee and Georgia Union Associations.

Grover Cleveland Sullivan
Birth:
Oct. 31, 1893
Dooly County, Georgia
Death:
Jan. 27, 1986
Perry
Houston County, Georgia
Burial:
Snow Methodist Church
Cemetery
Unadilla
Dooly County, Georgia

Was a minister in Georgia Union Association.

John Taylor
Birth:
Feb. 14, 1818
Emanuel County, Georgia
Death:
Jan. 12, 1896
Worth County, Georgia
Burial:
Old Shiloh Cemetery
Tift County, Georgia

He was a clergyman in the Chattahoochee Assn according to its minutes in 1891-92.

J. L. Tedder
Birth:
Jul. 18, 1886
Death:
Dec. 6, 1960
Burial:
Sowhatchee Cemetery
Blakely
Early County, Georgia

From 1923 until 1960 he was a minister in the Midway and Martin Associations.

James Alfred Thompson
Birth:
Sep., 1849
Appling Co, Georgia
Death:
1910
Burial:
Bethel Free Will Baptist
Church Cemetery
Appling County, Georgia

He preached in the Ogeechee and South Georgia associations in the early part of the 1900s.

Allen L Thornton
Birth:
Dec. 5, 1872
Death:
May 18, 1953
Burial:
Satilla Freewill Baptist Church
Cemetery
Hazlehurst
Jeff Davis County, Georgia

He was a preacher in the South Georgia Association and is recorded in most of the minutes from 1919 until 1953.

A J Tomlinson
Birth:
Aug. 6, 1870
Death:
Mar. 18, 1951
Burial:
Pine Level Cemetery
Cairo
Grady County,
Georgia

He was a minister in the Liberty and Martin associations from 1921 until 1950.

Moutrie H Touchton
Birth:
Aug. 22, 1876
Death:
Feb. 3, 1961
Burial:
Boney Bluff Cemetery
Echols County, Georgia

He was a preacher in the Little River Association.

Thomas J. Touchton
Birth:
Sep. 28, 1905
Death:
Jul. 15, 1907
Burial:
Macedonia Baptist
Church Cemetery
Mayday
Echols County,
Georgia

He was a minister in the Union Association.

Willie Gus Turner
Birth:
Jun. 29, 1922
Sale City
Mitchell County,
Georgia
Death:
Aug. 9, 2012
Cairo
Grady County, Georgia
Burial:
Carter-Banks Cemetery
Grady County, Georgia

Rev. Turner was born to the late David Glenn Turner and Blanchie M. Johnson Turner. On March 23, 1946, he married Nancy Elizabeth Banks Turner. Rev. Turner was a minister for 66 years (32 years at First Freewill of Cairo, Georgia). He served his country in the U. S. Army, as an honorable veteran, fighting on the front line in the European Theatre of WWII. His ministry was spent in the Martin and Union associations.

James Edwary Usury
Birth:
May 6, 1935
Graham,Appling County, Georgia
Death:
Mar. 16, 2013
Jeff Davis County,
Georgia
Burial:
Satilla Freewill
Baptist Church Cemetery
Hazlehurst,Jeff Davis County,
Georgia

He graduated from Jeff Davis high school. He desired for education and took correspondence courses after graduation, including some courses from Welch College (then Free Will Baptist Bible College). After graduation from High School he worked at a news agency. He married Janice Quinn who was a real asset and blessing in his Christian Ministry.James was called to the ministry at the age of 21 and was ordained the next year. He was ordained in the South Georgia Association and those serving on the Ordaining Committee were: Dr. Tom Hamilton, Dr. Ralph Lightsey and Rev. C. D. Rentz.His first pastorate was at the Oak Hill Church and then at the Corinth Church both in the South Georgia Association. In 1967 he was called to the Midway Church, Moultrie, in the Union Association and was there until 1976. The Lord led him to the First Church in Columbus, Twin Cities Association until 1982. Then they went back to the South Georgia Association, First Church in Jesup until 1990. He then served the New Home Church in the Martin Association until 1999 when he officially retired from active ministry because of health problems and went back home to Hazlehurst. During his ministry there were at least five young men called to ministry: Rev. Steve Hughes, Dr. Billy Lewis, Rev. Irvin Murphy, Rev. Ken Murphy and Rev. Curtis Alligood. James was totally involved in Free Will Baptist ministry. In the districts where he pastured he served in various capacities including committees and moderator. At the State level, he was on the Resolution Committee; served as music director for the State Meeting; served on Board of Christian Education; Budgeting Committee; was Chairman of the Board of Mission and in 1985 was elected Clerk of the State. Officiating the services were Rev. Paul Smith, Rev. Herbert Waid and Rev. Steve Hughes.

Julian Vickers
Birth:
Dec. 20, 1923
Death:
Mar. 27, 2002
Burial:
Hebron Cemetery
Coffee County, Georgia

He preached in the Union and Little River associations.

Edgar Jackson Wade
Birth:
Jan. 1, 1881
Georgia
Death:
Jan. 11, 1952
Cordele
Crisp County, Georgia
Burial:
Sunnyside Cemetery
Cordele
Crisp County, Georgia

He preached in the Georgia Union conference.

Frank W Wade
Birth:
Feb. 22, 1884
Death:
Nov. 12, 1954
Burial:
Colquitt City Cemetery
Colquitt
Miller County, Georgia

He was a preacher in the Martin Association.

Samuel Watkins, Jr
Birth:
1779
Richland County, South Carolina
Death:
Apr. 15, 1855
Columbus
Muscogee County, Georgia
Burial:
New Providence Baptist Church
Cemetery
Muscogee County, Georgia

Rev. Samuel Watkins, Jr. was the son of Samuel Watkins, Sr,and Elizabeth (unknown). He married Charity (unknown) about 1808 in Richland Co., SC and they were the parents of six children: William, Zachariah, Samuel, Ervin, Epsey and George Washington Watkins. He migrated from Richland Co., SC to Muscogee Co., GA about 1833. He was an early pastor of the New Providence Freewill Baptist Church. The dates for Samuel and Charity were accidently reversed on the tombstone.

Benjamin Blanton Watson
Birth:
Aug. 24, 1829
Marion County, Georgia
Death:
Feb. 13, 1915
Taylor County, Georgia
Burial:
Trinity Freewill Baptist
Cemetery
Taylor County, Georgia

The 1842 Chattahoochee Assn minutes record him as a minister. He was the son of Richard William Ansley Watson (1803 - 1871) and Sealia R Waller Watson (1802 - 1870). He married Sarah Frances Rebecca Lawhorn Watson (1834 - 1921).

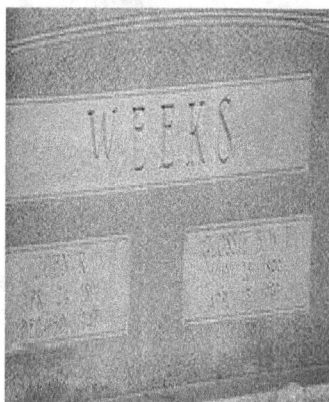

John R. Weeks
Birth:
Apr. 24, 1891
Death:
Dec. 30, 1947
Burial:
Weeks Chapel Cemetery
Norman Park
Colquit County, Georgia

He was a minister in the Little River conference.

John B Wheeler
Birth:
Sep. 29, 1875
Death:
Mar. 13, 1967
Burial:
Oak Ridge Cemetery
Tifton
Tift County, Georgia

He preached in both the Little River and South Georgia conferences.

Connie C White
Birth:
Oct. 27, 1878
Death:
May 22, 1975
Burial:
White Plains Freewill Baptist Church Cemetery
Lucile
Early County, Georgia

Son of Andrew Jackson White (buried at Blakely City Cemetery) and Linton Ann Malinda Mills White. Married Ola Barbrie on 17 Aug 1899 in Early County, Georgia.The minutes of the Midway Association beginning in 1916 record him in most all minutes until 1971.
Inscription:
In thee o Lord have I put my trust

A. G. Windham
Birth:
Jul. 19, 1927
Death:
Jul. 22, 2014
Reynolds,Taylor County, Georgia
Burial:
Mount Olive Freewill Baptist Church Cemetery
Potterville,Taylor County, Georgia

He was a member of Mt. Olive Free Will Baptist Church and for over 43 years he had pastored several churches in the Chattahoochee Association of Free Will Baptists, including Little Bethel, Turners Chapel, Mt. Olive, Spring Hill and New Liberty. He retired from Robins Air Force Base after 31 years. He served in WW II as a merchant Marine.

James L. "Jim" Whitley
Birth:
Mar. 11, 1883
Death:
Sep. 5, 1968
Burial:
Pine Level Cemetery
Mauk, Taylor County, Georgia

He was a minister in the Chattahoochee Association. He was the son of James M. and Polly Whitley, who married Fannie Lucinda Lee Hayes Whitley (1882 - 1956).

L B Whitley
Birth:
1855
Death:
1929
Burial:
Brushy Creek Cemetery
Adel, Cook County, Georgia

He is recorded in the Liberty minutes in 1895.

Green Thomas Wiley
Birth:
Apr. 10, 1845
Death:
Sep. 14, 1917
Burial:
Sowhatchee Cemetery
Blakely
Early County, Georgia

His ministry began in 1879 in the Chattahoochee Association where he served until 1885. Afterwards, he joined the Martin Association in 1892 and remained there until 1902. He joined the Midway Association in 1902 and served there until 1909. He was the husband of Margaret (Walter) Wiley and son of Jacob Wiley, Jr and Mary D. (Lane) Wiley.

William T Wiley
Birth:
Sep. 6, 1868
Georgia
Death:
Jun. 26, 1952

Burial:
Sowhatchee Cemetery
Blakely
Early County, Georgia

He joined the Martin Association in 1887 and in 1902 he united with the Midway Association and remained there until 1948 as a clergyman. He married Ella G. Alston Wiley (1873 - 1975).

Samuel Longstreet Wilkinson
Birth:
May 13, 1933
Death:
Apr. 11, 1988
Burial:
Ebenezer Cemetery
Glennville
Tattnall County, Georgia
Plot: Section B2

His name appears in the South Georgia minutes on a regular basis from 1954 until 1985. He was a Minister, Missionary in Brazil 19 years, and a professor at Hillsdale FWB College. Husband of Volree June Goode.
Inscription:
Children: Kevin, Kimberly, Kenan

E. C. Williams
Birth:
Jan. 8, 1879
Death:
Feb. 16, 1970
Burial:
New Enterprise Freewill Baptist
Church Cemetery
Seminole County, Georgia

He served in the Midway and Martin Association's from 1919 until 1969. He was married to Abbie Rebecca Williams (1887 - 1947) and to them had the following children; Infant Son William (1905 1905), Anderson Williams (1906 - 1971), Nita Williams Tyler (1907 - 1998), J. T. Williams (1913- 1934) Modainer R. Williams (1914 - 1930).

233

Kinnebrew Willis, Sr
Birth:
1812
Morgan County, Georgia
Death:
Dec. 12, 1880
Lee County,, Alabama
Burial:
Emmaus Baptist Church
Cemetery
Muscogee County, Georgia

His name appears in the Chattahoochee minutes of 1879. It is SPECULATIVE that this individual is buried at Emmaus Baptist Cemetery - at least two of his children, one who died during the Civil War in 1864 and another who died in 1934, are buried here. Said to be son of Robert L. Isabel (Frazier) Willis, Sr. Married ca. 1837, probably in Muscogee County, Georgia, to Nancy Motley. Father of fifteen children.

Harvey J. Wilson
Birth:
Dec. 28, 1902
Death:
Aug. 24, 1932
Burial:
New Hope Free Will Baptist
Church Cemetery
Madray Springs
Wayne County, Georgia

He was a member of the Union conference.

Riley H Windham
Birth:
Feb. 12, 1908
Death:
Jun. 22, 1987
Burial:
Mount Olive Freewill Baptist
Church Cemetery
Potterville
Taylor County,
Georgia

The Chattahoochee minutes record him from 1930 until 1948.

Needham Graham Yarbrough
Birth:
Nov. 28, 1842
Williamsburg County, South
Carolina
Death:
Mar. 10, 1928
Wayne County, Georgia
Burial:
George Cemetery
Wayne County, Georgia

Rev. Yarbrough's parents were: Needham Madison and Rebecca Wright Yarbrough. He enlisted in Clarendon County, South Carolina with Co. H 26th Regiment, South Carolina Volunteers along with his brothers John Edward, William, his brother in law John McCaskill and his uncle John Yarbrough during the War Between the States. Before the war he was working as a farm hand on the

Jones farm in Clarendon, South Carolina where he met and fell in love with Eliza McCaskill. Family members said he came to the field one day and ask her to marry him and off they went to Charleston, SC and was married that very day Dec. 24, 1860. During the war his father Needham Madison Yarbrough went to South Carolina and brought his sons family to his home in Liberty Co., Georgia. After the war Needham G. moved his family from Georgia to Starke Florida. In a letter he wrote back to his father, he wrote it took 3 months by ox and cart to get there and they had to fight off Indians during the journey. Years later he and the family moved back to Georgia and settled in Wayne County, Georgia. The Ogeechee minutes showed him as a clergyman in their Association in 1903 and later the South Georgia minutes in 1905 through 1907 showed him as a minister.

Thomas Patrick Young
Birth:
Jan. 15, 1843
Death:
Dec. 18, 1908
Columbus
Muscogee County, Georgia
Burial:
Riverdale Cemetery
Columbus
Muscogee County, Georgia
Plot: Section 7, North
1/2 of Lot 93

Son of Marmaduke N.and Elizabeth (McSWAIN) YOUNG. The local newspaper said:."MR. T. P. YOUNG DIED YESTERDAY: Was 66 Years of Age and a Confederate Veteran--Funeral Tomorrow Morning. The deceased was a member of the Free Will Baptist church and was held in high esteem by all who knew him. The news of his death will bring sorrow to many homes in the community in which he lived. He was a gallant soldier in the service of the south during the civil war and the following page from an old family record bears out the fact of his loyalty to his state: Enlisted in Company B, Captain R. F. PARDY, (of Muscogee county) Thirty-first Georgia regiment, volunteers, October 4th, 1861. Was captured at Appomattox, Va., May 12th, 1864, carried to Fort Delaware. Paroled March 10th, 1865. During the war he served under Generals A. R. LAWTON, John B. GORDON, Clement A. EVANS, Jeb. A. EARLY, and a member of JACKSON's corps, Army of Northern Virginia. Was wounded on the 13th of December, 1862, and afterwards joined the ranks.' Besides his devoted wife, he is survived by five children, as follows: Messrs. F. B. YOUNG, of Chattanooga; F. R. YOUNG, Jr., of the United States navy; W. L. YOUNG, C. L. YOUNG, of Columbus, and G. N. YOUNG, of Milledgeville. He is also survived by two brothers, Messrs. F. R. YOUNG, of Columbus, and O. C. YOUNG, of Girard. The funeral will take place tomorrow morning at ten o'clock from the late residence, and 'Taps' will be sounded over the grave by Messrs. Marion Schley DAVIS and Gurlin F. DAVIS, of the Columbus Guards." [Columbus (GA) Enquirer-Sun newspaper, Saturday, 19 DEC 1908, p. 3.]" Sunday morning at 10 o'clock, the services being conducted by the Rev. Mr. KIDD. The funeral was largely attended by relatives and friends of the deceased. Camp Benning was also represented at the funeral, as Mr. YOUNG was a member of the camp and served the south well during the civil war. Interment was in Riverdale cemetery and the following members of Camp Benning acted as pallbearers: Probably the most impressive feature of the ceremony at the grave was the sounding of 'taps' immediately after the services by Mr. Marion Schley DAVIS, leader of the Columbus Guards drum and bugle corps." [Columbus (GA) Enquirer-Sun newspaper, Tuesday, 22 DEC 1908, p. 8..Entry in Sexton's Card File for Riverdale Cemetery:

Idaho

Rev William Henry Berreman

Birth:
Apr. 24, 1852
Iowa
Death:
Jul. 12, 1949
Southwick
Nez Perce County
Idaho
Burial:
Normal Hill Cemetery
Lewiston
Nez Perce County, Idaho
Plot: IOOF, R 43, L 224, G 07
GPS (lat/lon): 46.40582, -117.02589

Ordained 1884 and ministered in Missouri, West Fork Q.M.

Romanzo Alexander Coats
Birth:
Jul. 3, 1842
Fabius
Onondaga County, New York
Death:
Mar. 17, 1927
Ontario
Malheur County, Oregon
Burial:
Canyon Hill Cemetery
Caldwell, Canyon County, Idaho

UNION WISCONSIN VOLUNTEERS 23rd Regiment, Wisconsin Infantry Romanzo Alexander CoatsRegiment Name 23 Wisconsin Infantry. Side Union Company K Soldier's Rank_In Fifer Soldier's Rank_Out Fifer also...He was an ordained minister in Spencer, Iowa .He was a teacher and a school superintendent in Idaho. He was a farmer in Minnesota."Rev. R.A. Coats, son of Rev. D. N. Coats was born in Chenango Co., NY, July 3, 1842. He studied at Spring Green Academy, Wis., and served three years in the 23d Wis. Vol Infantry at Vicksburg, New Orleans, etc. He was converted Jan. 1, 1863, and ordained June 23, 1872. As missionary for the Little Sioux

Valley Quarterly Meeting in the winter of 1871-72, he was engaged in revivals at Lost Island, Iowa, and Elm Creek and Freedom, Minnesota. In April 1883, he entered upon a seven years' pastorate with the Spencer, Iowa church, during which he served the Minnesota Southern Yearly Meeting in soliciting funds at the time of the famous "grasshopper scourge."In 1880 he became pastor of the Mitchell, Burr Oak and Lincoln churches, enjoying a gracious revival with the latter, and three years later returned to Spencer. In 1887, he removed to Idaho. Rev. Coats was a member of the General Conferences of 1874 and 1880; has served as superintendent of schools in Clay Co. IA, two terms; has been a member of the Iowa Home Mission Board six years and an assistant editor of the *Free Baptist* from commencement. His varied labors have been very helpful to the cause in that region, and he is widely known and respected. His parents were David N Coats (1815 - 1889) and Elizabeth Eleanor White Coats (1822 - 1910)and his spouse was Lephe H Wells Coats (1844 - 1924).

Rue Thomas
Birth:
Apr. 15, 1907
Arkansas
Death:
Jul. 17, 1992
Twin Falls
Twin Falls County, Idaho
Burial:
Sunset Memorial Park Cemetery
Twin Falls
Twin Falls County, Idaho

Thomas, was converted when Oklahoma preacher Jake Gage conducted a revival in Idaho. He soon answered the call to preach, left his farming career in 11953 and invested the next 39 years as a Free Will Baptist minister. Although he did not organize any of the Idaho Free Will Baptist churches, Rue Thomas had a part in each of them. He was a charter member of the Buhl Church, formed the nucleus of the Jerome Church and preached in the Boise church.Born in Kingston, AR, he pastored the only Free Will Baptist church that ever existed in the state of Nevada. He also pastored churches in Midland and San Angelo, TX., and at Artesia, N.Mex. While pastoring small, struggling churches, Bro. Thomas earned a living working for the C.R. Anthony Co. where he received numerous awards as top manager and salesman.He retired from the C.R. Anthony Co., at age 66, then spent more than 15 years on occasional special assignments with the Home Mission Dept. going into churches where a missionary had become discouraged and left. Every time Bro. Thomas left a church, the congregation was debt-free with money in the bank and a larger membership than when he came. His last pastorate was in Rupert, Idaho.

If God called you to preach- Preach!!

Illinois

A L Asberry
Birth:
Oct. 17, 1827
Death:
Aug. 23, 1876
Burial:
Glenn Cemetery, Glenn
Jackson County, Illinois

Early Free Will Baptist Church in western Illinois.

D. W. Ashby
Birth:
January 7, 1851
Hopkins County, Kentucky
Death:
Unknown
Burial:
DeSoto Cemetery
De Soto, Jackson County, Illinois
APlot: Second Addition Row 7
He experienced religion in January, 1869 and received license to preach in 1871. He was

ordained on April 4, 1875 with his connection first being with the General Baptist. About 1885 he united with Freewill Baptist. And began to minister churches in the Makanda Quarterly Meeting in Illinois.

Rev Richard Ashcraft
Birth:
Dec. 3, 1803
Hardin County, Kentucky
Death:
Nov. 12, 1879
Burial:
Pittenger (Ashcraft) Cemetery
Schuyler County, Illinois

Rev. Richard Ashcraft, was born in Hardin Co. Ky, in 1803. In 826 he moved to Vigo Co. Ind., where he was converted three years later and joined the Free Baptists. Later in Illinois he was a colleague of Rev's Samuel Shaw, and J.B. Fast, in laying the foundation of the denomination in the state. He was among the earliest ministers in the Walnut Creek Association, org. in 1839, by Rev. Samuel Shaw and others. Rev. John B. Fast, was a licenate and made clerk of this new association. Rev. Ashcraft traveled quite extensively as an evangelist, aiding the brethren in revivals, laboring as a Free Baptist for twenty-six years.

J. H. Bagwill
Birth:
1874
Death:
1936
Burial:
Looney Springs Cemetery,
Campbell Hill,
Jackson County, Illinois

Early Free Will Baptist minister in Southwest Illinois.

Matthew Baker, Jr
Birth:
Oct. 21, 1791,
Stamford,
Bennington County, Vermont
Death:
Jan. 19, 1852,
Coles County, Illinois
Burial:
Hurricane Cemetery,
Hutton Township,
Coles County, Illinois

Matthew was a prominent minister, marrying many of the local couples in Coles County.

Stephen Bathrick
Birth:
May 27, 1810
New York
Death:
Sep. 26, 1880
Frankfort, Will County, Illinois
Burial:
Pleasant Hill Cemetery
Frankfort, Will County, Illinois

A native of Cayuga Co. N.Y. He died at Frankfort, Ill, aged 70 years. In 1830 he commenced preaching and in 1832 married Miss Cynthia M. Bartholomew. He was ordained Sept. 28, 1833, a Free Will Baptist minister, and became pastor of the N. Parma church, N.Y. He was successful in his efforts in other places. After nine years, he settled at Conneaut, Ohio, where many were added to the church. His labors in the Ashtabula Q.M. were greatly profited by his earnest efforts. After spending some time in his native State, he spent time in Saco and Biddeford, ME, and with the exception of a short period at Lexington, MI, most of his last twenty years were spent in Central New York.At the urgent request of the church at Frankort, Ill, where he had recently pastored, he settled there some two years before his death. His beliefs were positive; his preaching practical and earnest. He loved truth and condemned error. It is thought by many that he preached over 7,000 sermons, and they were remembered by thousands who felt a loss at his death.

Loren Bixby
Birth:
1810
Death:
1900
Burial:
Bloods Point Cemetery
Boone County, Illinois
Plot: 108
Parents: Ebenezer and Hannah Tracy (Flint) Bixby, both bur. VT. His bro., Newell W, also a FWB minister, is bur. in Iowa.

Rev Thomas H Blanden
Birth:
1820
Ohio
Death:
Mar. 12, 1870
Randolph
McLean County, Illinois
Burial:

Arrowsmith Township
Cemetery
Arrowsmith
McLean County, Illinois
Plot: Sect. 13

Thomas H. Blanden, a native of Ohio, died near Cheney's Grove, IL, aged about 50 years. He labored some years as a licensed preacher in the Northern Ohio Y.M., and later as an ordained minister in the Licking Q.M., Ohio,, of the Marion (OH) Yearly Meeting, where he was connected with the St. Albans church. His later years were spent in Illinois, where he did good service in the Livingston Q.M., and aided in organizing several churches. He was known throughout that region as a man of God."
He was married to Louisa Myers, Jan. 21, 1840, in Licking, OH.

Rev William Bodine
Birth:
Mar. 8, 1820
Southwold
Ontario, Canada
Death:
Aug. 19, 1910
Harrison
Winnebago County
Illinois

Burial:
Oakland Cemetery
Durand
Winnebago County
Illinois

His parents were Abram and Zelah (Taylor) BODINE. He was ordained in the Free Baptist church in 1851, and soon after his ordination his voice failing, he preached but little, but has been active in the work of the Laona (Ill.) church, of which hs is a member."
First wife was Harriet Sophronia Babcock (1 Jul 1827 - 5 Aug 1846). Second wife was Frances Elizabeth Albright.

Rev William Bonar
Birth:
Nov. 4, 1814
Coshocton County, Ohio
Death:
Aug. 11, 1875
Kewanee
Henry County,Illinois
Burial:
Cosner Cemetery
Henry County
Illinois
Age of Death - 60 Years, 9 Months, 7 Days.

Richard A. Bradley
Birth:
1802
Death:
1859
Burial:
Looney Springs Cemetery,
Campbell Hill,
Jackson County, Illinois

Richard A. Bradley was born in Sumner Cty, Tennessee. Richard was in his mid-teens when the family moved to Randolph County, Illinois. At age 22 Richard was a member of the survey party that finalized the disputed county line between Jackson and Randolph County. The Bradley's found the majority of their land was now in Jackson County, Illinois. The Black Hawk war broke in the early 1830s and Richard served as a Corporal in the 3rd Regiment, Illinois volunteers commanded by Gabriel Jones. From 1838 to 1840 Richard served as a County Commissioner, and in 1842 he was elected a Representative to the Illinois State Legislature. He served in this capacity until 1846 and then again from 1848 to 1852. During his first term in the State Legislature he Chaired the Elections Committee and presented the bill that moved the Jackson County seat to Murphysboro. In 1848 he chaired the Committee on Public Buildings and Grounds and presented the bill which reduced the fees of many county officials and also presented the bill that chartered the Chester and Wabash Railroad. Richard joined the Looney Springs Free Will Baptist Church in 1850 and was ordained a minister in 1852. For many years he served as Pastor at Looney Springs, as well as at the Campbell Hill Free Will Baptist Church. Richard died on April 16, 1859.

William Bradley
Birth:
Feb. 13, 1814
Death:
Aug. 10, 1887
Burial:
Holliday Farm Cemetery,
Murphysboro,
Jackson County, Illinois

William Bradley was born in Sumner County, Tennessee. Through his early years he studied on his own and acquired a liberal education. In April 1839 William was one of the 32 men who pooled their funds to purchase 80 acres of land to be used in establishing Shiloh School and Meeting House to serve both Jackson and Randolph Counties. In December he, along with his brothers James,

Benjamin, and Richard and six other men, was elected Trustee for the incorporation of Shiloh College which was approved on January 8th, 1840 by the Illinois House and Senate. He remained a trustee for several years and was a member of the committee which drafted the resolutions which governed the board of the college. He was appointed postmaster of the town of Bradley from its formation in 1846 until 1853. He served as Associate county Judge from 1849 to 1853 and County Judge from 1853 to 1857. In 1858 he unsuccessfully ran for the State Legislature. In October 1852 he was ordained a Freewill Baptist Minister by Reverend Henry S. Gordon. He served as Pastor at Looney Springs Baptist Church near Campbell Hill and at Sato Baptist Church. In 1860, he and Reverend Gordon organized the Ava Free Baptist Church, where William served as pastor until 1864. In 1869 William and Serena moved to the growing city of Murphysboro where they lived the rest of their lives. From 1869 to 1873 William once more served as County Judge and through his remaining years stayed active in the church.

He Is The Beginning And The End

Samuel S. Branch
Birth:
Dec. 27, 1801
Vermont
Death:
Jan. 29, 1862
Geff, Wayne County,
Illinois
Burial:
Pleasant Grove
Christian Church Cemetery
Geff, Wayne County
, Illinois

He had 11 children by three wives, the first two wives dying in childbirth in Meigs Co, Ohio. He moved his family and congregation to Wayne County, Illinois in 1852 and started the Oak Valley Free Will Baptist Church. The HISTORY OF WAYNE CO: Free-Will Baptists, pg 121-122-- The first church organized in this county about two miles west of Jeffersonville, Sept 2 1854, by Rev. S. S. Branch, and consisted of six members: S.S. Branch, Elizabeth Branch, Densy TUBBS, Samuel BRANCH, Jacob S. HAWK AND Mary HAWK.

S.S. Branch was chosen pastor; J.S.Hawk clerk, and Samuel Branch, deacon a cousin to S.S. Branch, his wife is Phoebe and they had no children. He is buried in the Geff cemetery]. The Saturday before the third Sabbath of each month, was appointed for covenant meetings. Regular services were held on the Sabbath. Rev. S.S. Branch was born in Vermont in 1794 [bible records say 27 Dec 1801], removed to Ohio in 1802; professed religion April 1831; baptized by Rev. Eli STEADMAN, his brother-in-law, was ordained 1841, removed to Illinois 1853; and died leaving a wife and eight children. His widow Elizabeth Branch lived in Big Stone Co. Minnesota with her son Joseph. The membership of the church was 92.

Henry Brown
Birth:
Mar. 4, 1843
Virginia
Death:
Mar., 1928
Illinois
Burial:
Harvel Cemetery
Harvel, Montgomery County,
Illinois

He was converted in 1859 and married in 1878. And received his license to preach in 1886 and at one time ministered the church in East St. Louis, Illinois.

Obed W Bryant
Birth:
Mar. 9, 1815
Death:
Aug. 2, 1882
Burial:
Wyoming Cemetery
Paw Paw, Lee County, Illinois

Bryant, a native of New Vineyard, Me., was converted when about nineteen years of age and went to reside in Illinois two years later. He joined the Baptist church and later the Free Baptist, near Lamoille. Later, he moved to Four Mile Grove, where he was instrumental in raising a church. He was ordained at that place in August 1859, and remained a member until his death, when 67 years of age. He labored zealously and successfully. He was faithful in his care of the widely separated churches, punctual at the general meetings, persistent in revival efforts, true in positions of public trust and active in moral interposes..

William Riley Burton
Birth:
Sep. 21, 1881,
Ewing, Franklin County, Illinois
Death:
Nov., 1963,
Ewing, Franklin County, Illinois
Burial:
Shiloh Cemetery
Ewing, Franklin County, Illinois

Rev. W. R. BURTON, 82 of Whittington, retired minister, died at his home after an illness of a was a member of Rescue Free Will Baptist Church at Whittington. W.R. Burton was the main missionary, evangelist and pastor in Illinois when they were trying to get the FWB back together following the merger in 1910. Everyone called him "Brother Riley". David Shores said, "He started the church I pastor in 1930 following a revival of 53 nights."

Byford Lee Campbell
Birth:
Jun. 3, 1927
Spring Garden
Jefferson County, Illinois
Death:
Oct. 17, 2014
Ina
Jefferson County, Illinois
Burial:
Kirk Cemetery
Ina
Jefferson County, Illinois

Byford Lee Campbell and Wastina Faye Campbell passed away at their home in Ina. The couple were extraordinary individuals that had just celebrated their 67th wedding anniversary on April 21 of this year. Both Byford and Wastina had a great love for God, their

family and will be greatly missed. Byford Lee Campbell was to former Trellie and Lillian Allen Campbell in Spring Garden. He was an ordained Free Will Baptist minister and pastored several southern Illinois churches over the years. He was also a transformer designer at Dowzer Electric for 20 years plus. In his later years, he served the village of Ina in numerous capacities. He loved the community of Ina in which he lived his entire life.

Preceded in death by parents; an infant sister, Thelma Campbell; brother in law, Junior McCann; and brothers-in-law, Charles Webb and Robert Montgomery.

Wastina Faye McCann Campbell (1927 - 2014) and he were killed at their home in Ina, Illinois as a result of a natural gas explosion. He had been in the ministry for over 50 year. He was the historian for the village of Ina and for the FreeWill Baptists of Illinois.

Lyman Chase
Birth:
Oct. 2, 1839,
Rutland, Ohio
Death:
1918
Burial:
Tamaroa Cemetery,
Tamaroa, Perry County, Illinois

He began his new life in 1857, and received license in 1859, and ordination in 1868, having graduated from Hillsdale College (Michigan) in 1866. He became principal of Atwood Institute in Ohio, the year of his graduation, and was there five years. He has also served as editor of the Huntington, West Virginia., *Independent*, and as superintendent of the city schools.

His pastorates were at Conneaut, Sheffield and Madison, Ohio; Fairview, Ill, and Mt. Pleasant, Kan. He was superintendent of the work in the northern Kansas and southern Nebraska Yearly Meeting, and in connection with his ministerial duties prepared a book entitled, *Contending for the Faith.*

Claude B Childers
Birth:
Jun. 17, 1882
Death:
Mar. 29, 1962
Burial:
Wakefield Cemetery,
Wakefield,
Richland County, Illinois

Early preacher in Illinois.

Rev Peter Christian
Birth:
Dec. 23, 1817
Plattsburgh
Clinton County, New York
Death:
Jul. 31, 1899
Fulton County, Illinois
Burial:
Fiatt Cemetery
Fiatt
Fulton County, Illinois
Rev. Peter Christian was the son of Joseph and Frances (Stanthill) CHRISTIAN.
He was married to Mary J. Johnson, June 26, 1841 in Ill. Rev. Christian was ordained June 24, 1854, by Rev's S. Shaw, L.Driscoll, of Walnut Creek Free Will Baptist Quarterly Meeting, Illinois.

Rev Oscar T Clark
Birth:
1832
Essex, Vermont
Death:
Aug. 8, 1891
Iowa
Burial:
Riverside Cemetery
Prophetstown
Whiteside County, Illinois

He married Miss Caroline Fielding in 1854. He professed religion in 1850, he having moved to Illinois in 1836. He served three years in the Army, Civil War: Co F 28th Ia, and while there decided to obey the call to the ministry.

Returning home to Iowa, he joined the Free Will Baptist church, and served as layman until 1870; he was licensed in 1871, and ordained the next year. He served churches in Iowa, and for eight years in Kansas, and was instrumental in gathering several churches in Norton Co. His name is mentioned in church history as being there in 1880. After eight years, he returned to Iowa where he was faithful until his death.

Charles Dwight Dame
Birth:
Jan. 15, 1922,
Waltonville,
Jefferson County,
Illinois
Death:
Oct. 9, 2009
Burial:
Maple Hill Cemetery,
Sesser,
Franklin County,
Illinois

Dwight was ordained a Free Will Baptist minister in 1952 and served as a minister for over 50 years at several different churches. He was the chaplain for the Sesser VFW and American Legion, giving the Memorial Day address every year. He attended grade school at White Oak and high school in Sesser. He entered the United States Army on Sept. 8,1942, serving until Jan. 1,1946, with two years, 11 months and 24 days overseas, serving in battles at Ardennes, Rhindland and Central Europe. He received six overseas service bars, one service stripe, American Campaign, European and African and Middle East Theater Ribbons, three Bronze Battle Stars, Asiatic Pacific Theater Ribbon, Good Conduct Medal and a World War II Victory Medal, while becoming a sergeant.

Dwight raised cattle and farmed his entire life and loved to hunt quail. He worked at Valier Coal Company before World War II and at Freeman United Coal for 30 years after the war. He worked as a United Mine Workers Association member, a supervisor and plant superintendent. He was also a college mining instructor at Rend Lake College for five years before retiring. He served on the Sesser School Board for eight years and as president for four years. He was also the mayor of Sesser for four years and got the city hall built during his term in office. Military rites were conducted by the Sesser VFW and American Legion.

Tracy Dees
Birth:
Aug. 21, 1907
Death:
Jan. 18, 1980
Burial:
South Hickory Hill Cemetery
McClellan Township
Jefferson County, Illinois

Tracey pastor numerous FWB churches including Waltonville, Nason, and Rescue. He also pastored South Hickory Hill Christian Church and Howard's Chapel (Pentecost).

He was the son of Robert Lee Dees and Sarah Cansada Bean.

Rev Howard S. Flota
Birth:
Jul. 16, 1920
Death:
Unknown
Burial:
Bethel Memorial Cemetery
Mount Vernon
Jefferson County, Illinois
An ordained Free Will Baptist minister/pastor.

James Charles Gilliland
Birth:
1874
Death:
1958
Burial:
Grandview Cemetery, Freeport, Stephenson County, Illinois

Free Will Baptist minister in Illinois.

George Alexander Gordon
Birth:
Apr. 14, 1842,
Alton, Madison County, Illinois
Death:
Aug. 25, 1922,
Ava, Jackson County, Illinois
Burial:
Calvary Cemetery,
Campbell Hill,
Jackson County, Illinois

Active early leader and church builder in Illinois. Respected and looked to for guidance by other ministers in his area in southern Illinois.

Rev Henry Smith Gordon
Birth:
Jun. 19, 1816
Franklin County, Pennsylvania
Death:
Jan. 10, 1898
Percy
Randolph County, Illinois
Burial:
Lickiss Cemetery, Steeleville
Randolph County, Illinois

Henry Smith Gordon married Susan Rebecca Young on October 18, 1835, when he was 19 years old.

His father gave him 100 acres of land of which he later sold for $1,200 and left for S. Illinois."Abt. 1837 at Age 21 he operated a large grist mill driven by cattle or horses on an incline wheel. He also was ordained minister of the Missionary Baptist Church. Realizing he needed further education to be a minister he took his wife and one child and entered Shurtleff College.

When he was 36 years old in the year of 1852 and because of failing health he felt that compelled him to make a long and tedious trip across the plains defined gold. So with a team of milk cows and two of his neighbors. Namely Westley Higginson and Noah Guymon they were gone for six months to California.

In 1855 he began a mercantile business until this health approved in O'Fallon, St. Clair County, Illinois. After which he returned to his farm and because the man who had rented it would not give it up he enlarged is farm to 400 acres between the years 1856 and 1885. He was a strict vegetarian and became a republic when it was first organized but later became a Democrat. In 1880 he became an Advocate to the principles of the Prohibition Party.

In 1892 he built a new home and he and Nancy lived there until he died.

He was the founder of the Free Communion Baptist denomination in southern Illinois, some of which still exist and continue as active churches affiliated with the State Assn. of Illinois Free Will Baptists.

Leo Kivett Grider
Birth:
Feb. 26, 1926
West Frankfort
Franklin County, Illinois
Death:
Aug. 29, 2016
Marion
Williamson County, Illinois
Burial:
Egyptian Memorial Gardens
Herrin
Williamson County
Illinois

Leo Kivett "Pete" Grider, 90, of Marion went home to be with his Lord and Savior at his family home with his children by his side.

Leo was the son of Leo Adolphus and Laura Margaret (Mayberry) Grider. He was united in marriage to Joyce Ardelle Ehnert on January 12, 1946 in Marion. Leo was retired, having been a journeyman lineman for IBEW Local #702 for 22 years.

He was a veteran of the United States Navy, having served his country honorably during WWII. He was a member of the Freedom Freewill Baptist Church south of Marion. He was an ordained Freewill Baptist Church Minister for over 50 years.

He liked to tinker on cars and tractors. He had a passion to read the Bible on a daily basis. Leo's family and serving his Lord was the love of his life.

Funeral services was in Pyle Funeral Home in Johnston City with Rev. Ivan Ryan officiating.

Gladys Alene Pitchford Hanna
Birth:
Sep. 16, 1914
Death:
Dec. 26, 1987
Burial:
Old Baptist Cemetery,
Waltonville Jefferson County,
Illinois

She was a lady minister of many that were in the state of Illinois. In 1960 when the state assn. was formed they grandfathered the license for them but no women have been ordained since.
Married Louie Barrett Hanna November 7, 1931 who was also a FWB minister in Illinois.

Rev Louie Barrett Hanna
Birth:
Jan. 29, 1911
Scheller
Jefferson County, Illinois
Death:
Jan. 3, 2005
Mount Vernon
Jefferson County, Illinois
Burial:
Old Baptist Cemetery
Waltonville
Jefferson County, Illinois

The Rev. Louie Barrett Hanna, 93, of Scheller died in Good Samaritan R.H.C. in Mt. Vernon. Services were held at Brayfield-Gilbert Funeral Home in Sesser, with the Rev. Kent Dunford officiating. The Rev. Hanna was pastor of many Free Will Baptist churches all over Southern Illinois.
His wife was also a FWB minister.

Floyd Harley
Birth:
Unknown
Death:
Unknown
Sesser,
Franklin County, Illinois
Burial:
Maple Hill Cemetery,
Sesser,Franklin County, Illinois

Missionary Evelyn Lawrence Hersey
Birth:
Mar. 2, 1930,
Vroman,Otero County,Colorado
Death:
Oct. 4, 1993,
Nashville,
Davidson County, Tennessee
Burial:
Zion Cemetery,
Ozark, Johnson County, Illinois

She served many terms as a missionary to Japan under the International Mission Board of Free Will Baptists. She was married to Fred Hersey.

Rev Clifford Leon Hicks
Birth:
Jan. 17, 1928
Waltonville
Jefferson County, Illinois
Death:
Jul. 7, 2015
Waltonville
Jefferson County, Illinois
Burial:
Knob Prairie Cemetery
Waltonville
Jefferson County, Illinois

Rev. Clifford Leon Hicks age 87 of Waltonville passed away at his home in Waltonville. Clifford was born in Waltonville, Illinois the son of Traves and Sadie (Dees) Hicks. He married Wilma Maxine (Young) on March 24, 1948 at the home of Rev. Tracy Dees in Waltonville and she survives in Waltonville. Clifford Served his Country in the United States Navy during WWII. He worked for the Missouri Pacific Railroad, Vernois Stove Foundry in Mt. Vernon, Freeman Coal Mine #3 in Waltonville, and then last for Good Samaritan Hospital in Mt. Vernon. During this time Rev. Clifford Hicks was serving as pastor for various Free Will Baptist Churches in Jefferson, Franklin, and Wayne Counties.

He served as Illinois State Treasurer and on the Executive Board for the Illinois State Association of Free Will Baptist. He was a member of the Waltonville Free Will Baptist Church where he served as pastor on two separate occasions. Funeral services for Rev. Clifford Hicks will be held at the Waltonville Free Will Baptist Church in Waltonville with Rev. Ivan Ryan and Rev. Curtis Smith officiating.

James Walter Hicks
Birth:
Sep. 18, 1930
Jefferson County, Illinois
Death:
Sep. 9, 1987
Burial:
Knob Prairie Cemetery
Waltonville, Jefferson County,
Illinois

Hicks, a son of Travis and Sadie (Dees) Hicks. On Dec 4, 1954, in Mt. Vernon, he married Anna Marie Fairchild. Services were at the Waltonville Free Will Baptist Church with the Rev Geraldine Lewis officiating. Hicks was a U. S. Navy veteran of the Korean War and a member of VFW 9153 and Disabled American Veterans of Mt. Vernon. He was a Free Will Baptist minister in the Waltonville area for several years and was a member of the Free Will Baptist Church in Nason.

Ellamae Harrelson Hiltibidal
Birth:
May 13, 1921
Hamilton County, Illinois
Death
Dec. 1, 2013
Mt. Vernon,
Illinois
Burial:
Mount Olivet Cemetery
McLeansboro
Hamilton County, Illinois

Ellamae Harrelson Hiltibidal, 92, was the daughter of Edgar and Lou (Bennett) Harrelson. She married the Rev. John Hiltibidal on Oct. 26, 1941, and he preceded her in death on March 9, 1999.

She was a licensed Free Will Baptist Minister. She served 10 years as Illinois State President & Field worker for Illinois Free Will Baptist Woman's Auxiliary (Women Active for Christ). She graduated from McLeansboro High School in 1941, where she played violin in the symphony. She was a member of Pleasant View Free Will Baptist Church since 1941, and attended Mt. Vernon First Free Will Baptist Church in later years.

She has always been gifted with lots of talents; singing, sewing, crafting, painting, quilting, den mother for Boy Scouts, church work and a good friend to lots of people.

Bro. David Shores and Bro. David Burgess officiated.

John J. Hiltibidal
Birth:
Jan. 24, 1908
Death:
Apr. 21, 1973
Burial:
Old Covenanter Cemetery
Marion County,
Illinois,
Plot: Back of church

He was a retired Carmen and welder for the Illinois central railroad and a retired minister in the Free Will Baptist denomination. For 50 years he served as a minister for several Free Will Baptist Churches throughout southern Illinois. He was a member of the Pleasant View Free Will Baptist Church where he established his original membership in 1934.

John W Hiltibidal
Birth:
Jun. 18, 1916
Death:
Mar. 9, 1999
Burial:
Mount Olivet Cemetery
McLeansboro
Hamilton County, Illinois

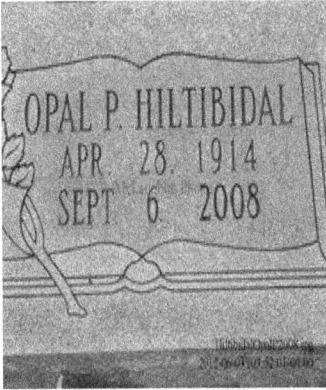

Opal P. Hiltibidal
Birth:
Apr. 28, 1914
Illinois
Death:
Sep. 6, 2008
Walnut Hill,
Marion County, Illinois
Burial:
Old Covenanter Cemetery,
Marion County, Illinois

Opal passed at the age of 94 years. Opal was a resident of Walnut Hill, Illinois at the time of her passing. She was a student of the first class of FWB Bible College of Nashville, Tenn. She was also a minister in the state of Illinois.

On That Bright And Cloudless Morning When The Dead In Christ Shall Rise

Rev Daniel G Holmes
Birth:
Apr. 5, 1812
Death:
May 2, 1902
Burial:
Oak Woods Cemetery
Chicago
Cook County, Illinois

Rev. D.G. Holmes, received license from the Boston Q.M. (Mass) in 1844. Three years later he was an ordained minister connected with the Fairport, N.Y. church. About 1848 he became pastor of the Walworth church, to which he ministered some ten years, after which he served the Fairport a like term. He was highly esteemed for his work's sake.

About 1868, he moved to Chicago, and from there he made yearly visits to certain churches in Missouri, and greatly aided them by his counsel. He continued to reside in Chicago.

He married Huldah B. Currrier, in N.H.

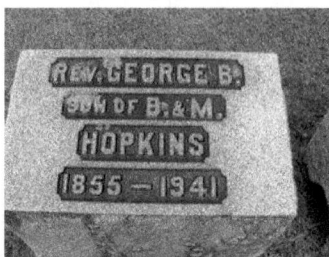

George B. Hopkins
Birth:
April 11, 1855
Oakfield, New York
Death:
Nov. 13, 1941
Illinois
Burial:
Oakwood Cemetery
Geneseo, Henry County, Illinois

He graduated from the Pike Seminary in 1879, from Hillsdale College in 1884, and completed the theological course in Bates College in 1887. He made a public confession of Christ in 1876 and received his license to preach for the Genesee, New York Quarterly Meeting in January 1886. He served churches in Maine and New York before coming to Illinois.

Andrew J. Hoskinson
Birth:
August 4, 1816
Athens County Ohio
Death:
1892
Illinois
Burial:
Peaceful Valley Cemetery
Odin, Marion County, Illinois

He experienced religion in 1837, and in 1843 was ordained by Rev. S. S. Branch and others in South East Ohio. He labored as an evangelist among the destitute churches and has organized several churches and baptized about 80 converts.

George H. Hubbard
Birth:
Feb. 16, 1823
Burlington, New York
Death:
1911
Burial:
Oakwood Cemetery
Waukegan, Lake County, Illinois

He was converted in 1836, receiving baptism at the hand of Elder Wm. Hunt, and united with the Free Communion Baptist church. He studied at Clinton Seminary, received license from the Otsego QM, about 1852, and was ordained June 28, 1857, at Libertyville, Ill. Since October, 1855, with the exception of one year, his ministry has been with the churches of the Wisconsin YM, the longest pastorate being with the Honey Creek and Caldwell churches. He has been clerk of the Honey Creek QM seventeen years, and has held other positions of trust for long terms. The sermons preached number 3,700, and have resulted in much good. The assistance of his faithful, consecrated wife, Mary Wilbur Hubbard, since their marriage, Jan. 6, 1848, has aided him materially amid the toils and trials incident to a minister's life, and will ever be remembered with appreciation.

of all ages attended. A huge fireplace that was kept filled with great logs heated the cabin.On April 3rd, 1850, Enoch Huggins and wife deeded a piece of ground eight rod square in the N. W. corner N.W. Quarter of Section 36, Radnor Township, to School District No. 5. A short time thereafter, a schoolhouse was built which has always been known as Glendale.

Inscription:
ORVILLE. HUGGINS
DIED Sep. 14, 1855
23Ys,7Ms,14Ds.

Orville E. Huggins
Birth:
Jan. 31, 1832
New York
Death:
Sep. 14, 1855
Illinois
Burial:
Mount Hawley Cemetery
Peoria,
Peoria County,
Illinois

Huggins, removed in 1847 from Penfield, N.Y., to Illinois, where he united with the Osceola church in 1852, and was soon licensed to preach by the Walnut Creek Quarterly Meeting. He was a young man of much promise, and his death, Sept. 14, 1855, at the age of 23, was much lamented."The Glendale School, though not known in the beginning by that name, was opened in the fall of 1849 in a little log cabin. Orville Huggins was the first teacher, and pupils

Rev Willis Marshall Jones
Birth:
Oct. 30, 1870
Illinois
Death:
Oct. 25, 1943
Illinois
Burial:
McCann Cemetery
Franklin County
Illinois

An ordained Free Will Baptist minister, who worked in and attended the Cooperative General Association, before it merged with the Eastern Conference and they became the National Association of Free Will Baptists.

Arthur W Kern
Birth:
May 4, 1919
Death:
Aug., 1992
Illinois
Burial:
Oak Hill Cemetery,
Ewing,
Franklin County
, Illinois

He pastored the Plasters' Grove Free Will Baptist Church, Thompsonville, Illinois and the Aiken Grove church, Benton, Illinois. He was the founding pastor of the Belle Rive Free Will Baptist Church in Belle Rive, Illinois.

Columbus Jackson "Jack" Ketteman
Birth:
Apr. 3, 1899
Death:
Jan. 10, 1994
Burial:
Liberty-Ridlin Cemetery,
Macedonia,
Franklin County, Illinois

He was a very active Free Will Baptist pastor and minister in southern Illinois. He preached his first sermon in 1938 and pastored at least 14 churches in southern Illinois. He was 94 at his passing. He was the father of Jack Ketteman and Mrs. Bobby Jackson.

Rev Elnation Lewis
Birth:
Sep. 16, 1804
Ludlow
Windsor County
Vermont
Death:
Dec. 22, 1853
Grundy County, Illinois
Burial:
Stevens Cemetery
Grundy County, Illinois

Rev. Elnathan Lewis, a native of Vermont, was converted in New York, and united with the Free Baptists in Illinois in 1845. He preached to destitute churches with devotion and success, was ordained in 1849, and died Dec. 21, 1853, aged 49 years, having been the means of gathering two churches in the south part of

Grundy County, Illinois. His loss was deeply felt.

H. Wallace Malone
Birth:
Jan. 16, 1917,
Mulkeytown,
Franklin County, Illinois
Death:
Nov. 29, 2006,
Decatur, Macon County, Illinois
Burial:
Greenwood Cemetery,
Coello, Franklin County, Illinois

Throughout his 66 years of ministry, the Rev. Malone was pastor of several Free Will Baptist Churches throughout the state of Illinois and was the founding pastor of Bethel Free Will Baptist Church in South Roxana. He pastored Decatur Free Will Baptist Church in Decatur until his retirement. He was a member of IBEW, a former member of Illinois Mission Board, and a member of the Alumni Association of Free Will Baptist Bible College in Nashville, Tenn. The Rev. Malone was co-founder of Illinois Free Will Baptist Youth Camp, now known as Camp Hope. He was on the Executive Committee of the National Association of Free Will Baptists. He was the father of two Free Will Baptists ministers. One was pastor of the South Roxana and one the President of Free Will Baptist Baptist Bible College.

Rev John W. Marvel
Birth:
Oct. 26, 1789
Rhode Island
Death:
Feb. 5, 1856
Illinois
Burial:
Sharon Cemetery
Spring Hill
Whiteside County
Illinois
Plot: Row 3 Lot 74 A

Rev. John W. Marvel was born in Rhode Island in 1796, and converted at twenty-four years of age and soon commenced preaching. He was ordained about 1834 and labored with the Second China (NY) church until 1839, then for four years with the church at Aurora, NY, after which he removed to Illinois and was connected with the Rock River Quarterly Meeting.

His death occurred in 1856. He was active and useful in winning souls

He spent most of his life in the Centralia area. He served in the Army Air Force during World War II in the South Pacific. Upon returning home from war, he farmed the family farm near Walnut Hill. Leon was a minister and pastor of several Free Will Baptist Churches, including Johnsonville, Bear Point in Sesser, Blue Point and Oak Valley in Cisne, First Free Will Baptist Church in Johnston City and Zephyr Hills in Asheville, N.C. Celebration services of his life will be conducted by Rev. Tom Malone and Rev. David Shores. Graveside military rites will be conducted by the VFW and American Legion of Mount Vernon.

E Leon McBride
Birth:
Dec. 29, 1917
Death:
Apr. 21, 2006
Burial:
Zion Grove Cemetery
Kell,
Marion County, Illinois

George McMillan
Birth:
May 23, 1832
Belfast, Ireland
Death:
1902
Burial:
Woodlawn Cemetery
Creston
Ogle County, Illinois

His studies were pursued at Grand River Institute, Austinsbourgh, Ohio and in 1855 he graduated from Oberlin College, Oberlin, Ohio. He was a professor of the Greek language and literature at Hillsdale College, Michigan, from 1860 until 1876 and later held a similar position in the University of Nebraska. He married Josephine young in 1858 and they had two children. One son received a Master Of Arts from the University of Nebraska and later was an instructor in Botany at the University of Minnesota.

John W. McMillan
Birth:
Jun. 16, 1844
Death:
Jan. 12, 1912
Burial
Calvary Cemetery, Campbell Hill, Jackson County, Illinois

He was an early Free Will Baptist minister and served with Co A 80th Illinois Infancy during the Civil War.

Thomas O. McMinn
Birth:
Dec. 20, 1869
Death:
Feb. 13, 1936
Burial:
Tamaroa Cemetery, Tamaroa, Perry County, Illinois

He was baptized at age 17 (by his future father-in-law) and later ordained 10 Nov 1875 by Rev. W. H. Blankenship, J. C. Gilliland, J. S. Gullege at Cottage Home, T.O. founded the Cottage Home Baptist Church. It was built in 1883.Those who followed the leadership of McMinn organized themselves into the Cottage Home Baptist Church a Free Will Baptist Church. He was a member of the 1883 General Conference at Minneapolis and in 1895 at Winnebago MN.
In the early days he was a real circuit rider, serving several churches at the same time going from church to church and farm to farm on horseback. He helped start or grow several churches. Some churches he was involved with: Campbell Hill Free Will Baptist Church, 1886 helped

reorganize Ava Free Will Baptist Church, 1897-1900 Scheller Church,1901 Murphysboro Church. He had 3 main churches where he served for many years: Tamaroa IL, Little Cedar IA, and one in Nebraska. In his later years, Thomas worked for the American Baptist association of churches after returning to IL in 1918. His earlier association with the Free Will Baptists were thought an aid to convert people to the new association. He retired in the 20s as he became quite forgetful.

George W Minton
Birth:
Jul. 16, 1860
Union County, Illinois
Death:
Jan. 21, 1904
Burial:
Friendship Cemetery
Union County

He was ordained in 1884 and was connected with the Rock Springs Church of the Looney Springs Quarterly Meeting.

William J. Mishler
Birth:
1916,
Colville, Stevens County,
Washington
Death:
Oct. 20, 1995,
Johnston City,
Williamson County,
Illinois
Burial:
Lakeview Cemetery,
Johnston City,
Williamson County, Illinois

He was a Free Will Baptist minister for 61 years pastoring 11 churches in five states: Missouri, Tennessee, Michigan, Arkansas and Illinois. He was the State Moderator in both Arkansas and Illinois. He was a member of the national Sunday School Board and later served as the first Promotional Secretary beginning in 1954. He set up the first Sunday School Department in the National Offices in Nashville, Tennessee. He served 17 years on the Board of Trustees at Free Will Baptist Bible College being Chairman 14 years. He served 18 years on the General Board of the National Association. He was a graduate of Free Will Baptist Bible College.

Samuel Reddick Modlin
Birth:
May 28, 1828
Davidson County,
Tennessee
Death:
Mar. 10, 1904
Blue Mound
Macon County, Illinois
Burial:
Hall Cemetery
Blue Mound
Macon County,
Illinois

His record was taken from death certificate; there is no grave stone.

Rev Schooley Lemmon Morris
Birth:
Apr. 5, 1856
Plantsville
Morgan County
Ohio
Death:
May 16, 1922
Spring Garden
Jefferson County
Illinois
Burial:
Ashley Cemetery
Ashley
Washington County
Illinois

Son of David MORRIS & Rachel JAMES. Married first, in Morgan Co., OH, 30 April 1879, Millie J. DANIEL, daughter of John W. DANIEL & Elizabeth Ann TORBERT. Married second, in Pocahontas, Cape Giradeau Co., Missouri, 4 March 1891, Belle FULBRIGHT. Married third, in Ashley Twp., Washington Co., IL, 24 March 1901, Grace Irene TOPPING, daughter of Dandamus 'Daniel' TOPPING & Indiana Zane WATKINS. Schooley is father of 3 children by his first marriage- Carlos 'Carl' William MORRIS [1880-1946]; Hallie Elizabeth MORRIS PIPER [1883-1952]; and Nellie E. MORRIS MEADOR [1886-1965].

FREE-WILL BAPTIST MINISTER. MORRIS, Rev. S. L., FREE-WILL BAPTIST Born in Ohio in 1856. Converted at 13 years of age; entered the ministry at 28, and later joined the Free Baptist Church at Ava [Jackson Co., IL] in 1896. Ordained in 1897, at Tamaroa, Ill. [Perry Co.], and has done pastoral work ever since; organized Lone Oak church; pastor of Tamaroa church. Source: Jackson County, Illinois THE LIFE AND LABORS OF REV. HENRY S. GORDON By REV. GEO. A. GORDON, Campbell Hill, Illinois (1901) Death due to heart failure/ over extertion while preaching per inquest/coroner's certification of death.

Inscription:
Rev S.L. MORRIS 1856-1922.
Only "Good-night" beloved, not farewell

Jacob Overocker
Birth:
Jul. 5, 1795
Minden
Montgomery Count, New York
Death:
Feb. 28, 1877
Franks
DeKalb County, Illinois
Burial:
Cronktown Cemetery
Kirkland
DeKalb County, Illinois

Ordained in 1826, a Freewill Baptist minister, and preached extensively in this vicinity, as his health would permit until "called to his reward. "Married 1/8/1815 in NY State to Anna Delavigne, and was the father of nine children.

Kevin Payne
Birth:
Aug. 19, 1956
Mount Vernon,
Jefferson County, Illinois
Death:
Aug. 18, 2012
Franklin,
Williamson County, Tennessee
Burial:
Kirk Cemetery,
Ina, Jefferson County, Illinois

He was bi-vocational and had been pastor of the Cornerstone Free Will Baptist Church in Murfreesboro, Tn. shortly before his death. Dr. W. Stanley Outlaw and the Rev. Brad Ryan officiated

Orrin D Patch
Birth:
Jan. 23, 1861
Eaton, New Hampshire
Death:
Oct. 16, 1915
Burial:
Roseville Cemetery
Roseville
Warren County
Illinois

When he was 18 years of age he moved to Illinois and was

educated in his hometown at Prairie city Academy, Illinois, where he also taught for two years and studied theology under a private instructor. His life was consecrated to God in 1861; licensed to preach was granted in 1865, and ordination received in July, 1867. Prof. Ransom Dunn preached the sermon of his ordination. He ministered the church and Kewanee, Illinois until 1874 when under the direction of the home mission board he took charge of the work at Cleveland, Ohio were under his direction the church reorganized and a house of worship was erected in a new location and an interest became greater.

In 1881 he moved to Greenville, Rhode Island and had a successful pastorate. Then at the Main Street Church in Lewiston Maine as well. But the Cleveland church demanded is labor and he returned to Cleveland in 1884. He was for many years a member of the home mission board and is now a member of the conference Board in one of the corporators for the Free Will Baptist Printing Establishment.

Peter Wells Perry
Birth:
January 24, 1830
Stockbridge, Massachusetts
Death:
1916
Burial:
Bronswood Cemetery
Oak Brook
DuPage County, Illinois

He was educated at Ohio University, Athens, Ohio. He licensed on November 3, 1855 and was ordained at Canaan, Ohio on September 14, 1856. In June, 1861, he was married to Julia Hall. His pastorates in Ohio with the Free Will Baptist were at Chester, Mainville, Rutland, Blanchester and Pleasant Plain. He also pastored in Jackson, Michigan, Lowville, New York and Great Falls, New Hampshire. For about seven years he was connected with the Congregationalists. He was the principle of Cheshire Academy for five years at Cheshire, Ohio, and a member of the Free Baptist Foreign Mission Board for six years. He baptized more than 500 converts

Jacob B Prickett
Birth:
October 30, 1834
Springfield, Ohio
Death:
May 11, 1886
Belvidere, Illinois
Burial:
Davis Cemetery
Winnebago County, Illinois

In 1836 his parents moved to Indiana where he united with the Washington church in 1846. He received his licensed to preach in 1856 and after serving the Fifth-Fifth Illinois infantry and honorably discharged, he was ordained in 1863 at the Noble County Quarterly Meeting. His ministry was confined primarily in that quarterly meeting in Indiana and the Fox River Quarterly Meeting in Illinois.

Andrew Jackson Rendleman
Birth:
Mar. 3, 1867
Williamson County, Illinois
Death:
Oct. 2, 1940
East Saint Louis
St. Clair County, Illinois,
Burial:
Mount Hope Cemetery
Belleville
St. Clair County, Illinois

Early Free Will Baptist, preacher, principal, supervisor and County Superintendent of Schools in Jackson, Perry, Williamson and Madison Counties, and newspaper editor. He was a member Illinois State Teacher's Assn. and Historical Secretary of the Illinois Baptist State Convention- 1938-39. He researched and wrote several historical papers.

George Edward Ritter, Jr
Birth:
Jul. 21, 1923,
Johnston City,
Williamson County,
Illinois
Death:
Nov. 18, 2009,
Marion,
Williamson County, Illinois
Burial:
Sunset Lawn Cemetery,
Harrisburg, Saline County,
Illinois

He served in the U.S. Air Force from 1943 to 1949. Rev. Ritter pastored churches in Illinois, Arkansas and Alabama until he retired in 1993. He was former owner of Ritter's Custom Cabinets and a member of the Scottsboro Baptist.

Wiley L. Smart
Birth:
1833
Wilson County, Tennessee
Death:
Aug. 6, 1891
Saline County, Illinois
Burial:
Ward Cemetery
Saline County, Illinois

He married Mary A. Allison in 1854, KY, and they had eight children. He was converted in 1859, began to preach the next year and was ordained in 1865. His pastorates have been Oak Grove and Bell City, KY; and Harmony, Mt. Pleasant, Pleasant Ridge, Mt. Moriah, Mt. Zion and Freedom, Illinois. He was active in the work of the ministry until about 1884, when he was unable to bear the burdens longer.He has baptized 530 converts.

Caleb Marsh Sewall
Birth:
Nov. 6, 1811
Maine
Death:
Nov. 21, 1875
Hamilton, Illinois
Burial:
Greenwood Cemetery
Hamilton
Hancock County,
Illinois

He was converted when 19 years of age and ordained in Chesterfield, Maine on April 13, 1842. The same year he was sent by the Home Mission Board to Illinois, where he labored with great devotion 33 years within the bounds of the Hancock and Quincey Quarterly Meetings he was a man of strong faith and fix purpose and was instrumental under God interning many souls to Christ.

Emma Serena *Snider* Uhles
Birth:
Sep. 25, 1863
Campbell Hill
Jackson County Illinois
Death:
Jun., 1914
Illinois
Burial:
Cottom Cemetery,
Denmark, Perry County,
Illinois

She was an early Free Will Baptist preacher in Southern Illinois.

Rev William Roshier Spurlock
Birth:
Jul. 12, 1882
Death:
Aug. 31, 1965
Jefferson County, Illinois
Burial:
Hope Cemetery
Spring Garden
Jefferson County, Illinois

This record is found in the "Saga of Southern Illinois" quarterly on page 40 of the April-June 1975 issue.

Jonathan Noel Thigpen
Birth:
Dec. 17, 1951
Death:
May 20, 2001
Burial:
Wheaton Cemetery, Wheaton,
DuPage County, Illinois

Dr. Thigpen was president emeritus of the Evangelical Training Association. He had ministered in various church and Para-church organizations for 34 years. He was a member of College Church in Wheaton.

Born in Nashville, Mr. Thigpen graduated from Free Will Baptist Bible College and earned degrees from Tennessee Temple Theological Seminary in Chattanooga, Tenn. and Trinity Evangelical Divinity School in Deerfield, Illinois. Before joining the association, Mr. Thigpen was an editorial manager for Randall House Publications and a professor at Free Will Baptist Bible College. His last job before the association was as an advertising manager for Christianity Today.

Dr. Thigpen was an innovator who helped modernize the delivery of Christian educational materials as president of Evangelical Training Association in Wheaton.

He died in his home of amyotrophic lateral sclerosis after a six year battle with Lou Gehrig's disease.

Now We Know That If The Earthly Tent We Live In Is Destroyed, We Have A Building From God, An Eternal House In Heaven, Not Built By Human Hand

George Douglas Ward
Birth:
Mar. 5, 1831,
Tennessee
Death:
Nov. 4, 1915,
Bradley Twp, Jackson Co. Il.
Burial:
Evergreen Cemetery, Ava,
Jackson County, Illinois,
Plot: Lot #52, Bl #4

Early Free Will Baptist minister in southwestern Illinois.

India

Missionary Marie Hanna
Birth:
Plattesville, Wisconsin
Death:
April 23, 1998
Buried:
India

Missionary Hanna suffered a heart failure in mid-April in North India, departing this life at 70 years of age. When her body arrived at the mission station, Christians started ringing the church bell. Hindu and Muslim shops in the market closed out respect for her. Her body was placed on the veranda and thousands of people filed past. Due to the conditions in India, and the lack embalming, she was to be buried that evening, but a large crowd caused them to wait until Friday morning, when she was buried in the church compound in Sonapurhat near

the bell tower.
She attended Harris Teachers College in St. Louis, Mo. and was the first woman to graduate from Free Will Baptist Bible College. Memorial services were conducted at the First Free Will Baptist Church in Florence, South Carolina, and Free Will Baptist Bible College in Nashville, Tennessee.

Death is
a trade-in.

One day we will trade in our broken down bodies for a new body. Look what Paul says about that new body.

It is from God.
It is not made with hands.
It is eternal.
It is heavenly, not earthly.

Indiana

Rev William Bonar
Birth:
Dec. 12, 1814
Death:
Sep. 10, 1890
Burial:
Rose Hill Cemetery
Albion
Noble County
Indiana
Plot: A-15

Rev. William Bonar, was in the early beginning of the organization of the Walnut Creek Freewill Bapt. Quarterly Meeting, in Illinois, southeast, with Rev. Samuel Shaw, who laid the foundation of the work there, with Rev's J.B. Lewis, Richard Ashcraft, L. Driscoll, and P. Christian, Rev. Wm. Bonar being one." He later resided in Indiana where he died.

Caleb W. Collett
Birth:
May 1852
warning County, Ohio
Death:
1926
Burial:
Maplewood Cemetery
Anderson, Madison County,
Indiana

He was educated at Ridgeville college in Indiana. He turned to God in 1870 and receive license to preach in 1886 and thereafter became the clerk of the Salem Quarterly Meeting in Indiana.

John E. Cox
Birth:
October 14, 1850
Posey County, Indiana
Death:
Dec. 5, 1932
Evansville
Vanderburgh County, Indiana
Burial:
Stewartsville Cemetery
Stewartsville
Posey County, Indiana

His conversion took place in 1872 and he was ordained in September 1878 by the Liberty Association, Indiana. In 1879 he founded, edited and published *The Golden Rule* at Evansville, Indiana and later *The Open Door* Enfield, Illinois; and in 1884 The *Free Will Baptist Herald* was established by him to aid his work in the Kanawha Valley and in the South generally.
He held pastorates in Indiana and Illinois and in the spring of 1883 settled in the Kanawha Valley, West Virginia where he was the acknowledged leader in founding the West Virginia Yearly Meeting and from which place he has made several journeys South exerting a wide influence. He organized 10 churches and assisted in organizing many others and baptized about 400 converts since 1885. He was aVeteran of service in the Indian Wars. And a minister of over 40 years in Owensville, Oakland City and Evansville. He left a legacy through his children namely Daughters: Eva   Grace Cox. Sons: Dr. James E Cox, Dr. Harvey C Cox and Arthur S Cox.

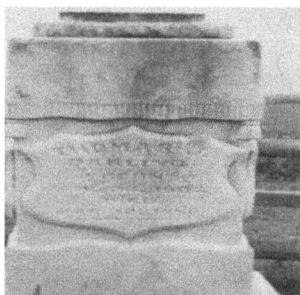

Thomas Jefferson Darling II
Birth:
Nov. 20, 1807
Essex County, New York
Death:
Jan. 12, 1881
Dearborn County, Indiana
Burial:
Darling Family Cemetery
Bonnell
Dearborn County, Indiana

Son of Thomas J. Darling Sr. (1784 - 1865) and Ruth Ann Beech Darling (1785 - 1866). DARLING, Rev. Thomas J., a native of New York, died at aged 73 years. He moved with his parents to Wright's Corners, Ind., married Julia A .Martin in 1829, received license from the Miami Quarterly Meeting Oct. 18, 1839, and was ordained at the Second Creek church,Aug. 20, 1841. He preached to churches in the vicinity of his home, was earnest in exhortation, fervent in prayer, zealous in preaching and hence useful in his calling.

Ichabod S. Jones
Birth:
February 23, 1833
Niles, New York

Death:
Indiana
Burial:
Woodland Cemetery
Wolcottville
Lagrange County, Indiana

When quite young, with his parents, he moved to Indiana. In 1861 he enlisted in the Union Army, and was appointed sergeant, and in two years he was promoted to the office of a major. He began preaching in 1871 and was ordained in 1872. For some time he preached at churches in the Lagrange Quarterly Meeting.

M H Jones
Birth:
unknown
Death:
Dec. 21, 1876
Burial:
Oak Park Cemetery
Ligonier, Noble County, Indiana
Plot: 2-3

Elder Benjamin Leavitt
Birth:
Apr. 10, 1765
Death:
Dec. 26, 1835
Burial:
Reul Cemetery
Jefferson County
Indiana

An ordained minister of the Free Baptist church.
Inscription:
Elder Benjamin Leavitt, of the ___ Baptist order, b. in

Charlestown, State of Rhode Island, 10 Apr 1765, d. 26 Dec 1835, age 94 yrs

Note: This information is from the DAR transcription, published in 1941.

Israel Luther
Birth:
Mar. 29, 1810
Canaan, Vermont
Death:
Oct. 1, 1888
New Haven, Indiana
Burial:
Eel River Cemetery
Dunn
MillAllen County, Indiana

He was converted in 1835 and ordained in 1851 by the Noble Quarterly Meeting in Indiana. He traveled in the early part of his ministry through Ohio, Indiana and Michigan holding revival meetings and organizing churches. He baptized over 300 people.

Death is not the end of the story for those who know the Lord

Ives Marks
Birth:
Jan., 1812
Connecticut
Death:
Sep. 9, 1884
Scipio, Jennings County, Indiana
Burial:
Cave Springs Cemetery, Jennings County,Indiana

Parents: David Marks (1778 - 1852)- Rosanna Merriman Marks (_- 1821). Spouse: Emily Leaming Marks (1810 - 1902). Children: Jared Marks (1842 - 1883), William Marks (1851 - 1900), Ives J. Marks (1856 - 1933).
Preacher in Freewill Baptists, brother of Rev. David Marks, noted FWB in NH, then Ohio. Rev. Ives helped build several churches in Kansas and Nebraska with son Rev. William

Marks.

Thomas J Mawhorter
Birth:
Dec. 10, 1852
Noble County, Indiana
Death:
1921
Indiana
Burial:
Cosperville Cemetery
Wawaka
Noble County, Indiana
Plot: 3-5

Mawhorter, was the son of William and Prudence (Pierson) Mawhorter, of Scottish descent, an early family in Noble Co. Indiana. He attended local schools, graduated from Fort Wayne College, 1872. He was converted in June 1873, and baptized by Rev. Dodge. He felt his need to do more, but also felt he was unqualified. He married Arminda "Mindie" Rendel in May 17, 1874, in Noble Co. Ind. To this union was born ten children. He served as deacon, SS Supt., and other offices in his church, but in 1885, he entered Hillsdale College, MI, to pursue more education, having worked on the Railroad to obtain funds. Soon after, however family sickness called him home. He began to preach in local churches and his church asked that he be ordained. He was ordained to the Freewill Baptist ministry, May 15, 1887. Several ministers, including Rev. Rendel, Prof. Ransom Dunn, and others were on his ordaining council. He immediately began pastoring the Wawaka Church, (now Cosperville Freewill Bapt). Other pastorates included Pleasant Ridge, Haw Patch, S. Milford, and he served Jones Chapel and Rome City churches, as well .He attended the Gen. Conference when held at the Minneapolis; and in 1897 he was delegate to the Gen. Conf. at Lowell, Mass; then delegate to Ocean Park Gen. Conference, 1898, and a delegate to Harpers Ferry Conference in 1901. He was recognized as a strong and forceful speaker, and in Noble County was an advocant in the cause of temperance.

Wilton R McKee
Birth:
1830
Shelby County, Indiana
Death:
1899

Burial:
Liberty Cemetery
Martinsville
Morgan County, Indiana

He was converted in December, 1849, and ordained in 1858. From 1856 to 1870 he was a member of the Separate Baptist. He then united with the Free Baptist Church, and during his ministry witnessed many revivals and organize several churches. In 1852 he married Kathryn Hawkins, and after her death, he married Elizabeth Bock, August 15, 1860. He was the father of 13 children. All the churches he pastored were in the state of Indiana.

Michael Mills
Birth:
May 28, 1787,
Death:
May 17, 1864
Burial:
Liber Cemetery
Portland, Jay County, Indiana

Mills was born in Pennsylvania and the year 1817 began a life unto God. He soon began to preach with the Calvinistic Baptists; but having Arminian views finally became a Free Baptist. In 1838 he moved to Jay County, Ind., and continued his work, being ordained at about this time, and aided in building upthe Salem Q. M. His native talent made him a close reasoner with a firm purpose.

Jared H Miner
Birth:
Feb. 27, 1795
Death:
May 26, 1863
Otsego, Indiana
Burial:
Clark Cemetery
Steuben County, Indiana

He was ordained in 1829 and labored successfully for many years in Sheldon, New York and in adjacent towns and later in northern Indiana and southern Michigan where many were converted and churches were gathered under his labors. He baptized about 400 converts of whom several entered the ministry.

Eli Noyes
Birth:
Apr. 24, 1814,
Jefferson,
Lincoln County, Maine
Death:
Sep. 10, 1854,
Lafayette, Tippecanoe County,
Indiana
Burial:
Greenbush Cemetery,
Lafayette, Tippecanoe County,
Indiana,
Plot: Section 3, lot 208

His parents were deeply pious and taught their children religion, missions, and stories of missionaries. He pursued an education, and taught a few months and studied till he commenced preaching in 1834. In Jan. 1836, he offered himself to the Foreign Mission Board of Freewill Baptists as a candidate for missionary service to Orissa, India. He and his wife were accepted and on 22nd of Sept. 1835, they sailed to Calcutta, India, along with Rev. Jeremiah Phillips, who sailed in the same vessel, and took charge of the bazaar schools connected with the General Baptist mission in Balasore. In a few months, their bright hopes were succeeded by suffering and disappointments. They lost a 16-month old daughter, as well as Rev. Jeremiah Phillip's wife. They became prostrated by disease and his became of a chronic type. Mr. Noyes made rapid progress in the language, and became a ready and able preacher, and for a time encouraging results attended his ministry. But, he was not able to shed the disease, and in 1841, they returned to their native home. For a time, he pastored small churches in Maine, and Lynn, Mass., then went to Roger Williams church in Providence, R.I. Here the congregation grew until they had to add a balcony of seats. His health failed and he retired from the pastorate forever. He did recover enough to make a trip to England with Rev. Jonathan Woodman, to visit the General Baptists of England.

His knowledge of languages exceeded all but few, and he was an able theologian, lecturer and a writer. He was taken with consumption and in his debilitated state, he went to Lafayette, Indiana where his brother-in-law, Mr. M.L. Pierce, had generously provided a home for him and his family. He died the 10th of Sept. 1854, age 40 years. *"A Hebrew Reader," "Strength of Hindooism", "Lectures on the Truth of the Bible;"* and two or three sermons,

were published before his death. He instructed what would be inscribed on his tombstone: ELI NOYES First Freewill Baptist Missionary To India, and it was carried out.

William C. Parson
Birth:
May 6, 1933
Morehead, Kentucky
Death:
Feb. 7, 2011
Anderson,
Madison County,Indiana
Burial:
Carthage Cemetery,
Carthage, Rush County,Indiana

The Rev. Parson was an ordained Free Will Baptist minister for more than 40 years. He pastored several churches, retiring in 2007 from East 16th St. Separate Baptist Church in Muncie. His secular occupation was as a machinist and grinder, retiring from Delaware Tool and Machinery after 19 years of service. Prior to that, he had worked at Nicholson File. He was a member of the 38th Street Free Will Baptist Church in Anderson.

John Prickett
Birth:
1811
Death:
Oct. 24, 1856
Indiana
Burial:
Metz Cemetery
Noble County, Indiana
Plot: 11

A native of Ohio, he was converted under the labors of Rev. Elias Hutchins in 1831 and was ordained in Indiana in 1842. He preached in the Noble Quarterly Meeting for his untiring labors were blessed to the conversion of many.

Rev Ebenezer Redlon
Birth:
Oct. 15, 1799
Buxton
York County
Maine
Death:
Sep. 5, 1874
Pierceville
Ripley County
Indiana

Burial:
Prattsburg Cemetery
Delaware
Ripley County
Indiana

Rev. Ebenezer, a native of Buxton, Maine, moved to Indiana in 1837, and died at Pierceville, Sept. 5, 1874, aged 74 years. He was converted when fifteen years of age, and ordained in 1865. Both before and after ordination he was active for God. The churches of the Ribley Quarterly Meeting, where his ministry was spent, held him in high esteem   *

John W Rendel
Birth:
March 24, 1849
Wayne County, Ohio
Death:
1917
Burial:
Lake View Cemetery
Kendallville
Noble County,
Indiana
Plot: Section D
Row 3 Circle 11

He was converted in 1865 and attended Auburn and Kendallville high schools for two years. Received ordination on June 2, 1878. His pastorates were all in the state of Indiana. In these churches he had many good revivals resulting in a large number of conversions.

Rev William Henry Sayler
Birth:
Mar. 22, 1844
Ohio
Death:
Oct. 18, 1923
Jasper County, Indiana
Burial:
Weston Cemetery
Rensselaer
Jasper County, Indiana
Plot: Section E, Block 10,
Lot 2, Space 1

Rev. W. H. Sayler, son of Henry and Catharine (Klindfielder) SAYLER, was born in Marion OH, in 1844. He was married in 1865 to Miss C. Keazee. He was educated at Renasselaer, Ind., and Wheaton, Ill. In 1880 he was converted, and two years later was licensed to preach. In 1884, he received ordination. He has had two pastorates, one of two years at Troy Grove, Ill, and his present one [1888] at Elburn, Ill

Fredrick Stovenour
Birth:
Oct. 18, 1834
Morrow County, Ohio
Death:
Mar. 6, 1923
Burial:
Green Park Cemetery
Portland
Jay County, Indiana

He began his religious life in 1863 and in the following year was ordained by the Richland and Licking Quarterly Meeting, Ohio. He was a pastor also in the Saline Quarterly Meeting in Indiana.

We will have a new body - not the same as before.

William Tucker
Birth:
Oct. 7, 1820
Beaver County, Pennsylvania
Death:
Dec. 21, 1905
Ripley County, Indiana
Burial:
Union Flat Rock Cemetery
Ripley County, Indiana
Plot: Row 7 Lot 24

David A. Tucker
Birth:
May 20, 1845
Jennings County, Indiana
Death:
Jul. 10, 1927
Burial:
Union Flat Rock Cemetery
Ripley County, Indiana

He was a student one year at Moores Hill college and one year at Hillsdale. His conversion was in 1859 and he was licensed in 1870. He was ordained in 1872 to the gospel ministry. He pastored a number of churches in Indiana. He was also a veteran of the Civil War serving in Co. K 18th Ind. Inf. He enlisted in 1861 as a private in reenlisted on January 1, 1864. He mustered out in all this 1865 at Savannah Georgia as a Sgt. He married first, Susanna Dorsh Tucker (1845 - 1888) and after her passing Sarah A. Snow Tucker (1861 - 1949)

He married Mary Oldham (1816 - 1894) with whom they had nine children. Three of whom served in the Civil War. And David was also a Free Will Baptist preacher. When he was one year old his father died leaving four children to the mother's care. There were no free schools where he lived at the time and hence his education was very limited. His family moved to Indiana and there and his early years were spent in clearing the wildland by day and studying the Bible by fire-light at night. He was converted in 1843 and in 1873 he was ordained to the ministry. He preached in several churches in the Ripley and other quarterly meetings and his labors were blessed with the conversion to larger number of converts.

Henry W. Vaughn
Birth:
May 31, 1820,
East Greenwich, Kent County,
Rhode Island
Death:
Aug. 13, 1900
Burial:
Greenwood Cemetery, Lagrange,
Lagrange County,Indiana,
Plot: Big Old

His conversion took place in 1842 and his ordination to the ministry in 1856, the council being composed of Freewill Baptist Elders Seth Parker, E. Root and Thomas Dimm. He had the care of several churches in Ohio, Indiana and Michigan. He was twice a member of the General Conference, and he organized two churches and had several revivals.

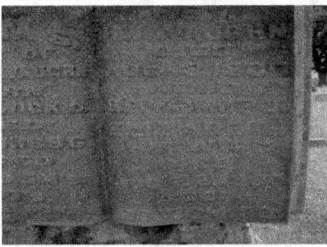

Joseph Winch
Birth:
unknown
Death:
February 10, 1854
Galena, Indiana
Burial:
Foster Cemetery
Hesston
La Porte County, Indiana
Plot: 1-4-8

The last two years as his life were the only years devoted to the ministry. His death was one of the most triumphant every witness. His early life was spent in Massachusetts, Vermont and Ohio.

Rev Edward Wooley
Birth:
1817
England
Death:
Jul. 31, 1857
Wrights Corner
Dearborn County, Indiana
Burial:
Wrights Corner Baptist
Cemetery
Wrights Corner
Dearborn County, Indiana

Rev. Edward Wooley, born near London, Eng., labored six years in Jamaica, West Indies, as a missionary of the General Baptists, when, on account of failing health, he came to the United States and labored with the Free Baptist churches of Ohio and Indiana until his death, July 31, 1857, at the age of forty. He was highly esteemed as a clear reasoner and an unflinching defender of the truth.
A record from "Gentlemen's Gazeeteer" shows that he d.(same date as is in Cyclopedia) in Wright's Corner, Indiana, and that after his name is "M.D."
Nothing is known of his family...he possibly was a medical missionary/preacher to the W.Indies? His name was not among the recorded stones in

this cemetery, but given the old dates and broken as they are, and the "Wooley" info showed where he died, this being of same church with which he was affiliated, this is most likely where he is.

Iowa

Oscar E. Baker
Birth:
Jan. 9, 1826,
Marion County, Ohio
Death:
Jul. 31, 1893,
Minneapolis,
Hennepin County,
Minnesota
Burial:
Elmwood Cemetery,
Waterloo,
Black Hawk County, Iowa,
Plot: C E Lot 17 E

Oscar was in the 141st Regiment, Ohio Infantry, during the Civil War. Born at Marion, Ohio, the son of Rev. George Washington Baker. Oscar's grandfather, was one of the founders of the town of Marion, OH. He, as his father, were Free Will Baptist ministers. Oscar was licensed to preach when he was 17 yrs old. And by his nineteenth birthday, he was ordained by the Free Will Baptist church, because of his work and dedication. From time to time he endeavored to go to college, but the demands of the churches interfered with his plans. Meanwhile he applied himself to study and with the aid of private teachers acquired at length an elective collegiate and theological course. Rev. Baker preached in Ohio, moved to Iowa and became pastor of Wilton Junction church, and took charge of the Seminary at that place. The Seminary grew into a college of which he became president. His health failing, he resigned. Then he took charge of the church at Waterloo, IA. In 1881 he was called to the church in Marion, OH, his native city. In 1884, he accepted a call to the Roger Williams church, Providence, R.I. where he remained until 1888, when he was called to Lincoln, Nebraska. He served his denomination for many years through the several benevolent societies and as a member of the Board of Corporators of the Printing Establishment. He was a frequent contributor to the denominational papers.

Tappan Batchelder

Birth:
Jan. 25, 1817,
Bridgewater, Grafton County
New Hampshire
Death:
Oct. 29, 1885,Linn
County, Iowa
Burial:
Jordan's Grove Cemetery,
Central City,
Linn County, Iowa

Rev Batcheler was a Methodist minister but ordained a Free Will Baptist minister in 1841 in R.I. In 1855 he moved from Taunton, Mass. to Olive Twp, Clinton Co, Iowa. In 1865 he moved to Clay Twp, Jones Co, Iowa. In 1876, he moved to Linn Co, Iowa and farmed near Central City, and served as pastor at Free Will Baptist churches in Central City and Waubeek.

Newell Willard Bixby

Birth:
Jan. 18, 1809
Death:
Jan. 31, 1903
Burial:
Edgewood Cemetery

Edgewood,
Delaware County,
Iowa

Son of Ebenezer Bixby and Hannah Flint. Husband of Ruby Knapp, married 09 Nov 1842 Vermont. Was an ordained Freewill Baptist minister, prominent and successful among the pioneer ministers of Iowa.

Ruby Knapp Bixby

Birth:
1818
Death:
Jan. 5, 1877
Burial:
Edgewood Cemetery
Edgewood
Delaware County,
Iowa

Both she and her husband, Rev. N. W. Bixby, where prominent Free Will Baptist ministers in the early days of Iowa.

He was converted when sixteen years of age, and baptized by Rev. I. Eaton. He was licensed to preach by the Freewill Baptists, while connected with the Fox River Q.M. (Ill), about 1856. He remained a few years with the Ohio Grove church which was much increased during his connection with it. About 1860, he moved to the Waterloo Q.M., IA, and was connected with the Oxley Grove, Pleasant Valley, Spring Creek and Waterloo churches. He was in the organization and the first pastor of the Waterloo Freewill Baptist church, which was organized with twelve members. The church grew but in 1896, all 49 members joined the regular Baptist church, just before the Freewill Baptist denomination was merged with the American Baptist. Rev. David Champlin, was a zealous, faithful laborer, an advocate of all moral reform, and active in the work, until a brief illness carried him away from the earth.

David E. Champlin
Birth:
1825
Ohio
Death:
Feb. 20, 1871,
Waterloo
Black Hawk County, Iowa
Burial:
Fairview Cemetery, Waterloo
Black Hawk County, Iowa,
Plot: Block 19, Lot 100

David N Coats
Birth:
Dec. 7, 1815
Litchfield
Tioga County, New York
Death:
Jan. 20, 1889
Spencer
Clay County, Iowa
Burial:
Riverside Cemetery
Spencer, Clay County, Iowa

He was converted under the labors of Elder David Marks. While yet a young man he moved to Wisconsin, where he was ordained in 1859. At about this time he became a pioneer in northwestern Iowa, and made his home at Spencer, where he died. He was an untiring worker and his labors were blessed to the good of many. The results of his labors in Iowa will be manifest for years to come. He was married to Miss B. E. White. They have two children, Rev. R.A. Coats, and Mrs. Frank Wells.

Rev Cyrus Coltrin
Birth:
Dec. 10, 1813
Le Roy
Genesee County, New York
Death:
Nov. 13, 1872
Marshalltown
Marshall County, Iowa
Burial:
Unknown

An ordained Free Will Baptist minister whose name recorded in list of its ministers who had died since last General Conference. "Rev. Cyrus Coltrin, Waltham, IA, d. Sept. 13, 1872, age 60" was given to clerk.

Rev Andrew Donaldson
Birth:
Mar. 24, 1807
Youngstown
Mahoning County,
Ohio
Death:
Mar. 13, 1883
Burial:
Mattingly Cemetery
Garwin

Tama County,
Iowa

The following is from the "History of Tama County, Iowa" by Union Publishing Company, Springfield, Ill, 1883, from Chapter 21, Carlton Township, p. 641.

In the "Hist. of Jones Co. IA, Clay Twnsp, a FWBapt church was organized in 1853 by Rev. Donaldson, and for many years continued prosperous. An organization of the Free Will Baptist Church was effected in 1856 by Rev. Andrew Donaldson, with the following membership: Rev. A. Donaldson and wife; Sampson Strong, wife and daughter. Soon after membership increased to twenty. Meetings were generally held at private residences. The organization was discontinued in 1860.

Rev. Andrew Donaldson, who was the main worker in the church, is a native of Youngstown, Trumbull county, Ohio, born March 24, 1807, removing with his parents, when he was three years old, to Cuyahoga county, which was one vast wilderness. Here Andrew spent his boyhood days attending the pioneer schools, which consisted of log cabins with slab benches. In those days the best recommendation for a teacher was his muscular powers, consequently Andrew's early instruction was very limited, but after years of reading and study he acquired a good practical education. In 1828, he experienced religion and united with the Congregational Church, remaining a member of that organization until 1837, when he united with the Free Will Baptist Church and served as a minister of that denomination for twenty-three years. In 1860, owing to age and infirmities, he retired from active life. Mr. Donaldson has been earnest in his religious work and thinks it wrong for a pastor to receive compensation, referring with pride to the fact that he has never accepted one cent for his services. In politics he was originally a Democrat, but when the slavery question began to enter into politics he advocated freedom for all and worked with the Anti-Slavery party, casting his first vote as a Free-Soiler in 1844. Since the organization of the Republican party he has been one of its warm supporters and has held several local offices. Mr. Donaldson came west to Jackson county, Iowa, in 1845, and in 1853, came to Tama county, locating on section 25, in Carlton township where he still resides. He was united in marriage with Roxana Norton, in 1829, who was a native of Vermont. Eleven children have been born to them, ten of whom are now living. His wife died in Carlton township, March 23, 1869, aged sixty-three years, one month and two days. Mr. Donaldson's father died in the spring of 1883, aged seventy-five years, eleven months and seventeen days.

Isaac W Drew
Birth:
May 11, 1823,
Quebec,
Canada
Death:
1893,
Black Hawk County
Iowa
Burial:
Fairview Cemetery,
Waterloo,
Black Hawk County,
Iowa

He was converted about 1850 and soon began to preach, receiving ordination by the Freewill Baptists in 1858 while connected with the Coaticook church of the Stanstead QM. His later ministry has been chiefly with churches of the Waterloo, Ia., and the Fond du Lac, Wis., QM's.

Edward Dudley
Birth:
Dec. 11, 1811.
Brentwood,NH
Death:
Feb. 19, 1890
Burial:
Agency Cemetery
Agency, Wapello County,
Iowa
Plot: Section 36

Son of Daniel Dudley and Jane Campbell; m. 10 Jun 1841 Eliza A. Dudley; Free Will Baptist minister, ordained 1844. Did a good work and passed to his reward.

L. D.. Felt
Birth:
1821
Death:
Nov. 29, 1889
Burial:
Greenwood Cemetery
Masonville,
Delaware County, Iowa

He experienced the new birth in 1837 and was ordained in 1863. He held pastorates in the state of Wisconsin and Iowa. In these fields he enjoyed a good degree of prosperity and that churches was strengthened. He was a delegate to the General Conference of 1866.

Marcus B Felt
Birth:
October 3, 1832
Brutus, New York
Death:
unknown
Burial:
Osage Cemetery
Osage, Mitchell County, Iowa

He was a brother of L. D. Felt. He was converted in January, 1855 he was ordained in February, 1866 and spent the first nine years of his ministry was churches and Root River Quarterly Meeting in Minnesota. During his ministry he served the churches in Nebraska, three churches in Illinois and in Burnett, Wisconsin. He was very efficient in the pastorate and organized four churches. Marcus served in Company H 6th Minnesota Infantry then served as a 2nd Lt in Company E 121 United States Colored Infantry and then transferred to Company I 13 United States Colored Heavy Artillery.

Henry Elijah Gifford
Birth:
Dec. 18, 1809
Pawlet, Rutland County, Vermont
Death:
Jun. 26, 1881
Burial:
Elkader Cemetery
Elkader, Clayton County, Iowa

Gifford, died at his residence near Elkader, Iowa. aged 72 years. He was baptized by Rev. S. Howe at Otselic, N. Y., and later received license at Portage. He moved to Iowa in 1842, and was ordained May 27, 1849, at the fifth session of the Delaware and Clayton Q. M. His was the first ordination in Iowa among the Free Baptists, and in this vicinity his ministry was spent. The Boardman Grove (later Farmersburg), West Union, Cox Creek and Volga Bottom churches enjoyed his labors. He was a man of good natural abilities, a close student of the Bible and hence sound in doctrine. His wife, who had toiled with him more than fifty years, survived at his death. He was chaplain of the Old Settlers' Association, whose president pronounced a fitting eulogy at the grave.

Yea, saith the Spirit, that they may rest from their labours; and their works do follow them.

Abel Gleason
Birth:
Jun. 4, 1795
Rome
Oneida County, New York
Death:
Jan. 3, 1874
Burial:
Oakview Cemetery
Clinton County, Iowa

He went in his youth to Genesee County, New York where was baptized at the age of 13 and ordained when he was about 28. Then on to Michigan in 1838, and two years later he was found in Illinois continuing on to Iowa in 1853. He was a gentle and affectionate gifted man of prayer and faithful in the Lord's vineyard

David Demaree Halstead
Birth:
Feb. 24, 1811
New Paltz,
Ulster County,
New York
Death:

Dec. 3, 1887
Fort Dodge,
Webster County,
Iowa
Burial:
Oakland Cemetery,
Fort Dodge,
Webster County,
Iowa,
Plot: lot 95

He was converted in 1831 and in 1853 united with the Free Will Baptist and soon was ordained. He pastored churches in Greene and Mecca, Ohio and also preached in other places. In 1859 he moved to Marion County, Ohio, where he labored with success. In 1872 he moved to West Fort Dodge, Iowa where he died.

Erastus C Harvey
Birth:
Mar. 8, 1789
East Haddam
Middlesex County,
Connecticut
Death:
Aug. 27, 1872
Castalia, Winneshiek County,
Iowa
Burial:
Pleasant View Cemetery
Castalia,
Winneshiek County,
Iowa

Erastus Harvey, sixth child of William and Jane (Beebe) Harvey. In the year 1807, he enlisted in the regular army and was in the War of 1812. He played the tenor drum in the battle of Plattsburg, in September, 1814. At the close of the war he returned to Lyndon, Vermont, and in the year 1816 he married Betsey Bettis, who was born September 27, 1798.

Erastus Harvey was a member of the Free Will Baptist church at Cabot, Vermont, in 1821. The Wheelock Q. M., licensed him to preach in 1822. In 1825 he was ordained. From the time of his marriage until he entered the ministry he had farmed at Lyndon, Vermont. His obituary speaks of his preaching first in Vermont; then he went to Littleton, New Hampshire, for one year, returning to Vermont. Thence to Barnston, in Stanstead county, Canada, Province of Quebec. A call came to Rev. Erastus Harvey to preach to a congregation at Woodstock, Champaign county, Ohio which was gladly accepted and he moved his family to that place sometime about the year 1838. He purchased a farm in the woods and soon a log house was built and some land cleared.

He preached to Baptist congregations in Champaign and Union counties, and for a while at Pitchin, in Clark county. After six or seven years he sold this farm and purchased one in Perry township, Logan county, Ohio, near North Greenfield. He continued to preach and acted as Q. M. clerk "making full proof of his ministry." After a residence of about five years, he sold this farm and purchased another near Walnut Grove. After a long illness from dropsy the wife and mother died on the Walnut Grove farm July 31, 1855. In a month or two the father sold the farm and with his sons, William and Albee, he moved to Castalia, Winneshiek county, Iowa. In 1857 he married Mrs. Hannah Sargent, who was a native of Vermont. He preached to a number of congregations in northern Iowa and did so occasionally till a few days before his death. "As a preacher Brother Harvey was earnest, animated and spiritual. He had received and had retained the Holy Anointing which gave him strength and boldness in the presence of the people. His sermons were eminently Scriptural, evangelical, and comforting to the saints. He succeeded well as a pastor. He died of bilious diarrhea and was first buried in Mt. Grove cemetery; but was later removed to Pleasant View cemetery, Castalia, Iowa.

Orrin Hix
Birth:
September 11, 1807
Montpelier,
Vermont
Death:
Mar. 5, 1880
Benton, Iowa
Burial:
Brooks Cemetery
Hedrick,
Keokuk County,
Iowa

He went to Ohio in his youth and married Sally Gregory in 1831 and commenced ministerial work in 1840 receiving his ordination five years later. He continued to labor in Ohio until 1854 and then took up the work in Van Buren Quarterly Meeting, Iowa.

Charles Holroyd
Birth:
1823
England
Death:
Oct. 22, 1875
Iowa
Burial:
Campton Cemetery
Lamont,
Buchanan County, ,Iowa

Charles Holroyd was born in England. He came to the United States in 1850 with his wife, Mary (Patch) and their family. Holroyd was a stone mason and carpenter by trade. On Nov. 20, 1858, he received his license to preach in the United States at the Union Free Will Baptist Church of Wingville, Grant County, Wisconsin. When he moved to Delaware County, Iowa, he helped build the Campton schoolhouse and the Campton church where Free Will services were held. He preached there and everyone loved him. The little children used to sit around his feet while he was preaching.

Enoch Jenkins
Birth:
1808
Death:
1892
Burial:
Fairview Cemetery
Waterloo
Black Hawk County, Iowa
Plot: blk. 16 - lot 41

Rev. Enoch Jenkins, was born in western New York. He was son of Rev. Herman and Nancy (Brown) Jenkins, and grandson of Rev. N. Jenkins. He was licensed by the Chautauqua Q.M. [Freewill Baptist] and ordained about 1855, his first pastorate being with the Heart Prairie, Wis., then recently organized. His ministry continued in Wisconsin and Iowa, being characterized by great loyalty to the denomination.

John Lucius Lesher
Birth:
Sep. 20, 1830
Batavia
Genesee County, New York
Death:
Oct. 28, 1890
La Porte City
Black Hawk County,
Iowa
Burial:
Pleasant Hill Cemetery
Ireton,
Sioux County, Iowa
Plot: Block 3, Lot 3

He was converted in his early life and received ordination on November 22, 1863 periods to churches were organized by him and more than 100 converts were baptized.He married Nancy Jane Allred of Perrysville, Indiana on 24 Apr 1852.

Amaziah Loomis
Birth:
Aug. 8, 1800
New York
Death:
April 30,1873
Riceville, Mitchell County, Iowa
Burial:
Riverside Cemetery
Riceville, Mitchell Count, Iowa

Loomis, died at age 72 years. He was licensed by the Catlin church, August 21, 1830, and ordained by the Chemung Q. M. (N. Y.), Sept. 7, 1834, continuing his labors with this and adjoining Q. M's until 1855, when he removed to Iowa. He was a pioneer preacher, and devoted himself to the work with great perseverance.

James Cram Marston
Birth:
Aug. 14, 1804
Parsonfield, Maine
Death:
Jun. 25, 1865
Iowa
Burial:
Postville Cemetery
Clayton County, Iowa

Son of James Marston and Elizabeth Cram.He first married Cordelia Sutton who died before 1850. then he married Nancy Maria Fisher. He emigrated to western New York at an early age. In 1854 he went to Iowa and the following year united with the Postville church, where he became deacon. He received license from the Elgin Quarterly Meeting in 1859 and ordination in 1861, serving the Postville and Bloomfield churches as pastor until his death in 1865. All the benevolent enterprises of the day received his hearty co-operation.

Thomas Proctor Moulton
Birth:
Apr. 19, 1808
Hatley
Quebec, Canada
Death:
Feb. 25, 1893
Newell
Buena Vista County, Iowa
Burial:
Newell Cemetery

Newell
Buena Vista County, Iowa

In January, 1840, he was married to Louisa Moore who he shared fifty years of happy life together. In early life they entered upon the work of the Christian ministry, being connected with the Freewill Baptist denomination. His father was a Rev. Avery Moulton, who was the ancestor for many Free Will Baptist preachers. For more than forty years. Thomas Proctor continued in the active ministry in the following places: Walden and Lyndon, Vt. Conneaut, Ohio, Pelham, N. H., Coaticook, .P. Q., and West Derby, Vt. At Coaticook P. Q., he organized the first church and labored there for fifteen years. His active ministry was closed at West Derby, Vt., in 1873, at which time he came to Newell to be near his daughter, Mrs. S. A. Parker.

John Russel Mowry
Birth:
Oct. 30, 1853
Lyons

Clinton County, Iowa
Death:
Feb. 14, 1908
Des Moines
Polk County, Iowa
Burial:
Woodland Cemetery
Des Moines
Polk County, Iowa

He was the son of Rev. Juni Mowry. He was converted in 1871 and studied at Wilton Collegiate Institute and at Hillsdale College. He was ordained of by President Durgin at Hillsdale in April 8, 1883. He ministered to churches Michigan and Ontario, Canada, and was later employed as the state evangelist for Michigan. He was successful in pastoral and revival work can baptized over 100 converts.

Junia Smith Mowry
Birth:
Jul. 18, 1805
Smithfield,
Providence County,
Rhode Island
Death:
Apr. 27, 1890
Calamus,
Clinton County, Iowa

Burial:
Mowder Cemetery,
Clinton County, Iowa

In 1829 he was licensed by the Free Baptist Church to preach, and that year commenced his ministerial labors. In 1832 he was licensed by the Elders of the Free Baptist Conference, and in August of that year was ordained at North Taunton, and was pastor there and in Rehoboth until the spring of 1835. He then went to Tiverton and served as pastor of a congregation in that place until the fall of 1840, when he went to Apponaug and continued his ministerial labors for a year and a half. From Apponaug, Mr. Mowry went to Johnson, R.I., where he preached for some eleven months, being at the same time an agent for the Smithville Seminary, located in North Seituate. He then received a call from a congregation at Georgiaville, in Smithfield Township, and there resided until the spring of 1847. He next went to Hebronville, Mass., where he preached for two years and taught school one winter and again returned to Georgiaville and preached to different congregations in that region until 1851. He was also on the School Board of the town of Smithfield.

Rev. Mr. Mowry was first united in marriage Dec. 2, 1835, to Rev. Salome Lincoln. She was born in Raynham, Mass., Sept. 13, 1807. She was a good, kind-hearted, Christian woman, and, as well as her husband, was engaged in ministerial labor. She died July 21, 1841.

The second marriage was solemnized Dec. 2, 1841, when Miss Nancy Manchester became his wife. She died Feb. 24, 1868. She was a woman of superior abilities, both as a wife and mother, and had few equals. A son, John R. attended Wilton Institute, Iowa, and Hillsdale College, Mich., and is a preacher of the doctrines of the Free Baptist Church.

The third marriage was solemnized July 15, 1869, when Mildred M. A. Holmes, widow of Rev. Luther Holmes, became his wife. She died March 11, 1879, and June 8 of that year he was married to Susan Mott. She was born in Ohio, and they lived together as man and wife until the 15th of March, 1885, the date of her demise. Oct. 11, 1885, our subject was married to Nancy Dubois, who came to Iowa with her husband in 1841. She was a native of Pickaway County, Ohio.

Benjamin F Morrill
Birth:
1848
Blanchard
Ontario, Canada
Death:
1913
Burial:
Lawn Hill Cemetery
Stanhope
Hamilton County, Iowa

His conversion to Christ was in 1874, and his marriage to Miss Mary O'Dell was in 1875. He received licensed to preach the following year and was ordained in November, 1886, taking pastoral charge of the Fostoria and Buffalo Valley churches in Kansas. His ministry later took him to Iowa.

Joshua Gaskill Newbold
Birth:
Sep. 30, 1802
Fayette County, Pennsylvania
Death:
Aug. 31, 1887
Burial:
Hillsboro Cemetery
Hillsboro
Henry County, Iowa
Plot: Row 18

Ordained to the Freewill Bapt. ministry Sep. 10, 1826; He ministered in western Penn, organizing churches, until 1854, when he moved to Iowa, and organized the Hillsboro church there and pastored as long as his health would permit. He baptized over 800 converts and ministered sixty years.He was first married to Rebecca Davis who passed away in 1855. After which he married Mrs.'s Susannah Dudley Hoyt, sister of Rev. Edward Dudley who died in 1881.

Nathaniel A Odell
Birth:
1816
Wayne County, New York
Death:
Aug. 19, 1882
Elliott, Montgomery County,
Iowa
Burial:
West Point Cemetery
Bremer County, Iowa

Rev. Nathaniel Alvah ODELL, was the son of Augustine Odell, and Lydia Odell. When a young man, he emigrated to Newton, Calhoun Co. Michigan, in 1835. He joined the Freewill Baptist Church in 1844, and soon began to preach, being connected to Barry Co. Quarterly Meeting. After opposing the wave of spiritualism then sweeping over the vicinity, he moved to Delhi, IA, where he was ordained, May 25, 1856.He labored with good success, especially in Revivals, nearly 20 years, when he went to Montgomery Co. where the closing years of life were spent.He married Mahala May Bruce and they raised a large family.

Asahel Palmer
Birth:
1835
New York
Death:
Dec. 6, 1879
Horton

Bremer County, Iowa
Burial:
Horton Cemetery
Horton, Bremer County, Iowa

Palmer, a Free Will Baptist minister, was a worthy man, well loved and respected, and lamented by his untimely death. His death was caused by a fall from a staging while assisting in repairing the house of worship. This is noted in the "Butler and Bremer Counties, IA History" as also being the eighth pastor of Horton Church.. He and his wife were converted under the labors of the Rev. Mrs. Ruby Bixby in 1866 and united with the Madison church. He was ordained in 1873 having served with a license for two years. He pastored many churches in the Delaware, Clayton, and Cedar Valley Quarterly Meetings.

Rev James Reeve
Birth:
1812
Susquehanna County
Pennsylvania, USA
Death:
Aug. 18, 1871
Cedar County, Iowa
Burial:
Wright Cem
etery
Cedar County, Iowa

Rev. James Reeve, born in Susquehanna Co. PA, died near Tipton (Cedar Co) Iowa, Aug. 18,

1871, aged 60 years. He became connected with the Free Baptists in Washington, Ohio, where he was ordained in February 1847, and remained until 1852, when he moved to Iowa. He was a man of intellect, an acceptable preacher, an exemplary Christian and a pioneer in all reforms.

Live So Death Will Have Its Reward.

Samuel Shaw
Birth:
May 3, 1793
Rockingham County
New Hampshire
Death:
Oct. 15, 1879
Washington
Washington County, Iowa
Burial:
Woodlawn Cemetery
Washington
Washington County, Iowa

Shaw was a native of Epping, NH. He died at his home Oct 15, 1879, age 86 years. About 1819, he made his home in Ohio and was there about ten years. Later he began to preach, and was ordained in 1830. In 1837, he went to Illinois, being probably the first minister of the denomination to settle in the state. He gathered a church at Walnut Creek, and was largely instrumental in gathering the Walnut Creek Quarterly Meeting.

In 1850 he became pastor of Fiatt Church, which prospered under his care, while at the same time he was also ministering to other churches. In 1865, he moved to Iowa. Father Shaw was a positive man, but affectionate, faithful in his work, and self-sacrificing. He was held in high esteem among his brethren.

William Small
Birth
1812
Death:
Jun. 17, 1883
Burial:
Upper Bay Cemetery
Delhi, Delaware County,
Iowa

Small, Rev. William, was born in Scarboro', Me., in 1812. He and his brother James were ordained to the ministry in the Exeter Q. M., Jan. 13, 1842. He continued to labor in the Exeter and Montville Q. M's until 1855, when he went to Wisconsin and preached at Monticello and other places in the La Fayette Q. M. In 1868 he moved to Manchester, Ia., and continued to preach in various churches of the Delaware and Clayton O. M. until his last sickness. His death occurred at the residence of his son, near Earlville, Ia., in his 71st year, His earnestness and love for the work seemed to increase as he approached the close of life. He had baptized over two hundred converts.

Justus H Steward
Birth:
Aug. 4, 1819
Erie County,
Pennsylvania
Death:
Jan. 8, 1877
Tama County,
Iowa
Burial:
Rock Creek Cemetery
Tama County,
Iowa

He was the fifth son of Lemuel Steward and Elizabeth Roush. Justus studied for the ministry and was licensed with the larger Baptist body before uniting with the Free Baptists soon after his marriage to Amanda Main on August 29, 1846. They made their home in Ashtabula County, Ohio, where they settled on a homestead. He was ordained on September 28, 1863 and soon after moved to the state of Iowa where he pastored a number of churches as well as organizing the Fairview church where he remained its pastor until his death. He also taught school many years. The family consisted of three sons, and two daughters. Rev. Justus H. Steward was stricken with typhoid fever in the fall of 1876 at his home in Tama County, Iowa, suffering many weeks, then the infection settled in one leg, necessitating an operation, and the leg amputated.

He was licensed by the Cook's town quarterly makes the meeting, Pennsylvania and in two years he was ordained in September, 1845 where he labored with some churches in the Somerset quarterly meeting, Pennsylvania. Their after he moved to Iowa and assisted in forming the Van Buren quarter meeting in that state. Minister of the Free-Will Baptist Church. He and his wife both died in a typhoid epidemic.

Inscription:
Rev. D. SmutzDied May 6 1858AE. 44 Yrs 1 Mo 6 Ds Not lost blessed thought But gone before Where we shall meet to part no more.

David Smutz
Birth:
Mar. 30, 1814
Washington County, Maryland
Death:
May 6, 1858
Van Buren
Jackson County, Iowa
Burial:
Hillsboro Cemetery
Hillsboro
Henry County, Iowa

Spencer Summerlin
Birth:
May 27, 1828
Norwalk, Ohio
Death:
Feb. 1, 1907
Burial:
Horton Cemetery

Horton
Bremer County, Iowa

He married Sarah P Cook (1830 - 1921) in April 1858. He was ordained in 1861 and pastored a number of churches in Ohio as well as many churches in Iowa. He was active in the work of the denomination serving offices in the quarterly and yearly meetings. He was a member also of the Home and Foreign Mission Boards. His been a general missionary for the yearly meeting and was a member of the General Conference of 1883. He conducted many revivals which produced the organization of at least five churches.

John Sweatt
Birth:
1806
Gilmanton, New Hampshire
Death:
December 18, 1884
Toledo, Iowa
Burial:
Woodlawn Cemetery
Toledo
Tama County, Iowa

He was ordained on September 30, 1841 at Orange, New

Hampshire. In January 1843 he moved to Fort Jackson, New York where he organized a church and remained until 1856 when he returned to New Hampshire. Here he held official positions in the town and served in the legislature. In 1865 he settled on a farm in Iowa but continued be faithful to the end.

Rev Charles H True
Birth:
Aug. 19, 1847
Scales Mound, Ill,
Death:
1937
Burial:
Edgewood Cemetery
Edgewood
Delaware County
Iowa

Son of Charles True & Esther Rhodes; he married Luthera

Bixby in 1874.

He was converted in 1859, attended Hillsdale College, Michigan, 1864-1865, and Prairie City Academy, Illinois, 1866-67, and received license to preach in September 1868. He taught ten years in the Illinois schools, and had charge of the church at Prairie City, Ill., 1875-76. (His father, Charles True, had been taking care of it).

His estimable wife, Thera I., to whom he was married Aug. 19, 1874, is a daughter of Rev. N. W. Bixey.

Robert T Valentine
Birth:
1812
North Carolina
Death:
unknown
Burial:
Pleasant Hill Cemetery
Fayette
Fayette County, Iowa
Plot: Row 9 Lot 22

Because of his race he enjoyed no advantages in his birth state. He was ordained in Fairfield, Iowa in May, 1877 and ministered to the all but the church. He was a good man and faithful to his Lord. Unmarked grave near wife .

Joseph Whittemore
Birth:
Sep. 10, 1813
Salisbury
Merrimack County, New Hampshire
Death:

May 9, 1891
Iowa
Burial:
Harlington Cemetery
Waverly
Bremer County, Iowa

His parents were Eleazer and Lydia (Richards) Whittemore, of a well-known New Hampshire family. He was a brother of Rev. David Richards Whittemore, bur. in R.I. He studied medicine in Concord, N.H., and in 1834, and theology in Dr. Mott's school at Nashua. He was licensed by the Congregationalists in 1836, and ordained in Freewill Baptists about 1841, at Tiverton, R.I., by a council of the Rhode Island Quarterly Meeting. His pastorates were Tiverton, Pawtuxet, Pawtucket, and South Providence, R.I., Grafton and Taunton, Mass., and Randolph and Charleston, VT. He baptized about three hundred converts, and served as delegate to the General Conference. About 1865, he went to Iowa. NOTE:Zorn Family Tree shows he married Sarah M. Williams, Dec. 1876

William Wright
Birth:
1803
Otsego County, New York
Death:
Aug. 11, 1877
Delaware County, Iowa
Burial:
Spring Branch Cemetery
Delaware County, Iowa

Wright was converted at the age of seventeen years. He was connected with the Erie Quarterly Meeting, and after his ordination in 1842, with the Chautauqua and French Creek Q.M's. Later he resided in Iowa, being in feeble health, and died at age 74 years. He was a Free Baptist minister. He married Lovica (Unk) abt 1824 in NY; [Louisa: 1808-1884]

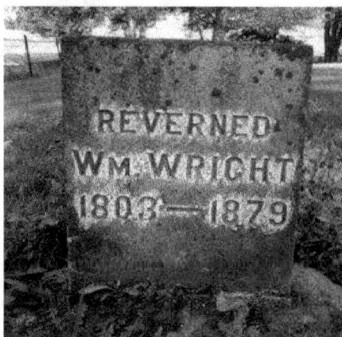

Amos C .Zabriskie
Birth:
Nov. 17, 1836
La Porte County,Indiana
Death:
Aug. 6, 1915
Stanley,
Buchanan County, Iowa

Burial:
Stanley Cemetery, Stanley
Buchanan County, Iowa

Amos C. served in the Iowa 32nd Inf., Co. K, Union Army until the close of the War. Throughout his life, he retained a great interest in the Grand Army. For years he was in great demand as a speaker at encampments throughout the state and the few remaining comrades in the vicinity were his chosen pall bearers. He was converted in 1867, and labored as a licentiate among the United Brethren, engaging in itinerate work. In 1886, having united with the Free Will Baptists, he was ordained and became pastor of the Buffalo Grove and Madison churches in Iowa. For more than thirty-five years he preached the gospel in the pulpits of various denominations in country places and in villages and towns. For although thoroughly orthodox he was broad in his sympathies and understanding of religious principles. For a number of years he conducted revival meetings during the winter. The saving power of Christ was his great theme---On account of his clear thinking and his deep moral conviction, he was a extemporaneous speaker. The power that he processed was an inheritance and a special "inducement from on high" rather than the result of education. He performed weddings and funerals in the hundreds. It was said, "he was a friend maker and a faithful and helpful friend to many of all classes. For forty years he was a poplar auctioneer. And for 35 years he was an agent for the Hawkeye Insurance Co. He was highly esteemed by both his company and patrons.

Kansas

Rev Orrin E. Aldrich
Birth:
Oct. 29, 1825
Orleans County
New York
Death:
Feb. 8, 1890
Greenwood County
Kansas
Burial:
Twin Grove Cemetery
Severy

Greenwood County
Kansas

He studied at Brooklyn Academy and four years at Geauga Seminary, OH, where he was classmate of President James Garfield. The Granville College, OH, conferred upon him the degree of Master of Arts. He commenced the christian life in 1843; and the year following he was ordained a Freewill Baptist minister. He has ministered to the churches at Spencer, Lagrange, Troy, and Pittsfield, Ohio; and at Clay, Pleasant Hill, Central City, Delhi, Olin, and Welton, Iowa, and Piedmont, Kansas, devoting part of his time to ministerial work. He has baptized about 400 converts during his ministry, and has assisted in building four houses of worship, and served seven years as Superintendent of Public Instruction in Jones Co. Iowa. He was married to Emma Adeline Post, 27 March, 1850, Lorain, Ohio.

Joseph E. Bayless
Birth:
Nov. 13, 1835
Huron County, Ohio

Death:
Sep. 20, 1921
Kansas
Burial:
Elmwood Cemetery
Chanute
Neosho County, Kansas

Joseph was the son of Jacob and Sally Bayless. He was born in Ohio, but by age 15 he was living in Fulton County, Illinois. He came to Christ in 1848 in the Fiatt, Illinois church. He married Laura O. Tharp, and in 1860 the couple was living on her parents' farm. He was a licensed in 1861; and stated for three years at the Prairie city Academy, and was ordained in 1869. Except for three years in Wisconsin, which was of between 1872-75, he ministered with the church there in Illinois. His ordination came in 1882 when he moved to Kansas and organized the Village Creek church and labored to build up the cause in the vicinity. By 1880 Joseph had become a minister and was the father of three. In 1895 he and Laura were living in Wilson County, Kansas. By 1905 they had moved to Chanute, Neosho County, Kansas.

Willard L Bastow
Birth:
1869
Death:
1941
Burial:
Haddam Cemetery
Haddam
Washington County
Kansas

He was a delegate to the first Co-Operative General Association of Free Will Baptists representing the Northern Kansas Yearly Meeting which met in Plattsburg, Missouri that ended on Dec. 31, 1916.

Rev Orion Beldon
Birth:
1857
Death:
Jul. 9, 1889
Burial:
Wheatland Cemetery
Horton
Atchison County, Kansas

A Freewill Baptist minister. Died young.

Rev Israel T Bradbury
Birth:
1815
Pennsylvania, USA
Death:
1890
Kansas
Burial:
Burr Oak Cemetery
Burr Oak
Jewell County, Kansas

When he began his ministerial

career is not known for certain, but prob. in Penn. or Ohio. The "History of Summit Free Will Baptist Church," shows that Rev. I.T. Bradbury, "a venerable and worthy man, organized the Summit FWB church, Cloud Co. KS, in 1882." Their first pastor was Rev. E.A. Phillips.

He was represented in Cloud and Republic Quarterly Meeting) in 1886 conference, working in John's Creek Mission, Cloud County. An agricultural tax record showed he and his sons engaged in farming, and Isaac in "stock raising and farming." Most of the pioneer ministers did not consider 'ministry' as an occupation, for they received very little funds to help them, and they made their living another way.

He probably was not long in Kansas until he passed away.

Milo William Dodge
Birth:
Mar. 14, 1851
Erie, Erie County, Pennsylvania
Death:
1919
Great Bend, Barton Count,
Kansas
Burial:
Great Bend Cemetery
Great Bend, Barton County,
Kansas

Milo married (1) Annie E. Morey 01 March 1871. She died 04 April 1890. He married (2) Harriet Aurelia 'Hattie' Buffum 01 October 1890 in Manila, Erie

County, New York. Dodge, was the son of Rev. Calvin and Sharlotte Dodge. He was educated at Pike Seminary, New York, and in 1871, married (3) Annie E. Mowry. .His conversion took place in 1864, and his ordination in 1880. With the exception of two years at Bliss, where he assisted in organizing the church, and one year at Odessa, his ministry has been with the churches of the Owego Quarterly Meeting (PA). In 1886 extensive revivals resulted from his labors with the Warren and Windham Churches. After Annie died., he married (4) Hattie Buffon in 1890.

John Blosser Fast
Birth:
Oct. 12, 1814
Pennsylvania,
Death:
May 1, 1897
Burial
Columbus City Cemetery,
Columbus, County, Kansas,
Plot: Section 10

He went to Orange, Ohio where he joined the Freewill Baptists in 1835, and received license to preach the next year, and was ordained in Adams Co. Ill, April 3, 1840. He took a prominent place among the early workers in Illinois, and did much good in the work of the church. He was instrumental in gathering some fifteen churches and assisted in establishing other church Quarterly and Yearly meetings. The Prairie City Academy was established largely through his instrumentality. Many years he served as clerk of Quarterly and Yearly meetings, and in 1859, he represented Illinois Y.M. in the General Conference of Freewill Baptists in Lowell, Mass. His later years were spent in Kansas and the pastor of Ness City Church.

Kan Rev Joseph A. Hale
Birth:
Nov. 15, 1836
Kennebec County
Maine, USA
Death:
1922
Burial:
Yates Center Cemetery
Yates Center
Woodson County
Kansas
Plot: Section 8, Lot 58

Rev. J. A. Hale, son of Aaron and Hannah A (Kenney) Hale, was born in Kennebec Co. Maine, NOv. 15, 1836. The following year his parents moved to Indiana, where he was educated in Laporte and Lake Counties.
He married Julia A. McCann in December, 1861, and five years later moved to Yates Centre, Kan., where they have since resided, and have four children [1889]. He received license to preach in 1875---thirteen years he has been with the Pleasant Valley and other churches in the vicinity.

Rev Ewin E. Harvey
Birth:
Aug. 8, 1835
Stanstead
Quebec, Canada
Death:
May 17, 1904
Kansas
Burial:
Nelson Cemetery ,Rice
Cloud County, Kansas

Rev. E.E. Harvey is the son of a Freewill Baptist minister, and removed to Ohio in 1840 and to Iowa in 1855.

He married Miss Lucy Polley, March 31, 1857. He was converted in 1866 and united with the Bloomfield Centre Freewill Baptist church.

He removed to Kansas in 1872, was licensed in 1873, and ordained in 1876, by Revs. R.D. Preston, J. Palmer and I.T. Bradbury.

He has been pastor of the Fairview church two years, of the Montana five years and supply preacher two years. He organized the Buffalo Valley church, and was its pastor four years; has been pastor of the Dry Branch for more than three years altogether as well as of the Miller church, recently organized by him.

He says: "I never kept any memoranda, and cannot tell how many conversions or additions to the church I've had."
---from *"Four Years of Cooperation,"* by Rev. A.D. Williams, D.D., pub. 1886.

Arlie Z. Hoover
Birth:
Feb. 24, 1903
Death:
Oct. 19, 1978
Burial:
Grinnell Cemetery,
Grinnell,
Gove County, Kansas

He was active both of Missouri and Kansas and serve both states in its early ministries. He was an early contributor to the *Free Will Baptist GEM.*

David Marks Inman
Birth:
Dec. 25, 1833
Medina County, Ohio
Death:
Oct. 16, 1924
Neosho County, Kansas
Burial:
East Hill Cemetery
Erie
Neosho County, Kansas

He was named for a Freewill Bapt. noted minister, Rev. David Marks, and his family were all involved in this church; he owned an old FWB hymnal and inscribed his name inside, printed abt. 1834, which is in my hands. I researched his name and found his memorial here. Thank you, D.M. Inman.

David Marks Inman, one of Wright County, Iowa's leading and well-known citizens, came to this county in the fall of 1866.

He was born in Medina County, Ohio, December 25, 1833, a son of Stephen and Sophronia (Robbins) Inman, who were natives of York State. They had six children that grew to man and womanhood, David M. being the oldest son and the second child.

David M. grew to manhood in Medina County, where he received his education. At the age of twenty-one he went to Jefferson County, Wisconsin.

He was married at Farmington, Wisconsin, to Miss Sarah E. Green, who was born in Yates County, New York, December 23, 1835, a daughter of William and Elizabeth (Mann) Green.

In 1862 our subject enlisted in the 29th Wisconsin Infantry, Company F, leaving a wife and four children to go in the defense of the old flag. He participated in the battles of Magnolia Church, Champion Hill, Vicksburg, Jackson, Mississippi; Spanish Fort, and Ft. Blakely, and was with General Banks up the Red River. He was in twenty-two engagements altogether. He was honorably discharged as a Sergeant, June 22, 1865. He was appointed by Wyman Spooner, acting Governor, as a First Lieutenant.

Our subject lived in Wisconsin until 1866, when he came to Vernon Township; he came by team, and his family by rail, as far as Iowa Falls. The first year he lived on section 12, and in 1867 he moved on to his present farm of 160 acres in section 16. He now has 340 acres of as fine a land as there is in the country. Improved by a good house and barn and other good farm buildings.

He has served eight years as county supervisor in a very credible manner.

David Johnson
Birth:
June 16, 1822
Bethany, New York
Death:
1903
Burial:
West Cedar Cemetery
Phillips County, Kansas

His conversion took place in 1839; he received license to preach in 1846, and years later was ordained in Wisconsin. After preaching for some time in the state of Wisconsin, he moved to the state of Kansas where in 1886 he organized the Plum Creek church in Phillips County, Kansas. He baptized more than 180 converts during his ministry and accomplished much good.

Samuel Keyes
Birth:
May 5, 1819
West Boylston, Massachusetts
Death:
Feb. 13, 1901
Burial:
Fairview Cemetery
Fulton,
Bourbon County,Kansas

In 1843 he married D. E. Johnston. He spent his early years in DeKalb, New York and was converted in 1843 receiving license to preach in 1858. He was ordained by the Cherokee Quarterly Meeting in Kansas on September 27, 1870. He organized the West Liberty church. He baptized 60 the year following his ordination and continued his labors in that vicinity.

George S Latimer
Birth:
Nov. 7, 1864
Iowa
Death:
Feb. 19, 1958
Vinland, Douglas County, Kansas
Burial:
Blocker Cemetery,
Haddam,
Washington County, Kansas

He was an ordained Free Will Baptist minister, who pastored the FWB Church at Hadden, KS, and in 1900, in Elm, Putnam Co. Missouri, as well as others. Rev. G.S. Latimer, and Rev. John H. Wolfe, planned the organization of a Western Conference of FWB after the 1911 merger of FWB with the Northern Baptists. They met with the Missouri State Association with their proposal, and perfected the organization, with representatives from Kansas, Nebraska, Missouri, Oklahoma and Texas, in Old Philadelphia Church, Plattsburg, MO. on Dec. 16, 1916. He represented the North Kansas Yearly Meeting. This became the Co-Operative General

Association. Rev. Latimer was a faithful minister with a vision for his denomination and carried out the work he was called to do.

Willis Jackson "Jack" Ledbetter
Birth:
Apr. 5, 1913
Drakes Creek
Madison County, Arkansas
Death:
Feb. 24, 1995
Wichita
Sedgwick County, Kansas
Burial:
Wichita Park Cemetery and Mausoleum
Wichita
Sedgwick County, Kansas

He was a retired minister, founding pastor and pastor emeritus of the Westside Freewill Baptist Church. He was licensed as a FWB minister in 1951 and ordained in 1952. He pastored four churches, three in Arkansas and one in Kansas. Of his 44 years in the ministry, 24 was invested at the Westside FWB church, that he founded. He was a leader in Kansas and served 16 years on the state Executive Board and chaired the Examining Board also for 16 years. He was father of the 'Singing Ledbetter Family' who recorded more than 30 albums and tapes. His close preacher friends nicknamed him 'Tig' short for Tiger, because of his boldness for Christ. At the time of his death the Ledbetter family number 62 members, eight of whom are ministers.

Henry S. Limbocker
Birth:
Sep. 10, 1807
Death:
Jan. 28, 1893
Burial:
Sunset Cemetery, Manhattan, Riley County, Kansas

Entered the Gospel Ministery January 28 1839 as Freewill Baptist ordained minister from NY to Mich, then Kansas. Honored and esteemed by many. A true pioneer.

Horace Washington Morse
Birth:
Jan. 24, 1822
Williamsfield
Ashtabula County, Ohio
Death:
May 23, 1894
Fostoria
Pottawatomie County, Kansas
Burial:
King Cemetery
Pottawatomie County, Kansas

He was a son of Rev. Horace Morse, who is buried in Ohio. He began his religious life as a young boy and was baptized by Rev. Ransom Dunn on January 17, 1839, as was also Melvinia Prindle whom he married on March 30, 1842. He was ordained in 1861 having served as a licensed minister for two years and ministered to churches in the Ohio and Pennsylvania Yearly Meeting until this removal to Illinois in 1864. Later he moved from Illinois to Kansas in the year 1870 and organized the Fostoria and other churches and was the founder of the Blue Valley Quarterly Meeting.

Francis P. Newell
Birth:
Feb. 9, 1813
Boston
Suffolk County, Massachusetts
Death:
Dec. 23, 1899
Cedar
Smith County, Kansas
Burial:
Cedar Cemetery
Cedar
Smith County,Kansas
Plot: Section 4, Row 1-9

Rev. Francis P. Newell, was born in Mass. and educated at Whitestown Seminary, NY, and New Hampton College, New Hampton, NH. He married Miss Hannah B. Ramsey, in New Hampton, on 30 May 1847. He was ordained a Freewill Baptist minister, and after school he moved west to Iowa, where he was the the fourth pastor of a church in Butler Co. Some years later, he moved to Smith Co. Kansas, where he was minister and lived with his family. It was written in Butler and Bremer Co. Iowa Histories, that he was an able man and preacher.

In 1856 he received his licensed to preach and settled in Kansas in 1872 where he was ordained by the Blue Valley Quarterly Meeting on November 20, 1876.

William H Northrup
Birth:
September 4, 1826
Otsego County, New York
Death:
Oct. 20, 1878
Burial:
Womer Cemetery
Womer
Smith County, Kansas

Chad Russ
Birth:
Sep. 2, 1918
Bladenboro
Bladen County, North Carolina
Death:
Jun. 7, 1992
Burial:
Sumner Memorial Gardens,
Wellington,
Sumner County, Kansas
Plot: C L25

Chadwick Beauford Russ, was the son of Evander Hayes Russ and Lizzie G. (Hester) Russ of North Carolina.

Besides Chad, they had several children, one of which was "Lenorah" or Norah Russ, who married Rev. Walter L. Jernigan, of Bladenboro, North Carolina, the parents of Rev. Dr. Wade T. Jernigan, noted Free Will Baptist evangelist, pastor, educator and church planter.

Chad was ordained a deacon before he entered the ministry.

He married Inez (maiden name unknown) in North Carolina, and they had four children.

They moved from North Carolina, to Oklahoma in about 1955, to assist his nephew, Rev. Wade Jernigan in a new church in the panhandle of Oklahoma, at Guymon, Oklahoma, close to the Kansas border. He worked there and was ordained a minister. He pastored at Commanche, Oklahoma (Stephens Co), and churches in Kansas that were newly organized works.

Chad was an affable person, who believed in the golden rule. He and Inez worked hard and were well-liked and esteemed.

Charles Smith
Birth:
Jul. 26, 1824
La Roy, New York
Death:
Jun. 25, 1904
Burial:
Powhattan Cemetery
Powhattan
Brown County, Kansas

He was converted very early united with the Protestant Methodist Church. In March 1852 he was married to Maria E. Fish in Mason, Michigan. In 1856 he moved to Kansas uniting with the Free Baptist denomination, and was licensed and began preaching. He was ordained in 1874 and traveled and preached in the states of Kansas and Nebraska doing pioneer work.

George W Thompson
Birth:
1846
Wisconsin
Death:
1918
Burial:
Mound Valley Cemetery
Mound Valley
Labette County, Kansas
After serving in the Civil War he

was brought to God in 1872 and united with the United Brethren in Kansas receiving from them license to preach. Three years later he united with the Free Baptist receiving ordination soon after. In 1882 he moved to Clearwater, Nebraska where he assisted in organizing several churches and continued to minister to them baptizing 50 converts.

Charles True
Birth:
Nov. 6, 1813
Maine, USA
Death:
Sep. 16, 1867
Fort Scott
Bourbon County
Kansas
Burial:
Twin Springs Cemetery
Linn County
Kansas

Rev. Charles True, formerly of Prairie City, Illinois died of typhoid at or near Fort Scott, Kansas. It was thought an appropriate coffin was prepared, but it was necessary to bury him at Twin Springs, KS on September 16, 1867. Border Sentinel, Mound City, Kansas dated Sept. 16, 1867.

Rev James Raymond Wylie
Birth:
Aug. 10, 1834
Eden
Lamoille County, Vermont
Death:
Dec. 28, 1932
Oswego
Labette County, Kansas
Burial:
Oswego Cemetery
Oswego
Labette County, Kansas
Plot: Sec 5

Son of Peter and Sally (Stowell) WYLIE. On Sept. 4, 1855, He was married to Miss Achsah Griffin. In 1853 he entered the ministry and was ordained in 1882, by the FWB Blue Valley Quarterly Meeting of Kansas. Note: Married September 4, 1855 in North Bangor, Franklin, New York

---

Jules Legender Williams
Birth:
Mar. 2, 1841
Merthyr
Tydfil, Wales

Death:
Jul. 14, 1878
Jefferson County, Kansas
Burial:
Pleasant View Cemetery
Oskaloosa
Jefferson County, Kansas

When he was quite young his parents emigrated to Canada. His father died when he was about seven years of age. He early prepared himself for a teacher, and in 1859 went to Hillsdale College, Michigan, expecting to remain there until he graduated, but in '61 he enlisted in the 4th Michigan Infantry regiment and was sent immediately to the front. He was in both battles at Bull Run, and other engagements. He remained with the regiment only a year being discharged for disability, having contracted a lung disease. He remained at home until he partially recovered, and then enlisted in the 137th Pennsylvania Volunteers. The 137th enlisted for nine months and were discharged at the expiration of that time. The ensuing fall he enlisted for one year on board the U. S. Receiving ship "Grampus." He was promoted to Master's Mate. When he left the Navy he received a commission at Lieutenant in the U.S. colored Infantry, but was not assigned to duty. He then returned to college and remained during the winter tern of 1864-5, and in May 1865, was ordered to report for duty in the 42nd Regular Colored Infantry stationed at Chattanooga, Tenn. In November 1865 he obtained leave of absence, came north and was married to Lovina A. BATES of Spring, Crawford Co., Penn., who returned with him to his Regiment, then stationed in Huntsville, Ala. In Feb. '66, he was discharged from the Army. He came to Kansas and settled in Sarcoxie township, Jefferson County, May 4, 1866. He taught school in the Tibbots district, Pleasant Valley and Stringtown. He commenced to preach during the first years of his residence in Sarcoxie. He was a member of the Free Will Baptist Church, having professed religion before he entered the army and lived true to his profession through all the temptations of army life. When the Mud Creek Baptist Church was organized he walked to Brown county, Kansas, sleeping on the prairie, with his shoes for a pillow, to get an ordained Minister to administer the church ordinances. He was himself soon after ordained by Rev. Keniston, of Walarusa. He was elected Probate Judge of Jefferson county in 1872, and re-elected in 1874. From October 9, 1873, to April 11, 1878, he was connected with a paper as Editor, which he assisted in establishing. He was buried July 15 and followed to the grave by a very large procession of friends and mourners. The funeral services were conducted by Rev. L.D. Price, in a most appropriate manner.

Kentucky

Rev Bobby Blevins
Birth:
Aug. 14, 1934
Death:
Apr. 25, 201
7Michigan
Burial:
Davidson Memorial Gardens
Ivel
Floyd County
Kentucky

Rev. Blvins age 82 died in Linclon Park, Michigan.His funeral services were held at the Fellowship FWB in Taylor, Michigan where he pastored.

He was transfer to Martin, Kentucky for his burial.

Roger Lee Blair
Birth:
Sep. 21, 1959
Death:
Oct. 9, 1993
Burial:
Highland Memorial Park
Cemetery
Staffordsville
Johnson County, Kentucky

He was a FWB minister and a member of the John-Thomas Association.

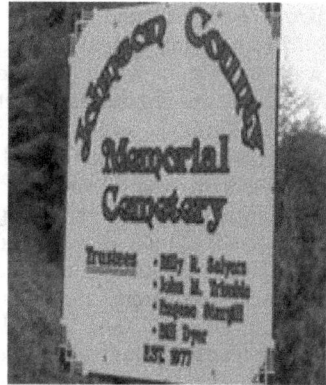

Steve Branham
Birth:
Aug. 15, 1901
Johnson County, Kentucky
Death:
Apr. 7, 1978
Prestonsburg,
Floyd County, Kentucky
Burial:
Johnson County Memorial
Cemetery,
Staffordsville
,Johnson County, Kentucky

Rev. Steve Branham, 76, died at Highland Regional Medical Center. Rev. Branham was born the son of Turner and Martha Engle Branham. He was a resident of Sitka, a retired coal miner, and an ordained minister since 1969. Rev. Branham was pastor of the Collista Freewill Baptist Church for four years. Funeral services were held in the Sitka Freewill Baptist Church with Reverends Richard Williams, Herb Arms, and Mark Daniel officiating. Paintsville Herald Wednesday April 12, 1978

Scott Castle
Birth:
Jul. 7, 1902
Johnson County, Kentucky
Death:
Nov. 29, 1997
Salyersville,
Magoffin County,
Kentucky
Burial:
Staffordsville Church Cemetery,
Staffordsville,
Johnson County, Kentucky

C Z Cavin
Birth:
1875
Death:
1956
Burial:
Rose Hill Park and Mausoleum,
Ashland,
Boyd County,
Kentucky,

Plot: D

Lawrence E Colliver
Birth:
1899
Death:
1999
Burial:
Crown Hill Cemetery,
Sharpsburg,
Bath County, Kentucky

Harvey Burns Conley
Birth:
Sep. 3, 1861
Paintsville
Johnson County, Kentucky
Death:
Feb. 1, 1941
Paintsville
Johnson County, Kentucky
Burial:
Conley Cemetery
Johnson County, Kentucky

Family genealogy states "he had always lived in Paintsville, managed several hotels in the city and had been interested in several business enterprises. He was a poplar man with a large following, elected Judge at one time. He was a leading minister of the Free Will Baptist church and did much to advance its cause. He has probably married more couples than any man living in the county. He officiated at many, many, funerals. Rev. Conley, was a son of the Judge Hiram E. and Clerinda Rice Conley. He was the County Judge for 5 years, served 1 term as County Assessor, 1 term as Master Commissioner, 2 terms as a member of the Board of Education of Paintsville City Schools, and was a Baptist minister for the Freewill Baptist Church for 58 years. site. Rev. Burns Conley helped lead the Kentucky FWB into organization of that State's Association in 1939, at Tom's Creek church, where he explained the purpose of the organization.

Rev Joe Conley
Birth:
Feb. 24, 1938
Johnson County,
Kentucky
Death:
May 30, 1978
Lexington
Fayette County, Kentucky
Burial:
Conley Cemetery
Johnson County,
Kentucky

Rev. Joe Conley, 40, died in University of Kentucky Medical Center, Lexington, after an extended illness. He was a resident of Davis Branch, was ordained minister at North Ridge Freewill Baptist Church, Dayton, OH, in 1965, and moved his letter from there to Rockhouse Freewill Baptist Church, and was an employee of American Standard. Funeral services were held in Rockhouse Freewill Baptist Church with Reverends Don Fraley and Richard Williams officiating.

John Elliott Conley
Birth:
Nov. 30, 1856
Johnson County, Kentucky
Death:
Jan. 6, 1945
Auxier
Floyd County, Kentucky
Burial:
C C Meade Cemetery
Hagerhill
Johnson County, Kentucky

An early FWB minister of note who came out of Toms Creek church who with others, offered leadership and counsel to the denomination for a number of years. His name is mentioned in History of FWB in KY. Conley married Susan James January 17, 1877, Johnson Cty, Kentucky.

Scott Daniels
Birth:
Feb. 13, 1884
Thealka
Johnson County, Kentucky
Death:
May 23, 1975
Johnson County, Kentucky
Burial:
Greenlawn Cemetery
Louisa
Lawrence County, Kentucky

Rev. Scott Daniel was in the Tri-State Association organized on Oct. 4, 1919, and included the Scioto Yearly Meeting, Ohio; the Big Sandy Yearly Meeting in KY, in the early movement in Johnson Co. KY. and the West Virginia Yearly Meeting. Rev. Scott Daniel was listed as one of several leaders for that year. He worked as a coal miner.

Wilda Nelson Davis
Birth:
Nov. 13, 1923
Muhlenberg County
Kentucky
Death:
Dec. 30, 1993
Owensboro
Daviess County
Kentucky
Burial:
Owensboro Memorial Gardens
Owensboro
Daviess County
Kentucky

She surrendered to the call of the Ministry on March 18th 1955.

First message was John 12:31 on March 20, 1955 at the First Free Will Baptist Church, 1534 East 18th St. Owensboro, Ky.
Licensed at First Free Will Baptist Church in Owensboro on June 5th 1955.
Ordained at First Free Will Baptist Church in Owensboro on Dec. 16th, 1962. Rev. E.L. Hall message was Isa. 6: 1-8
Charge by Rev. K. L. McGuyer
Prayer by Rev. Roy W. Westerfield
She was born in Muhlenberg County, Ky and was a member of the First Free Will Baptist Church. She was the daughter of Elmer and Jenny Bruce Nelson.
Survivors include her husband, Walter H. Davis, a son Carroll Davis of Henderson, a grandson John C. Davis of Henderson and three brothers, Orville Nelson of Calvert City, S.R. "Buck" Nelson and Gene Nelson of Owensboro.
Her funeral was performed by Rev. Tim Hall in 1993 and her husband, Walter in 2000.

John B Dills
Birth:
1890
Death:
Jan. 5, 1972
Paintsville,
Johnson County, Kentucky
Burial:
Sycamore Cemetery, Nippa,
Johnson County, Kentucky
He was a retired miner and was affiliated with the Freewill Baptist church by Revs. Millard VanHoose and Claude Preston at the Mouth of Rush Freewill Baptist Church.

Rev Clyde Lowell Eldridge, Sr
Birth:
Aug. 2, 1927
Boyd County
Kentucky
Death:
Mar. 20, 2016
Dayton
Montgomery County
Ohio
Burial:
Byron Smith Cemetery
Swampton
Magoffin County
Kentucky

Rev. Clyde Lowell Eldridge Sr., age 88, of Fairborn, at Hospice of Dayton . He was born the son of John Henry & Mattie Mae (Lewis) Eldridge 1927 in Ashland, Kentucky. He is preceded in death by his parents, his loving wife Mary Francis Eldridge whom he married on March 4, 1949, sons Phillip and Andrew, grandson Chris, and brothers Claude, Carl, Johnny, Avery, and Billie Joe. He served his country proudly with the United States Air Force during WWII. He served his Lord, ministering to many fine Christians at several churches in the community. He was loved by all the lives he touched. Clyde will be missed. Funeral services were held at Fairborn Enterprise Baptist Church with Pastor Bobby Jenkins officiating.

Rev Herbert Winfield French, Sr
Birth:
May 8, 1902
Boyd County, Kentucky
Death:
Jul. 25, 1951
Boyd County
Kentucky
Burial:
Hazlett Cemetery
Catlettsburg
Boyd County, Kentucky

Ted Greene
Birth:
Jan. 21, 1916
Floyd County, Kentucky
Death:
Sep. 1, 1996
Morehead
Rowan County, Kentucky
Burial:
Lee Cemetery, Morehead,
Rowan County, Kentucky

He was a Free Will Baptist pastor for nearly 50 years pastoring four churches, organized 10 churches and was a full-time evangelist. He pioneered radio and television ministries in the Morehead area. He organized the Kentucky Bluegrass Association and moderated it often and the Kentucky State Association for six years. For seven years he represented Kentucky on the General Board of the National Association of Free Will Baptists. Seventy-five men answered the call to preach under his ministry. He attended Booth Business College, Free Will Baptist Bible College and Emmanuel Bible Seminary.

Death is not the greatest loss in life.

James A. Hayes
Birth:
Dec. 29, 1931
Georges Creek Kentucky
Death:
Apr. 25, 2012
Louisa, Key
Burial:
Pine Hill Cemetery,
Louisa,
Lawrence County, Kentucky

James A. Hayes was a Freewill Baptist minister having been ordained in 1955. He had served the Louisa Free Will Baptist Church for 25 years stepping down in 1997. Before that he had pastored the Columbus First Free Will Baptist Church in Columbus, Ohio. He is well-known for his leadership and participation. Funeral service was at the Louisa Freewill Baptist Church and the burial with military honors.

Jesse Eugene Meade
Birth:
Jun. 27, 1941
Magoffin County, Kentucky
Death:
Jan. 18, 2000
Paintsville, Johnson County,
Kentucky
Burial:
Meade Cemetery, Flatgap,
Johnson County, Kentucky

He was the son of Rev. Wayne Meade, Sr. Jesse. A graduate of Free Will Baptist Bible College, and Army veteran. He pastored in Tennessee and Kentucky.

The South-Central Q. M. of Tennessee's Cumberland Assn, where Meade had pastored for 15 years, established a Memorial scholarship in his honor at the Free Will Baptist Bible College. He was a man of powerful and deep held convictions carried through with his magnetic personality and a sense of humor, which were legendary. Besides his father, he had 3 brothers who were Free Will Baptist ministers. His funeral was held at the Southside Free Will Baptist church in Paintsville, Ky.

Tommy Moore
Birth:
Sep. 19, 1928
Adams, Lawrence County
Kentucky
Death:
Sep. 23, 1967
Columbus,
Franklin Co., Ohio
Burial:
Yatesville Cemetery,
Louisa, Lawrence County,
Kentucky

He was born to Hubert and Delphia Adams Moore. The obituary of Rev. Moore notes that he was 39 years of age at his passing in his home in Columbus following a long illness. He had been a Free Will Baptist minister for 21 years. The service was conducted at the Welch Avenue Church in Columbus where he was its third pastor..

Earlist Mullins
Birth:
Apr. 29, 1921
Pike Co., Kentucky
Death:
Jun. 9, 1994
Burial:
Salem Cemetery
Irvine
Estill County, Kentucky

A FWB minister, retired sheet metal worker and a World War II veteran. He attended Hylton Freewill Baptist church, Ashcamp, Ky.

Charlie Pennington
Birth:
1888
Death:
1970
Burial:
Dixon Cemetery, Westwood, Boyd County, Kentucky

Jay Francis Preston
Birth:
Feb. 15, 1893
Death:
May 27, 1994
Lawrence County, Kentucky
Burial;

Preston Family Cemetery
Georges Creek
Lawrence County, Kentucky

He was ordained as a Free Will Baptist minister in 1926. The picture of Rev. Preston was taken at his 100th birthday gathering being celebrated by his children. At his party he preached a sermon for about 10 minutes. He married first Marie Burgess who died in a home fire in 1966. His second wife was Gladis R. Preston who died in 1992. He was a veteran of World War I. His funeral was held at the Bell's Chapel Free Will Baptist Church, where he at one time had been pastor. The ancestry of the Preston family in Kentucky and Virginia is quite large and one of his ancestors was Moses Preston who was born in 1700. There are eight Preston Cemetery's in Lawrence County where he also is buried. He was the father of 13 children of which 10 lived to adulthood. One of his daughters, Helen, taught Sunday school for more than 73 years before retiring at age 90. These were in Free Will Baptist churches.

Oliver W Privett
Birth:
Mar. 12, 1918
Death:
Sep. 29, 1983
Burial:
Mill Creek Cemetery
Sawyer
McCreary County,
Kentucky

Well-known Free Will Baptist preacher in West Virginia and Kentucky. Helped organize a Chapman Memorial Free Will Baptist Church in Chapmansville, West Virginia. He was the first moderator of the West Virginia State Association when it reorganized in 1949. His parents were James Harmon Privett (1895 - 1957) and Hannah Perry Privett (1898 - 1956) His spouse was Ella Rose Privett (1923 - 1997). He was a PFC in the US Army during WW II.

Carl Lee Senters
Birth:
Aug. 14, 1901
Death:
Apr. 27, 1969
Burial:
Davidson Memorial Gardens,
Ivel, Floyd County, Kentucky

Joe Slone
Birth:
1941
Death:
Aug. 24, 2009
Prestonsburg
Floyd County, Kentucky

Burial:
Annie E. Young Cemetery
Pikeville, Pike County, Kentucky

Joe was born to the late John M. and Stella Thacker Slone. Joe worked as a coal miner for many years and was a member of the Chapter 166 Disabled American Veterans Society of John's Creek KY .Joe was a minister for the lord for 30 plus years and loved to preach the Gospel to all. He was a member of The Owsley Freewill Baptist Church.

Rev Isaac Solomon Stratton
Birth:
Feb. 12, 1874
Floyd County
Kentucky
Death:
Nov. 6, 1964
Floyd County
Kentucky
Burial:
Jones Family Cemetery #1
Allen City
Floyd County
Kentucky

Son Of Allen Monroe & Mary Williams Stratton. He Married Apr. 19, 1900

A Minister For 61 Years and Preached More Than 3000 Funerals and Officiated More Than 3000 Marriages.

A Member Of The Prestonsburg Lodge No. 293 For 70 Years

"The Lord Is My Shepherd I Shall Not Want."

A Faithful Servant Of The Lord Called Home For Rest.

Inscription:
"THE LITTLE SHEPHERD OF THE HILLS"

Rev Thomas M Tinsley
Birth:
May 11, 1857
Death:
Dec. 27, 1918
Burial:
New Bethel Missionary Baptist Cemetery
Maynard
Allen County, Kentucky

Early Kentucky FWB preacher. He married Kittie A York Tinsley (1860 - 1920).

Eliphas Preston VanHoose
Birth:
Feb. 29, 1836
Floyd County, Kentucky
Death:
Oct. 5, 1911
Johnson County, Kentucky
Burial:
VanHoose-Fairchild Cemetery,
Tutor Key,
Johnson County, Kentucky

A Free Will Baptist minister in the early days in the Paintsville, Johnson Co. KY area. He was a farmer. He served in the Civil War, the 10th KY Calvary, Co B.

Frew Stewart VanHoose
Birth:
Sep. 4, 1883
Johnson County,Kentucky
Death:
Apr. 6, 1967
Johnson County, Kentucky
Burial:
Wells Buckingham Cemetery,
Paintsville,
Johnson County,
Kentucky

F. S. VanHoose, 83, president and manager of VanHoose Lumber Company for the past 50 years, died in Paintsville after a long illness. Mr. VanHoose was born Sep. 1, 1883 in Johnson County, a son of the late Harry and Elizabeth Dixon VanHoose.

He was an active Republican, a member of the Paintsville Rotary Club, a member and minister of the Third Street Freewill Baptist Church. His company had outlets in Louisa, Prestonsburg, and Paintsville.

Millard VanHoose
Birth:
Jun. 24, 1883
Johnson County,
Kentucky
Death:
Sep. 16, 1973
Johnson County,
Kentucky
Burial:
Highland Memorial
Park,Staffordsville
,Johnson County,
Kentucky

An ordained Free Will Baptist minister, pastor and leader, who served mostly in Johnson Co. in early times.

Rev Nathan VanHoose
Birth:
Feb. 22, 1908
Johnson County
Kentucky
Death:
Dec. 7, 1978
Lowmansville
Lawrence County
Kentucky
Burial:
Sycamore Cemetery
Nippa
Johnson County
Kentucky

Rev. Nathan VanHoose was a retired miner and a member of the Freewill Baptist Church.

Funeral services were Mouth of Rush Freewill Baptist Church at Nippa, with James Kelly Caudill and Ellis Hamilton officiating.

Richard Scott VanHoose
Birth:
Oct. 30, 1977
Ashland,
Boyd County, Kentucky
Death:
Apr. 9, 2004
Johnson County,
Kentucky
Burial:
Johnson County
Memorial Cemetery,
Staffordsville,
Johnson County, Kentucky

Owned VanHoose Funeral Home and in the later stages of his life became a Free Will Baptist Pastor and preacher.

Rev Lincoln Varney
Birth:
Mar. 23, 1923
Kentucky
Death:
Jul. 1, 2015
Mount Washington
Bullitt County
Kentucky
Burial:
Brookland Cemetery
Brooks
Bullitt County
Kentucky

Reverend Lincoln Varney departed this city for a new city, not made with human hands. He looked into the eyes of the One that gave him eternal life, King Jesus. As the Lord greeted him the Lord asked, "What did you do before dinner?"

Lincoln, Abe, Dad, Grandpa, Papaw Great, Uncle Abe, Uncle Lincoln, Preacher or Brother Varney, as he was lovingly known as, proudly served our country in World War II from October 5, 1940 until August 28, 1945. He served the Lord in the office of pastor for over 60 years. He was ordained into the Gospel ministry on March 12, 1955. He organized three churches, preached countless revivals and led thousands to a saving knowledge of Jesus Christ. He served for 17 years on the Free Will Baptist Board of Retirement, and served as the denominational moderator for the state of Kentucky and the Green River Association.

Rev Thomas B. Wheeler
Birth:
Dec. 13, 1923
Saint Albans
Kanawha County
West Virginia, USA
Death:
Mar. 17, 1986
Westwood
Boyd County
Kentucky
Burial:
Rose Hill Burial Park and
Mausoleum
Ashland
Boyd County
Kentucky, USA
Plot: D

The Rev. Thomas B. Wheeler, 62, of Ky. 5, pastor of Hoods Creek Freewill Baptist Church, died Monday at his home. Rev. Wheeler was born Dec. 13, 1923, in St. Albans, W.Va., a son of the late Thomas Albert and Flora Cyrus Wheeler. He was a retired electrician and a member of Local 317, International Brotherhood of Electrical Workers. He was on the credentials and executive committee of the Freewill Baptist Association of Boyd County and was a Kentucky colonel. Survivors include his wife, Mrs. Dorothy Louise Yutzy Wheeler; three sons, Thomas B. Wheeler Jr. and Sheldon Ray Wheeler of Ashland, James Vincent Wheeler of Woodbridge, Va.; three daughters, Connie Lou Kapteler of Greensburg, Pa., Mrs. Lark Annabelle McKinney and Mrs. Hope Arlene Fraley, both of Ashland; one brother, Vincent James Wheeler; four sisters, Mrs. Mildred Escue of Hurricane, W.Va., Mrs. Hazel Sanson of Columbus, Ohio, Mrs. Virginia Crouch of St. Albans, and Mrs. Lucy Borune of Florida; 10 grandchildren. Funeral arrangements are incomplete. The family has asked that flowers be omitted and contributions made to the building fund of Hoods Creek Freewill Baptist Church. Note: FM1 US Navy WWII

Louisana

Rev Richard N Hinnant
Birth:
Aug. 17, 1900
Death:
Jun. 11, 1981
Burial:
Denham Springs Memorial Cemetery
Denham Springs
Livingston Parish
Louisiana

His name appears in old church minutes and other records.

HINNANT, REV. R.N.
Died at 8:05 p.m. Thursday, June 11, 1981, at Dixon Memorial Hospital, Denham Springs. He was 80, a native of Macro, N.C. and a resident of Denham Springs. He was a retired minister. Visiting from 9 to 11 a.m. Saturday at Seale Funeral Home, Denham Springs. Religious services at 11 a.m. Saturday at the funeral home, the Rev. George Duerson officiating. Burial in Denham Springs Memorial Cemetery. Survived by a daughter, Mrs. Harold R. (Doris Faye) Hine, Denham Springs; a grandson, Christopher Hine, Denham Springs; a granddaughter, Karen Abedinzadeh; a great-grandson, Shaun Abedinzadeh, both of Baton Rouge; a number of nieces and nephews. Preceded in death by his wife, Stella Faye Hinnant. He was a Free Will Baptist minister and was a graduate of Moody Bible Institute of Chicago, Ill.

Robert Martin
Birth:
Dec. 29, 1814
Union County, South Carolina
Death:
Dec. 25, 1899
Bossier Parish, Louisiana
Burial:
New Bethel Baptist Church
Bossier Parish, Louisiana

His parents moved to Georgia when he was a child, where he was raised.In 1839 he was married to Miss Indiana Dillard, and was ordained to the ministry in 1840. In 1852 he moved to Louisiana, and settled six miles from Rocky Mount, where he lived until 1886, when he moved to Fisher county, Texas, residing there six years, when he returned to his old home in Louisiana, where he remained to his death. The deceased raised nine children, seven. Full of years and honors Rev. Robert Martin was on Christmas morning gathered to his father. He was a man of positive force of character, and ever exerted that force for the cause of his God, and

his country and his people. He was one who [sent] luster to the citizenship of his country and inspired those who came in contact with him to greater effort in the struggle to reach higher ideals.-> From the Bossier Banner, Thursday, December 28, 1899, page 3a. He was one of four brothers that preached the gospel, one of which was the founder of the Martin Association in the state of Georgia as well as one other association. Since there were family roots into South Carolina one of which had been buried in the Cemetery of the Horse Branch Free Will Baptist Church that I am assuming that the other three brothers that went on west also carried the Free Will Baptist doctrines.

Rev Guy Watson
Birth:
Jan. 1, 1833
Virginia
Death:
Apr. 2, 1902
Burial:
Chalmette National Cemetery
Chalmette
St. Bernard Parish, Louisiana
Plot: Sec 154 Grave 12481

His parents were Robert and W. (Wiliams) WATSON, and his early years were spent in slavery. In 1861 he escaped to the Union lines and enlisted in the navy. He was discharged at New Orleans, LA, in January 1865, after more than three years' service. He united with the First Freewill Baptist church there, having been converted in 1857. He was made a deacon the same year, and continued in that position until he was called to the pastorate of the church, and ordained in August 1884. Since then the church has enjoyed continued prosperity under his care. He is highly esteemed by his people.

Maine

George J Abbot
Born
Dec. 3, 1830
Death:
Nov. 3, 1883
Burial:
Pond Cemetery 1, Unity, Waldo County, Maine, Plot: row 6

He was baptized by the Rev. Dexter Waterman, under whose labors he was converted about 1852. He joined the church in South Jackson, Maine and in June of 1856 he was licensed by the Unity quarterly meeting. Soon after this, he went to the theological school at new Hampton, New Hampshire where he was highly esteemed by his teachers and fellow students. He was ordained in June of 1858 during a session of that same quarterly meeting. His pastorates were in South Montville, Wayne, and Dover, Maine and also In Bristol, Hampton, New Hampshire. He was pastor of the Apponaug church in this state of Rhode Island. The Rev. E Knowlton, a well-known Free Will Baptists at the time, knew him in his first church and said of him that he was one of the best spirited man he had ever known and for a young man his sermons were both spiritual and instructive.

John Quincy Adams
Birth:
Jan. 19, 1848
Death:
Apr. 16, 1897
Burial:
Riverside Cemetery, Lewiston,
Androscoggin County, Maine

He graduated from Bates College 1876 and from the Divinity school in 1881. He was baptized by the Rev. Elisha Purington, his pastor. In April, before his graduation, he accepted the call to the South Parsonsfield, Maine church. He also pastored a church in Dover, Maine, but due to failing health he resided in Lewiston and supplied the Kennebunk and Kennebunk Port churches for one year. In 1883 he was a delegate to the General Conference from the Maine Western quarterly meeting. In 1885 and 1886 he was the corresponding secretary of the Maine Association and delivered addresses at its annual meetings.

William Abbott
Birth:
1793
Livermore
Androscoggin County, Maine
Death:
Jul. 16, 1877
New Portland
Somerset County, Maine
Burial:
East New Portland Cemetery
New Portland, Somerset County,
Maine

He became a Christian when about 26, was baptized by Rev. Samuel Hutchins and united with the church in New Portland. He was a faithful minister for over fifty years and instrumental in bringing many to Christ. He was a strong advocate of education and reforms. He won the affection of his brethren by whom he was venerated.

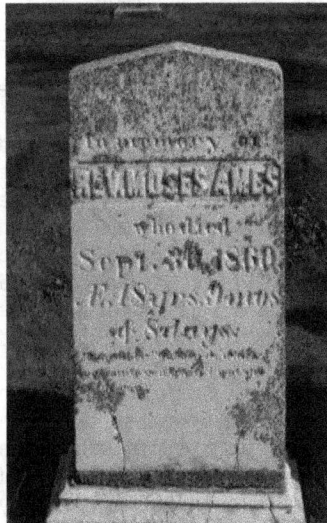

Moses Ames
Birth:
Dec. 8, 1812
Dover-Foxcroft,
Piscataquis, Maine
Death:
Sep. 30, 1860
South Dover, Me.
Burial:
South Dover Cemetery
Dover-Foxcroft
Piscataquis County, Maine
Plot: North Section, Row 2

Moses Ames was a FWB clergyman, At the age of 4, the family moved to Bradford, where after twelve years his parents were reclaimed, and he had the conviction strongly forced upon his heart that he was a sinner. In the spring of 1834, through a protracted meeting, he and others were converted, and in July following he began preaching. He had been baptized by Rev. Nathaniel Harvey, uniting with the church in Bradford. The destitute churches in the Sebec Q. Y. were objects of his labor. He was licensed by the Quarterly Meeting September, 1838, and labored in Garland and Danville. Sept. 22, 1839, he was ordained. In May 1838, he began his ministry at Corinth. In 1840 he saw from his preaching a great revival at Garland, and in a short time baptized over twenty. His work in Bradford was blessed. In 1841 he saw revivals both in the Wellington and in the Springfield Q. M's. In October he was present at the eleventh General Conference at Topsham. He moved his family to Corinth in December, where for some months he had preached half the time. In January 1842, in a revival at Hunting's Mills, in Corinth, twenty-three were added to the church. A revival attended him in Garland where he preached part of the time. During the summer he baptized there forty-six. and in 1845 moved there. He attended the thirteenth General Conference in Sutton, Vt., in October 1847, as a delegate from the Penobscot Y. M. The next year he moved to Veazie for a pastorate of two years. Here a church was organized. In November 1850, he began his labors with the Dover and Foxcroft church, where his strength failed him. During the last year of his ministry seventy were added to the church. He was a man highly gifted in natural talent; he possessed good business ability. His devotion to the ministry cost him his health. He was a gifted speaker and drew multitudes after him.

"His Power Is Infinitely Strong,

So Is His Wisdom Infinitely Clear,

And His Will Infinitely Pure."

Otis Andrews
Birth:
Mar. 14, 1817
Livermore Falls
Androscoggin County, Maine
Death:
May 5, 1897
Industry
Franklin County, Maine
Burial:
Weeks Mills Cemetery
New Sharon
Franklin County, Maine

He studied in the common schools and was converted on January 1, 1836. He was licensed in 1838 and then ordained by the Bowdoin Quarterly Meeting In 1843. He pastored a number of churches and enjoyed many revival meetings. He saw 100's converted, married over 100 couples and attended over 200 funerals.

Inscription:
REV. OTIS ANDREWS
MAR. 14, 1817-MAY 5, 1897

Hezekiah Atwood
Birth:
unknown
Death:
Dec. 26, 1870
Burial:
Gibbs Mill Cemetery
Livermore
Androscoggin County, Maine

He studied at the Farmington Academy and served his denomination for many years in the state of Maine. He organized the church at Barkers Island, Booth Bay, Maine. He had a son A. C. Atwood that was a pastor in Cape Sable Island, Nova Scotia.

Inscription:
HEZEKIAH ATWOOD
Died
Dec. 26, 1870
AGE. 72

Aaron Ayer
Birth:
Apr. 3, 1802
Buxton, York County, Maine
Death:
Oct. 8, 1866
Naples
Cumberland County, Maine
Burial:
Naples Village Cemetery
Naples, Cumberland County,
Maine

Ayer was a Freewill Baptist Minister. He filled pulpits in Maine and New Hampshire, and was widely known and beloved. (His stone says 1866).

Inscription:
AARON AYER
Died Oct. 8, 1866
Age. 64 yrs. 5 mos.
Blessed are the dead that die in the Lord.

Rev James M. Bailey
Birth:
Mar. 3, 1817
Andover, Merrimack County
New Hampshire
Death:
1899
Burial:
Hillcrest Cemetery
West Buxton
York County, Maine

Rev. J.M. Bailey, D.D., was ordained a gospel minister in the Freewill Baptist church in Feb. 1847. He was an active and useful minister.

John M Bailey
Birth:
1764
Death:
Oct. 5, 1857
Burial:
Grover Cemetery
Woolwich, Sagadahoc County,
Maine

He was born in Woolwich in 1764, and was converted by the preaching of Benjaman Randall and baptized by Rev. E. Lock about 1787. In 1798, when the denomination had less than a score of ministers, he was ordained by Timothy Cnnningham and Dea. Daniel Dunton, neither of whom were then ordained ministers. He entered upon a long ministry. In 1823, the best of feeling was restored by the aid of a council between him and his church, and with the help of Rev. Allen Files a revival sprung up in which over 100 were converted. He retained his mental faculties to the end of his long and useful life, and died in peace, fully resigned to his Master's will. Revolutionary War veteran.An ordained Freewill Baptist minister, died at age 93 years.

Rev Nathaniel Bard
Birth:
Sep. 2, 1814
Sumner
Oxford County
Maine
Death:
May 30, 1874
Lisbon
Androscoggin County
Maine
Burial:
Hillside Cemetery
Lisbon Falls
Androscoggin County, Maine

Rev. Nathaniel Bard, was a resident of Lisbon about forty years. When about 20 years of age he became a Christian, was baptized by Rev. Charles Bean, and united with the Second church of Lisbon. He was licensed by the Bowdoin Quarterly Meeting (QM) in 1840, and at the end of that year, was ordained.

He preached in Webster, Wales, Oak Hill, Litchfield two years, Litchfield Plains two yrs. Durham 8 yrs., Richmond Corner several yrs. North Freeport three different times, eight yrs in all; and lastly at Monmout, where an attack of paralysis disabled him and finally terminated his life. Ordained Freewill Baptist minister of Maine. Death listed in the minutes of the 22nd Gen. Conference.

Quite a number were added to the Litchfield churches: many were converted at Durham, and a house of worship was built. At Freeport he had frequent conversions and forty were baptized in one year. Two small churches in Bowdoinham were united by him; the Lisbon Falls church was organized mostly by his labors.

What he may have lacked in early educational mental culture was largely made up for by prayerful study of the Bible, and general reading. He was a man of superior judgment, and a sound gospel preacher. He occupied a prominent place in his Quarterly Meeting, and achieved that distinction by faithful and persistent labor. He was also esteemed for his integrity, kindness and hospitality.

John J. Banks
Birth:
Dec. 20, 1826
Levant, Penobscot County, Maine
Death:
Mar. 13, 1917
Burial:
Corinthian Cemetery, Penobscot County, Maine, Plot: Div. 9 Lot 8

He became a Christian at the age of 26. He was two years a member of a Baptist church. He received license on Sept. 29, 1855, and on Jan. 3, 1857, was ordained by the Free Will Baptist Springfield Quarterly Meeting. He had a revival in Lincoln, Me, in 1856, and raised up a church of thirty-six members of which he was chosen pastor. In 1858, he had a revival in Chester. He had a revival in Kenduskeag in 1866. A church was organized there two years later of which he has been pastor. He supplied the Congregationalist church of Kenduskeag part time eight years.

Favel Bartlett
Birth:
Apr. 12, 1792
Plymouth, Mass.
Death:
Mar. 22, 1873
Auburn, Me
Burial:
Norway Pine Grove Cemetery
Paris, Oxford County, Maine

In early manhood he was an active minister in Franklin County, Me., but disease of the throat and lungs forced him to turn aside and engage in business. He became a merchant, but preached occasionally as long as health permitted. Fifteen years before his death he moved to Auburn, where he soon retired from business, in still feebler health. He lived a quiet, cheerful, Christian life till his departure, and was much respected and beloved.

John Batchelder
Birth:
Feb. 15, 1813
Rhode Island
Death:
Jun. 21, 1865
Burial:
Evergreen Cemetery,
Garland,
Penobscot County, Maine

John Batchelder moved to New Hampshire at the death of his father in 1823, and went out as a tanner's apprentice. At the age of 21 he was baptized, joining the Free Baptist Church. Having moved to Garland, Maine, he united with the church there in April 1842. He was licensed by the Exeter Q.M.in March 1854 and for a while was connected with the Biblical School at New Hampton. He was ordained in Parkman, Maine in January 1858, in which field he organized a church and became it's pastor. During the last four years of his life his work was crippled through ill health. His last season was spent with the church at South Dover. He was a good preacher and was much beloved.
Inscription:
Died at age 53 yrs. and 4 mos.

Rev Isaac N Bates
Birth:
Dec. 25, 1830
Waterville
Kennebec County
Maine
Death:
Mar. 28, 1902
Maine
Burial:
Old Cemetery
Oakland
Kennebec County
Mainne

Rev. Isaac N. BATES, was he son of Isaac and Betsy Bates.
He studied in schools at Norridgewock and Waterville, Maine. Converted in March, 1846, he was licensed in 1862, and ordained in 1864. He has had] nine revivals, organized six churches and baptized over 300. He is now settled with the church at Fairfield, Maine.

The Burial Locations of Free Will Baptist Ministers

Rev Charles Bean
Birth:
Jan. 3, 1811
Limerick, Maine
Death: Jun. 18, 1889
Burial:
Highland Cemetery
Buxton
York County
Maine
Plot: Ordained as evangelist Nov 21, 1833

He received licensed to preach in 1831, and at age 20, was ordained by a council of the Parsonfield Quarterly Meeting. After itinerat ministry for some years, he became pastor of the Falmouth church and remained three years. He was pastor of several other churches, following this, and after sixty years of ministerial work made his name familiar in western Maine. He preached up to the advanced age of 78, and was noted for a remarkable 'verbatim knowledge of the Bible.
He died at the residence of his daughter, Mrs. Simon Libby, in Scarborough, ME, June 18, 1889, in his 79th year.

Rev George Winthrop Bean
Birth:
Feb. 8, 1819
Readfield
Kennebec County
Maine, USA
Death:
May 4, 1893
Burial:
Readfield Corner Cemetery
Readfield
Kennebec County
Maine

Ordained in June 1843 as a Free Will Baptist minister at Milton, ME.
Inscription:
His Stone Reads:
God's Church They Lead
Her Stone Reads:
With God They Dwell

Rev Selden Bean
Birth:
1825
Death:
Jul. 6, 1883
Burial:
Seavey's Corner Cemetery
Vienna
Kennebec County
Maine
Age 58 yrs at death. An ordained Freewill Bapt.

338

Rev Leroy S, Bean
Birth:
Jan. 12, 1860
Quebec, Canada
Death:
Jul. 12, 1903
Maine
Burial:
Laurel Hill Cemetery
Saco
York County
Maine

He was only 43yrs, and a promising young minister. Pastored in Canada, VT and ME.

Charles E. Blake
Birth:
Unknown
Death:
Jan. 8, 1892
Burial:
Riverside Cemetery
Farmington
Franklin County,
Maine

He was a Free Baptist Minister and the father of Rev. Edwin Blake of the same denomination.

Edwin Blake
Birth:
1843
Death:
1915
Burial:
Riverside Cemetery,
Farmington,
Franklin County, Maine
Freewill Baptist minister. He served Co. A 8th Me. Vol. Sept. 1861 to Nov. 1865 during the Civil War. His wife was Elsie W. Cross, who lived between 1842-1926.

Stephen S Bowden
Birth:
Oct. 18, 1806
Penobscot, Maine
Death:
Nov. 3, 1878
West Waterville, Maine
Burial:
Old Cemetery
Oakland
Kennebec County,Maine

He was converted in 1829, when 22 years of age, under the labor of Rev. Cyrus Stilson and baptized by him on November 22 and joined the church. He was chosen clerk of the church and served it for 12 years. He was licensed on January 15, 1842. His ordination occurred at the Pittsfield church in June 1844. While not specifically an evangelist, he did have a circuit of some 12 towns in the Waterville Quarterly Meeting and was graciously favored by his ministry. For 30 years before his death he rarely spent a Sunday at home, though few loved home more ardently or more fully honored the relationship of husband and father. His preaching was sound, clear, and persuasive. He attended many funerals and solemnized many marriages. At the time of his death he was clerk of the Quarterly Meeting and had served in this office 17 1/2 years out of the last 20 attending every session. He was chosen delegate to the last General Conference before his death but yielded his place to his alternate.

Rev David Boyd
Birth:
1781
South Berwick, Maine
Death:
Dec. 11, 1855
North Berwick, ME
Burial:

Boyd Plot, South Berwick
York County, Maine

He was one of the Fathers in habits, views of duty, doctrine, styles of communication, and sympathies. He was frequently called to positions of public trust; was a member of the Massachusetts Legislature from Maine, and a member of the convention which framed Maines's Constitution. See "Constitution of Maine" of which Rev. David Boyd was a member in 1820 when it was adopted.
He was familiar with probate matters and other technicalities of law. He was an esteemed Christian.

Rev David Boyd
Birth:
Mar. 2, 1836
Maine, USA
Death:
Mar. 7, 1900
Burial:
Riverside Cemetery
Newport
Penobscot County
Maine

Ordained a Freewill Bapt. minister May 12, 1861.

Aldolphus Eugene Boynton
Birth:
Aug. 5, 1833
Plymouth
Grafton County
New Hampshire
Death:
Sep. 24, 1889
Shapleigh
York County
Maine
Burial:
Pleasant Hill Cemetery
Newfield
York County
Maine

Adolphus Eugene Boynton, Free Baptist, son of John and Phebe (Batchelder) Boynton, was born Aug. 5, 1833. Preparatory studies at New Hampton Institution. Studied for the ministry at Bates (Me.) Theological School. Licensed to preach, Canaan, 1870. Ordained, Newport, Canada, June 21, 1874, and pastor there, and at Eaton, Jan. 1874-5; Daniel's Mills, Newfield, Me., Aug. 1875-8; Kittery Point, Me., June 1878-80; Bow Lake, Strafford, April 1880-1 ; Nottingham, April 1881-2; Barrington and West Notting ham, May 1882-3; North Shapleigh, Me., March 1884-6. Died there, Sept. 24, 1889.From Native Ministry of New Hampshire by Nathan Franklin Carter page 74. Available from FWB Publications.

The resurrection of the body is the final step in our salvation.

Rev James Boyd
Birth:
Nov. 26, 1830
South Berwick, ME
Death:
Oct. 14, 1907
Burial:
Boyd Plot
South Berwick
York County
Maine

His parents were Charles and Margaret (David) BOYD. His education was received in common and select schools. He became a Christian at the age of twenty-one, and was baptized by

Rev. C.B. Mills. He received license to preach in December, 1855, and was ordained in December, 1856, by Rev. E. Knowlton, and others at the Unity Quarterly Meeting (Q.M.). He held pastorates in Bangor (Second Church), Sabattus, Booth Bay, Biddeford, ME; Taunton, Mass; Bangor ME, (First Church), and Pittsfield, ME. He was a state missionary of Maine, New Hampshire, Massachusetts, Rhode Island, New York, and Wisconsin. He was a missionary pastor at several churches including Cape Sable Island, and Halifax. N.S., and Manchester, N.H. He has baptized over 300, with more than that number converted. Helped ordain Rev. V. D. Sweetland in 1879.

He was married Sept. 4, 1851, to Miss Mary M. Cuttings. Of eight children, four are living [1889]. His son, Charles S. Boyd was a member of the class of 1881 in Bates Theological School when he died.

Rev David Brackett
Dirth:
Feb. 1, 1837
Jackson
Waldo County
Maine
Death:
1922
Burial:
Grove Cemetery
Belfast
Waldo County
Maine,

Rev. David Brackett, Jr., son of David and Olive (Trueworthy) Brackett, was born in Jackson, ME in 1837. He was converted at the age of forty-three. The next year, 1881, he received license to preach, and in 1882 was ordained at the Quarterly Meeting. He had a revival in the Brooks church in 1881, and in the Thorndike and Knox churches in 18882-83, of which he became pastor of the Thorndike church.

Levi Brackett
Birth:
1813
Westbrook, Maine
Death:
1890
Burial:
Growstown Cemetery
Brunswick
Cumberland County, Maine

He was converted at age 26, and graduated from the Theological School at Whitestown, New York about 10 years afterwards in 1849. He received license to preach in 1844 and was ordained by the Bowdoin quarterly Meeting in 1849. After pastoring in New Hampshire for many years he moved to West Lebanon, Maine and supplied in Northfield and elsewhere. He also pastored in North Parsonsfield. Revivals and baptisms he enjoyed in nearly in all his pastorates. On December 20 field, 1852 he married Mrs. Nancy J Cram, of Brownfield, Maine. He had four children and the oldest was a professor at the Colorado State University. The older daughter was a teacher in the Classical Institute at Hallowell, Maine, and the second daughter is Librarian of the Spear Library at Oberlin College. These three were graduates of Bates College, Lewiston Maine.

Nancy Jane Cram Brackett
Birth:
1827
Death:

1897
Burial:
Growstown Cemetery
Brunswick
Cumberland County, Maine

She had been a Free Will Baptist preacher prior to the marriage to Rev. Levi Brackett.

Me Rev Allen W Bradeen
Birth:
Feb. 27, 1859
Maine, USA
Death:
1915
Springvale
York County
Maine
Burial:
Mount Pleasant Cemetery
Dexter
Penobscot County
Maine

Rev. Allen W. Bradeen, son of Isaac and Philena C. (Billington)

Bradeen, was born at Byron ME, Feb. 27, 1859. He studied at the Wilton Academy 1882-84, and at Cobb Divinity School 1884-88. In the winter of 1878 he was converted, and licensed Jan 11, 1887. He has supplied at Hallowell, ME, and during one year five were baptized and seven admitted into the church. In 1888 he became pastor at Dexter, ME, and was ordained.

Rev Frank C. Bradeen
Birth:
Jun. 29, 1840
Maine
Death:
Nov. 4, 1923
Burial:
Highland Cemetery
Buxton
York County
Maine

An ordained Free Will Baptist minister and pastor in Maine and New Hampshire; ordained ca 1873, after which he ministered to the Dexter Village, Exeter and St. Albans churches, and in 1877, went to Parsonfield. He pastored in Concord N.H. the Curtis Mem.

Rev Roscoe E Bradford
Birth:
Sep. 8, 1857
Death:
Jul. 29, 1889
Burial:
Knox Station Cemetery
Knox
Waldo County
Maine

Ordained Free Will Baptist minister/pastor in Maine 1883); studied (1887 to ?) in Bates Theological School, Lewiston ME.

Rev Otis W Bridges
Birth:
Jan. 26, 1806
Penobscot, ME
Death:
Oct. 24, 1903
Burial:
Mount Pleasant Cemetery
Dexter
Penobscot County
Maine

His parents were Rev. Abiezer and Deborah (Stores) Bridges. He was converted at the age of seventeen. He received license to preach in 1830, and was ordained in 1834, by Rev's Clement Phinney (who preached the sermon), Benjamin Thorn, and A. Files, of the Bowdoin Quarterly Meeting. He lived in Sangerville, ME, forty-two years, where he labored in a number of revivals, and assisted in organizing two churches. He resided at Ft. Fairfield, and was pastor of the church there. He was married Oct. 11, 1833 to Margaret W. Owen, and has three children; his oldest son is a deacon of the Dexter church

Rev Albion C Brown
Birth:
Jan. 13, 1859
New Portland
Somerset County
Maine
Death:
1944
Burial:
Oak Grove Cemetery
Bath
Sagadahoc County
Maine
Plot: South 4

Son of Israel and Flora A. (Emery) Brown. They mar. Nov. 1, 1857, at New Portland, Somerset Co. ME.
Rev. A.C. Brown was ordained to the ministry June 29, 1887, and pastored Vienna Church, Weeks Mills, and First Mount Vernon Church.

Ebenezer Brown
Birth:
1771
Death:
Mar. 27, 1838
Wilton, ME,
Burial:
East Wilton Cemetery
Wilton
Franklin County, Maine

Rev. Ebenezer BROWN, d. at age 67 yrs. He was ordained a minister of the Freewill Baptist church May 19, 1805. He was married to Hannah, who d. May 29, 1852, age 76. Their daughter, Hannah (Brown) Fletcher, m. Asa Fletcher Jan. 27, 1877. Brown, after a pastorate of the First church at for many years died after a hurtful and distressing Illness. He was excellent as a counselor, and zealous in his work for the Savior.

Jonathan Brown
Birth:
1772
Death:
Sep. 10, 1850
Burial:
Curtis Cemetery, Bowdoinham,
Sagadahoc County, Maine

Jonathan Brown was born in Phippsburgh, ME. At the age of twelve he was converted and baptized. About the year 1803 he began to preach. He was ordained to the Free Baptist ministry in 1808. He was afflicted through much sickness in his family, but as far as possible, he prosecuted his holy calling.

Georges E S Bryant
Birth:
October 28, 1818
Dover-Foxcroft,
Piscataquis, Maine
Death:
1871
Burial:
South Dover Cemetery
Dover-Foxcroft
Piscataquis County, Maine
Plot: North Section, Row 8

George married Nancy S Dexter on 21 Nov 1844 in Dover-Foxcroft, Piscataquis, Maine. He became a Christian at the age of 15 and joined the church. He was ordained about 1860 and license several years before. He was 12 years clerk of the Penobscot Yearly Meeting and preached at Milo and other places. He had an excellent mind and was a good scholar and for a time a student in the biblical school. His sermons were carefully prepared, were instructive, suggestive and plain. He was an acceptable preacher until his health failed. He was a radical supporter of reforms, but was a kind and accommodating person. He was very efficient in the business affairs of the church. In him the churches and institutions of the denomination had a true friend and helper.

Rev Porter S Burbank

Birth:
Mar. 13, 1810
Newfield
York County
Maine, USA
Death:
Jul. 21, 1883
Limerick
York County
Maine
Burial:
Baptist Society Church Cemetery
Limerick
York County
Maine

Rev. Porter S. Burbank, was a bro. of Rev. Samuel Burbank, (1792-1845), and 3rd in family to enter the ministry, and son of Samuel Burbank, a native of Rowley, Mass., and Susanna (Graves) Burbank, of Brentwood, NH.

He graduated Dartmouth, College in 1832, but took 3 yrs of his course in Waterville, College, ME. He prepared for college at Limerick Academy and Parsonfield Seminary.

Self-reliance and courage were required in procuring his education. At age 16 he was employed as apprentice under Wm. Burr in the "Morning Star" printing office at Limerick, and helped set type for the first number of that paper.

During his three yrs apprenticeship he became possessed with an intense disire for an education.

While fitting himself to teach he felt the call to the ministry. He preached some while at Waterville College, and was licensed by Waterville Q.M., at Industry, ME, 1836.

During his active ministry he probably taught a score of high schools. He loved to teach but at the close of his 3 yrs as principal of Stafford Academy, NH, he longed for the active work of the ministry.

He was ordained at a session of NH Yearly Meeting, June 13, 1840. He afterwards taught a few terms at Parsonfield Seminary. A call to take charge of Clinton Seminary, NY and Whitestown Seminary was declined.

He was corresponding seretary of the Education Society six consecutive yrs. He was frequently on its board, and often made chairman of committees on education at General Conference. He was one of the committee that compiled the *"Psalmody."*

He was heartily interested in Temperance and Anti-slavery causes and the benevolent causes of the denomination, especially, the "Morning Star," newspaper, with which he was corresponding editor from 1833-1866.

He held pastorates in Hampton, Deerfield, New Hampton, and Danville, NH and in West Buxton and Lemerick, ME.

His ministry was eminently

347

successful' several efficient Free Baptist ministers were converted in revivals in churches he pastored.

At the close of his last pastorate at Danville, NH, he purchased a home in So. Parsonfield, ME, where he spent the last ten yrs of his life. He supplied the church there one year and preached occasionally afterward.

Almira Wescott Bullock
Birth:
1797, USA
Death:
Apr. 25, 1859
Maine,
Burial:
Forest Hill Cemetery
Bridgton
Cumberland County, Maine
Plot: Chap. 19
Wife of Andrew Cobb married 1st: Rev. Jeremiah Bullock. She was an ordained minister of the Free Will Baptist, and went with her first minister husband, and later, her second husband, Dea.

Cobb. Her son, Wescott Bullock, was also a minister. It is written she was a successful and much loved speaker, a Christian in all areas of her life.

Jeremiah Bullock
Birth:
1797
Death:
Dec. 16, 1849
Maine
Burial:
Forest Hill Cemetery
Bridgton
Cumberland County, Maine
Plot: Chap. 19

An ordained Free Will Baptist minister.

Wescott Bullock
Birth:
Jul. 7, 1818
Limington
York County, Maine
Death:
1900
Burial:
Greenwood Cemetery
Biddeford
York County, Maine

He received his education in the common schools and at Parsonsfield Academy, and was a teacher in early life. He began to preach soon after he embraced religion in 1842. He was ordained in Aug. 1856, in Saco, ME, his mother preaching the sermon to a vast assembly of people in the town hall. He was of fine build, very distinctive voice, with both his father and mother's qualities intertwined. He preached in N.H. and Maine with good success, was loved and esteemed by many.

The twofold and wonderfully woven mantle of his parents had fallen on him; that part received from his father, coarse, hard twisted and substantial, proved a panoply of security amid the storms that sometimes gathered about the minister's pathway; that inherited from his saintly mother and dyed by her gentle spirit, was of soft and silken texture designed to keep the heart warm and tender. This sacred mantel was "reversible" and sometimes changed in the pulpit, alternating between the rough and silken sides. He was ordained at Saco, in August 1856, preaching the sermon to a vast assembly of people in the town hall. He says "I have preached in various towns of Maine and New Hampshire, sometimes in a fine pulpit, sometimes in school house and sometimes standing on stone walls; wherever I had a thus saith the Lord." He has always preached what he believed and lived as he preached. In personal appearance both commanding and attractive; his voice pleasant and melodious, and his language plain and pure. He has been a very useful man, who was widely known and much beloved; now passing the snowy years of venerable age, cheered by the sunshine of the Christian's undying hope. He has been incapacitated for active service from paralysis, and says he "lives by praying"; resides in Biddeford, Maine. indicates Ord. 1856. Son of Jeremiah Almira (Wescott) Bullock..

Asa Burnham
Birth:
Aug. 9, 1789
New Hampshire
Death:
Aug. 9, 1852
Garland, Maine
Burial:
Sebec Corner Cemetery
Sebec Piscataquis County, Maine

He was ordained, 1819 and pastored in Maine.

Inscription:
LIVERMORE

(back)
Rev. Asa Burnham
Died Aug. 9, 1852 Æ 63.
Hannah
His wife, died
May 14, 1887 Æ 99.

Oliver Butler
Birth:
Feb. 25, 1809
Berwick, York County Maine
Death:
Dec. 6, 1897
Chelsea,
Suffolk County,
Massachusetts
Burial:
Woodlawn Cemetery,
Biddeford,
York County, Maine

A graduate of Bowdoin College and for year's publisher of the "Biddeford Journal," a member of the Maine Legislature, two yrs president of the Senate, and at present (1889) attorney at law in Boston, Mass. Rev. Oliver Butler studied with a tutor and at Parsonfield Seminary in theology in 1843. He was licensed in June 1840 and ordained Jan. 28, 1842 a Free Will Baptist clergyman at Great Falls, N.H., by a council from the Rockingham Q.M., with Rev. Silas Curtis as Chairman. His first pastorate was at Effingham Falls where he organized a church and built a meeting house, adding during fourteen years, about 100 to the membership. He pastored Middleton, Wolsbourough, East Andover and at Parker's Head,

ME, and for twelve years at Meredith Centre, N.H., where a hundred were baptized. He also pastored at Buxton, and Lyman, Me. He went into the publishing business in 1872, but continued preaching until 1880. When enfeebled by disease he moved to Chelsea, Mass, where he has served three yrs in a Baptist city mission. At nearly 80 years, he retired active service. He was three years a member of the Home Mission Board, and a member of Gen. Conference at Sutton, VT, in 1847, and Lowell, MA in 1852.

John Buzzell
Birth:
Sep. 16, 1767
Barrington, Strafford Cty
New Hampshire,
Death:
Mar. 29, 1863
Parsonsfield,
York County,
Maine
Burial:
North Parsonsfield
North Parsonsfield,
York County
Maine

Rev. John Buzzell, a Free Will Baptist clergyman, married Anna Buzzell, b. 1770, d. 1839. They had 11 children. His attainments were above average, early becoming a teacher of common schools. He along with Dr. Moses Sweat, and Rev. Rufus McIntire, founded the Old Parsonsfield Seminary, the first school in the denomination.

He, with Elder Benjamin Randall founder of FWB in NH, came to Maine before 1800, and he is known to have pastored churches in Maine for more than 50 years. He was a noted and powerful preacher, dignified in his demeanor, yet in spirit humble. He did as much as any in extending the work and influence of the FWB church. It was said that he also had a talent for painting, 'as good as the old masters' and even painted a portrait of a young couple a week after their marriage as a gift to them. He had a far-reaching view of education, and had a commanding influence in exerting and molding political and religious opinions of the people. He was first editor of his denomination's "Morning Star" paper, which position he held seven years; He was instrumental in establishing the Orissa Mission (India.) He wrote a biography of his mentor, *"Life of Rev. Benjamin Randall."* He died at his home in North Parsonsfield at the advanced age of ninety-five years, and 6 months.

Cyrus Campbell
Birth:
Sep. 29, 1817
Bowdoin
Sagadahoc County, Maine
Death:
Jun. 13, 1893
New Sharon
Franklin County, Maine
Burial:
Weeks Mills Cemetery
New Sharon
Franklin County, Maine

He was converted 25 years of age. He was a student of

Whitestown, New York. On October 7, 1846 at the age of 29, he received license to preach and was ordained the following year in September. He pastored a number of churches in the area. On December 8, 1846 he married Adaline Lenpest.

Joseph Chadbourne
Birth:
Jun. 28, 1807
Greene
Androscoggin County, Maine
Death:
Nov. 20, 1877
Bradford
Penobscot County, Maine
Burial:
Corner Cemetery
Bradford, Penobscot County
Maine

Joseph Chadbourne, at the age of nineteen, while a student in the Seminary at Kent's Hill, became a Christian. Ten years afterwards he became a member of the church in Bradford. He was for a time the efficient deacon of

the church. In 1858 he took a letter and joined the Christian denomination, by which he was ordained March, 1859. He was highly esteemed among them.Four years before his death, he again became a member of the church in Bradford. He was much interested in education and a successful teacher. He was frequently elected to officesof trust and responsibility.
Inscription:
JOSEPH CHADBOURNE died
November 20, 1877
age 70 years   4 months
22 days

Edward R. Chadwick
Birth:
Jun., 1861
China
Kennebec County, Maine
Death:
1926
Burial:
Chadwick Hill Cemetery
China
Kennebec County, Maine

He was converted in 1878 and later graduated at the Maine Central Institute in 1880 and then from Bates College in 1884. He was of the class of 1888 of the Cobb Divinity School. In July, 1888 he settled in Milton, New Hampshire and on August 23 he was ordained by the New Durham Quarterly Meeting.
His parents were: Abner D. Chadwick (1831-1911) and Drusilla Newcomb Chadwick (1836 - 1920)

Rev S. Freeman Chaney
Birth:
1819
Death:
Oct. 13, 1843
Burial:
Hillcrest Cemetery
West Buxton
York County
Maine

Oren Burbank Cheney
Birth:
Dec. 12, 1816
Ashland, Grafton County,
New Hampshire
Death:
Dec. 22, 1903
Lewiston,
Androscoggin County, Maine
Burial:
Riverside Cemetery, Lewiston,
Androscoggin County, Maine

Dr. Cheney attended Parsonfield Seminary and New Hampton Institution, and graduated from Dartmouth College in 1839. He was converted in the spring of 1836 and, walking from Dartmouth to his native place, he was baptized by Rev. Simeon Dana, and united with the Ashland church. After graduation he became principal of the Farmington ME Academy in the autumn of 1839. He became principal of the Strafford Academy in 1841. Then he taught the Greenland, N.H., and Academy near Portsmouth and was licensed by the Portsmouth church. He was ordained in the Effingham Hill, N.H. church, in the autumn of 1844, by Rev. John Buzzell, Rev. Benj. S. Manson, and others. He held anti-slavery sentiments, and this pastorate was laid down because of opposition to his views. In 1851-52, he was sent to the Legislature by the Whigs and Free-soilers, and voted for the original Maine Temperance Law. In 1852, he went to Augusta for five years as pastor of the church. On Sept. 22, 1854, he received a letter from Rev. J. A. Lowell, principal of Parsonfield Seminary, announcing that the Seminary building had been burned the day before. From that day Dr. Cheney consecrated himself to build for the Free Baptists an efficient literary institution in a more central place. President Cheney held many important positions of confidence and trust in this denomination. Twice was moderator of General Conference, and occupied important position on the Conference Board. He represented his denomination as delegate to the General Baptists of England. He has been recording secretary of both the Foreign and Home Mission Societies, and president of the

Education and Anti-Slavery Societies. He was foremost in vision to merge the Free Baptists with the larger open-communion Baptist, and worked to that end not only with Baptists but with Christian and other denominations until his demise. He is best known for being the founder and first president of Bates College in Lewiston, Maine. The college was chartered in 1862 and was founded as the Maine State Seminary in 1855.

Rev. Chandler was converted and baptized before age 20 by his mother's brother, Rev. Jeremy Bean. He then began to preach and connected himself with the Second Wilton church, preaching in all the towns around and doing evangelistic work, holding revivals with great success. He was ordained at Phillips, ME, June 9, 1822, by Rev's Samuel Hutchins and John Foster. His travels as an evangelist in Maine extended to 120 towns and plantations. All the while, he supported himself, not receiving $50 a year for his labors. Though he was not favored with an extensive education, yet, he was gifted by nature. He was very conversant with Scripture. As a speaker, he was dramatic and was mighty in persuasive powers to move sinners. His earnestness and consecration enabled him to accomplish a great work. He raised up quite a number of churches in the new settlements he visited.

Hubbard Chandler
Birth:
Jan., 1798
Death:
Nov. 5, 1866
West Poland,
Androscoggin County,
Maine
Burial:
Highland Cemetery,
West Poland,
Androscoggin County,
Maine

Blessed *are* the dead which die in the Lord

George Colby Dyer Chase
Birth:
Mar. 15, 1844
Death:
May 27, 1919
Burial:
Pond Cemetery 1,Unity,
Waldo County, Maine,
Plot: row 22

Professor of Rhetoric and English Literature in Bates College, Lewiston, Me., was born in Unity, Me. He prepared for college at the Maine State Seminary (afterwards Bates College), and immediately, entered Bates College, where he graduated in 1868.The next two years he was teacher of Greek, Latin and Mental Philosophy, at New Hampton Institution, N.H.
He then spent a year in Bates Theological School, and was at the same time a tutor of Greek in the college. He was at this time elected a professor in the college, and after taking a post-graduate course of one year at Harvard College, entered upon the work of the professorship. He was a member of the Lewiston School Board and twice chosen. President in 1883 and 1887. In 1894 George Colby Chase, Class of 1868, succeeded President Cheney. Known as "the great builder," He oversaw the construction of eleven new buildings, including Coram Library, the Chapel, Chase Hall, Carnegie Science Hall, and Rand Hall. Chase tripled the number of students and faculty, and the endowment. He discontinued the Cobb Divinity School and Nichols Latin School departments of the College. In 1907 at the request of Chase and the Board, the legislature amended the college's charter removing the requirement for the President and majority of the trustees to be Free Will Baptists; this change to a non-sectarian status allowed the school to qualify for Carnegie Foundation funding for professor pensions He was for several years a contributor to the *"Morning Star."*

Uriah Chase
Birth:
Sept. 28, 1810
Death:
Aug. 1, 1888
Waterboro, Maine
Burial:
Elder Grey Cemetery
Waterboro
York County, Maine

He began to preach in 1848; licensed by the New Durham QM 1848; ordained at East Parsonfield, Me., 1850. All of his ministry was in Maine.

Rev Roger W Churchill
Birth:
Jul. 30, 1847
Shapleigh
York County
Maine
Death:
1914
Burial:
Mount Auburn Cemetery
Auburn
Androscoggin County
Maine

Rev. Roger W. Churchill, son of Nathaniel and Abigail W. (Stevens) Churchill, was born at Shapleigh, ME, Aug. 30, 1848. He first studied for the law. He studied theology at Bates Theological School, and was converted in 1869, licensed in 1881, and was ordained in 1883, at Richmond, ME. He labored successfully there five years; he had two rivivals; sixty-four were added to the church. He is settled at Belmont, NH, where in one year twelve have been added. He married Maggie A. Archibald, Dec. 13, 1883, and has one daughter.

He was a brother to Edgar W. Churchill, 1858-1929, also a clergyman, per New Hampshire death records.

Aaron Clark
Birth:
Unknown
Death:
Dec. 11, 1880
Hennon, Maine
Burial:
Light Cemetery
Knox County, Maine,

He was converted at the age of thirteen. When seventeen years of age, he was licensed by the Methodists as an exhorter. He afterwards united with the Free Baptists, by whom he was ordained about 1840. He preached in several places within the limits of the Montville Q. M. His name appears in the Register in connection with the Washington church from 1848 to 1869; then as pastor of the Second Montville church till 1872; then as pastor of the Washington church till 1875; then as pastor of the South Montville church one year. He remained a member of the latter church till his death.

John Clark
Birth:
Unknown
Newcastle. Me.
Death:
Aug. 8, 1871
Prospect
Waldo County, Maine
Burial:
Clark Cemetery
Prospect, Waldo County, Maine

He married and moved to Monroe in early manhood, and in 1824, during a great revival in that section, he was converted and united with the church. He was licensed in1832, and ordained as an evangelist in 1838. He worked hard to support his family, and preached Sabbaths. He was in the ministry about forty years, and traveled in that time about forty thousand miles, at least one half of the distance on foot. He baptized 125, attended 100 funerals; and. Married sixty couples. He preached till within a few days of his death. Though born of poor parents and with limited education, his willing mind enabled him to do a good work Reverend John Clark for whom the Cemetery was named. He was a Veteran of the Battle of Hampden, War of 1812 and began the Clark Settlement, in Prospect, Maine. His broken gravestone is down and buried and no flag marks him as a veteran. He died at age 78 years 8 months, 19 days.

Death is the crown jewel for the Christian.

Jonathan Clay
Birth:
December 13, 1775
Buxton
Maine
Death:
Feb. 20, 1849
Maine
Burial:
Highland Cemetery
Buxton
York County,
Maine

He was converted in 18 and five and was one of the early members of the Buxton church. He began to preach soon after his baptism and was ordained in 1815. His labors were mostly confined to Buxton and in 1831 he took his destination from his church and united with a few others who constituted a church near his home.

Rev Tisdale D. Clements
Birth:
Dec. 7, 1810
Monroe
Waldo County
Maine
Death:
Jul. 12, 1881
Burial:
Mount Rest Cemetery
Monroe
Waldo County,
Maine

Rev. T.D. Clements was ordained a Free Baptist minister in Maine; he was one of the first members of the Cooperation of Bates College, in Lewiston, and gave $1,000 to the endowment fund. His death was noted in the 25th Gen. Conf. of Freewill Baptists list of ministers' deaths, since "last session of Gen. Conf. 1880.

Edward Lindley Cleveland
Birth:
Nov. 6, 1813
Camden
Knox County, Maine
Death:
Mar. 9, 1897
Rockport
Knox County, Maine
Burial:
West Rockport Cemetery
West Rockport
Knox County, Maine

He became a Christian at the age of 24 and was ordained in 1845 by Rev. John Hampton and others. He has preached an evangelist and labored in many revivals. He was a member of the Rockville Church, Camden, and preached as opportunity was offered him.

William G. Cobb
Birth
1779
Otisfield
Oxford Co., Maine
Death
Jun. 2, 1850

Otisfield
Oxford Co., Maine
Burial:
Cobb Hill Cemetery
Otisfield
Oxford Co. Maine

He was converted to at the age of 22 and was baptized by Rev. Zachariah Leach and after preaching considerably for 16 years was ordained in March, 1824. Ill health confined his labors near his home. Note: Age 70 yrs

Rev. Almira Wescott Cobb
Birth:
Oct. 2, 1795
Gorham
Cumberland County, Maine
Death:
Apr. 25, 1859
Maine
Burial:
Forest Hill Cemetery

Bridgton
Cumberland County, Maine
Plot: Chap. 19

She was the wife of Andrew Cobb Married 1st: Rev. Jeremiah Bullock 1797 - 1849) and mother of Rev. Wescott Bullock (1818 - 1900).

Greenleaf H Coburn
Birth:
Mar. 7, 1839
Turner
Androscoggin County, Maine
Death:
Jul. 11, 1865
Maine
Burial:
Gray Village Cemetery
Gray
Cumberland County, Maine

Died aged 26 years.He early showed a fondness for books. At fourteen he went to Boston, here he was employed till he was seventeen. He was converted in 1857, at Gray, ME, under the labors of Rev. W. T. Smith. He was baptized at once uniting with the church (Freewill Baptist) at Gray. In the spring of 1858, he returned to Boston for another year. Early in 1859, he went to Lewiston and entered Bates College, enjoying the love and esteem of his instructors, graduated from his preparatory course in July 1862. He then entered the Theological School at New Hampton (NH) and after three years graduated being ordained there July 17, 1865. A fortnight later he came to Lewiston and arranged with President Cheney to enter the Junior Class of the College. But in two weeks he was dead from a fever. A gentleman offered to start him in business in Boston, and give him half the profits. "No," young Coburn replied. "I must get an education and enter upon a higher calling." President Oren B. Cheney, Bates College, preached his funeral sermon.

George Warren Colby
Birth:
Dec. 8, 1836
Vassalboro
Kennebec County, Maine
Death:
Jan. 22, 1913
Augusta
Kennebec County, Maine
Burial:
Mount Hope Cemetery
Augusta
Kennebec County, Maine

He was converted to the age of 23. He received license to preach from the Montville Quarter Meeting in March 1874 and was ordained on June 20, 1875 by Rev. Aaron Clark and others. In his many revivals he had between three and 400 conversion, baptized 73. Records show that he married 23 couples and attended 75 funerals.He married Ayrobine DAMON on 16 JAN 1879 in Vassalboro, Kennebec Cty, Maine.

Inscription:
COLBY /CONANT
George Warren Colby1836-1913

Joshua B. O. Colby

Birth:
Jan. 13, 1808
Maine
Death:
Mar. 27, 1891
Denmark
Oxford County, Maine
Burial:
Colby Cemetery
Denmark
Oxford County, Maine

He studied for a time at Fryeberg Academy. He became a Christian at the age the 26 and was baptized by Elder Jonathan Tracy and joined the church at Denmark. He was first ordained as a Deacon but soon after on

October 6, 1852 was ordained by Rev. James Rand and others. The church in Denmark was under his care for 40 years.

Inscription:
Rev. J. B. O. Colby
Born Jan. 13, 1808
Died Mar. 27, 1891

Jacob D. Couillard

Birth:
Nov. 24, 1815
Frankfort, Maine
Death:
Jul. 18, 1888
Maine
Burial:
Smith Cemetery
Palermo
Waldo County, Maine

He was converted in 1832, and an in Exeter, Maine was licensed in 1834. Two years later he was ordained. He had an itinerant ministry in which he baptized a good number of people and assisted in organizing several churches. After driving for some time in Massachusetts he moved to North Palermo, Maine and did a good work among the destitute churches. He also served during the Civil War.

Rev Gideon Cook

Birth:
Nov. 5, 1787
Eastham
Barnstable County
Massachusetts
Death: Dec. 7, 1869
Kennebunk
York County
Maine
Burial:
Pine Grove Cemetery
West Kennebunk
York County
Maine

Ordained Freewill Baptist minister in 1826, and ministered in Maine.

Inscription:
Rev. Gideon Cook Nov. 3, 1787 - Dec. 7, 1869

John Cook

Birth:
May 7, 1809
Alton, Belknap, New Hampshire
Death:
Jan. 4, 1891
Burnham, Waldo, Maine
Burial:
Burnham Village Cemetery
Burnham, Waldo County, Maine

His obituary appeared in the *Morning Star* published on 2 Apr 1891. Mary Jane (Adams) Cook married Rev. John Cook on 8 Nov

1846. His parents were Jacob and -- (Hubbard) Cook. His education he received from the common school Before he was sixteen his father moved on a new lot in Exeter, Me., where, in the midst of "black logs and flies," he was educated to work with his hands so effectively, that he could support himself and family' by working half the time and have the rest for preaching in destitute places without hire. He found a region of four towns without a preacher. In a town where there had been no religious meetings for ten years, he proclaimed the" glad tidings."He was converted at the age of twenty, received license to preach in 1833, and was ordained June 26, 1837, by Rev's Nathan Robinson, Roger Copp, and John B. Copp. He had revivals, baptized 141 converts in twelve different towns, assisted in organizing seven or eight churches, and married ninety-eight couples. He was chosen pastor of the Burnham church at its organization, July 2, 1857. During the war their church edifice was built. Though his pastorate ceased some time ago, he supplied the church from time to time,. He attended every monthly conference since 1860, and can tell how many times each member had been present for the last eighteen years. He was married Dec. 29, 1833, to Miss Sally P. Kenisten on Nov. 8, 1846, he was married again.

Lavina Carr Coombs
Birth:
Nov. 23, 1849
West Bowdoin
Sagadahoc County, Maine
Death:
1927
Burial:
Woodlawn Cemetery
West Bowdoin, Sagadahoc
County, Maine

Coombs, Miss Lavina C., daughter of David and Sarah Coombs, She commenced the Christian life in 1862; attended Litchfield Academy 1864-66, the Normal School at Farmington 187273, and the Lewiston High School in1880. She taught ten years in the schools of Maine, and in November, 1882, was sent by the Woman's Missionary Society as a missionary to India. She located at Midnapore, and took charge of the Zenana work and the Ragged Schools at that place. Was a Free Will Baptist missionary in India for forty years, teaching in a school and helping the team there. 1882- 1922.

Roger Copp
Birth:
unknown
Death:
Feb. 16, 1860
Burial:
Detroit Village Cemetery
Detroit
Somerset County
Maine

A Freewill Baptist ordained minister, who pastored churches in Maine; his son, John B. and grandson, Prof. John Scott Copp, were also FWB ministers.

Freeman Cooper
Birth:
February 6, 1835
Wakefield, Maine
Death:
Apr. 11, 1900
Maine
Burial:
Oak Hill Cemetery
Windsor
Kennebec County, Maine

He was converted to the age of 35 and send began to preach the gospel. He received his license on February 15, 1873 and was ordained by the Montville quarterly meeting on September 20, 1874. He pastored many of the churches in that area of Maine and held revivals throughout the region.He was a Member of Co.F 21st Me. Reg during the Civil War.

Rev David B. Cowell
Birth:
Dec. 20, 1807
West Lebanon, York County
Maine
Death:
Apr. 15, 1884
Maine
Burial:
Cowell-Corson
West Lebanon, York County
Maine

He studied in the Academy at Limerick, and also at Wolfborough, NH. He taught fifteen terms of school, mostly in his native town. His townsmen honored him with most of the offices in their power to bestow. He had an aptitude for mercantile pursuits, and at the age of seventeen began to keep a store in West Lebanon. After some years he went to Great Falls, where his trade became extensive. During this time he became a Universalist and then an infidel. But in 1833 he became clearly convinced of his error. Making his way through a crowded assembly, he stood upon the pulpit stairs and renounced his infidelity. He became a class leader in the Free Baptist church at Great Falls and an earnest worker. His conversation from house to house and over the counter was the means of many conversions. He soon felt called to preach, but was loth to give up his business. Finally, he yielded and first went to Barnstead, NH. He went then to Northwood, NH, North Berwick Me (Beach Ridge), Lebanon and Springvale. Others ministers baptized the converts during this time. In 1837, he was ordained. He traveled almost constantly for seven years and was associated in the ministry with Rev's Caverno, Thurston, Woodman, Place, Buzzell, Hobbs and others of the fathers. He was instrumental in the conversion of many, some of whom became ministers, and missionaries. In 1848 he suggested to Rev. O.B. Cheney, then pastor at West Lebanon, the idea of founding the Lebanon Academy and offered the land and one hundred dollars. One of his sons, educated in this flourishing school, became successful principal of Arms Academy, at Shelburne Falls, Mass. His last fields of labor were in Walnut Grove, N.H., a year or more, and six months in Gorham and Standish, ME.

In 1841, he married Miss Christiana B. Coffin, daughter of Rev. Stephen Coffin. She was talented, educated and zealous. She often accompanied him on his preaching tours, and aided him much, and in the Academy her influence on the students led many of them to Christ. Mr. Cowell was afflicted with heart disease many hears and kept close at home, but he was able to say, "It is alll clear now; the hope of other days sustains me still."

He and Christiana had three children: Hosea C. Cowell (1849 - 1853), Christiana M. Cowell (1853 - 1854), Eugene C. Cowell (1858 - **1862).**

Rev Simon Cox
Birth:
Apr. 14, 1800
Lincolnville
Waldo County
Maine
Death:
Jan. 28, 1851
Rockland
Knox County
Maine
Burial:
Achorn Cemetery
Rockland
Knox County
Maine

Rev. Simon Cox, died in Rockland, ME, aged 51 years. He was converted when about nineteen, and united with the Methodists, by whom he was licensed to preach. After about fifteen years, he united with the Free Baptists, and by them was recognized as an elder. While consumption was wasting his life, he was sustained by the gospel he preached to others."

He was married to Rachel Philbrook, with whom they had children: Deborah H. b. 1826; Aurelius Augustus, 1828; James Warren, 1829; Ruhama F. 1832; George Washington,1836; Hollis Monroe, 1837.

Charles T. D. Crockett
Birth:
Mar. 15, 1833
Woodstock
Oxford County,
Maine
Death:
Jun. 25, 1899
Maine
Burial:
Hunts Corner Cemetery
Albany
Oxford County,
Maine

He Was A Student At Gould's Academy In Bethel, Maine. After His Conversion On February 8, 1875 He Attended Bates Theological School, Lewiston, Maine. With his wife he was baptized at Mechanic Falls on May 16 1875 by Rev. B Menard.

He was licensed to preach on January 27th, 1876 and ordained at Canton on June 8, 1877 by Rev. J. M. Pease, and others. He preached at West Paris where the church was revived and the next four years at Canton. After preaching at many churches in the area he settled at Jackson, New Hampshire where a house of worship was thoroughly repaired and well-furnished and the church strengthened by the addition of excellent members. In 1888 he became the pastor of the church at Steep Falls, Maine and served branched churches..

Their works do follow them.

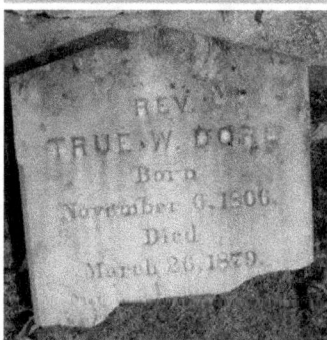

True W. Dore
Birth:
Nov. 6, 1806
Death:
Mar. 26, 1879
Garland, Maine
Burial:
Hathaway Cemetery
Garland
Penobscot County, Maine

Converted in early man hood, he soon began to hold meetings. Gifted in prayer and song he labored as an evangelist with success. He first united with the Methodists, but it Ripley, Maine, he joined the Free Baptists and was ordained by them in June 1842. He preached at Ripley, Garland, and in the vicinity for other.
Inscription:
I have kept the faith.

Death is the entry to Life Evermore

Rev George Douglass
Birth:
Aug. 16, 1816
Bowdoin
Sagadahoc County, Maine
Death:
Aug. 25, 1845
Fairfield

Somerset County, Maine
Burial:
Litchfield Plains Cemetery
Litchfield Plains
Kennebec County, Maine

Rev. George Douglass experience religion at age twenty, was baptized in spring of 1836, and united with the church, and soon after began to preach. He was licensed in 1840 by the church, and was ordained in 1842 when he was engaged at Pittsfield, while engaged in a meeting there, by visiting ministers from the Waterville and Exeter Quarterly Meetings (QM). His work was blessed throughout the Waterville Q.M., in the addition of over one hundred within two years. He moved to Fairfield in 1843, and died there in the summer of 1845, in his 29th year.

Dr Daniel Dyer
Birth:
May 25, 1827
Charleston
Penobscot County
Maine
Death:
Oct. 2, 1892
Burial:
Mudgett Cemetery

Burnham
Waldo County
Maine
Plot: 14

His parents were Benjamin and Louisa (Sylvester) DYER. Converted at fourteen years of age, he studied at Litchfield Academy and at the Bowdoin Medical School, and has been successful as a physician.

He was licensed to preach in 1851, and afterwards ordained at North Anson. In 1852-53 he engaged in a revival to which over one hundred were converted. He has preached with needy churches. After three years' service his health failed.

He married in 1849 Miss Abby Weston.

Joseph Dyer
Birth:
1774
Boston
Suffolk County,
Massachusetts
Death:
Jan. 31, 1859
Phillips
Franklin County,
Maine
Burial:
Riverside Cemetery
Phillips
Franklin County
Maine

Rev. Joseph DYER, was the son of a sea-captain, and was one of the memorable party who threw the British tea into Boston harbor.

His mother's was Elizabeth Nichols, of Malden, MA. At the age of eight years, Joseph's father died, and Joseph was bound out to learn the Morocco shoe trade. He married Miss Sally Merritt, of Malden, where he resided till he removed to Hallowell, ME, in October 1806. He had already experienced religion and joined the Calvinistic Baptist church in Massachusetts. He was ordained in 1810, and when the Free Baptist church which had been established by Benjamin Randall in 1795, was reorganized, Nov. 12, 1819, Rev. Dyer was one of the eleven included in the reorganization. With this church he was worthily connected until Sept. 17, 1831, when with others he organized a new church in Madrid, where his labors had been blessed. Over this flock he watched with ceaseless interest for more than a score of years, when failing health induced him to resign the charge to a younger brother.Though engaged in pioneer work in this section, making his way with his precious message on horseback through the wilderness, guided by spotted trees and preaching the gospel chiefly in log cabins, yet he was progressive and was practically interested in the moral and educational enterprises. He was devout and eminently spiritual in prayer. He lived to see his great-great-grandchild. He was universally esteemed.

Ebenezer G Eaton
Birth:
Jul., 1808
Death:
Aug. 13, 1883
Lewiston, Me.
Burial:
Oak Hill Cemetery
Auburn,
Androscoggin County, Maine

Eaton died at age 76 years. He was thoroughly converted in1831. He studied at Parsonfield Seminary and held meetings in Freedom, N. H., where sixty were converted. He was ordained at Freedom July 14, 1833, by Rev's Hosea Quinby and John Buzzell. He was for a time a missionary in the Otisfield Q. M., being the first preacher in the Q. M. who received a salary. He preached in Otisfield, Harrison, Bridgton, Brunswick, Auburn, Buckfield, Canton, Livermore, Greene, Poland, South Lewiston, Bethel and Sabattus. He also preached three years in Nova Scotia, and in a great revival there one hundred and seventy-five were added to the churches. During his ministry, he baptized 1000 persons. He was a schoolmate of President Cheney, who wrote of Eaton, "He was a good man and full of the Holy Ghost and of faith, and much people was added unto the Lord."

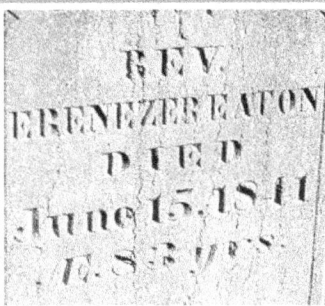

Ebenezer Eaton
Birth:
Unknown
Death:
Jun. 15, 1841
Androscoggin County, Maine
Burial:
Sedgwick Rural Cemetery
Sedgwick
Hancock County, Maine

Rev. Ebenezer Eaton Died June 15, 1841 (Age 83 years.). Ebenezer Eaton was the son of Theophilus Eaton and Abigail Fellows. He was married about 1777 to Abigail Herrick, the daughter of Joshua Herrick and Huldah Brown. Abigail is buried in Southwest Harbor, Maine, where Reverend Ebenezer Eaton was the town's first established minister. He was converted in 1831 after which he stated to

attend Parsonfield Seminary and held meetings in Freedom, New Hampshire, where 60 were converted. He was ordained at Freedom on July 14, 1833, by Rev. Hosea Quinby and John Buzzell. He was for a time a missionary in the Otisfield Quarterly Meeting being the first preacher in the quarter meeting who received a salary. He preached in the churches at the following towns of Otisfield, Harrison, Bridgton, Auburn, and numerous other places in the area. He also preached three years in Nova Scotia and in the and in a great revival where 175 were added to the churches during his ministry he baptized 1000 people. He was a schoolmate of Pres. Cheney, who wrote of him, "he was a good man and full of the Holy Ghost and of faith, and much people were added unto the Lord.

Death Is The Setting Free From The Warfare Of The Soul

Rev John Farnham
Birth:
1784
Death:
Oct. 6, 1847
Burial:
Woodside Cemetery
Belgrade
Kennebec County,
Maine

Ordained 1826, Freewill Bapt. minister. Labored in Maine.(Free Bapt. Cyclopedia, pub. 1889).

Josiah Farwell
Birth:
Unknown
Death:
Mar. 10, 1872
Burial:
Pittsfield Village Cemetery,
Pittsfield,
Somerset County, Maine

Ordained a Free Will Baptist minister in 1817 in Maine, but after a time he left the church.

Rev Ebenezer Nichols Fernald
Birth:
Mar. 10, 1833
West Lebanon
York County
Maine
Death:
Jan. 15, 1898
Acton
York County
Maine
Burial:

Joseph Fernald Cemetery
Lebanon
York County
Maine

"Rev. Ebenezer N. FERNALD, was the son of Joseph and Polly (Nichols) Fernald. He was converted in 1842. He was fitted for college at New Hampton, NH, from 1855-58. In Aug. 1858, he entered Amherst College (MA) and graduated in 1862. After teaching four years he entered Andover Theological Seminary, and graduated in 1869. He was licensed to preach in 1868, and ordained by a council of the Boston Quarterly Meeting (QM) in Dec. 1869. He was pastor of a church which he organized at Winthrop, Mass, from 1868 to 1870. From 1870-1874, he was pastor of the church in Auburn, Maine. The next two years he was corresponding secretary of the Education Society. From 1876 to 1883 he was financial secretary of the Home Mission, Foreign Mission, and Education Societies [Freewill Baptist], and treasurer of the same societies until 1885.

He then became publisher of "The Morning Star.

He was married Dec. 27, 1863, to Miss Anna B. Tuxbury. Two of their five children are living. Mrs. Fernald has been for some years a member of the board of managers of the Woman's Missionary Society.

Rev Allen Files
Birth:
1791
Gorham
Cumberland County, Maine
Death:
Mar. 20, 1864
Benton, Maine
Burial:
Grover Cemetery
Woolwich
Sagadahoc County, Maine

He was born in Gorham. Me., in 1791, where he was converted, and soon entered upon an itinerant ministry, in which many mere converted. In 1819, the revival in Lincolnville, under his labors, continued until a hundred accepted Christ. He was then ordained. In 1823, with Rev. J. M. Bailey, in Woolwich, he saw more than a hundred converted. In the extensive revival in Richmond, in 1825, he, with Rev. Clement Phinney, led a hundred to the Saviour. He became pastor for five years at Topsham, ME. He married about this time Miss Susan Shaw, of Woolwich, and purchasing a small farm, moved to Wales, and united with the church there. He preached with this church, or in an adjacent town, for thirty years. He was mild in his address yet firm and unflinching for the truth. His upright life won for him a large circle of friends. Having suffered from feeble health for years, he went from work to reward.

Charles W. Foster
Birth:
Feb. 3, 1836
Harrison, Maine
Death:
Sep. 16, 1902
Burial:
Evergreen Cemetery
Phillips
Franklin County,Maine

He attended the Bridgeton Academy and Westbrook Seminary. He was converted on May 30, 1870 in the Methodist Church at South Harrison. After three years he yielded to a call to the ministry and preached his first sermon in the Grand Hill schoolhouse in York. He was licensed in 1874 and ordained by the York and Cumberland Christian conference on October 19, 1875. On June 21, 1878 he united with the Free Baptist Church in Bridgeton. He was also treasurer of the town of Bridgeton for three years. In the Civil War he served in Battery A 1st. Reg. Me. Vol. Lt. Art._Regt.

Rev Thomas Flanders
Birth:
1780
Alton, New Hampshire
Death:
1889
Burial:
Knowlton Mills Cemetery
Piscataquis County, Maine

Ordained 1825. Itinerated in Maine and New Hampshire.

Rev Jabez Fletcher
Birth:
Jul. 2, 1800
Gray
Cumberland County, Maine
Death:
May 13, 1878
Dixmont
Penobscot County, Maine
Burial:
Simpson's Corner Cemetery
Dixmont
Penobscot County, Maine

Rev. Jabez Fletcher at age 24 was converted, and after about three years, he began to hold meetings. He was ordained by the Freewill Baptist at the June session of the Prospect Quarterly Meeting (QM), in 1833, at Dixmont. His early ministry was blessed in Dixmont, Prospect, Waldo, Monroe, Brooks and on the islands of the coast. He was an advocate of all moral enterprises and a man of excellent spirit.
Fletcher who more than 50 years ago, drove his ox-team from New Hampshire 160 miles to Dixmont, in Maine and cleared a farm there, toiling all the week

and preaching without compensation on the Sabbath. He died after a long and useful life, aged 78 years.

Joseph Foss
Birth:
1765
Lee,
Strafford County,
New Hampshire,
Death:
Dec. 28, 1852
Brighton,
Somerset County, Maine
Burial:
Mount Rest Cemetery,
Athens,
Somerset County,
Maine

An ordained Free Will Baptist minister. He went west to Brighton, ME, in 1812, and began holding meetings. He became pastor there and stayed pastor for forty years, doing much ministerial work in towns that had no regular minister. He preached more than fifty years and died in his 88th year of age.

William E. Foy
Birth:
1818
Death:
Nov. 9, 1893
Burial:
Birch Tree Cemetery
East Sullivan
Hancock County, Maine
Plot: Very back of the cemetery
on the right

William was born a free black. His parents were Joseph and Betsy Foy. His home was near Augusta, Maine. Even though slavery was not tolerated in the north, free people of color were not considered equal to whites. There isn't a lot of information about Foy's parents, but seems that Foy was allowed to read books and attend school. William Foy had a friend whose name was Silas Curtis. Silas was an ordained Freewill Baptist. It was through the ministry of Silas that Foy became converted at the age of 17. Foy continued to study and followed his mentor's footsteps in becoming a minister. Foy was an unusual black man. Foy was tall and light skinned. He was gifted as an eloquent speaker. Witnessing for God, however, wasn't always easy for Foy. He worked hard among both the blacks and whites and led many people to know Jesus. Early in 1842, Foy had experienced two visions about Christ's second coming and the reward of the righteous. Because of the visions, he joined the Millerite movement. However, he was reluctant to relate the visions publicly because he was aware of the prejudice displayed toward blacks. Foy was attending ministerial school in Boston at the time. A fellow pastor of the Episcopal Methodist Church encouraged Foy, and he began relating the visions to large audiences throughout New England.

The third and last vision Foy experienced was in 1844. That vision showed three levels. #1...God guiding his people from truth to truth; #2...testing the truths God's people had discovered; and #3...ultimate victory when the saved reach the Holy City because they believed and followed God's messages. Foy was experiencing financial pressures and there were things about the vision that he could not understand. Therefore, he stopped recounting them. Foy moved back to Maine and continued to minister to the FW Baptist and Methodist congregations. William Foy is considered as a prophet for the time prior to the Great Disappointment.

Inscription:
Rev. William E. Foy.
Died in Plantation at Age 74 years. Also buried here is his daughter, Laura, age 7 years

Rev Charles S. Frost
Birth:
1849
New Hampshire, USA
Death:
1933
Burial:
Laurel Hill Cemetery
Saco
York County
Maine

A Freewill Baptist minister, ordained 1878. A graduate of Bates College in 1874, and Bates Theological Seminary in 1878.

Rev Harold Ionel Frost
Birth:
Nov. 13, 1886
New Hampshire
Death:
Mar. 4, 1976
Auburn
Androscoggin County
Maine
Burial:
Mount Auburn Cemetery
Auburn
Androscoggin County
Maine

Jarius Fuller
Birth:
May 27, 1805
Maine
Death:
Jan. 23, 1877
Maine,
Burial:
Harding Cemetery
Brunswick,
Cumberland County,
Maine

Jarius married Sophia (Cargill) Fuller. He was an ordained minister/pastor in the Freewill Baptist church in Maine, and pastored in Greene, ME, where in 1826, revival was seen in that church, resulting "in twenty being added to the church." He also pastored at So. Monmouth, and other places, and was known to be a faithful man.

He was the son of Rev. Robert D. and Hattie (Parrott) Frost, born in 1886, in NH.

His father moved to different states going to school, pastoring, etc.

On this cemetery record, it gives the title, "Rev" with his name, and also shows his wife, Mabel's m/n. His WW I Draft Registration,[1918] states that he was a Missionary to India in 1917 for the American Baptist Foreign Mission [prev. to 1911, Free Baptist], and was on furlough from Balasore, Orissa, India, arriving in USA in 1918.

He lived to the age of 89 years.

Rev Robert D. Frost
Birth: 1846
Monroe County
New York
Death: 1921
Cumberland County
Maine
Burial:
Bay View Cemetery
South Portland Gardens
Cumberland County
Maine
Plot: Sec. 7 Lot 24

Rev. Robert D. Frost received license to preach in Iowa, 1866. He graduated from the Cedar Valley Seminary, Osage, IA in 1871, from Hillsdale College, Mich. in 1873 and from Bates Theological School, Lewiston, ME in 1881. Upon graduation, he was accepted as a missionary to India, and was ordained at Dover, NH in Feb. 1874, by the Freewill Baptist Foreign Mission Society. He sailed for India March 18, and was located in Midnapore. He acquired the native language rapidly and soon engaged in bazar and itinerant preaching and supplied the Bhimpore station for a time.

In late 1875, he sent his resignation intending to start for America the next year, but by March 1, 1876, two ladies of the mission, disabled by sickness-- one of them helpless--were sent home, and with the advice of his colleagues he accompanied them. He was himself suffering with fever.

After his return, he preached in Limerick, ME, and then in 1877, he entered the Theological School, studying the original languages of the Bible and afterwards completed the progressive course of the Correspondence School of the American Institute of Hebrew.

He was married to Miss Hattie G. Parrott of Cape Elizabeth, ME, on Oct. 1, 1885. They have a son, bn Nov. 13, 1886. After about two years he, pastored churches in ME and NH, and beginning in Aug. 1877, he entered upon pastorate at Block Island, R.I.

He was delegate to General Conference in 1889.

He was a useful minister, pastor and theologian.

John Fullonton
Birth:
Aug. 8, 1812
Death:
Apr. 17, 1896
Burial:
Riverside Cemetery
Lewiston
Androscoggin County
Maine
Plot: 0605W

He graduated from Dartsmouth College, 1840. He was a teacher at Parsonfield, Whitestown Seminary and studied for the ministry at Whitestown Biblical School. He was ordained at Whitestown, Jan. 5, 1845. Then he became a professor of Hebrew and Church History, and after 1851 of Ecclesiastical History and Pastoral Theology at Whitestown Biblical School, 1850-4; New Hampton Theological Institution, 1854-77; and Bates Theological School, 1877-98. Delegate to the General Conference, 1847.Editor of The Dartmouth, 1839-40. Assistant Editor o the Morning Star 1839-98. D.D. from Dartmouth College, 1869.

William F Gallison
Birth:
Windham,
Me,
Jan. 14, 1799
Death:
Mar. 9, 1858
Burial:
Dover Cemetery,
Dover-Foxcroft,
Piscataquis County,
Maine,
Plot: North Section, Row 3

At age eighteen, he professed Christ, and was baptized by Rev. C. Phinney in Feb. 1817. He moved to eastern Maine at age twenty-five, and settled in Charlotte. He united with the Christian church in that place and maintained an outward life beyond reproach. He served his townsmen as officer in the militia and as magistrate. In 1832, he was a member of the State Legislature. In 1834, moving to Dover, Me, he joined the Free Will Baptist church, and the next year began his gospel ministry. He had in early life received a good academic education. He was licensed by the Sebec Quarterly Meeting, in January, 1840, and was ordained in Dover, July 8, 1841. His labors in the ministry were confined mostly to the Sebec Q.M. Fourteen ministers attended his funeral.

Rev Danville A Gammon
Birth:
Jul. 20, 1861
Canton, Maine
Death:
Dec. 26, 1910
Burial:
Roxbury Village Cemetery
Roxbury
Oxford County
Maine

Rev. Danville A. Gammon, son of Charles E. and Matilda T.(Brown) Gammon. He studied at Maine Central Institute. He was licensed to preach Dec. 9, 1886, and ordained Jan. 1, 1889. He was pastor of the Weld church from November, 1886 to April, 1888. He then became pastor of the Second Wilton and Chesterville churches. He married Carrie A. Locke, on May 6, 1891, in Maine.

Mark Gatchell
Birth:
May 17, 1812
Litchfield
Kennebec County Maine
Death:
Jul. 28, 1887
Burial:
Litchfield Plains Cemetery,
Litchfield Plains,
Kennebec County, Maine

He became a Christian under the labors of the Rev. Dexter Waterman and was baptized at the age of 16. He began to preach at the age of 20 and was licensed two years afterwards. He was ordained by a council at the Bowdoin Quarterly Meeting at 24 years of age. He pastored many churches in Maine and records show that he was asked 25 times to harmonize difficulties in churches. He was a member of the legislature the year that a grant was made to the Maine State Seminary.

Rev Benjamin S Gerry
Birth:
May, 1821
Freedom
Waldo County, Maine
Death:
Feb. 19, 1885
Dexter
Penobscot County, Maine
Burial:
Mount Pleasant Cemetery
Dexte, Penobscot County, Maine

He was born in Freedom, Waldo Co. ME, where he lived until six yrs of age, when his parents moved to Dover. He lived there until 1864 when he bought a farm near Dexter where he resided until his death.

In 1846, he married Miss Maranda Rowe, of South Dover, in whom he found a worth companion and helper. He was converted at the age of thirteen and baptized at the age of nineteen and united with the Methodists.

He afterwards, from doctrinal conviction, joined the Free Baptist church at South Dover, and later the West Sangerville church, of which he was pastor many years and a member at the time of his death. In 1853 he began to preach. He was ordained in 1858 at So. Dover, Rev. E. Harding preaching the sermon. His ministry was mostly within the limits of the Penobscot Yearly Meeting (Y.M.) and especially in the Exeter and Sebec Quarterly Meetings (Q.M.) and especially in the Exeter and Sebec Q.M's. He held pastorates in Corinth, First and Second Sangerville, Corinna, Bradford, LaGrange, Charleston, Abbott, Atkinson, and Ornesville. He also preached at Nmber Eight (Willimantic). Revival interests followed his labors and many were converted. He was deeply interested in missions, temperance and education, and a father in his Q.M. For twenty-one consecutive years he was its clerk, and during that time he was absent but once. He was a good and faithful man.

William Getchell
Birth:
Dec. 6, 1793
Vassalborough, Me.,
Death:
Oct. 30, 1867
Pittsfield, Me.
Burial:
Carr Cemetery
Pittsfield, Somerset County,
Maine

He married, Aug. 22, 1814, Miss Mary Leavitt, of Clinton. In the summer of 1818 he was converted and united with the Christian church at East Pittsfield. In August, 1823, having moved to another part of Pittsfield, he was instrumental in organizing a Freewill Baptist church and was chosen one of its deacons. In September 1826 he was ordained by a council from the Exeter Q. M. as pastor of the church with which he was connected. This relation he held till death. He also acted as pastor of the Second Pittsfield church and of the Burnham church for over twenty years. He solemnized over one hundred and fifty marriages and attended hundreds of funerals.

Rev Orison L Gile
Birth:
Oct. 22, 1857
Bennington
Hillsborough County
New Hampshire
Death:
May 31, 1892
Burial:
Ridge Road Cemetery
Bowdoinham
Sagadahoc County
Maine

"Rev. Orison L. Gile, was the son of P.S.H. and Mary B. (Dodge) Gile, and was born in Bennington NH, Oct. 22, 1856. He became a Christian at the age of sixteen. He prepared for college at New Hampton Institution, NH, from 1875-1878, graduated from Bates College, Lewiston, ME, in 1883, and from Bates Theological School in 1886. He received license to preach from the Weare Q.M., NH, Feb. 1880, and was ordained at Richmond,

ME June 8, 1886, by Rev's C.F. Penney, J.B. Jordan, A.B. Drew, R.W. Churchill, C.E. Cate and others.
He was pastor at Lisbon Falls during his course of study, also of the Pine Street church, Lewiston, two years. He has been instrumental in a large number of conversions and has received sixty-two persons into the churches. He was in 1887 pastor at Richmond Village, ME, and in 1888 at Cape Elizabeth.
He was married, Jan. 1, 1884, to Miss Linda E. NELSON, who died. In June, 1887, he married Miss Sarah E. Libby, or Richmond Village."

Harry O Gidney
Birth:
July 9, 1829
Cambridge
New Brunswick
Canada
Death:
Nov. 11, 1895
Maine
Burial:
South Amity Cemetery
South Amity
Aroostook County, Maine

He became a Christian at the age of 20. In 1860 he moved on Houlton, Maine, where he lived 16 years and then moved on to Amity where he resided for some time. He received license in 1868 and was ordained in the same year. His pastorates were at the Glenwood church, a Littleton, second Hodgdon, and other churches in that area of Maine. He had revivals in each of the churches where he pastored and baptized over 100 converts. He organized a Littleton and Haynesville churches.

Capt Philip Gilkey, Sr
Birth:
Jan. 25, 1788
Islesboro
Waldo County, Maine
Death:
Jan. 5, 1872
Searsport
Waldo County, Maine
Burial:
Gordon Cemetery
Searsport, Waldo County, Maine

He lived in Islesborough till forty years of age, and the rest of his life in Searsport. He was converted in youth, but did not decide to preach till he was more than fifty years of age. He was then a Baptist. His first efforts were in the town of Eden, Mt. Desert, where some were converted. He was then ordained by the Free Baptists, and preached mostly in Eden. Philip was married to Jane Pendleton (1789 - 1821) They had 7 children. After Jane died, Philip married Deborah Cushing (1787 - 1865). They had 6 children. Deborah was the widow of Philip's brother Jacob. After Deborah died, Philip married Judith Pendleton (1794- 1892), they had no children.

Rev Arthur Given
Birth:
Feb. 27, 1841
Wales Corner
Androscoggin County,Maine

Death:
Feb. 22, 1925
Maine
Burial:
Riverside Cemetery
Lewiston
Androscoggin CountyMaine
Plot: 0267

His father bore the same name, and was a highly esteemed citizen, whose occupation was that of a farmer. Previous to the age of eighteen the son was employed part of the time on the farm, attended the district school, spent one term at the Litchfield Liberal Institute, and another at the Maine State Seminary at Lewiston.

At this age he was released from further service at home, and commenced his perparation for college at the last named institution. He secured the means to pay his expenses by teaching and manual labor. Subsequent to the completion of this preparatory course of study, in 1862, he served nine months in the army.

In the fall of 1863 he entered Bates College, and graduated in 1867 in a class of eight, the first graduating class of the college. He was its valedictorian.

He became at once principal of the New Hampton Literary Institution, and after a year of successful service, resigned, and was for two years principal of Maine State Seminary at Lewiston.

From 1870 to 1872 he was a student in the theological department of Bates College, and during part of the time was a tutor in the college.

In September, 1872, he became pastor of the Essex Street church at Bangor, and was ordained in the December following by the Unity Quarterly Meeting. He continued in this relation until March, 1875, when he became pastor of the church at Greenville, R.I. In February, 1881, he resigned this position to become the joint pastor of the church at Auburn and of a mission of the Rogers Williams church at Arlington. In 1883 he relinquished Arlington, and in 1885 he resigned his Auburn parish to become general treasurer of the benevolent societies of the denomination. During his pastorate at Auburn there was begun the erection of a large and commodious house of worship which was dedicated early in 1889.

Since 1873 he has been one of the board of overseers of Bates College, and in 1880 was chosen its secretary. For several years he has been a member of the executive board of the Education Society, and 1880-85 its corresponding secretary. He was till 1885 the secretary of the Rhode Island Sunday-School Union, and for several years clerk of the Rhode Island Association.In July, 1889 he was elected a corporator of the "Star." He married Dec. 22, 1868, Miss Lura Durgin, sister to Mrs. John Malvern, of Sanbornton, N.H., and has one daughter.

He had a brother, Rev. Lincoln Given, b. 1827, who was a

teacher/minister to Maine Freewill Baptist churches.

Lincoln Given
Birth:
Nov. 7, 1827
Wells, Maine
Death:
Oct. 8, 1894
Maine
Burial:
Pond Road Cemetery
Androscoggin County
Maine

He was a brother of the Arthur Given. He was converted at the age of 15 and was baptized by Rev. E. J. Eaton and United with the church in Wales in the spring of 1843. He received his early education at Litchfield Institute, and his theological in the Biblical School at New Hampton. In June 1854 he received license to preach from the Bowdoin Quarterly Meeting and in June 19,1859 he was ordained at a session of the Springfield Quarter Meeting At Weston by Rev. L. M. Hagget and others. Most of his pastorates was in Maine and New Hampshire. However he did spend 18 months in Minnesota and six months in Illinois where many were converted for his efforts. He was a member of the General Conference three different times. He taught 15 terms of school and served as a supervisor 15 years. In 1851 he married Miss Lucy A. Colby who died in 1869 and afterwards he married in December 1873 Miss Carrie Weymount.

Rev Cleaveland B Glidden
Birth:
Sep. 28, 1822
Woolwich
Sagadahoc County, Maine
Death:
May 15, 1864
Gardiner
Kennebec County, Maine
Burial:
South Gardiner Cemetery

South Gardiner
Kennebec County, Maine

Rev. Cleaveland B. Glidden, died after an illness of three days in Gardiner, ME, May 15, 1864. He was born in Woolwich, ME, Sept. 28, 1821(sic). At sixteen he was converted, baptized by Rev. C. Quinnam and united with the church in his native place. After a struggle he yielded to God and began his ministry. He was ordained in Gardiner, July 5, 1855, and settled with the First church there. He was also pastor at West Gardiner, Jefferson, Whitefield, and five years of the Monmouth church.
His funeral services were conducted by Rev. J. Mariner in the meeting-house at South Gardiner. He was an upright Christian and a humble, devoted minister of the gospel.

Barnard Goodrich
Birth:
1800
Nottingham, N. H.
Death:
Mar. 20, 1883
Burial:
Ripp Cemetery
West Gardiner
Kennebec County, Maine

He became a Christian in early life. About 1831 he moved to Maine. He preached and baptized in Monmouth, West Gardiner, Greene, Litchfield, South Gardiner and Richmond. He supported himself at the trade of blacksmith and preached as opportunity
Offered.

Joseph Goodwin
Birth:
Jul. 10, 1788
Death:
Mar. 21, 1850
Wells, Maine
Burial:
Goodwin Cemetery
Oxford County, Maine

He was converted in 1801, and on August 28 joined the Baptist church. The next year his name appears as one of the committee who transcribed the articles of faith and records of this newly organized church. Later difficulties some years distracted the church and the radical preaching of the election by the pastor caused some to question the doctrine. He and 13 others were expelled on June 4, 1807. They associated themselves for worship with himself as the leader. In 1808 a revival followed and a Free Baptist church was organized over which he was ordained as pastor in 1812 and for 13 years this relationship existed. He supported his family by labor in the ship-yards but his excellent gift of exhortation frequently gave him wholely to the Lord's work.

Oh! How precious is the dust of a believer!

Rev William Gowell
Birth:
Mar. 6, 1808
Androscoggin County
Maine
Death:
Jan. 1, 1884
Poland
Androscoggin County
Maine
Burial:
Mount Auburn Cemetery
Auburn
Androscoggin County
Maine

Spouses: Abigail Penny Gowell (___ - 1845), Prudence Moulton Gowell (___ - 1886)*

Inscription:
75 years 8 months 26 days

John Grant
Birth:
Unknown
Death:
Oct. 25, 1882
Bucksport
Hancock County,
Maine
Burial:
Oak Hill Cemetery
Bucksport
Hancock County, Maine

He was a native of the Province of New Brunswick, but moved to Maine in 1839. He was converted to the age of 16 and publicly professed Christ eight years later and in 1842 was baptized uniting with the Hodgdon church. He was licensed by this church in 1859 and ordained a few years later. His preaching was characterized by interesting expositions of Scripture.

Andrew Gray
Birth:
Sep. 2, 1823
Brooksville, Maine
Death:
Mar. 24, 1901
Burial:
Otter Creek Cemetery
Hancock County, Maine

He was converted at the age of 28, and was licensed to preach on December 12, 1854 and ordained on June 17, 1872. He had for pastors and baptize 83 converts at four churches.

Stephen Gross
Birth:
unknown
Death:
Nov. 27, 1887
East Bucksport
Hancock County, Maine
Burial:
Granite Cemetery
Orland
Hancock County, Maine

He died at age 85 and his wife only two days later. Throughout his earnest early ministry many of the churches in the Ellsworth Quarterly meeting were strengthened, if not planning. He was loyal to his denomination and an early subscriber and devoted reader of *The Morning Star*. He was earnest in securing the salvation and especialty of the young, and in urging them to seek good learning as an advantage for their life work. Throughout his faithfulness many found their saviour.

S. M. Haggett
Birth:
Nov. 8, 1818
Edgecomb
Lincoln County, Maine
Death:
Aug. 23, 1878
Springfield
Penobscot County, Maine
Burial:
Mills Cemetery
Springfield, Penobscot County, Maine

At the age of seventeen he became a Christian and united with the church in his native town. Soon he felt called to the ministry, and received encouragement from the church.In 1840, he went to Parsonfield Seminary, and was a student there three years. The Edgecomb Q.M. gave him license in 1842. He traveled and preached in New Hampshire and Vermont with good success. From 1845 to 1849, he preached in Penobscot. In 1849 he settled at Monroe. The next year, in June, he was ordained by the Prospect Quarterly Meeting. After several years at Monroe he went to North Bangor, where many were converted under his labors. At this place in 1852, he married Miss Delia H. Rollin.The next year he preached in the Springfield Q.M. At Chester he held meetings and where he organized a church. He was a delegate to General Conference in 1856. The same year he became pastor of the Springfield church. He served as clerk of the Q.M. sixteen years and attended all its sessions and all the Yearly Meetings. He was the town clerk nine years. In 1871, he resigned the pastorate of the Springfield and Carroll church, and in 1873 he served as missionary in the Springfield Q.M. The next two years he preached in Gardiner, ME, and then returned to Springfield. He baptized over four hundred, and attended over eight hundred funerals.

Rev Turner Hanson

Birth:
May 27, 1810
Death:
Apr. 3, 1876
Burial:
Saint Albans Village Cemetery
Saint Albans
Somerset County
Maine

An ordained Free Baptist minister in Maine, whose death was in the list of names of ministers who had died. He was listed as being from St. Albans.

Ephraim Harding

Birth:
December 23, 1809
New Sharon, Maine
Death:
1892
Burial:
Corinthian Cemetery
Corinth
Penobscot County, Maine
Plot: Div. 3 Lot 25

His father was Jedediah Harding M.D. who was buried at sea when Ephraim was only 13 months old. At the age of seven he was sent away on among strangers. He was converted on October 25, 1825, at the age of 13 and was baptized by Rev. Samuel Hutchins, united with the church in his native town. In 1838, he began to preach and on October 13 received his license. January 29, 1843, he was ordained at New Portland by the Anson Quarterly Meeting. He was pastor of 14 churches and had revivals in 15. He baptized over 150 people. He organized eight churches during his ministry. Five times he was a delegate to the General Conference and wants to the Free Christian Baptist Conference of New Brunswick.

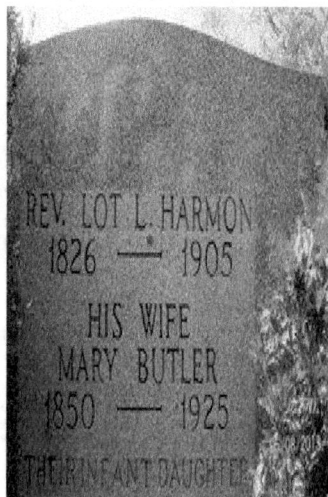

REV. LOT L. HARMON
1826 — 1905
HIS WIFE
MARY BUTLER
1850 — 1925
THEIR INFANT DAUGHTER

Lot L Harmon
Birth:
1826
Madison, New Hampshire
Death:
1905
Burial:
Mount Auburn Cemetery
Auburn
Androscoggin County, Maine

He became a Christian when 10 years old and studied at Parsonsfield Seminary and Bangor Theological Seminary. He was licensed in 1856, and was ordained March 5, 1857 by Rev's. M.J. Steere, P. S. Burbank and J. R. Cook. He pastored churches throughout the area and after graduating from the Seminary he continued to pastor the North Bangor church and made a specialty of Sunday school work, mostly in Maine. Being a gifted musician and singer, sometimes for weeks he talked and sang with the children three or 3 1/2 hours a day. He was a member of the Maine legislature in 1866 and assisted in getting the charter of

the Maine Central Institute. He was a general agent of the Sunday School Union from 1868 to 1883 and recording Sec. of Free Baptist Sunday School Union from 1877 to 1882. Before he entered the ministry he was a justice of the peace and had charge of schools in Madison, New Hampshire.

Ephraim H. Hart
Birth:
June 11,1809
Death:
Jan. 4, 1877
Lynn, Mass.
Burial:
Hiram Village Cemetery
Hiram
Oxford County
Maine

He studied at Parsonsfield Seminary and Strafford Academy. He was licensed in 1838 and ordained at Brownfield, Me. Dec. 23, 1840.

Most of his ministry was in Maine. Spouse: Frances B. Hart (1815 - 1897)

Samuel Hathorn
Birth:
Sep. 14, 1794
Bowdoinham
Sagadahoc County,
Maine
Death:
Dec. 13, 1858
West Gardiner
Kennebec County,
Maine
Burial:
Ridge Road Cemetery
Bowdoinham
Sagadahoc County,
Maine

Rev. Samuel Hathorn was converted in 1817 in revival conducted by Asa Foster. He was active and consecrated, and 1819, in connection with Andrew Rollins and one other, he purchased a tract of land and began clearing it. In Jan. 1821, Rollins began to preach, and Hathorn soon sold the land and began his labors with the Rock River church in the vicinity in Sept. 1825. The First Church in town grew from this church. He was licensed by the Bowdoinham Quarterly Meeting, in Oct 1825, and Jan. 12, 1826 was ordained. After an itinerant ministry of five or six years in his QM, he extended labors over the state. Late in 1836 he went to Indiana and after a brief visit to Maine in the summer of 1837, he returned and settled at Milan, Ripley Co. Indiana with his wife, and lived there three years. Finding the climate ill suited to their health, they returned to the home of their early years. Before 1844, he had made four tours through the Western States. In 1852, his wife died of consumption. In July 1853 he married Cordelia Clough, who survived him. They spent the following winter in the Western States and on their return to Maine they purchased a farm at West Gardiner. He preached his last sermon May 30, 1050 at Bowdoinham Ridge from Hosea 6:3. He spoke of his uninterrupted peace and joy, and of the brightness of his hope beyond. During his ministry he baptized 1350 persons. Many churches were gathered and organized.

George W Haskell
Birth:
Dec.9, 1814.
Poland,ME.
Death:
Dec. 31, 1874
Hodgdon, Aroostook County, Me.
Burial:
Hodgdon Cemetery
Hodgdon,
Aroostook County, Maine

He became a Christian in early life, and resisted for some time a call from God to the ministry. He was ordained in 1840, and after three years of very successful evangelistic work, moved to Aroostook County. In 1844 he married Miss Hannah M. Smith, of Hodgdon, and resided in the town of Hodgdon the remainder of his life. His labors in Aroostook County were very extensive, and resulted in the conversion of about one thousand, the most of whom he baptized. His last work for the Master was the erection of the house of worship at Hodgdon. He identified himself with the anti-slavery movement, and represented his district in the Legislature in 1855, 1866, and 1867. As the result of his benevolence and large heartedness, he had great popularity.

Inscription:
In Memory of
Rev George W Haskell
Died Dec. 31, 1874 AE 60 yrs
He being dead yet speaketh

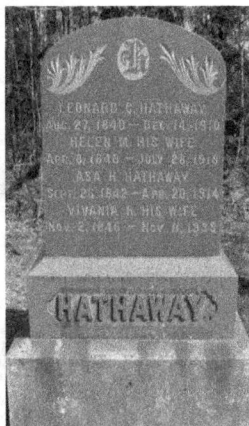

Asa Hathaway
Birth:
Sep. 26, 1842
Atkinson, Maine
Death:
Apr. 20, 1914
Burial:
Hathaway Cemetery
Garland
Penobscot County, Maine

He was educated in the public schools of his time and converted in 1875 and ordained in September, 1884. He was the father of Rev. Leonard Hathaway who also served in Maine. He married Vivania R. Batchelder Hathaway (1846 - 1933) on January 5, 1869.

Leonard Hathaway
Birth:
1802
Middleborough, Mass.,
Death:
Nov. 7, 1876
Burial:
Hathaway Cemetery
Garland, Penobscot County,
Maine

A preacher in the F.W.Baptist Denomination fifty-one years. Ordained in 1826. His labors have been in Maine. Died at age 74 yrs.29 ds.

*Inscription:
Front *I have finished the work which thou gavest me to do.*
Back:*The gospel which he preached for more than fifty years sustained him to the last.*
Right:*Faithfully he done the work of the ministry Firmly he kept the faith Surely he wears the crown. Sacred is his memory.*

Rev Wilson Warren Hayden
Birth:
Apr. 28, 1856
Maine
Death:
Jan. 7, 1932
Burial:
South Dover Cemetery
Dover-Foxcroft
Piscataquis County, Maine
Plot: South Section, Row

"Hayden, Rev. Wilson Warren, son of H. W. and Cynthia A. (Bigelow) Hayden, was born in Corinna, Me. He was converted when eleven years of age. He prepared for college in the Corinna Union Academy and the Maine Central Institute, finishing in 1876. He graduated from Bates College, Lewiston, in 1881, and from Bates Theological School in 1884. June 7, 1882, he received license to preach from the Exeter Q. M., and Aug. 14, 1884, was ordained by the Lisbon Q. M., N. H., and became pastor of the Whitefield church. June 17, 1884, he married Miss Cora R. Lambert.

Benjamin Francis Hayes
Birth:
Mar. 28, 1830
New Gloucester
Cumberland County, Maine
Death:
Feb. 27, 1906
Lewiston
Androscoggin County, Maine
Burial:
Riverside Cemetery
Lewiston
Androscoggin County, Maine
Plot: 0304

Rev. Benjamin Francis Hayes, D.D. son of Rev. Jesse and Mary (Harmon) Hayes. He fitted for college at the Lewiston Falls Academy (Edward Little Institute), Auburn, ME. He graduated from Bowdoin College in 1855, and from the Theological Seminary at New Hampton, N.H. in 1858. He was a teacher of sciences and German in New Hampton Literary Institution 1855-59. Converted in 1843, he was baptized in August. He was ordained in 1859 by the Rhode Island Association and May 1st entered upon a pastorate at Olneyville, R.I.

August, 1863, he became principal of Lapham Institute, which office he filled till July 1865. Since that date he has been professor in Bates College (professor of modern languages 1865-69, of intellectual and moral philosophy since 1869); and since 1873 he has been also professor of exegetical theology in the theological department of the college.

He studied at Halle, Germany, with Ulrici, 1873-74. He was appointed acting president of the college 1877-78, during the absence of the president in Europe. He has been connected with our schools or colleges as teacher or superintendent ever since his graduation in 1855.

He has been vice-president and acting president of the Foreign Mission Society, member of the Home Mission, Education, and (since 1873) the Printing Establishment boards. In 1862 he was a delegate to General Conference, and in 1880 preached the centennial sermon at Weir's. He married Aug. 12, 1856, Miss Arcy Carry, dau. Of Francis and Sally Cary, of Turner, ME. (From ME Birth records).Of Prof. Hayes' three children, Rev. Francis L. Hayes is pastor at Boston, and Elizabeth is wife of Rev. A. E. Cox." Another son, is Elwood Cary Hayes, b. 1868, m. Annie Lee Bean, 21 Oct. 1895.

Rev Jesse Hayes
Birth:
1797
Death:
1865
Burial:
Riverside Cemetery
Lewiston
Androscoggin County
Maine

Father of Benjamin Francis Hayes who was a noted theologian and once president of Bates College.

Joseph Higgins
Birth:
1776
Death:
1837
Burial:
Thorndike Center Cemetery
Thorndike, Waldo County,
Maine

Rev. Joseph Higgins of Thorndike, Maine, aged 91 years, and his wife, Betsey Higgins, aged 89 years, both died on the 5th of February, 1867, and within ten hours of each other, by no especial sickness except the gradual breaking down of old age. Father Higgins was born in Eastham, Mass., in 1776. Mother Higgins, whose maiden name was Files, was born in Gorham, Maine, in 1778. He came to Thorndike, then called Lincoln Plantation, and felled the first tree on the farm where he ever afterwards lived, in 1797, being one of the very first settlers in town. They were married in 1804, were blessed with eight children, all of whom lived to have families of their own. One of the two sons, Joseph Higgins, Esq., has always lived on the farm with his father and had three children. Still there had never been a death on that dear old homestead until father and mother Higgins passed over the Jordan together. He retained his mental faculties and physical strength in an unusual manner - enjoying life, and contributing to the enjoyment of others till the last days of his life. She was a devoted and cheerful Christian and a most affectionate wife and mother, and although her memory failed, and she was quite childish for the last few years, yet her happy disposition and social, buoyant spirit continued with her to the end. Father Higgins had a good education for his time and taught the first three schools ever taught in Thorndike.

He experienced religion in 1803 and joined the Freewill Baptist Church organized there in that year. He commenced preaching in 1806 and was ordained in 1811. He was an honor to his profession to the day of his death. He worked on his farm through the week and preached on the Sabbathentirely without salary, as was the custom in those days. His preaching was candid, Practical, and very scriptural, the Bible being his chief book of study. The Freewill Baptist Church in Thorndike owes much of its strength and prosperity to father Higgins. For years he preached and lived when many ministers would have been discouraged. And for many years last past, having voluntarily resigned the pastorate, his life, advice, sympathy and means have been a great help to those who have ministered to that church and people. He was a most conscientious and exemplary man in his daily life, showing love to God, man and his country. He was prompt and accurate in his business affairs and quite successful in temporal as well as spiritual things. They gave their eight children a good home and school education, so that they are among the most respectable and influential members of society. Seven of them are living, and they were all present at the funeral, and the aged parents lived to see all their children worthy members of Christian churches. Their life work so perfectly done, there is a pleasing sublimity in the fact that these venerable parents were taken together from earth to heaven. And it adds to the moral grandeur of the scene when we remember that it can literally and truthfully be said of them in the language of scripture, "And they were both righteous before God, walking in all the commandments and ordinances of the Lord blameless." (Written by E. Knowlton in *the "Morning Star"*

Albert G. Hill
Birth:
Apr. 27, 1838
Newfield
York County, Maine
Death:
Jan. 26, 1907
Garland
Penobscot County, Maine
Burial:
Mount Pleasant Cemetery
Dexter
Penobscot County, Maine
He attended the Parsonfield Seminary and New Hampton Institution. In 1858 he was converted and was licensed in 1867 and ordained by the Cumberland Quarterly Meeting in 1869.

Elder Henry Hobbs, Sr
Birth:
Mar. 3, 1768
Berwick
York County
Maine
Death: Mar. 20, 1848
Waterboro
York County
Maine
Burial:
Hobbs/Knights Cemetery
Waterboro
York County
Maine

Rev James W. Hinckley
Birth:
Mar. 12, 1827
Industry
Franklin County
Maine
Death:
Aug. 22, 1908
Burial:
Mount Rest Cemetery
Athens
Somerset County
Maine

"Rev. James W. Hinckley, son of Josiah and Mercy (Williams) Hinckley. He was converted on this thirtieth birthday, and Jan. 3, 1862, received license. He was ordained Dec. 25, 1863, and has been pastor of the Brighton, Athens, Harmony, Cambridge, and Parkman churches, where in eight years he baptized thirty converts. He now (1887) resided at Athens and supplies as occasion requires. On Jan. 23, 1850, he married Miss Mary J. Ladd.

Rev. Henry Hobbs, Sr., began to preach in 1798, and strengthened the church in Waterborough, which had recently been reorganized with eight members by P(elatiah) Tingley. The rest of the church had gone with their pastor to the Baptists.

In January, 1800, he visited the Farmington Q.M. with John Buzzell, and assisted in quieting the Locke trouble. He was ordained in Standish, May 22, 1801.

He was one of the original peitioners in 1804 to the Legislature of Massachusetts for a recognition and incorporation of the "Freewill Anti-pedo

Baptists" of Maine. It was his sonorous voice which was heard over a mile distant during the grove reformation in August 1808, and which brought Rev. Henry Leach to a sense of his sin. He was clerk of the Parsonfield Q.M.(Quarterly Meeting), and treasurer of the "Maine Freewill Baptist Charitable Society" from its organization, Nov. 27, 1824.

In 1825 he was one of the nine who assumed financial responsibility for the publication of the first "Morning Star." In February, 1826, he was chairman of the meeting at which the legal company was organized for the publication of the paper. The printing house was known as Hobbs, Woodman & Co. From this press John Buzzell issued his "Life of Benjamin Randall," in 1827.

H. Hobbs was six years a proprietor of the "Morning Star," and in 1832 was on the publishing committee for a year. He was one of the committee of twelve to whom the call for a General Conference of the denomination was referred by the Y.M.(Yearly Meeting) at Parsonfield in November, 1826. He was a member of the Second General Conference in 1828, and chairman of the business and standing committees. He was moderator of the third General Conference and preached the opening sermon. He also sat in the fifth and sixth sessions of the General Conference.

He represented the district of Maine in the Massachusetts Legislature, and was a member of the convention which drafted the constitution of Maine. He subsequently served in the Legislature, and was on the Governor's council several times. He was a man of strong mind and good business tact. He was an exellent presiding officer. Rev. O.H. Tracy is a great-grandson."

Andrew Hobson
Birth:
Sep. 10, 1795
Buxton,
York County, Maine
Death:
May 1, 1877
Cambridge,
Middlesex County,
Massachusetts
Burial:
Steep Falls Cemetery,
Steep Falls,
Cumberland County, Maine

He was converted at age 21, under the labors of Rev. Clement Phinney, was baptized by Rev. Jonathan Clay, and united with the Free Baptist church in Buxton. He began to preach in 1821, and was ordained two years after. He pastored several churches, including So. Gorham,

Buxton, fifteen yrs and built a new meeting house there, Fort Hill, Steep Falls, ten yrs. He returned to Steep Falls in 1862, and in ten years baptized over fifty. In 1871, he entered upon his last pastorate which was at Hollis. He was one of a committee of twelve in favor of establishing a General Conference, and was a member of the first and of several other General Conferences. He was one of the original trustees of the "Morning Star" (newspaper). Every genuine interest received his sympathy. He had one son, Pelatiah M. who became a Free Will Baptist minister.

Pelatiah M. Hobson
Birth:
Jul. 20, 1818
West Buxton,
York County, Maine
Death:
Jan. 8, 1888
Steep Falls,
Cumberland County, Maine
Burial:
Steep Falls Cemetery,
Steep Falls,
Cumberland County, Maine

He was educated at Parsonfield Seminary (later Bates) and Gorham Academy, and was a member of the first class in the Biblical School at Parsonsfield. He received license from the Gorham Quarterly Meeting in 1842, and was ordained by the Bowdoin QM, at Bath, ME, in July, 1843.He was pastor of the North Street church, Bath, and remained two years, baptizing about twenty. He engaged in business with his father at Steep Falls. He helped build up the church there, which was organized in 1847. Beginning in the spring of 1856, he was pastor of this church three years, and added sixty to its membership, forty by baptism.

Alphonso L Houghton
Birth:
May 3, 1847
Weld, Me
Death:
Oct. 2, 1881
Weld, Me
Burial:
Oak Grove Cemetery
Bath, Sagadahoc County, Maine

He was the eldest child of Azel E. and Betsey (Hawes) Houghton. "When about sixteen years of age he became a Christian, was baptized by Rev. Orin Pitts and united with the church. He graduated from Bates College in 1870, as valedictorian of his class, and at once entered the Theological School. During this course he was a tutor in the college. In May, 1872, he received a unanimous call to the church in Lawrence, Mass. He accepted the call and began his labors there in July ; was ordained and installed Sept. 4. Jan. I, 1873, he married Miss Hattie B. Mallet, of Bath, Me., in whose death, three years later, he was grievously afflicted. He held the pastorate eight years, when broken health compelled him to resign. As a minister, the scholar and pastor were most finely blended. He was an organizer. Besides the addition of nearly three hundred members to the church during his pastorate, he trained the church into such order and efficiency that, when he was cut off, the church went on steadily with its work. For several years he served on the school committee in Lawrence. He was a member of the executive board of the Foreign Mission Society, and a trustee of Bates College. He left his excellent library and $1,000 to this institution, $500 to the permanent fund of the Bible School in India, and a microscope and cabinet of minerals to Maine Central Institute. After seeking recovery in Europe and in Colorado, he returned to his native place shortly before his death.

Francis Howard
Birth:
Nov. 2, 1810
Ward, Maine
Death:
Feb. 11, 1892
Washington
Knox County, spaceMaine
Burial:
Howard Cemetery
Knox County, Maine

His conversion happened when he was 13 years of age. In 1843 he was licensed and the same year ordained. He labored in many revivals and was a pastor eight years. He has baptized 74 and attended 412 funerals.

Rev. Richard L. HOWARD
Birth:
Mar. 24, 1824
Oxford
Chenango County
New York
Death:
Dec. 11, 1902
Limerick
York County
Maine
Burial:
Highland Cemetery
Limerick
York County
Maine
Plot: Tier 10--3

"Rev. Richard L. HOWARD was the brother of Rev. Geo.H. Howard, His parents were Anson M. and Bershabee L. (Lawrence) HOWARD. His father was clerk of the Susquehanna Y.M.., and of the Owego Q.M. He was baptized by Rev. Asa Dodge, at the age of ten, and reclaimed when thirty-two years of age, beginning to preach the next year. He received an academic education in the town of Union, N.Y. In June 1857, he was licensed, and in December was ordained by the Boone Co. Q.M., Ill., to preach for the Freewill Baptists. He organized two churches in Moniteau Co. Missouri, and baptized thirty or more, among whom was his brother, Rev. G.H. Howard.

He labored with the churches in the Quincy Q.M., Ill, and was pastor of all its churches, organizing two and baptizing over two hundred.

He enlisted in the summer of 1862, as first Lieutenant in the 124th Ill. Infantry, and had command of his company through the Vicksburg campaign under Grant; was promoted to the chaplaincy in Sept. 1863, and served till the close of the war.

In 1865 he became pastor of the Commerce church, Mich. In 1870 he took chqarge of the "*Christian Freeman,*" Chicago, and after a year settled with the Mt. Pleasant church at Racine, Wis. He was called to Fairport, N.Y., in 1873; to the Pine St. church, Lewiston, ME, in 1876; to Bangor in 1879, and in March 1885, he entered pastorate at Franconia, N.H. In these churches he has baptized over five hundred. He raised the debt of the Bangor church, of $3,000, in his last winter there. He is a member of the executive committee of the Home Mission Society, and has been a member of General Conferences in 1868, 1874, 1880 and 1886. He was trustee of Hillsdale College ten years, of Maine Central Institute six years, a trustee of the New Hampton Institution, N.H. While in Maine he was president of the Maine State Sunday-School Association two years, and chaplain of the Grand Army in Maine eight years.

He has published a history of his regiment. He was on the school board of Bangor five years, the last three chairman, and done similar service at Franconia. Sept. 3, 1853, he married Miss Clara J. Nelson, it being his second marriage, and had three children. Among whom was the Rev. George N. Howard."

Rev James A Howe
Birth:
Oct. 10, 1834
Massachusetts
Death:
Dec. 29, 1918
Lewiston
Androscoggin County, Maine
Burial:
Riverside Cemetery
Lewiston
Androscoggin County, Maine
Plot: 0643

Rev. James A. Howe, D.D., (Hillsdale College, 1876) brother of Rev. Geo. W. Howe, was raised near Centralville, by pious parents, serving in the Lowell church for over forty-two years as most useful members. Their home was known for its Christian hospitality. James A. was converted under the labors of Rev. O.T. Moulton, and soon after united with the church. He studied a term at Smithville Seminary and another at North Hampton, NH. He prepared for college with his elder brother under the able teacher, and in 1856 entered the sophomore class of Bowdoin College, graduating in 1859.He studied in the Biblical School at New Hampton, and at Andover Seminary, and accepted the church at Blackstone, Mass., where he was ordained by the Rhode Island Association. The next year he married Miss Rachel E. Rogers of Upper Stillwater, ME.After a pastorate of eighteen months he was pastor for over eight years at Olneyville, R.I. Here he added 104 to the church, sixty-two of them by baptism. He resigned in 1872, to accept a chair of theology in the theological department of Bates College.

John Hull
Birth:
unknown
Death:
Aug. 19, 1829
Livermore
Androscoggin County
Maine
Burial:
Turner Village Cemetery
Turner
Androscoggin County
Maine

In Freewill Baptist records as a minister. Aged 31. He was of Nova Scotia.

Eld Samuel Hutchins
Birth:
Nov. 29, 1790
New Portland, Me.
Death:
Apr. 9, 1876
West Waterville, Me.
Burial:
East New Portland Cemetery
New Portland, Somerset County,
Maine

He was converted when twelve years of age, and began to preach at the age of nineteen. In 1810, at the age of twenty, he was ordained and became the first settled minister in New Portland. Previous to his marriage, he taught school and preached in Madison. He witnessed several revivals there. In Mt. Vernon many were converted under his labors. He also preached in Boston, Mass., Portland, Bangor, and Augusta. He was pastor at Norridgewock several years. He then moved to Belgrade, and was pastor of the church there and at the same time at Smithfield, till his death. He baptized more than 1,000 persons, and his labors "were widely known and appreciated throughout the Kennebec Y. M. For several years he was military chaplain. He was a representative in the Legislature two or three years, and while there preached in Portland. He was a member of the Second and Third General Conferences. Inscription: Age 85y 4m 10d.

Leonard Hutchins
Birth:
April 20, 1828
New Portland, Maine
Death:
1915
Burial:
East New Portland Cemetery
New Portland
Somerset County, Maine

His mother died when he was 12 years old and three years later he was converted. He studied in the schools near him, and dwelt with his father until the father's death in May, 1868. He had been licensed in June, 1853 and was ordained September 21, 1856. He entered Bangor Theological Seminary in 1869. He pastored a number of churches in the area and had revival interest in each of his churches, baptizing 50 in Garland, and about 150 and other pastorates. From 1883 through 1887 he was employed in missionary work by the Maine State Mission Society in Anson Quarterly Meeting having under his care the churches in Stark, Freeman and Salem, Lexington and Dead River. He was the clerk and treasurer of the Anson Quarterly Meeting and also was a trustee of the Maine Central Institute.

Asa Foster Hutchinson
Birth:
Aug. 1, 1824
Buckfield, Maine
Death:
Dec. 2, 1893
South Portland, Maine

Burial:
Mountain View Cemetery
Auburn
Androscoggin County, Maine

His parents were Rev. Samuel and Mercy (Randall) Hutchison, and a cousin to Rev. C. T. Keen. He was converted at 15 and studied in North Bridgeton Academy, Maine and in Strafford Academy and in the Biblical School at Whitestown, New York. He was licensed in September, 1845 and ordained in September, 1850. He pastored many churches in that area and baptized 185 converts. He was on school committees in various towns and in 1865 he represented the towns of West Garndiner, Farmingdale, and Pittston in the legislature.

Rev Ebenezer Hutchinson
Birth:
Mar., 1818
Scarborough
Cumberland County, Maine
Death:
Sep. 29, 1865
Maine
Burial:
Bay View Cemetery
South Portland Gardens
Cumberland County, Maine

Rev. Ebenezer Hutchinson, bro. of Rev. Asa F. Hutchinson, was born in Scarborough, ME..
At age nineteen he united with the Baptist church in Dover ME. He entered the Parsonfield Seminary under Hosea Quinby soon after where he joined the the Free Baptists. He was licensed by the Otisfield Quarterly Meeting and saw many converted in an itinerant ministry.
In 1843 he married Miss Frances Dyer, of Cape Elizabeth, and for several years gave his attention to teaching. In 1856 he was ordained as pastor of the Cape Elizabeth church and in five years which followed many were converted, and the meeting-house enlarged and improved. He now completed a course of medicine which he had left unfinished years before, and prosecutd successfully that practice, preaching only occasionally.
He enlisted early in the Civil War in the Twenty-fifth Maine Regiment, and served nine months He contracted consumption, from which he died in camp in 1863,

Elder Joseph Hutchinson
Birth:
1755
Penobscot County
Maine
Death:
Feb. 24, 1801
Hebron
Oxford County,Maine

Burial:
Bog Brook Cemetery
Hebron
Oxford County
Maine

Rev. Joseph Hutchinson moved with his father to Windham about 1780.
He married Rebecca, daughter of Joseph and Ann Legro, of Marblehead, Mass, in 1778, and had eleven children.
He was the first minister of the denomination to die. As early as 1790, he was ruling elder and an unordained preacher, and nine years later he was ordained. He was present at the Y.M. at Anson, ME, in 1800, and chairman of an important committee. At the beginning of the year 1801, he visited with a friend the members of the church, and seemed impressed with the necessity of diligence. He would call upon a family, speak to them of Christ, kneel and pray, and hasten to the next house. The church was revived, but in the midst of the interest he was taken sick, and on the 24th of February, 1801, in the vigor of manhood, at the age of 40, he passed away.
His funeral was attended by Elder Stinchfield. During twenty years of the denomination, they had increased to thirty in the ministry without a death.

NOTE:
He was the first minister to die in the Free Will Baptist denomination.

Rev Joseph Hutchinson
Birth:
Apr. 11, 1811
Gorham
Cumberland County
Maine
Death:
Jan. 25, 1889
Maine
Burial:
Lane Cemetery
Freeport
Cumberland County
Maine

Rev. Joseph Hutchinson, of East Otisfield, ME, was born in Gorham, ME, April 5, 1811. He was an older brother of Rev's Asa F. and Ebenezer Hutchinson: [all sons of Rev. Samuel and Mercy (Randall) Hutchinson.]
He preached his first sermon on Bailey Hill, Poland, April 1, 1856, and was ordained July 8, 1858. His pastorates have been in Poland, Danville, Sumner, Buckfield, N. Freport, Otisfield, Bridgewater, and Miinot. He has had revivals at each place, and baptized 125 converts and organized two churches.
After three years of suffering he passed to his reward. He married Miss Martha J. Tobey, and has five children living. Two sons served honorably for three years in the war.

Benjamin Jaques
Birth:
1790
Death:
Jul. 16, 1878
Lisbon, Me
Burial:
Riverview Cemetery
Topsham, Sagadahoc County
Jaques died at aged 87 years and 8 months. He was converted in April, 1825, and baptized the next year. He was in the ministry more than forty years.

John B Jordan
Birth:
September 30, 1850
Auburn, Maine
Death:
1925
Burial:
Oak Hill Cemetery
Auburn
Androscoggin County, Maine

He was converted as a boy, and at the age of 16 was baptized. He united with the Court Street church, Auburn. His early education was with a business life and view. In March, 1868, when 17 years of age he accepted the position of messenger and bookkeeper in the First National Bank of Auburn, and was promoted in 1871 to the position of Teller, and in February, 1874, was elected cashier, which office he held until 1882, when he resigned and accepted a call to the pastorate of the Pine Street church, Lewiston, Maine. For a number of years he was active in evangelistic work in connection with the YMCA. He received license to preach June 11, 1878 and was ordained on may 25, 1882. During his pastorate with the Pine Street church 122 were added to its membership, 100 by baptism. In August 1883, he accepted a call to the first church, in Minneapolis, Minnesota. He remained with this church until October,, 1885 but not before 53 had been added to the church. There after he became pastor of the Augusta church in July, 1886. During the first year, 30 were added to the church. In December, 1886 he was elected chaplain of the Maine Insane Hospital. He was a member of the General Conference in 1886. He was the corresponding Sec. of the Maine Home Missionary Society and clerk of the Maine Central Yearly Meeting. He was a member of the city Council of Auburn for two.

Rev Columbus T Keene
Birth:
Feb. 21, 1832
Death:
Jul. 22, 1901
Burial:
Buckfield Village Cemetery
Buckfield
Oxford County
Maine

Rev. Columbus T. Keen, son of Nathaniel and Lydia (Hutchinson) Keen, was converted in the winter of 1857-58. Licensed in November 1881, he was ordained by the Otisfield Q.M. in September, 1884. He has held pastorates at West Mt. Vernon, Wells Mills, East Buckfield, and from 1886 at E. Hebron, a church reorganized in 1838 from the old First church founded by the grandfather of Mr. Keen, the Rev. Joseph Hutchinson. He has labored a number of years in the Y.M.C.A., and in 1884 was engaged as Minnesota state missionary for six months. He married Martha M. Boody, Nov. 16, 1855, and has five children.

William P. Kinney
Birth:
Mar. 7, 1833
Queensberry
New Brunswick, Canada
Death:
1916
Maine
Burial:
Old Baptist Cemetery
Yarmouth
Cumberland County, Maine

He became a Christian at the age of 16 and was educated in the Houlton Academy and Bangor Theological Seminary. His license to preach was granted on March 15, 1873, and on March 17, 1881 he was ordained. He held eight pastorates and several revivals and baptized 20 convert. He helped organize four churches. He was clerk of the quarterly meeting for a number of years and was a trustee of the Maine Central Institute and a member of the legislature of 1876.

Rev Charles L Kirkland
Birth:
1843
New Brunswick, Canada
Death:
Apr. 15, 1912

Burial:
Mattawamkeag Cemetery
Mattawamkeag
Penobscot County
Maine,

Note: "Buried at Sea" He was lost on the "Titanic"

Elder Ebenezer Knowlton, Sr
Birth:
unknown
Death:
Nov. 18, 1841
Burial:
Pine Grove Cemetery
South Montville
Waldo County, Maine

He was a Freewill Baptist minister, per town records: Descendants of Jonathan Towle : "They lived in Chichester and had twelve children." *Town Records - Vol.2 - p.68: "Pittsfield, March 22, 1808. This may certify the Selectmen of Chichester and all others whomsoever it may concern; that Mr. Joshua Towle of

Chichester doth belong to the freewill-Baptist Society and doth attend meeting with us when it convenient - given under my hand. El. Ebenezer Knowlton of Pittsfield"

He was married to Abigail True Knowlton (___ - 1868)

Ebenezer Knowlton
Birth:
Dec. 6, 1815
Pittsfield, N. H.
Death:
Sep. 10, 1874
Montville, Me.
Burial:
Pine Grove Cemetery
South Montville, Waldo County,
Maine

His father moved to Montville in 1828. He obtained a thorough academic education and became a teacher in early life. He was converted in 1832, and united with the church in Montville. The day that he decided to preach the gospel was the day he was elected speaker in the Legislature of his state. He preached his first sermon at Hallowell, Aug. 9, 1846, from the words" We love him because he first loved us." He was ordained Dec. 17, I848. His labors covered a wide territory in eastern and central Maine. He preached in Rockland two years at different times. The rest of his ministry was in connection with the Montville churches. He went far and near to solemnize marriages, attend funerals and deliver temperance and Sunday-school addresses. At the close of 1852, he wrote in his journal: "number' of funerals attended during the year, sixty; sermons preached, 171; religious meetings attended, 332; temperance and Sunday school lectures, twenty-three." In I853 the Legislature elected him State Treasurer, but he declined the honor. He consented, however, in 1854, to be elected to Congress, upon the advice of his brethren, but declined a re-electiion in order to devote himself to the work of the ministry and also to work for the Maine State Seminary. When he accepted the nomination to Congress he informed the convention that nominated him, that if elected, he should go to Congress as a Christian minister devoted to the interests of humanity; that he would accept the nomination only as from freemen desiring to be represented by a freeman; that he should allow no allegiance to any clique or party in any way to interfere with a strict adherence to freedom, country, and God.

While in Congress he wrote weekly letters to the *Morning Star*, subscribing himself "Daniel" This correspondence attracted considerable attention. He took an interest in the colored people and preached the gospel to them. He preached one half of the Sabbaths during the time he was in Congress. In 1869, there was a general desire among the Republicans of Maine that he should be their candidate for Governor. But although great pressure was brought to bear upon him and he was himself disposed to consent for the sake of the principles of temperance, he finally refused to allow his name to be used. Mr. Knowlton had all the mental and moral qualities that go to make up the real statesman, such as ability, strength, foresight, decision, honesty, integrity, love of humanity, and fear of God; and the only reason he did not rise to higher positions in the affairs of state was because he declined to do so, believing that, as a minister of Christ, he was holding the highest office on earth. When urged to become a candidate for Governor, he wrote to a leading religious politician saying, among other things: "You urge me to be Governor so as to enforce prohibition. I know rum-selling is a crime and grog-shops are a nuisance. A radical law with front teeth and grinders should be kept on the statute book and be lived up to. But a correct moral sentiment among the people is the only means to secure this end. This moral sentiment grows only out of the gospel. The Christian ministry is the leading agency in spreading the gospel. So do let me alone, that what there is left of me may be devoted to the appropriate work of my profession. It is easier to find good and suitable material to make governors of, than it is to find good and suitable material to make ministers. It is but little I can do anywhere, but I would rather see one young man in my congregation soundly converted to Christ than to have any office in the gift of man." He was often appointed to preach at denominational gatherings, but accepted with extreme diffidence. He was desired as pastor in Lewiston, Auburn, Augusta, Portland, Boston, New York and other places, but accepted none of these positions. He was very firm in his denominational loyalty. He was one of the projectors of the Maine State Seminary, which grew into Bates College. Other positions of responsibility were as follows: Trustee of Colby University, trustee of Bates College, president of the Foreign Mission Society, corporator of the Printing Establishment, and moderator of three General Conferences. He died suddenly while taking a bath in a pond near his home, where he was accustomed to fish and swim. His death was conspicuously noticed by resolutions in town meeting, and by the denomination in which he was a pillar of strength.

Elliot Sawyer Lamb
Birth:
May 26, 1810
Vermont
Death:
Jun. 17, 1888
Weld
Franklin County, Maine
Burial:
West Leeds Cemetery
Leeds
Androscoggin County, Maine,

Zina Knowlton
Birth:
Sep. 20, 1813
Swanville
Waldo County, Maine
Death:
Sep. 7, 1885
Monroe
Waldo County, Maine
Burial:
Mount Solitude Cemetery
Monroe
Waldo County, Maine

Married Nov 2 1833 in Swanville and was a Free Will Baptist minister.

Elliot was the son of Luther and Lucretia (Lamb) Lamb. He had at least three siblings. Though his death record and census records say he was born in Vermont, his biographical sketch in the "Free Baptist Cyclopedia" says he was born in Canaan, New Hampshire, but his family moved to Vershire, Vermont shortly after his birth.
When Elliot was 17, his family moved to Leeds. He was converted at the age of 20 and baptized by Rev. Silas Curtis.
On May 27, 1832 he married Julia A. Stanley. Julia had been a founding member of the Free Will Baptist Church in North Leeds, when established in 1829.

Elliot and Julia lived in West Leeds on River Road, in a house almost immediately across the road from the entrance to this cemetery. They had two children: Orissa and a son born in 1848. Vital records say his name was William Elliot, however the census records say his name was Hurbert (or similar name spelling). This son likely died young, as the Cyclopaedia said Orissa was Elliot's only child.

Elliot was ordained in 1842. The 1850 census said he was a minister for the Free Will Baptist Church, though the 1860 census said he was a house carpenter. According to the Cyclopedia he preached most of the time, and participated in revivals in numerous Maine towns.

After Julia died Elliot moved to Weld to help his brother care for their father. There Elliot remarried to Rozillah Lawrence on May 15, 1874. They lived on the farm her father had owned in Weld. He organized a church in Weld, and baptized 40 converts.

George Lamb
Birth:
1788
Lincolnville,
Waldo County, Maine
Death:
Dec. 14, 1836
Brunswick,
Cumberland County, Maine
Burial:
Growstown Cemetery,
Brunswick,
Cumberland County, Maine

He became interested in religion when but a boy, and was converted and joined the Free Will Baptist Church. His circumstances afforded him little advantage of an education, but he had an inquisitive and well-balanced mind, he worked with a clergyman in his preaching endeavors, and his success was such that he was licensed and ordained in 1813. He gathered a church in Bangor Me, but he declined settlement. His brethren wanted him to go to Topsham where the church was waning. There was a remarkable revival commenced and he baptized about 40. (It was here that the later eminent scholar, Prof. John J. Butler, was influenced by good from Rev. George Lamb, with whom he stayed while a student there.

John Lamb
Birth:
Jun. 7, 1776
Nova Scotia, Canada
Death:
Jun. 4, 1828
Waldo County, Maine
Burial:
Center Lincolnville Burying
Ground
Waldo County, Maine

In 1805 he was ordained and for 20 years he had a useful ministry. He preached the gospel without any salary and at the same time supported with hard labor a large family. For some time his public ministry was hindered by asthma.

journey he had among the churches of the Sandy River country. He made the ordaining prayer while Joseph White preached the sermon at the ordination of Clement Phinney at Standish Neck in 1816. In 1834 he added forty-six to his church by baptism and the next year twenty-nine.

Zachariah Leach
Birth:
Jun. 7, 1765
Raymond
Cumberland County, Maine
Death:
Nov. 3, 1841
Raymond
Cumberland County, Maine
Burial:
Raymond Village Cemetery
Raymond
Cumberland County, Maine

He was ordained a Free Will Baptist minister on Nov. 6, 1794 by Rev. Benjamin Randall, and others. In 1799 he became clerk of the Edgecomb Q. M. In 1808 he had an extensive reformation at Standish, in which Joseph White was converted and soon became an efficient minister. He preached three times at the Y. M. at Edgecomb in September 1811. He was followed by John Buzzell and John Colby. March 18, 1812, he wrote to the *Religous Magazine* of an agreeable

Rev Daniel Blaisdell Lewis
Birth:
Mar. 1, 1804
Cornish
York County
Maine
Death:
Oct. 16, 1859
Waterville
Kennebec County
Maine
Burial:
Pine Grove Cemetery
Waterville
Kennebec County
Maine

His parents moved with him to Waterville, where, at the age of twenty, he publicly convessed Christ, and the next year was baptized by Rev. L. Lewis. He soon saw his duty clearly, and after deep conviction, began to preach. He was licensed, and in 1831 was ordained by the Exeter Quarterly Meeting in Pittsfield, ME.

For thirty years the Sabbath nearly always found him at his post preaching Jesus. His evenings he gave to study and to preparation for his ministry. In Sydney, Waterville, Smithfield, Belgrade, Mt. Vernon, Readfield, Unity and Thorndike he went organizing churches and baptizing converts. He has been called "quite the father of the Waterville Q.M." He was a modest, unassuming preacher, firm and unwavering in his faith, earnest and effective in his appeals.

Samuel Lewis
Birth:
1825
Buxton, Maine
Death:
Oct. 12, 1850
Burial:
Hackett-Notch Cemetery
New Vineyard
Franklin County, Maine

At the age of 24 he married Phepe Irish. He was converted at the age of 28 and was baptized by John Buzzell. He moved to Chatham, New Hampshire and began to preach and some years later he moved to Harrison,

Maine where he had great revivals. He was ordained in Sebec Quarterly Meeting in 1832 and was instrumental in promoting revivals in this new section and organizing and sustaining several of the hurches that composed Springfield Quarterly Meeting.

Rev Stephen Lewis
Birth:
Jan. 5, 1781
Boothbay
Lincoln County
Maine
Death:
Mar. 14, 1856
Burial:
Highland Cemetery
Jefferson
Lincoln County, Maine

Rev. Stephen Lewis, died at his residence in Augusta, ME, aged 77[sic] years. He was licensed to preach April 17, 1830, by the Edgecomb Quarterly Meeting and ordained in Whitefield Nov. 7, 1834. He spent most of his ministerial labors in Windsor, and in the Edgecomb Q.M.

He was devoted to the spiritual welfare of his people and deeply intrested in all the benevolent enterprises of the day.

Almon Libby
Birth:
Oct. 10, 1816
Minot, Maine
Death:
Nov. 1, 1895
Burial:
Stroudwater Burying Ground
Portland
Cumberland County, Maine

He became a Christian at the age of 16 and was a student in the Parsonfield Seminary. In 1837 he was ordained by the Cumberland Quarterly Meeting. All of his pastorates were in the state of Maine. He labored in many revivals and baptized a large number of converts. In 1886 he was an agent for the Androscroggin County Bible Society. He has been a member of the General Conference. He had two sons that graduated from Bates College; one is a civil engineer, and the other is a district attorney in Colorado. His youngest daughter was on the staff of the Lewiston Journal.

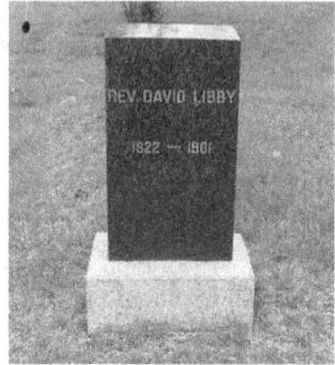

David Libby
Birth:
Jun. 2, 1822 Portland,
Cumberland County,
Maine
Death:
1901
Burial:
Lisbon Cemetery, Lisbon,
Androscoggin County, Maine
He was a younger brother of Rev. Almon Libby. He became a Christian when fourteen years of age; was licensed in June 1845, and ordained by the Bowdoin Quarterly Meeting, two years later. He had pastorates in South Lewiston, Harrison, Harpswell, Freeport, Poland and Lisbon. He baptized a large number of converts.

James Libby
Birth:
Oct., 1796
Auburn,
Androscoggin County, Maine
Death:
Mar. 6, 1884
West Poland,
Androscoggin County, Maine

Burial:
Highland Cemetery,
West Poland,
Androscoggin County, Maine

Rev. James Libby, became a Christian at the age of twenty, was baptized by Elder Leach and joined the church in that vicinity. In 1828, after serious conviction, he consecrated himself to the ministry, and was ordained at Danville by Rev's Z. Jordan, J. White and J. Clay. In 1832, he moved to West Poland, and for thirty-three years was pastor of that church. Early in his pastorate a meeting house was erected. There were several extensive revivals with large additions to the church. The Second Poland church grew out of this church. In the course of his ministry of more than sixty years, he baptized about one thousand converts, married several hundred couples and attended the funerals of 1500 persons. His valuable labors were frequently sought by various pastors in protracted meeting.

What A Day That Will Be When My Saviour I Shall See!

Elder Ward Locke
Birth
1784
Death:
Nov. 25, 1828
Chesterville, Maine
Burial:
Chesterville Center Cemetery
Chesterville
Franklin County, Maine

He began to preach in 1806 and was ordained in 1818. His ministry was in Maine. He was a delegate to the General Conference in 1827.

Jason Mariner
Birth:
November 14, 1824
Lincolnville, Maine
Death:
Nov. 18, 1891
Burial:
Union Cemetery
Lincolnville Center
Waldo County, Maine

He was converted through the Ministry of Rev. John Stevens who baptized him at the age of 18 when he fully gave his heart to God. He preached his first sermon on 14, 1843 in the same church where he was converted. He was a student at Whitestown, New York after which he was licensed at Montville Quarterly Meeting and ordained at Lincolnville with Rev. Ebenezer Knowlton preaching. He held numerous pastorates in New York, Maine, Massachusetts, and Rhode Island. He was a trustee of the Maine State Seminary and Bates College for 25 years.

Moses McFarland
Birth:
Unknown
Death:
Nov. 1, 1865
Burial:
Mount Repose Cemetery
Montville
Waldo County, Maine

He was ordained in 1806 and nine in May. In 1818, 40 were converted under his labors and the Second Montville church was organized. Early in 1827, he was charged with preaching Universalism. Rev. Ebenezer Knowlton of Pittsfield, New Hampshire had moved to the area in time to save the church from defection. At the June Quarterly Meeting a charge was brought against McFarland. In September a committee of seven was appointed, with Rev.

Benjamin Thorn as chairman. McFarland finally separated from the quarter meeting in December, 1827.

Elbridge L McKindsley
Birth:
1839
Whitefield, Maine
Death:
1911
Burial:
Whitefield Cemetery
Whitefield
Lincoln County,, Maine

He was converted to the age of 13 and studied at Pittston Academy he was licensed in September 1883 and was ordained in September 1886. He preached as an evangelist most of his ministry.

Death Is The Setting Free From The Warfare Of The Soul

Rev George Zeigler Mears
Birth:
Feb. 2, 1799
Bristol,
Maine
Death:
Mar., 1881
Washington
Knox County,
Maine
Burial:
Morrill Village Cemetery
Morrill
Waldo County, Maine

Listed in minister's roll of deceased ministers in 1881, Maine Freewill Bapt. ministers.
1st Wife Abigail Wentworth (mar. Oct. 6, 1821; 2nd wife Elizabeth Rust Neal (ME mar. records) Married: Aug. 18, 1860.

John Miller
Birth:
May 13, 1806
Durham
Androscoggin County, Maine
Death:
Dec. 5, 1869
Durham
Androscoggin County, Maine
Burial:
Union Cemetery
Auburn, Androscoggin County,
Maine

He was converted in 1829 and began to preach with the Methodists in 1837. He afterwards joined the Free Baptists and continued a good and acceptable minister with them until his death. He felt especially called to preach to the poor, and his labors were fruitful. He was a man of much prayer, strong faith, fervent love, and deep piety. He was married to Hannah, dau. of Samuel and Catherine (Clark) Robinson on 2 Dec 1830.

David Moody
Birth:
December 3, 1804
GilmanTon, New Hampshire
Death:
Mar. 7, 1878
Burial:
Mount Solitude Cemetery
Monroe
Waldo County, Maine

He was converted at age 18, and received his license the following of May, 1824 and was ordained two years later by Rev's. Enoch Place, S. B. Dyer, and Moses Bean, Ebenezer Knowlton and Arthur Caverno. He was in the ministry more than 63 years. The first 10 years was spent in evangelism, with his ministry beginning at Bethlehem, where he had an extensive revival. He helped numerous churches throughout New Hampshire and during this time baptized 171 converts, married 197 couples and attended 572 funerals. On March 19, 1827, he married Miss Sally Bean.

Samuel Plummer Morrill
Birth:
February 11, 1816
Chesterville,
Maine
Death:
1892
Burial:
Chesterville Hill Cemetery
Chesterville
Franklin County, Maine

He was a student at the Farmington Academy, and was converted at the age of 18, licensed in 1839 at the age of 23, and ordained in 1841 by the Rev. Dexter Waterman. He held many pastorates in the state of Maine after his ordination, but in 1885 he settled in Vienna, Maine where a good revival was enjoyed. In his 11 pastorates he baptized in all 75. In 1886 he lay aside an active ministry due to poor health. He was a member three times at the Gen. conference; and assisted in organizing several churches. He was elected to the 41st Congress of the United States and served during 1869-70. On November 28, 1838, he married Mary J. Chase.

The body was found and buried in June on the lake shore. His funeral was attended by Rev. Moses Ames of Garland. He experienced religion about 1834 and was baptized by the Rev. Samuel Lewis, after which he joined the church at Lee. This Sebec Quarterly Meeting granted him a license in January, 1838 and ordained him the following July. He was blessed by revivals in his tours through the Springfield Quarterly Meeting. He had a deep love for the Bible, and was a friend of the Bible school at Whitestown and especially advocated the cause of the slave.

Levi Moulton
Birth:
1812
Death:
May 10, 1846
Burial:
Academy Cemetery
Lee
Penobscot County, Maine

He drowned while crossing a lake in a boat with others coming out of the woods from a lumber drive, when a squall hit the boat.

They preached about this time and the hereafter

Rev James Nason
Birth:
Mar. 29, 1829
Lyman
York County,
Maine
Death:
Nov., 1894
Burial:
Oak Grove Cemetery
Wells
York County,
Maine

Rev. James Nason, son of Nehemiah and Olive (Davis) Nason. He received his education in the common schools and in private study. He was converted in March, 1839; licensed by the York County Quarterly Meetinng (QM) in June 1859 and ordained by the Cumberland QM June 7, 1860. He has held pastorates at White Rock, two years; Shapleigh, one year; North Berwick, Beach Ridge, twelve years; Meredith Centre, NH one year; Wells Branch, ME six years; Ross' Corners, two years; Kennebunk, two years; Wells Branch, two years, where he still resides. From four general revivals he has baptized about one hundred. He has assisted in the ordination of four, attended over two hundred funerals and solemnized over one hundred marriages. He was a delegate to the General Conference at Providence, R.I. He married Alice L. Edgecomb, Oct. 8, 1848, and has four sons.

Joseph Nickerson
Birth:
Apr. 10, 1833
Litchfield. Maine
Death:
Feb. 27, 1909
Burial:
Litchfield Plains Cemetery
Litchfield Plains
Kennebec County, Maine

Converted at 17. In December, 1878 he received his licensed to preach and on October 11, 1883 was ordained by Rev. Mark Getchell and others. His pastorates were in the vicinity of his conversion.

Joseph N. Noble
Birth:
Apr. 29, 1847
New Brunswick, Canada
Death:
Feb. 2, 1912
Burial:
Evergreen Cemetery
Houlton
Aroostook County, Maine
Plot: Section 6, Block 13, Grave

He was converted on September 27, 1866 in Canning, Nova Scotia under Rev. Charles Knowles. He yielded the call to preach in May 1882. He was licensed to preach at Upper Woodstock, New Brunswick. In October he began working with the Bridgewater, Maine church, where upon his labors he was ordained by the Houlton Quarterly Meeting on December 18, 1886.

Lemuel Norton
Birth:
Jun. 21, 1785
Edgartown
Dukes County, Massachusetts
Death:
Sep. 18, 1866
Burial:
Hillrest Cemetery
West Tremont, Hancock County, Maine

Son of Noah and Jerusha (Dunham) Norton. (Noah served in Revolutionary War and died in Mass.) He married Mary "Polly" Norton. Rev. Lemuel Norton, was ordained in 1817, in the Calvinist Baptist, but after ten years preaching, changed his views and united with the Freewill Baptist in 1828, and organized a church at Mt. Desert. In 1840, he became pastor of the Belmont Church, and served in the ministry faithfully until his death from cancer of the stomach, at the home of his daughter, Mary. He requested to be "buried on Mt. Desert Island," where he had organized the first Freewill Baptist church in Hancock County, ME.

Rev Chandler Noyes
Birth:
1818
Maine
Death:
Jun. 12, 1878
Waldo County, Maine
Burial:

Highland Cemetery
Jefferson
Lincoln County, Maine

Rev. chandler Noyes, died of consumption. He was the older brother of Rev. Eli Noyes, one of the First Free Baptist missionaries to India, and sons of Moses and Sarah Noyes.
He became a Christian early in life, and at his death had been forty years in the ministry. He preached mostly as an evangelist and saw many revivals. His labors were mostly within the limits of the Montville and Prospect Quarter Meetings. While he had health, he was a faithful worker. He left a devoted wife.-On 14 Nov. 1829, he married Abigail Perkins in Lincoln Co. He married 2) Mary Bailey, 27 Nov. 1843, Johnson, Maine.

Albert Pease
Birth:
Oct. 21, 1811
Norridgewock, Maine
Death:
Jul. 16, 1898
Burial:
Pease Cemetery
Avon
Franklin County, Maine

He came to Christ in 1830 and in 1832 was licensed. In 1843 he was ordained by the Farmington Quarterly Meeting. At first he was an itinerant preacher preaching mostly in Maine. However, thereafter he preached in Massachusetts and Rhode Island, but due to his health he lived with his father in Maine and therefore held many pastorates at the time while his health was poorly. He finally engaged in farming and became a successful writer for agricultural papers. He also wrote the *History Of Phillips*, the city where he lived. He married on February 24, 1830 Ms. Ann Huntoon. His eldest son was a captain of the 17th Regiment New York volunteer's.
Inscription:
"Preacher - Poet - Farmer"

Ezekiel Gilman Page
Birth:
Dec. 25, 1814
New Sharon
Franklin County, Maine
Death:
Jun. 17, 1909
Kennebec County, Maine
Burial:
Litchfield Plains Cemetery
Litchfield Plains
Kennebec County, Maine

His parents were Reuben and Elizabeth (Jackson) Page...He married in March, 1837, Miss Mary G. Bursley, deceased, and has one son living. He married Mrs. Mary Bates, of Oakland, Sept. 12, 1885. He was ordained Dec. 10, 1839" according to "Ordinations" on page 164 of Volume II, Number 1, June 1840, the *Freewill Baptist Quarterly Magazine.* He has been pastor in Edgecomb, Booth Bay (sic), Woolwich, Westport, Brunswick, Georgetown, Richmond Village,

West Gardiner, Winnegance, Bowdoinham, Richmond Corner, Litchfield Plains and West Bowdoin. During his ministry he had charge of two churches at the same time and never without a pastorate or appointment in his 47 years of ministry. Baptized between 400-500, and married 211 couples.

Inscription:
Rev.E. G. Page
Died June 17, 1909
age. 94 yrs.

John Page
Birth:
Feb. 11, 1787
Wentworth
Grafton County, New Hampshire
Death:
Aug. 17, 1834
Garland
Penobscot County, Maine
Burial:
Hathaway Cemetery
Garland
Penobscot County, Maine

He was converted in 1805 and began to preach in 1808. On March 20 of that year he was married by the Rev. Hezekiah Buzzell to Susan Clark and moved to Alton where he served the church at East Bridge. He was ordained they are in 1811 and was pastor of the church 12 years engaging at the same time successfully as an evangelist in the country around assisting in the organization of several churches. In 1820 he moved Maine and begin preaching in that area and organized a church at Garland where he was the pastor for 10 years.

Inscription:
That gospel he preached for twenty two years triumphantly supported him in the hour of death

Page, Rev. John, was born in Wentworth, N. H., Feb. 11, 1787. He removed early in life to Gilmanton, where he was converted in 1805. He began to preach in 1808. March 20 of that year he was married by Rev. Hezekiah Buzzell to Susan Clark, and moved to Alton, where he served the church at East Bridge. He was ordained here in 1811, and was pastor of the church twelve years, engaging at the same time successfully as an evangelist in the country around, and assisting in the organization of several churches. In the winter of 1823-24 he removed to Maine, and began preaching at Corinna and Exeter, but settled in Garland in 1825, where a church was organized, and he had a pastorate for ten years. He labored extensively in revivals in the neighboring town. While on an errand of mercy in 1832 he was severely chilled by a rain, and took a severe cold, which ended in consumption. He died Aug. 17, 1834, in his 48th year. He was a man of robust health and commanding appearance, and his upright life gave power to his words, which were especially blessed in the winning of souls.

William Paine

Birth:
Nov. 19, 1760
Woolwich
Sagadahoc County, Maine
Death:
Oct. 14, 1846
North Anson
Somerset County, Maine
Burial:
Gray Cemetery
Embden
Somerset County, Maine

He was converted under the preaching of Reverent Edward Locke after which he joined the Free Baptist Church. Two years later his wife was converted and united with the church. He was ordained as a minister in the Anson church in October, 1808, with which he remained till death. He was a husband for 60 years and the father of 15 children. He fought in the Revolutionary War as a private in Capt. Wiley's company, Col. Michael Jackson's regiment in 1777. He enlisted at age of 17 and served about three years. Lived in North Anson, Maine. A son of John Payne. A headstone marks his grave. Ref: *Daughters of the American Revolution Magazine, Vol 36 January-June, 1910*

Rev George Parcher

Birth:
Sep. 18, 1781
Saco
York County
Maine
Death:
Jan. 8, 1834
Maine

Burial:
Laurel Hill Cemetery
Saco
York County
Maine

An early Maine Freewill Bapt. minister, said that he was "an ornament to his profession."

Rev Thomas Park

Birth:
Jun. 24, 1795
Maine
Death:
Feb. 23, 1882
Burial:
Bowditch Cemetery
Searsport
Waldo County
Maine

From his bio in "Cyclopedia of Free Baptists," pub. 1889, he was ordained in 1823, and ministered in Maine.

Benjamin P Parker
Birth:
May 16, 1835
Kittery, Maine
Death:
Aug. 3, 1924
Burial:
Hillside Cemetery
North Berwick
York County, Maine

His father was ordained as a Christian minister about 1867. When he was about two years of age, his parents moved to Newburyport, Massachusetts, where his early life was spent in study in the public schools. He was converted on April 18, 1852 and on his 17th birthday was baptized by Rev. Daniel Pike, joining the Christian church there. In the spring of 1859 he united with the First Baptist Church at Greenwood, Maine and on June 2, was licensed at the Otisfield Quarterly Meeting. His first pastorate was at New Gloucester, Maine; in 1862 he moved to Kittery, his birthplace, and was employed at the Navy Yard for six years. Thereafter, he held a number of pastorates in Maine, New Hampshire and Vermont.

He was the first vice president of the Maine Home Mission Society, clerk of the Strafford, Vermont Quarterly Meeting and attended one of the General Conferences.

Rev Alfred Patterson
Birth:
Oct. 5, 1808
Maine
Death:
Mar. 22, 1875
Exeter, NH
New Hampshire
Burial:
Gilman Cemetery
Sangerville
Piscataquis County
Maine
Plot: Row 2 Lot 5

Ordained in March 1839, by Free Will Baptist Sebec Quarterly Meeting. He continued to preach until just before his death cause by heart disease. He Left the denomination and joined the Free Christian Baptists in Cambridge.He was married to Mary P. Gilman.

Rev Charles Sumner Perkins
Birth:
Oct. 25, 1836
Auburn
Androscoggin County
Maine
Death:
Oct. 11, 1905
Maine
Burial:
Riverside Cemetery
Lewiston
Androscoggin County
Maine
Plot: 0845

Rev. Charles Sumner PERKINS, son of Rev. Gideon and Mary (Dunham) Perkins. He prepared for college at the Lewiston Falls Academy, Auburn; graduated from Bowdoin College in 1860, and from Bangor Theological Seminary in 1864. He became a Christian in 1857, was licensed by the Bowdoin Quarterly Meeting in 1863, by a council of Rev's J.A. Lowell; J. Mariner; C.F.Penney, and D.M. Graham. After his graduation from the theological seminary, he supplied the Free Baptist church in New York City one year; then in 1865-66 he supplied the Roger Williams church, Providence,

nearly a year, during the absence of Dr. Day. In this year his labors were rewarded with nearly one hundred conversions. His first settlement was with the Park Street church, Providence. During this pastorate of six years the church was reorganized, its location changed from N. Main St., and the present edifice on Park St. was built. He then became pastor of Greenfield, R.I., over two yrs, and next of the Portland, ME church five years. Then he was called to the Boston church, Mass. He remained six years and secured the permanent establishment of the church in its present location on Shawmut Ave. He was pastor of the church at Lyndon Centre, VT. He has baptized over two hundred persons.

He has held several public and denominational positions as recording and corresponding secretary of the Foreign Mission Society, member of the Foreign Mission and Home Mission Boards, also of the executive committee of these and of the Education Society, overseer of Bates College, and member of four General Conferences. He is superintendent of schools in Lyndon Centre. He married Nov. 30, 1864, Mary S. Murray, of Brunswick, ME. Their oldest son, Albert T., graduated from Harvard, class of 1887. Martha graduated from the Lyndon Institute in 1886. Osborn in the latter school.

Rev Gideon Perkins
Birth:
Nov. 28, 1801
Woodstock
Oxford County,Maine
Death:
Jan. 25, 1884
Lewiston
Androscoggin County, Maine
Burial:
Riverside Cemetery
Lewiston
Androscoggin County, Maine
Plot: 0362

Rev. Gideon Perkins resided in his native town until after he entered the ministry. His father, Cornelius Perkins, was one of the earliest settlers of the town, having come from Carver, Mass, when he was a young man. A devoted Christian and a deacon in the Baptist church, he brought up his children in the fear of the Lord and saw all eight of them converted. Three became preachers, Gideon was one. His opportunities for education were very limited, but he made the most of them, gaining information easily by natural aptitude, where most young men would have remained ignorant. He was converted at the age of thirty and was baptized by Rev. Aaron Fuller. Previous to his conversion he had married Mary Dunham--a most worthy and helpful Christian wife through life---and had settled on a farm.

His conviction was to preach the gospel and he very soon began to hold meetings. His license to preach is dated Aug. 21, 1831, and is signed by Andrew Hobson, Clerk of then Gorham Q.M. He was ordained Sept. 27, 1832, by Rev's Joseph Hutchinson, Clement Phinney and James Libby. Clement Phinney preached the sermon, and according to the testimony of an eye witness, he preached upon his knees, mingling his words of address to the people with petitions to God.

Like all our ministers of that period Mr. Perkins traveled much from place to place; but he was located for considerable periods in Otisfield, Hebron, Bridgton, Danville, W. Gardiner, Wayne, and Sabattsville. He had everywhere marked sucess. Upon his own testimony not less than two thousand were converted under his preaching, of whom twenty-seven entered the ministry. During his pioneer ministry his salary was seldom sufficient.

He was a man of fine natural

ability and of excellent acquirements. He was a good preacher, thoughtful, clear, earnest, tender and persuasive. He was especially gifted in prayer. When he prayed everybody felt that he was speaking to God, and that he was really bringing those for whom he prayed into God's very presence.

He was among the first in Maine to espouse the anti-slavery and temperance causes. He was the first abolitionist sent to the State Legislature by the town of Lewiston. His home was a rendezvous for anti-slavery lecturers and escaped slaves. He was often threatened with violence, but escaped personal injury.

One of his children, John W. Perkins, was one of the most prominent both in counsels and benefactions among the founders of the Maine State Seminary (now Bates College). Another is the Rev. Charles S. Perkins, and another Miss Sarah A. Perkins. In the home of another son, Joseph W. Perkins, many years a merchant in Lewiston, he passed away peacefully and trustfully"

What A Day That Will Be When My Saviour I Shall See!

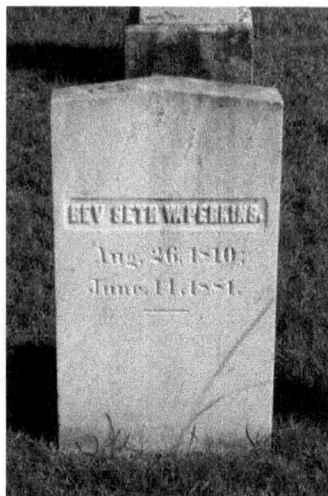

Seth W Perkins
Birth:
Aug. 26, 1810
Death:
Jun. 14, 1881
Hollis,
Me.
Burial:
Riverside Cemetery
Dixfield,
Oxford County,
Maine

About the year 1866 he settled in South 'Wheelock, Vt., and remained three years; then he was pastor of the Eaton and Newport church, Province of Quebec, three years. After this he was pastor one year in each of the following places in Maine: Canton, Wiltoll, Weld, New Sharon, South Montville and New Gloucester.

Rev John Pettengill
Birth:
Feb. 7, 1834
Sandwich, Carroll County
New Hampshire
Death:
1919
Maine
Burial:
Fairview Cemetery
Jefferson
Lincoln County, Maine

Rev. John Pettengill, son of John and Sally (Hatch) Pettingill was converted at the age of twenty-three. He received license to preach in 1861, and was ordained Jan. 17, 1875. His pastorates have been in North Lisbon, Jackson, Thronton Gore, East Holderness, Moltonboro, Eaton, NH, and South Gorham and Scarboro, ME, where he preached in 1887. Leaving the latter interest in 1888, he took in its place the South Buxton church. He has had hundreds of conversions in his ministry.
He married in 1855, Miss Laura A. Read, and has two children [1889].
Rev. John married Fannie Wescott 11 Sept 1894, at Portland, ME.

Clement Phinney
Birth:
Aug. 16, 1780
Death:
Mar. 2, 1855
Burial:
Western Cemetery,
Portland
Cumberland County,
Maine

He became a minister in the early 1800's. He served at the Free Will Baptist Church, Standish, Maine from 1816-1825. Had a talent for singing, and frequently used it in meetings and at school. He had an unusual wit, won many friends and could hold the undivided attention of large audiences. A book on his life was written by D.M. Graham.

Joseph Phinney
Birth:
Unknown
Death:
December 3, 1869
Harrison, Maine
Burial:
Saint John Cemetery
Pembroke
Washington County, Maine

He died in his 81st year and for many years he preached the gospel with a particular power and success until he was trouble with ill health.

John Pike

Birth:
Aug. 25, 1793
Cornish,York County, Maine
Death:
Nov. 29, 1877
East Fryeburg
Oxford County, Maine
Burial:
Pike Cemetery
Fryeburg, Oxford County, Maine

He was the son of John and Nancy (Thurston) Pike He married Hannah (Hubbard) Pike March 23, 1819, East Fryeburg, Oxford County, Maine. He was in the ministry about fifty years, and preached in Fryeburgh, Brownfield, Harrison, Chatham, Conway, Sweden, Hiram and Sebago. He usually preached to more than one church at a time. His ministry was successful in the conversion of souls. In his former years he did much justice and probate business. He was an earnest advocate of reforms, including abstinence from tobacco.

Inscription:
Age: 84 yrs, 3 mos

The dead in Christ will rise first.

John Pinkham

Birth:
Jan. 25, 1808
Death:
Jan. 18, 1882
Burial:
Cook Pinkham Cemetery, Casco, Cumberland County, Maine

He was converted at the age of sixteell and joined the church. When about eighteen years of age, he began to hold meetings in his own and adjoining towns with good results. At the request of his church the Q. M. licensed him. In 1830, at the age of twenty-two, he was ordained in Freedom, N. H. His pastorates were, Sandwich seven years, Gilford eight years, and Alton five years. He lived at Dover two years, and preached as an evangelist at Great Falls and Portsmouth. In the latter place a Church was organized. His health became impaired so that he ceased to preach. He then moved to Casco, Me., and cared for his aged parents while they lived. As soon as health permitted he entered into the work again and preached to churches in the Otisfield and Cumberland Q. M's. As formerly, his labors were very fruitful. The Second Poland church, of which he was a member when he died, held him in high esteem, as did also the community in which he lived.

Inscription:
REV JOHN PINKHAM
BORN
JAN 25 1808
DIED JAN 8 1892
Rest, sweet rest

Rev Orrin Pitts
Birth:
Unknown
Sidney
Kennebec County,Maine
Death:
Nov. 18, 1884
Gilmanton Ironworks
Belknap County
New Hampshire
Burial:
Riverside Cemetery
Farmington
Franklin County,Maine

His father died when he was three years old, and he lived with Mr. Joseph Butterfield, of West Farmington, ME until his twenty-first year, when he began a course of three years at the Farmington Academy, during which he was employed as assistant teacher and lived in the family of the preceptor. He taught about forty-five terms of school several of them in high schools, and continued his work as an educator till near the close of his life.

At the age of thirty-two he was converted, and not long after united with the church in New Portland (Free Baptist).

He was a licentiate one year and then was ordained by the Anson Quarterly Meeting, June 9, 1861. He preached in a number of places in the Anson Q.M; then in 1862, he moved to West Farmington, and lived there six years where he preached in Farmington Falls, New Sharon, and Bean's Corner, where he witnessed a good revival.

After going to Weld with Rev. R. Ely, where they witness a good revival he was soon called to settle there, and remained six years.

A good house of worship was built and many added to the church.

He was twice elected delegate to General Conference.

There is no sting when you die in the Lord.

431

George Plummer
Birth:
Apr. 7, 1826
Durham
Androscoggin County,
Maine
Death:
Jun. 17, 1897
Lisbon Falls
Androscoggin County,
Maine
Burial:
Hillside Cemetery
Lisbon Falls
Androscoggin County,
Maine

He was the son of Henry and Wealthy (Estes) Plummer. He was licensed to preach in the Free Baptist Church, March 1856, and ordained 22 Dec. 1861.He was pastor in Durham five years, at Lisbon Falls five years, at Freeport one year and W. Bowdoin one year. He baptized 60, married 190 couples, and attended 636 funerals.He was a Member of Maine Legislature in 1859.

Albert Pratt
Birth:
unknown
Death:
Oct. 19, 1886
Sebec, Maine
Burial:
Foss Cemetery
Piscataquis County, Maine

He was converted it to age of 31 and was baptized for the Reverend E. Harding on his 32nd birthday and united with the Sebec church. Three years after, in 1856, he was licensed by the Sebec Quarterly Meeting and at the next annual session was ordained. He preached several years, mostly within the limits of this quarterly meeting with good success.

Rev Benaiah Pratt
Birth:
Mar. 4, 1773
Plymouth County
Massachusetts
Death:
Aug. 26, 1846
Maine

Burial:
Grove Cemetery
Belfast
Waldo County, Maine

Ordained in 1807, preached all over Maine with success. His first wife d. 1819, and March 10, 1825, he married Rachel Heal. He studied medicine, for support, but preached with any rescued time he had. Attended all meetings, and d. age 73. He org. many churches and baptized about 500 person Very successful Freewill Baptist minister, in Maine, where in abt 1816, Topsham, Bristol and Woolwich, he preached 3 times daily for three wks with over 100 conversions.s.

Rev Cyprian S Pratt
Birth:
Aug. 14, 1806
Hebron
Oxford County
Maine
Death:
Jul. 8, 1858
Harmony
Somerset County, Maine
Burial:
Libby Cemetery
Harmony
Somerset County, Maine
Maine Records: His parents were William and Martha (unk) Pratt. He was converted about the year 1831, on Fox Island, and subsequently joined the Free Baptists. Licensed by the Exeter Quarterly Meeting (QM) in Brighton, he devoted several

years to an itinerant ministry. After the organization of the Wellington QM, his labors were confined mostly to its limits. His health failed while preaching at Richmond. He soon after moved to Harmony and engaged in secular pursuits for five years, when consumption caused his decease.. He married Lovina H. Whittier 10 Jan. 1828, at Brighton, ME.

Henry Preble
Birth:
January 9, 1815
Norridgewock,
Maine
Death:
May 5, 1892
Burial:
Maplewood Cemetery
Fairfield
Somerset County,
Maine

He was licensed to preach in 1841 and was ordained the next year. For some years he was an evangelist in the Farmington Quarterly Meeting. For nearly 20 years he spent his time pastoring within this body. Thereafter, he labored in the Anson Quarterly Meeting and the Bowdoin Quarterly Meeting as well. He organized a number of churches within the confines of these associations. During his ministry of 46 years he has traveled over 80,000 miles with his own team, not having received as much as four cents a mile for his services. But he served over 40 churches and hundreds were converted and baptized. He was firm in moral reforms and genuine in his loyalty to his denomination.

Nehemiah Preble
Birth:
Sep. 15, 1819
Death:
Jan. 6, 1891
Waterville,
Maine
Burial:
Litchfield Plains Cemetery,
Litchfield Plains,
Kennebec
County,
Maine

In 1849, he was ordained to the gospel ministry in the Free Will Baptist church. He labored with remarkable results wherein many hundreds were converted and baptized. He was much loved and very successful as a pastor, having held that position in the Free Baptist churches in Gardiner, Manchester, West Gardiner, Richmond Corner, Bowdoinham and Litchfield Plains. Of the last mentioned church, he was pastor for eighteen years. In Litchfield, where a large portion of his work was accomplished, he is held in loving remembrance by hosts of friends who recall his faithful labors. Elder Preble was a residence in the town of Richmond for nearly half a century.

Elijah H Prescott
Birth:
Feb. 14, 1831
Death:
Sep. 14, 1872
Burial:
Whitaker Cemetery
Albion
Kennebec County, Maine,

Rev. Elijah H. Prescott was a Free Will Baptist minister, noted in the History of the town. He pastored Candia Village, NH FWB church.

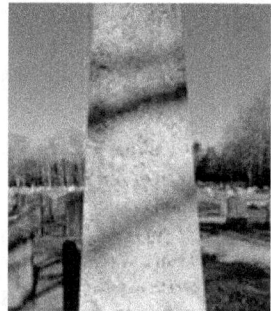

Albert W Purinton
Birth:
Jun. 2, 1811
Bowdoin, Sagadahoc County,
Maine
Death:
May 10, 1878
Maine
Burial:
West Bowdoin Cemetery
West Bowdoin,
Sagadahoc County, Maine

He was the oldest son of Rev. Nathaniel Purinton. He became a Christian when about twenty-two years, influenced by a sermon of Rev. Joseph White. He was baptized by his father and joined the Second Lisbon church, where he was elected a deacon. After a great struggle, he consented to preach, and was licensed by the Quarterly Meeting in 1841. He preached first to his own church and in other places in his own and adjoining towns. His labors were fruitful, and Jan. 8, 1843, he was ordained. His pastorates were E. Bowdoin, Freeport, two years; Sabattusville, Freeport a second time six years, Bowdoin in all nine years, and Woolwich five years. In 1865 he returned to his native place, where his wife and two daughters died. He then became pastor at Bath four years and afterwards settled at Lisbon, where at the close of an address on Decoration Day in the cemetery, May 30, 1874, he was stricken with paralysis, and after four years of patient waiting he passed to be with his Saviour. In all his pastorates he had marked religious interest, and at Freeport and Bath, houses of worship were build. His second wife, who had faithfully cared for him, was called away seven months before his death

Charles W Purinton
Birth:
Apr. 27, 1849
Bowdoin, Sagadahoc County, Maine
Death:
Oct. 21, 1910
West Bowdoin, Sagadahoc County, Maine

Burial:
West Bowdoin Cemetery
West Bowdoin, Sagadahoc County, Maine

He became a Christian at the age of 15 and graduated from state normal school in 1870 and was a student at Lewiston, Maine for three years. In March 1875 he was licensed by that Bowdoin quarterly meeting and on December 27, 1877 he was ordained. He was a member of the General Conference in 1880 and on October 4, 1882 he married Hattie Newman. He pastored churches in the area.His father was Joseph C. PURINTON, and his mother was Octavia,

Humphrey Purinton
Birth:
Aug. 16, 1758
Bath, Sagadahoc County, Maine
Death:
Jan. 25, 1832
Bowdoin, Sagadahoc County, Maine
Burial:
Old Bowdoin Cemetery
Sagadahoc County, Maine

He was converted at 17 uniting with the Congregationalists at Harpswell. He was a Revolutionary War Patriot from

Prov. of Maine serving during 1 Jul 1775-31 Dec. 1777. After his service in the war of the Revolution, in about 1779, he settled in Bowdoin, then a wilderness. He was active in supporting divine worship, and preached some. It became evident that an Arminian element existed in the Baptist church. In the separation which occurred, Bro. Purinton and others united under the name of "Christian Band." Through his ministry large accessions occurred. When the Freewill Baptist movement reached Bowdoin, Purington and his followers joined them. He was ordained in December, 1807. His labors were especially blessed as a revivalist. Finally, with mind bright and soul tranquil, he fell asleep in his 75th year. He was married to Thankful Snow, and they had a large family. Many of his descendants were ministers, deacons and workers in the Free Baptist Church, especially, the West Bowdoin Free Baptist, Bowdoin, ME.

Nathaniel Purinton
Birth:
Aug. 20, 1787
Maine
Death:
Jun. 12, 1862
Bowdoin, Sagadahoc County, Maine
Burial:
West Bowdoin Cemetery
West Bowdoin,
Sagadahoc County, Maine

First pastor of West Bowdoin Free Baptist church. Ordained June 4, 1818. Rev. Nathaniel Purinton was the son of Rev. Humphrey Purinton and Thankful Snow. He was converted in December 1808, when he entered at once upon a faithful Christian life. He commenced a membership for life with the Second Lisbon church at its organization in May, 1818, and the next month he was ordained as its pastor. This relation he sustained till death with but slight interruptions. He was married to Pricilla Wilson, 20 Sept. 1810, Lincoln, ME.

He was frequently absent to serve destitute churches, and sometimes had two or three under his pastoral care. He possessed a discerning mind, clearness of utterance, a warm, true heart, and was progressive in regard to the benevolent enterprises of his day.

He was constant in his attendance of the Quarterly Meetings, and was frequently engaged on ordination councils and at church organizations. At times he took up the mason's trowel (He was a mason by trade) to enable him to preach the gospel to the poor. He died respected and beloved. One son (Rev. A. W. Purinton), one brother and two nephews entered the Free Baptist ministry.

Constant Quinnam
Birth:
Feb. 9,1807
Wiscasset, Me.
Death:
Apr. 24, 1865
Bowdoinham, Me.
Burial:
Ridge Road Cemetery
Bowdoinham,
Sagadahoc County, Maine

At the age of eighteen, while listening to Rev. E. Hutchins, he decided to accept Christ and was baptized by Hutchins. The woe rested upon him by day and by night, at home and abroad, till he began to preach. He was licensed by the Edgecomb Q. M., Jan. 16, 1830, and was ordained in Whitefield, N. H., Nov. 17, 1831. After an itinerant ministry of several years, during which he saw many converted, teaching school frequently at the same time, he settled as pastor. He was one year each in Georgetown, Booth Bay, Harpswell, Waterville, Hallowell, Richmond and Bowdoin. In 1851 he was pastor of the interest at Litchfield, till in 1855 he entered upon a pastorate at Bowdoinham Ridge which terminated with his death some ten years later. He

had good natural abilities, rendered efficient by a good academical training. For several years he served on school committees, and represented both Litchfield and Bowdoinham in the State Legislature. Spouses: Betsey Quinnam (1807 - 1835), & Sarah Swett Quinnam (1809 - 1893).

John Holmes Rand
Birth:
Aug. 3, 1838
Parsonfield,
Maine
Death:
Nov. 7, 1907
Burial:
Riverside Cemetery
Lewiston
Androscoggin County,
Maine

He was a nephew of Rev. James Rand and was fitted for college at Limerick Academy, Parsonfield Seminary and Maine State Seminary. He was a member the first class of Bates College, graduating in 1867. He at once became a teacher of mathematics and of mental and moral philosophy in the New Hampton Institution and continued in that position until 1876 when he was elected to the professorship of mathematics at Bates College. In 1868, he made a public profession of religion and united with the Free Baptist Church at East Parsonfield, Maine. He was married on November 24, 1881 Miss Emma J. Clark of Lewiston a graduate of Bates College in the class of 1881.

Walter Eugene Ranger
Birth:
Nov. 22, 1855.
Wilton,
Maine
Death:
Nov. 4, 1941
Burial:
Evergreen Cemetery
Portland
Cumberland County
Maine
Plot: Sec-I Lot-152 Grv-1

Prof. Walter E. Ranger, son of Peter and Eliza (Smith) Ranger graduated from Wilton Academy, and from Bates College in 1879. He taught in Nichols Latin School. In 1883, he became principal of Lyndon Centre Institute. He has been an earnest worker for Christ. During the past five years as opportunities have sought him, he as delivered sixty sermons and addresses,

supplying the Congregational pulpit at one time at Lyndonville, VT, for three months. He labored in the revival of 1885-86, when eighteen students of the Institute found Christ. During five years at the school some fifty have been converted.

Appleton W Reed
Birth:
Jul. 16, 1821
Albion, Maine
Death:
1911
Burial:
Whitaker Cemetery
Albion
Kennebec County, Maine

He was a student at read to feel Seminary. Converted in August, 1835 he was sliced Sunday in 1840, and ordained that Skowhegan, February 8, 1843. He was for 20 years pastor of the Christian denomination and has been 20 years pastor with the Free Baptists. His pastorates were in New Hampshire and Maine.

John N Rines

Birth:
Apr. 3, 1807
Maine
Death:
Dec. 16, 1874
South Thomaston
Knox County,
Maine
Burial:
Pine Grove Cemetery,
Appleton,
Knox County,
Maine

Rines was married to Mercy Dunham (Pease), daughter of James PEASE and Abigail Dunham. He became a Christian when about twenty-six years, and after a long struggle with duty, he entered the ministry. His fields of labor were Lincolnshire, Dixmont, Plymouth, Carmel, Mt. Desert, Thorndike, Brooks, Montville, Monroe, Waldo, ME. He had great success in most of these places. About 1859 his health failed after which he preached only occasionally. He was an earnest and effective speaker, and a devoted Christian.

Joseph Robinson

Birth:
1774
Death:
Mar. 3, 1858
Burial:
Litchfield Plains Cemetery
Litchfield Plains
Kennebec County, Maine

He was ordained in Maine in 1818. After of which he assisted in many of the churches and revival seem to follow him in most places he went in Maine.

Andrew Rollins

Birth:
Sep. 5, 1799,
Topsham, Maine
Death:
Aug. 15, 1859
Burial:
Growstown Cemetery
Brunswick
Cumberland County, Maine

Feeling a call to the ministry in January 1821, he went into the Sandy River country and began holding meetings, and the next year he was ordained by the Gorham Quarterly Meeting at Danville, and had a useful itinerant ministry of eighteen or twenty years. On May 17 1829, he married Miss Huldah Freeman. He accepted a call to Brunswick, and a revival at once beginning over one hundred were baptized. Some four years later, in a protracted meeting of twenty-one days, assisted by Rev. Clement Phinney, he saw another revival in which a hundred were baptized, mostly among the young. In 1841 he became pastor of the church at Topsham, and after two or three years returned to his itinerant ministry. He journeyed preaching through southern New England.

John Alvin Rogers
Birth:
Apr. 29, 1830
Ossipee
Carroll County, New Hampshire
Death:
Feb. 6, 1866
West Newfield, York County, Maine
Burial:
Rogers Family Graveyard
York County, Maine

He was baptized at Lowell, Massachusetts by Rev. A. K. Moulton. At the age of 22 with his family he moved to West

Newfield where he married Miss Julia Nealey in 1854. In June 1863, he was licensed up by the Parsonfield Quarterly Meeting. He was ordained at is home on June 21, 1864.

Varnum S Rose
Birth:
Nov. 23, 1810
Islesboro, Maine
Death:
Dec. 14, 1865
Burial:
Islesboro Cemetery #2
Islesboro, Waldo County, Maine

Converted at the age of seventeen, he united with the Baptist church. Ten years later, feeling called to the ministry, on the ground of doctrine he united with the Free Baptists and in 1831 was ordained. He moved later to Monroe on the mainland, seeking for greater usefulness.

Rev Ashmun T Salley
Birth:
Sep. 16, 1848
Madison
Somerset County
Maine, USA
Death:
May 21, 1931
Burial:
Riverside Cemetery
Lewiston
Androscoggin County
Maine, USA
Plot: 1152E

Rev. Ashmun T. Salley, was born of Christian parents, richer in the grace of God than in the wealth of the world.

He completed his preparatory studies at Maine Central Institute, and overcoming many obstacles, graduated at Bates college in the class of 1875. Having been converted two years preceding his entrance into college, he worked as a Christian student accepting a call to the ministry of the gospel. After teaching one year at Lapham Institute, R.I., he returned to Bates College, graduating from the Theological School in 1879. While yet a student he supplied the church at Lawrence, Mass., for a time, and later the Roger Williams church of Providence, R.I., and he was ordained pastor of the latter church in the fall of 1879. He continued in this relation, doinig useful substantial work, until called to the chair of Sacred Literature at Hillsdale College, Mich. in 1883, which position he filled acceptably. He was invited the same year to supply the Hillsdale College church. These double duties not proving too arduous for him.

On 18 Aug. 1880, he married Miss Ellen Clark, sister to Mrs. John H. Rand, and two children now bless their home.

Nathaniel Kennard Sargent
Birth:
Mar. 23, 1797
Wells
York County, Maine
Death:
Jan. 13, 1876
Kennebunk
York County, Maine
Burial:

Hope Cemetery
Kennebunk, York County, Maine

He was born in the southern part of Wells, and was married Sept. 17, 1818, to Miss Susan Brooks, of Sanford, with whom he lived fifty-four years. He moved to Wells Beach in 1826, became a Christian in 1827, and united with the church in that place. He was ordained at Acton June 8, 1837, by Samuel Burbank and others. In the same year he moved to Kennebunk, and was one year pastor of the church. After this, he preached as he had opportunity in destitute places. He was clerk of the York County Q. M. four years. He was a pioneer in the temperance and anti-slavery causes.

His zeal, conscientiousness and sterling integrity gave him influence in these enterprises. He was appointed collector of customs by President Lincoln in 1861, and held the office till 1875. His wife Susan is recorded as being blind. He was the son of William SARGENT{born - 2 June 1752 at York, Maine who died - 13 November 1824 at Wells, York, Maine Occupation - Farmer; Owner of schooner 'Elmira' Served in the Revolutionary War}. and wife Susannah ALLEN {born - 26 March 1757at York, York, Maine}.

Inscription:
NATHL. K. SARGENT
died January 13, 1876
aged 78 years 10 months.

Edward Savage
Birth:
Nov. 21, 1766
Woolwich
Sagadahoc County, Maine
Death:
Aug. 27, 1856
Solon
Somerset County, Maine
Burial:
Murphy Cemetery
Embden
Somerset County, Maine

Reverend' Edward Savage moved to Embden, where he was converted in March 1789, and was baptized the same month, being the first person baptized in Seven Mile Brook. A church was organized at Anson in August and united with the Farmington Quarterly Meeting. In 1801, he was ordained, and was devoted to the spiritual welfare of his people and deeply interested in all the benevolent causes of the day.In June 1838, he removed his standing to the Embden and Concord church. He died in his 90th year at the residence ofhis son, at Solon, Maine. Edward and Sarah married on 8 June 1790 at Woolwich, Sagadahoc, Maine left thirten children, seventy-five grandchildren and twenty-five great-grandchildren.

There is no sting when you die in the Lord.

442

Rev Ebenezer Scales
Birth:
Nov. 6, 1766
Nottingham
Rockingham County
New Hampshire
Death:
Feb. 18, 1855
Wilton
Franklin County
Maine
Burial:
Wilton Old Town Cemetery
Wilton
Franklin County
Maine

He had been converted and licensed to preach whenin1803 he moved to Farmington, Me. On Oct 21 1804 he was ordained by the Quarterly Meeting at Anson, Me, preaching his own ordination service. He moved to Wilton, Me., in 1805. He endured many inconveniences traveling to and breaking the bread of life with settlers. His hard labors provided enough property to support and educate a family of eleven children. He was useful in promoting revivals and establishing churches.

At the August Q M in Farmington, in the barn of Rev Asa Libby, he preached the Sabbath in company with Moses Dudley. At the Yearly Meeting at Weare, NH, in 1821, he preached with Rev's John Buzzell and Clarissa H Danforth. A revival followed and sixty were converted. In 1828, he preached at the Rhode Island QM.

He possessed a strong mind, good native talent and spoke with boldness and energy. When the Biblical School was established he looked upon it's success with pleasure and was one of many friends who gave $100 for it's endowment.

Stricken with paralysis he lay for over a year waiting for the summons that would set him free.

Sargent Shaw
Birth:
Dec. 16, 1791
Standish, Me.
Death:
Mar. 4, 1866
Burial:
White Rock Cemetery
White Rock, Cumberland
County, Maine

His father left Congregational church for the Free Baptist church, and he early became acquainted with Randall, Tingley, Buzzell and Stinchfield, as they made his father's house their home. In the revival of 1808-09 in Standish, in which Z. Jordan, A. Files, C. Phinney and J. White found the Saviour, he was converted. After deferring his call to the ministry for years, he was ordained in September, 1828, through the encouragement of Joseph White. He still labored with his hands, preaching as opportunity offered. He was a safe counselor and a true friend to the slave.

Moses Shepard
Birth:
Jan. 18, 1802
New London
Merrimack County
New Hampshire
Death:
Jun. 6, 1860
Bangor

Penobscot County, Maine
Burial:
Mount Hope Cemetery
Bangor
Penobscot County, Maine

He was a clergyman who wanted to preach the gospel in its simplicity, and he went into the wilds of Maine to do so. In 1848, Moses became the guardian to the minor children of Asa Tibbetts of Glenburn, ME. Following his death, Moses' estate was administered by his wife Phebe, and son-in-law Edwin Drew. The birth places of his children given an indication of the various places in which Moses lived and worked: New London, New Hampshire, Sutton, NH, Corinth, Maine, and Hermon, Maine.

This memorialist had an old daguerreotype or tin-type of a man that was not labeled and whose identity was unknown. However, a picture of Moses and his wife Phebe was found in the "History of New London, New Hampshire" and the man pictured in the book was identical to the one in the old framed photo, which is reproduced here.

You Are Home At Last!

Humphrey Small
Birth:
July 26, 1828
Bowdoin, Maine
Death:
1910
Burial:
Rose Cemetery
Brooks
Waldo County, Maine

He was converted when he was 12 years of age and for four years was a member of a Methodist church. He was licensed by the Prospect Quarterly Meeting on June 25, 1858 and then ordained March 10, 1860. He pastored many churches in the area for many years.

James Small
Birth:
1821
Death:
Feb. 26, 1885
Montville, Maine
Burial:
Halldale Cemetery
West Montville
Waldo County, Maine

He accepted Christ as an early age and was baptized by Rev. J. B. Copp and united with the Exeter church. He began to preach at the age of 19 and was ordained in the Exeter Quarterly Meeting. He preached in countless churches during his 45 years of ministry and baptized a large number of converts

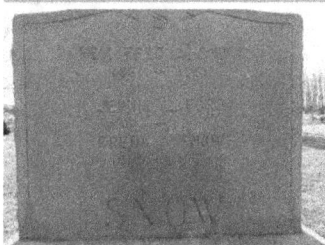

Fred Albertis Snow
Birth:
Nov. 23, 1861
North Berwick
York County, Maine
Death:
Oct. 9, 1931
Islesboro
Waldo County, Maine
Burial:
Burr Cemetery
Freeport, Cumberland County,
Maine

Rev. Snow was the first member of his church, the Freewill Baptist Church of North Berwick, to go to divinity school and to be ordained as a Baptist preacher. He went to Colby College, Waterville Maine and later to Newton Seminary, Andover Massachusetts. He was known as a Hebrew and Greek scholar.

Henry F Snow
Birth:
Nov. 25, 1831
Effingham
Carroll County
New Hampshire
Death:
Jan. 1, 1908
Burial:
Riverside Cemetery
Cornish
York County, Maine

He prepared for the ministry at New Hampton Institution and was licensed to preach there. He was ordained 1858 at the Merrimack Street Church, Manchester. Most of his ministry was in Maine but he moved to Tallapoosa, Ga. Devoting most of his time among four colored churches during 1898-1903 before returning back to Effingham Falls where he was to be found in 1908.

Thomas Spooner
Birth:
Feb. 4, 1852
Death:
March 6,1895
Lawrence, Mass.
Burial:
Riverside Cemetery
Lewiston
Androscoggin County, Maine
Plot: 0254W

He studied at St. Johnsbury Academy. Ordained, Graduated at Bates College, 1874 and Cobb Divinity School 1877. Ordained in North Berwick, Me. 1877. He was the first business manager of the Bates Student. Delegate to the General Conference 1883; member of the Executive Board of the Foreign Missionary society; recording secretary of the Education Society; trustee of Bates College.

Elder James Stevens
Birth:
Jun., 1799
Wells
York County
Maine
Death:
Oct. 21, 1886
Boston
Suffolk County
Massachusetts
Burial:
Maple Grove Cemetery
Vassalboro
Kennebec County
Maine

James was a son of Theodore Stevens & Mary Boyd. Older Bro. of Rev. John and Rev. Theodore Stevens,Jr.

Inscription:

Eld.
JAMES STEVENS
DIED
Oct. 21, 1886
AEt. 87ys. 4ms.

Blessed are the dead which Die in the Lord.

Rev John Stevens
Birth:
Jun. 18, 1801
Maine
Death:
Apr. 5, 1878
Biddeford
York County
Maine
Burial:
Laurel Hill Cemetery
Saco
York County
Maine

He was convinced to preach after his marriage, he having excused himself because of lack of education. But he renewed his covenant and at once his preaching resulted in many conversions. He returned to Limington and taking charge of his father's farm, he labored in the several districts so effectively that the church increased to over three hundred members. He was ordained in June 1823. In 1825, he accompanied Rev. B.S. Manson, friend from boyhood, on a tour through upper NH and VT to Canada. A collection of $7 was raised in the Parsonfield Q.M. to send them on this mission. He was a member of the second General Conference, held in Sandwich, NH.
Name is in Minutes of 24th General Conference of Freewill Baptists, of 88 ordained ministers who had died since last meeting in Oct. 1877.

Moses Stevens
Birth:
1794
Death:
May 28, 1866
Burial:
West Mills Cemetery
Industry,
Franklin County,
Maine

He was converted in early life, joining the Christian Connection. He united with the Free Baptists from doctrinal preferences, and was licensed *by* the Sebec Q. M. He was ordained in 1832 at Bradford, Me. He joined the Springfield Q. M. at its organization, and for many years was a itinerant ministry.

Rev Theodore Stevens
Birth:
Oct. 10, 1812
Maine
Death:
Oct. 20, 1880
York County
Maine
Burial:

Laurel Hill Cemetery
Saco, York County, Maine

A Free Bapt. ordained minister who labored in Maine. He had two older brothers who were also ministers.

Son of Theodore, Sr, and Mary (Boyd) STEVENS. He was mar. to Susan Brackett, 18 March 1836, ME. Their children: Milton T., b. 1845, d. 14 Sep 1911, Waltman, MA; Eunice V., d. 28 Feb. 1868, 24y, 3m.; Theodore Jr. d. 25 June 1862, 20y, 2m, and 15d.Newell T, b. ca 1850 Clara, b. ca 1852, Charles, b.ca 1854; Belle, b.ca 1856; Fanny, b ca 1859.In 1870 census HH was also a dau,Mary Hasty, 33y, with 2 sons, Frank L. age 9, and James E. age 4.

Never More To Roam.

Freelon Starbird
Birth:
September 14, 1841
Woodstock, Maine
Death:
Jan. 29, 1910
Burial:
Riverside Cemetery
Farmington
Franklin County, Maine

In February, 1877, he was licensed to preach and on June 3, 1880 he was ordained at Milton, Maine by the Otisfield Quarter Meeting. He organized the Carthage church on May 5, 1880 and became it's pastor. He later pastored a number of churches in the area. He was married to Myra C. George and after her passing married on January 30, 1864 to Miss Mary Oldham.

William S Stevenson
Birth:
Feb. 3, 1818
Montville,
Maine
Death:
May 2, 1891
Burial:
Halldale Cemetery
West Montville
Waldo County,
Maine

His father, the Col. William Stevenson, was born in Liverpool, England. He was converted at age 13 and joined the church in North Montville. He yielded his call to the ministry in 1868 at the age of 50 and was ordained in June, 1871 at a session of the quarterly meeting at his church. Rev. Ebenezer Knowlton preached the sermon. He has preached mostly as an itinerant and has seen many revivals.

Joseph Stinson
Birth:
October, 1798
Bowdoin, Me.
Death:
Feb. 27, 1864
Burial:
Tilton Corner Cemetery
Pittsfield, Somerset County,
Maine

Stinson, Rev. Joseph, son of Rev. William Stinson of the Christian Connection. He married in 1823 Miss· Mary Whittemore, after which for several years he resided in Litchfield, where he was converted and baptized by Rev. S. Hathorn, uniting with the Free Baptist church there in 1838. In March, 1842, he was ordained by Rev's N. Purington, C. Quinnam and M. Getchell. In 1844 he moved to Pittsfield of the Exeter Q. M., and joined the church there, a relation which continued during life. He served this church with acceptance to their edification. He was deeply interested in the Sunday-school of which he was superintendent.

Cyrus Stilson
Birth:
1801
Sydney, Maine
Death:
Oct. 17, 1894
Burial:
New Sharon Village Cemetery
New Sharon
Franklin County,
Maine

William C Stinson
Birth:
February 14, 1803
Richmond,
Maine
Death:
Jul. 20, 1886
Pittsfield,
Maine
Burial:
Pittsfield Village Cemetery
Pittsfield
Somerset County,
Maine

He was converted in a revival under Rev. Dexter Waterman. He was ordained in 1857 and in 1861 became pastor away from that area until 1870 when he returned back to Pittsfield where he remained until his death. He was an important factor in the establishment of the Maine Central Institute at Pittsfield. He helped to raise the first $10,000.

He was ordained in 1828 and the next year with Leonard Hathaway, entered New Brunswick, Canada, by way of Houlton and for a month preached to large and attentive audiences up and down the St. John's River. At Hodgdon, where a revival was in progress before they arrived, a church was organized and Stilson remained till August. In the meantime making a tour 100 miles further into the Providence where he not only preached but baptized. Age 93 yrs. 7 mo. 25 days at his death.

Alvah Strout
Birth:
Apr. 28, 1810
Limington
York County, Maine
Death:
Aug. 24, 1881
Burial:
Mills Cemetery
Bradford
Penobscot County, Maine

His ministry extended over 45 years and he did much for the cause of Christ in the Sebec Quarterly Meeting.

James Strout, Jr
Birth:
Apr. 24, 1800
Limington
York County, Maine
Death:
Sep. 25, 1878
Exeter Center
Penobscot County, Maine
Burial:
Chamberlain Cemetery
Penobscot County, Maine

Rev. James Strout died in Exeter, ME. At the age of seventeen he was converted but lapsed. While in Harrison he lost his wife and a child, and in his affliction he turned to God. After removing to Bradford, ME, he united with the church in March 1834, and soon began to preach. About 1835 he was licensed, and was ordained in March 1839. He traveled extensively, often on foot, and preached mostly without compensation. He was a workman that needed not to be ashamed. He was a good citizen and elected to offices of trust. He was clerk and treasurer of the Penobscot Yearly Meeting. Though the church where he lived was broken up, he continued a zealous supporter of the denomination. His health and hearing failed a few years before his death.

Elder Nathaniel Sturgis
Birth:
Sep. 3, 1774
Gorham
Cumberland County
Maine
Death:
Oct. 29, 1825
Pejepscot
Sagadahoc County
MaineBurial:
Fitz Cemetery
Auburn
Androscoggin County
Maine

Elder Nathaniel Sturgis, while sick abed in 1801, thinking he would die, became a Christian and later entered the ministry and was ordained 1821, in the Freewill Baptist church. Soon after this, he took a journey of some 400 miles into the British Provinces to preach free salvation.

He was a man of clear mind and strong judgment. He was married to Betsy Woodman 5 Jan. 1806. They had several children, some who died at a young age.

Virgil D Sweetland
Birth:
Sep., 1837
Palmyra,
Maine
Death:
unknown
Burial:
Warren Hill Cemetery
Palmyra
Somerset County,
Maine

His grandfather was a Revolutionary War soldier and a native of Providence Rhode Island. Virgil studied at the Academy and was a member of the First Main Heavy Artillery in the Civil War serving two years. He took part in the desperate charge of May 18, 1864 at Spottsylvania and was wounded. His conversion, which was sudden and radical, occurred in the autumn of 1862. He began to preach in 1876 and was licensed on June 9, 1877 and ordained at Palmyra by Rev's. James Boyd, John Cook, M. H. Tarbox and others on June 18, 1879. He pastored many churches in the area and at one time even pastored four churches at once.

He is attended about 200 funerals and married 61 couples. He has been supervisor of schools, the town clerk, and represented his town in the legislature.

David Swett
Birth:
Jun. 22, 1792
Gorham, Me.
Death:
Jul. 13, 1869
Burial:
Libby Hill Cemetery
Albion, Kennebec County,
Maine
Plot: row 1

He was ordained in 1822. In the Montville Q. M. in 1824 at Dixmont and Newburg, he baptized 106 during three months. His ministry was confined to Maine, New Hampshire and Vermont.

Jesse Swett
Birth:
1807
Gorham, Maine
Death:
Mar. 15, 1840
Burial:
Ridge Road Cemetery
Bowdoinham
Sagadahoc County, Maine

He was converted in 1827 and baptized by the Rev. Clement Phinney and united with the church at Windham. In 1828, while in Dover, New Hampshire, with his brother, trying to advance the cause of Christ, he became to consider the duty of the ministry. He already had three brothers in the ministry at that time. He continued to exhort at home until 1830 when he spent some time in Bowdoinham and Litchfield. His work with blessed and in January, 1831 he was licensed by the Gorham quarter Meeting and in June 1832 was ordained by the Bowdoin Quarter Meeting. In September of the following year he formed the Second Richmond church with 15 members and resided there until the spring of 1837 during which time the church and had grown to 50 members. He died at the home of his father-in-all Capt. Sanford in Bowdoinham where his sermon was preached by the Rev. Stephen Purington.

Rev Josiah Spooner Swift
Birth:
Feb. 28, 1813
Wareham
Plymouth County
Massachusetts
Death:
Mar. 26, 1883
Wilton
Franklin County
Maine
Burial:
Riverside Cemetery
Farmington
Franklin County
Maine

Son of Josiah and Eleanor (Spooner) Swift. Married Martha Coney Flint in Sep 1834 at Bath, Maine.
He was a Freewill Baptist minister, an orchardist and nurseryman, and an amateur artist. He is best known as a publisher, characterized as "the father of journalism in Franklin County [Maine].
Bates College in Lewiston, Maine holds his early papers as part of the Edmund S. Muskie Archives

and Special Collections Library

Bradbury Sylvester
Birth:
Nov. 19, 1815
Leeds,
Maine
Death:
Aug. 31, 1889
Burial:
Evergreen Cemetery
Wayne
Kennebec County, Maine

He was licensed in 1868 and on September 29, 1877 was ordained by the Bowdoin Quarter Meeting.

Rev Moses H Tarbox
Birth:
Sept. 8, 1824,
Kennebunk Port
Maine
Death:
Apr. 13, 1907
Burial:
Riverside Cemetery
Lewiston
Androscoggin County
Maine
Plot: 0442

His parents were Daniel and Susan (Hanscom) TARBOX. He prepared for college at Farmington, ME, and Lewiston Falls Academy, and graduated from Waterville College in 1849, and Bangor Theological Seminary in 1855.

He was ordained by the Kennebec Quarterly Meeting in 1851, and was pastor at Sabattus, ME, three years; at Bangor, ME, seven years, where a house of worship was built, revivals being enjoyed at both these places; at Kendall's Mills, ME, one year; at Amesbury, Mass. three years; at Cornishville, ME, one year; at Dover, ME, four years, and at Houlton, ME, three years. Revivals resulted from his labors at Dover and Houlton, a church being organized at the latter place and a house erected. He was also missionary in the city of Lewiston three years, and in the Penobscot Yearly Meeting for a like period.

Subsequently moving to Minnesota, he became pastor of the Elk River church, and did much to strengthen it.

He was married in 1856 to Adrianna Weymouth, and in 1882, to Mrs. M.E. Nash. He has five children, one of whom, O.C. Tarbox, graduated from Bates College in 1880 and practice medicine in New York City.

Ebenezer Tasker
Birth:
Unknown
Death:
Sep. 24, 1839
Burial:
Mudgett Cemetery
Dixmont
Penobscot County, Maine

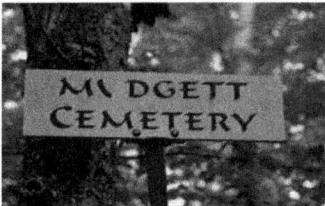

Friend D. Tasker
Birth:
Jul. 31, 1850
Jackson, Maine
Death:
Oct. 24, 1904
Burial:
Mount Pleasant Cemetery
Dexter
Penobscot County, Maine

He became a Christian at 28 and on January, 1879 he was licensed, and in December, 1880 was ordained. He held several pastorates in Maine.

Sophia Thomas
Birth:
December 14, 1814
Limerick, Maine
Death:
Jan. 22, 1888
Burial:
Woodlawn Cemetery
Biddeford
York County, Maine

On April 30, 1836 she married Samuel Thomas. She was converted in her childhood and early felt the call to preach. She made a resolute struggle for an education and was greatly interested in God's word. In 1845 she gathered all the Free Will Baptist she could find in Biddeford to her home, where January 15, 1848 a Free Will Baptists church was organized. Her husband became its first Deacon. After many years of devoted ministry she died at her daughter's home.

Thomas W Thompson
Birth:
181
Litchfield
Kennebec County, Maine
Death:
Apr. 26, 1894
Sumner
Oxford County, Maine
Burial:
Fields Hill Cemetery
Oxford County, Maine

His parents were Joel and Rachel (Wilson) Thompson. He became a Christian at the age of eighteen, and was Ordained Freewill Baptist by Rev. C. W. Goule. He had been pastor of the Carthage, Weld, and Livermore churches, and from 1880, of the Summer church. He has organized one church and had three revivals. He was married in 1837 to Miss Hannah Hammond.

Rev Benjamin Thorne
Birth:
Mar. 30, 1779
Cumberland County,Maine
Death:
Dec. 4, 1864
Auburn
Androscoggin County,Maine
Burial:
Herrick Cemetery
Lewiston
Androscoggin County,Maine

Parents: Samuel Thorne and Hannah (Hoyt) Thorne. Married: 1) Alice Dresser, dau of Aaron and Alice Dresser. On Aug. 1804, ME.
Bio taken from Eminent Preachers, by Selah H Barrett, and FWB Cyclopedia, pub. 1889.]
Rev. B. Thorne, appears to have been interested in religion at an early age. He listened to the first Freewill Baptist minister, Eld. Benjamin Randall, who preached in Lewiston. Eld Randall's sentiments, doctrine, etc, were embraced by Benjamin, his parents and quite a number of others, and formed substantially the basis of his life and ministry. In the year 1800, a few persons with himself were organized into the First Freewill Baptist Church in Lewiston, and in 1809, he was

ordained to the gospel ministry. Eld. Thorne was a self-educated man, having very limited educational advantages at that time. He studied, and acquired a commendable knowledge of the Latin and Greek languages, knew something of the Hebrew and mastered the French after he had passed his eightieth year. He was generally prepared to give a satisfactory reason of views he entertained. While his hands were employed in daily toil, his mind was equally industrious upon difficult questions in both theology and philosophy, which enabled him to acquire a larger and more useful fund of knowledge than not-a-few persons acquired.

His ministry was centered in the area round about for over 57 years, and he was the oldest inhabitant of the town at the time of his death with a longer residence than any other person of eighty-five years. He was permitted to see great changes-- from a wilderness to cultivated farms; a few log houses displaced for large, convenient ones; a few families grown to a population of eight thousand souls; schools, churches, banks, mills, public buildings, a seminary and at last, Bates College, honoring the town, in which he manifested a lively interest.

The private Christian character of Mr. Thorne was formed by the sterling piety of his mother and Freewill Baptists of those days. His integrity to Christian principles was never questioned. His hospitality and kindness were large and liberal, and honesty was never questioned.

He was one of the best and most talented ministers of his time. His extreme modesty left many unconscious of his superior ability, unless some special occasion made it manifest.

Few persons were ever blessed with a stronger memory, and chapters, if not entire books in the Bible, could be repeated by him verbatim in his last years, and with surprising skill and accuracy. This talent no doubt, was a source of much power.

He had a large family of ten children to support entirely dependent upon his own labors. He did not receive in all his life, one hundred dollars for his services in preaching.

Born in the midst of the Revolutionary War, he imbibed its patriotism until the last. His five grandsons fought in the Civil War.

He labored and enjoyed revivals of religion both in the villages and in his own neighborhood, and never better than in his last days. His vigor of mind and body continued unabated until he looked the age of a sixty-five year-old man, rather than eighty-five. Some of his best discourses were preached only a few days before his death.

His last sickness was short, his work was done and he was ready to depart. Peaceful and trusting he fell asleep on Sabbath eve, Dec. 4, 1864, aged 85yrs, 9m, calm as the setting sun of mid-summer.

He left an aged and infirm widow of eighty-three years, who had been in very deed a most devoted wife and mother for nearly sixty-five years; kind and faithful children, and many grand and great-grandchildren, to mourn their loss.

One of the earliest ministers in the Benjamin Randall Freewill Baptist New England church. He was a useful and faithful man. May he be remembered here.

Pelatiah Tingley
Birth:
Jan. 3, 1735
Middlesex
County,Massachusetts
Death:
Sep. 3, 1821
Waterboro,York County, Maine
Burial:
Woodward/Tingley,
Waterboro,York County, Maine

At age sixteen, he had serious reflections regarding religion and was encouraged to obtain a collegiate education. so he went through the preparatory studies, and in 1757, at the age of twenty-two, entered Yale College, in New Haven, Conn. He graduated in

1761. His class at the time of graduating, consisted of thirty young men, of whom ten afterward became ministers, and one of them, several years later, was chosen governor of the state of Georgia. He heard Rev. Benjamin Randall, founder of the Free Will Baptist in NH, preach and felt he had the same sentiments for a general atonement and other biblical doctrines. He joined that church and was ordained a Free Will Baptist Minister in 1764, which he followed until his death. He was the first FWB minister of Waterboro, ME. On Dec. 26, 1787, the town of Waterboro, voted to send the first representative to the Convention in Boston, to ratify the Constitution. The person they chose was Rev. Pelatiah Tingley. (Some info from *Memoirs of Eminent Preachers in the Freewill Baptist Denomination--1874* by Selah Hibbard Barret

Edward Toothaker
Birth:
May 20, 1813
Bowdoinham
Sagadahoc County, Maine

Death:
Feb. 12, 1879
Rangeley
Franklin County, Maine
Burial:
Evergreen Cemetery
Phillips, Franklin County, Maine

His parents moved to Rangeley when he was eight years of age. He became a Christian and a member of the church there in early life. He began to preach when about twenty-one, and was ordained at the June session of the Farmington Q. M. in 1849. His ministry was mostly within the limits of the Farmington and Ansoil Q. M's. His last pastorate was with the Phillips church. He was highly esteemed by those among whom he had faithfully preached the gospel forty-five years and lived an exemplary Christian life.

Christopher Tracy
Birth:
Oct. 2, 1758
Falmouth,
Cumberland County,
Maine
Death:

Nov. 12, 1839
Burial:
Littlefield Cemetery,
Lisbon Falls,
Androscoggin County,
Maine

Eld. Tracy was baptized by Eld. Benjamin Randall in 1781, and was one of the original members of the Free Baptist Church of Durham, organized 1790, of which he remained a member until his death. He was ordained a minister of the gospel, Aug. 31, 1808, by Elders Ephraim Stinchfield, Adam Eliot, and Benjamin Thorn. Rev. Tracy was an evangelist; a well-read and educated man for his time, of excellent judgment; earnest and forceful as a public speaker. He had four sons who were licensed to preach: Jonathan, Asa, Christopher, Jr., and Daniel.

Etta G Goodwin Tracy
Birth:
Oct. 8, 1865
Kennebec County, Maine
Death:

Oct. 17, 1917
Skowhegan,
Somerset County, Maine
Burial:
Mount Auburn Cemetery,
Auburn,
Androscoggin County, Maine

Etta was the daughter of Charles N. and Emma C. (Ellis) Goodwin, both of Maine. She attended Bates College and became a teacher before she was ordained a minister in 1910. She served churches at So. Berwick, ME; Pittsfield and Meredith Center, N.H. churches. She was a resident of New Hampton, NH.

Olin Hobbs Tracy
Birth:
Jul. 4, 1857
Minot,
Androscoggin County, Maine
Death:
Aug. 7, 1944
Stoneham,
Middlesex County,
Massachusetts
Burial:
Mount Auburn Cemetery,
Auburn,
Androscoggin County, Maine

Olin H. Tracy was the son of Ferdinand Tracy and Sylvia J. (Hobbs) Tracy. (He was grandson of Rev. Jonathan and Abigail (Small) TRACY). He was a resident of Lewiston Maine in 1857, where he attended Nichols Latin School, a preparatory school. He then went to Bates College, Lewiston, where he was graduated in 1882. On 3 Nov. 1884, he married Miss Susan Elizabeth Barbarick, at Ossippee, Carroll Co. NH. He was ordained to the Free Will Baptist ministry on 24 June 1885, by Prof. J. Fullerton, D.D. In 1885, he was graduated from Cobb Divinity School. He moved to Oakland, Alameda Co. CA. after his graduation, and there his wife, Susan died in childbirth in 1891. He moved to Minneapolis, MN, where he was found in 1891. In 1896, he was married to Rev. Etta Gertrude Goodwin, in Kennebec, ME. (She was not ordained until 1910, some years after her marriage). In 1901, at age 44 years, he was awarded the D.D. degree from Hillsdale College, MI.

In 1910, he was a resident in Pittsfield, Merrimack, NH, age 63...probably a pastor. Cem., Auburn, Androscoggin Co. Maine.

Jonathan Tracy
Birth:
Dec. 28, 1782
Durham,
Androscoggin County, Maine
Death:
Jan. 24, 1864
Wales Corner,
Androscoggin County, Maine
Burial:
Mount Auburn Cemetery
Auburn,
Androscoggin County, Maine

Jonathan; Christopher, Jr; Asa, and Daniel. Jonathan and his father, Christopher, Sr., were ordained Free Will Baptist ministers in that part of Maine and did great work. (Hist. of Durham, ME, by Everete Stackpole, Lewiston, 1899.)Rev. Jonathan was named for is grandfather, Jonathan Tracy of Gouldsboro. It was said he was a good type of his ancestors and showed his Norman origin in his extremely light hair and blue eyes. He had a sturdy and powerful frame, though only of medium height. Rev. Jonathan moved to Minot, now Auburn, when a young man. Ordained 24 Feb. 1828. Was called "Scripture Tracy" for his remarkable familiarity with the Bible. He baptized between 700-800 converts, and one time 45 through a hole cut in the ice. He was an earnest advocate of temperance and anti-slavery. He d. at Wales, aged 81 yrs. The text at his funeral was I Cor. XV 58, "Steadfast and unmovable always abounding in the work of the Lord." Two of his grandsons, Rev. A.P. Tracy of VT and Rev. Olin H. Tracy of Boston, entered the ministry of the Free Bapt. Church.

Rev Isaac Tripp
Birth:
Dec. 14, 1770
Bristol
Lincoln County
Maine
Death:
Sep. 18, 1827
Maine
Burial:
Orchard Hill Cemetery
Temple
Franklin County
Maine

Rev. Isaac Tripp was an early Maine Freewill Bapt. minister, ordained in 182_.

Me Rev Joseph Trueworthy
Birth:
May 12, 1816
Hancock County
Maine
Death:
Oct. 29, 1881
Ellsworth
Hancock County
Maine
Burial:
Dollardstown
Ellsworth
Hancock County,Maine

Rev. Joseph Trueworthy, was the son of Amaziah and Hannah Trueworthy. He married Mrs. Margery Paine (Brown) Dollard, widow of William Dollard, 04 Nov. 1842. She was the dau. of Samuel Hinckley Brown and Margery (Paine) Brown.

Joseph was converted when young and united with the Baptist church in Ellsworth. When he became acquainted with the views of the Free Baptists, he joined the West Ellsworth church, of which he remained a member during life. In 1859 he was licensed by Ellsworth Quarterly Meeting and in March 1862, ws ordained. He spent a few years in Aroostook County, working with his hands and preaching as he was able. The rest of his ministry was within the limits of the Ellsworth QM. He was an earnest worker. Family Records/genealogy state he and his wife were buried on the Dollard 35-acre estate, in Ellsworth that Margery was willed by her former husband, William Dollard.

Abel Turner
Birth:
14 Mar 1811
Death:
1878
Burial:
South Dover Cemetery
Dover-Foxcroft,
Piscataquis County, Maine
Plot: South Section, Row 9

He moved to Foxtrot, ME, among the early pioneers. Eld.Turner heard of Baptist meetings in the area when a young man, went to hear, and began his life as a Free Will Baptist, rejecting his Calvinistic upbringing. There is a book, *The Life and Travels of Abel Turner, Minister of the Gospel--* Written by himself, Written for his Wife, dated 1839----------
"His father, Abel Turner, it said, was born in Pembroke, Mass, a descendent of John Turner, one

who came over with the Pilgrims. He moved to Foxtrot, ME, among the early pioneers, where the last two of his eight children, Adam B., ca 1817, and Betty B, late 1818, were born. Eld. Abel Turner heard of Baptist meetings in the area when a young man, went to hear, and began his life as a FreeWill Baptist, rejecting his Calvinistic upbringing. He was ordained at age 21 yrs, in about 1832. His ministry was in Maine, Vermont, and Western New York. He lived out his life as a FWB preacher in Chester, Penobscot Co. ME.

Matthias Ulmer
Birth:
1809
Death:
Jun. 24, 1878
Appleton, Me.
Burial:
Pine Grove Cemetery
South Montville, Waldo County, Maine

Ulmer died at age 69 years and 9 months. His father died when he was young, and being the oldest, the care of his mother and a large family devolved upon him. He fulfilled his trust well. He early became a Christian and was a pioneer worker in every good cause. He organized the first temperance society in that part of the state, in March, 1828. His bold stand against slavery gave him a prominent position in political matters. He lost a son in the war. His labors were mostly with the people of the Montville Q. M., and for fifty years he spared neither time nor money for their advancement. His fine business talent made him efficient in the management of churches.

Sidney Wakely
Birth:
Oct 7, 1850.
Trowbridge Wiltshire, England
Death:
1937
Burial:
New Village Cemetery
Clinton
Kennebec County, Maine

He came to the United States in 1869, when about eighteen years old. He was converted when sixteen and joined the Wesleyan Methodist church in Trowbridge. He joined the Free Baptist church at Lisbon Fallls, ME, and was baptized by immersion. His early education was in the English Church school. He was licensed by his church Feb. 1, 1879, and by the Bowdoin Quarterly Meeting June 1881, and was ordained at West Poland, Maine, by the Cumberland Quarterly Meeting, Oct. 4, 1882. He was pastor at West Bowdoin over a year, West Poland one year,

Casco two years, at the same time a year at East Otisfield, and Bow Lake, N.H., three years. He settled at Kittery Point, Maine, March 1, 1855.He was married Aug. 22, 1870, to Miss Emma White and had eight children.

John B. Wallace
Birth:
Jan. 31, 1787
Mystic, Massachusetts
Death:
Aug. 19, 1851
Freeman
Franklin County, Maine
Burial:
North Freeman Cemetery
Farmington
Franklin County, Maine

After his birth he was carried by his parents the next year to New Brunswick, Canada. In 1809 he experienced religion with the Baptists. Two years later he married a pious lady, and in 1814 he moved to Marmashe. In 1818, having moved to Belgrade, Maine, he became interested in the reformation there prevailing, and joined the Free Baptist Church. In 1830, he moved to Freeman, near the kingfield line, and by his labors a small church was revived and strengthen till it became large and flourishing. August, 1838 he was licensed by the Anson Quarterly Meeting and on May 11, 1845 he was ordained. He helped organized a church in the center of the town of Freeman where he afterwards lived till his death.

Dexter Waterman
Birth:
Jun. 13, 1807
Litchfield, Me.
Death:
Feb. 8, 1890
Burial:
Growstown Cemetery,
Brunswick,
Cumberland County, Maine

In Jan. 1828, he was licensed to preach for the Free Will Baptist. He was ordained in July 1828, by Rev's Robbins, Joseph Robinson, and Silas Curtis, and for six years led an itinerant ministry, witnessing many revivals in the Bowdoin and Edgecomb Q.M's. In the twenty-five churches he served, as many as 375 were converted and baptized. Four churches were organized by his help. He became interested in the temperance and anti-slavery movements, preaching, lecturing and voting; has been two years president of the Foreign Mission Society, a member of the board of corporators of the Printing Establishment since 1844, nine times a delegate to General Conference. He was one of the four brethren that originated the call for the convention that organized the Education Society, Jan. 18, 1840, and joined in the efforts to endow that society. His two winters, of seven months

each, at Harper's Ferry, were especially blessed. He is now trustee of Bates College and of Storer College. During more than fifty years of active labors at over eighty years of age he was still active, conducting the preaching service every Sunday, and attending the other meetings of the church.

Elder Samuel Weeks
Birth:
Nov. 21, 1746
Greenland
Rockingham County
New Hampshire
Death:
Jun., 1832
Parsonsfield
York County, Maine
Burial:
East Parsonsfield Cemetery
Parsonsfield
York County, Maine

Rev. Samuel, son of Matthias and Sarah (Sanborn-Ford) Weeks. In February, 1783, he removed from Gilmanton to Parsonsfield, and soon afterward began preaching there and elsewhere in that vicinity. With the assistance of Elder Randall he organized the church in Parsonsfield in 1785 and continued to preach and cultivate his farm in that town until January, 1793, when on returning to his home from a meeting in Porter he lost his way in the woods and was so severely frozen that he never afterward regained his full health. During the earlier years of his life Elder Weeks was a mechanic, but always of pious mind, he fitted himself for the ministry, and was ordained pastor of the Baptist church at Gilmanton, June 15, 1780. He accepted the teachings of the Free Will Baptist church after his removal to Parsonsfield. He stood six feet four inches in height, was broad shouldered and possessed a very strong voice: and indeed he was a powerful man in every sense and was not wanting in physical courage, as may be inferred from the following anecdote which is related of him: "On his way to meet an appointment in Limerick he came to a bridge upon which two men were standing. They told him to 'go home, for he was no minister, and could not pass.' He quietly turned his horse, but soon returned, bearing aloft a stake, calling out: 'The Lord told me to go to Durgin's and preach. If you attempt me I will split your heads.'" He was permitted to pass without further molestation. Elder Weeks married (first) Mercy Randlett, and by her had twelve children. Married (second) Mrs. Sarah Barnes, whose family name was Guptail. She bore him one child.

Nathaniel F Weymouth
Birth:
Oct. 3, 1818
Gray, Maine
Death:
Oct. 1, 1887
Burial:
Rogers Cemetery
Troy
Waldo County, Maine

He was licensed in September, 1852 at the age of 34. After this, he was a student five terms at New Hampton, New Hampshire mostly during his 38th year. He was ordained June 18, 1857 by the Exeter Quarterly Meeting. His pastorates were basically in the Exeter area. The Exeter church was organized during his pastorate there. He also assisted in the organization of several churches and had revivals at Exeter, Pittsfield and Burnham. He gave liberally in the building of churches and for the Maine Central Institute of which he was a trustee. He was also clerk of the Exeter Quarterly Meeting for 12 years. He married Judith P. (Simons) in 1843.

Samuel Wheeler
Birth:
May 20, 1801
Chesterville, Maine
Death:
Apr. 6
Burial:
Chesterville Center Cemetery
Chesterville
Franklin County, Maine

His grandfather came to the United States from England about 1770 and served in the Revolutionary War with courage and gallantry under Commodore John Paul Jones. Mr. Wheeler became a Christian at the age of 17 and was licensed in June, 1841. He was Ordained at Vienna, Maine the following year in June by a Council of the Farmington Quarterly Meeting. He pastored numerous churches in the area. However, he was the most successful as a pastor that Chesterville church which he pastored for 40 years. In 1864 he represented his town in the legislature. He married to November 11, 1823 to Miss Nancy W. Keniston.

Simeon Coffin Whitcomb
Birth:
Jan. 16, 1845
Thorndike, Waldo County,
Maine
Death:
Feb. 24, 1918
Bangor, Penobscot County,
Maine
Burial:
Mount Hope Cemetery
Bangor
Penobscot County, Maine

He was a student at Hampden, Maine where he studied at the Academy and later at Maine State Seminary. In 1862, he enlisted in the Army as a private and rose to a second sergeant before the close of the war. At age 22, he was converted and soon felt called to preach. He was licensed in September 1874. He graduated from Bangor Theological Seminary and was ordained at Dover, Maine on July 1, 1875. He held a number of successful pastorates and became a trustee of the Maine Central Institute, Pittsfield, and was clerk of the Maine Central Yearly Meeting. On August 1, 1877 he was married to Miss Celestia Cates.

Joseph White
Birth:
May 24, 1789
Standish, Maine
Death:
May 17, 1837
Burial:
Harding Cemetery
Standish
Cumberland County, Maine

At the age of 20 he witnessed a baptismal of 150 in his town by the Rev.'s Z. Leach and Silas Hutchison. As Leach was coming up out of the water, he noticed a young man of serious face gazing earnestly and said, "come now and let us reason together saith the Lord." These words God blessed to the conversion of Joseph White. In 1814, he became deeply impressed with Colby's petition for help in Rhode Island, and in company with Rev. George Lamb on May 1, 1815 he set out for this field, which for the next 10 years was to be so richly blessed by his ministry. He joined John Colby and for three months they preached together there and in surrounding towns. He returned to Maine and was ordained on November 4 at a session of the yearly meeting held in Fort Hill in Gorham. During the next 22 years of his ministry he was engaged in the Master's work. By June, he left the state to visit the yearly meeting in New Hampshire and make a tour in Maine, at his home administering his first baptism. A little previous to Colby's death in 1817, Colby urgently solicited White to re-visit Rhode Island. A revival attended his efforts at Parsonsfield, Maine. For the next six years he spent most of his time in Rhode Island. On May 16, 1820 he organized the First Smithfield church at Greenville which prospered greatly under his care. At the Rhode Island meeting in October, 1821 the church numbered 144 members. He presented the organization of the quarterly meeting and at that time assisted in the ordination of the first Free Baptist minister ordained in the state. He was greatly used in his state and neighboring states. He was a member of the sixth and seventh General Conferences. With John Buzzell, Henry Hobbs, Enoch Place and Hosea Quinby. He was chosen by the General Conference on the committee of revision for the denominational treatise published in 1834. Two days before his death he said, "I find support in the Christian religion, my soul rest in the bosom of God." And also, "life is none too good to wear out in the service of God." He first married Elizabeth White (1796 - 1863) day next year after their marriage leave you a baby child. Thereafter he married her sister, Catherine White (1798 - 1822).

Thomas White, II
Birth:
1806
York County
New Brunswick, Canada
Death:
Dec. 19, 1859
Hodgdon, Maine
Burial:
Hodgdon Cemetery
Hodgdon
Aroostook

He was converted in 1822 uniting with the Christian church in his location. In 1829 he married and moved a Hodgdon where he joined the Free Baptist church under the evangelistic labors of Elder's Leonard Hathaway and Stillson. In 1840, he was called to God and entered the Christian ministry. He was ordained in 1853. Note: Marker placed beside stone by GAR.

Rev John Ansel Wiggin
Birth:
Jul. 2, 1859
Baldwin
Cumberland County
Maine, USA
Death:
Jul. 20, 1930
Burial:
Eastern Cemetery
Gorham
Cumberland County
Maine, USA

Rev. John Ansel Wiggin, son of John and Martha A. (McKenney) WIGGIN, was born at North Baldwin, Maine. In January 1875, he was converted. He graduated from Nichols Latin School in 1882, and from Cobb Divinity School in June 1887. In July 1884, he was licensed, and was ordained July 21, 1887, by the Anson Quarterly Meeting as pastor of the church in Madison. At the same time Rev. R.B. Hutchins, at the request of the Lexington church was ordained, the Rev. A.T. Salley preaching the sermon.

Because He Lives All Fear Is Gone

Stephen Williamson
Birth:
Feb. 16, 1795
Maine
Death:
Jul. 2, 1873
Stark
Somerset County, Maine
Burial:
Tupper-Williamson Cemetery
Starks, Somerset County, Maine

Ezra Winslow
Birth:
Apr. 13, 1808
New Vineyard, Franklin County,
Maine
Death:
Jul. 27, 1884
New Portland, Somerset County,
Maine
Burial:
West New Portland Cemetery
New Portland,
Somerset County, Maine

Williamson, died in Stark, Me., his native town. When twenty-one years of age he became a Christian and united with the First church in Stark. He was licensed to preach Aug. 10, 1822 and again by the Farmington Q. M. Feb. 5, 1824. Dec. 4, 1826, he was ordained. He labored successfully in many revivals, particularly at New Portland, Anson, Mercer and Stark. In business he was wise and successful and the benevolent causes found in him sympathy and support. He was a friend of freedom and temperance. His name is frequently found on the records of Q. M's, Y. M's and General Conferences.

He was the son of Rev. Howard, an M.E. minister, and Polly Winslow. He was an acceptable teacher for many years. His conversion in early life was thorough. He joined the M.E. class and was soon licensed by "camp-meeting" John Allen. Having become convinced that baptism should be by immersion only, he took a letter and joined the Free Baptists.He was united in marriage with Miss Mary Thomas, of Farmington, March 24, 1831.He was ordained by a council appointed by the Anson Quarterly Meeting in June 1850. His labors were in many towns in Somerset and Franklin counties, and were abundant and fruitful.He remembered each of the benevolent causes of the denomination in his will. He died at age 76 years, 3 months.

Lewis H Witham
Birth:
July 6, 1817
Milton, N. H.
Death:
Jan. 26, 1880
Biddeford, Me.
Burial:
Woodlawn Cemetery
Biddeford, York County, Maine

His father was Obadiah Witham, of Wakefield, N. H., and his mother, Abigail Hanson, of Milton. He was a teacher in a large number of schools. In 1834 he became a Christian, and three years later began to preach. He was licensed the next year, and was ordained Sept. 13, 1839, by the Waterboro Q. M. Rev. H. Hobbs preached the sermon. In 1840 he was married to Miss Martha A. Richardson, of Limington. He spent some time in missionary work in his Q. M., and supported himself by teaching. During his ministry he baptized 182 persons: fifty in Saco, forty-one in Biddeford, twenty-six in South Buxton, and the others in Kennebunk, Kennebunk Port, Hollis, Lyman, and Lebanon, Me., Portsmouth, and Contoocookville, N. H., and two in Bristol, Pa., while connected with the army. He enlisted in the Thirty-second Maine Volunteers in February, 1864, and finally acted as chaplain. Through ill health he

was mustered out of service in July, 1865. He was pastor at Shapleigh two years, and South Buxton six years. He preached six months at Kittery, and was supplying at Kennebunk Port when he was prostrated by the disease which resulted in his death. He was clerk of the Maine Western Y. M. twelve years.

John Whitney
Birth:
Unknown
Death:
Mar. 9, 1851
Burial:
Elmwood Cemetery
Dexter
Penobscot County, Maine

In June 1785, to attend the Q. M., and there related his Christian experience and call to the ministry. The question of his ordination was referred to the next Q. M., when it was decided in the affirmative, and he was ordained at Westport, Sept. 7; Randall himself preached the sermon, Tingley made the consecrating prayer, and Hibbard gave the hand of fellowship. He was the first to be ordained to the ministry in the denomination, and for thirty years he was successful especially in awakening sinners in his evangelistic work. He frequently met with opposition in his preaching tours. He visited the frontier settlements with Tingley the year of his ordination, and souls were saved and a few churches organized. He went to reside at Edgecomb, where a church of twenty members was organized by the aid of Hibbard. In 1787 a remarkable revival was enjoyed by him at Royalsborough. In 1788 he baptized several at Lewiston and visited the "Eastern country." He moved his family to Leeds, where they resided for several years. He organized churches at Canaan, Bristol, aild at the present Camden. In 1791 from the revival in Kittery, a church, vas embodied. In September, 1793, with Randall, Tingley, Hibbard, and Deacon Otis he went from the Y. M. to answer the call for help from the churches in the Sandy River valley. In 1813 he moved to Newfield, and through faithful labors the place of death soon bloomed as a garden. One hundred and fifty were converted during the year. Samuel Burbank, the teacher, with many pupils was among the number.

William Woodsum
Birth:
Feb. 1, 1792
Saco
York County, Maine
Death:
Jul. 24, 1872
Dickvale
Oxford County, Maine
Burial:Dickvale Cemetery
Dickvale
Oxford County, Maine

He was converted at the age of sixteen and soon felt called to preach, but being an orphan and having little education he put it off until he should be settled in life.In January, 1814, he married Miss Rosannah Woodman, of Leeds, Me. They had eleven children.He soon began with trembling to preach the gospel. He was ordained in Sumner, Sept. 20, 1823 (and there for about 17 years). Many were led to Christ through his efforts. In 1831 he settled in Peru, and resided there till his death. History shows that he founded the Free Baptist Church there, and he was its pastor for nearly 40 years. He also preached in various places in Maine and New

Hampshire, attending about four hundred funerals.He repeatedly served his town in public offices, and in 1833, he represented his district in the Legislature.

Samuel Wormwood
Birth:
Jun. 24, 1793
Saco, York County, Maine
Death:
Mar. 25, 1865
North Berwick
York County, Maine
Burial:
Mount Pleasant Cemetery
North Berwick, York County,
Maine

He was converted and baptized by Rev.John Buzzell when about eighteen years old, and at the age of twenty-one was ordained. Meeting with opposition in his early Christian life, he yet stood firm and -remained true. His labors were confined mostly to the Wellington Q M. on the St. John River. In Brighton seventy were converted under his labors

in about three weeks. At that time another baptized the candidates, as Brother Wormwood was afflicted with lameness from which he never afterwards was free. His life was characterized by the spirit of true piety, sound doctrine, and indomitable perseverance. He moved his family to North Berwick two years before his death, where his health gradually declined.

Psalm 90:5-6, "You sweep men away in the sleep of death; they are like the new grass of the morning- though in the morning it springs up new, by evening it is dry and withered."

Maryland

Dr Richard I. McKinney
Birth:
Aug. 8, 1906
Live Oak
Suwannee County
Florida
Death:
Oct. 18, 2005
Norfolk
Norfolk City
Virginia
Burial:
Unknown
Cumberland
Allegany County
Maryland

African American philosopher Richard I. McKinney was born on August 8, 1906 in Live Oak, Florida on the college campus of Farmer Institute (later named Florida Memorial College). The son of educators, he graduated from Morehouse College in 1931 with a major in philosophy and religion. Following his graduation from Morehouse, McKinney enrolled at Newton Theological Seminary and he completed his Bachelor of Divinity degree in 1934 with a thesis entitled, "*The Problem of Evil and its Relation to the Ministry to an Under-privileged Minority.*" In 1937, he also earned the Masters of Sacred Theology degree at Newton. Celebration of his life held Nov. 12, 2005, at Union Baptist Church, Baltimore, MD.

Freedom Prospers When Religion Is Vibrant And The Rule Of Law Under God Is Acknowledged

Massachusetts

John C Ball
Birth:
unknown
Death:
Feb. 7, 1872
Leverett,
Franklin County,
Massachusetts
Burial:
Gardner Cemetery
Leverett,
Franklin County,
Massachusetts

Ball, Rev. John C., died at age 33 years. He became a Christian when quite young and united with the church in Ashfield, Mass. He began to preach in 1862 and was ordained at the September session of the Rensselaer Q. M., in 1867. His ministry was mostly in that Quarterly Meeting. He preached as he had opportunity in Leverett, Shutesbury and Ashfield, Mass. till 1868 when he became pastor of the, church in Stratton, Vt., and preached also for the West Jamaica church. His death was most painful. While watching with a sick daughter, he fell asleep and overturned the lamp. The oil saturated his clothes so that he was fatally burned before he could be relieved. He was a devoted and consistent Christian, and willing to do what he could.

Isaiah M. Bedell
Birth:
Jul. 11, 1820
Springvale,
York County, Maine
Death:
Feb. 9, 1893
Massachusetts
Burial:
Pine Grove Cemetery,
Lynn, Essex County,
Massachusetts,
Plot: Catalpa Path-Section-C,
Lot-33,Grave-8

He studied at Parsonsfield Seminary, and in the Biblical School at Whitestown, N. Y. Converted in 1834, he was licensed in 1850 and the next year ordained by Rev's G.P. Ramsey, W. H. Littlefield, C. B. Mills, and L. H. Witham. His pastorates were Woolwich, Farmington and Topsham, ME, and Meredith, Belmont and Strafford Centre, N.H. He has seen revivals in seven of the churches with which he has labored.

Coming Home,

Coming Home

Never More To Roam.

Rev William Badger
Birth:
Apr. 4, 1804
Farmington
Franklin County, Maine
Death:
May 14, 1865
Medford
Middlesex County,
Massachusetts
Burial:
Oak Grove Cemetery
Medford
Middlesex County
Massachusetts
Plot: Oak Ave, Lot 113.

His parents [Joseph Badger and Hannah (Webster) BADGER] lived in Gilmanton, NH. Both died when William was four years old, leaving seven children, of which he was the youngest but one. He was bound out to Jonas Green, who soon settled on the northern frontier in Byron, Oxford Co., Maine. He moved to Brunswick, ME on reaching majority age, where his brothers and sisters resided, and began work as a farm laborer. Here in the summer of 1825, he was converted.

A few months later he returned to Byron, settled on a tract of land and married Rebecca Taylor [12 April 1827] of that place, who survived him with six children.

After some hesitation, but urged by his brethren, he began his ministry. On supplying when a minister was absent, he came to the rescue and with such satisfaction, that he was urged to appoint further services. The next year he was licensed and received a call to preach at Phillips, where his labors were signally blessed, and scores saved. He was ordained by a council from the Farmington Quarterly Meeting in 1833. He still resided in Byron, traveling over rough roads from thirty to fifty miles, frequently on foot, to preach in Phillips and in Weld. In 1835, he became pastor of the church in Wilton, ME where he made his residence, and working on the farm to support his family. With assistance of his three boys, he was able to go out from six to twenty miles on Saturday to be present at the Saturday conference.

He preached in several places in Maine, and his services were always well-attended and churches always prospered under his labors.

His wife attested that she remembered but very few Sabbaths when he did not preach somewhere, from the time of his removal to Wilton in 1836 to 1861, when his health failed.

He had a protracted sickness, and visited Boston in 1862, seeking medical relief. He sold his place and moved to Medford, Mass, in Sept. 1863, where his daughter resided.

His funeral was attended by Rev. A.W. Avery, of Haverhill.

Rev Harvey Brewer
Birth:
Aug. 10, 1812
Death:
May 12, 1894
Burial:
Ashley Cemetery
West Springfield
Hampden County,
Massachusetts

He started and was first pastor of the Walnut Grove Free Will Baptist Church in Rochester, N.H.in 1863. It started after a Revival and with the baptizing many people. The church joined the New Durham Quarterly Meeting and was organized into a church June 29, 1864.

Spouse: Julia Brewer (1810 - 1892).

Rev Caleb Eastabrooks
Birth:
Sep. 5, 1784
Swansea
Bristol County, Massachusetts
Death:
Aug. 25, 1855
Swansea
Bristol County, Massachusetts
Burial:
Mount Hope Cemetery
Swansea
Bristol County, Massachusett

Rev Willard Fuller
Birth:
Dec. 27, 1798
Sutton
Worcester County,
Massachusetts
Death:
Dec. 8, 1875
Worcester
Worcester County
Massachusetts
Burial:
Fuller Cemetery
Sutton
Worcester County
Massachusetts

Rev. Willard Fuller, died in Sutton, Mass, his native town, , aged 76 years, 11 months. He was baptized by his father, at age twenty-two, joining the Third Baptist church in Sutton.

In 1826 he moved to Pascoag, R.I., and united with the Free Baptist church. In 1831, he began to preach, and by request of the church he was ordained in 1834. He organized a church in Sutton, Mass., and a house of worship

was built. Continued prosperity attended his labors. After twenty years the infirmities of age compelled him to cease in a measure, from the work."

Stephen Gibson, Jr
Birth:
Mar. 29, 1745
Massachusetts
Death:
Feb. 12, 1812
Massachusetts
Burial:
Ashby First Parish Burial Ground
Ashby
Middlesex County
Massachusetts

He was a farmer in Ashby, and a prominent man in town affairs, holding the more important town offices. In early middle life he accepted the Baptist belief, and became a lay preacher with little if any salary, but in later years he became Rev. Stephen Gibson. He was ordained in 1807 in the Free Baptist and labored in Massachusetts and New Hampshire. He served in the Revolution.

SOURCE: The History of New Ipswich, New Hampshire 1735-1914, Charles Henry Chandler, p 438.

He served as First Lieutenant under Captains John Jones and James Bennett, and Colonels James and Oliver Prescott, Massachusetts Militia

SOURCE: National Society Daughters of the American Revolution databas

Rev Lucien Chase Graves
Birth:
Feb. 14, 1849
Vienna
Kennebec County
Maine
Death:
1917

Burial:
Woodland Cemetery
Granville Center
Hampden County
Massachusetts, USA

Ordained Freewill Bapt. Minister pastor in 1882.

Rev George H. Horton
Birth:
Jan. 29, 1862
Rehoboth
Bristol County, Massachusetts
Death: 1930
Burial:
Thomas Cemetery
Swansea, Bristol County
Massachusetts
Rev. Geo Horton was licensed

to preach Sept. 29, 1881, and ordained June 7, 1883. He became pastor of the church at Barneyville. From the fruit of a revival in May, he organized the South Rehoboth church.

Rev George Wilson Howe
Birth:
Jan. 5, 1833
Dracut
Middlesex County
Massachusetts
Death:
Mar. 21, 1894
Burial:
Hildreth Cemetery
Lowell
Middlesex County
Massachusetts

Ordained Free Baptist minister and pastor, and principal of school, in Lowell, Mass. Active in his denomination and useful in service.He embraced religion in 1851, completed preparation for college at New Hampton NH, in 1855, and graduated at Bowdoin College in 1859. Three years later, 1862, he graduated from Andover Theological Seminary. Nov. 12, 1863, he was ordained by the Cumberland Q.M., Maine. He was was pastor of the West Buxton church three years, and

other pastorates in Maine. He was principal of the Colburn Grammar School, Lowell, Mass. He was a member of the executive committee of the Education Society, and was for a time agent of the Maine State Home Mission Society. He was superintendent of schools in Buxton, ME.
He was first married to Annie E. Bean. They wed Aug. 20, 1862 in Sandwich, NH. She died in 1865. He then married Emily R. Hobson. They wed in Portsmouth, NH, on Sept. 12, 1866.

Larkin A. Lang
Birth:
February 17, 1822
Brighton, Maine
Death:
Jun. 23, 1894
Massachusetts
Burial:
Pine Grove Cemetery
Lynn
Essex County, Massachusetts
Plot: Bignonia Path
Lot-3,Grave-8

He studied at Conway, New Hampshire and in 1841-42. He was converted in March, 1837, and was licensed at Conway in 1845 and ordained the same year by the Conway Quarterly Meeting. During his pastorate of 16 years at Conway, he enjoyed frequent revivals, baptizing about 120. He also was engaged in the practice of medicine. In September 1845, he married Harriet W Leavitt.

Lewis Malvern
Birth:
Jun. 9, 1846
England
Death:
May, 1939
Burial:
Pine Grove Cemetery
Lynn
Essex County, Massachusetts
Plot: Plot-C,Lot-118 ,Grave-1

He studied in the school at Cheltenham with Rev. H. H. Hayman, D.D., as head master, and at New Hampton, N.H. He was converted in 1867, and the same year licensed. He was ordained June 3, 1874, by the Sandwich Quarterly Meeting and supplied at Barrington, Ashland, and Dover. His pastorates have been Bristol, Manchester, and Laconia, where he is now located [1889]. He has had important positions of trust on the state Home Mission board, as Q.M. chairman, and on committees of the Yearly Meeting [Y.M.]. He has been on the Laconia school board, and is Grand Master of Odd Fellows in N.H.

Rev Lowell Parker
Birth:
Nov. 11, 1811
Fayette
Kennebec County, Maine
Death:
Jul. 25, 1878
Burial:
Hillside Cemetery
Attleboro
Bristol County, Massachusetts

Rev. Lowell Parker began to preach when age 30, was ordained in the June session of the Farmington Quarterly Meeting at New Sharon, ME.

The early part of his ministry was spent in Maine, then he went to Rhode Island, and about 1853, he settled at Rehoboth, Mass, and remained about six years.

He was pastor of the Portsmouth N.H. Church, then preached in Maine at Mechanics Falls and elsewhere.

He moved to Attleboro, MA (in 1870 census) bought a house and lived there the last 12 years of his life.

Isaiah Pinkham
Birth:
Aug. 10, 1803
Death:
Mar. 15, 1884
Lynn, Mass.
Burial:
Pine Grove Cemetery
Lynn
Essex County, Massachusetts
Plot: Yucca Path,Lot-2,Grave-4

He was licensed by the York Cty Maine QM in 1843 and ordained by South   Lebanon, Me. On Nov. 9, 1858.He labored in Maine and New Hampshire. He was a brother of Rev.John Pinkham also a FWB minister. Spouse: Mary D. Murray Pinkham (1804 - 1890).

John H Roberts
Birth:
April 17, 1860
Providence, Rhode Island
Death:
Mar. 23, 1925
Burial:
Meeting House Hill Cemetery
West Springfield
Hampden County,
Massachusetts

He was converted in 1873 and 10 years later, while employed at a hardware store which was in Lowell,   Massachusetts, where he was a member of the Paige Street Church, he felt called of God to the ministry. He lay aside his secular occupation and spent some six months as an assistant secretary of the YMCA. The year later he was called to be acting secretary, but in the spring of 1886 he entered Cobb Divinity School. And later was a pastor

Warren Chase Stafford
Birth:
1823
Death:
May, 1857,
Burial:
Pine Grove Cemetery
Lynn
Essex County, Massachusetts
Plot: Dahlia Path, Lot-478,Grave-8

He is known for the work he did as a minister in the Free Baptist Church, in ME, NY, VT, NH and MA.

Edmund March Tappan
Birth:
Sep. 3, 1824
Sandwich
Carroll County, New Hampshire
Death:
Dec. 12, 1860
Lawrence
Essex County, Massachusetts
Burial:
Bellevue Cemetery
Lawrence
Essex County, Massachusetts

Edmund was the son of Jonathan and Dorothy (Beede) TAPPAN, was the eldest of ten children.In the Autumn of 1841, went to high school in Douglas, MA, and taught his first school the following winter in Uxbridge with success and satisfaction. In 1846, he entered Smithfield Seminary as a pupil, then under the charge of Rev. Hosea Quinby, also from Sandwich, and a Freewill Baptist educator, he remained until August 1847, when he entered Dartmouth College. The year before, he was converted and was baptized by Rev. H. Quinby at which time he announced his Christian purpose, and united with the Freewill Baptist Church, at North Scituate, R.I. At Dartmouth, he and his wife, Lucretia Logee, whom he had married Aug. 15, 1849, by practicing rigid economy while they both taught, he graduated 29 July 1852, from Dartmouth, free of debt. He accepted the Principalship of Geauga Seminary in Ohio. He was ordained Aug. 18, 1852, only a few days before starting his work in Ohio.He then went to pastor Waterford Church in May 1853...then to Lawrence, MA in 1857, his last sphere of labor. He enjoyed a pleasant revival and added a goodly number to the church.Here his health began to fail, and in May 1860, retired for a season. In Sept. 1860, he preached once more, his last, with great feebleness, that he did not attempt again. He passed away at 36 years of age, leaving a wife and daughter of six years.Rev. Dr. George T. Day, D.D., Providence, R.I., delivered the sermon; Rev. Ransom Dunn, D.D., of Boston, followed with a brief and touching address to the bereaved family, friends, and church. The services closed with singing of Hymn 322 in the "Choralist" that Rev. Tappan, himself, had composed. He had for some years, beem an efficient co-laborer in sustaining the literary department of the "Quarterly," and had contributed material for the "Morning Star," a leading denominational paper, and had actively co-operated in all the great general enterprises.He was esteemed by his peers, twenty ministers attending his funeral, along with many in the town who had great respect for his dedication and work....taken from *Memoirs of Eminent Preachers in the Freewill Baptist Denomination, (1874)* by Selah Hibbard Barrett of Ohio. Some info from state records; more info in Tappan Family Genealogy, Sandwich, NH.

No One Understands Life Until He Knows God

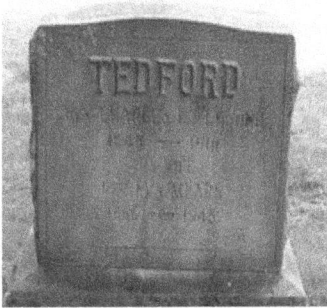

Charles Tedford
Birth:
September 24, 1850
Topsham
Minot
Androscoggin County, Maine
Death:
Jan. 12, 1911
Boston
Suffolk County, Massachusetts
Burial:
Rock Hill Cemetery
Foxboro
Norfolk County, Massachusetts

He prepared for college at Nichols Latin school and was a student at Bates College. He was licensed in June 1872 and was ordained February 22, 1887 by a Council called by the church at Limerick, Maine. He pastored a number of churches in Maine and also served as superintendent of schools in Limerick for three years. He married December 10, 1885 minutes Eva M. Mears.

Rev Benjamin Tolman, Jr
Birth:
Apr. 15, 1782
Marlborough,
Cheshire County
New Hampshire
Death:
May 21, 1863
Fitchburg, Worcester County
Massachusetts
Burial:
Laurel Hill Cemetery
Fitchburg,
Worcester County
Massachusetts
Plot: Lot 74: Side Hill

He was born in Troy, N.H.... In 1810 he was ordained. His name appears as pastor of the Ashby and Fitchburg church of the Weare Q[uarterly] M[eeting] from 1833 till 1850; from this time till 1858 as pastor of the Fitchburg church. He preached but little for eight or ten years before his death on account of ill health.

Inscription:

REV.
BENJAMIN TOLMAN
Died May 21, 1863.
AE. 81.

SARAH
his wife.
Died May 13, 1862.
AE. 77.

Michigan

Charles P Walker
Birth:
May 14, 1832
Scituate, Rhode Island
Death:
Jan. 31, 1877
Johnston, Rhode Island
Burial:
Jonathan Wheeler Cemetery
Rehoboth
Bristol County, Massachusetts

In 1850 he married, and about 18 months after he was converted and united with the church at Johnston. He was ordained in installed pastor of this church on November 28, 1061. He received only donations for his services and worked in a cotton field, of which he became superintendent. He preached neighboring districts in his zeal for winning souls characterize him both as a layman and as a pastor. He was faithful in diligent in business in his Christian life was uniform and exemplary.

James Ashley
Birth:
Nov. 18, 1850
Toronto, Ontario, Canada
Death:
Mar. 23, 1882
Cass County, Michigan
Burial:
Adamsville Cemetery,
Adamsville,
Cass County, Michigan,
Plot: Row 7

In 1826 the family removed to Huron County. Ohio, where his father followed farming. In 1841 he was ordained and commenced preaching as a Free Will Baptist minister in the Huron Quarterly Meeting; but most of his pastoral and evangelist work for fourteen years was in new fields where churches were gathered and the Seneca Q.M. was organized. In 1855, he removed to Mason township, Cass county, MI, where he preached at Summerville for twelve years and organized the church at Berrien Center, and preached there nine years. He also did much missionary work and was never idle, working as a carpenter to supply his needs. Through his instrumentality the churches at Adamsville and Mason were built. He labored mostly in the St. Joseph Valley Yearly Meeting where he spent the remainder of his useful life. He was a Representative in the legislature of 1869-70 as a Republican.

REV Franklin Page Augir
Birth:
Oct. 14, 1818
Schuyler
Herkimer County, New York
Death:
Jul. 3, 1893
Springfield
Greene County, Missouri
Burial:
Oak Grove Cemetery,Hillsdale
Hillsdale County, Michigan
Plot: SECTION 14 ROW 3
Franklin, at the age of seventeen, took charge of the transportation of his father's household goods from Sandusky, Ohio, to Racine, Wisconsin, via the lakes, the rest of the family going overland by team. That was before the days of steam navigation, and the boat being unable to make harbor at Racine on the down trip, kept on to Chicago. There Franklin made inquiry at the ferry, the only means of crossing the Chicago river at that time, and found that his father's party had crossed only a few hours before. Hurrying on he overtook them and spent the night with the family. .

He frequently remarked that Chicago at that time was mostly a marsh, and that government land in that locality would hardly be taken as a gift. His father's family made their home in Racine County, Wisconsin, near Honey Creek. .

Franklin was educated at Western Reserve Seminary, Ohio; Whitestown Seminary, NY; and Hillsdale College, Michigan. He was ordained by a Council of the Honey Creek Quarterly Meeting in April 1847. His forty years of active ministry were spent in Rhode Island, Wisconsin, Illinois, Michigan, Iowa, Minnesota, and Kansas. .

For several terms he was on the Board of Trustees of Hillsdale College. .

The leading characteristic of "Elder Augir" as he was familiarly called, was his logical turn of mind. He was abolutely fearless in his search for turht. He was years in advance of his time on many questions, having no fear for religion in the acceptance of newly discovered facts. He strongly combatted the doctrine of the literal resurrection of the body, and believed the second coming of Christ was a spiritual and not an earthly kingdom. He taught the spiritual and not the literal Inspiration of the Scriptures. .

In political opinions he was also a leader and not a follower, and was prominent Abolitionist in every community he served during the years of the agitation of that issue. He was a supporter of the Republican Party for thirty years. For the last few years of his life, however, his conviction of the growing domination of the "money power" in the councils of that party and its failure to thoroughly enforce temperance legislation, even when enacted, led him into the Prohibition Party.

He believed and asserted that when men were elected on the issues thus presented they would know that a majority were supporting them and could be relied upon to enforce the laws. History and policitical economy were his favorite subjects of thought and study. He clearly foresaw many issues that have come up for settlement long in advance of their becoming popular, and advocated the right public policy in regard to them. Haven, Connecticut,

He married Lavina Lillie Bixby Augir (1821 - 1909) and they had the following children: Arvilla Leila Augir (1848 - 1871), Newell Galusha Augir (1849 - 1918), Emmer Estella Augir (1851 - 1871), Wayland Bixby Augir (1853 - 1926), Viola Juliett Augir (1855 - 1954), Addie B Augir (1861 - 1861).

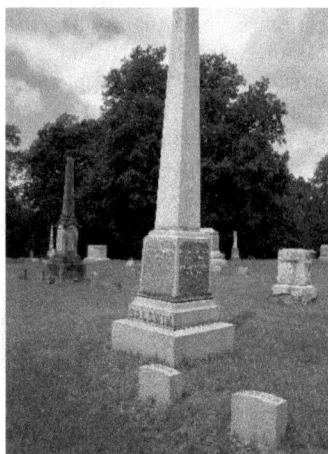

Rev Jeremiah Baldwin
Birth:
1798
Vermont
Death
March 8, 1878
Oakland Co. Michigan
Burial:
Oak Grove Cemetery
Hillsdale
Hillsdale County, Michigan
Plot: SECTION 5 ROW 6

Rev. Jeremiah Baldwin, was born in Strafford, VT, in 1798. At the age of nine years he went with his grandfather, Rev. N. Brown, to Bethany, NY. At Ellington, NY, in 1832, he turned out his liquors from his hotel, and soon began to preach. He was licensed the next year, and ordained in 1840. At Ellington he was interested in every good work, especially education, temperance, and the anti-slavery cause. He was a half-brother of Rev. Wm. Johnson, and the father-in-law of Pres. Fairfield, of Hillsdale College, Michigan, to which place he moved about 1861. A man of great energy and force of character, he was always in earnest, and his convictions were strong and positive.

Rev George E. Barnard
Birth: 1860
Death: 1949
Burial:
Oak Grove Cemetery
Coldwater
Branch County
Michigan, USA

Pastored in Ohio and reported of the Bible Institute in the Central Ohio Yearly Meeting in 1907.

George T. Baxter
Birth:
Jul. 11, 1837
Long Island City
Queens County, New York
Death:
Jul. 16, 1912
Oceana County, Michigan
Burial:
Otto Township Cemetery
Rothbury
Oceana County, Michigan

He was converted in 1878 and labored with success as a licensed preacher among the United Brethren in the White River mission. Afterwards he united with the Free Baptists being connected with the East Otto church of the Holton and White River Quarterly Meeting in the state of Michigan.

His first wife was Mary Mason whom he married in 1859/60?. On May 13, 1866 in Defiance County, Ohio he married Mary Jane Morgan (1847-May 20, 1891 Otto, Oceana Co., Michigan). Mary Jane was born November 22, 1847 Ohio and died May 22, 1891 in Otto, Oceana County, Michigan. Mary's parents were Richard S. Morgan & Margarette A. Then George T. Baxter married Margaret (Harjes) Schmiedeknecht, widow of Phillip.

Archibald Bennet
Birth:
Jan. 22, 1807
Otsego, N.Y.
Death:
Oct. 22, 1889
Waverly, Michigan
Burial:
Covey Hill Cemetery
Van Buren County, Michigan

Archibald Bennet married Harriet C. (Whitcher) Bennet when 25 years of age and began to preach at age 29 receiving his ordination two years later. He labored as a revivalist for seven years in Columbus and vicinity and for four years in North

Clarkson. In about 1849 he moved to Michigan where he ministered and organized Free Will Baptist churches. He was engaged in about 20 revivals and saw over 1000 conversions and baptized several hundred.At his death he was 61 yrs, 9 mos.

Rev James Bignall
Birth:
1799
Pittstown
Rensselaer County, New York
Death:
Aug. 3, 1869
Lyons
Ionia County, Michigan
Burial:
Lapham Cemetery
Salem
Washtenaw County, Michigan

Rev. James Bignal was baptized by Eld. Wire [Samuel] in 1820, and in 1828, he was ordained by the Holland Purchase Y.M. of Freewill Baptists, at Potter, NY. His early labors were in western New York and northern Pennsylvania. The esteem in which he was held is evinced by his serving as a delegate from Holland Purchase Yearly Meeting to the General Conference of 1831 and 1835 from NY and PA, Yearly Meetings in that of 1844. One of the two last named he was made ass't moderator. The Conference Hymn Book was published by him in the early years and ran through several additions. In 1844, he moved to Ingraham Co. MI where he labored ten years. After this he continued the work until his death. Bro. Bignal associated with Revs David Marks, Samuel Wire, and others, enduring the hardships of the itinerant period joyfully that he might win souls. He was a safe counselor, a good disciplinarian, sometimes pronounced "ahead of the times" and never a laggard in any good work. His children are useful members of the church."

He was married to Sarah KNAPP. She was in the Free Will Baptist Church in Barrington, NY, which her father, Matthew KNAPP, was instrumental in organizing. He served as a deacon and then later, was voted by Y.M.(Yearly Meeting) to license him to preach.

Rev George P. Blanchard
Birth:
Dec. 28, 1835
Vermont
Death:
Jun. 10, 1907
Alma
Gratiot County
Michigan
Burial:
Riverside Cemetery
Alma
Gratiot County
Michigan
Plot: P

Rev. G.P. Blanchard, was born in Vermont, Dec. 28, 1833. He married Mary A. Beers, Sept. 27, 1860, and has two children.

He studied at Whitestown Seminary 1856-57, also later at Hillsdale College, in the College and Theological departments. He received license to preach in 1853, and was ordained in 1860. His pastorates were at Rome and Cambridge, Mich.; Chicago, Ill; Paw Paw, Mich; Providence (Roger Williams church), R.I., and Harrisburg, PA. He also held revival meetings in Pittsford, Mich, and Hamlin, N.Y., and baptized 238 converts." Civil War Veteran. (GAR)
53rd Massachusetts infantry, Co. Sergeant) Enlisted 15 Sept 1862. is charged 17 July 1863.
Son of Abijah Blanchard and Eda Nurse. m 27 Sep 1860 Lenawee Co., MI. Mary Ann Beers (15 Feb 1839 MI - 10 Dec 1920 Alma, MI)dau of Jabez Beers and Sarah Langden

Rev Lucius Darwin Boynton
Birth:
Oct. 20, 1846
New York
Death:
Apr. 7, 1917
Pontiac
Oakland County
Michigan
Burial:
Oak Hill Cemetery
Pontiac
Oakland County
Michigan
Plot: Section 9

Married twice, first to Marnlla Marks Reyolds, second to Armintha Pugsley.

Lucius was a Baptist Minister and migrated from New York, living at times in Ohio, Illinois, and mostly in Michigan.

Boynton, Rev. Lucius D., was born Oct. 20, 1846, at Bethany, N. Y., where his parents, Ezra and Mary (Darwin) Boynton, resided. He consecrated his life to God in May, 1863; was educated at Hillsdale College; received license in 1872, and was ordained Sept. 17, 1876. His pastorates have been at Blackberry, (Elburn) Ill., Auburn, O., Wellsburg, Pa. Colebrook, O., and Paw Paw, Mich. He is now ministering to the Gliddensburg, Arlington, and Oshtemo churches, of the Van Buren Q. M., Mich. He has baptized forty-nine converts. Dec. 31, 1874, he was married to Marilla M. Reynolds; they now have three children to brighten their home.

George Bradley
Birth:
May 28, 1830
Death:
Aug. 8, 1900
Hillsdale,
Michigan
Burial:
Oak Grove Cemetery
Hillsdale
Hillsdale County,
Michigan

Attended Michigan Central College, and was a professor at Oberlin College and Hillsdale College. Ordained at North Parsonsfield , Me., July 5, 1860. He pastored in Maine, Wisconsin, Iowa, Indiana and Kansas. He was a trustee of Hillsdale College and western editor of *The Morning Star.* Spouse: Sally Ann Weaver Bradley (1834 - 1913).

David Daniel Brown
Birth:
1822
Ontario, Canada
Death:
Aug. 3, 1869
Macomb County, Michigan
Burial:
Centennial Cemetery
New Haven, Macomb County,
Michigan

Rev. Brown was an ordained Freewill Baptist minister, baptized by Rev. S. Griffith, and ordained in 1845, after which he moved to Lexington, MI and preached in the Oxford Quarterly Meeting, with considerable success, and in June, 1867, settled as pastor of the Bruce Church, where he remained until his death in Bruce Twp of Macomb County, Michigan, when forty-seven years of age. He is recorded as having served in Michigan's 22nd Reg. Inf., Co. K, from 1864-1865, mustering out at Murfreesboro, TN, from the 29th Inf. Reg. having previously transferred from 22nd to 29th. It's possible he contracted his "consumption", i.e. TB, while exposed in the War.

Inscription:
Died Aug 3, 1869
Aged 47 yrs. 4 mos. 29 days
Here he will sleep till that great day when Heaven and earth shall pass away when saints with joy their graves forsake.

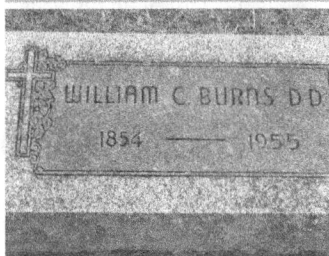

William C. Burns
Birth:
1854
Death:
1955
Burial:
Macon Cemetery
Macon
Lenawee County, Michigan

He was converted in 1868 and was ordained to the ministry in 1880 and was a minister to the churches at Paw Paw, Michigan and Fairport, New York. He baptized 35 converts during his ministry and has been active in the Young Peoples Society Of Christian Endeavor and served as an instructor in history at Oak Park Seminary in Paw Paw, Michigan. On September 9, 1885 he married Alice Collins. His education was received at Hillsdale College and the Theological School. He also did postgraduate work at Auburn Theological Seminary in New York.

Because He Rose, We Too Shall Rise.

John Jay Butler
Birth:
Apr. 9, 1814
Berwick,
York County, Maine
Death:
Jun. 16, 1891
Hillsdale,
Hillsdale County,
Michigan
Burial:
Oak Grove Cemetery,
Hillsdale,
Hillsdale County,
Michigan,
Plot: Sect. 15 - Row 5

Prof. John J. Butler, when quite young became interested in politics and religion. He united with the Free Will Baptist church of Great Falls, NH. When the Free Will Baptists established a Seminary at Parsonsfield, ME, he became a student and prepared for college. While there he lived with the family of Rev. George Lamb, an eminent minister of the village, for whom he formed a deep attachment and under whose direction he began holding meetings and delivering addresses. John was ordained a minister in 1846. He was Professor Emeritus of Systematic Theology in the early Free Will Baptist movement in New England. He graduated at Bowdoin College in 1837. Following his graduation, he began teaching as an assistant teacher in the Seminary in Parsonsfield. In Dec. 1839, he entered Andover Theological Sem. Mass. The highlights of his teaching career included holding the professorship of systematic theology in the Whitestown Seminary at Whitestown, New York for 10 years, as well as holding the professorship of systematic theology in the Seminary at New Hampton, New Hampshire for 16 years, and in Bates College at Lewiston, Maine for 3 years. In 1860, Bowdoin College gave him the degree of Doctor of Divinity. In 1873, Butler took the chair of Hebrew Language and Literature at Hillsdale College, in Michigan. A large number of his pupils became worthy ministers and missionaries abroad. No less than fifteen hundred pupils were under his instruction, and a third prepared for the Gospel ministry. He retired from teaching in Hillsdale in 1883.He was the author of: Natural and Revealed Theology (Dover, New Hampshire, 1861) Commentary on the Gospels (1870) Commentary on the Acts, Romans, and First and Second Corinthians. (1871) Lectures on systematic theology: embracing the existence and attributes of

God, the authority and doctrine of the scriptures, the institutions and ordinances of the gospel (with Ransom Dunn, 1892) In 1834, Dr. Butler became the assistant editor of The *Morning Star,* a Free Will Baptist publication.

Missionary Julia Emma *Phillips* Burkholder
Birth:
Jun. 5, 1845,
India
Death:
1931
Dickinson County, Michigan
Burial:
Oak Grove Cemetery,
Hillsdale,
Hillsdale County, Michigan

Julia Emma was the daughter of Jeremiah Phillips, D.D., and Hannah (Cummings) Phillips, missionaries for the Free Will Baptist church. She was one of six of their children to serve in India. She was born in Jelasore, India, Orissa Province. She was married to Thomas Wesley Burkholder, M.D., Nov. 8, 1879, by her brother, James Liddell Phillips, M.D., in India. She and her husband as a physician served many years in India, where he died and is buried, as well as her brother, Dr. James L. Phillips, and her mother, Hannah Cummings Phillips. Julia E. studied at Hillsdale College, Michigan, and served as missionary in India from 1865-1917. Her father, Jeremiah, is bur. in Oak Grove, as well as sisters, Ida Orissa, Mary Anne Platt(s) and bro.-in-law, Dr. Richard Gilbert Platt(s), M.D., and other kindred.
Inscription:
Missionary to India
1865-1917

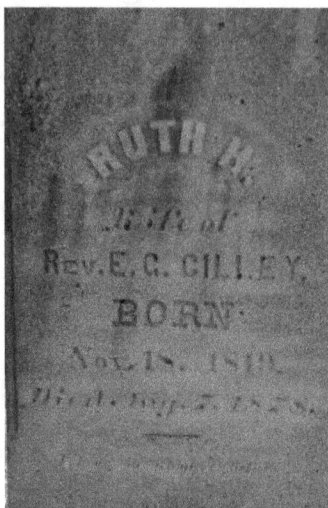

Rev. Ruth Hunt Cilley
Birth:
Nov. 18, 1819
Vermont
Death:
Aug. 7, 1878
Burial:
Idlewild Cemetery
Kent City
Kent County, Michigan,

Wife of Rev. Elbridge G Cilley b. NH 1818. It was written of her that "she was a helpmeet indeed, sharing the joys, sorrows and burdens of a pioneer minister's life, being especially active in Sabbath-school work." She was mother of five children, four living to adult-hood, one, "Mrs. Z.F. Griffin of India."
Children:
Calvin B b. VT 1846 (This might also be D. Dexter from the 1860 census)-Elizabeth (Libbie) b. MI 1851-Naomi S b. MI 1855 Simeon H b. MI 1861

Dudley E Clark
Birth:
Jul. 18, 1855
Ashtabula County, Ohio
Death:
Nov. 24, 1884 Arlington,
Rhode Island
Burial:
Northlawn Cemetery,
North Adams,
Hillsdale County, Michigan

He was graduated at Hillsdale College, Mich., in 1879, and from the Theological Department of this college in 1881. He was ordained in 1880, and preached while in school, at Woodstock, Mich., where he witnessed a revival and a score of conversions. After his graduation he preached and taught school at Davison Station, Mich., where his labors were highly esteemed. In 1883, he was called to Arlington, R.I., where he endeared himself to many in the short time before his early death.

Elijah Cook
Birth:
Jul. 17, 1793
Rensselaer County,
New York
Death:
Jan. 31, 1872
Eckfor, Calhoun County,
Michigan
Burial:
Cook's Prairie Cemetery
Clarendon,
Calhoun County,
Michigan

Cook, Rev. Elijah, of Cook's Prairie, Mich., died aged 78 years. He was converted when fourteen, and soon moved from Oneida County; N. Y., to Clarkson, where his home welcomed the fathers of those times.

In 1835 he moved to Michigan, locating at Cook's Prairie, where he saw the need of ministerial labor and took up the work. He was ordained in 1845, and his zealous labors were crowned with success. About 1858 he united with the Girard church. He and his companion of fifty-seven years, were highly esteemed.

Ellen A Cross Copp
Birth:
1849
Death:
December 23, 1924
Waterloo, N. Y.
Burial:
Oak Grove Cemetery
Hillsdale
Hillsdale County, Michigan
Plot: SECTION 16 ROW 1

Rev. Ellen A. Copp died at the home of her daughter, Mr. A. C. Price, at seventy-five years and 9 months of age. She was buried in Hillsdale, Michigan beside her. She was a pastor of the Free Baptist Church in this city for a time and has many friends in Evansville.

January 8, 1925, *Evansville Review*, p. 3, col. 5, Evansville, Wisconsin.

Her spouse was Rev. John Scott Copp (1843 - 1896).

Mrs. Copp was a teacher and religious leader, well respected. Taught for a time in the Freewill Baptist College in Tecumseh, OK, in 1920's. Randall University has a Latin New Testament, with her name on inside cover showing it was from her "Home Library."

495

Rev John Scott Copp
Birth:
Jan. 17, 1843
Saint Albans
Somerset County, Maine
Death:
Jun. 19, 1896
Hillsdale
Hillsdale County, Michigan
Burial:
Oak Grove Cemetery
Hillsdale
Hillsdale County, Michigan
Plot: SECTION 16 ROW 1

Prof. John Scott Copp, A.M., was the 2nd of four children of John B. and Cyrena Mills COPP, both of Maine. His mother, Cyrena, was sister of Judge C.B. Mills, of Tuscola Co. MI. Rev. Copp's parents resided in ME until 1847, when they moved to Ohio, Ashtabula Co. His father and grandfather [Roger Copp] were both faithful ministers in the Freewill Baptist denomination. John B. Copp, father, died in Genesee Co. MI in 1855 and his mother had died after a short illness, in Ohio in 1852.
Rev. J. S. Copp had labored with others in the abolition of slavery. He joined the 16th Mich Inf., Co. C, in the Civil War, and served until he suffered severe wounds at Battle of Bull Run, which soon after he was discharged. His superiors cited him for bravery and good conduct.
After his discharge he returned to Mich., and was ordained in 1868. He and entered Hillsdale College taking classical courses and graduated in 1869. He then entered Andover Theological Seminary near Boston, MA, and graduated in 1872.
He then accepted a professorship at Hillsdale College, MI, taking charge of the Dept. of Hebrew Languages, Literature and Church History, which position he held 3 yrs. During 1882-83, he attended lectures at Universities of Berlin and Heidelberg, Germany, on Literature, Philosophy and Theology. He also was professor of Systematic Theology of Hillsdale Theology Dept.
He was married in 1874 to Miss Ellen A. CROSS, of Wis. They had three children, 2 sons, 1 daugh.
Prof. Copp was elected in 1886 a member of the Modern Language Ass'n of America.
--from Univ.of Mich County Histl., Portraits & Biography Album...of Prominent and Representative Citizens, Pub. Ann Arbor, Mich, 1888.

The Divine Power Appears Fearful In Its Holiness

Rev Jairus Eaton Davis
Birth:
Feb. 13, 1813
Quebec, Canada
Death:
Dec. 2, 1870
Reading
Hillsdale County
Michigan
Burial:
Oak Grove Cemetery
Hillsdale
Hillsdale County
Michigan
Plot: SECTION 2 ROW 5

Ordained 1834 in Ohio Ashtabula Q.M. and was active in western states and engaged for years in the Freewill Baptist work.

Rev James Harvey Darling
Birth:
Dec. 2, 1828
Spafford
Onondaga County
New York
Death:
Jul. 31, 1916
Paw Paw
Van Buren County
Michigan
Burial:
Covey Hill Cemetery
Van Buren County
Michigan

Died at age 87 yrs, 7 months and 29 days. His parents were Rev. Jacob W. Darling (1800-1868) and Mary (Buffington) Darling. He studied at Cortland Academy, Homer, N.Y., and at the Biblical School at Whitestown, a Free Will Baptist institution. His father was also a FWB minister, having died in Eleroy, Ill.
James' life was consecrated to God in 1848, and the same year license to preach was granted. He was ordained a Free Will Baptist

minister by Rev. R. Ide and others, Sept. 20, 1853. After ministering to the Spafford and Summerhill churches, N.Y., he moved to Michigan, where the remainder of his ministry, except three years at Prairie Centre and Homer, Ill., has been spent. He has ministered to the Summerville, Paw Paw, Waverly, Oshtemo, Gliddengurg, Arlington, Gobleville, Porter and Ortonville churches, enjoying revivals in them all. He has (by 1889) organized three churches and baptized over one hundred converts. On March 26, 1851, he was married to Mary M. French, and has three children, three having died.

Mary died sometime after 1890, and he married Lavella (or Lovenel) in 1894, and had a son, Jacob W, 2 yrs in the 1900 census.

Rev Egbert Oakley Dickinson
Birth:
Aug. 31, 1844
Ellenville
Ulster County
New York
Death:
Mar. 26, 1928
Hillsdale
Hillsdale County
Michigan
Burial:
Oak Grove Cemetery
Hillsdale
Hillsdale County, Michigan

Son of Phineas/Finis and Julia Ann Melendy/Maloney Dickinson

Civil War Veteran-Pvt,Co C 4th MI CAV

Dickinson, Rev. E. O., son of Finis and Julia An n (Melendy) Dickinson, was born at Ulchester, N. Y., Aug. 31, 1844· He was married to J. Ella Cook June 22, 1875. After a preparatory course of education at Paw Paw, Mich., he entered Hillsdale College and was graduated from the classical and theological departments in I 875· His pastorates have been Bedford, Wixom and Greenville, Mich., and Haw- patch, Wolf Lake and Ridgeville, Ind. The churches were blessed with revivals, and many were baptized during his pastorates. In the war of the Rebellion, he served three years in the Union army. He became president of Ridgeville College, Indiana, in June, 1886.

Edward John Doyle
Birth:
Nov. 11, 1831
Nova Scotia
Canada
Death:
Oct. 27, 1889
Burial:
Capac Cemetery
Capac
St. Clair County
Michigan
Plot: CAPAC-OLD-20-4

His parents were M.S. and Sarah (Tuffs) Doyle. He was given a license to the gospel ministry in August 1861, and in July 1862, he received ordination in the Freewill Baptist church. He labored with the Oxford Quarterly Meeting in Mich., twenty-six years, eight years acting as clerk; he has also been a member of the Mission Board fifteen years. He has conducted a large number of revivals, baptizing about two thousand converts, and has organized nine churches. His eldest son, A.F. Doyle, is principal of a high school.

Cyrena Emery Emery Dunn
Birth:
Feb. 20, 1824
Maine
Death:
May 20, 1896
Hillsdale
Hillsdale County
Michigan
Burial:
Oak Grove Cemetery
Hillsdale
Hillsdale County
Michigan
Plot: SECTION 5 ROW 3

Cyrena Emery mar. Rev. Ransom Dunn, in 1849, in Dover, New Hampshire. They had several children, some died as young children. She was hostess many times at Hillsdale College where her husband was professor and then President. She was eulogized as a woman who was devoted to her husband's success and to her home. She was a quiet and gracious lady in her church and in the Hillsdale College circle.

(She shares a double stone with her husband, and a footstone with "Mother" inscribed on it.

Inscription:
"Together They labored Here-
They Rest Together There--
Forever With The Lord."

Dr Ransom Dunn
Birth:
Jul. 7, 1818
Bakersfield,
Franklin County, Vermont
Death:
Nov. 9, 1900
Scranton,
Lackawanna Cty,
Pennsylvania,
Burial:
Oak Grove Cemetery,
Hillsdale, Hillsdale County,
Michigan,
Plot: Sect 5, Lot 150

He grew up in Vermont one of ten children of John and Abigail Dunn. All four of their sons became ministers, including Ransom. His eyesight was poor but he never ceased to study. He became an orator, writer and sought-after pastor in the northeastern Free Will Baptist movement. He came west to preach and teach in the newer states, finally lending his time and influence to the growth of Hillsdale College in its formative years, and forward. He became

the "Grand Ole Man" of Hillsdale College, serving the College in various capacities (professor, fund-raiser, and president) from 1852 to 1900. From 1853 to 1855, he obtained over $10,000 of the original college funding by travelling 6,000 miles by carriage through frontier Illinois, Wisconsin, Iowa and Minnesota. Dr. Dunn was a long-time anti-slavery activist. In 1891, a book of lectures by Prof. Dunn, and co-educator Prof. Butler entitled, *"Butler and Dunn's Systematic Theology"*, was published, which instantly became a favorite of scholars interested in biblical doctrines, and is still a sought-after volume. Within the cornerstone of Central Hall is the prayer of Ransom Dunn: "May earth be better and heaven richer because of the life and labor of Hillsdale College." He had extensive work in Ohio at Geauga Seminary and Rio Grande College where he was the first president.

The second son of Rev. Dr. Ransom Dunn. He graduated from Hillsdale College in 1862, and went into the 64th Reg. of Illinois Volunteers for the War, along with his brother, Newell Ransom. They served in Mississippi, going thru several battles, and when his brother died of typhoid fever, he was with him and took responsibility to ship the body back to Hillsdale. After the war he became editor of *The Christian Freeman,* a denominational publication. His health continued to decline from the exposures of war. 'He accepted the chair of belles letters at Hillsdale, but it was only a matter of months until his brief professorship would end.' He suffered from tuberculosis and died in 1874, an outstanding young man, loved by his family and college friends.

Francis Wayland Dunn
Birth:
Jan. 29, 1843 Ohio
Death:
Dec. 13, 1874
Hillsdale
Hillsdale County
Michigan
Burial:
Oak Grove Cemetery Hillsdale
Hillsdale County
Michigan

Wellington DePuy
Birth:
Aug. 20, 1849
Mount Morris
Livingston County, New York
Death:
Mar. 22, 1919
Grand Ledge
Eaton County, Michigan
Burial:
Oakwood Cemetery
Eaton Rapids
Eaton County, Michigan

He graduated from Hillsdale College, Michigan in 1878. He had been converted in 1872 and license by the Hillsdale Quarter Meeting in 1876. In 1880 he graduated from Bates Theological School, Lewiston, Maine and in April 1881 he settled in Ortonville, Michigan. On December 11, 1881 he was ordained to the Free Will Baptists ministry. In 1882 he became the pastor of the Grand Ledge, Michigan church and thereafter became a Congregationalist in 1885.

Gilbert G. Durfee
Birth:
Unknown
New York
Death:
Dec. 23, 1868

Burial:
Forest Home Cemetery
Greenville, Montcalm County,
Michigan, Plot: sec 7

He affiliated with the Free Baptists in Michigan in 1865, but due to failing health, soon had to retire from active ministry. Ordained Freewill Baptist minister, bn NY, abt 1819, moved to Michigan, where he died relatively young.

Rev Abner C Eggleston
Birth:
1808
Ulysses
Tompkins County
New York
Death:
Jun. 16, 1864
Lawrence
Van Buren County
Michigan
Burial:
Wildey Cemetery
Paw Paw
Van Buren County
Michigan
Plot: Section A Row 8 Position 4
Lot A35

Rev. Abner C. Eggleston, died aged 56 years.

He was licensed while in NY, but in about a year moved to Illinois, and was ordained by the Walnut Creek Quarterly Meeting (QM). He traveled as a pioneer minister in the southwestern part of the state, where he gathered several churches. In 1849 he removed to the Van Buren QM (Michigan), and organized other churches. He was devoted and successful in his work for the Master.

Nathaniel Ewer
Birth:
1800
Death:
Aug. 9, 1836
Burial:
Perry McFarlen Cemetery
Grand Blanc
Genesee County, Michigan

An ordained Freewill Baptist pioneer minister from Vermont. Died young.

Micaiah Fairfield
Birth:
Apr. 3, 1786
Vermont
Death:
Feb. 19, 1858
Burial:
Oak Grove Cemetery
Hillsdale
Hillsdale County Michigan

Micaiah Fairfield graduated Middlebury College, VT, with highest honors, and studied theology at Andover, Mass. His roommates there were Judson, Newell and Rice, and no one of the number was more devoted to missionary work than he. One of their children was Rev. Edmund Burke Fairfield, D.D., LL.D, who became president (1848) of Hillsdale College, Hillsdale, MI. Rev. Micaiah Fairfield, was for fifty years engaged in the work of the ministry, and whether missionary or pastor, his aim was for the promotion of the gospel.

Rev Jessie Calvin Ferris
Birth:
Dec. 31, 1817
Smyrna
Chenango County
New York

503

Death:
Jul. 17, 1901
Lansing
Ingham County
Michigan
Burial:
Mount Hope Cemetery
Lansing
Ingham County
Michigan

His parents were Robert R. and Abigail (Lindley) Ferris. He experienced religion in December, 1837, was licensed to preach in 1847; studied at the Biblical School at Whitestown, N.Y., and received ordination Feb. 15, 1849. His pastorates have been with the Smyrna and Galen and Savannah churches, in New York, and the Lansing and Orange churches in Michigan. The DeWitt church was gathered through his instrumentality, and he has assisted in revivals at Bath, Elsie, Delta, and other places with good results. He now [1889] resides at North Lansing, Mich.

William Penson Fifield
Birth:
Jul. 7, 1813
Salisbury,
Merrimack County,
New Hampshire
Death:
Feb. 12, 1880
Jackson County, Michigan
Burial:
Fifield Cemetery,
Blackman Township,
Jackson Cty, Michigan

William P. Fifield came to Michigan with his parents, Enoch and Abigail (Stevens) Fifield, in 1830, locating on a farm near Jackson. He united with the Baptists in 1834, but shortly afterward became connected with the Freewill Baptists. He firmly maintained the principles he so dearly loved to the end. He was deeply interested in all the denominational work.

Ebenezer Fisk
Birth:
Oct. 1, 1802
Death:
Oct. 5, 1890
Jackson, Michigan

Burial:
Oak Grove Cemetery
Hillsdale
Hillsdale County, Michigan

He studied at New Hampton institution and was ordained there in 1836. His ministry was mainly in NH and area before moving to Michigan. He was s revival preacher and good pastor. He was president of the Anti-slavery Society, 1848. Trustee of the Printing Establishment and one of the Corporators. He was a member of the Executive Committee for seven years. He was one of the founders of the New Hampton Literary Institution and first president of its Board of Trustees. He was twice a member of the General Conference. He represented New Hampton in the Legislature.

Henry Mead Ford
Birth:
Apr., 1853
Hillsdale
Hillsdale County,
Michigan
Death:
Jun. 3, 1946
Brooklyn
Jackson County,
Michigan
Burial:
Oak Grove Cemetery
Hillsdale
Hillsdale County,
Michigan
Plot: SECTION 19E
ROW 19EW

His spouse was Sarah Beecher Searle Ford (1856 - 1933) and they has son Robert Darwin Ford (1888 - 1931).

Rev Spencer J. Fowler
Birth:
Feb. 1, 1825
Groveland
Livingston County
New York,

Death:
Aug. 28, 1875
Saco, York County, Maine
Burial:
Oak Grove Cemetery
Hillsdale
Hillsdale County, Michigan
Plot: SECTION 2 ROW 4

Stimulated by the kind words of a lady from Oberlin, OH, assuring him that it was possible, he without aid beyond the gift of a single dollar, fitted for college, and spent two years at Hamilton, one at Yale, where he distinguished himself in mathematics, and one at Union, graduating in 1849. The next year he was married in Geneva, OH, to Miss Elizabeth M. Crawford.

He was connected with Geauga Seminary, OH, for a time, and in 1850 took charge of the academy in Kingsville, OH, continuing there four years. He had consecrated himself to God when eleven years of age and was ordained in 1857.

The chief work of his life was in connection with Hillsdale College. In 1856 he entered upon his duties as professor of mathematics and natural philosophy, a position which he filled with credit until his death. Casting his lot with the college in its infancy at a time when its existence depended upon the sacrifice of its servants, it may be truly said his life was given to the cause of Christian education. He was a man of more than ordinary energy and consecration to his life work. He never shirked any duty, but in the class room, in the faculty meeting, as a trustee and as member of the prudential committee, was always prompt, accurate and efficient, respected by his associates and loved for his kind helpfulness. Added to his manifold duties in the college, the meager salary then paid compelled him to serve also as pastor of neighboring churches, and in this capacity also he was useful. He acted also as solicitor in raising funds for the college and added more than $20,000 to its endowment funds. These incessant labors so affected his health that, in 1875, he requested leave of absence from college duties, and seeking rest near the sea, after a short illness he died at Saco, Maine, Aug. 28, in the fifty-first year of his age. In his early death the students, the college and the denomination sustained a great loss."

Retire W. Frees, Jr
Birth:
Jan. 2, 1864
Wisconsin
Death:
Feb. 5, 1937
Ypsilanti
Washtenaw County
Michigan
Burial:
Sand Creek Cemetery
Lenawee County
Michigan

FREES, Rev. R. W. [Retire W. Jr], 1864-1937, b. Wisconsin, d. Mich. He is bur in Sand Creek Cem. Lenawee Co. MI. He was an ordained minister, and a dth cert.

Newton Preston Gates
Birth:
Feb. 18, 1894
Clay County, Arkansas
Death:
Nov. 1, 1977
Detroit,
Wayne County, Michigan
Burial:
Roseland Park Cemetery,
Berkley, Oakland County,
Michigan

He was the founder of the First Free Will Baptist Church in Hazel Park, which was the very first Free Will Baptist Church in the state of Michigan after the 1935 merger of the present FWB Natl'

Association. He was the founder of the Liberty Association of Free Will Baptist churches in the state and was founder of the Free Will Baptist Temple in Detroit. He was widely known as a song writer and singer. He was awarded the Professor of Music degree from the Arkansas State Normal Music College. His daughter, Winona, married Raymond Riggs which continued a large legacy of FWB ministers.

Alba A Glovier
Birth:
Dec. 23, 1856
New Hampshire
Death:
Dec. 7, 1933
Chicago
Cook County
Illinois
Burial:
Mount Evergreen Cemetery
Jackson
Jackson County
Michigan
Plot: Sec C Lot 107

Death Certificate
Name: Alba A. Glovier
Event Date: 07 Dec 1933
Event Place: Oak Park, Cook, Illinois
Gender: Male
Race:

Age: 76
Birth Year (Estimated): 1857
Birth Date: 23 Dec 1856
Birthplace: Easton,   New
Hampshire
Father's Name: Ivory H. Glovier
Occupation: Minister
Residence Place: Chicago, Ill.
Spouse's Name: Mary Elizabeth
Burial Date: 09 Dec 1933
Burial Place: Jackson, Jackson,
Mich.Family links: Spouse:
Mary Elizabeth Glovier (1861 -
1940)*
Parents, J.H. and L.S. (McCullock)
Glovier, b. in East Landaff, NH,
Dec. 22, 1856. He mar. Miss Etta
P. Farr, who d. two yrs later. "Bro.
Glovier is now pursuing a course
of theological study at Hillsdale
College with the ministry in
view."

Thomas Grinnell
Birth:
1794
Exeter
Washington County, Rhode
Island
Death:
Feb. 4, 1882
Bethel
Branch County, Michigan
Burial:
Snow Prairie Cemetery
Bethel
Branch County, Michigan

A native of Exeter, R. I., died at
age 89 years. Shortly after his
marriage he made his home in
Genesee County, N.Y., where he
was ordained in 1826. Two years
later he moved to Chautauqua
County, where his ministry was
marked by persevering efforts

for the cause he loved. Later he
labored in Wisconsin and Illinois,
making his home in Michigan.
Note: *Chautauqua Co. NY history:*
The Free-Will Baptist Church, in
the town of Cherry Creek, was
formed about the year 1826, by
Rev Thomas Grinnell; and is said
to have been the earliest
religious organization in the
town.

John W Hallack
Birth:
Oct. 27, 1844
New York
Death:
Jan. 26, 1901
Sparta

Kent County, Michigan
Burial:
Greenwood Cemetery
Sparta
Kent County, Michigan

Ordained in June 1872, by the Michigan Yearly Meeting, after his return from the army.
John Hallack served in Co.L, 8th Michigan Cavalry during the Civil War.

Elisha Wesley Harding
Birth:
Jan. 15, 1852
Warsaw
Jefferson County, Pennsylvania
Death:
Jan. 3, 1951net
Corunna
Shiawassee County, Michigan
Burial:
Yerian Cemetery
Vernon
Shiawassee County, Michigan

He died at the age of 44. He was converted when he was 16 years of age, licensed by the Leicester church in 1838 and ordained 10 years later in 1848. He preached at Warsaw, New York for six years and in the Elk County

Quarterly Meeting in Pennsylvania. In 1855, they moved to Michigan where he was pastor at Venice and Vernon until his death.

Rev Lyle Henry Hatfield
Birth:
Aug. 14, 1885
Wisconsin
Death:
Oct. 26, 1956
Alpena
Alpena County
Michigan
Burial:
Evergreen Cemetery
Alpena
Alpena County
Michigan
Plot: 24-69 S

Son of William E. HATFIELD, and Wealthy (Rowley) HATFIELD.
He was a student living at Osseo, Hillsdale Co., Mich., when he mar. Nellie May Harter, 20 June 1912. (Her father: Isaac Harter, and mother: Sophia C. Crane.

In 1917 WW I Draft, he was at Sandusky, Sanilac, Michigan, and his occupation was "ordained minister." His Michigan death record stated his occ. was "Ret. Bapt. Minister."

Rev Julius Perry Hewes
Birth:
Mar. 30, 1851
Wisconsin
Death:
Feb. 22, 1907
Hillsdale
Hillsdale County
Michigan
Burial:
Oak Grove Cemetery
Hillsdale
Hillsdale County
Michigan
Plot: SECTION 13 ROW 17

Son of David and Sarah Thompson Hewes, was born at Clayton, Wis., March 30, 1851. His father was killed in the battle at Corinth, Miss., in October, 1862, and his invalid mother was dependent on her only son. With commendable perseverance he applied himself to the work, studying at Lawrence University, Wis., and at Hillsdale College, Mich., graduating from the Theological department at Hillsdale in 1885. He received license to preach in 1872, nine years after his conversion, and was ordained March 8, 1876. His pastorates have been at Pittsford and Bankers, Mich., and Hortonville, Fairwater and Waupun, Wis. These pastorates have been successful, those at Hortonville and Pittsford having been attended with extensive revivals.

Rev Jonathan Niles Hinckley
Birth:
Jun., 1772
Death:
Jun. 27, 1855
Breedsville
Van Buren County, Michigan
Burial:
Breedsville Cemetery
Breedsville
Van Buren County, Michigan

Rev. Jonathan N. Hinckley, was ordained at Russia, NY, in 1806, and settled in Parma, Ohio in 1816. He soon found nine others at Ogden who were ready to unite with him, and a church was organized which soon numbered nearly one hundred. Among the original members of this church were John Hill and Oliver A. Willard, the grandfathers of Miss Frances E. Willard. In 1819 he gathered the Harrisville, Ohio church, which though not itself

permanent, was the germ of the Medina Quarterly Meeting. At Milan he organized another church, which stood as a moral light until the Huron Q.M. was built up. He soon returned to New York, however, and continued to labor with the churches of the Monroe Q.M., until 1847, when he removed to Michigan, and remained with the Anthwerp church (Van Buren Q.M.) until his death. He was for many years a leader and a father among the people of his choice."
Inscription:
Rev. Jonathan N. Hinckley
Died
June 27, 1855

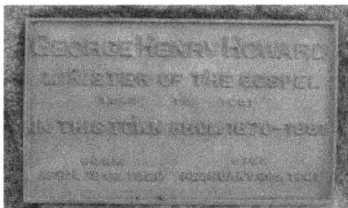

George Henry Howard
Birth: Apr. 18, 1829
Union
Bloome County, New York
Death:
Feb. 3, 1907
Michigan
Burial:
Ortonville Cemetery
Brandon Gardens
Oakland County,
Michigan

He consecrated his life to God in November, 1857 and received ordination on June 16, 1867 in the Wolf River Quarterly Meeting, Wisconsin. He began his work with the Rosendale, Wisconsin church and then removed to Ortonville, Michigan and later to Lisbon, Michigan. He baptized at 200 converts.

Edward J. Howes
Birth:
Oct. 17, 1838
Ontario County, New York
Death:
Mar. 16, 1906
Michigan
Burial:
Knauss Cemetery
Kinderhook
Branch County, Michigan
Plot: Lot 92

The family moved to Hillsdale County, Michigan in 1848, and nine years later Howe was converted and united with the North Reading church. He was ordained by the Hillsdale Quarterly Meeting at Cambridge in 1864. His pastorate was with the Salem and Green Oak churches of the Oakland Quarterly Meeting In 1865. He was married in 1870 and the next year became pastor of the Fairfield, Michigan church. After 12 years as a faithful leader there he was again compelled to abandon the work because of poor health.

Thomas Huckins
Birth:
1795
Lee, New Hampshire
Death:
1853
Lexington, Michigan
Burial:
Huckins Cemetery
Croswell
Sanilac County, Michigan

Left an orphan in early life, after serving in the war of 1812, he married and moved to Canada where he joined the first Free Will Baptist church organized in that locality. In 1819 he moved to Dunwick, and later to London. In these places churches were organized and the latter he served as a Deacon until 1827, when he was ordained to the ministry, which occurred soon after. He labored in that vicinity for 10 years gathering three churches and then moved to Lexington, Michigan where his

remaining years were spent. Here he soon organized a church to which about 60 members were added during his pastorate.

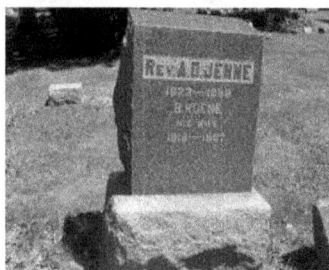

Alonzo O. Jenne
Birth:
1822
Hartland, Vermont
Death:
1892
Michigan
Burial:
Needmore Cemetery
Needmore
Eaton County,
Michigan

He was converted in 1837; received license to preach in 1847, studying at Whitestown Seminary, New York and was ordained in April, 1853. Much of his ministry was done in the Grand River Quarterly Meeting.

Oh! How Precious Is The Dust Of A Believer!"

Samuel Lamson Julian
Birth:
Sep. 16, 1804
Portsmouth
Rockingham County
New Hampshire
Death:
Mar. 29, 1876
Wayne County, Michigan
Burial:
White Cemetery
Dowagiac
Cass County, Michigan
Plot: Row 6

Samuel Lamson Julian is the eldest child of Andrew Julian and Catherine Lamson. His family was poor and made an honest living by hard work and industry in Portsmouth, New Hampshire. SLJ had distinct recollections of news of significant events of the War of 1812. His father, Andrew, sailed his last voyage during this war. Events recalled were the looming British Fleet off New Hampshire's coast, at Rye Beach, Perry's victory on Lake Erie, the Battle of Plattsburg, Hall's defeat at Detroit, Andrew Jackson's victory at New Orleans and finally the Declarations of Peace. While he was young 2 brothers died young. Shortly thereafter,

his mother, Catherine Lamson, passed away in 1814. These deaths made a significant impression on young Samuel regarding the subject of death. On her deathbed, his mother impressed upon him to seek the Lord. It is something he never forgot and ultimately, he became a traveling preacher.

His father married Mary Muchmore who became his step-mother. At her urging,

As a young adult man, he became acquainted with the Free Will Baptist Church and became a traveling minister for congregation. His journeys took him through New Hampshire, Maine, Illinois and Michigan.

Began to preach in 1830, ordained Brookfield, Nov. 6, 1833. Pastored several churches, and organized churches in Van Buren Co. Mich, and also in Illinois.

He met Nancy L. Hill, daughter of Joshua Hill, Limerick, Maine and was married by Elder S. Burbank on November 2, 1831. They initially set up their home in Shapleigh, Maine.

Samuel had a falling out with the Free Will Baptist Church around 1861. On page 44 of his unpublished autobiography (1875), Samuel says he was "cast out of the synagogue" on the grounds of his "teaching false doctrine such as the non-immortality of the soul and annihilation of the wicked...and other pernicious doctrine contrary to the views of ...the Free Will Baptists denomination.

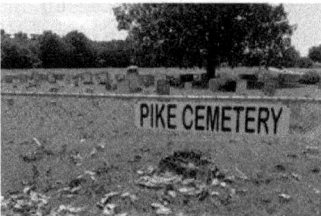

Anson Green Kalar
Birth:
Nov. 8, 1833
Stamford, Ontario,Canada
Death:
Jan. 31, 1902
Richfield Center,
Genesee County,Michigan
Burial:
Cottage Cemetery
Richfield Center,
Genesee County, Michigan

Parents were William Kalar and Winifred Hawley. A minister of the Freewill Baptist, licensed in April 1877, and pastor in Genesee Quarterly Meeting, Michigan.

Ada Montgomery Kennan
Birth:
Jun. 4, 1839
Madison
Lake County, Ohio
Death:
Apr. 14, 1894
Hillsdale
Hillsdale County, Michigan
Burial:
Oak Grove Cemetery
Hillsdale
Hillsdale County,
Michigan

Freewill Baptist minister and pastor. Wife of Rev. George Kennan (1832 - 1905). She was also the mother of Ralph Kennan who was also an effective Free Will Baptist minister.

Moses Rice Kenny
Birth:
Sep. 6, 1816
Townshend
Windham County, Vermont
Death:
Mar. 25, 1905
Hillsdale
Hillsdale County, Michigan
Burial:
Oak Grove Cemetery
Hillsdale
Hillsdale County, Michigan

An ordained Free Will Baptist minister and pastor, born in VT but lived in mid-west for many years. Married Elizabeth "Betsey" Ross, -16 Nov. 1843- Ashtabula County, Ohio. Married Caroline Gage-15 April 1863- Ashtabula County, Ohio.

Samuel Ketcham
Birth:
Feb. 2, 1807
Chautauqua, New York
Death:
May 6, 1889
Mason, Cass County, Michigan
Burial:
Five Points Cemetery
Edwardsburg
Cass County, Michigan

He was converted in early manhood and went to Michigan about the time of his marriage to Abigail Pullman, which was consummated on March 13, 1831. She was his companion for more than half a century. On July 15, 1848 he was ordained at Gillead and his ministry was spent in the St. Joseph Valley Quarterly Meeting.

Elijah Kingsbury
Birth:
Unknown
Death:
Aug. 16, 1862

Oakland County, Michigan
Burial:
Kingsbury Cemetery,
Oxford, Oakland County,
Michigan
Plot: Lot 8 Grave 1

Minister and also the father of Rev. Leonard Kingsbury.

Leonard Kingsbury

Birth:
1794
Death:
Oct. 19, 1879
Oakland County, Michigan,
Burial:
Kingsbury Cemetery, Oxford,
Oakland County, Michigan,
Plot: Lot 8 Grave 2

He was converted under the labor of Rev. E. Hannibal. He began to preach and was licensed by the Free Will Baptist Church in Clarkston, New York. He continued to labor in that vicinity until 1834. After which, he moved to the state of Michigan where he was ordained and was accepted into the Oakland quarterly meeting with

the Bruce church. His labors were well known since the established several churches in the Oxford quarterly meeting. He loved the denomination and carefully gave of his time and money and aiding its evangelistic work and benevolent enterprises.

Kingsbury, Rev. Leonard, son of Rev. Elijah Kingsbury, was born in Boonville, N. Y., June 4, 1794, and died at Addison, Mich., Oct. 19, 1879. When quite young he moved to Clarkson, N. Y., where at the age of seventeen he was converted under the labors of Rev. E. Hannibal. He soon began to preach and was licensed by the church. He continued to labor in the vicinity until 1834, when he took up the work in Michigan. In the report for 1834, he appears as an ordained minister coming into the Oakland Q. M. with the Bruce church. In this vicinity his life was spent. God blessed his labors in building up several churches and in organizing the Oxford Q. M. He continued true to his trust till death, though in advanced years he was not active in consequence of the infirmities which came with age. He was a man of perseverance and strong faith in God. He loved the denomination, and cheerfully gave his time and money in aiding its evangelistic work and its benevolent enterprises.

Arnold D. Knight

Birth:
Apr. 8, 1803
Oneida County, New York
Death:

Mar. 18, 1889
Burial:
East Hill Cemetery
Osseo
Hillsdale County, Michigan
Plot: Sec. A, Lot 161

On January 2, 1823 he married Harriet M. Knight. At the age of 18 he was converted and before 1840 he was ordained at the Pittsfield church. He held long pastorates with the Pittsfield, Spencer, and Rochester churches along with some other churches for a brief time. In all these pastorates there were revivals. He baptized over 200 converts and assisted in gathering's six churches.

John Beal Lash
Birth:
Jan. 25, 1841
Athens County,
Ohio
Death:
Jul. 17, 1901
Hillsdale,
Hillsdale County, Michigan
Burial:
Oak Grove Cemetery,
Hillsdale,
Hillsdale County,
Michigan

An ordained Freewill Baptist minister from Ohio, who moved to Michigan and was a great warrior for Christ.

J. B. Leavenworth
Birth:
Jun. 5, 1820
Sandgate, Vermont
Death:
Sep. 20, 1905
Michigan
Burial:
Novi Cemetery
Novi
Oakland County, Michigan

He was born of Puritan ancestry in Vermont but later settled in Novi, Michigan about 1844 and received ordination 18 years later and his ministry was in this vicinity.

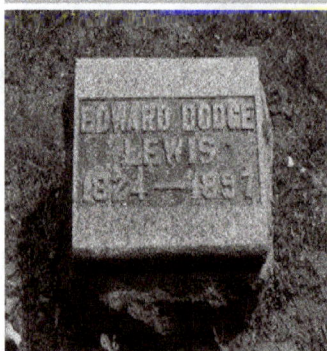

Rev Edward Dodge Lewis
Birth:
Feb. 9, 1823
West Windsor
Broome County
New York
Death:
Oct. 2, 1897
Burial:
Oak Grove Cemetery
Hillsdale
Hillsdale County
Michigan
Plot: SECTION 16 ROW 8

Rev. Edward Dodge LEWIS, son of Solomon and Hannah (Weeks) LEWIS, was educated at Farmington Academy and Geauga Seminary, Ohio. Soon after his conversion in 1841, he began to preach, and May 23, 1847, was ordained in Bazetta, Ohio. His first pastorate was as Williamsfield, O., commencing in 1844. After this he labored in Crawford Quarterly Meeting Penn, and the Lake Co. QM, in Ohio. In 1848 he entered the work in Wisconsin, with pastorates at Rutland and Cookville three years; Oregon, three years, organizing a church at Bellville, Johnstown three years; Honey Creek seven years; Warren, Ill, two yrs; Rock Creek three yrs; Prairie City two yrs; Strong's Prairie, Wis, several yrs while regaining health; Bradford 1875-77; Oakfield five yrs; Gobleville, MI, five yrs; and Burnett, Wis.. These churches have been blessed under his labors, with many additions to the membership.
He has held various positions of

responsibility, and was a member of the Centennial General Conference.

On April 3, 1844, in Ashtabula, O, he was married to Mary P. Woodworth, who received from the Ashtabula, QM, Ohio, license to preach, and engaged with him in the work.

She died in 1863, and in 1865, he was married to Miss Eliza A. Cole, of Providence, R.I., who was graduated from Hillsdale College, Mich, in 1863.

Rev Rick L. Locklear
Birth:
Nov. 5, 1959
Death:
Mar. 28, 2017
Michigan
Burial:
Michigan Memorial Park
Flat Rock
Wayne County, Michigan

He passed away at the age of 57, and had been a resident of Trenton. He was the dear son of

Rev. Lloyd and Lois Marie. Cherished husband of Donna. They were married for 36 years. Devoted father of Jessica (Dan) Corne, Jonathan (Stephanie), and Hannah Locklear. "Big Poppy" of Brooks, Vivian, Rickey, and Beckett. Loving brother of Rev. Michael, Bruce, the late Lona, and Towonica. He will also be missed by other dear family members, his church family, and many loving friends. He served as Pastor for the Woodhaven Free Will Baptist Church for 30 years.

David H Lord
Birth:
Aug. 9, 1814
Rumney
Grafton County, New Hampshire
Death:
Jun. 14, 1889
Hillsdale
Hillsdale County, Michigan
Burial:
Oak Grove Cemetery
Hillsdale
Hillsdale County, Michigan

Rev. D.H. Lord was the son of Thomas H. and Louisa (Avery) Lord. He consecrated his life to God in Aug. 1832, and soon began to preach, studying at Parsonfield Seminary, ME, in

1835-36, and on Sept 28, 1836, was ordained to the gospel ministry in the Free Will Baptist Church. He ministered successively to churches in Portsmouth, NH, Springvale, E. Lebanon, and others in Maine, and Newport and Pascoag in RI, in Medina, OH, and in Howard City, MI. He baptized over five hundred converts. His voice having failed, he studied medicine at Brunswick, ME, and Vermont Medical College, graduating in 1849. In Sept. 1838, he married Elmira Clark of Dover, NH, who died seven years later. In 1848, he married Annette M. Merrill, of Parsonfield, ME. After a brief illness at Hillsdale, MI, he died and was buried there. By his wide and benevolent life, he exerted a wide influence for God.

Rev John Stewart Manning
Birth:
Apr. 3, 1813
Whitehall
Washington County
New York
Death:

Jun. 25, 1893
Cairo, Alexander County
Illinois

Burial:
Oak Grove Cemetery
Hillsdale
Hillsdale County, Michigan,
Plot: SECTION 7 ROW 2

John Stewart Manning, son of Ziba Manning and Rachel Polley. He married Maryette Hammond on May 24, 1844. She was born on Jan 24, 1822 in Perrysburg, Cattaraugus, New York, USA. She died on Oct 11, 1899 in Hillsdale, Hillsdale, Michigan,
He founded the Manning Bible Institute in Cairo, Illinois for the Freeman coming up the Mississippi and Underground Railroad.

Joseph William Mauck
Birth:
Aug. 17, 1852
Cheshire
Gallia County,
Ohio
Death:
Jul. 7, 1937
Hillsdale
Hillsdale County,
Michigan
Burial:
Oak Grove Cemetery
Hillsdale
Hillsdale County,
Michigan

Inscription:
President of Hillsdale College
1902-1922

Dr. Mauck was a graduate of Hillsdale College, Class of 1875, after which he became Professor of Classical Languages at the college. He later served as Chancellor of the University of South Dakota. Dr. Mauck was President of Hillsdale College for 20 years, retiring in 1922 to his beloved home, Sunnycrest, with the title President-Emeritus.

John H Maynard
Birth:

November 29, 1830
Junius, New York
Death:
1905
Burial:
Greenwood Cemetery
Sparta
Kent County, Michigan

After his marriage to Mary Williams in 1853, years later they moved to the state of Michigan. He was ordained in the Hillsdale Quarterly Meeting in January, 1866 with Rev. John Thomas, who had baptized him, preaching the sermon. Most of his pastorates were in the state of Michigan where he served as the Michigan Yearly Meeting clerk for many years and for three times a delegate to the General Conference.

Rev Charles Blunt Mills
Birth:
May 5, 1823
York County, Maine

Death:
Mar. 11, 1896
Mayville
Tuscola County, Michigan
Burial:
Fremont Township Cemetery
Mayville
Tuscola County,Michigan,

Rev. Charles Blunt Mills at his home in Mayville while sitting in his chair during the temporary absence of his wife in attendance at their weekly prayer meeting. He received a good common and high school education, and at an early age he became a minister in the Free Baptist denomination. He was a close student and gave frequent lectures in addition to his regular pastoral work. He removed to Ohio, and from there, in 1856, to Tuscola County, where he bought a farm. He was a State senator in 1869-70 and a representative in 1877 and was judge of probate for Tuscola County eight years. He had been a trustee of Hillsdale College for many years and several years acted as its secretary and treasurer, and was one of the incorporators of the Free Baptist printing house at Dover, N. H. From his close resemblance, both in features and actions to Henry Ward Beecher, he was frequently mistaken for that individual in his earlier days. His address made at Caro in September, 1895, to the large outdoor gathering of the Tuscola County Sunday School Association will long be remembered and his memory cherished by all present on that occasion. He married Ann M. Morrison in 1851.

(Michigan Pioneer & Historical Collections, Vol. 27, 1896.)

Rev Ollie Lafferty, Jr
Birth:
Sep. 7, 1936
Prestonsburg
Floyd County, Kentucky
Death:
Feb. 19, 2016
Ypsilanti
Washtenaw County Michigan
Burial:
Highland Cemetery

Ypsilanti
Washtenaw County Michigan

Lafferty Jr., Rev. Ollie Ypsilanti, MI (Formerly of Prestonsburg, KY, Age 79, went home to be with the Lord following an extended illness. He was the son of Ollie and Lack (DeRossett) Lafferty Sr. On June 1, 1957, he married Peggy S. Day and she survives. Ollie was a former pastor of both Whittaker and Trinity Free Will Baptist Churches, a former member of First Free Will Baptist Church and a current member of Trinity Free Will Baptist Church. He was employed as a machine operator at Ford Motor Company, Ypsilanti plant for 33 years, retiring in 1988 and was a longtime member of the U.A.W. He loved his Lord, family, church, fishing and hunting. The funeral service was at Trinity Free Will Baptist Church, with Pastor Calvin Brown officiating.

Rev John Meighan

Birth:
Mar. 6, 1871
Glasgow City,
Scotland
Death:
Jul. 16, 1928
Hillsdale
Hillsdale County
Michigan
Burial:
Oak Grove Cemetery
Hillsdale
Hillsdale County
Michigan
Plot: SECTION 19E
ROW 13EW

Note: 1904-1921 Minister - 1921-1928 Professor Of Religion At Hillsdale College.

Rev. Thomas Ross McCullough
Birth:
Dec. 22, 1950
Royal Oak
Oakland County
Michigan

Death:
Aug. 11, 2017
Michigan,
Burial:
White Chapel Memorial Park
Cemetery
Troy
Oakland County
Michigan

THOMAS ROSS, born at 11 p.m. to Calvin and Grace McCullough.
Tom grew up in Royal Oak and graduated from Kimball High School in 1969. He attended Oakland University for 2 years playing golf and hockey for the University. Through the influence of Pastor Raymond Riggs, Assistant Pastor Bill Robinson, and Youth Pastor Leroy Welch, Tom accepted the Lord on January 25, 1970. His life now took a new direction and Tom attended Free Will Baptist Bible College (1971-74) in Nashville studying Bible and Pastoral Training, where his senior year he served as Student Body President.
He worked at Central school and Church with Patty Underhill whom he married in March, 1977. In 1979 Tom and Patty were approved for missionary service. They spent the 1980's in language school and serving on the mission field in France. In 1988-89 while on deputation he completed his thesis and earned a MA at CIU. Then they returned to France to serve at the church in St. Nazaire.
Tom and Patty separated from the Missions Department in 1994. Ian Ross was born

February 14, 1994 and joined the McCullough Family June 20, 1994. Tom worked at Central Church as an assistant to the Pastor.

In 1996 Tom joined the faculty of his alma mater, FWBBC, where he taught Missions until 2002. In October, 2002 Patty, Ian and Tom returned to Michigan to begin his pastoral career at Central. In his selfless love for the growth of the church and the building of the Kingdom of God, Tom encouraged the congregation at Central to hire a younger man of God. He helped to transition the leadership role of Pastor to Jacob Riggs and in 2015 retired from Central. In March, 2015 he joined Riverside Fellowship Church in Clinton Township as assistant Pastor to Steve Thrasher, II.

In his never ending commitment to the Great Commission, Go into all the world and preach the Gospel. . ., Tom has set up "The Tom and Patty McCullough scholarship fund for mission students at Welch College" (formerly known as FWBBC). To honor his final request a contribution to the Foundation, instead of flowers, would be greatly appreciated.

Spouse:Patty J. Underhill McCullough (1953 - 2004)

Patty J. Underhill McCullough
Birth: Mar. 7, 1953
Detroit
Wayne County
Michigan, USA
Death: Dec. 18, 2004
Royal Oak
Oakland County
Michigan, USA
Burial:
White Chapel Memorial Park
Cemetery
Troy
Oakland County
Michigan

Patty J. Mc Cullough, age 51, died at William Beaumont Hospital, Royal Oak, Michigan. Mrs. Mc-Cullough earned a Bachelor Degree. She and her husband, The Rev. Thomas McCullough, were former missionaries in France for 15years.

Rev John Bascom McMinn
Birth: 1873
Illinois
Death: Oct. 11, 1949

Flint
Genesee County
Michigan Burial:
Rich Township Cemetery
Mayville
Lapeer County
Michigan

Married 4-1897 Mary Rice Chaplain in World War I Veteran. Rev. J. B. McMinn, 76, passed away Tuesday Oct. 11th, at Hurley Hospital, Flint, as the result of injuries received Friday afternoon, Oct. 7th, when his car and one driven by Walter H. Smithling, of Davison, collided on M-15 at Lapeer Road, just south of Davison.

John Bascom McMinn was born in Illinois, the son of Mr. and Mrs. Thomas O. McMinn. In. April 1897, he was united in marriage to Mary Rice, and to this union five children were born, one son Randall, died in infancy.

Mr. McMinn had been pastor of the Baptist Church here for the past 15 years, and resigned only a month ago. He was active in civic affairs and was the (first president of the local Rotary Club when it was organized in 1942. He was a Chaplain in the U, S. Army in France in World War One. He held pastorates in Illinois, Kansas, Nebraska and Wisconsin before coming to Michigan.

Funeral services, were held at the Mayville Baptist Church, Rev. Orviie Williams of Dearborn officiated, assisted by Rev. William Collier, local Pastor.

Samuel A. J. Moody
Birth:
Feb. 25, 1825
Chautauqua County, New York
Death:
1891
Michigan
Burial:
Fairfield Cemetery,Adrian
Lenawee County, Michigan

He was born in Chautauqua Co. New York, Feb. 26 1825. His parents were Samuel and Martha (Thompson) Moody. He married Roxey E. Emmery in 1859, and had six children. He was converted in 1839, and received ordination May 26, 1861.He ministered to the Liberty and First and Second Augusta churches in Michigan and engaged in revival work at Rose, but for several years was hindered in the work because of disease. He also received certification to teach school in

1855, in the Lenwanee Co. schools.

Inscription:
"In God's Care"

Marcus Mugg
Birth:
Aug. 12, 1809
Yates County, N. Y.
Death:
Jun. 23, 1865
Mason, Mich.
Burial:
Five Points Cemetery
Edwardsburg, Cass County, Michigan
Plot: Section 1, Row 8, Stone 2
Marcus was the son of Rev. John Mugg, and died at aged 56 years. His conversion took place in York, Ohio, where he soon began to preach and was ordained June 6, 1840. He spent most of his ministerial life with the churches of the Huron and Seneca Q. M's, Ohio, where his general influence and exemplary life were appreciated. Some twelve years before his death he moved to Michigan, where bereavement and sickness awaited him. His wife passed to a better world and his eldest son was slain in the war. But the sustaining grace of God was present.

Rev A. A. Myers
Birth:
1838
Death:
1924
Burial:
Oak Grove Cemetery
Hillsdale
Hillsdale County, Michigan
Plot: SECTION 18 ROW 32EW

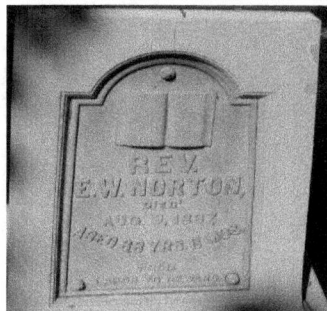

Erastus W Norton
Birth:
Sep. 9, 1818
Richmond, Ontario County, New

York
Death:
Aug. 9, 1887
Sparta, Kent County, Michigan
Burial:
Greenwood Cemetery
Sparta Kent County, Michigan
Plot: O-2-1

Rev. Norton's parents were John and Norma (Short) NORTON. He married 1) Minerva Gardener, Feb. 14, 1839, and 2) Laura A. Compton, July 17, 1851.He was converted when twelve years of age, and ordained in the Freewill Baptist church in Michigan when twenty-three years (ca 1841). He went to Kent County in 1850, where his principal work in the ministry was done. The Sparta and Lisbon churches enjoyed his services many years, and both built houses of worship during his pastorate. He was strongly denominational, a good preacher, and an energetic business man. His wife and ten children were left to mourn his passing.

William R Norton

Birth:
February 12, 1822
Richmond, New York
Death:
1902
Burial:
Rose Cemetery
Bath
Clinton County, Michigan

He was converted in 1843 and the same year received licensed to preach. He moved to Michigan in November of that year and commenced to labor in the Oakland Quarterly Meeting where he was ordained in 1848. In 1854 he moved to Clinton County and also the Lansing Quarterly Meeting where he organized the Bath church which he served for 22 years. He later became a missionary in the vicinity of Boyne City in the northern peninsular of Michigan. He had two sons both of whom graduated from Hillsdale College with Walter E., being a soldier in the Civil War and William A., a successful lawyer.

Rev Benjamin E Parker
Birth:

Feb. 26, 1806
Brutus
Cayuga County
New York
Death:
Mar. 20, 1877
Addison
Lenawee County
Michigan
Burial:
Hillside Cemetery
Addison
Lenawee County
Michigan

Son of Thomas and Sarah Elliott Parker and Brother of Rev Seth C Parker.

Linus S Parmelee
Birth:
August 20, 1815
Spafford, New York
Death:
1895
Burial:
Maplewood Cemetery
Old Reading
Hillsdale County, Michigan
Plot: Old Part Sec E Lot 30

On May 3, 1835 he married Julia A. Jones and their son, Horatio, became a trustee of Hillsdale College, Michigan. Linus was converted the year following his marriage. In 1847 he received licensed to preach and that next year was ordained. He ministered the Salford, Ontario, Canada church for seven years, and two years the Innerskip church which he organized. He then moved to Reading, Michigan and assisted in organizing that

church and was its pastor for 21 years. He also assisted in organizing the Woodbridge and West Reading churches and served them also as pastor. Four of these churches build houses of worship during his pastorates and he had baptized more than 210 converts. He also spent some time in Chicago and raised several thousand dollars for the interest of Free Will Baptist. He also raised $18,000 for the Hillsdale College from which he also served as a trustee for 15 years.

Michael G Pett
Birth:

1836, England
Death:
Apr., 1901
Michigan
Burial:
Carson City Cemetery
Carson City
Montcalm County
Michigan

PETT, Rev. M.G. (Michael G.), The children from their births, parents could have lived in Illinois. A dau, Anna (Pett) Gamble, 1871-1904 d. in Calif. Calif Dth record states her parent's names. A christening record of 04 Nov. 1836, Trinity, Ely, Cambridge, Eng.   for Rev. Michael G,   states his parents were Henry and Mary ? PETT. His tombstone has the title "Rev" on it.

Dr. Jeremiah Phillips
Birth:
Jan. 5, 1812
Plainfield Center,
Otsego County, New York
Death:
Dec. 9, 1879
Hillsdale,
Hillsdale County, Michigan
Burial:
Oak Grove Cemetery,
Hillsdale,
Hillsdale County, Michigan

He studied at Hamilton Literary and Theological Seminary, N.Y; ordained at Plainfield, NY, Sep. 2, 1835. Was among the very first missionaries for Free Will Baptists, going to India in 1835, aged twenty-three, with his colleague, Rev. Eli Noyes, and founded the Free Baptist Mission in Orissa, India. He began work among the Santals, an aboriginal tribe, reduced their language to writing, and also prepared a dictionary and grammar, and translated the gospels and other portions of the Bible. He married Mary Spaulding Beede in 1835, who died soon after arriving in India. In 1839, he married Mary Anne Grinditch, Serapore, India, who also died. Thirdly in 1841, mar. Hannah W. (Cummings) who had gone to India at twenty-two years of age, died there in her ninetieth year, having had but two furloughs during the intervening sixty-seven years.
Dr. Jeremiah Phillips was the father of fourteen children, eleven of whom lived to mature age, six of whom and three granddaughters became workers in the same field, while five remaining in America were nearly, or quite all active workers for missions.

On his retirement from the field in 1879, with health completely shattered by privations and strenuous labors during one of India's terrible famines, the Lieutenant-Governor of Bengal addressed to him a letter in which he said he could not allow him to retire without expressing his high appreciation of the valuable service he had rendered to India.

His eldest son, a medical doctor, James L. Philips, spent twenty-five years in the same field and was the Field Secretary of the India Sunday-School Union, in whose service he remained until in 1895.

Also, a daughter, Dr. Nellie M. Phillips, and Dr. Thomas Wesley Burkholder, a son-in-law, were medical missionaries. Eleven of Dr. Phillips' family are buried in India, including his last wife, Hannah Cummings Phillips, while Dr. Phillips himself, and those of two missionary daughters and one daughter-in - law, rest in Oak Grove Cemetery. One daughter, Mrs. Julia P. Burkholder (widow of Dr. T.W. Burkholder), served 50 years as a missionary in India. A fine brick church now stands in Khargpur, India, a memorial to Dr. Phillips, erected in 1906-07 by Mr. and Mrs. I.L. Stone, (Harriet Phillips Stone) of Battle Creek, the latter a daughter of Dr. Phillips, and for twenty-six years a member of the mission. This family did great service for God in helping the poor and down-trodden, and gained for themselves, a great reward.

Nor pain, nor death can enter there.

Dr.
Nellie Maria Phillips
Birth:
Jun. 15, 1852,
India
Death:
Mar. 7, 1906
Rochester,
Olmsted County,
Minnesota
Burial:
Oak Grove Cemetery,
Hillsdale,
Hillsdale County,
Michigan

She graduated from Hillsdale College, MI in June 1875. She engaged in teaching and the study of medicine until 1881, graduating at that time from Adelbert Medical College, Cleveland, Ohio. She served with her parents and a rather large, extended family as a medical missionary to India, from 1881 to 1903. Dr. Phillips died in Rochester, MN.

Ida Orissa Phillips
Birth:
Jan. 24, 1856
Death:
Jul. 5, 1889
Winnebago,
Faribault County, Minnesota

Burial:
Oak Grove Cemetery, Hillsdale,
Hillsdale County, Michigan

Daughter of Jeremiah L. Phillips, DD, and Hanna (Cummings) Phillips, Free Will Baptist missionaries to Orissa Province India. She graduated from Hillsdale College, MI. in 1877 and was a missionary to India from 1877-1889, at the time of her death, at age 32 yrs and 5 months. She came from an extended family of medical missionaries and ministers. Her mother lies buried in India with other family members there. Ida came to U.S. at age 16, probably to attend college, in Dec. 30, 1870 with a clergyman's family, Rev. Obadiah B. Batchelder, M.D., who worked with the Phillips family in India. Most info is from a book, pub. 1912, "Jeremiah Phillips, DD, Family Missionaries to India" by Harriet Phillips Stone.)

Mary R *Sayles* Phillips
Birth:
Unknown
Death:
Feb. 6, 1911
Battle Creek,
Calhoun County, Michigan
Burial:
Oak Grove Cemetery, Hillsdale,
Hillsdale County Michigan

Married James L. Phillips, M.D., at Pasoag, R.I., Aug. 10, 1864, a Free Will Baptist missionary to India. She died at 73 years, after serving with her husband in India. He died there in 1895.

Mary Anne *Phillips* Platts
Birth:
Feb. 20, 1842,'
India
Death:
Apr. 25, 1911
Winnebago,
Faribault County, Minnesota
Burial:
Oak Grove Cemetery,
Hillsdale,
Hillsdale County, Michigan,
Plot: Row 3

Mary Anne was the daughter of Free Will Baptist missionaries to India, Dr. Jeremiah Phillips, and Mary Anne (Grimditch) Phillips She married R. Gilbert Platts, MD, Dec. 15, 1866, in Brittany NY. She studied at Whitestown Seminary, NY and Prairie City Academy, Illinois, and New Hampton Seminary, N.H. They served at missionaries with her extended family in Orissa Province, India, where her husband died at the early age of 34 yrs.

Richard Gilbert Platts

Birth:
Nov. 4, 1838
Old Saybrook,
Middlesex County, Connecticut,
Death:
Jan. 3, 1873,
India
Burial:
Oak Grove Cemetery,
Hillsdale,
Hillsdale County, Michigan,
Plot: Plot: Row 3

Gilbert Platts, M.D. was a student of Hillsdale College, MI, and was graduated at Buffalo Medical College, N.Y., Feb. 1866, as a physician. He married Mary Anne Phillips, the daughter of Jeremiah Phillips, D.D., and Mary Anne Grimditch Phillips, Free Will Baptist missionaries to India, on Dec. 15, 1866, at Bethany, NY. Death occurred in India in January 1873, and presumed re-interment in 1874, in Oak Grove Cem. as Feb. 1, 1874, is shown as date of burial He died a young man at 34 years of age. His wife is also interred in Oak Grove. The children are buried at the Riverview Memorial Cemetery in Ft. Pierce, Florida.

Rev Freedom Randall

Birth:
Apr. 10, 1842
Burlington, Michigan
Death:
May 21, 1915
Tekonsha
Calhoun County
Michigan
Burial:
Riverside Cemetery
Tekonsha
Calhoun County
Michigan

His parents were Gilbert and Alma (Howe) Randall. He consecrated his life to God in Jan. 1868, and received ordination in Dec. 1877. He had pastoral care of the Penn church two years, the Hadley's Corners church three years, and the Leslie church two years, and in 1881, settled with the Cook's Prairie church, to which thirty-eight were added under his ministry the past year. July 3, 1866, he was married to Melissa S. Downs, who died in 1872. They had a son, Hazen C. Randall, 1870-1936, MI In 1874he married Mary O. Smith.

Rev Delavan B Reed

Birth:
Jun. 12, 1855
Sardinia
Erie County, New York
Death:
Sep. 27, 1932
Manton
Wexford County, Michigan
Burial:
Fairview Cemetery, Manton
Wexford County Michigan
Plot: Section 2, Lot 525

Rev. Delevan Bloodgood REED, was the fifth child and only son of Lewis B. and Hannah (Quackenbush) REED. His parents were members of the Free Baptist Church in NY and in 1879 He entered the ministry. After study in Griffith Institute, Springville, NY, He entered Hillsdale College in Mich. in Jan. 1881, and graduated from the classical course in 1888, and from the theological course in 1889.

He was president of the Theadelphic Society in the spring of 1886 and won the prize in he oratorical contest of 1885.

In 1888 he was elected to the Chair Of Ecclesiastical History in the theological department of the college, and pursued a post-graduate course of study with that work in view.He was ordained at Wheatland, Mich, about 1881, and has ministered to the Pittsford, Wheatland, and Pittsford Village churches in Michigan while pursuing his studies; and also, for a brief time, to the Johnstown and Oakland churches in Wisconsin.

Chauncey Reynolds
Birth:
August 28, 1805
Argyle, New York
Death:
1890
Burial:
Oak Grove Cemetery
Hillsdale
Hillsdale County, Michigan

In the winter of 1819 the family moved to Bethany, New York. During that first year he became interested in religion, but delayed baptism until 1827. He went to Michigan in 1828 and was married to Sarah Harper, October 30, 1828. He was ordained at the Grand River Quarterly Meeting in October, 1845 and soon organized the church and Shiawasasee County. He also organized a church and Du Plain, Clinton County, and another in North Plains, and assisted in the work in other places. He was a trustee of Michigan Central College at Spring Arbor and served also as a trustee at Hillsdale College for 20 years and he served as a delegate to the Gen. Conference in 1853.

William T. Risner
Birth:
1847
Prussia
Death:
1919
Burial:
Novi Cemetery
Novi
Oakland County,
Michigan

He married Sarah Hammond in 1868. In 1874 he was led to Christ's and licensed to preach was granted four years later. He received his ordination on February 14, 1883. His pastorates were in Michigan.

J. C. Robinson
Birth:
April 14, 1836
Harrison County,
Ohio
Death:
1922
Burial:
Oak Grove Cemetery
Coldwater
Branch County
Michigan

His parents migrated from Virginia to Ohio where he turned of God in August, 1851. Seven years later he was licensed to preach having received his education Albany University, Ohio. On August 24, 1862 he was ordained by Rev. H. J. Carr and others. His labors have been in Ohio, Minnesota, Illinois, Wisconsin and Michigan. He has organized five churches and baptized 125 people.

E B Rolf
Birth:
Vermont
Death:
Nov. 16, 1872
Bristol,
Indiana
Burial:
East Union Cemetery
Union
Cass County,
Michigan

After his conversion he joined the Sodus, New York church. The Holland Purchase Conference granted him a license to preach in 1843 and his ordination took place on July 12, 1844. 21 years of his ministry was spent with the Galen and Savanna churches of Wayne Quarterly Meeting, New York. About 1865 he assisted in organizing the church at Porter, Michigan and remained its pastor until he died.

Charles A Shattuck
Birth:
Feb. 19, 1815
Leyden,
Mass.,
Death:
Apr. 9, 1887
Burial:
Mount Hope Cemetery
Litchfield,
Hillsdale County,
Michigan
Plot: Section 9 Row 1 Lot 3
His manhood was spent in Hillsdale County, Mich., where he engaged in the work of the ministry for some twenty years before his death. He was faithful in duty, and none could leave a better reputation for sincere piety.

John Silvernail
Birth:
November 17, 1828
Greene County, New York
Death:
1917
Burial:
Brigham Cemetery
Monroe County, Michigan

He was brought to Christ in 1852 and was ordained in April 1867. His ministry was mainly in Michigan.

Nor pain, nor death can enter there.

Tilton E. Smith
Birth: 1840
Death:
Feb. 4, 1890
Lapeer
Lapeer County
Michigan,
Burial:
Mount Hope Cemetery
Lapeer
Lapeer County
Michigan

Free Will Baptist Minister and Civil War Veteran, Corporal 33 New York Infantry Company-F. Enlisted: May 9, 1861
Discharged: June 2, 1863
Enlisted In: Yorktown, New York

Rev Sheldon Smith
Birth:
Apr. 14, 1836
Elbridge
Onondaga County
New York
Death:
May 17, 1892

Van Buren County
Michigan
Burial:
Arlington Hill Cemetery
Bangor
Van Buren County
Michigan
Plot: Sect. 1

Rev. Sheldon Smith, son of Bliss and Priscilla (Rounds) SMITH, was married to Miss Emily Hakes Feb. 14, 1856.

In 1882, she died, and he afterwards married Miss Susan Stevens, May 29, 1883, Van Buren Co. MI.

In September 1873, he was ordained by the church of God. In 1885, he united with the Free Baptists, and was pastor of the church at Corey Hill, Van Buren County, Mich. In 1882 he was elected department chaplain of the G.A.R. of the state of Michigan, having served in the late war in Co. H, 19th NY H.A. Regiment.

O Thou Who
Choosest For Thy
Share
The World, And
What The World
Calls Fair,
Take All That It Can
Give Or Lend,
But Know That
Death Is At The End

Lonnie H. Sparks
Birth:
Dec. 14, 1930
Davis
Murray County, Oklahoma
Death:
Jun. 26, 2014
Edwardsburg
Cass County, Michigan
Burial:
Edwardsburg Cemetery
Edwardsburg
Cass County, Michigan

No one could have foreseen this second child of Lewis and Linnie Sparks, now deceased, Lewis Sparks Jr., would travel the world working to break the spiritual and financial poverty of those living in the jungles of West Africa (Cote d'Ivorie); in the cities of Europe (Alcala de Henares and Santurce Spain); and in the U.S., (primarily in Elkhart and briefly in Oklahoma and South Carolina) before making his home in Edwardsburg. He was born in the

Depression Era in Davis, Oklahoma. His 56 years of ministry were preceded by a time of rebellion against God, when Lonnie, wanting to escape his own family's poverty, went to school to assure himself a financially secure future. Ironically, Lonnie, who was studying to be an automobile engineer, was brought back to obedience to Christ by an automobile accident that nearly took his life. Lonnie then and there surrendered himself to God's will, embracing the cross and whatever sacrifice, financial and otherwise situation, that might cost him. In the summer of 1954, after having secured a B.A. from Free Will Baptist College (now Welch College) in Nashville,TN and in Winona Lake, IN for a summer scholarship course, surrendered to a call to the mission field after hearing a message by Oswald J. Smith, in the Billy Sunday Tabernacle. That decision sealed the deal for Anita J. Kaminsky, who made the decision to break up with Lonnie, and not accept his proposal of marriage, since he had never mentioned the mission field, and she knew in her heart of hearts that she had to be a missionary. They were married that summer on Aug. 15, 1954 in Elkhart, IN. They pastored two churches in Oklahoma in 1954-1955, before moving to Columbia, SC, where they attended Columbia Bible College (now University) in the 1955-1956 school year, where they pastored two churches

while Lonnie was securing a Masters in Missions. On Dec. 22, 1956, they left from New York Harbor for language study in Switzerland, where they spent a whole year learning the French language. In Jan. 1958, they left for the Ivory Coast, studying and learning the Twi language (Ghana) and then Koulango (Ivory Coast). On Feb. 14, 1959, their son Paul was born (since deceased) in Dembrokro. During their stay in Africa, Lonnie established a church in Goumere, and had many more preaching points. Also, sensing the need for the Koulango Tribe to have the Word of God in their language, he came back to the U.S. on a furlough, where son Noel was born in 1962, and studied at Wycliffe Summer School of Linguistics on the campus of the University of Oklahoma in Norman, OK, before moving on to get his Masters in Linguistics from the University of Michigan, Ann Arbor in 1963. Lonnie, back in Africa, reduced the language to writing, wrote a school primmer, so the children could study in their native language, and, most importantly, translated the New Testament into the Koulango language. From 1974-1997, they served as missionaries to Spain, where they opened two churches in Alcala de Henares (Madrid) and Santurce (Vizcaya), and was the case with Africa, saw many people come to faith in Jesus Christ. In 1997, Lonnie and Anita came home to "retire", but through work in the now defunct La Vanture Plastics Corporation, came into contact with a burgeoning Hispanic community. What started as a home Bible Study, ended up becoming the Primera Inglesia Bautist Libre of Elkhart, IN, where he served as pastor until Alzheimer's forced him to truly retire.

A Service at the Primera Inglesia Bautista Libre (their church), of a Life Well Lived began with some of his co-pastors officiating, including, but not limited to, his son, Pastor Noel Sparks, the church pastor, Pastor Robert Helms and other associates, Pastor Lonnie Palmer and Pastor Mark Riggs. The funeral procession went to Edwardsburg (MI) Cemetery, where was laid to rest next to his deceased son, Pastor Paul Sparks.

Paul M. Sparks
Birth:
1959
Ivory Coast, West Africa
Death:
1992
Indianapolis, Indiana
Burial:

Edwardsburg Cemetery,
Edwardsburg,
Cass County, Michigan

He was the minister of the Antlers Free Will Baptist Church in Oklahoma at the time of his passing. He had formerly served churches in Winona Lake and Elkhart, Indiana and before was a missionary to Spain.

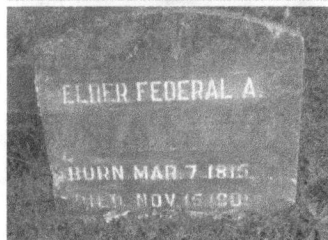

Federal Alcander Stanford
Birth:
March 15, 1815
Oneida County,
New York
Death:
1901
Burial:
Mount Hope Cemetery
Middleville
Barry County,
Michigan

He was married to Miss Sophia Hicks in 1838. His conversion took place in 1832 and he was ordained in February, 1854. His ministry was spent in Pennsylvania, Ohio and Michigan with the longest continuous pastorate being in watch in Michigan. In September 1873, he was ordained by the church of God. In 1885, he united with the Free Baptists, and pastor of the church at Corey Hill, Van Buren County, Mich. In 1882 he was elected department chaplain of the G.A.R. of the state of Michigan, having served in the late war in Co. H, 19th NY H.A. Regiment.

Norman Starr
Birth:
Unknown
Death:
Sep. 16, 1865
Burial:
Hart Cemetery
New Baltimore
Macomb County
Michigan

He was an ordained minister connected with the Southfield church of the Oakland Quarterly Meeting, Michigan as early as 1856. He remained with this church until about 1859 when he became pastor of the Chesterfield and Lenox church of that Oxford Quarterly Meeting where he remained until his death. Note: age 42 yrs.

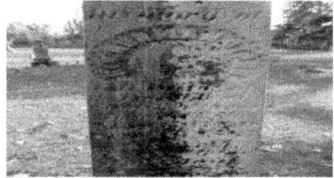

Rev Henry T. St Clair
Birth:
Aug. 26, 1824
England
Death:
Jan. 13, 1908
Fenton
Genesee County
Michigan
Burial:
Oakwood Cemetery
Fenton
Genesee County,Michigan

Henry was a Minister. Father is Howard St Clair from England, mother unknown.
ST CLAIR, Rev. Henry T. I could find few records. But there is a death cert on his memorial which gives his occ: Minister;

John Thomas
Birth:
Unknown
Death:
Oct. 10, 1874
Burial:
Fairfield Cemetery
Adrian, Lenawee County,
Michigan

Thomas, a native of New York, while yet young consecrated himself to God and his work. Soon after receiving license in Royalton, N. Y., he commenced laboring in Michigan, receiving ordination at the Michigan Central Q. M. Feb. 23, 1839. There were then few Free Baptist churches in the state, but giving himself, soul and body, time and talents, to his work, neither the poverty of the churches nor the. Roughness of the roads weakened his courage or

diminished his fervor. Many log cabins were cheered by his genial presence, many rough school houses were made houses of God and gates of heaven to converted souls. After laboring several years as an evangelist, he settled as pastor and spent nearly twenty-five years with the Wheatland and Fairfield churches of the Bean Creek (later Hillsdale) Q. M. His sermons were short and earnest, sprinkled at times with a little natural eccentricity and wit, and full of love. His sermons were practical and forcible, his life godly and earnest, and the whole enveloped in a cheerful, affectionate spirit, which seemed to be the most forcible element of his nature. After spending a little time in labor at Blackberry, Ill., he returned to the scenes of his former labors, and died Oct. IO, 1874, aged 58 years. He was an early and constant friend of Hillsdale College, and for some time a trustee. He was the Pastor of Fairfield Baptist Church from 1864-1870.

Nelson Thomas
Birth:
1820
Death:
Aug. 7, 1848
Constantine, Michigan
Burial:
Five Points Cemetery
Edwardsburg
Cass County, Michigan
Plot: Section 1, Row 8, Stone 10
He was 27 years old at his death which came only three years after his ordination. However during that three years he organized three churches and was a preacher of much promise.

Joseph Harvey Walrath
Birth:
Jan. 14, 1847
Canajoharie
Montgomery County, New York
Death:
Aug. 31, 1892
Michigan
Burial:
Oak Grove Cemetery
Hillsdale
Hillsdale County, Michigan
Plot: Section 14

In 1847 he married Miss L. M. Mount. Entering Hillsdale College in 1871, he passed through both the academicals and theological departments graduating in 1878. He was ordained by the Hillsdale Quarterly Meeting in September, 1876 and had the pastoral care of many churches within this state of Michigan, Iowa, South Dakota and Wisconsin. For four years he was secretary treasurer of the

Wisconsin Home Mission Board. Other positions which he occupied were: agent of the Free Baptist Western Association, State Agent and Evangelist of the Iowa Yearly Meeting, and was the Corresponding Editor of *The Free Baptist* from its beginning to February 15, 1888. In pastoral and evangelistic work and in his life of official work for the denomination he was successful.

Death Has No Strength

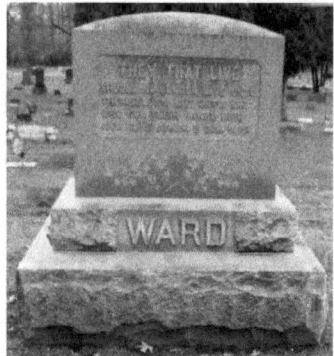

John T. Ward

Birth:
Jan. 20, 1847
Norway,
Herkimer County, New York
Death:
Dec. 9, 1918
Yokohama, Kanagawa, Japan
Burial:
Oak Grove Cemetery, Hillsdale
Hillsdale County, Michigan

He graduated from Whitestown Seminary in 1867, from Hillsdale in 1870, and from Andover Theological Seminary in 1873. While a student in Hillsdale he was a member of the Amphictyon society and the Hillsdale chapter of Delta Tau Delta fraternity, being one of the seven charter members of the latter when it was founded in 1867. He received ordination to the ministry in the Freewill Baptist church on Dec. 14, 1873. As pastor, Dr. Ward served several of the leading Free Baptist Churches in Ashland, NH; Georgiaville, R.I; Park Street, Providence, RI, and Jackson, MI, and was prominent in the activities of the denomination. He was elected as delegate to the national conference and was on educational boards, and served six years on the Home Mission Board. He was also a member of the General Conference Board and trustee of Hillsdale College from 1889-1898. He became editor and manager of "The Free Baptist" at Minneapolis, the first religious paper in the northwest, founded by Rev. A. A. Smith, a former pastor of the College Church in Hillsdale. He managed and edited the paper with distinct efficiency for a number of years, and was instrumental in merging it into "The Morning Star" in Boston. During his service as pastor and editor he and two fellow clergymen edited "The Free Baptist Encyclopedia," a large volume of significant ecclesiastic and historic value, which passed to the sole control of Dr. Ward shortly after he and the one surviving collaborator received it from the press and bindery. He had positive convictions on the doctrines and practices of the Church, but was of a practical vision, and was one of the most consistent advocates of co-operation of the denominations in their foreign missions, federation and union at home and abroad, openly supporting the organic union of the Baptists and Free Baptists which was wrought out while he was in Hillsdale. He entered the faculty of Hillsdale College in 1898 where he served until 1913, with one intervening It is knowing that God WILL!year of leave of absence which he and his wife spent with Mrs. Phelps in Japan. His subjects were theology and homiletics. During a part of the residence of the family in Hillsdale, the daughter Mary, the only child and a graduate of the University of Minnesota, was an instructor in Hillsdale College, and was active in the religious and club life of the college and city. On her marriage to Mr. Phelps they went to Japan, where he is one of the most prominent of the international secretaries of the Young Men's Christian Assn. Probably remembered now more as the co-author of *"Free Baptist Cyclopedia"* with Gideon Burgess, pub. 1889.

Abraham H Whitaker
Birth:
June 9, 1845
Kirklin, Indiana
Death:
1917
Burial:
Bankers Cemetery
Hillsdale County, Michigan
Plot: Sec 1 Row 2 Lot 16

On January 1, 1868 he married Sarah Ellen Balcom. Brother Whitaker was converted11 years of age, was a student at Centerburg Academy, Ohio and four years at Hillsdale College in Michigan and received his ordination in January, 1871. He pastored many churches in Michigan, and, also churches in Ohio and Wisconsin. He nearly all of these revivals were enjoyed under his labor. He organized three churches and baptized about 200 converts. He was active in temperance and every good work, and was highly esteemed among his brethren both as a preacher and a pastor.

Elder Samuel Whitcomb
Birth:
June I, 1788
Lisbon, N. H
Death:
April 7, 1867
Clarendon, Mich
Burial:
Cook's Prairie Cemetery
Clarendon, Calhoun County, Michigan

Aug. 5, 1813, he married Miss Nancy Jacobs. In 1816 he was thoroughly converted. Soon after he moved to Lyons, N. Y., and joined the Presbyterian Church. Disagreeing with them in doctrine, in December, 1819, he united with the Free Baptist church in his place. He moved to Hartland in April, 1822, and soon to Shelby, where he organized a church in 1824, and was its pastor till he moved to Michigan in 1838. Here the next year he organized the Cook's Prairie church in Clarendon, where he retained his membership till death. Oct.10, 1844, his wife died, and he afterwards married Miss Lydia Cowles, of Burlington,

Mich. He was in sympathy with all denominational enterprises, a safe counselor, a practical preacher. He was once a member of General Conference.

William E. Whitney
Birth:
1812
Penfield, Monroe County,
New York
Death:
Sep. 17, 1893 Leslie
Ingham County,
Michigan
Burial:
Woodlawn Cemetery Leslie
Ingham County Michigan

He began his Christian life in 1832, moved to Canada in 1834, commenced to preach in 1844, and was ordained a Free Will Baptist minister in 1846. He moved to Michigan in 1849, and worked with various churches there. He served as a soldier in the Civil War in the Mich. 12th Infantry, Co G, in the early part of the war, and re-enlisted in 1864. He lost a limb, but on his return resumed the work of the ministry and was a faithful servant of God.

Samuel Wire
Birth:
1786
Goshen, Conn
Death:
Jun. 6, 1870
Commerce, Mich.
Burial:
Wixom Cemetery,
Wixom, Oakland County
Michigan

His father served in the British army and was present at the defeat of Braddock; he also served in the army of the Revolution. Brother Wire moved to western New York in early manhood, and was baptized with his wife by Elder Z. Dean in May, 1819. Immediately he began to preach and was ordained the same year. In July of that year he and Elder Dean sought out David Marks and introduced him to his life of usefulness, and from that time Brother Wire was active in carrying forward the work. His labors were abundant and successful in western New York and northern Pennsylvania until 1833. When he removed to northeastern Ohio, and labored in the Ohio and Pennsylvania Y. M. Subsequently he returned to New York, where in 1843 his companion of thirty-eight year was parted from him. He afterwards married 'Widow Colby of Sodus. N. Y., and removed to Michigan, where his remaining years were spent. Brother Wire was a man of unusual natural ability and of extraordinary energy. Which made his life an exceedingly active one. For many years he is prominently mentioned in the field of his labors, and he did much to strengthen the denomination. His love of preaching was intense, and in the days of his strength, his soul burning with holy zeal, there was sometimes a power in his sermons which was well-nigh irresistible.

Elder Joseph Woodman
Birth:
Feb. 12, 1790
Barrington
Strafford County
New Hampshire
Death:
Apr. 2, 1879
Paw Paw
Van Buren County
Michigan
Burial:
Bangs Cemetery
Paw Paw
Van Buren County
Michigan

Elder Joseph Woodman was born in Barrington, N. H., Feb. 12, 1790. When quite young, his father, John Woodman, with his family, became a pioneer settler in Caledonia Co., Vt. Joseph was the second child, and eldest son in the family, and in early life he developed those active qualities of labor, perseverance, and prudence, which crowned his life with success and honor. He was married to Tryphena Johnson, of the same county, Jan. 1, 1810, with whom he lived a happy union fifty-three years, she dying June 14, 1863, in the seventy-second year of her age, having had ten children, six of whom still survive. Riley, the eldest son, resides in Powhatan, Kan., the other five, viz.: David Woodman (2d), J. J. Woodman, Mrs. Joseph Luce, Mrs. Freeman Ruggles, and Mrs. H. P. Nelson, are residents of Van Buren County.

Soon after his marriage he, with his wife, joined the FreeWill Baptist Church. Earnest in his religious convictions, he soon to the labor of his hands joined that of the ministry, and engaged in preaching the gospel. In the spring of 1831 he sold the farm (among the hills) in Sutton, on which he had lived several years, and which he cleared and improved with his own hands, also the saw-mill which he built on the stream near his residence, and in July of that year emigrated to Western New York, and settled on a farm in Riga, Monroe Co., where he resided until the spring of 1835, when he with his family moved to Michigan, and settled upon the land which he located and which became his future home, on the Territorial Road in the township of Antwerp, east of and adjoining the village of Paw Paw. He was the first white settler, and built the first log house and the first frame barn in the township. His

log house, built in three days and finished ready for occupancy, and into which he moved his family on the 10th day of May, 1835, was built on the spot now occupied by the fine residence of his youngest son, Hon. J. J. Woodman, to whom he sold all of his farm in 1861, except forty acres on which his residence stood, which he built in 1838, and in which he lived forty-one years, and until his death, April 2, 1879, at the advanced age of eighty-nine years, one month, and twenty-one days.

When he settled upon his farm there was but one small frame house, three log cabins, and a saw-mill on the territory now occupied by the beautiful and flourishing village of Paw Paw. There being no church of his faith near him at the time, he united with the Protestant Methodists, and was soon after ordained, and was actively engaged in the ministry until within a few years of his death, when advancing age compelled him to retire from the pulpit and active duties of a long and useful life, and seek the quiet and comfortable surroundings of his home and fireside. His second wife, Mrs. Mary Osmer, to whom he was married in the winter of 1883, faithfully ministered to him in his declining years.

Minnesota

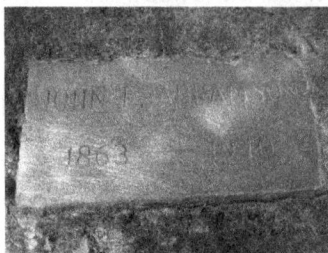

John Edward Abramson
Birth: 1863
Death: Jan. 29, 1940
Hennepin County
Minnesota
Burial:
Lakewood Cemetery
Minneapolis
Hennepin County,Minnesota
Plot: SECTION 26 LOT 42
GRAVE 5.5

ABRAHAMSON, Rev. J.E. (John Edward), His wife, Louise E. (Johnson), also there, They mar. 25 Aug. 1887, Houston, Houston Co. MN.   Found an obit of Polly Osborn, a Free Bapt. in Janesville, WI, 1798-1891, with her obit stating "Rev. J.E. Abrahamson" assisted in her service.   Then, in 1900, Bird Island, Renville, Minn census, John E. was 37y, Louise and son, Earl 10, b. IL. Occ: Bapt. clergyman. The 1930 Fed census, Hennepin MI, he was 67y, stated he was 'retired minister' with   Earl, a son, age 36, single.

John D. Batson
Birth:
Feb. 16, 1835
Otsego County, New York
Death:
Jan., 1919
Farmington,
Dakota County, Minnesota
Burial:
Corinthian Cemetery
Farmington,
Dakota County, Minnesota

Batson,was born of English parents. He united with the Free Will Baptist Church at Fairwater, Wis., where he was ordained Sept 29, 1861. He settled in Dakota Co. Minn., and began to preach in that new country as congregations could be gathered. He served in the Civil War, in the 4th Minn. Vols., Co. I. until the close of the war. He continued this work and in 1869 organized the Castle Rock church, and later the East Castle Rock church, both of which have been continually favored with his efficient ministry. His education was obtained at Ripon and Carleton Colleges. His sister, Mrs. W.I. Price, was a missionary in Burma. He served for years as clerk of Minnesota YM and a member of the State Mission Board.

A P Corey
Birth:
October 6, 1795
Amherst, Massachusetts
Death:
October 14, 1882
Minnesota

Burial:
Money Creek Cemetery
Money Creek
Houston County, Minnesota

He was ordained by a Council of the Winona and Houston Quarterly Meetings in Minnesota on December 11, 1857. His ministry was largely spent within the bounds of this quarterly meeting having moved there at a very early day. He worked earnestly to establish sabbath schools and churches and he was very highly esteemed for his devoted Christian life.

Frank Llewellyn Durgin
Birth:
1851
Maine
Death:
Sep. 23, 1935
Winnebago,
Faribault County,Minnesota
Burial:
Rosehill Cemetery,
Winnebago,
Faribault County,Minnesota

He married Lucy M. Phillips, dau.of Dr. Jeremiah and Hannah C. Phillips, in Hillsdale, MI, Aug.6, 1877, by Prof. Ransom Dunn, D.D., of Hillsdale College, of

which he graduated. He also was graduated from Adelbert Medical College, Cleveland, OH, Mar. 15, 1882.

Many of Lucy's family (eleven siblings) served as Freewill Baptist doctor, missionaries to Orissa Province, Belasore,India. Inscription:Frank L. Durgin, M.D.

Lucy Marilla *Phillips* Durgin
Birth:
Sep. 6, 1854
New Hampshire
Death:
Mar. 6, 1938
Winnebago,
Faribault County, Minnesota
Burial:
Rosehill Cemetery,
Winnebago,
Faribault County, Minnesota

Lucy M. Durgin was the daughter of Dr. Jeremiah Phillips, Sr., and Hannah (Cummings) Phillips. She, as well as most of her siblings, were medical missionaries with the Freewill Baptist church, her father going to the Orissa area in India when he was 23 yrs of age. Her mother died in India and is bur. there, as well as several other of her family. Lucy married Dr. Frank L. Durgin in Hillsdale, Michigan, Aug. 6, 1877, by Prof. Ransom Dunn, D.D., Hillsdale College, from which she was graduated. Frank Durgin became a medical doctor. Lucy was Lady Principle of Parker College, Minnesota, from 1889-1897.

Rev John Foster
Birth:
unknown
Massachusetts
Death:
Nov. 29, 1870
Oregon
Burial:
Minneapolis Pioneers & Soldiers
Memorial Cemetery
Minneapolis
Hennepin County
Minnesota
Plot: LOT 86 BLOCK D

Wentworth Hayden
Birth:
Oct. 28, 1813
Skowhegan,
Somerset County, Maine
Death:
Feb. 8, 1886
Minneapolis, Hennepin County,
Minnesota
Burial:
Champlin Cemetery, Champlin,
Hennepin County, Minnesota

He was ordained at Mayfield, ME in 1838, ten years after his conversion. In Maine he labored for some time as a home missionary. His ministry was attended with many revivals and several churches were organized. In 1856. Because of impaired health he went to Minnesota, where he organized a church at Champlin and was pastor of the Minneapolis church. He served in the Maine Legislature in 1854, and later in the Minnesota Territorial and State Legislatures, and was the only member of the Minnesota Constitutional Convention that voted against excluding the black man from the ballot.

Josiah Lorenzo Heath
Birth:
1822
New York
Death:
Apr. 12, 1864
High Forest, Olmsted County,
Minnesota
Burial:
High Forest Cemetery
High Forest,
Olmsted County,
Minnesota
Plot: Section 1SW 16

He married Candace Louise Fisher She was b: Feb 05, 1820 in

Jefferson County, New York and died Oct 28, 1907 in Bangor (LaCrosse) Wisconsin.A native of NY, he moved to Wisconsin about 1844, where in 1859, he was ordained by the Saulk Co. Q.M, among the churches of which he labored, when because of failing health he moved to High Forest, MN, where he died. He was a man of excellent spirit.

Charles Augustus Hilton
Birth:
Jul. 22, 1845
ParsonsfielD
York County, Maine
Death:
Oct. 24, 1912
Minneapolis
Hennepin County, Minnesota
Burial:
Lakewood Cemetery
Minneapolis
Hennepin County, Minnesota

He was converted in 1856. He served two years in the Civil War and returned with an impaired health, in 1868 he was licensed and soon after was ordained. He helped many pastorates including Maine, Illinois, New York, and Massachusetts before coming to Minnesota.

Samuel Kendall Hovey
Birth:
Nov. 30, 1823
Brookfield
Orange County
Vermont
Death:
Feb. 10, 1890
Rock County
Minnesota
Burial:
Maplewood Cemetery
Luverne
Rock County
Minnesota
Plot: 1st Division, North Section

His name is shown in old church records in Wis. as a Bapt. minister. He m. Rebecca Bostic(k), b. NY. S.K's stone is in plot with Robt. J. Cobban, shown, a son-in-law, m. to his dau Mary Melvina (Hovey) Cobban, b. 1859, Wis, d. 1947, Los Angeles.Parents: Samuel Willis Hovey, b. 1801, VT; and Betsey Kendall, b. 1795.   Wife: Rebecca Bostic(k);   Lived in

Wis, served in Union Army from Wis. 42nd Reg. Inf., Co. C. Drew pension in 1880.
Children:

Betsy Ann Hovey Pokett (1868 - 1955)*

Amy Jane Hovey Bullis (1871 - 1934)*

Inscription:
S. K. Hovey
Co. C,
42nd Wis. Inf.

Phineas Edward Jaquith
Birth:
Apr. 16, 1902
Jefferson County
Wisconsin
Death:
Mar. 26, 1947
Minnesota
Burial:
Oakley Cemetery
Littlefork
Koochiching County
Minnesota

Parents: John Franklin JAQUITH, and Lillie Walrath, died in Minn.

Inscription:
Age 44

Ruth J *Canney* Keith
Birth:
Feb. 7, 1827
Farmington, Strafford County, New Hampshire
Death:
Nov. 11, 1898
Minneapolis, Hennepin County, Minnesota
Burial:
Lakewood Cemetery, Minneapolis, Hennepin County, Minnesota

She united with the Free Will Baptist church and was connected with the "Mission Column" of the 'Free Baptist.' In 1883-86. She was a member of the Foreign Mission Board, and for several years has been a member of the board of managers of the Woman's Missionary Society, holding other responsible positions in it. In her service to the cause of missions, especially in connection with the 'Free Baptist, she has been widely known among the FWB people and universally appreciated.

Albert Josiah Marshall
Birth:
Nov. 3, 1847
Death:
Jul. 30, 1924
Burial:
Wadena Cemetery
Wadena
Wadena County, Minnesota

MARSHALL's parents were Josiah H. MARSHALL, and Elizabeth O (Wood) MARSHALL.In January, 1864 he entered the army (WI) and was with Sherman's army on its famous march to the sea and thence north, to the end of the war.He was converted in 1869 while at Rochester Seminary, Wisconsin. After this he studied at Evansville Seminary and at Hillsdale College, Mich., where he completed the theological course and the larger part of the college course. He received license to preach in 1870 and ordination April 26, 1872, in the Freewill Baptist denomination. While at Hillsdale he was pastor successively of the churches at Butler, St. Joseph River, gathered by his labors, and Cook's Prairie, where a considerable revival resulted. While in the Junior class at Hillsdale, the needs of the foreign work were so great that he devoted himself to it, and set sail for India in September, 1873. He was accompanied by his wife, Emily L., a daughter of Rev. Jeremiah Phillips, and a graduate of Hillsdale in the class of 1870, whom he married July 15, 1871. On reaching India they were located at Balasore, where they labored with success until their return in 1882. After a period of recuperation, Brother Marshall was called to the pastorate of the Evansville, Wis., church, and a year and a half later he became principal of Rochester Seminary, which prospered under his direction. He then served a year as editor of the Free Baptist, and entered upon his duties as president of Winnebago College.

Rev Theodore Moses
Birth:
Nov. 17, 1812
Harmony
Somerset County
Maine
Death:
Nov. 23, 1869
Minneapolis
Hennepin County
Minnesota
Burial:
Unknown

He was a member of the Hampton, N. H., (Freewill Baptist) church, and was ordained as an evangelist about three years previous to his death. He was on his way to Wyoming, and was found in the streets of St. Paul (Minnesota), insensible from a shock of the palsy. He was conveyed to the residence of his son, where he closed his career, and went to his reward. He did good service for the Master, and, though called so soon, has left abundant evidence of his readiness to meet Him. -- Register, for the Year of our Lord 1871, Freewill Baptist Association, Dover, New Hampshire.

Franklin B. Moulton
Birth:
Feb. 15, 1835
Adams, New York
Death:
Jun. 20, 1902
Minnesota
Burial:
Pleasant Prairie Cemetery
Rochester
Olmsted County, Minnesota

Soon after his conversion in 1849, he united with the Methodist Church and entered large university, Wisconsin. His first learning of the Free Will Baptist was in 1855 and he united with this denomination for they held his own doctrinal views. In the March session, 1858, of the Zumbro Quarterly Meeting, Minnesota, he was licensed and excepted the call as the quarterly meeting missionary of the Hennepin Quarterly Meeting which was then on the extreme frontier. In 1861, he assumed the pastorate of the Rolling Prairie church, Wisconsin. The Americans Sunday school Union in 1866 called him to engage in their work which he did for several months. He resigned this work traveling in the interests of the Western Freeman's Mission. In the spring of 1867, he took the pastorate of the Stockbridge church, Wisconsin. His next pastorate was with the Vineland church where a church of 110 members was organized and a church building erected. For many years he labored in Wisconsin, but in 1884 he returned to Minnesota and ministered with some churches there and organizing the Winona church. In 1887, he removed to Diamond Bluff and engage in mission work under the direction of the state home mission board.

Thomas Corrollo Partridge
Birth:
Aug. 26, 1816
Pennsylvania
Death:
Oct. 4, 1902
Fairhaven
Stearns County
Minnesota
Burial:
Fairhaven Cemetery
Fairhaven
Stearns County
Minnesota

In 1858, Rev. Thomas Partridge, a Methodist minister and 5 other men arrived in Minneapolis, MN from Ohio, with the intention of settling somewhere in Minnesota. During a year's stay in Minneapolis, they heard about land described by Indians as "the most beautiful in the area" to the north of the city. They set out, following the Mississippi River north to the Clearwater River. There they decided on a nearby spot to stake claims. Rev. Partridge acquired enough land to establish the town and a family farm. A surveyor was hired to plat the city, complete with blocks, streets/names, a church, school, town square and cemetery. Rev. Partridge then provided the land and plans to a designated committee to begin building Fair Haven.

He was ordained by the New Durham FWBapt. Quarterly Meeting at Canterbury, N.H., May 29, 1845. While continuing in business life, he has had the charge of several churches and served as Q. M. clerk

Nathan J. Robinson
Birth:
Unknown
New Brunswick, Canada
Death:
Sep. 20, 1871
Burial:
Minneapolis Pioneers and
Soldiers Memorial Cemetery
Minneapolis, Hennepin County,
Minnesota
Plot: LOT 34 BLOCK P

C. L. Russell
Birth:
April 21, 1824
Brighton, Maine
Death:
Oct. 25, 1891
Burial:
Lakewood Cemetery
Minneapolis
Hennepin County, Minnesota
Plot: Section 6, Lot 188, Grave 2

He was converted when 12 years of age and on August 16, 1848 married Tryphen Hutchins, who died on January 8, 1885. He

was ordained on March 8, 1863 and was pastor at Wellington, Maine for five years, as Sangerville, Maine, three years; at Champlin, Minnesota for 12 years. Revivals were enjoyed in all these places and some have been baptized every year church being materially strengthened he was the quarterly meeting clerk many years and president of the state mission board.
Spouse: Tryphena D. Russell (1829 - 1885)

Levi N Sharp
Birth:
Mar. 18, 1831
New Brunswick, Canada
Death:
Oct. 19, 1894
Minneapolis, Hennepin County,
Minnesota
Burial:
Lakewood Cemetery
Minneapolis, Hennepin County,
Minnesota

He was born in New Brunswick, March 18, 1832. He was married to Miss E.A. Fenwick {Ellen

Adelaide Finwick, Can]. He pursued his preparatory studies at Sackville, N.B., and graduated at the Pennsylvania Medical College. After a short practice in his native place, he graduated at the Royal College of Surgeons of Physicians in Edinburgh, Scotland.Dr. Sharp was converted when a child and has been active in religious work. In 1882, he moved to Minneapolis, Minn., and uniting with the First church there, he has taught in the Sunday-school and serves it as clerk. Since the organization of the Western Free Baptist Publishing Society, he has held, with credit, the responsible position of treasurer. He has moved in political life in New Brunswick and has held many important positions of trust in the community. He is now a lecturer in the Minnesota State Medical College and also in the Winnebago City College.Mrs. Sharp has served jointly with Mrs. H. C. Keith in editing the department of the Woman's Missionary Society.

Andrew A Smith
Birth:
Nov. 5, 1840
North Randolph
Orange County, Vermont
Death:
Jan. 5, 1887
Minneapolis
Hennepin County, Minnesota
Burial:
Lakewood Cemetery
Minneapolis
Hennepin County, Minnesota
Plot: Sec. 7, Lot 115, Grave 5.5

He was married to Laura A. Chubb in 1864, whom he survived less than two years, leaving a son and daughter at his death.Converted to Christ in 1857, he entered New Hampton Institution with the preparation afforded by the North Randolph schools, and fitted for the ministry. His first pastorate was at Topsham, ME, where he was ordained in 1865. His earnestness, fervor, passion for saving souls, and a felicitious way of meeting men won their hearts and their acceptance of the saviour. Leaving Topsham he held a successful pastorate of three years at Portlan, ME, when he was called to the responsible duties as pastor of the college church at Hillsdale, Michigan, in 1873. Here his lively sympathy for the young found full play, his genial temperament gaining for him a ready welcome to the rooms and meetings of the students. During this pastorate he led a large number into the baptismal waters. Accepting a call to the First Free Baptist church of Minneapolis in 1878, his old-time zeal broke forth into a flame that rapidly consumed his expanding life. He deeply felt the need of organization and concentration in that vast field where churches were many miles from each other. He was a leader in uniting the brethren in the ministry by correspondence, and cooperation, among the churches, until a general organization of the churches was agreed upon, and the "Association of the Free Baptist Churches of the Northwest," was the direct result. He saw the need for a Western paper to help unify the churches, and his conviction and tenacity resulted in "The Free Baptist" paper at Minneapolis. Soon after resigning the pastorate of the First Church in Minneapolis, he continued his labors with a mission Sunday-school which he organized in a store building in 1881. He hoped this would be the nucleus for a second church, which was realized in January 1884, when he organized the

Stevens Avenue church, of which he became the pastor in connection with editorial and other work, and continued in these relations until his death, when he left a self-supporting church, moved with much of the missionary zeal of their leader and pastor.

Freeborn W Straight
Birth:
1806
Washington County, New York
Death:
Dec. 23, 1878
Monroe County, New York
Burial:
Beach Ridge Cemetery
Brockport,
Monroe County, New York
Plot: B.R. II 165

Soon after his birth, with his father, William Straight, moved to Walworth, Wayne Co. NY. When about twenty-one years of age he ws converted under the labors of Elder Lyon and united with the Walworth Free Baptist church. In about a year he was licensed to preach and soon after, with Elder David Marks, he went to Ontario, Canada, where they traveled and labored with great success. Marks, returning, but Straight remained in Canada and supplied the Woodstock and London churches, forty miles apart, and preached at intervening points. More than a hundred were converted during the winter, and he was sent to New York for ordination in March 1828. He remained in Canada several years and churches were formed which grew to become the Ontario Yearly Meeting. Returning to New York, he was inactive for a time. In 1841, he took up the work and a year later he assisted Brother Bathrick at Conneaut, Ohio, and Bro. Dunn at Mecca, with many being converted at each place. He was pastor at Conneaut two years and assisted in a great revival in Pennfield, N.Y., and later settled as pastor of the church at Fairport for eight years. In the winter of 1851-52 he assisted Bro. Bathrick again at Saco, Maine and more than four hundred were converted in the congregation with the revival being one of unusual power and extending also to other congregations and towns. He seemed almost inspired in his labors there. A part of the following winter was spent in revival work in Saco. After a year at Brockport, he settled at Manchester, New Hampshire., where he remained for three years, and eighty were converted the first winter. After one year at Boston, Massachusetts, and two at Saco ME. he went to Conneaut Ohio in 1861, and two years later to Jackson, Michigan. He remained there nine years,

reorganizing the church and carrying it through many difficulties. He then made his home in Lansing, intending to rest, but could not.

He gathered fragments of several churches together at Grand Ledge, encouraged them to build their beautiful brick church, and by his visits aided the churches at Reading, Cambridge, Paw Paw, Bath, Macon, Delta and Leslie. Then in 1877, visiting the scene of his early labors in Ontario, he took charge of two churches in Zorra, and worked with the zeal and ardor of his youth until his sudden death. Straight was a man of large and commanding form, and of robust health, rather diffident unless aroused by some exigency, pre-eminently social and companionable. His intellect was of a high order, quick, discriminating and logical. He was several times a member of the General Conference. He died at the post of duty near where he preached his first sermon fifty-one years before, and was buried at Brockport, N.Y., near the scenes of his early ministry.He was married to Sarah (unk) Straight,(said to be born in Canada?)and their Family Tree says they married in Lowell, MA. His wife, died on Mar. 4, 1855, at age 43. He was then married to Miriam F. Jenkins, on 27 May 1856, Lowell, MA.

subsequently labored in Hebron, Gardiner, Minot and Canton. Going in May, 1862, to reside in Minnesota, he soon organized a church, and aided in building up the Minnesota Southern Y. M. His baptisms numbered 231. He was a safe counselor and a good preacher, enforcing both with an exemplary life.

Austin Wheeler
Birth:
unknown
Death:
Feb. 7, 1873
Burial:
Rice Lake Cemetery
Delavan, Faribault County,
Minnesota

Wheeler, a native of Gilead, Me., died in Prescott, Minn., aged 72 years. He was licensed at the age of twenty-six, and ordained the following year. He moved to Otisfield in 1837, and

Mississippi

Matthew Ranson Allen
Birth:
Oct. 5, 1888
North Carolina
Death:
Jul. 21, 1953
Mississippi,
Burial:
Sherman Cemetery
Sherman
Pontotoc County, Mississippi

Minister, teacher; who pastored churches in Monroe Co. MS. His name is listed in book by Rev. G. C. Lee, Sr., in 1949. College educated he taught school after college. As a minister of the gospel it was said that he served the Lord in pastoring several churches in N. E. MS including Pearce's Chapel in Monroe County near Smithville, MS. Allen married Lillian L. Brasfield, 19 Dec 1914. Born to that union included sons: Doyle, Thomas, an Eustace Dorsey Allen.

Rev James Earl Cosby
Birth:
Jul. 29, 1947
Canton
Madison County
Mississippi
Death:
Mar. 1, 2015
Ashland
Ashland County
Ohio
Burial: Andrews Chapel
Cemetery
Kearney Park
Madison County
Mississippi

Rev. James Earl COSBY, 67, was born Elex and Beulah (Allen) Cosby in Canton, Mississippi and had lived in Mansfield, Ohio the past 47 years. James was employed in the steel industry first with DSL where he served as the first African American Union President of Steelworkers Local Union #7597 serving for 20 years, and retiring from Empire Detroit Steel Mill in 2004 after 21 years of service.

James became an ordained minister in 1993 and pastored several churches in the Mansfield and Willard, Ohio area. In his ministry Rev. Cosby continued to break barriers by being the first African American to either join or pastor in the following conferences and churches: joined and ordained through the Ohio Northern Conference Free Will Baptist, pastored the Free Will Baptist Church in Clyde, current pastor of Paradise Free Will Baptist Church in Mansfield, and joined the Lorain-Cuyahoga Conference Free Will Baptist. Rev. Cosby was very involved in his community, and church as a member of the Mansfield Interdenominational Ministerial Alliance where he was former vice president, NAACP where he held numerous positions, Richland County Democratic Party, founder of the Cosby Educational Heritage Center located in the Ocie Hill Building. His accomplishments were many and too numerous to name them all.

William Fondren
Birth:
Dec., 1855
Alabama
Death:
Mississippi
Burial:
Gauley Cemetery, Pittsboro,
Calhoun County, Mississippi

He came to Mississippi sometime between 1870 and 1880, where records show him as performing a number of marriages. He was a Free Will Baptist minister, but it is unknown where and when he was ordained.

Luther D. Gibson
Birth:
Aug. 20, 1920
Mississippi
Death:
May 2, 1992
Booneville,
Prentiss County, Mississippi
Burial:
Tuscumbia Baptist,
Old Hwy 145, Booneville,
Prentiss County, Mississippi

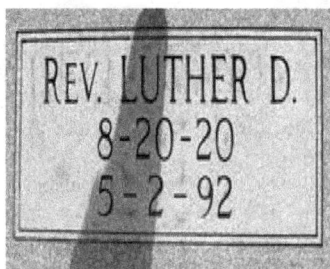

A well-known Free Will Baptist pastor and denominational leader. He pastored for 49 years in Mississippi except for 5 years in Missouri. As a leader, he was the moderator of two district associations and for 25 years served on the Board of Trustees of the Free Will Baptist Bible

College in Nashville Tennessee. *The Lumen*, the college yearbook, was dedicated to him in 1976. A Navy veteran serving in World War II. He was a pastor's pastor and a role model for many. He held a Bachelor of Arts degree from Free Will Baptist Bible College and did graduate study at Columbia Bible College in Columbia, South Carolina.

Jesse Heath was 22 years old when he and four of his brothers served with Stanford's battery at Shiloh. Here, he poses years after the war with his wife, Sally Little, who became the oldest living person in Mississippi in the 1930s when she reached the age of 102.

Jesse Heath
Birth:
Unknown
Death:
Unknown
Inscription:
Burial:
Calvary Cemetery
Carroll County, Mississippi

Plot: Unknown Dates Stanfords Battery Miss E Arty. CSA

M. L. Hollis, Sr.
Birth:
Sep. 1, 1898
Death:
Feb. 18, 1974
Amory, Mississippi
Burial:
Masonic Cemetery
Amory, Monroe County,
Mississippi

The 17 year old saw mill worker had only completed eight years of school, but God had called him to preach and for several years he fought that calling. Mr. Hollis was licensed to preach in June, 1918. He began holding services and revivals, but somehow he just couldn't shake the conviction that God wanted him to finish school. He tried several ways to get the money to further his education, but each time the door was closed. Finally, Damascus Free Will Baptist Church near Meridian, Mississippi asked Brother Hollis to come to their church for a revival. Meridian seemed to be very far from his home in Vernon, Alabama, yet, he realized this was a call from the Lord. He soon found himself standing on the train depot in Meridian waiting to be met by two men from the church. However, these two men mistook him for a young boy and they left without the evangelist! Brother Hollis finally managed to get to the church - just in time for the service. As he walked to the pulpit, an elderly man with a beard stroking his belt, said in tones loud enough for that frightened 17 year old to hear, "lf that is our chance for a preacher, we are out!" But God hadn't struck out. At the close of the revival the church offered to call the teenage preacher as pastor of the church and pay his expenses while he finished school. So, Mr. Hollis started back to school in the ninth grade. He finished high school graduating second in his class. The Damascus Church then sent Brother Hollis to Beason Jr. College in Meridian for two

years. Several years later, in 1927, Brother Hollis received a scholarship from the John D.Rockefeller Foundation to attend Vanderbilt School of Religion in Nashville, Tennessee. He attended six weeks a year for four years. He later went to Moody Bible lnstitute in Chicago, lllinois. After God had called and prepared His vessel, He began to open doors of service. In 1927 he went to a full time church in Bryan, Texas. He then returned to Red church Bay, Alabama in 1929, where he served as it's pastor for 21 years. Following his five year ministry at the Damascus church, Mr. Hollis accepted the pastorate of five country churches in Alabama for four years. However, during these churches he was already serving, he also had the times the newly organized churches had the responsibility of simultaneously having services on Saturday night or Sunday ministering in five to eleven other mornings at nine o'clock, or Sunday churches, preaching five to six sermons in the afternoon to enable Brother Hollis to pastor or preach every weekend. This schedule was maintained as a typical story repeated 24 times during these years of his ministry Brother Hollis organized many Free Will Baptist churches. As far as is known there were no Free Will Baptist known who organized more churches as he did. He began as a Free Will Baptist minister in extensive evangelistic endeavors and organizing churches. Because of his ability and dedication, he was elected chairman of the National Home Missions Board in 1938. Not only is Mr. Hollis known for his pastoral and organizational work. but he has been one of the most widely used evangelists in 20th century in Free Will Baptist history. Whether the revival was held in brush-arbors, tents, churches, or auditoriums, God blessed the revival work of M. L. Hollis. One of the best remembered revivals in this evangelist's ministry was held at Pearce Chapel Free Will Baptist Church in Smithville, Mississippi. At the close of the week 78 converts were baptized. Because of the large number of baptismal candidates several hundred people gathered at the river to watch. Many doubted that the short evangelist could accomplish the strenuous task by himself. However, he not only baptized all 78, but he did it in exactly 32 minutes! Many called Mr. Hollis again and again as evangelist. The Damascus Church where he first pastored has had him in revival 33 times. Brother Hollis' ministry spanned over 55 years with his longest pastoral tenure being 35 years at the Pearce Chapel Church. During these years he had become well-known for his prophetic messages. One of the highlights of his ministry was his visit to he Holy Land. Even though in his 70s he thrilled to see the area where many Biblical prophecies, of which he has so long preached, will be fulfilled. It

is impossible to fully realize what this veteran preacher has meant to the Lord's work. A numerical summary of his work is given in his own words: "l have organized 24 churches, held revivals in 23 states, baptized more than 6,000 converts, received into Free Will Baptist churches over 10,000 members, and married numerous couples and average over 100 funeral a year. His spousd were Effie Mae Hollis (1898 - 1969) who married in 1922 and Helen Streety who he married have the death of Effie..

Inscription:
A Devoted Husband, A Loving Father.And A Faithful Soldier Of The Cross Of Jesus Christ

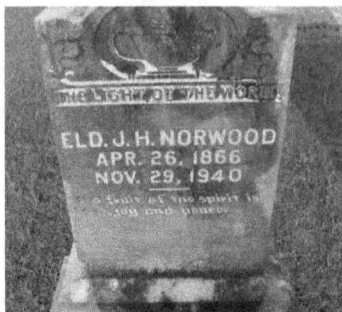

James H. Norwood
Birth:
Apr. 26,1866
Death:
Nov. 29,1940
Mississippi
Burial:
Antioch Cem.,
Toccopola
Pontotoc Co. MS

Parents were Washington Pinkney Laben NORWOOD, and Mary (Farrar) NORWOOD.
He married Margaret "Maggie" (Carr) NORWOOD, 4 Mar 1886 in Pontotoc Co., MS.
He was an ordained Free Will Baptist minister, who worked in several localities in northeastern Mississippi, including counties, Calhoun, Kemper, Lee, Lafayette and Pontotoc, as well as Hood Co. TX in 1900, and Atascosa Co., TX in 1910.
His name is listed with the old pioneer ministers in these Mississippi areas before 1900 and afterward, who went many times without any remuneration for their services. He established the Stetson's Chapel church before 1909, in Lafayette Co. and he pastored throughout the area,

as well as doing the work of of an evangelist with great success in his meetings. A friend, Rev. G.C. Lee, Sr., wrote of him, "...he was a mighty power in the ministry of the gospel of the Lord." He was always ready to help another minister whenever he could, but was loyal to his church.
He was beloved and esteemed by the many friends and minister brethren he worked with.

Daniel Wyatt Jones, Jr
Birth:
Mar. 23, 1930
Death:
Apr. 20, 2011
Burial:
Little Brown Cemetery,
New Site,
Prentiss County, Mississippi
He was a member of New Lebanon Freewill Baptist Church, a retired Freewill Baptist preacher and a sheet metal mechanic. He was the son of Rev. D.W. Jones Sr.

Rev Norlin Dencil Jones, Sr
Birth:
Feb. 3, 1928
Death:
Mar. 16, 2003
Burial:
Jones Chapel Cemetery
Prentiss County
Mississippi
Plot: Section behind the church

A Free Will Baptist minister, he pastored the Randall Memorial and First Free Will Baptist Churches in Memphis from 1955 to 1966. He served as home missionary/church planter for the State of Tennessee and the National Association of Free Will Baptists. He founded the First Free Will Baptist Church of Jackson, Tenn. He then moved to Daytona Beach, Fla., where he founded the Daytona Beach Free Will Baptist Church. He also pastored several Free Will Baptist Churches in Mississippi. He served in the U.S. Army from 1946-1948 and was stationed in Tokyo, Japan. After his marriage he moved to Memphis and worked as a tool and die pattern maker for International Harvester Corp. until entering the ministry full time.
Services with the Rev. Terry Booker and the Rev. Leonard Ball officiating. WW II U.S. Army Veteran.

John A. Killingsworth
Birth:
Dec. 5, 1852
Mississippi
Death:
Jan. 4, 1925
Calhoun County, Mississippi
Burial: Pittsboro Cemetery, Pittsboro, Calhoun County, Mississippi

A Free Will Baptist pioneer minister/pastor in Mississippi.

George Cullen Lee
Birth:
May 3, 1887
Calhoun County, Mississippi
Death:
Jul. 12, 1971
Calhoun County, Mississippi
Burial:
New Gauley Cemetery, Calhoun City, Calhoun County, Mississippi
A Mississippi FWB minister for

over 62 year and a man of faith. From the Calhoun newspaper, "Rev Lee was one of Calhoun County's best citizens and in addition, is a forceful, eloquent and successful preacher. If we were called on to name most valuable citizen of Calhoun City, Rev. Lee would be among those who would come to our mind. He lives his religion every day of his life; he meddles with no person's affairs, but is ever ready to help and advise when there is trouble or sorrow. He is not the spectacular, egotistical type of preacher--he goes about his work quietly, confidently, full of high purpose. George Lee is a product of Calhoun and we are proud of him." He was called to preach in his home church of Gauley Free Will Baptist Church west of Calhoun City, MS and pastored there from 1909 until the late 60's or approximately 60 years. He married Estelle Whitworth in 1909 and they had 8 children. Clara Mae, who died in infancy, Marie, Lillian, Lora, Nellie Helen, Wanda and G.C., Jr. followed.

He pastored country churches in Mississippi during his ministry and a partial listing of them were: New Gauley, New Life, Priceville, Antioch, Bethlehem, Lee's Chapel, Stetson's Chapel, Beech Springs, McGregor's Chapel Springdale. Those are some of the ones I recall going to with him but this is an incomplete list. (GC Lee,Jr.)

He married hundreds of couples and conducted at least 500 funerals.

Rev George Pardon Mayo
Birth:
Jun. 27, 1875
Tishomingo
Tishomingo County
, Mississippi
Death:
Oct. 12, 1957
Booneville
Prentiss County,
Mississippi
Burial:
Little Brown Cemetery
New Site
Prentiss County,
Mississipp

Mississipi Free Will Baptist minister, who served as assistant moderator in 1923, and name appears in minutes of Northeast Mississippi Association.

William Garland Prude
Birth:
Nov. 22, 1895
Death:
Jun. 12, 1966
Burial:
Tupelo Memorial
Park Cemetery
Tupelo
Lee County,
Mississippi
Plot: Section C - Row 19

Iris Lyndon Stanley
Birth:
Mar. 19, 1906
Saltillo, Lee County, Mississippi
Death:
Sep. 27, 1993
Saltillo, Lee County, Mississippi

Burial:
Spring Hill Cemetery,
Saltillo,
Lee County, Mississippi

He was the first Superintendent of the Free Will Baptist Home for Children in Greenville, Tennessee. He served in this position for 25 years. He started the Harris Memorial Free Will Baptist Church in Greenville so the children would have a Free Will Baptist church to attend. He was a World War II veteran of the U.S. Army and a former school teacher with the Lee County school system. He was a well-known music director assisting the late Rev. H. L. Hollis in starting many Free Will Baptist churches in Mississippi and Alabama. He was frequently used as the song leader of the National Association at its annual sessions.

George W. Wages
Birth:
May 5, 1886
Death:
Jun. 27, 1972
Burial:
Blue Mountain Cemetery
Blue Mountain
Tippah County, Mississippi

Rev. Geo. Washington Wages, was a FWB minister, mentioned in a book pub. in 1949, by Rev. G.C. Lee, Sr., who had association with him. In the 1940 census he states his occupation. as 'minister.' He was esteemed by those who knew him. George W. Wages married Viola Sewell on September 15, 1907. They had 6 children.

To Call His Soul To The Life Immortal Where Souls A-Weary Shall Rest With God.

Randy Wright
Birth:
Aug. 13, 1960
Amory
Monroe County
Mississippi
Death:
Feb. 7, 2015
Fayette
Fayette County, Alabama
Burial:
Masonic Cemetery
Amory
Monroe County, Mississippi

Bro. Randy Wright, 54, of Guin, Ala., passed away in Fayette Medical Center in Fayette, Ala.
He is the son of Henry Grady Wright and the late Mary Mildred Schumpert Wright. He was pastor of Piney Grove Free Will Baptist Church for the past 25 years. He was Chairman of the Home Mission Board and had served on the Trinity Youth Camp Board and ALCAP Board. He was a former Chairman of the Acts 1:8 Committee, and he served 11 years as Chaplin of Hospice of Northwest Alabama. He loved music, was a trumpet player, and had also been a DJ since he was 15 years old.
Services were at the Guin First Baptist Church with Bro. Mickey Crane, Bro. Rick Cash, Bro. Danny Williams, Bro. David Crowe and Bro. Jack Whitley officiating.

To Be Cursed By God, One Need Not Do The *Wrong* Thing, Just *Nothing*.

Missouri

Rev Ocia Leonard Allen
Birth:
Oct. 6, 1896
Hartville
Wright County
Missouri, USA
Death:
Jun. 1, 1955
Springfield
Greene County
Missouri
Burial:
Greenlawn Memorial Gardens
Springfield
Greene County
Missouri

Ocia Leonard Allen was the son of James "Maudy" Allen, an Iowa Civil War veteran, and Amanda Smith Burton, an Indiana native who moved to Wright County as a child. Both were married before, had families and were widowed.

Ocia served in Europe in WWI, and upon his return in 1920, married Thelma Davis. Their first child was born in Wright County, then by 1923, he moved his family to Fresno, California, where several Burton siblings had already relocated. About 1928, the Allen's returned to Wright County, and eventually moved to Springfield. The Allen family included four sons and a daughter.

In the Mountain Grove, Wright County, Missouri obituary, he was listed as Rev. Allen, having been pastor of churches of Willow Springs and Mansfield, as well as a rural mail carrier.

O. T. Allred
Birth:
Sep. 12, 1895
Death:
Apr. 29, 1976
Burial:
Bethel Cemetery, Masters,
Cedar County, Missouri

Well-known Free Will Baptist preacher and pastor in the Southwest region of the state of Missouri. He was one of the early writers for the Free Will Baptist Gem and was a contemporary with B.F. Brown the first editor. He, with John Rollins, Ken Turner and Winford Davis, were all the early pastors in the Indian Creek Association.

Earl Edward Altis
Birth:
Mar. 14, 1933
Death:
Apr. 12, 1986
Springfield
Greene County, Missouri
Burial:
Providence Cemetery, Cabool,
Texas County, Missouri

He received his bachelor's degree from Southwest Missouri State University in 1961, his Master's degree from the University of Denver in 1964 and an advanced studies certificate in 1974. He was a teacher and librarian in Missouri and Oklahoma colleges and schools. He also served as a Free Will Baptist pastor in Missouri and Colorado. He helped organize the Church Training Services organization in Missouri and served as the editor of the Free Will Baptist Gem. He married Judy Shrewsbury in Nashville, Tennessee in 1979.

Rev Floyd "Bud" Arnold
Birth:
Unknown
Missouri
Death:
Aug. 4, 2016
Springfield
Greene County, Missouri
Burial:
Ozarks Memorial Park
Branson
Taney County, Missouri

Rev. Floyd Arnold, 88 of Branson, died at the Cox South Medical center in Springfield. The

services was held at the Friendship FWB church in Branson with Military honors provided by the Vietnam Veterans of American #913 and the United States Army. He ministered many churches in the St. Louis area and Southwest Missouri including the Friendship church where he retired. He also served as Envoy of the Salvation Army in Branson for over 10 years. He is also remembered for his service at Camp Niangua.

Rev James Barker
Birth:
Dec. 17, 1920
Desloge
St. Francois County,
Missouri
Death:
Nov. 6, 2014
Park Hills
St. Francois County
Missouri
Burial:
Hillview Memorial Gardens
Farmington
St. Francois County
Missouri

He was a long time Free Will Baptist minister in the St. Francois QM and one of the most knowledgeable of the history of the oldest conference in Missouri. He pastored many of the churches in this conference and at his death was a member of the Gospel Light Free Will Baptist church. He was married to Geneva, His wife for 73 years. The service was officiated by Rev. Larry Allison and Rev. Herb McMillian.

Lewis P. Barker
Birth:
1913
Death:
Nov. 24,2002
Oklahoma City,
Okla.
Burial:
Licking Cemetery,
Licking,Texas County, Missouri

He was a member of the First Free Will Baptist Church in Moore, Okla. He pastored FWB churches in Arkansas and Missouri. Surviving are one daughter, Willie Jean Deeds, retired missionary to Brazil, of Moore, Okla.; two sons, Charles Berton Barker of Licking and Dr. Robert Lewis Barker of Oak Park, Calif.

Garland Alexander Barrett
Birth:
Jan. 17, 1854
Ozark County,
Missouri
Death:
May 17, 1900
Ripley County,
Missouri
Burial:
Macedonia Cemetery
Doniphan
Ripley County,
Missouri

He was the co-author with G.W. Million of *A Brief History of the Liberal Baptist People in England and America from 1606 to 1911.*
He was a licentiate at the first meeting of the Social Band thaws was held with the Sugartee Grove church in Ripley County, Missouri on Sept. 17, 1875. This was the first General Free Will Baptists west of the Mississippi. He was ordained the next year at second association that met with the Brier Crteek church. This Assn. consisted of churches in both Missouri and Arkansas from FWB and General Baptists churches. Barrett was an active member of this conference until his death. He was a noticed writer, preacher, leader and one remembered for his contribution to the denomination. He was the son of John Barrett (1812 - 1883) and Mary Jane Ivy Barrett (1816 - 1870). He married a widow Louisa Jane Flanigan King (1835 - 1894).

Rev David E Bates
Birth:
Mar. 21, 1946
Ironton
Iron County, Missouri
Death:
Dec. 30, 2014
Farmington
St. Francois County, Missouri
Burial:
Hillview Memorial Gardens
Farmington
St. Francois County, Missouri

Reverend David E. Bates of Farmington, departed this life and entered into eternity on Tuesday, at his residence at the age of 68 years with his heart prepared to meet his Savior and his guitar in hand. He was born the son of Iva "Aline" (Henson) Bates and the late Paul Elwood Bates. In addition to his father he was preceded in death by a son Jonathan Bates.

David grew up in the Bismarck area and graduated from Bismarck High School in 1964. At the age of eight he met Miss Marilyn Barnes. David and Marilyn quickly became best friends and started a relationship that soon grew into love and the two were married on May 17,1967. He proudly served his country in the Army as an Artillery Sergeant Specialist serving overseas during the Vietnam War. Following his service David returned home, and began a career working as a salesman, and eventually a sales supervisor and trainer for the Bunny Bread Co. then later the Holsum Bakery Co. During this time David attended night school for Business Management, and later enrolled in Bible College by correspondence at Hillsdale College. In 1977 he received the call to the Gospel Ministry and was ordained in the Free Will Baptist Church. He served at the Free Will Baptist Church in Farmington as an associate pastor and music director and in Santa Paula, CA. as senior pastor. In 2008, he became the pastor of Grace Community Church in Knob Lick where he served until the time of his death.

David was an amazingly talented musician and enjoyed singing and playing music for church, his family, and friends. While serving as Music Director at Farmington First Free Will Baptist Church, he was also the director and a member of the Gospel Quartet "Master Peace" performing at various local churches and community events. A memorial service at Grace Community Church at the Nelson Music City Theater at Knob Lick. Interment with full military honors was at Hillview Memorial Gardens in Farmington.

Harry Howard Beatty
Birth:
Aug. 16, 1911
Oregon County, Missouri
Death:
Feb. 27, 1994
Owasso,
Tulsa County, Oklahoma
Burial:
Thayer Cemetery, Thayer,
Oregon County, Missouri

Beatty was converted at the age 19 and began his ministry in the Thayer area. He was a well-known Freewill Baptist minister for many years in Missouri and Oklahoma as a pastor and church planter. He was the first Missouri Promotional Secretary of Free Will Baptist and served in that capacity from 1961 until 1975. During his tenure led the state of Missouri in becoming one of the strongest co-operative giving states in the denomination.

Lue Bequette
Birth:
Apr. 16, 1922
Death:
Jan. 4, 2008
Burial:
Mine La Motte Cemetery,
Mine La Motte,
Madison County,
Missouri

He was an early Free Will Baptist minister and pastored in the St. Francois Association in Southeast Missouri.

Manuel Eugene Bingham
Birth:
May 7, 1924
Death:
Apr. 22, 2007
Burial:
New Home Cemetery, Falcon,
Laclede County, Missouri
He worked as a cattle farmer and in the timber. Manuel followed the Free Will Baptist faith throughout the years.

K. Breshears and Mary Ann McDonald. According to his death certificate, he died of apoplexy and hypertension. His occupation was minister.

Miles Evans Brasher
Birth:
Sep. 6, 1855
Death:
Feb. 23, 1948
Burial:
Crossroads Cemetery,
Lebanon,
Laclede County, Missouri

Nathan Joseph Breshears
Birth:
Jun. 15, 1863
Missouri
Death:
Dec. 11, 1936
Springfield
Greene County, Missouri
Burial:
Greenlawn Memorial Gardens
Springfield
Greene County, Missouri

Benjamin F. Brown
Birth:
Jan. 6, 1870
Death:
Aug. 29, 1964
Barry County, Missouri
Burial:
Purdy Cemetery, Purdy,
Barry County, Missouri

Rev. B. F. Brown was the second president of Tecumseh College in Tecumseh, Oklahoma until after 1927 when the school burned. At that time there was a committee considering a publication that would be located in Missouri, but a publication for everyone in the denomination. This committee offered B. F. Brown the opportunity to be the first editor, even though he still resided in Tecumseh. The first issues of the *Free Will Baptist GEM* were published in Tecumseh, beginning January 1929. In May of 1930 the paper was moved to Purdy, Missouri. Rev. Brown moved to Purdy and continued as editor until 1939 when he retired. At that time, the publication was moved to Monett, Missouri. However, in 1946 he was called upon to rescue the magazine and became the acting editor from December of 1946 until August of 1947. B. F. Brown during the time between 1929 until 1935 had become a leader in the Cooperative Association which existed throughout the Midwest. It later was to merge with the General Conference, a conference mainly in the Southeast, in 1935 at Nashville, Tennessee. Rev. Brown would sign for the

Cooperative Association to accept the agreement with the General Conf. This agreement in 1935 formed the National Association of Free Will Baptists. Rev. Brown was a member of the executive board and served as its secretary. Later, he became a member of the Home Missions Board of the National Convention. Records revealed that he attended the national convention until about 1946.

Claude R Bryan
Birth:
May 13, 1884
Death:
Nov. 26, 1981
Burial:
Thayer Cemetery, Thayer,
Oregon County, Missouri

He was an early Free Will Baptist preacher in the south-central part of the state of Missouri.

Rev George Bullock
Birth:
Jan. 31, 1837
Ontario, Canada
Death:
Jul. 19, 1932
Pierce City
Lawrence County
Missouri

Burial:
Pierce City Cemetery
Pierce City
Lawrence County
Missouri

He received license to preach in 1874, and was ordained in 1875. His work was in Michigan, Iowa, and Missouri. He assisted in organizing four churches. He pastored the Clay and Delhi churches.

Rev. George BULLOCK, was the son of William and Nancy (Heten) BULLOCK. He was married July 28, 1861, to Sarah Aldrich, daughter of Jefferson and Eliza ALDRICH.

James Eli Burney
Birth:
Dec. 20, 1879
Wright County
Missouri
Death:
Mar. 10, 1951
Mountain Grove
Wright County
Missouri
Burial:
Steele Memorial Cemetery
Hartville
Wright County
Missouri

James "Eli" Burney was the son of William Lafayette Burney and Sarah Ann [Cope] Burney.
He married Ora Alice Claxton, daughter of James Edward Claxton and Phoebe Carolina [Palmer] Claxton, 14/Jan/1900 in Wright County, Missouri.

Cecil Herbert Campbell
Birth:
Sep. 28, 1910
Stella,
Newton County,
Missouri
Death:
Jul. 18, 1999
North Little Rock,
Pulaski County, Arkansas
Burial:
Jones Chapel Cemetery,
Stella,
Newton County, Missouri

He served churches in Missouri and North Carolina. He conducted revivals in Texas, Oklahoma, Missouri, North and South Carolina. He was an active denominational leader on state and national levels, with a good ministry where ever he served.

John M Carnahan, Sr
Birth:
Jun. 7, 1877
Death:
May 3, 1954
Burial:
Maple Park Cemetery
Springfield
Greene County, Missouri

Early FWB Preacher.

Rev Jacob Newton Carner
Birth:
Dec. 8, 1838
Indiana
Death:
Apr. 13, 1919
Howell County, Missouri
Burial:
Merideth/Meredith Cemetery
Lanton
Howell County, Missouri

He was a was a preacher of the General Baptists of Kentucky when he as accepted as a minister in the Social Band Assn. in Arkansas where he was a leader. He did a great work as he remained but afterwards moved to Howell county, Missouri and rejoined the General Baptists. He was a veteran of Co H 8 Ky Cav Union Army. He was married twice to Francis Prudence

Tackett Carner (1841 - 1925) and Nancy E Jones Carner (1841 - 1904).

Elijah Carpenter
Birth:
1858
Illinois
Death:
1941
Seymour
Webster County, Missouri
Burial:
Liberty Cemetery Seymour
Webster County, Missouri

Mike S. Cleaver
Birth:
Nov. 21, 1897
Death:
Dec. 6, 1971
Burial:
Oakside Cemetery,
Summersville,
Shannon County, Missouri

Rev Marion Benjamin Clift
Birth:
Mar. 17, 1873
Webster County
Missouri
Death:
Dec. 1, 1926
Webster County
Missouri
Burial:
Black Oak Cemetery
Marshfield
Webster County
Missouri

Early Free Will Bapt. minister, ordained in Sept. 1909.

Fred E Comber
Birth:
1857
Canada
Death:
1917
Galveston
Galveston County. Texas
Burial:
Weiss Cemetery
Doe Run
St. Francois County, Missouri

Born in Canada; immigrated to Bonne Terre, Mo. to work as an engineer at about 18 years of age. Married Elizabeth Weiss of Doe Run about 1885. About 1895 he began preaching and helped to organize Free Baptist Churches. He had served the Free Baptist Churches at Doe Run, MO, Murphysboro and Ava, IL and various other localities in this area as well as southern Illinois.He was preceded in death by his wife Elizabeth early in 1915, after which he located in the Galveston, TX area for health reasons and where he had accepted a pastorate.

Funeral Services were conducted by his friend and co-worker of many years, Reverend George Gordon of Ava, IL.

Note: per Gib Weiss - a neighbor's team of Percheron horses were used to skid the tombstone up to the cemetery.

Tombstone was donated by some of his parishioner's (from another state) and shipped to the Weiss farm in Doe Run..

Rev. Fred E. Comber was in a list of ministers who had pastored the First FWB Church in Bryan, TX; he from 1915-1917.

Archie Stanley Cooper
Birth:
Jul. 10, 1907
Mystic
Sullivan County, Missouri
Death:
Apr. 27, 2003
Kirksville
Adair County, Missouri
Burial:
Green Grove Cemetery
Novinger
Adair County, Missouri

Reverend Archie Cooper, 95, passed away at Kirksville Manor Care Center in Kirksville.

The son of Byron Isaac and Cleo Virginia (Muncy) Cooper. On October 16, 1927, Archie was united in marriage to Verdie Summers and to this union two daughters were born. Verdie preceded Archie in death in 1945. In 1946 he was united in marriage to Gladys Wellman Peterson who preceded Archie in death on January 30, 1997.

Reverend Cooper lived most of his life in Adair County and was a preacher of fifty-three years. Archie was ordained for the ministry by the Free Will Baptist Association at Hazel Creek Church in Adair County on September 4, 1937. He served at the New Harmony Baptist Church from 1938 to 1947 and at age eighty-two, returned to Pastor from 1966 until the early 90's. He also ministered at Low Ground, Baring, Refuge, Jewel and Sublette church's. Archie also spent thirty-two years every morning, six days a week at 6:15 a.m. serving many counties on KIRX with his morning meditations that he thought of from scripture, prayer and often a poem. Throughout Archie's amazing career, he ministered over 900 weddings and 2800 funerals.

Archie was recently recognized as the KTVO Heartland Hero.
Reverend Archie was a devoted member of the New Harmony Baptist Church.
Funeral services was held at in Kirksville with the Rev. Daniel Eloe officiating.

Rev W. H. Copas
Birth:
Sep. 9, 1836
Ohio
Death:
Jul. 23, 1904
Missouri
Burial:
Niangua Cemetery
Niangua
Webster County, Missouri

The St. Francois County, Fed U.S. Census in 1880 Fth VA Mth Pa
Wife Mary A 40 OH, Son William He stated his Occupation as Shoe Maker which most ministers had a trade in which to a living. In 1890 Mo. Vets. Census, it showed W.H. Copass, a native of Ohio was working in Missouri with Rev O.S. Harding of Iowa and Dr. E.H. Hunt in beginning new churches in Missouri. His SON Charles K. Copas IS BURIED IN THIS Cemetery.

And with unfaltering lip and heart, I call the Saviour mine.

Henry Clay Crase
Birth:
1865
Death:
1966
Burial:
Garfield Cemetery,
Garfield,
Oregon County, Missouri
He had a long ministry in the Free Will Baptist denomination and was very active as a district and state leader.

Grover Cleveland Cravens
Birth:
Feb. 3, 1885
Wright County
Missouri
Death:
Nov. 22, 1958
Mansfield
Wright County
Missouri
Burial:
Steele Memorial Cemetery
Hartville
Wright County Missouri

William Elvin Crews
Birth:
Sep. 22, 1893 Alton,
Oregon County,
Missouri
Death:
Aug. 24, 1946 Oregon
County, Missouri
Burial:
Shiloh Cemetery, Alton,
Oregon County, Missouri

He was a Veteran of the U.S Army (Pvt; Btry D, 342 Inf) serving in World War I. Minister of the Freewill Baptist Church.

Rev John H Culley
Birth:
Jan. 29, 1839
Jackson County
Illinois
Death:
Apr. 23, 1907
St. Francois County
Missouri
Burial:
Doe Run Memorial Cemetery
Doe Run
St. Francois County, Missouri
Plot: Sect. C

Rev. John H. Culley, was an ordained minister of the Freewill Baptist Church. He married Clarinda Rhodes. Oct. 9, 1861, and served in various offices of trust in the town of Murphysborough, Ill., until his conversion in 1876. He then devoted himself to ministerial work, receiving ordination Dec. 27, 1878. He has ministered to the Beaver Pond, Mt. Nebo.
Drura, De Soto, Rock Springs and Cedar churches, all in the Looney Springs Q. M., Ill., the three first named having been organized by himself; and in the St. Francois Q. M., Missouri.
He was in the sixth session of the Missouri State Conference of FWB, which minutes are dated Oct. 8, 1896, when convened at the Casteel Church in Clinton Co.

MO, and his name is listed as being from Doe Run. During the 1890 session of the State Conference Rev. John H. Culley, was re-elected as president. This old conference was affiliated with northern Randall movement.

There is a Civil War record of John H. Culley, as Commisary Sgt, Pvt. Illinois 18th Inf., Co. CFS.

Rev Jack C. Day
Birth: May 26, 1934
Niangua
Webster County
Missouri
Death: Feb. 9, 2016
Springfield
Greene County
Missouri
Burial:
Marshfield Cemetery
Marshfield
Webster County
Missouri

He was born to Orville and Mabel Whitehead Day. Jack was the eighth child born unto a family of nine children.

On May 21, 1955, he married

Freda Mae Sell, and to this union was born one daughter, Carolyn. Jack and Freda were married for 60 years.

Jack was a loyal servant for Jesus Christ. He learned as a young adult that he had been called to spread the Gospel of our Lord. In addition to a career at Custom Trailer/Polar, He pastored Black Oak Freewill Baptist Church in Marshfield for over 48 years. While he tirelessly served the members of Black Oak, he also was a spiritual comfort to many others in the community.

Rev Henry B Davis
Birth:
Jun. 30, 1819
Warren County
New York
Death:
Jul. 4, 1879
Warren County
New York
Burial:
Highland Cemetery
Hamilton
Caldwell County
Missouri

He commenced preaching in 1847. His labors were mostly in the Caldwell and other churches of Lake George Quarterly Meeting except two years at Ashfield, Mass, where he was ordained [Freewill Baptist], Sept. 13, 1857, by a council of the Renesselear, Q.M. He was well received as a minister and quite successful.

Death Before Life

Eliphaz Davis
Birth:
Aug. 23, 1845
Jackson County, Illinois
Death:
Aug. 9, 1925
Everett
Snohomish County
Washington
Burial:
Ledbetter Cemetery
Pottersville
Howell County, Missouri

An early FWB Minister serving in the General Free Will Baptist Assn.
His parents were Van B. and Eliza Crawford Crawshaw Davis. He wed Elizabeth Crawshaw on 4 Feb 1872 in Briar Creek, Ripley Co, MO.

And their children were Grace Davis Burlison (1838 - 1890), Samuel W Davis (1839 - 1885), Eliphaz Davis (1845 - 1925), Van Crawshaw Davis (1847 - 1928), Daniel L. Davis (1849 - 1917), and Joshua Dial Crawshaw Davis (1854 - 1934).

Samuel W Davis
Birth:
Aug. 13, 1839
Death:
Mar. 4, 1885
Burial:
Shirley Cemetery
Briar
Ripley County, Missouri

An Early FWB minister serving in the General Free Will Baptist Assn. which was an association of General Baptists and Free Will Baptists in Missouri and Arkansas.He was a brother to Eliphaz Davis who was also a preacher in this movement.

Winford C. Davis
Birth:
Dec. 8, 1904
Death:
May 5, 1997
Burial:
Bethel Cemetery, Monett, Barry County, Missouri

Davis lived to be 93 years old and had been a Free Will Baptist preacher for more than 70 years in which time he was a very active leader in the denomination.
He was converted at age 12 at a brush arbor revival. He preached his first sermon in the Macedonia Free Will Baptist Church in 1926 and was a member of that church at the time of his death. He pastored churches for 60 years including 40 years at the Macedonia church in various tenures. He served for 19 years as Secretary-Treasurer of the Missouri State Association. He was a member of the National Board Of Education that led the denomination to establish the Free Will Baptist Bible College. He was Secretary-Treasurer of the Foreign Missions Board and made three trips to Cuba: in 1942; in 1944; and in 1946. He helped to establish Missouri's magazine, *THE GEM*, and served 3 1/2 years as its editor and manager from a printing office in Monett. He kept a comprehensive record of his ministry which recorded he had preached 9,100 sermons, won 2,170 souls to the Lord, and received 1,385 members into the church. He traveled 330,772 miles, not counting three trips to Cuba and three trips to Israel. He conducted 159 revivals, officiated at 173 weddings, and conducted 621 funerals. He organized 13 churches, baptized 40, and ordained 30 deacons. He attended the organizational meeting of the National Association in 1935 and was a member of the Treaties Committee. He was truly a pioneer within the Free Will Baptist denomination.

The Burial Locations of Free Will Baptist Ministers

Christian Benjamin Dees

Birth:
Jun. 28, 1902
Fredericktown,
Madison County, Missouri
Death:
May 19, 1973
St. Louis City, Missouri
Burial:
Woodlawn Cemetery,
Leadington,
St. Francois County,
Missouri

An active pastor and leader in Missouri. He was editor of the Free Will Baptist Gem, serving in that position for a number of years. He was a member of the St. Francios Association in South East Missouri.

Alice M Dickey

Birth:
1907
Death:
2001
Burial:
White Chapel Memorial Gardens, Springfield, Greene County, Missouri

She was a longtime minister and known for founding the First Free Will Baptist Church of Kansas City, Missouri.

Claude A. Dotson

Birth:
Aug. 23, 1891
Death:
Apr. 29, 1954
Burial:

Huddleston Cemetery,
Alton,
Oregon County, Missouri

An early Free Will Baptist pastor in south central Missouri.

William Duponit Dowell

Birth:
Oct. 5, 1880
Philadelphia
Philadelphia County,
Pennsylvania
Death:
Feb. 25, 1950
Camden County
Missouri
Burial:
Hopewell Cemetery
Tunas
Dallas County, Missouri

Early FWB preacher in the General Free Will Baptist Assn.

589

William Driver, Sr
Birth:
1859
Jefferson City, Missouri
Death:
1934
Burial:
Iberia Cemetery, Iberia
Miller County, Missouri

Was born in in 1859, the son of a slave woman named Amanda/Mandy Dixon. At an early age he was adopted by a black family named Driver and carried that name the rest of his life. William Driver, Sr. moved to Laclede Co., MO in the early 1880's and located near the small town of Eldridge. He became a preacher in the Free Will Baptist Church and traveled around central Missouri as an evangelist. About 1916 he moved his wife and children to Miller County and located southwest of Iberia near the Pleasant Hill community and the old Rankin Wright Cemetery. Driver was a well-known minister in the area as he traveled around preaching the Holy Word and playing loudly on his large drum. When he died in 1934, his funeral was held at the Iberia Nazarene Church, conducted by Rev. Otto Shearrer. He was buried at the Iberia Cemetery (per his obituary) but no stone marks his grave today.

Eunice S. *Jenkerson* Edwards
Birth:
Jan. 5, 1912
Death:
Jul. 30, 1997
St. Francois County, Missouri
Burial:
Parkview Cemetery,
Farmington,
St. Francois County, Missouri

She served as pastor at the Leadington Freewill Baptist Church in Missouri and then she served the National Free Will Baptist Women's Auxiliary for seven years as Director. A great leader and servant of God.

Rev William B. Fadely
Birth:
Dec. 8, 1865
Death:
Aug. 1, 1946
Burial:
Hopewell Cemetery
DeKalb County
Missouri

Rev. William B. Fadely, was an ordained Free Will Baptist minister.
He attended the 1924 session of the Cooperative General Association of FWB, in Tecumseh, OK, and listed his home as 'Weatherby, MO'. [DeKalb Co].

Thomas Campbell Ferguson
Birth: Jan. 10, 1870
Ontario, Canada
Death: Mar. 28, 1957
Gallatin
Daviess County
Missouri
Burial:
Alta Vista Cemetery
Alta Vista
Daviess County
Missouri

Thomas Campbell Ferguson, was the son of William Ferguson, and Jessie (McFarland) Ferguson. He departed this life at the Sullivan Rest Home in Gallatin, MO, March 28, 1957, at the age of 87 years, 2mos, and 17 days.

His early life was spent between farmhand, sailor, miner and railroading.

At the age of 26 years he was converted and took an active part in Christian work, from that time he attended the Moody Bible school in Chicago. From there he went to Wisconsin, and while there he united with the Freewill Baptist Church in which he was ordained a minister in the year, 1900, at Lincoln, Neb., and spent the most of his life in evangelical and pastoral work. He baptized more than 2000 people and aided in many ordinations.

He was a friend and associate of Rev. John H. Wolfe, Neb., and he joined with Wolfe in leading in the formation of the Cooperative General Association, and before that, the Southwestern Free Will Baptist Convention (of Texas, Oklahoma, and Missouri). Rev.

Ferguson, as a delegate from Texas at the time, joined with Wolfe in opposing the merger of the Randall movement Freewill Baptists with the Northern Baptists in 1910. Rev. Ferguson was on the original Board of Trustees of Tecumseh College, Oklahoma, when it was founded by the Cooperative General Association in 1917, and Rev. John H. Wolfe was elected president.

Rev. Ferguson also helped to organize the Missouri State Association of Free Will Baptists, and was elected moderator of it for several years, as well as serving as State Evangelist of Missouri FWB for some time.

He held revival meetings in several states and in parts of Canada. The most of his work was done in Missouri, Kansas, Texas and Nebraska.

He was united in marriage to Miss Myrtle Henderson in 1900. To this union three children were born. He was later united in marriage April 25, 1932, to Miss Odessa Reid. Funeral services were conducted by Eld. John D. McKown, of Daviess Co., March 30, at the Alta Vista church after which he was laid to rest in the cemetery nearby. [Alta Vista Cemetery].

Charley David Findley
Birth:
Jul. 25, 1891
Death:
Sep. 17, 1972
Burial:
Pleasant Hill Cemetery
Hartville
Wright County

Rev William Henry Ford, Sr
Birth:
Nov. 18, 1838
Warren County
Tennessee
Death:
Jun. 27, 1905
Pea Ridge
Benton County, Arkansas
Burial:
Jane Cemetery
McDonald County, Missouri
Brothers who were FWB ministers in Arkansas and Texas. George Harvey Ford (1827 -

1896).
Richard E. Ford (1835 - 1922).
William Henry Ford (1838 - 1905).
James Alexander Ford (1842 - 1912). Josephus Wesley Ford (1848 - 1898). Markley Stanford Ford (1852 - 1917).

Warren Franklin
Birth:
Mar. 12, 1879
Osseo, Wisconsin
Death:
May 25, 1957
Burial:
Lone Rock Cemetery,
Plad,
Dallas County, Missouri

He was an early Free Will Baptist minister.

Jerry William Fields
Birth:
May 19, 1934
Springfield

Greene County, Missouri
Death:
Oct. 1, 2014
Greene County, Missouri
Burial:
Robberson Prairie Cemetery
Ebenezer
Greene County, Missouri

Jerry William Fields, departed this life surrounded by loved at Mercy Hospital in Springfield, Mo. He was 80 years and 4 months old.

Jerry was born to Ernest E. and Bernice (Tidwell) Fields at their home in Springfield. Jerry married Dorlene Deeds on May 10, 1951 in Harrison, Ark. and to this union four children were born.

While at a rodeo Jerry met Dorlene, the love of his life, beside an old watering pump. Years later the eyes of his understanding were opened in a little hotel room as he read a Gideon Bible. Jerry's love of God, family and his commitment to every good work laid a foundation for his children and succeeding generations. Jerry was described by his family as a servant, teacher, a man of great love, a pastor and father devoted to the truth and speaking the truth in love. In his words, "I am too blessed to be depressed".

He created a lifetime of memories that will be treasured in the hearts and minds of his family and those he pastored for over fifty years.

Rev Thomas A Gaines
Birth:
May 15, 1846
Washington
Wilkes County,
Georgia
Death: 1907
Missouri
Burial:
Hickory Creek
Jameson
Daviess County,
Missouri

Rev Perry Thomas Gardenhire
Birth:
Feb. 10, 1908
Death:
Oct. 6, 1997
Burial:
Idumea Cemetery
Laquey
Pulaski County
Missouri

A Free Will Baptist minister who pastored churches in Calif. before he retired. His name appears from Exeter, CA, in the 1967 Southern Association No. 1. Remembered here.

Levi Jackson Gearing
Birth:
Apr. 17, 1881
Missouri
Death:
Oct. 30, 1945
Burial:
Coldwater Cemetery

Manes
Wright County
Missouri

Spouse: Sophia Elizabeth Long Gearing (1882 - 1939)

Rev Ken Goff
Birth:
Oct. 16, 1939
Savonburg
Allen County, Kansas
Death: Nov. 15, 2014
Bonne Terre
St. Francois County, Missouri
Burial:
Three Rivers Baptist Church
Cemetery
Farmington
St. Francois County, Missouri

He retired in 2011 from being and active minister for 41 years, and also being the superintendent at the Free Will Baptist Youth Camp in Niangua, Missouri, for 16 years. He was a member of the Parkview Free Will Baptist Church in Desloge,

Missouri. The Rev.'s Gary Parker, Lindell Richardson and Ron DeGonia Officiated.

Ross H. Green
Birth:
May 7, 1929
Death:
Apr. 28, 1989
Burial:
Parrack Grove Cemetery,
Macks Creek,
Camden County, Missouri
He was a veteran and Cpl in the US Air Force. He was a minister & pastor in the Free Will Baptist denomination.

Virgil R. Greenway
Birth:
Mar. 4, 1906
Missouri
Death:
Mar. 27, 1993
Joplin,
Jasper County, Missouri
Burial:
Leann Cemetery,
Leann, Barry County, Missouri,
Plot: Row 30, Plot 419

Early Free Will Baptist preacher in the state of Missouri serving mostly in the region around Monett and southeast Missouri.

Rev J. S. Handyside
Birth:
Aug. 13, 1853
Death:
Mar. 2, 1920
Burial:
McBride Cemetery
Competition
Laclede County
Missouri

Rev. John S. Handyside, was ordained to Freewill Baptist ministry in Missouri, in 1885, having served with the Methodists before.

Archibald Millard Halford
Birth:
Feb. 29, 1888
Dora
Ozark County
Missouri
Death:
Dec. 10, 1961
Norwood
Wright County
Missouri
Burial:
Brushy Knob Cemetery
Vera Cruz
Douglas County
Missouri

SPRINGFIELD DAILY NEWS
Springfield, Greene Co., MO
Wednesday, 13 December 1961

The Rev. Archie M. Halford, 73, of Norwood, died in his home.

He was a minister of the Freewill Baptist Church and had lived in Norwood seven years. He was a native of Douglas County.

Survivors are a brother Thomas C. Halford, Norwood; a stepson

Kenneth Pennington, and a stepdaughter Mrs. Hollace Oxley, Mountain Grove; four step-grandchildren and three step-great-grandchildren. Spouse:

Ethel Margaret Anderson Halford (1895 - 1961)*

Benjamin F Henderson
Birth:
1874
Death:
1950
Burial:
Bethel Cemetery, Monett,
Barry County, Missouri

Early Free Will Baptist preacher in southwestern Missouri.

George Washington Henderson
Birth:
Feb. 17, 1840
Death:
Nov. 10, 1919
Burial:
Shiloh Cemetery
Shook
Wayne County
Missouri

Minister of the Free Will Baptist church, as was his son, James W.M.Henderson.

Rev James Woodrow Monroe Henderson
Birth:
Dec. 30, 1878
Bonne Terre
St. Francois County, Missouri
Death:
Dec. 2, 1944
St. Louis County, Missouri
Burial:
Big River Cemetery
Irondale
Washington County, Missouri

Rev. James W. M. Henderson, was converted in 1919 at the Free Will Baptist Church at Cherryville, St. Francois Co, and was a member of Fredericktown

FWB church in Madison Co. It was said that he learned how to read and write by studying the Bible. He was also a pastor of a Mission on South Broadway in St. Louis. He and his wife were injured, he seriously, enroute to church. His wife, Martha/Mattie, suffered a broken wrist, but he died shortly after the accident. Martha lived to age 95 yrs. She is bur. next to her husband in this cemetery."
--from "Henderson History of Southeast Missouri," by E.M. Carroll.

Rev G. W. Hensley
Birth:
1840
Death:
1932
Burial:
Fletchall Cemetery
Grant City, Worth County,
Missouri

He represented the Northwest

Missouri Yearly Meeting at the Co-operative General Assn of Freewill Baptists in Plattsburg, Missouri December 1916.

William C Hill
Birth:
Jul. 22, 1920
Death:
Jul. 8, 1986
Burial:
Polk Memorial Cemetery
Ellington
Reynolds County, Missouri:
He served as pastor of the Flat Woods Free Will Baptist Church in St. Francois QM.

Elmer Hodges
Birth:
May 7, 1883
Alton,
Oregon County, Missouri
Death:
Sep. 19, 1960
Alton,
Oregon County, Missouri
Burial:
Smyrna Cemetery, Alton,
Oregon County, Missouri

He was a pastor and minister in southcentral Missouri serving in the early days of the denomination in that region.

Rev James T. Holcomb
Birth:
Sep. 23, 1849
Death:
Jun. 21, 1936
Webster County, Missouri
Burial:
Saint Luke Methodist Church
Cemetery
Marshfield, Webster County
Missouri

James W Housley
Birth:
1855
Death
: 1937
Burial:
Oak Grove Cemetery
Norwood
Wright County
Missouri

Spouse:
Rebecca Butcher Housley
(1855 - 1912)

King David Hudgens
Birth:
Sep. 16, 1847
Phipps County, Missouri

Death:
Jul. 16, 1920
Burial:
Dunkard Cemetery
Saint Robert
Pulaski County, Missouri

He entered the ministry among the Presbyterians in 1875 and a few years later became a Free Will Baptist with the Big Creek Quarterly Meeting, Prosperity Assn, Missouri ministering to the Liberal church.

Rev George Henry Huffman
Birth:
Feb. 26, 1913
Buckhorn
Madison County
Missouri
Death:
Sep. 24, 2001
Farmington
St. Francois County
Missouri
Burial:
Huffman-McKelvey Cemetery
Buckhorn
Madison County
Missouri

Parents: William Pink Huffman (1883 - 1966) - Cora E Stroup Huffman (1884 - 1968)
Spouse: Ruby Alma Gipson Huffman (1912 - 2005)

Truman Huffman
Birth:
Feb. 2, 1922
Death:
Oct. 26, 2006
Fredericktown
Madison County
Missouri
Burial:
Twin Oak Cemetery
Madison County
Missouri

Spouse: Amy Lee Huffman (1923 - 2006) Children: Judy Huffman Latham (1957 - 2009)

Rev Elihu H. Hunt
Birth:
1814
Burial:
Boyd Cemetery
Holt County
Missouri
Death: 1890
Burial:
Boyd Cemetery
Holt County
Missouri

His name and title(s) are shown in old records where he was a great help to other prominent ministers as they organized churches--i.e. Rev's John and Jeremiah Wood, O.S. Harding, W. H. Copas, and probably others. Note: Rev. E.H. Hunt was a M.D.

E. Marie Hyatt
Birth:
1920
Death:
April 1, 2002
Burial:
Warrensburg Memorial Gardens Cemetery,
Warrensburg,
Johnson County, Missouri,
Plot: Section 2
Lot 147 Space 1

Rev. E. Marie Hyatt, and Myron E. Hyatt were married at the Free Will Baptist Church, Monett. She served 40 years in church ministry, with the first 12 years with the Free Will Baptist Church. She was a member of Professional Women, Chaplain of AARP and the Western Missouri Medical Center

Lloyd T. Jeffrey's
Birth:
Apr. 23, 1917
Death:
Mar. 4, 1972
Burial:
Monett IOOF Cemetery,
Monett,
Lawrence County, Missouri

He was a retired Army officer and pastored in the Indian River Association of Free Will Baptist in Southwest Missouri. His wife was the Rev. Opal Jeffrey's and they both pastored Merl's Chapel Free Will Baptist Church near Cassville.

Opal Ethel McClerren Jeffrey's
Birth:
Jul. 8, 1921
Death:
Oct. 2, 2000
Burial:
Monett IOOF Cemetery,
Monett,
Lawrence County, Missouri

She was a well-known Free Will Baptist minister and pastor in southwest Missouri serving for many years the Merl's Chapel Free Will Baptist Church near Cassville. She was married to the Rev. Lloyd Jeffrey's a retired Army officer. A minister's reward is out of this world!

Rev Harry S Johns
Birth:
Jul. 30, 1901
Missouri
Death:
Jul. 1, 1976
Springfield
Greene County
Missouri
Burial:
Ragsdale-Harmony Baptist
Cemetery
Seymour
Webster County
Missouri

Harry is the son of Alexander and Louvada Johns.
He married Beulah Francis Miller on December 20,1930 in Webster County, Missouri.
Four known children were born to this union:
Arthur Doyle Johns
Lawrence David Johns
Marvin G. Johns
Ralph Johns

Rev Bill Jones
Birth:
Sep. 30, 1929
Grove spring
Wright County
Missouri
Death
:   Mar. 12, 2016
Lebanon
Laclede County
Missouri
Burial:
McBride Cemetery
Competition
Laclede County
Missouri

Brother Jones was born to George Ralph and Opal Estelle Jones. On February 10, 1950, he married Wilma McClanahan and they were married for 66 years at the time of his passing.

He served in the United States Army and pastored the Pleasant view Free Will Baptist Church, Little Vine Free Will Baptist church, Cope, Happy Hill and Liberty Free Will Baptist churches. He was also employed with Ben Stephen construction, ran heavy equipment and loved farming and raising cattle. His services were officiated by Dan Talbot, Craig Perry and R. E. Helsley.

Arthur A. Kicenski
Birth:
Dec. 21, 1896
Death:
Dec. 29, 1970
Burial:
Clintonville Cemetery,
El Dorado Springs,
Cedar County, Missouri

He was active Free Will Baptist minister serving in the Missouri & Kansas region.

John Gilbert Koch
Birth:
Nov. 25, 1869
Death:
Sep. 27, 1952
Burial:
White Rock Cemetery
Texas County
Missouri

Early minister in Union Assn.
Parents:
Julius Koch (1833 - 1918)

Dialtha Pryor Koch (1840 - 1902)
Spouse:
Matilda Lou Daily Koch (1882 - 1953)*

Levi The

odore Koch
Birth:
Mar. 12, 1879
Death:
Aug. 6, 1947
Burial:
White Rock Cemetery
Texas County
Missouri

SFC 301 Wagon Co QMC WWI
Family links: Parents:
Julius Koch (1833 - 1918)
Dialtha Pryor Koch (1840 - 1902)
Siblings:
John Gilbert Koch (1869 - 1952)
Rhoda Koch (1871 - 1943)
Dora Elizabeth Koch (1873 - 1943)
Christian Julius Koch (1877 - 1961)
Levi Throdore Koch (1879 - 1947)

Absalom Sussdorf Lick
Birth:
Jul. 31, 1853

Illinois
Death:
Jul. 17, 1942
Springfield,
Greene County, Missouri
Burial:
Dixon Cemetery, Dixon,
Pulaski County, Missouri

He served in central Missouri.

Rev Julius Arthur LeRoux
Birth:
Sep. 9, 1841
Paris, France
Death:
Mar. 25, 1931
Doniphan
Ripley County
Missouri
Burial:
Oak Grove Cemetery
Ripley County, Missouri

George Million in his history of this area said "No man can jump higher, turn around quicker, squall louder, of get happier than Elder Leroux.

Before joining the General Free Will Baptists, he had been a preacher in the Missionary Baptists. He was ordained in 1884. He was of French extraction, a good man, tireless worker and few men did more for the advancement of the cause than he. He was a great revivalist. He went with the General Baptists later. He was married to Matilda Margaret Pennington LeRoux (1849 - 1911) and Margaret Louise Barnes LeRoux (1855 - 1948).

Inscription:
CPL CO D 188 OHIO INF CIVIL WAR

Rev Sylvester Bowman Lewis
Birth:
Mar. 22, 1846
Death:
May 23, 1921
Burial:
Muddy Cemetery
Pattonsburg, Daviess County
Missouri

Rev. S. B. Lewis, was an ordained Free Will Baptist minister/pastor in Missouri. He was in the early Missouri state work. In 1917, he was in attendance at the organization of the Cooperative General Association of churches and districts, (that did not go into the 1911 merger of the northern Free Will Baptists), held at the Philadelphia Church, Davies Co. MO., evidenced by his name appearing in the roster of ordained ministers present. He stated his home was Pattonsburg, MO. He was in Missouri State ministers list of Freewill Baptist in 1896.

Rev Claude V Lincoln
Birth:
Nov. 1, 1887
Mine La Motte
Madison County,
Missouri
Death:
Mar. 12, 1942
Esther
St. Francois County, Missouri
Burial:
Parkview Cemetery
Farmington
St. Francois County,
Missouri

Claude Lincoln passed away at his home in Esther after an illness of nearly two years with tuberculosis. His name is in the Hist. of Flat River FWB Church as then (1938) pastor in St. Louis church. Funeral services were held by Rev. James Miller of North Missouri, a former pastor of the church, assisted by Rev. Cecil Campbell, evangelist who is conducting revival services at the church. Mr. Lincoln had worked for the St. Joseph Lead Co. for the past 23 years.

He was converted when a young man and united with the Free Will Baptist Church at Mine La Motte, but had been a member of the Flat River Church for the past 21 years.

Rev John David Long
Birth:
Feb. 3, 1899
Death:
Jul. 25, 1976
Saint Louis
St. Louis City
Missouri
Burial:
Marcus Memorial Cemetery
Fredericktown
Madison County

Missouri pastor who spent most of his life in southeast Missouri, was pastor of the Parkview FWB church after Lizzie McAdams held a meeting in the former Second Missionary Baptist Church of Desloge changing their affiliation to Free Will Baptists. He was a leading minister in the St. François conference.

Rev Russell M Lowe
Birth
21 Nov 1942
Death
9 Sep 2017
McAlester, Pittsburg County, Oklahoma,

Burial
Saint Marys Cemetery
Saint Mary, Ste.
Genevieve County, Missouri,

Born to Gladys Ford Lowe and James Vincent Lowe. Russell lived his life in Clyde, North Carolina until he graduated from high school in 1961. He enlisted immediately in the U.S. Air Force where he served our country until 1965. He met Gracie Jane Hannah and on June 2, 1966 they were married and started their life together. They moved to Michigan that fall and that is where he came in contact with the gospel. His mother-in-law, Ruby and father-in-law, Paul, never failed to invite them to church and on Christmas of 1972, where Russell met the Lord and gave his heart to Him. Gracie rededicated her life that same day. This is where Russell became a soldier of the cross because, from the very first day he told everyone what the Lord did for him. When he went back into the car plant, where he worked they knew something had happened to him. He drove a Cushman truck to deliver parts and they nicknamed him the Holy Ghost express. It didn't upset him, it just made him smile. He surrendered to preach in October of 1973 and was ordained in November 1975 in Wayne, Michigan. He has served as Pastor in Church's in Michigan, West Virginia, Idaho (National Home Missionary), and last 29 years in Oklahoma. He attended Nashville Free Will

Baptist Bible College, Degree Graduate of Theology and Bachelor of Religious Education from Trinity College in Newburgh, Indiana in 1991, Masters of Theology from Andersonville Baptist Seminary in Camelia, Georgia in 1996, and Doctor of Theology with honors, Andersonville Baptist Seminary in 2010. He always said, "I just want to be the best that I can be for the Lord who gave His all for me!". He loved his Lord, his wife, his family, God's people and the lost. He was preceded in death by his mother, Gladys Lowe, father, Vincent Lowe, a brother, John David Lowe and a sister, Judith Ann Lowe. His Going Home Celebration was held at the First Free Will Baptist Church on Carl Albert Parkway in McAlester, Oklahoma.

Cora Ann Hamilton Mann
Birth:
Jun. 8, 1875
Schuyler County, Missouri
Death
Sep. 9, 1934
Schuyler County, Missouri
Burial:
Jimtown Cemetery
Queen City
Schuyler County, Missouri

She was a minister who represented the Northwest Missouri Yearly Meeting at the Co-operative General Association of Freewill Baptists in Plattsburg, Missouri December 1916. She was the daughter of John L. Hamilton and Addie Grimes. She was the wife of Rev. Charles Earl Mann (1875 - 1943).

Charles Earl Mann
Birth:
Jul. 8, 1875
Glenwood,
Schuyler County, Missouri
Death:
Mar. 20, 1943
Jackson County, Missouri
Burial:
Jimtown Cemetery,
Queen City
Schuyler County, Missouri
He was an early minister and pastor in central Missouri. He was the Clerk of the Missouri State Association and along with his wife represented the Northwest Missouri Yearly Meeting at the Co-operative General Association of Freewill Baptists in Plattsburg, Missouri December 1916. Son of Nathan Mann and Loreda Charlotte. Married (1st) on 4 October 1899 in Schuyler County, Missouri to Cora Ann Hamilton, and (2nd) on 18 December 1937 in Marshfield, Webster County, Missouri to Emaline Hightower (widow of Rev. Marion Benjamin Clift).

Thomas J. Mann
Birth:
1880
Death:
1943
Burial:
Pendleton Cemetery
Doe Run
St. Francois County, Missouri

He was pastor of the church in Flat River in 1918.

Samuel H Marcum
Birth:
Aug. 14, 1891
Death:
Mar. 19, 1975
Burial:
Evergreen Cemetery,
Cameron,
Clinton County, Missouri

An early Minister and active leader in the state of Missouri.
Parents:
William M Marcum (1860 - 1900)
Annalocka Jane Wisdom Marcum (1861 - 1950)
Spouse:
Daisy D Marcum Marcum (1900 - 1996)*

Rev Luke M. Marler, Jr
Birth:
Jun. 15, 1872
Douglas County
Missouri
Death:
Mar. 2, 1958
Missouri
Burial:
Fannon Cemetery
Ava
Douglas County
Missouri

Rev Elias Matney
Birth:
Apr. 17, 1871
Death:
Oct. 23, 1950
Burial:
Murray Cemetery
Squires
Douglas County, Missouri

Family links: Parents:
Uriah Matney (1834 - 1899)
Catherine Cobb Matney
(1837 - 1886)
Spouse:
Jane Manning Ecton Matney
(1856 - 1938)
Children:
John Matney (1891 - 1946)
Henry Everett Matney
(1892 - 1965)
Ruth J. Matney Hartley
(1899 - 1971)

Rev James Franklin McCall
Birth:
Nov. 18, 1857

Illinois
Death:
Jan. 22, 1933
Norwood
Wright County
Missouri
Burial:
Denlow Cemetery
Denlow
Douglas County, Missouri
Rev. J. F. McCall, 76 years old, passed quietly to his eternal rest at his home in Norwood early Sunday morning. Mrs. McCall had prepared breakfast and when she went to call her husband found him dead.

Short services were conducted at the home here by Rev. G. Chadwell Tuesday morning, after which the body was taken to Denlow for interment, Rev. Halford preaching the funeral sermon there. Rev. McCall has been in failing health for some time. He had spent many years in the ministry of the Freewill Baptist church, being a successful evangelist as well as a faithful pastor of many churches.

Rev W. L. McClanahan

Birth:
Jan. 30, 1884
Death:
May 5, 1974
Burial:
Eureka Cemetery
Rader
Webster County
Missouri

Evans Boyd McClintock
Birth:
Apr. 27, 1857
Milledgeville
McNairy County,Tennessee
Death:
Nov. 2, 1926
Springfield
Greene County, Missouri
Burial:
Greenlawn Memorial Gardens
Springfield
Greene County, Missouri
Spouse - Mattie T Painer
Father - Alexander H McClintock
(born TN) Mother - Cynthia
Evans (born TN)
Occupation - Retired minister
Info from MO death cert

Billy Gene McClintock
Birth:
Sep. 8, 1932
Doniphan, Missouri
Death:
Sep. 26, 2012
Poplar Bluff Regional Medical

Center
Poplar Bluff, Missouri
Burial:
Johnston Chapel
Ripley County
Missouri

Mr. McClintock, son of Raymond and Fay Ilene (Phillips) McClintock. He had been an auto mechanic and was minister and founder of Lingo Freewill Baptist Church. A minister of the gospel; served in New Mexico in the 1970's. Mr. McClintock enjoyed woodworking and had a special interest in the historical enactment of Ripley County Civil War Days and Timberfest.
On August 1, 1953, he was married to Joyce Marilyn Langlois at Detroit, Michigan. She preceded him in death on December 4, 2003.

John D McKown
Birth:
Apr. 29, 1892
Daviess County, Missouri
Death:
Mar., 1982
Jamesport,
Daviess County, Missouri
Burial:
Clear Creek Cemetery,
Lock Springs,
Daviess County, Missouri

His ministry was basically confined to Daviess County Missouri. Note: his life and ministry extended 90 years.

Wm. F. Millard
Birth:
Aug. 18, 1874
Death:
Aug. 15, 1958
Burial:
Lebanon City Cemetery,
Lebanon
Laclede County, Missouri,
Plot: 18-5 Blk 14

An early Free Will Baptist minister in Laclede County Missouri.

Rev William Henry McKown
Birth:
Aug. 2, 1846
Preble County, Ohio
Death:
1926
Daviess County, Missouri
Burial:
Clear Creek Cemetery
Lock Springs
Daviess County, Missouri

George Miller
Birth:
Sep. 3, 1834
Death:
Jan. 11, 1900
Burial:
Elmwood Cemetery,
Kansas City,
Jackson County, Missouri

One of the early Free Will Baptist ministers in western Missouri.

James F. Miller
Birth:
Sep. 3, 1894
Bollinger County,
Missouri
Death:
May 14, 1965
Farmington,
St. Francois County, Missouri
Burial:
Union Light Cemetery, Loyd,
Bollinger County, Missouri

During his ministry he pastored in four different states: Missouri, Texas, North Carolina and Tennessee. He was elected the Missouri State Moderator for Free Will Baptists in 1933 where he served eleven years.

He was elected as Moderator of the National Association of Free Will Baptists in 1938, a position he held for seven consecutive years. He served as a member of the Board of Trustees to the Free Will Baptist Bible College for sixteen years. The college yearbook was dedicated to him in 1963. He received a life time honorary membership in the college Alumni Association in April, 1965. He became a representative of the college in his later years and traveled in 16 states in the interest of the school. Funeral service were held at the Farmington Free Will Baptist Church by the Rev. Charles Thigpen, Dean of the college in Nashville, Tennessee. He was assisted by the Rev Everett Hellard, pastor of the church.

Brantly Sigle Moody
Birth:
May 28, 1884
Norwood
Wright County,Missouri
Death:
Jun. 7, 1963
Norwood
Wright County
Missouri
Burial:
Thomas Cemetery
Norwood
Wright County,Missouri
Plot: S-35 #5431
He is the son of Jonathan and Mary Jane (Barnett) Moody. On August 31, 1905 he was united in marriage to Elizabeth Zoella "Lizzie" Caudle. To this union four known children were born.
Family links: Parents:
Jonathan Moody (1858 - 1948)
  Mary Jane Barnett Moody (1866 - 1931)
  Spouse: Elizabeth Zoella Caudle Moody (1885 - 1972)*

Rev John W Moore
Birth:
1871
Death:
May 24, 1958
Burial:
Odd Fellows Cemetery
Neosho
Newton County
Missouri
Spouse: Anna Pendleton Callahan Moore (1876 - 1955)
Inscription: 87yrs

Glenn Edwin Murray
Birth:
Mar. 10, 1935
Doniphan
Ripley County
Missouri
Death:
Mar. 26, 2016
Hartville
Wright County
Missouri
Burial:
Howell Memorial Park Cemetery
Pomona
Howell County
Missouri

He was born to Jess Earl Murray and Clara Marie Crook Murray. He graduated from Doniphan High School with the Class of 1953. Reverend Murray was a veteran, having served with the United States National Guard. On September 24, 1955, he was married at West Plains, Missouri, to Rachel Victoria Adkisson. He worked at sawmills and restored antique furniture; having worked at Joplin Brothers Handle Factory and Smith Gas Company. While working at Cloud Oak Flooring, he answered the call to preach; he ministered for the next fifty-five years. On December 11, 1960 he preached his first sermon at the First Freewill Baptist Church, West Plains and where he was later ordained to preach on April 2, 1962 when his son, Jon, was ten days old. Susie Murray Stillwell was the first convert, at the Oak Grove Church of God, Doniphan, Missouri on January 1, 1961. He preached 9,700 sermons, saved 2,370 souls, officiated 1,900 funerals, 200 weddings, 700 baptisms and preached at over 700 revivals. Reverend Murray served at Pleasant Home Freewill Baptist Church, Alton Freewill Baptist Church, Hannon Freewill Baptist Church, Cabool Freewill Baptist Church, Oak Grove Church of God, First Freewill Baptist Church, Batesville, Arkansas, United Freewill Baptist Church, West Plains, State Line, Victory (Myrtle), Dry Creek and Hartville. He enjoyed turkey hunting, taking his 100th in the spring of 2015.

Death is a debt we all must pay.

Jesse Niswonger
Birth:
Apr. 6, 1848,
Millersville
Cape Girardeau County
Missouri
Death: Jul. 5, 1935
Cape Girardeau
Cape Girardeau County
Missouri
Burial:
Niswonger Cemetery
(Near Fruitland)
Cape Girardeau County
Missouri

Son of Joseph NISWONGER and Susana HAHS. Early FWB minister n the General Free Will Baptist Conference.

John H Noble
Birth:
Jun. 24, 1832
McMinn County, Tennessee
Death:
Jul. 13, 1903
Burial:
Ashland Cemetery
Saint Joseph
Buchanan County, Missouri

In 1861 he married Betty Tuck. His conversion took place in 1866 and ordination in 1872. He united with the Free Baptists in 1876 and has conducted several revivals and organized four churches. Besides pastorates in Tennessee he also pastored in Missouri where he died.

Benjamin Melton Owens
Birth:
Feb. 28, 1886
Norwood
Wright County
Missouri
Death:
Oct. 26, 1969
Mountain Grove
Wright County
Missouri
Burial:
Hopewell Cemetery
Texas County
Missouri

Family links: Parents: Isaac Owens (1855 - 1939) -   Sarah Catherine Bradshaw Owens (1852 - 1937)
    Spouses:
Arizona Cartwright Owens (1889 - 1960)
    Parlee Jane Reece Souder (1877 - 1970)*
    Children:
    Florence Owens Ratteree (1910 - 1984)*
Joseph Morris Owens (1918 - 1996)*
Fern Ratterree (1920 - 1991)*
Elijah M Owens (1928 - 1999)

James Coy Powell
Birth:
Dec. 25, 1923
Dunklin County, Missouri
Death:
Jan. 4, 1994
Flint
Genesee County, Michigan
Burial:
Mount Gilead Cemetery
Clarkton
Dunklin County, Missouri

His parents were Colombus Powell, and Luella Powell. He was one of several children. He married Sally Jane McFarland 8 Feb. 1943, in St. Louis, MO. A Free Will Baptist minister. He was pastor of the Friendship FWB in Flint, Michigan for many years.

John Postlewaite
Birth:
Apr. 5, 1926
Graff, Missouri.
Death:
Oct. 21, 2012
Sentera Leigh Hospital
Norfolk, Virginia
Burial:
Hillcrest Cemetery
Mountain Grove, Wright County, Missouri

He was the 8th son of the late John Jefferson and Lucy Jane (Crewse) Postlewaite. He was 86 years, 6 months, and 16 days of age at his death.John was saved at the age of 12 at the No. 1 Free Will Baptist Church near Huggins, Missouri, when his teacher dismissed school for the students to attend an 11:00 revival service. He answered the call to preach at the age of 19. After attending Free Will Baptist Bible College (now Welch College) in Nashville, Tennessee, he was ordained as a minister of the gospel in 1947. He married Leah Mae Scott on September 21, 1948 at the home of Rev. Homer B. Smith near Mountain Grove. To this union were born 4 children. John's first pastorate was at Faith and Hope Free Will Baptist Church near Willow Springs, Missouri. There John and Leah lived in a small log cabin, which was the church parsonage. Throughout the next 53 years, he pastored churches in Oklahoma, Arkansas, Illinois, and Missouri. He planted 7 churches in Washington and Oregon under the auspices of Free Will Baptist Home Missions. He was a well-known evangelist, soul winner, supporter of missions, and mentor to many young people. After moving back to Mountain Grove in his retirement years, he served as Senior Citizens' Pastor at First Free Will Baptist for almost 8 years. He had a lovely tenor voice and often sang in church and at home. He was also a lover of the Scripture and committed many passages to memory. Even in his last days, he spent several hours a day reading the Bible and could still quote many passages. He and his wife, Leah, shared 64 years. His four children were: Joe and Pauline Postlewaite of Florence, South Carolina; Sue and Earl Larson of Brentwood, Tennessee; Sam and Diana Postlewaite of Virginia Beach, Virginia; and Ruth and Donnie McDonald of Tokyo, Japan. Only eternity will reveal how many spiritual children were saved because of his faithful witness.

John Learner Ratteree
Birth:
Sep. 11, 1885
Death:
Apr. 8, 1962
Burial:
Hopewell Cemetery
Texas County
Missouri

Early minister in Union Assn. John was the son of David and Manerva Zirschky Ratterree. He married Florence Owens on February 24, 1929. This union 7 children were born. He was ordained as a minister in 1926. He was of the Free Will Baptist faith.

Family links:
Parents:David Lewis Gibson Ratterree (1849 - 1930)
Manerva Zirschky Ratterree (1852 - 1928)
Spouse: Florence Owens Ratteree (1910 - 1984)
Children:
David Benjamin Ratterree (1929 - 1991)
Donald Caleb Ratterree (1931 - 2014)
Delores Esther Ratterree Turner (1939 - 2012)
Siblings:

Sarah Margaret Ratterree Maxwell (1872 - 1954)
James Daniel Ratterree (1873 - 1949)
William Alexander Ratterree (1876 - 1935)
Mary Jane Ratterree Brooks (1878 - 1966)
Thomas Jefferson Ratterree (1880 - 1949)
Josie Ann Ratteree Wilson (1883 - 1951)
John Learner Ratteree (1885 - 1962)
Andrew Jackson Ratterree (1888 - 1966)
Joseph Ratterree (1890 - 1924)
Oma Lucinda Tanny Ratterree Scott (1891 - 1982)
Lola M Ratterree (1895 - 1983)

William T. 'Bill' Reeves
Birth:
Jan. 1, 1902
Death:
Sep. 15, 1994
Burial:
Big River Cemetery, Irondale, Washington County, Missouri

He ministered in central Missouri and was a regular contributor to the Free Will Baptist Gem. An influential officer and leader in the state Sunday school convention. In later years he was superintendent of the youth camp at Niangua which continues today as a beautiful and well attended camp for Missouri youth.

Elder Samuel Nelson Reid
Birth:
1868
Death:
1946
Burial:
Crossroads Cemetery, Lebanon, Laclede County, Missouri

He was an early pastor and minister in the central region of the state of Missouri.

William Haye Revelle
Birth:
Apr., 1845
Death:
Dec. 4, 1916
Burial:
Revelle Cemetery (Ebenezer) Cherokee Pass Madison County, Missouri

He was an early preacher in the General Free Will Baptist Assn. The son of Jackson and Cordelia (Lincoln) Revelle.

The Divine Power Appears Fearful In Its Holiness

Arthur Leroy Rich
Birth:
Aug. 22, 1883
Wright County, Missouri
Death:
Feb. 26, 1969
Wright County, Missouri
Burial:
Ashley Cemetery
Wright County, Missouri

Family links: Parents:
Robert Thomas Rich (1842 - 1918)
  Spouse: Arbella Moody Rich (1889 - 1968)
  Children: Dora Ione Rich Smith (1918 - 2014), Charles Clinton Rich (1920 - 1990)

John Byron Rollins
Birth:
Jul. 16, 1912
Stone County, Missouri
Death:
Jul. 6, 2003
Jefferson City,
Cole County, Missouri
Burial:
Hawthorn Memorial Gardens,
Jefferson City,
Cole County, Missouri

He was a 1932 graduate of Purdy High School in Purdy, Missouri. He was a Free Will Baptist minister who as early Minister and pastor began work with the Free Will Baptist GEM as a printer and writer.

When the founder B. F. Brown retired at age 70, he was succeeded by Rev. Rollins. In this position he traveled much of the State of Missouri.

He was a prolific writer, theologian, and well respected by his peers. He moved to Jefferson City where he united with the Southern Baptist, serving the Russellville Baptist Church, New Hope Baptist Church, Elston Baptist Church, Enon Baptist Church, Cole Springs Baptist Church, and the Little Flock Baptist Church in Vienna. He began to work with the *Word and Way* newspaper for the Missouri Baptist and by the time of his death at age 90 had performed 1648 weddings in the Jefferson City area.

Dee Roy Royster
Birth:
Jan. 6, 1892
Competition
Laclede County, Missouri
Death:
May 3, 1935
Wright County, Missouri
Burial:
Coldwater Cemetery
Manes
Wright County, Missouri

Source: History and Families of Wright County, Missouri, 1841-1991, page 529. ROYSTER - Dee Royster (Jan. 6, 1892, near Competition, MO) was the son of Sam and Laura Bohannon Royster. In 1902, his mother died of typhoid fever leaving six children, the youngest five months old. This sad experience never left Dee's mind and he often told his children to respect their mother at all times.

On March 17, 1914, he married Grace Wynn (March 14, 1895 near St. George, MO) daughter of John and Elmire Duncan Wynn. John owned three farms and Dee and Grace lived on one of them while Dee farmed John's land. While living in the St. George and Manes area Dee and Grace had two children: Norman (Sept. 5, 1915) and Erma (Feb. 25, 1917). Norman died of Pneumonia when one month old. The parents could never understand the "Why" but knew God always knows best.

In 1919 Dee and Grace lived in Idaho working to obtain extra money to buy their farm. In 1922, they bought a farm located near Grimes Mill on the Gasconade River. Two years later a son Doyle was born on May 5, 1924. Dee Royster was a very prosperous farmer and soon had his farm in excellent condition. When moving to this community, the family searched for a church of their choice and found it at Coon Creek Free Will Baptist Church. It was four miles from them which was quite a distance to travel in a buggy, but foul weather did not keep them from church. It was in that church that Dee preached his first sermon on July 7, 1924. He was the type of person that everyone he came in contact with knew him on a first name basis. That was quite an asset in his ministry. He would leave early on a Saturday morning to ride horseback many miles to the churches he pastored. That left his wife to care for the two children and do many farm chores, but she never complained. The family believed in always putting the Lord first. Riding so far in low temperatures, Dee must have suffered with the cold, but he never mentioned preaching being any hardship. In 1928, he bought a new Model A Ford car which kept him from enduring the cold going to the churches he pastored; but the roads were rough and the streams unbridged so trips by car were not always without unpleasant events. In 1935, he bought a new Ford V8 pickup, but he only drove it a few times to the churches he pastored. He was never very well, but he did not complain. His life ended on May 3, 1935 when he died from complications of an ear infection following the flu. His funeral at the Cope Church, was attended by the largest crowd which had ever assembled there.

Grace remained on the farm until 1962. She then sold it and bought a house in Mt. Grove where she lived until she had a fatal heart attack March 19, 1981.

John F. Schebaum
Birth:
Aug. 7, 1918
Death:
Jul. 7, 2000
Burial:
Big Creek Cemetery
Yukon
Texas County, Missouri

He was converted in 1955 and was ordained as a Deacon before answering his called to preach in 1963.

During his 37 years of ministry he pastored six Free Will Baptist churches in Missouri and one in Tennessee. He also served as a supply pastor for several churches and maintained an active tape ministry and Bible study at two nursing homes. At the time of his passing he was a member of the First Free Will Baptist Church in Waynesville, Missouri. He was married to Lorene Emeline Dixon Schebaum (1918 - 2011).

George Washington Scott
Birth:
Jun. 28, 1865
Ozark County, Missouri
Death:
Dec. 30, 1960
Wright County, Missouri
Burial:
Mountain Valley Cemetery,
Mountain Grove,
Wright County, Missouri
He pastored several churches in the area.

James W Sellards
Birth:
Jun. 28, 1835
Floyd County, Kentucky
Death:
Aug. 8, 1897
Missouri
Burial:
Barber-Whitener Cemetery
Zion
Madison County, Missouri

He was brought to God in 1861, and ordained by the larger Baptist body in 1864 laboring with them in Minnesota. He experienced much difficulty because of his open communion views; and, on moving to Missouri and learning of the Free Baptists at Fredericktown in 1885 where he united with the church.

Rev John Wesley Silvey
Birth:
Sep. 5, 1874
Clay County
Missouri
Death:
Mar. 8, 1954
Douglas County
Missouri
Burial:
Fannon Cemetery
Ava
Douglas County
Missouri
Per death certificate, parents Melvin Silvey and Mary Wolf, spouse. 1910-1930 Spring Creek, Douglas, MO.
Children: Lilith, Mabel E, Raleigh E, John L, Roy L, Melvin G, Lois F, Beulah C.

Elza Elisha Simpson
Birth:
Dec. 13, 1898
Wilderness,
Oregon County,Missouri
Death:

Sep. 25, 1994
St. Louis County,
Missouri
Burial:
Smyrna Cemetery, Alton,
Oregon County,
Missouri

Richard 'Milo' Standley
Birth:
Jun. 14, 1859
Pennsylvania
Death:
Dec. 31, 1935
Couch, Oregon County,Missouri
Burial:
New Salem Cemetery,
Couch, Oregon County,
Missouri

Son of William Richard Standley and Mary (Mathias) Standley. He first married Virgiline Crowell (1869-1932) on 07-Sep-1884 at Oregon Co., MO. Afterwards he married Caroline Mary Harder (1860-1892) about 1894. He was a farmer and preacher. Standley, of Cave Springs Association, gave his life for the cause of Christ. He traveled many miles in a buggy, pulled by a white mule named Maude. He preached in the Missouri and Arkansas Lapland: Many Springs, Walnut Grove, Bonds, New Salem, Hideout School House, Corning and Paragould, Arkansas, to name a few. Many were saved and baptized under his preaching. He and his wife, Caroline Harder, foster daughter to Judge John F. Harder of Many Springs, lived at Couch, Missouri.

William Preston Stogsdill
Birth:
Jan. 31, 1870
Oregon County, Missouri
Death:
Jul. 18, 1944
Oregon County, Missouri
Burial:
Cave Springs Cemetery,
Alton, Oregon County, Missouri

Free Will Baptist minister in south central Missouri.

John C Swaffar
Birth:
Jun. 19, 1904
Death:
May 31, 1996
Burial:
New Site Cemetery, Monett,
Barry County, Missouri

Minister in South west Missouri

John H Tally
Birth:
Dec. 25, 1878
Ash Flat,
Sharp County, Arkansas
Death:
Aug. 22, 1948 Thayer,
Oregon County,
Missouri
Burial:
Walker Cemetery,
Thayer,
Oregon County, Missouri

Ministry was mainly in southern Missouri.

Grover V Terry
Birth:
Apr. 7, 1913
Death:
Sep. 8, 1999
Burial:
Marshfield Cemetery
Marshfield Webster County,
Missouri

One of the leading Missouri pastors and very active in denominational affairs prior to his retirement.

Roena C Thomas
Birth:
1898
Death:
1959
Burial:
Worsley Cemetery,
Bronaugh,
Vernon County, Missouri

She was a Free Will Baptist Minister for 26 years in the state of Missouri.
Inscription:
Minister -
26 years

Lawrence Delmon Thompson
Birth:
May 16, 1925
Salem, Dent County, Missouri
Death:
Sep. 17, 1980
Saint Louis,St. Louis County,
Missouri
Burial:
Salem Grove Cemetery, Salem
Dent County, Missouri

Lawrence Thompson was a WWII Navy Vet, and was a pastor for 28 years. He was killed in a light plane crash along with 2 other pastors from the St. Louis area. He is remembered for his strong leadership in the state of Missouri.

United States raising funds for foreign missions. He served five years as president of the Free Will Baptist League and served in numerous roles in denominational offices during his 66 years of ministry.

Kenneth Turner
Birth:
Nov. 27, 1907
Death:
Feb. 8, 1998
Burial.
Jones Chapel Cemetery,
Stella,
Newton County, Missouri

Minister, pastor, and able denominational leader. He pastored churches in Missouri, Arkansas, Oklahoma and Kansas. He was on a Joplin TV station doing magic acts in the middle 50's. He went to Cuba three times filming the mission work there and traveled for 15 years in the

Rev Clarence Ussery
Birth:
Mar. 25, 1896
Norwood
Wright County
Missouri
Death:
May 9, 1949
Missouri

Burial:
Oak Grove Cemetery
Norwood
Wright County
Missouri

Clarence Ussery, son of Jospeh & Margaret (Tudors) Ussery, His age was 53 years, 1 month, 14 days. He was reared and educated in Blanchard School district, five miles north of Norwood, MO.

He was united in marriage to Cleo Lathrom on December 10, 1916. To this union five children were born.

He was united in marriage to Minnie Florence Adams on September 9, 1930. To this union was born two children.

Clarence professed faith in Christ on October 23,1916, and united with the Oak Grove Freewill Baptist Church where he remained a faithful member until his death. He was ordained as minister of the Gospel by the Union Association of Freewill Baptist at Pleasant Hill Church on august 30, 1918. He did pastorial work and conducted many revival meetings in Missouri and neighboring states for 31 years. It was his pleasure to witness many conversions. When he was called to rest, he was the pastor of the Freewill Baptist Church #1 near Huggins MO and Willow Springs Church #2 near Vanzant MO.

Services were held at Oak Grove with Rev Oliver Letterman and Rev Verle Tate officiating.

Herbert Steaven Vandivort
Birth:
May 20, 1909
Texas County
Missouri
Death:
Nov. 16, 2002
Phelps County
Missouri
Burial:
Hillcrest Cemetery
Mountain Grove
Wright County
Missouri
Plot: S.E. 1st 76-6

Herbert Steaven Hadley was the son of William Warren and Rosa Bell Meadows Vandivort. He married Bessie Jane Scott on February 28, 1934. To this union 3 sons were born. He became a ordained Free Will Baptist minister Sept. 27, 1935. For 21 years from 1937 to 1958, he served as a bi-vocational minister, pastoring rural churches in Texas and Wright counties.

Robert J Warner
Birth:
Mar. 16, 1941
Death:
Feb. 15, 1997
Fredericktown,
Madison County,
Missouri
Burial:
Mine La Motte Cemetery,
Mine La Motte,
Madison County,
Missouri

A minister, and denominational officer. He retired after 20 years in the military and returned to Missouri where he farmed and pastored. He was the Clerk of the Missouri State Association at the time of his death.

"Jesus Christ is in the noblest, and most perfect sense, the realized ideal of humanity."

Ira Waterman
Birth:
Nov. 6, 1873
Missouri
Death:
Nov. 23, 1926
Laclede County, Missouri
Burial
Hufft Cemetery
Eldridge, Laclede County,
Missouri

Free Will Baptist minister, evangelist and public school teacher. He was very active in the early stages of the Missouri State Association.

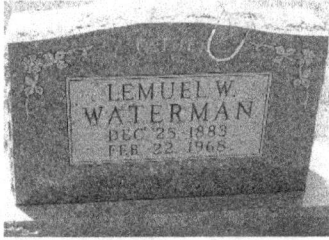

Lemuel W Waterman
Birth:
Dec. 25, 1883
Death:
Feb. 22, 1968
Burial:
Hufft Cemetery
Eldridge
Laclede County
Missouri

Family links:
 Parents:
 James Western Waterman
1839 - 1911)
 Mary Elizabeth Sanderson
Waterman
(1843 - 1906)
 Spouse:
 Dora Waterman
(1886 - 1912)
 Children:
 Naomi Waterman
(1904 - 1905)
 Siblings:
 Sarah Waterman Cochran
(1862 - 1916)
 Malissa B Waterman Butcher
(1865 - 1889)
 James Western Waterman
(1868 - 1938)
 Ira Waterman (1873 - 1926)
 Rachel Norton (1873 - 1926)
 Richard A Waterman
(1876 - 1951)
 John Andrew Waterman
(1879 - 1951)

Lemuel W Waterman
(1883 - 1968)
 Alice Delania Waterman
Kelley (1888 - 1960)

Mary Elizabeth *Retherford*
Wellbaum
Birth:
1887
Death:
1972
Burial:
Greentop Cemetery, Greentop,
Schuyler County, Missouri

She was a well-known and
respected Free Will Baptist
minister in central Missouri.

Willie K. Weston
Birth:
Sep. 30, 1904
Death:
Apr. 9, 1988
Burial:

Monett IOOF Cemetery,
Monett,
Lawrence County, Missouri

He was a well-known pastor and minister in Indian Association in southwestern Missouri and was a regular contributor to the Free Will Baptist GEM.

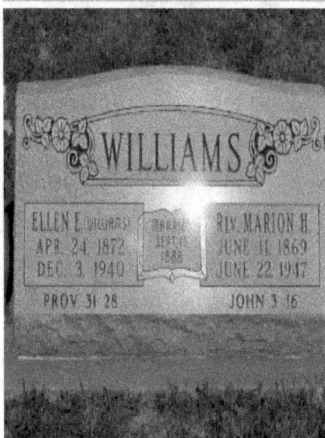

Rev Marion Henry Williams
Birth:
Jun. 11, 1869
Wright County, Missouri
Death:
Jun. 22, 1947
Wright County
Missouri
Burial:
Davis Cemetery
Wright County, Missouri,

Marion Henry Williams was the son of Henry McKinley Williams and Amanda Margaret Stevenson. He married Alcey Ellen Williams. He was a Free Will Baptist minister.

Paul Williams
Birth:
Feb. 9, 1918
Carterville,
Jasper County, Missouri
Death:
Jan. 12, 1963
Duquesne,
Jasper County, Missouri
Burial:
Carterville Cemetery,
Carterville,
Jasper County, Missouri,
Plot: Section 4A, Lot 48

He founded the Joplin Free Will Baptist Church where he served for eight years before an unexpected heart attack. Prior to this he pastored the Carterville Free Will Baptist Church. He was an active member of the Joplin Ministerial Alliance and the Niangua Youth Camp Board. He was also an officer on the State Executive Board and the Indian Creek Association Executive Board.

Jeremiah Wood
Birth:
Apr. 24, 1824
Virginia
Death:
Jan. 9, 1913
Doe Run,
St. Francois County, Missouri
Burial:
Doe Run Memorial Cemetery,
Doe Run,
St. Francois County, Missouri

Rev. Jeremiah, brother of Rev. John Wood, was born in Randolph County, Va. He was converted in 1847, was licensed to preach by the United Brethren in 1868, and ordained by the Freewill Baptists the next year. He assisted in organizing four churches, baptizing over one hundred converts. His labors have been in the St. Francois County, Mo., Q. M. which is the oldest in the state of Missouri. The results of his earlier work is still existent in that area.

Joshua Wood, Jr
Birth:
Apr. 12, 1857
Meigs County, Ohio
Death:
Jan. 11, 1928
St. Francois County, Missouri
Burial:
Cedar Falls Cemetery, Desloge,
St. Francois County, Missouri

He received license to preach Dec. 25, 1885. He has been for several years a student at Carleton Institute, Farmington, Mo., and was clerk of the St. Francois County Q. M. He is a part of the early Wood families that migrated to this part of Missouri from Ohio who were founders of the oldest existing quarterly meeting in Missouri.

John Wood
Birth:
Nov. 23, 1829
Virginia
Death:
Jan. 26, 1903
Doe Run, St. Francois County,
Missouri
Burial:
Doe Run Memorial Cemetery,
Doe Run, St. Francois County,
Missouri

John Wood was born Randolph County, Va. He was married in 1850 to Fidelia Nichols. Of their seven children one was commissioner of schools in California. His early education was limited. With commendable devotion he learned to read after his conversion, which took place in 1853. In 1871 he received license to preach, and three years later he was ordained. He has since engaged in revival and pastoral work. His labors have been largely instrumental in building up the St. Francois County Q. M., Missouri, all the churches of which, except two, he has either organized or assisted in organizing. He was a minister of the Free Will Baptist Church, having taken out his license in 1875. He was a member of the "Missouri Board", whose function is to secure a union between the Free Will Baptists and the General Baptists of Southeast Missouri.

Merl Wright
Birth:
Jun. 3, 1903
Cassville, Barry Co. Missouri
Death:
May 6, 1977
Wichita, Kansas
Burial:
Oak Hill Cemetery, Cassville,
Barry County, Missouri

She was born June 3, 1903, near Cassville. After her ordination, she and Winford Davis established Merl's Chapel Church on Nov. 14, 1929, north of Cassville.

A Minister's Reward Is Out Of This World!

Rev. John Lorn Yancey (1875-1948)

Rev John Lorn Yancey

Birth:
Jun. 11, 1875
Jasper County
Illinois
Death:
Jul. 27, 1948
Fredericktown
Madison County
Missouri
Burial:
United Methodist Church
Cemetery
Fredericktown
Madison County
Missouri

Family links:
Spouse:
Sarrah Clarenza Francis Yancey (1882 - 1962) Children:
Zelda Esther Yancey (1897 - 1913)- Grace Mae Yancey Coomer (1902 - 1981)- James Monroe Yancey (1907 - 1965)- Floyd R Yancey (1912 - 1968)- Woodrow Jessie Yancey (1916 -

1931)- William E Yancey (1918 - 2000)- Viola Margurite Yancy (1921 - 1922)

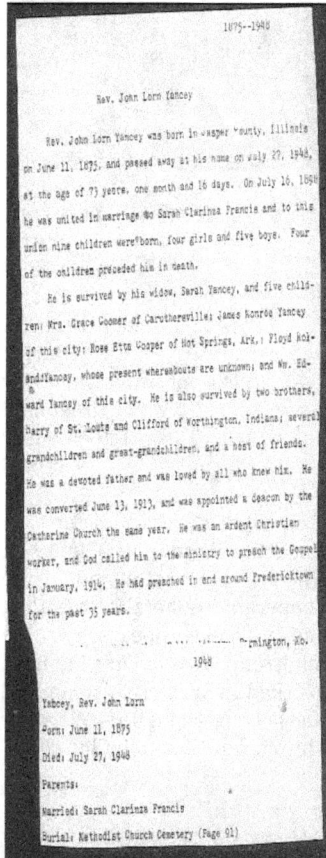

Rev William H York
Birth:
Jul. 25, 1897
Death:
Mar. 14, 1935
Burial:
Pleasant Grove Cemetery
Greenfield
Dade County
Missouri

A Free Will Baptist minister, who was from Hannon, MO, in 1925, when he attended the Cooperative General Association, and his name appears in in the ministers' list in its Minutes. Worked in Western Mo, and SE Kansas Associations--Wagoner Church, and Stockton Church.

Ferrell C Zinn
Birth:
Aug. 28, 1902
Death:
Mar. 24, 1984
Burial:
Brown Cemetery, Cedarcreek,
Taney County, Missouri

He was a Free Will Baptist minister and school teacher in southern Missouri. He was an active contributor to the *Free Will Baptist GEM* and served on various committees and boards of the state Association.

On that bright and cloudless morning when the dead in Christ shall rise,

And the glory of his resurrection share;

When his chosen ones shall gather to their home beyond the skies,

And the roll is called up yonder, I'll be there.

Nebraska

Rev Alonzo Curtis
Birth:
1814
Ohio
Death:
Dec. 9, 1876
Salem
Richardson County, Nebraska
Burial:
Maple Cemetery
Salem
Richardson County, Nebraska

His name is in a List of minister's deaths in Minutes of Centennial of Freewill Baptist, NH. Shows his name, place of death at Salem, NE, and death date, but nothing regarding his DOB or parentage, etc.
History of Salem Quarterly Meeting, southeast part of state and extending into part of Kansas, was org. in 1870 by Rev's H.B. Richey, A. Curtis, and K.R. Davis were with R. Dunn in the state for a brief time, the first ministers.

The Free-Will Baptist Church of Salem was organized in 1868, by Rev. A. Curtis, who was its first pastor, and remained with it until 1876. A church edifice was erected in 1872-73, at a cost of $1,600. It is forty-four by twenty-six feet on the ground floor, and has a seating capacity of 250.
Mr. Curtis was followed by Rev. M. Felt, who occupied the pulpit for one year, and was succeeded by Rev. Joseph Wesley, who held the position two years. O. V. Porter Supplied the Society for six months after this time, and was followed after a lapse of nearly a year, by Rev. J. D. Van Dorn, who performed service during the winters of 1881-82.
A Sabbath school was established in 1876, with D. A. Tisdel as its superintendent.

Kinsman R Davis
Birth:
Dec. 8, 1816
Quebec, Canada
Death:
Apr. 26, 1898
Burial:
Maple Cemetery
Salem, Richardson County, Nebraska

Parents: Silas L. Davis, b. VT, d. WI; and Phoebe (Bennett) DAVIS. Spouse: Sarah Ann Brooks, bn ME."Rev. Kinsman R. Davis, a brother of Rev. Jarius E. Davis assisted in gathering the LaFayette Quarterly Meeting at its organization, about 1850. His ministry was chiefly spent in Wisconsin, a part of the time in the Rock and Dane QM, until about 1869, when he moved to Nebraska, was connected with the Salem church.

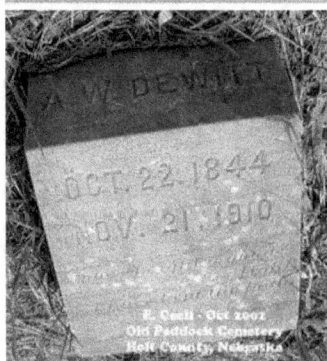

Rev A. W. DeWitt
Birth:
Oct. 22, 1844
Illinois
Death:
Nov. 21, 1910
Burial:

Old Paddock Cemetery
Holt County, Nebraska,

Listed in 1888 book on Nebraska Churches as a minister, along with his brother, Rev. W. R. DeWitt, in Keya Paha Co.

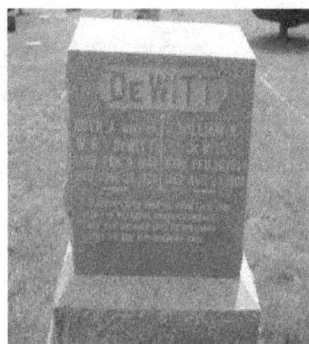

William Robert DeWitt
Birth:
Feb. 26, 1834
Pike County, Indiana
Death:
Aug. 23, 1903
MillsKeya
Paha County, Nebraska
Burial:
Olive Branch Cemetery
MillsKeya
Paha County, Nebraska

William Robert wed Ruth Jane Bartlett on Oct 27, 1869 in Knox co. Ill. he was brought to God in 1871, license in 1880 and ordained on February 19, 1886. He has since been actively engaged in revival work in Nebraska.

William Henry Edger, Jr
Birth:
Feb. 5, 1874
Wisconsin
Death:
Dec. 6, 1955
Central City
Merrick County, Nebraska
Burial:
Central City Cemetery
Central City, Merrick County,
Nebraska

He was the son of Rev. William H. Edger,Sr, and Elizabeth and himself a Free Will Baptist minister.

Rev George Washington Knapp
Birth:
Sep. 23, 1842
Cameron
Steuben County
New York
Death:
Apr. 19, 1921
Franklin
Franklin County
Nebraska
Burial:
Greenwood Cemetery
Franklin
Franklin County
Nebraska

Rev. George W. Knapp, was the son of William and Eliza J. (Osborn) KNAPP. He professed faith in 1851, and received license to preach in 1862, and ordained a Freewill Baptist minister in 1866. He pastored in Meredith Centre, and Contoocook, NH; Granville NY; and Aurora and Kenesaw, Neb. He was blessed in his ministry with over one hundred conversions in one year. In 1883, he was elected delegate to the General Conference.
He was educated in Hillsdale College, Mich, and Bates Theological school in Lewiston, Maine.
In Sept. 1865, he married Caroline [Carrie] Dennis, and had five children.

Peter Alexander Lansing
Birth:
May 9, 1808 Saratoga,
Saratoga County
New York
Death:
Sep. 7, 190
Saunders County, Nebraska
Burial:
Pleasant View Cemetery,
Leshara, Saunders County,
Nebraska

Rev. Lansing was converted in 1833, and ordained in 1844, taking charge of the Providence church and residing at Laurenceburgh, Indiana. In an anti-slavery article in the "Morning Star" he offended some of his parishioners, but also the same article became known to people of Mainville, Ohio, where he ministered to them until 1850. After spending three years in Jasper Co. Indiana, and organizing a church there, he settled in Wisconsin, where he remained thirteen years and organized seven churches. Then, after a revival in Iowa, he moved to Nebraska and organized two churches. During his ministry he has engaged much in revival work, and baptized 1,014 converts. He represented the Ohio Y.M. in the General Conference of 1844. He has served in several local offices and has always stood firm for temperance and every moral interest in the community. He was 92 yrs of age when he died.

William Marks
Birth:
Mar. 10, 1851
Death:
Oct. 26, 1900
Burial:
Shelton Cemetery,
Hall County, Nebraska
Plot: Lot 523

Free Will Baptist denomination in which Rev. Wm. Marks was ordained and labored until death. He was a nephew of David Marks the influenical minister of this denomination. His father was Rev. Ives Marks.

Marcus L. Morse
Birth:
Dec. 30, 1872
Death:
Aug. 15, 1938
Burial:
Shelton Cemetery
Hall County, Nebraska
Plot: Lot 552

His parents were Justus Elmer Morse (1842 - 1897) and Nancy Shroy Morse (1859 - 1896). He married G. Margaret Morse (1881 - 1959) and had George H. Morse (1902 - 1971); Fred W. Morse (1905 - 1964) and Lloyd J. Morse (1914 - 1998).

John Morrow
Birth:
Mar. 1, 1833
Pike County, Illinois
Death:
Feb. 4, 1912
Nebraska
Burial:
Mount Hope Cemetery
Scotia
Greeley County, Nebraska

He was ordained in 1887 and labored with the Bethel and Paddock Nebraska churches. He was also a veteran of the civil war serving and Sergt. Co. I 148 Ill. Inf.

Rev Joseph D Parkyn
Birth:
Jul. 27, 1812,
England
Death:
May 27, 1900
Nebraska
Burial:
Homerville Cemetery
Gosper County, Nebraska

Rev. Joseph Parkyn, was ordained a deacon in Methodists in 1834, and elder in 1837, and joined the Freewill Baptist at Ellington, New York in 1841; and was successful pastor for some years in southern NY of churches at Ashford, Otoe, Java, Napoli, and Little Valley; removed to Wisconsin in 1854, and preached at Hart's Prairie, Wayne, Oakland, Rome, Bradford and Johnstown; came to Nebraska in 1885, and he has preached at Homerville and vicinity, as health and circumstances permitted; has attended the last two sessions of the Nebraska yearly meeting, much to the satisfaction of the brethren; has kept no account, but thinks he has baptized some two hundred and married about as many."
--from "Four Years of Cooperation in Nebraska and Kansas, Free Will Baptist Associations," by A. D. Williams, D.D.
The following notes were found in the Family History file of Dorothy Grace (Hulce) Smith his great granddaughter.
Joseph Parkyn was born in England and came to this country as a missionary of the Moravian

Church. He walked 50 miles to get to the sailing vessel in which he made his journey to America. The last three days of the journey the travelers were without food. As he rode along a road in New Jersey, he saw a woman getting water at a well. Something seemed to say to him, "There's your wife". Six weeks later they were married. Her name was Rebecca Lake.

They lived in Maryland or Virginia and Joseph was teaching a negro woman to read. The people objected and planned to "tar and feather" him and "ride him on a rail", but a friend loaned him a horse so he could escape to New Jersey and promised to look after Rebecca and their baby, John.

They moved to western New York and made the journey on a horse-drawn boat on the Erie Canal. Later they moved to Michigan, where Joseph was chased by wolves that Rebecca scared away by a flaming pine knot. When they were in Michigan they helped runaway slaves get to Canada on the "underground railway". When they went to Wisconsin they got on the last boat to make the journey via the Great Lakes before winter halted lake traffic that year.

Inscription:
aged 87yrs 11m 8 days

Joseph H. Reeves
Birth:
Jan. 28, 1841
Burlington Island, Illinois
Death:
Dec. 7, 1927
Burial:
Greenwood Cemetery
Lexington
Dawson County, Nebraska

He was a son of Rev. M. D. Reeves, and like his father followed in the ministry. He was educated at M.E. Seminary and at Wasioja, Minnesota. His religious life began in 1860 and in September, 1879 he was ordained by the Root River Quarterly Meeting, Minnesota. He pastored numerous churches in Minnesota and in connection with his pastoral work he was a member they state home mission board, a trustee of the Western Association, an active supporter of the Free Baptists and a leading worker in founding the Winnebago City College.

Inscription:
39 IL Infantry Co. G

Rev Luster A Reger
Birth:
Sep. 13, 1900
Death:
May 13, 1950
Burial:
Maple Creek Cemetery
Beaver City
Furnas County, Nebraska

His father was Rev. Ellis F Reger (1877 - 1930) who married Olive

Arizona Smith Reger (1880 - 1957). He married Ada E Reger (1898 - 1981).

Edward Root
Birth:
Feb. 4, 1822
Litchfield County, Connecticut
Death:
Oct. 22, 1901
Weeping Water, Cass County,
Nebraska
Burial:
Oakwood Cemetery
Weeping Water, Cass County,
Nebraska
ROOT was the son of Anson and Sally (Brooks) ROOT, and was born in Litchfield Co. in 1822. Twenty years later, he was married to Lucy S. Palmer (15 Mqy 1842, Ohio). Brother Root received license from the Williamsfield church [Freewill Baptist] of the Ashtabula Quarterly Meeting (Q.M.) Ohio, in 1839, and two years later, was ordained by the Huron Q.M. He ministered ten years to the Greenfield and New Haven church, in Ohio; fifteen years to the church in Porter, Mich., and ten years to the church of Centreville, Nebraska, and to other churches for brief periods. He has engaged in many revivals and assisted in organizing ten or more churches. He was a member of the Executive Board of Nebraska and pastor of the Long Branch and Grand View churches..

George W. Sisson
Birth:
May 13, 1837
Bradford, Pennsylvania
Death:
Jul. 8, 1925
Burial:
Wyuka Cemetery
Lincoln
Lancaster County, Nebraska
Plot: Sec-17 Lot-47 Gr-5

In 1868 he married Miss Annie C. Griffith. He obtained his education at Kingsville, Ohio; Millersville, Pennsylvania and at Hillsdale College, Michigan. He was ordained in 1867 and

Latrope, Pennsylvania by Rev. J. S. Burgess preaching the sermon. He held pastorates in Pennsylvania and Ohio and conducted revivals in several other places. In 1862 he entered the Army and served with Co. F of the 169th PA Infantry, was stationed at Fort Keyes, Yorktown, Virginia nearly 6 months. He established Sunday schools for the freemen in the old Baptist Church of Yorktown. He was discharged from the army in 1863 engaging himself in the American Home And Foreign Mission Society of New York and was sent to Beaufort, South Carolina where he labored two seasons. In 1865 under the appointment of the Philadelphia Freeman's Aid Society he took up the work in Nelson County, Virginia before moving to Nebraska.

Samuel F Smith
Birth:
Aug. 2, 1825
Martinsburg
Lewis County, New York
Death:
Sep. 18, 1898
Brown County, Nebraska
Burial:
Grandview Cemetery
Long Pine, Brown County, Nebraska

He was educated at Geauga Seminary, OH, and at Whitestown Seminary, NY. He was converted in 1839 under the labors of Rev. Ransom Dunn. He was ordained July 4, 1844, by direction of the Ohio and Pennsylvania Yearly Meeting. He moved to Wisconsin in 1848, and assisted in revivals and in organizing churches at Fayette and Wayne, and preached at the Willow Springs church. He organized churches in Caledonia, and at Elgin, and McHenry, Ill. In 1853-55 where he worked assisted by Eld. Dunn, and a church at Racine, WI, was organized. He was seven years at

Fairwater, Wis. while assisting in a revival at Winnegago; four years at Berlin, WI, and one yr at Fairbury, IL, and five years commencing 1871, at Postville, IA. After this, moving to Nebraska he organized churches at Rose, Fairburg, Marshall and Dry Branch, Neb. and at DeWitt, KS. He covered a period of forty years, baptized move than four hundred converts, and assisted in organizing two Quarterly and two Yearly Meetings. He also manifested his benevolence and love for the cause of education by munificient gifts to Hillsdale College, Mich., of which he is an honored trustee.

Rev William Thatcher
Birth:
1815
Pennsylvania
Death:
1905
Nebraska
Burial:
Geneva Cemetery
Geneva
Fillmore County, Nebraska

Rev. William Thatcher, a native of Pennsylvania, came to Nebraska, exactly when is not known, but between 1870-1880, as his wife died in PA in 1870, and he was found in the 1880 census, Fillmore Co.,Nebraska, living with his foster daughter, Eliza J.(Mumford) and husband, James BORTNER. He was 65 years, and was widowed.(His wife was Lecretia (McFadden) Thatcher, is bur.in Crawford Co. Penn.)

In the 1900 Fillmore Census, he was in HH of James Bortner, and 2nd wife, Mary v. Bortner. He stated on this census he was born, March, 1815 in PA.

An excerpt from an 1888 book re Nebraska Freewill Baptists, by A.D. Williams, D.D., page 35, states: "In August, 1884, a visit was made to Father William Thatcher, living near Geneva, in Fillmore County. Father Thatcher had been a devoted member of the Freewill Baptists in western Pennsylvania, and had not lost his attachment to us on coming out West. He had attended the extra yearly meeting at Kenesaw and at that time joined the Kenesaw church, though living fifty miles distant.

Rev Alpheus Monroe Totman
Birth:
Apr. 2, 1835
New York
Death:
May 15, 1912
Omaha
Douglas County
Nebraska

Burial:
Mount Hope Cemetery
Omaha
Douglas County
Nebraska
Plot: Sect. D, Lot 32, Grave 14

Rev. A.M. Totman's parents were E. Samuel(1811-1895) and Anna Maria (Mcdole) TOTMAN (1813-1880). He was married to Phoeba Jannet (Newton) Totman - sometimes recorded as J. Phoeba.

Mr. Totman served in the Union NY 161st Inf. Co. K, in 1862 - ? from which service he later drew a pension.

Rev. Totman was ordained a Freewill Bapt. minister in NY, and moved west, to Illinois, then Iowa, and later to Nebraska.

He helped organized a FWB church in Aurora, NE, and served as its pastor in 1883. Church records show he pastored other churches. The Nebraska state census of 1890 showed the family in Rock Co.He was an effective minister in the early Neb. FWB church work, and his name showed up in old church records there.

Wilmetta Marks Wheeler
Birth:
Dec. 26, 1879
Death:
Dec. 18, 1973
Burial:
Shelton Cemetery,
Hall County, Nebraska

She was a niece of David Marks and a minister in Nebraska.

Alvin Dighton Williams
Birth:
Oct. 13, 1823 Smithfield,
Fayette County,
Pennsylvania
Death:
Dec. 31, 1894
Kenesaw,
Adams County, Nebraska
Burial:
Kenesaw Cemetery, Kenesaw,
Adams County, Nebraska,
Plot: Blk 2, Row 6

He was converted at age thirteen and commenced preaching two and a half years later, gaining some notoriety as the "boy preacher." He was ordained a Free Will Baptist minister at Carolina Mills, R.I. in May 1848, and graduated at Hamilton College, NY in 1849.

He was pastor of churches at Carolina Mills, and Pawtucket, R.I., Lawrence, MA, Minneapolis, and Fair Point, Minn., and Cheshire, and Middleport, Ohio, and has baptized nearly five hundred converts. He has assisted in organizing churches at East Killingly, Conn.; Elk River, Otsego, Ramsay, Iowa; Lebanon, Minn.; Flemington and Fairview W.VA; Kenesaw, Marshall, Pleasant Plain, Long Branch and Lincoln, Neb.; also, the Hennepin Q.M. Minn., the W.VA Ass'n and the Hastings, Autora and Nemaha River Q.M's in Nebraska. He has been superintendent of schools for Lawrence, Mass., and in W.VA, president of the Northwestern and West Virginia Colleges, principal of Nebraska State Normal School, and member of the Nebraska State Board of Agriculture. The degree of Doctor of Divinity was conferred in 1871 by Quincy, now Chaddock College, Ill. He did the *Freewill Baptist Quarterly* and is the author of "The *Rhode Island Freewill Baptist Pulpit*," "The Support of the Ministry," "*Memorials of the Free Communion Baptists,*" and of

"Four Years of Co-operation in Nebraska and Kansas." He was several times a member of the General Conference. From Kenesaw Cem. Neb cemetery records, it is stated that the first settlers to Kenesaw were Dr. A.D. Williams and his widowed sister, Mrs. Norton, with her four children. Other local history, tells that they lived in the wagon box for three weeks after arriving, a stove outside, and the horizon for the walls; that he had the first house, and the first well dug in Kenesaw. He bought up large tracts of land and left a sizeable estate when he died. He had a quest for learning that took him into many areas and avenues for service and progress.

John H. Wolfe
Birth:
Jan. 7, 1863
Olin
Jones County, Iowa
Death:
Dec. 30, 1954
Pawnee County, Nebraska
Burial:

Pawnee City Cemetery,
Pawnee City,
Pawnee County, Nebraska

He has served this denomination long and faithfully, having joined the Pleasant Hill, Iowa, Free Will Baptist Church on February 27, 1877. He entered College and the Theological Seminary in Hillsdale, Michigan, graduating in the class of 1897 with the degree of Bachelor of Divinity. He was ordained to the Gospel Ministry in Jackson, Michigan, January 10, 1897. After graduation, he accepted the call as pastor of the First Free Will Baptist Church at Lincoln, Nebraska. He has served as President of the Tecumseh (Oklahoma) College and for fifty years was Chairman of the Executive Board of Free Will Baptists [of Nebraska].

Wolfe was born to German immigrants near Olin, Iowa, on January 7, 1863, the only son of John and Barbara (Pferseke) Wolfe. His father died while serving the Union Army in the Civil War in 1864, but his mother stayed on to keep the land they had homesteaded. In 1877, at the age of fourteen, Wolfe and two of his five sisters were converted during a revival meeting at the Pleasant Hill Free Will Baptist Church in Olin. They and their mother, formerly a German Lutheran, joined the church at the time.

He married Delia Scriven, 14 Oct. 1884 in Marshall, Iowa. Both of them enrolled in Hillsdale College, a Free Will Baptist institution in Michigan, in 1889. Both took the same course of study in preparation for the ministry.

Their names appear in the Hillsdale Collegian for July 1, 1897, as having completed the "full theological" program— which included classical and Biblical Greek, Hebrew, and Latin.

There are other references to Wolfe in Hillsdale publications. The Hillsdale Collegian for January 26, 1894, reported that he was chosen "to publish next year's hand-book" for the Young Men's Christian Association on campus. The Hillsdale Herald for September 16, 1896, listed the results of "society elections," showing that he was elected vice-president of the Theadelphic Literary Society.

After graduation, he went to Nebraska, and was assistant pastor at Lincoln two years. He was President of the city Union C. E. for one year, and has been Chairman of the Nebraska Y.M. Executive Board since 1898.

Rev. Wolfe established churches in Nebraska and in their pastoral care, and in 1917, was called upon to be president of Tecumseh College in Tecumseh, OK. After the college burned in 1927, and was not rebuilt, they returned to Nebraska. He wrote articles for church magazines regarding FW Baptist work in the state of Nebraska, which is very helpful to church historians. He was one of the voices who tried to stem the decision to merge with Northern Baptists in 1911.

The Reveremd Mrs. Wolfe died in 1949 and the Reverend Mr. Wolfe in 1954, just eight days short of his ninety-second birthday.

Delia *Scriven* Wolfe
Birth:
Oct. 14, 1863
Fort Wayne
Allen County, Indiana
Death:
Jan. 7, 1949
Plattsmouth
Cass County, Nebraska
Burial:
Pawnee City Cemetery,
Pawnee City,
Pawnee County, Nebraska

Married John Wolfe on October 14, 1884, in Marshalltown, Marshall County, Iowa. They went to college together, took the same courses, and both graduated from Hillsdale College in Michigan in 1897. She was an ordained minister who taught and ministered beside her husband.

New Hampshire

Austin Wakefield Avery
Birth:
Nov. 18, 1838
Campton
Grafton County, New
Hampshire
Death:
Oct. 5, 1865
Haverhill
Essex County,
Massachusetts
Burial:
Blair Cemetery
Campton
Grafton County, New
Hampshire

At 16 he took a public stand for Christ in revival. He entered the New Hampton Institution to prepare for the ministry in 1856. Two years later he was licensed to preach. Shortly after he went to Paducah, Kentucky in early 1859 to visit his brother and to make a tour through nine of the southern states and saw slavery as it was. He returned to Dover, New Hampshire to supply for three months. And 51 requested interest in Christian prayers. For a while he served as an agent of the New York City church raising funds for building. When a revival broke out where he had settled. He resigned that job and settled in Parishville, where he was ordained at the age of 21 on March 24, 1860. In January 1861 he went to Boston to study with Rev. Ransom Dunn and on March 13 he became pastor of the Boston church. Through his four years of pastorate, a great interest continued till 1865 had been added to the church 156 of them by baptism. With the ministry of only six years he baptized 175, when an illness overtook him and he died in his 27th year. He was buried in his native state with the funeral being preached by Dr. Isaac the Stewart. Note: Additional information from *Native Ministry of New Hampshire.*

J. Franklin Babb
Birth:
May 20, 1873
New Hampshire
Death:
May 31, 1938
Laconia
Belknap County, New
Hampshire
Burial:
New Hampton Village Cemetery
New Hampton
Belknap County, New
Hampshire
Plot: 165

His parents were John W. Babb and Josephine H. (Damon) BABB. Was married to Candace Porter Ladd, 11 Oct. 1897, at Ladd's Hill, Belmont, NH. She was the dau of Arthur S. Ladd and Ellen M. (Porter) LADD. Rev. Babb was fondly called "the sporting parson" by editors and those who knew his affinity for the outdoors and his hunting and fishing expeditions. He was often called upon by groups to speak as he always drew a crowd for his entertaining way of presenting his subject. He was the last pastor of the New Hampton Freewill Baptist church, before it became the New Hampton Community church after 1911. It was originally built as a Freewill Baptist church in the 1800's and is now on the National Registry of Historic places.He pastored for some years in Mass. before the last one at New Hampton.

Wm. S Babcock
Birth:
Nov. 15, 1764
Death:
Aug. 29, 1821
Burial:
Babcock-Cate Cemetery,
Barrington,
Strafford County,
New Hampshire

Son of a wealthy merchant, who sent him to Yale College to prevent his being drafted as a soldier. After school, he settled in Springfield, VT, where he began a study of the Scripture to refute its teachings. But it mightily convinced him of its truth, and he was converted in 1800, and at once began to preach. Becoming acquainted with the Freewill Baptists, he found himself in agreement with them, was baptized and ordained by Rev. Jeremiah Ballard of NH. He gathered a church together, of 25 members, sent a letter to the Quarterly Meeting requesting instruction and fellowship, whereupon another church under Rev. Stephen Place, joined with Rev. Babcock's church and were in fellowship. These were pioneer days for the church in Vermont. Rev. Wm. Babcock and Nathaniel Marshall, convinced Rev. John Colby, the young FWB Vermont evangelist, to be ordained, before his trip to Ohio. Rev. Babcock's father's estate continued to yield him an annual remittance and he preached the word with acceptance. His life was cut short by consumption, but he died in the triumphs of faith,

Henry M. Bacheler
Birth:
Jun. 16, 1849,
India
Death:
unknown
Burial:
New Hampton Village Cemetery,
New Hampton, Belknap County,
New Hampshire,
Plot: #219

Henry M. Bacheler, M.D., was the son of Rev. Dr. Otis Robinson Bacheler and wife Sarah P. (Merrill) Bacheler. He was born in Balasore, India where his parents were medical and ministerial missionaries. He entered work in India at the close of 1886.

Otis Robinson Batchelder
Birth:
Jan. 17, 1817
Andover, Merrimack County,
New Hampshire
Death:
Jan. 1, 1901
New Hampton,
Belknap County,
New Hampshire
Burial:
New Hampton Village Cemetery,
New Hampton,
Belknap County,
New Hampshire,
Plot: Lot 219

In preparation to become a missionary he studied at Holliston & Wilbraham, MA and Kent's Hill, ME academies, 1835-

1839. He studied medicine at Dartmouth & Cambridge Medical colleges. He was licensed to preach by the Boston Quarterly Meeting, Lowell, MA, April 1839 and was ordained an evangelist in Lowell, May 7, 1840.He received his M D from Dartmouth College, 1850; and DD, Hillsdale College, 1881. He sailed for India, May 16,1840 where he was a missionary at Balasore, Orissa, India, October 1840-52; Midnapore, Bengal, 1865-83. Otis returned to the United States, September 1883 and was without charge in New Hampton, 1883-6. Again he sailed from Boston for India, January 23, 1886. He published "A Medical Guide in Oriya and Bengalee." The funeral services for Otis were held in the Free Baptist Church at New Hampton, with the Reverend Atwood B Meservey, DD, PhD, the venerable ex-principal of the New Hampton Literary institution, was to have preached the sermon, but was prevented by sickness, consequently his address was read by Reverend Professor Shirley J Case, of the institution. Others taking part in the services were the Reverend J Burnham Davis, late of Ocean Park, Maine, the Reverend Arthur Given, DD, of Providence, Reverend Robert Ford, of Campton, and Reverend George L White of New Hampton.

Benaiah Bean
Birth:
Jun. 30, 1793
Salisbury,
Merrimack County,
New Hampshire
Death:
Dec. 17, 1856 Colebrook,
Coos County,
New Hampshire
Burial:
North Road Cemetery,
Wilmot,
Merrimack County,
New Hampshire

He was converted under the preaching of John Colby and baptized in Feb. 1812, by Rev. Joshua Quimby. He moved to Whitefield in 1821 and became a member of the Freewill Baptist church in that place at its organization. In 1823, he was licensed to preach by the Sandwich Quarterly Meeting. He was ordained August 24, 1828, at Whitefield, where he was pastor for about ten years, witnessing several revivals. At one time he baptized forty-one, at another forty. During the revival which began July 1, 1832, ninety were hopefully converted. While in Whitefield, he labored in Concord, VT, Jefferson and Bethlehem, NH. In 1838 he moved to Bethlehem and was pastor of the church there for eight years. In 1850 he organized the Clarksville and Pittsburg church of fifteen members and became their pastor. Four years later the church numbered sixty. In 1855, the history of Colebrook give the account that Rev. Benaiah Bean organized a Freewill Baptist Church at Colebrook. A church about this time was also organized at Stewartstown, of which he was pastor till his death.

Rev Silas F. Bean
Birth:
Oct. 3, 1807
Death:
Mar. 6, 1890
Burial:
Bean Burial Ground
Tuftonboro
Carroll County
New Hampshire

Ordained Freewill Bapt. minister Dec. 28, 1834. He pastored several churches and until about 80 yrs of age, he preached regularly.
Pastor of First Freewill Baptist Church in Melvin Village from 1839-1866

Rev Hugh Beede
Birth:
Dec. 9, 1807
Sandwich
Carroll County, New Hampshire
Death:
Jan. 27, 1879
Sandwich
Carroll County, New Hampshire
Burial:
Skinners Corners
North Sandwich
Carroll County, New Hampshire

An early NH Freewill Baptist minister; featured in Carroll Co. NH History, and being pastor there.

Lewis P Bickford
Birth:
Oct. 4, 1844
Center Harbor,
Belknap County, New Hampshire
Death:
Aug. 3, 1917
New Hampton,
Belknap County, New Hampshire
Burial:
New Hampton Village Cemetery,
New Hampton,
Belknap County, New Hampshire

He experienced the new birth in 1857 and received license in 1868. He graduated from the New Hampton Institution In 1869 [later Cobb Divinity School, then Bates College]. He received ordination June 31, 1871.

Israel Blake
Birth:
1765
Death:
May 1, 1839
Grafton County,
New Hampshire
Burial:
Blake Cemetery
Stinson Lake
Grafton County,
New Hampshire

He was ordained in the Sandwich Quarterly Meeting in 1800. Here he continued to reside for 40 years. The year 1811 was one of marked revival for his church and quarterly meeting. In 1824 David marks visited him, and in the month of protracted meetings that followed, the church was revived and enlarged. In 1833, 27 members were added by baptism. On May 1, 1839, Brother Blake closed a long service for the master. The Rev. Thomas Perkins preached his funeral sermon from First Thessalonians 4:14.

Simeon Bolles
Birth:
April 16, 1830
Death:
Nov. 18, 1889
Burial:
Maple Street Cemetery
Bethlehem
Grafton County, New Hampshire

He studied at New Hampton Institution and was ordained in Concord, Vt. In 1866 where most of his ministry was. He wrote the History of Bethlehem in 1883.

Rev Hezekiah H Brock
Birth:
1819
Barrington
Strafford County, New Hampshire
Death:
Dec. 30, 1851
Dover
Strafford County, New Hampshire
Burial:
Pine Hill Cemetery
Dover
Strafford County, New Hampshire

Rev. Hezekiah H. Brock was born in Barrington, NH, and embraced the Saviour while young. He was baptized by Eld. Sherburne, and making Dover his residence, he united with the First Free Baptist church there. A year or two afterward, he preached his first sermon.

He did good work at Raymond and afterwards in Kennebunk, ME, where he was ordained in 1845. The next year, he entered the Bible School at Whitestown, NY. His lungs soon after began to fail, and being persuaded that he should not be able to preach further, he turned his attention to medicine.

His young wife died after a year of married life. In Utica, NY, later he married again. In failing health, he removed to Dover, N.H., where he sank rapidly. His last words were "Beautiful Jesus." He died Dec. 30, 1851, aged 31 years. He was amiable in spirit and winning as a preacher.

Rev Joseph Boody
Birth:
May 16, 1752
Barrington
Strafford County
New Hampshire
Death: Jan. 17, 1824
Strafford
Strafford County
New Hampshire

Burial:
Joseph Boody Burial Ground
Strafford
Strafford County
New Hampshire

Son of Azariah Boody (1720-1803) and Bridget (Bushbie) Boody (1720-1785). Children: John S Boody (1795 - 1874)* One of the converts of the revival that swept through his native town under Rev. Benjamin Randall's preaching.

Rev Joseph Boodey, Jr
Birth:
Apr. 12, 1773
New Hampshire
Death:
May 12, 1867
New Hampshire
Burial:
Old Boodey Place
New Durham
Strafford County
New Hampshire

He was aged 94 yrs. and 1 mo. He was the nephew of another Rev. Joseph Boodey or (Boody) bn 1752, who was shown as companion of Rev. Benj. Randall, whose house was where Eld. Randall and his group of Free Will Baptists organized their church by that name in New Durham.

Free Bapt. Cyclopedia, pub. 1889, records that this Eld. Joseph Boody was the first to preach free salvation in northern Vermont. He had good success but for six months he saw not a minister who gave him a word of cheer.

He was ordained Oct. 18, 1798, at a session of the QM in the New Durham Schoolhouse, with Eld. Benj. Randall, delivering the sermon and Eld. Daniel Lord giving the prayer. He helped organize Quarterly Meetings from the churches that had been organized. He was a worthy minister.

Nahum Brooks
Birth:
Jun. 11, 1811
East Wakefield,
New Hampshire
Death:
Mar. 17, 1883
Manchester,
New Hampshire
Burial:
Valley Cemetery,
Manchester,
Hillsborough County,
New Hampshire,
Plot: 973-3

He was baptized in Aug. 1834 by Rev Samuel Burbank, and joined the church in Wakefield. He acquired a thorough academic education at North Parsonfield under the instruction of the Rev. Hosea Quinby, D.D. He afterward went to Dover, New Hampshire, and was employed in the "Morning Star" office. He began preaching in 1837. Through his efforts a church was organized at Laconia, NH, March 17, 1838, which began with 9 members. He was ordained the following May in 1838 in a session of the Q.M. During this pastorate of six years, he baptized 166 persons. A fine house of worship was built and dedicated Jan 6th, 1841. His next pastorate was at Great Falls, where he baptized 192 converts. In all his pastorates he baptized 653 persons before he contracted a severe cold in a meeting in Candia, which caused partial paralysis of the vocal cords, and in consequence, he was obliged to cease preaching. After his ordination, he attended every session of the NH Yearly Meeting, except four. He was deeply interested in the benevolent enterprises of the denomination and contributed generously to their support. For twenty years, he was an active member of the Foreign Mission Board and two years treasurer of the society. He was also one of the founders of the Maine State Seminary at Lewiston, ME (now Bates)

Amos Brown
Birth:
Sep. 4, 1800
Bristol, Grafton County,
New Hampshire
Death:
Dec. 7, 1867
Eaton Center, Carroll County,
New Hampshire
Burial:
Homeland Cemetery,
Bristol, Grafton County,
New Hampshire,
Plot: Sec. 11E, Lot 3, Grave 7

Amos Brown was licensed to preach by the Sandwich Quarterly Meeting, of the Free Baptist denomination 16 Dec 1829, and was ordained at Alexandria, Grafton, New Hampshire, 30 Sep 1832, by council of elders of the Sandwich Quarterly Meeting, composed of Rev. John Hill, of Alexandria, Rev. Simeon Dana, MD, Rev. Thomas Perkins, of New Hampton, and Rev. Devi Smith. He labored one-half the time at Alexandria from 1837 till 1853, and had pastoral oversight of the church for thirty-seven years. During his labors there, 160 were added to the church. He also labored successfully in Nashua, Orange, Center Harbor, New Hampton, Hill, and Bridgewater.

He represented Bristol in the legislature of 1847 and 1848. In May 1867, he accepted a call to the pastorate of the Free Baptist Church at Eaton, where a revival of religion was very general.

William Burr
Birth:
Jun. 22, 1806
Hingham Center,
Plymouth County,
Massachusetts
Death:
Nov. 5, 1866
Dover, Strafford County,
New Hampshire
Burial::
Pine Hill Cemetery,
Dover, Strafford County,
New Hampshire

654

While in his early teens, he apprenticed with a Boston printer, learning the trade he would put to good use for the Free Will Baptist Printing Establishment. Their books included his name among those they hold in high esteem.

A biography, *Life of William Burr*, was written in 1871 by Rev. J. M. Brewster.

An inscription on the 12-ft marble monument erected over his grave reads: WILLIAM BURR, age 60. This Monument, erected by the Freewill Baptist Denomination stands as a tribute to his memory. He had charge of the Printing Office at the opening in 1826, and was Editor of the *Morning Star* and Agent of the Printing Establishment during a period of more than thirty years. By his integrity in business, his urbanity in social intercourse, His broad and philanthropic sympathies, especially by his

devout earnestness and as a Christian, he won and retained the high esteem of all who knew him.

He was a member of the City Government in Dover, the Legislature of New Hampshire; and for twenty-five consecutive years was elected Treasurer of the Benevolent Societies. He was a strong abolitionist and at a anti-slavery meeting sat beside President Abraham Lincoln.

Elder Hezekiah D Buzzell
Birth:
Dec. 16, 1777
Alton,
Belknap County, New
Hampshire
Death:
Sep. 6, 1858
Alton, Belknap County,
New Hampshire
Burial:
Hurd Cemetery, Alton,
Belknap County,
New Hampshire

Buzzell was ordained in Gilmanton, New Hampshire on Jan 25, 1803, then preached in Alton, Gilmanton and Weare for fifty years. He was a minister at the Free Will Baptist Church in Weare (established October 20, 1806) from March 8, 1812 to 1829. He served as a State Rep in the New Hampshire House of Representatives from 1814 to 1816 and again 1819-1820, and as a State Senator in the New Hampshire 3rd District 1822-1823.

Aaron Buzzell
Birth:
Dec. 31, 1764
Gilmanton,
Belknap County, New
Hampshire
Death:
Oct. 21, 1854
Barrington, Strafford County,
New Hampshire
Burial:
Pine Grove Cemetery,
Barrington, Strafford County,
New Hampshire

Rev. Aaron and his brother Rev. John Buzzell and Rev. Benjamin Randall were the people who started the Free Will Baptist Church of Middleton in 1790. The branches of both brothers and family members were all Free Will Baptists.

Alvah Buzzell
Birth:
Apr. 12, 1807
Parsonsfield,
York County, Maine
Death:
Apr. 2, 1888
Southborough,
Worcester County,
Massachusetts
Burial:
Lake View Cemetery,
East Andover,
Merrimack County,
New Hampshire

Reverend Alvah Buzzell, son of Reverend John Buzzell, was born in Parsonfield, Maine on April 11, 1807. He was converted at the age of eighteen and ordained as pastor of the church at Barnstead, New Hampshire in June 1834 by Reverend Enoch Place. He has had the care of twelve churches and helped organized six churches. He has baptized many hundreds. At the breaking out of the Civil War, when he was fifty-four, he followed his sons Frank and John to the front, caring for the sick and wounded, and preaching the gospel and helping the Negro to school privileges.

David Calley
Birth:
Nov. 8, 1815
Holderness, Grafton County
New Hampshire
Death:
Dec. 23, 1906
Bristol, Grafton County
New Hampshire,
Burial:
Green Grove Cemetery
Ashland, Grafton County
New Hampshire

David Calley's career as a clergyman was a remarkable one. At the age of 23 years he professed religion, and the next year, 1837, he received a license to preach. In May 1942, at a session of the Sandwich Quarterly Meeting he was ordained, and a month later became the pastor of the Free Baptist Church at North Tunbridge, Vermont, where he remained until 1847. In September 1852 he began his second pastorate at Bristol, which continued for seven years. He then returned to Tunbridge, Vermont. where he remained three years, and again assumed the pastoral charge of the church at Bristol and continued for another seven years. He thus served the Bristol church as pastor for sixteen years. To no other man does the Free Baptist Church of Bristol owe so much as to the Reverend David Calley. He was a man of great natural ability, an excellent preacher, devoted, godly and his pure life and labors endeared him to all classes in the community. He was of fine personal presence, standing six feet two inches. Mr Calley four times had a seat in the Legislature. He represented Holderness in 1853, Bristol in 1872, and 1873 and Sandwich in 1885.

Carter E Cate
Birth:
Aug. 26, 1852
Loudon
Merrimack County
New Hampshire
Death:
Jan. 18, 1927
Cranston
Providence County
Rhode Island

Burial:
Bayside Cemetery
Laconia
Belknap County, New
Hampshire

He graduated at Dartmouth College in 1876 and studied for the ministry at Boston University. His ministry was in the states of New Hampshire, Vermont, Mass., Maine and Rhode Island. His last pastorate was with the Roger Williams Church in Providence, Rhode Island 1897-1895. Spouse: Electa A. Dunavan Cate (1854 - 1929).

John Caverly
Birth:
Aug. 23, 1789
Barrington
Strafford County
New Hampshire
Death:
Mar. 23, 1863
Strafford
Strafford County
New Hampshire
Burial:
Caverly Hill Cemetery

Strafford
Strafford County
New Hampshire

Rev. John Caverly died of heart disease in his 74th year. He was the eldest son of Lieutenant John Caverly and his mother was a sister of Rev. Joseph Boody, all of Strafford. He was converted in the famous revival of 1824, and June 2nd was baptized and joined the Third Strafford church. About a later he began to preach and at the request from his church a council from the New Durham Quarterly Meeting (QM) met at his church and ordained him Sept. 6, 1827, as an evangelist in the presence of 1000 persons. He soon entered upon a life-long pastorate with the Fourth Strafford church. He had a revival gift. He loved his denomination and was true to her benevolent interests. He was trustee of Strafford Academy nearly twenty years at an expense to himself of over $300 besides his time. He was an agent for a large manufacturing company for many years, bearing large and responsible interests. The house of worship at Bow Lake was erected by his means and influence. His wife, Miss Nancy French of New Durham, died in 1855 leaving four children. For several years he bore up with patience and trust under the disease which caused his death. He selected Rev. Enoch Place to preach his funeral sermon.

Arthur Caverno
Birth:
Apr. 6, 1801
Strafford, Strafford County,
New Hampshire
Death:
Jul. 15, 1876
Dover, Strafford County,
New Hampshire
Burial:
Pine Hill Cemetery,
Dover, Strafford County,
New Hampshire

Caverno died at aged 75 years.
He was the son of Jeremiah and Mary Brewster Caverno, and great-grandson of Arthur Caverno (or Cavano), of Scotch Irish nationality, who came to this country soon after 1735.

He was born in Strafford (then Barrington), N. H., He was in a twofold sense one of the fathers of the denomination. He had been more than fifty-four years in its ministry, and, at a formative period of its history, he exerted a controlling influence.

When seventeen years of age he became a Christian, after a severe struggle with unbelief occasioned by deep conviction of sin. He was baptized by Rev.

Enoch Place, Oct. 11, 1818. He attended Gilmanton Academy six months, and afterwards studied in th academy at Newfield's village in New Market. He obtained what was, in those days, an excellent academic education and taught school successfully in various places. He yielded more cheerfully than many to the call to preach, and began at the age of nineteen. Aug. 23, 1822, at the age of twenty-one he was licensed by the New Durham Q. M. He was ordained June 17, 1823, in an oak grove on his father's homestead by a council consisting of Rev's Samuel B. Dyer, Moses Bean, David Harriman, Enoch Place and William Buzzell. David Harriman preached the sermon.

He was married December 23d to Mrs. Olive H. Foss of Strafford. The next year he taught school in Epsom.

Through his ministry there a church was gathered of which he was pastor till the autumn of 1827. The revival, the first year, was extensive. He also preached and baptized in Nottingham and Raymond. Rev. D. P. Cilley and two other ministers were converted ouring this time.

His second pastorate was at Contoocook. His first sermon there was published in the *Morning Star*. Text, "The Powers Of Heaven Shall Be Shaken."

The first year, 1830, a revival of remarkable power and extent was witnessed. People were converted at their homes, in their shops, on their farms, going to and returning from meetings.

The church more than doubled its membership and the good influence of the work lasted many years. He continued there five years. For three years, ending in 1836, he was pastor at Great Falls; the next two years financial agent of Strafford Academy; pastor of Roger Williams church, Providence, R. I. one year, eliding in the fall of 1839; assistant pastor in Lowell, Mass., six months; pastor in Charleston, Mass., two and a half years; pastor in Bangor, Me., three years, ending in the fall of 1845; stated supply in Portsmouth, N. H., at the Old South, until the spring of 1847; pastor in Candia two years; pastor in Dover three years, when the house of worship was changed to its present locality on Charles Street; stated supply in Concord several months in 1852, and several months in South Berwick, Me.; then pastor two years in Biddeford, Me.

His wife, who had helped him thirty-one years, died in Dover, N. H., Jan. 30, J854.

The next year he married Mrs. Isabel J. Sule, of Bath, Me.

He preached for the First church, Dover, a year, then in New Market a year. For two years, ending in 1860, he was pastor in Gardiner, Me. He then preached in Strafford Centre, Laconia, and Alton Corner, a few months in each place. For two years, ending in 1866, he was pastor at South Parsonfield, Me.

He next lived in Great Falls, N. H., and preached for the Baptist church at Little River Falls in Lebanon, Me., and in Berwick at Cranberry Meadow. Then he was pastor in North Berwick two years, and lastly in Candia again two years. In some places there were revivals, in others he trained the forces.

He was a preacher fifty-six years, an ordained minister fifty-three years. He preached 6,000 sermons, baptized 480 persons, married 320 couples, and attended 500 funerals. As a preacher, he was systematic in his presentation of truth, apt and forcible in his illustrations. He was a diligent student of the Bible and a careful observer' of men and things about him. His usual method was to preach from a well-prepared skeleton, and many of his sermons were afterwards 'written out in full. He possessed a voice of more than ordinary sweetness and power.

He was affable and courteous in manner, social in disposition, and a general favorite in all the families where he was known.

He helped forward every denominational enterprise.

He began to write for the *Morning Star* the first year of its existence, and contributed more or less every year during his life. His last article appeared in the number issued during the week of his death. He early published a series on the "Support of the Ministry," which helped to introduce the practice of stipulated salaries. He was himself the first minister in the denomination who received a stipulated. Salary.

He had great influence in

removing the practice of feet washing which prevailed in some measure.

He was a member of the first General Conference, and assisted in organizing the Home and Foreign Mission Societies. He was greatly interested in all the educational movements. Other good causes received his earnest support. He lectured often in many places on temperance, and helped in the organization of some of the earliest Total Abstinence Societies in New Hampshire. He labored much for the abolition of capital punishment.

His last years were spent in Dover. The Sunday before his death he preached in Alton. His funeral services were conducted by Rev. Joseph Fullonton one of his early converts.

Rev Daniel Plummer Cilley
Birth:
May 31, 1806
Manchester, Hillsborough,
New Hampshire
Death:
Nov. 14, 1888
Burial:
Pine Grove Cemetery
Farmington
Strafford County
New Hampshire

U.S., Civil War Soldier Records and Profiles, 1861-1865 Commissioned an officer in Company S, New Hampshire 8th Infantry Regiment on 28 Dec 1861.Mustered out on 17 Jan 1865.

A leading Free Will Baptist minister in the Northeastern movement

Peter Clark
Birth:
October 8, 1781
Upper Gilmanton, New Hampshire
Death:
November 25, 1865
Upper Gilmanton, New Hampshire
Burial:
Highland Cemetery
Belmont
Belknap County,
New Hampshire, Plot: D

He was born in Dialogue and had the example and instruction of a faithful mother who early told him the value of prayer. He was converted in June 1798 and was baptized by Elder R. Martin. In the next September he began his ministry in his native place. Elder Martin pointed them out to a bystander as a boy was hard to handle it in argument. In January 8, 1810 he was ordained by the Rev.'s Winthrop Young, R. Martin, and Hezekiah D. Buzzell. He became the pastor of the newly organized Third Gilmanton church. Great revivals followed and there were added on April 20, 24; August 22, eight; June 25, 1814, 22; October, 18, 31. In 1826 this independent church joined the New Durham Quarterly Meeting. In the 1829 session of the quarterly meeting a revival commenced which continued for months, spreading elsewhere, and in November there were 18 added to the church in others through the winter. A healthy growth existed in the church for years. And in its early days beginning in about 1830 the church began to have great interest in the cause of temperance. He represented his town in the legislature and was given to Christian hospitality.

Inscription:
Died in his 63rd yrs of Ministry.

Rev Stephen Coffin
Birth:
Mar. 8, 1792
Alton, Belknap County
New Hampshire
Death:
Mar. 4, 1867
Dover, Strafford County
New Hampshire
Burial:
Pine Hill Cemetery

Dover, Strafford County
New Hampshire
Plot: Sec 5 - Ave M

Ordained a Freewill Baptist minister in 1841, and was useful to the cause he loved, giving liberally of his means to its benevolent enterprises. His Daughter Christiana Cowell was an author and the wife of Rev. David Cowell.

Clefford Cole, Sr
Birth:
Jun. 11, 1772
Massachusetts
Death:
Sep. 15, 1852
Stark
Coos County
New Hampshire
Burial:
Percy Cemetery
Stark
Coos County
New Hampshire

Clefford was the son of Jonathon and Elizabeth [Crowningshield] Cole. His step-brother, John, was the very first man to settle in

Percy. Clefford followed shortly after and built a log cabin. Their elderly father joined them later in 1791.

He married Janet "Jint" Rowell, daughter of Capt. Daniel Rowell and Judith French. He was a farmer and a Free Will Baptist minister. They had eleven children

Inscription:
CLEFFORD COLE
June 11, 1772
Sept. 15, 1852

Rev Clefford Cole, Jr
Birth:
Feb. 16, 1813
Percy
Coos County
New Hampshire, USA
Death:
Jun. 10, 1882
Stark
Coos County
New Hampshire
Burial:
Percy Cemetery
Stark
Coos County
New Hampshire

Clefford is the son of Clefford Cole and Janet Rowell, daughter of Capt. Daniel Rowell. His father and uncle were the very first men to settle in Percy.

He was a shoemaker, station agent, Free Will Baptist preacher, and Fort Master. Licensed to preach 1842; 25-30 added to church first year. Ordained Jan 13,1845, became pastor of Milan & Stark Church.

On Sept 25, 1834 in Stark he married Almira Leavitt, daughter of Peter Leavitt Jr. and Mehitable Marden.

Inscription:
CLEFFORD COLE
DIED
June 10, 1882
AE. 69ys. 3ms.
& 22ds.

"He died rejoicing in that Jesus,
He had loved and labored for so long
Saying in his last hours,
It is blessed dying with Jesus."

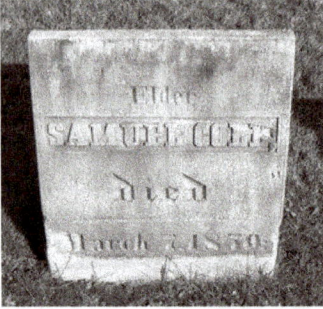

Samuel Cole
Birth:
Unknown
Salem, New Hampshire
Death:
Mar. 7, 1850
Lisbon, New Hampshire
Burial:
Sunny Side Cemetery
Grafton County, New Hampshire

In 1798 he moved to Landaff where at the age of 21 was converted. After deep conviction, he began to hold meetings and was ordained in 1827. His labors as a minister were confined mostly to Lisbon and Landaff. He supported a large family by diligence and yet found time to engage much in the labor for his master.

Solomon Cole
Birth:
July 8, 1821
Whitefield, New Hampshire
Death:
1902
New Hampshire
Burial:
Glenwood Cemetery
Lebanon
Grafton County, New Hampshire
Plot: sec a; Lot O

In a session of the New Hampshire Yearly Meeting about 1836, he was converted under the preaching of David marks and four years later was baptized by the Rev. Beniah Bean of Whitefield. At that time he felt called to the ministry, but put off the work for 20 years because of his lack of preparation. However, during this time he began holding meetings in needy places. He received license to preach about 1870 and was ordained in 1876 by Rev. C. N. Nelson and others. His early ministry enjoyed revivals and saw hundreds come to the Lord. He was a member of the firm of S. Cole and Sons Iron Founders and Machinists, Lebanon, New Hampshire, so he was able to preach the gospel to the needy without compensation. In 1846 he married miss Caroline F. Peasley. He also served four terms in the New Hampshire legislature.

Charles Corson
Birth:
1788
Lebanon, Maine
Death:
1860
New Hampshire
Burial:
Rochester Cemetery
Rochester
Strafford County,
New Hampshire

He was converted about 1820 and was baptized by Rev. David Blaisdell joining the Free Baptist Church in Lebanon. He began preaching soon after. After preaching several years he was ordained about 1840 and was associated with Rev. Blaisdell and Copp. He was not a revival preacher, but was instructive. His words were mighty through the excellent character of the man behind them.

Christ Has Led the Way

Thomas Cotton
Birth:
Nov. 16, 1766
Death:
Aug. 5, 1847
Wolfborough,
NH
Burial:
Cotton Mountain Cemetery
Wolfeboro
Carroll County,
New Hampshire

He was a farmer, deacon, and occasional preacher, "a man of very fervid religious Character." Family: Spouse: Martha Cotton (1768 - 1857), Children: Daniel Cotton (1803 - 1865), Saloma Cotton (1808 - 1823).

Arthur Elmes Cox
Birth:
May 25, 1858
Princes Risborough,
Buckinghamshire, England
Death:
May 21, 1942
New Hampshire
Burial:
New Hampton Village Cemetery

New Hampton
Belknap County New
Hampshire,
Plot: #182

Rev. Cox immigrated to the U.S. in 1872. He married Elizabeth Anna Hayes, daughter of Prof. Benjamin F. Hayes, of Lewiston, ME. Cox studied at Richmond College, Virginia, and theology at Cobb Divinity School. He was converted in 1869, and was ordained to the ministry June 24, 1883, by Rev's J.J. Hall, C.E. Cate, J. Fullerton, B.F. Hayes, and J.S. Burgess. He was a Freewill Baptist minister and held pastorates at Garner, W. Pike, Pennsylvania; Little Falls and Windham Center, Maine.

Jesse Cross
Birth:
June 9, 1790
Newbury,
New Hampshire
Death:
November 1, 1865
New Hampshire
Burial:
Church Place Cemetery
Wilmot
Merrimack County,
New Hampshire

In his early years he committed to memory, through the example in inspiration of the pious mother a large portion of the Bible. He acquired the rudiments of education in the common schools and when he was about 20 he was converted under the preaching of Rev. Timothy Morse and 10 years later was licensed by Weare Quarterly Meeting meeting. In 1840 he was ordained by the same body as pastor of the Springfield church, of which he had been many years a member. For 40 years he labored among the churches in Sullivan and Merrimack County and witnessed a precious outpourings of the spirit of God. His sermons were highly biblical, ernest and pathetic; his prayers were tender and suppository, yet wonderfully full of faith and power. He preached much in secret. He was a member of the Second Wilmot Church at the time of his death.

Silas Curtis
Birth:
Feb. 27, 1804
Minot,
Androscoggin County, Maine
Death:

Jan. 27, 1893
Concord,
Merrimack County,
New Hampshire
Burial:
Blossom Hill Cemetery,
Concord, Merrimack County,
New Hampshire

In the schools of Lewiston and Greene he laid the foundation of his education. He prepared for College in the Maine Wesleyan Seminary at Kent's Hill, but had health problems and could not continue. He was converted at age 17 was baptized by Rev. B. Thorn, and joined the Free Will Baptist church at Lewiston in May 1821. After his 21st year, he taught school several winters in Lewiston and Lisbon. In the spring of 1827, at age 23, he began to preach the gospel. He was ordained Oct. 4, 1827, when Bowdoin Q.M was in session at Topsham, Maine.

Ordaining members were Rev's Geo. Lamb, Aliezer Bridges, and Allen Files. He travelled and preached all around the area for the next three or four years. He pastored in Lynn, Mass, but the ocean air did not agree with his health, and thus, he became pastor of the Lowell church for five years. In Lowell. From 1852-1856, he pastored in Pittsfield, NH, and from there to Concord, NH, where he pastored. During his ministry he baptized 800 converts, assisted in organizing several churches and preached at the dedication of twelve church edifices. he was active and influential in every denominational enterprise.

He was foremost in the era of publication and educational institutions and organization of benevolent societies. In 1832, he was selected as one of the printing committee of the Printing Establishment and continued on that board for over 40 years, and was interim agent after William Burr's death.

He was appointed agent, and raised $17,000 for the New Hampton Institution, and gathered funds for Chapel Hall. He was corresponding Secretary of the Home Mission Society from 1839-1869, when he resigned. Also, he served on the Foreign Mission Society. In 1865, he spent several weeks in South Carolina and Virginia, superintendent of the work among the freedmen, and afterwards visited the schools and mission stations in Shenandoah Valley, and Storer College at Harper's Ferry. He was clerk of the General Conference in 1835 until 1868. He attended 20 of the 26 General Conferences. He made his home in Concord, New Hampshire for more than 30 years. In Concord, he was an esteemed member and Vice-President, of the "New Hampshire Bible Society" until his death. They recorded in their 1893 minutes at his death, "Rev. Silas Curtis, D.D., was removed by death"

Jacob Burnham Davis
Birth:
Oct. 6, 1830
Nottingham
Rockingham County
New Hampshire
Death:
May 29, 1905
New Hampshire Burial:
Homeland Cemetery
Bristol
Grafton County
New Hampshire
Plot: Sec. 16E, Lot 8, Grave 7

He was the son of Jacob and Anna (Davis) Davis and the husband of Mary Ann Perkins. They married on May 28, 1861

He studied at New Hampton Institution and graduated from its Theological School, 1859. He also attended Andover Theological Seminary May 1861-5. He was Ordained in Lawrence, Mass., June 21, 1861. He pastored in Mass., Rhode Island, Maine and Illinois.

He baptized over 400; solemnized 228 marriages; and officiated at more than 800 funerals.

Note: Additional information from *Native Ministry of New Hampshire.*

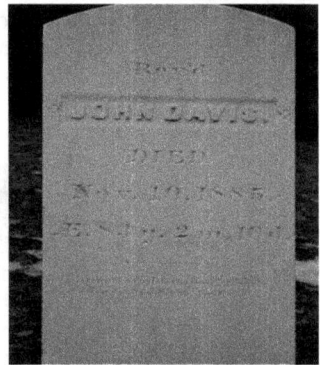

John Davis
Birth:
Sept. 1, 1802
Death:
Nov. 10, 1885
South Boston, Mass.
Burial:
Elkins Cemetery
Belmont, Belknap County,
New Hampshire
Plot: 10

Ordained 1830 at Bethlehem, and pastor 1830-8; the moved to Vermont where he ministered a number of churches until 1880 when he moved to Mass. And pastored two churches departing this life at South Boston while pastor.

Inscription:
I have fought a good fight, I have kept faith.

Robert Dickey
Birth:
Jun. 11, 1764
Boston
Suffolk County, Massachusetts
Death:
Jan. 2, 1849
Burial:
Bunker Hill Cemetery
Wilmot
Merrimack County,
New Hampshire

He was a member of Benjamin Randall's church and at New Durham, New Hampshire and went from Epsom, N.H. to Work as a laborer with a relative in Stafford, Vermont. The young man was touched by the spiritual needs of the place and began his preaching and witnessed over 30 converted. On September 10, 1791 a letter was addressed to the New Durham church desiring church orders. Benjamin Randall and John Buzzell and several times visited these brothers. It was the first Free Will Baptist church in Vermont to be organized in the spring of 1793. In june 1794 Robert Dickey was a delegate of this church with a letter to the New Hampshire Yearly Meeting for membership. He subsequently became a useful minister being ordained in 1814, but later his usefulness was lost when he joined the Shakers.

Because He Rose, We Too Shall Rise.

Samuel B Dyer
Birth:
March 21, 1779
New Market, NH
Death:
Nov. 19, 1846
Deerfield
New Hampshire
Burial:
Loudon Center Cemetery
Merrimack County
New Hampshire

When about three yrs of age his parents removed to Pittsfield where he grew up. He was trained from a child to hard work, which contributed to his possessing one of the best physical constitutions. He stood a little less than six feet, had a fine commanding form, with full, expressive eyes, and black hair, and was a fair-looking young man. He gave himself to God under the preaching of Rev. Aaron Buzzell, was baptized by Rev. Benj. Randall in 1798, and from then on he entered into the work of God.

He was married three times:
1) Mrs. Abigail Fogg, on 5th May, 1801. He set up his trade as a clothier, to support his rising family and his aging parents,

laboring in his mill from 12 to 14 hrs a day.

On March 7, 1804, he was ordained at Nottingham, and subsequently took charge of the FWB church in that town. He was blessed in this ministry.

He soon became extensively known to the public, and highly esteemed as an able minister, so that calls to funerals, marriages, baptisms, and other work, became so frequent he relinquished his clothing business and purchased a farm.

He was elected three times to the State Legislature. He left that place to devote his time to the ministry. He removed to Loudon in 1822, purchased a good farm and was well supported. He gathered a large church. Notwithstanding, the prosperity, he suffered the loss of hiswife, Abigail, Aug. 9, 1825, the wife of his youth, and the mother of twelve children---eleven who were then living.

He bore it with manly fortitude believing she was one of the most pious, amiable, and industrious women, but was in the end, her eternal gain.

2) On Feb. 21, 1826, he married Mrs Jemima Clough, a woman of good Christian character, benevolence of feeling toward his children, and was a good wife to him. But on the 18 of Nov. 1837, Jemima died, having helped raise nearly all his children. He resolved on visiting his children in Ohio, and declined a second term to state office.

3) After his return, he married Mrs. Betsey Morrill, of Gilmanton, the 12 of Dec. 1838. She was a lady possessing respectable accomplishments, and a good estate. In June 1839, they removed from Loudon to Deerfield, where God blessed his labors.

He was an ordained minister more than forty-two years, in which time he baptized many hundreds, solemnized between 700-1000 marriages and preached nearly 2,000 funeral sermons. He took great interest in the Deerfield/Nottingham QM, and attended for the last time in 1846, prayed at the ordination of two young ministers, which so affected many that it caused them to remark that they "would never hear Mr. Dyer pray again." He represented Nottingham in the Legislature, 1817-8. And was a State Senator, 1888..

He died from typhus fever which ended in quick consumption. Rev. Enoch Place preached his funeral, and the procession then went 18 miles to Loudon to lay him beside two of his wives.

Info taken from "Eminent Preachers" by Selah H. Barrett, printed in 1874.

Son of Samuel B. Dyer & Abigail Fogg; Samuel B. Dyer, died Feb. 9, 1897 in Hillsdale, Michigan. The source for this is found on Familysearch.org in Michigan Deaths, 1867-1897. The memorial for Samuel B. Dyer Jr.

shows his parents as Samuel Dyer, this Samuel Dyer was married to Lucretia Evans, they did have a son named Samuel who died at the age of 2 years.

Inscription:
Elder Samuel B. Dyer
Died Nov. 19, 1846 AE 67 ys 8
Ms.Abigail His Wife
Died Aug. 9, 1825 AE 42
Jemima His Wife
Died Nov. 18, 1837 AE 55
Side of stone;
Keziah B.
Died Sept. 17, 1831 AE 21
Edmund E.
Died at sea Feb. 1842 AE 21
Children of
Elder Samuel B. & Abigail Dyer

Andrew J. Eastman
Birth:
Jul. 23, 1846
East Parsonsfield,
York County, Maine
Death:
1918
Burial:
Blair Cemetery,
Campton Lower Village,
Grafton County,
New Hampshire,
Plot: A 85

He graduated from Bates College in 1974 and the Bates Theological School in 1977. He was ordained in the Steep falls, Maine Quarterly Meeting on November 1, 1877 by the Cumberland Quarterly Meeting. He held a number of pastorates in the state of Massachusetts and recorded many baptisms.

Daniel Elkins
Birth:
1760
Lee
Strafford County,New Hampshire
Death:
Jun. 4, 1845
Jackson
Carroll County,New Hampshire
Burial:
Jackson Village Cemetery
Jackson
Carroll County, New Hampshire

He moved to Gilmanton and in 1797. In 1799 he held meetings on Meredith Hill. In 1804 he had a revival in Jackson, and by request of the converts he was ordained at the quarterly meeting held at Sandwich, by Rev. Benjamin Randall and John Buzzell. He immediately returned to Jackson, where he baptized several, formed a church and soon made his home. Here he had a useful ministry for 40 years.

Rev Ebenezer Nichols Fernald
Birth:
Mar. 10, 1833
West Lebanon
York County
Maine
Death:
Jan. 15, 1898
Acton
York County
Maine
Burial:
Joseph Fernald Cemetery
Lebanon
York County
Maine

Rev. Ebenezer N. FERNALD, was the son of Joseph and Polly (Nichols) Fernald. He was converted in 1842. He was fitted for college at New Hampton, NH, from 1855-58. In Aug. 1858, he entered Amherst college (MA) and graduated in 1862. After teaching four years he entered Andover Theological Seminary, and graduated in 1869. He was licensed to preach in 1868, and ordained by a council of the Boston Quarterly Meeting (QM) in Dec. 1869. He was pastor of a church which he organized at Winthrop, Mass, from 1868 to

1870. From 1870-1874, he was pastor of the church in Auburn, Maine. The next two years he was corresponding secretary of the Education Society. From 1876 to 1883 he was financial secretary of the Home Mission, Foreign Mission, and Education Societies [Freewill Baptist], and treasurer of the same societies until 1885.

He then became publisher of *"The Morning Star,"*. He was married Dec. 27, 1863, to Miss Anna B. Tuxbury. Mrs. Fernald was a member of the board of managers of the Woman's Missionary Society.

Rev Jonathan Fletcher
Birth:
Feb. 22, 1002
Maine
Death: Jan. 17, 1881
New Hampshire
Burial:
Eaton Center Cemetery
Eaton Center
Carroll County
New Hampshire,

Rev. Jonathan Fletcher, received license for the ministry in 1838, and in 1839, he was ordained by the Sandwich

Quarterly Meeting (QM).

He was pastor of the Albany church till 1851, of the Third Eaton church the next three years, and of the Second Eaton church till 1871. From that year until his death he was pastor of the First Eaton Church. He preached also in Madison, Conway and Effingham.

He married Thirsa Allard, b. NH, and on 1850 census, they have daughters, Esther, 22, and Betsy, 13, both b. NH.

Timothy Flanders

Birth:
Jan. 12, 1787
Death:
June 17, 1849
Burial:
North Road Cemetery
Wilmot
Merrimack County
New Hampshire

Ordained Wilmot, Sept. 29, 1840. Timothy Flanders 63 yrs. and wife Abigail 77 yrs. Spouse: Nabby Abigail Robie Flanders (1788 - 1866).

Rev Nathaniel K George

Birth:
Apr. 2, 1816
Washington
Orange County, Vermont
Death:
Jun. 19, 1860
Franconia
Grafton County
New Hampshire
Burial:
Elmwood Cemetery
Franconia
Grafton County
New Hampshire

Nathaniel was the son of Joshua and Rhoda GEORGE. He was converted in Jan. 1831, and ws baptized in April by Rev. H.N. Plumb, and united with the Corinth (Freewill Baptist) church, where Rev. N. Bowles was pastor. He began to feel the call to the ministry and delivered his first sermon in a schoolhouse in the town of Bethlehem, in 1835. He travelled during the spring and summer preaching through the northern part of NH and VT, and in Warner, N.H, he spent the winter.

He saw many converted and added to the churches as he held meetings at various places.

Nov. 14, 1836, he married Sarah C. Kibbey, dau of Deacon John Kibbey of Lyndon, VT. Census shows he and his wife had two daughters, Sarah and Zillah George.

His first settled pastorate was in Washington, his native town, in May 1838. In 1839, he became pastor of the church at Franconia, NH. During four years of his six years pastorate one hundred were added to the church. He also pastored the Whitefield church, and Springvale, ME, church. Returning to Franconia for a visit, previous to a settlement at Bath, ME, while coming from the field on horseback, June 19, 1860, both himself and horse were killed by lightning. Only a week before he had attended a meeting of the Foreign Mission Board, of which he was a faithful member. He also met in the NH Yearly Meeting for twenty-three times.

Rev. Jonathan Woodman preached his funeral sermon from the text Matt 24:27, while six or eight of his intimate friends in the ministry, bore his remains to their last resting place. He died in his 45th year, twenty-five of which he had spent in the ministry. During this time between five and six hundred had been converted and added to churches. He was an ardent lover of truth, advocating all the benevolent enterprises of the denomination.

Joseph Granville
Birth:
Jan. 6, 1816
Death:
Jun. 8, 1897
Burial:
Village Cemetery
Fremont
Rockingham County
New Hampshire

Ordained by the New Durham QM 1865 and labored in New Hampshire, Maine, Nova Scotia and Vermont. Spouse: Abigail K. Allard Granville (1818 - 1893)

David Garland
Birth:
Dec. 18, 1791
Death:
Feb. 6, 1863
Burial:
Garland Family Cemetery,
Center Barnstead,
Belknap County, New
Hampshire

His ministry was confined to the New Hampshire area.

Orison Levi Gile
Birth:
Oct. 22, 1856
Bennington
Hillsborough County
New Hampshire
Death:

May 31, 1892
Bowdoinham
Sagadahoc County
Maine
Burial:
Sunnyside Cemetery
Bennington
Hillsborough County
New Hampshire

Studied at New Hampton Institution. Was a traveling agent for YMCA for a time and graduated from Bates College 1883 and Cobb Divinity School, 1886.His ministry was mainly in Maine. Married to Lina E. Nelson on Jan. 1, 1884 in Richimond, Maine. Born: Sutton, New Hampshire. Died: 25 Jan 1886 in Lewiston, Maine. Married to Sarah Eliza Libby on Jun. 22, 1887 in Richmond, Maine. Born: 13 Aug 1865. Died: 23 Jan 1931 in Bowdoinham, Penobscot, Maine.

Rev Edmund T. Gilman
Birth:
Feb. 21, 1844
Ossipee, NH
Death:

Jul. 7, 1925
Burial:
Gilman Cemetery
Tamworth
Carroll County
New Hampshire

He took the Methodist Local Preachers' course of three years, and was licensed by them at Great Falls, NH, in Feb. 1879. He taught and preached in neglected districts and Ossipee, NH. In 1885-86, he was a colporteur (seller/peddler of religious materials) of the New Hampshire Bible Society in Carroll and Coos Counties. On May 20, 1886, he was baptized by immersion and joined the Free Baptist church at Tamworth Iron Works. He was licensed by the Exeter Q.M. Dec. 11, 1887, ME. and was pastor at No. Guilford, in the same year. In 1888 he was engaged in missionary work in Willimantic, ME.

Moulton Hackett
Birth:
1772
New Hampshire
Death:
Oct. 10, 1830
New Hampton, Belknap County,
New Hampshire
Burial:
Chandler Cemetery,
New Hampton,
Belknap County,NewHampshire,
Plot: Grave 9

New Hampshire FWB Minister.

Ezra Ham
Birth:
Mar. 7, 1797
Farmington, Strafford County,
New Hampshire
Death:
Feb. 16, 1880
Gilmanton,
Belknap County, NewHampshire
Burial: Smith Meeting
House Cemetery,
Gilmanton,
Belknap County, NewHampshire

He became a Christian in early life, but did not enter the ministry till forty-three years of age. He was ordained a Freewill Baptist minister at Gilmanton Iron Works, New Hampshire, in 1840. He was instrumental in the organization of the church there and it was largely through his efforts that the meeting house was built. He was pastor of the church several years. In 1867-68, he represented his town in the Legislature; the latter term he served as chaplain of the House.

Moses Hanson
Birth:
Aug., 1792
Ossipee
Carroll County, New Hampshire
Death:
Nov. 21, 1868
Wolfeboro
Carroll County, New Hampshire
Burial:
Ossipee Town Cemetery
Ossipee, Carroll County,
New Hampshire

His father died when he was seven, and he was put out in a good home till he, reached his majority. In the war of 1812,as a musician, he served his country several months at Portsmouth. He married Oct. 1, 1815, Miss Joanna Hansom. At the death of his second child, in 1821, he was seriously convicted, but he did not yield his heart till the winter of 1829,and in 1830 was baptized by Rev. John Pinkham, joining the Second Ossipee church. The next year he was chosen deacon, and served the church well till he was dismissed with others to form the Fourth Ossipee church. He was licensed

in 1838, and ordained in 1840. In June,1842, his wife died; in 1843 he married Miss Hannah Seavey, who survived him.He preached in Effingham, N. H., andin Porter, Me., and finally came to Wolfborough,where he finished his course. He was earnest in reform and eminentlv a man of prayer.

Inscription:
"With heavenly weapons I have fought The battles of the Lord. Finished my course, and kept the faith, And wait the sure reward."

Pelatiah Hanscom
Birth:
1796
Kittery, Maine
Death:
Apr. 20, 1857
Epping, New York
Burial:
South Hampton Cemetery
South Hampton
Rockingham County,
New Hampshire

Early in his life he went to Barnstead, where he was converted and baptized by the Rev. n. Wilson. Receiving a license to preach, he moved to Lyman, Maine where he enjoyed a good revival. In 1837, he moved to Exeter, New Hampshire and connected himself with the Stratham church and did a good work in that locality. On July 5, 1839, he was ordained by a Council consisting of the Reverends John Kimball. S. P. Fernald, E. True, and J. Fullonton.

He soon had the satisfaction of baptizing his wife and his only daughter. After moving to Epping, he organized a church there in 1840.

Joseph Morrill Harper
Birth:
Jun. 21, 1787
Limerick
York County, Maine
Death:
Jan. 15, 1865
Canterbury, Merrimack County, New Hampshire
Burial:
Canterbury Village Cemetery
Canterbury, Merrimack County, New Hampshire

He attended Fryeburg Academy, studied medicine, and in 1810 began a practice in Sanbornton, New Hampshire, later moving to Canterbury, where he was a physician for 30 years. Converted in October 1810 he was baptized uniting with the church in Canterbury. He was ordained on April 11, 1838 and preached for more than 27 years. He was the moderator of the Ninth General Conference at Greenville, Rhode Island in October 2018; of the 10th at Conneaut, Ohio in October 1837; of the 11th, at Topsham, Maine, in October 1841. Harper was a veteran of the War of 1812, serving as Assistant Surgeon of the Fourth Infantry Regiment. He served in the New Hampshire House of Representatives from 1826 to 1827, and was Canterbury Justice of the Peace from 1826 until his death. Harper served in the New Hampshire Senate from 1829 to 1831. He was President of the Senate and became Governor ex officio upon the resignation of Matthew Harvey, serving from February to June 1831. In 1830 Harper was elected to the U.S. House of Representatives as a Jacksonian and served two terms, 1831 to 1835. He then returned to his Canterbury medical practice, and also became involved in banking, serving as President of Mechanics' Bank of Concord from 1847 to 1856.

David E Harriman
Birth:
November 11, 1788
Plaistow, New Hampshire
Death:
Dec. 1, 1844
Hillsborough County, New
Hampshire
Burial:
Hadley Cemetery
Weare
Hillsborough County,
New Hampshire

He was converted in 18 and seven and baptize by Rev. Timothy Morse in May. He soon began to teach and to preach. Then in 1808 he taught at Bangor, Maine and saw a good revival. Early in 1809 he returned to his hometown and married. He then moved to Candia where he was ordained on November 30, 1817.

John Sherman Harrington
Birth:
Dec. 17, 1846
Woodstock
Ontario, Canada
Death:
Dec. 30, 1911
Burial:
Pine Grove Cemetery
Farmington
Strafford County,
New Hampshire

He received an academic education, was converted at the age of 12, licensed March 5, 1870, and ordained by Rev's J. Ingram and George Donmocker on May 12, 1872. He graduated from Hillsdale Theological Seminary in 1880, and in July, 1881 took charge of a mission in Elmira, New York. Besides this church he pastored churches in New Hampshire, Michigan and had revivals in all of his pastorates.He was the father of Virgil Dewitt Harrington who ran the Oceanwave Hotel in Rye, NH.

Rev Josiah B Higgins, Sr
Birth:
Jan. 19, 1830
Livermore
Androscoggin County
Maine
Death:
May 16, 1878
Canterbury
Merrimack County
New Hampshire
Burial:
Canterbury Village Cemetery
Canterbury
Merrimack County
New Hampshire

Josiah B. Higgins, Chaplain for 12th Reg. NH Inf., received an invalid pension in December 1866, and his wife, Elizabeth M. Higgins received a widows pension, July 20, 1885. His service was from 1862-1865.

He was married May 1, 1852 to Eliza M. Cobb, and had two children, Josiah B., and Phebe E., who died young. His wife survived him a few years, dying in 1893, and leaving only one survivor of the family, John B., Jr. He had one brother, Franklin M., in the Army, who served in Co. "B" 5th NH Vol, and was mortally wounded at Fredericksburg, VA. The following sketch was penned by Chaplain Higgins'son: Chaplain Higgins was converted in 1850 and baptized the following year in Biddeford, ME, by Rev. J.L. Sinclair. He became deeply interested in Christianity and the Sabbath school work at Bartlett. He was ordained in Feb. 1865, at Alton, by a special council called for that purpose, and was soon appointed Chaplain of the 12th Regiment in place of the lamented Ambrose. After the war he preached at Barnestead and Wolfeborough and moved to Canterbury in 1867 and became the minister of the Free Baptist Church there for three years. The rest of his ministerial labors were at Canturbury Centery and preaching to the scattered brethren at Northfield at the same time. He spent most of his later life with feeble and destitute churches, getting nor asking but a small salary and of time without any at all.

As a man he was cool and deliberate, persistent in what he thought was right and sueful, industrious and purdent in all his efforts and habits. He maintained himself and family chiefly by manual labor. He was a kind husband, indulgent father and was patriotic and highly esteemed by his fellow citizens. As a Christian he was sincere and devout. He cherished personal piety and practiced personal effort in his Christian work. His emotional manifestations were of a subdued, tearful character rather than noisy and ephemeral. As a minister he excelled at finding fields of destitution and want, where he bestowed the best efforts of his life. He was a reliable minister; his preaching was expository, though, spiritual and was not in vain.

Rev John Hill
Birth:
1790
Strafford
Strafford County
New Hampshire
Death:
Feb. 28, 1837
Burial:
Meredith Village Cemetery
Meredith
Belknap County
New Hampshire
Plot: Section 2, Range 9
Lot 4

Free Will Baptist Minister of Meredith. Married a Polly Watson born in Northwood, NH and mother of Elizabeth.
Ordained in 1822 to gospel ministry in the Free Baptist, and resided in Meredith. A faithful minister, being true to the benevolent enterprises of the day. He was seen to fall, and before medical attendance could arrive, he had died.

Samuel Hill
Birth:
1784
Death:
Dec. 27, 1852
Loudon, New Hampshire
Burial:
Hill Cemetery
Loudon
Merrimack County,
New Hampshire

He was converted at the age of 18 and baptized at Canterbury, July 12, 1803 by Rev. Winthrop Young and remained a worthy member of the church there for 50 years. He was chosen a deacon in 1819 but was an ordained to the Free Will Baptist ministry in 1821 by the New Durham Quarterly Meeting. He held offices of trust in his town; was a member of the legislature during Jackson's administration. Many were baptized by him. He died respected and honored.

Rev True Worthy Hill
Birth:
Nov. 8, 1825
Loudon
Merrimack County
New Hampshire
Death:
May 10, 1864
Ossipee
Carroll County
New Hampshire
Burial:
Canterbury Village Cemetery
Canterbury
Merrimack County
New Hampshire

His father moved to Canterbury when he was four years old. He remembered the helpful prayers of his pious mother. At the age of sixteen he was converted, and September 7, was baptized by Rev. M. COLE. After ten years of wavering he began to preach in July, 1852, having received a license from the Canterbury church with which he was connected. During the fall he labored with Rev. Uriah Chase in Buxton, ME.

January 1, 1853, he married Miss E. A. Mason of Canterbury. He moved with his wife to North Parsonfield in March, to study, meanwhile supplying the Brownfield church, at first fortnightly. The church revived, requested the Quarterly Meeting to ordain and settle him, which was done Feb. 22, 1854. During three years fifty-seven were added to the church. In April, 1857, he began the pastorate with the First Ossipee and Wakefield church which

terminated with his death. Eighty were added to the church. He was a good mechanic and faithful preacher.

He was instantly killed in a saw-mill and was buried in Canterbury.

Marilla *Turner* Marks Hills
Birth:
Mar. 20, 1807
Vermont
Death:
Nov. 28, 1901
Dover,
Strafford County,
New Hampshire
Burial:
Pine Hill Cemetery, Dover,
Strafford County,
New Hampshire

She married Rev. David Marks, 20 Sep 1829, a Free Will Bapt. minister. They were involved in evangelizing, book publishing, and many works of the church.

then married Mr. Hills, who preceded her in death. She continued to live in Dover to the age of 93, a respected Free Will Baptist church woman.

She was elected treasurer of the Woman's Mission Society in 1848, and after the office of the treasurer was dissolved she became the corresponding secretary and remained such till the society dissolved. She edited and had published a Memoirs of David Marks, in 1846, taken from his diary and journals. She and her husband adopted and raised a niece, Julia Marks. Rev. David Marks died at age 44 in Oberlin, Ohio, where he is buried in Westwood Cemetery, Oberlin. Marilla and her husband were both active in the abolition causes at the Oberlin College. Marilla then married another esteemed FWB minister, Rev. Elias Hutchins, 26 Dec. 1846, a widower, in New Hampshire, where he pastored the Washington Street church in Dover. This union was not to endure for long as Rev. Hutchins' health failed in a few years and he died Sept. 11, 1859. Marilla

Abiel W. Hobbs
Birth:
1824
Death:
Feb, 6,1899
Burial:
Lakeview Cemetery
Freedom
Carroll County
New Hampshire

His ministry was in Maine.

Hiram Holmes

Birth:
October 3, 1806
Rochester, New Hampshire
Death:
May 1, 1863
Merrimack County, New Hampshire
Burial:
Presbury Cemetery
Bradford
Merrimack County,
New Hampshire

He consecrated himself to the Savior on November 8, 1827 and the next August was baptized at Crown Point by Rev. Enoch Place. Thereafter, he began to have meetings and appointments and on January, 1830 the New Durham Quarterly Meeting licensed him. He was ordained in Strafford, February 8, 1831 with Rev. B. S. Manson preaching the sermon. October 19, 1837 he married Miss Susanna Brown of Weare and in 1838 settled in Raymond. In 1839 he went to Bradford. During the next 20 years he made tours among the destitute churches of the Weare Quarterly Meeting. He was a member of the sixth, seventh, and eighth sessions of the General Conference.

John C. Holmes

Birth:
Oct. 1, 1804
Death:
Sep. 13, 1866
Burial:
Old North Cemetery
West Nottingham
Rockingham County
New Hampshire

He was ordained in Maine, Dec. 24, 1840 where he spent the majority of his ministry before moving to Barrington in 1853 near where he died. Spouse: Hannah F. Felker Holmes (___ - 1867).

Rev Leland Huntley

Birth:
Dec. 3, 1790
Marlow
Cheshire County
New Hampshire
Death:
Jun. 16, 1861
Campton
Grafton County
New Hampshire

Burial:
Blair Cemetery
Campton
Grafton County
New Hampshire

He was ordained in 1820, and ministered in Vermont and NH. Son of Isaiah & Elizabeth (Church) Huntley
Married 1st, Sarah Thomas in Brattleboro, Vermont on December 12, 1813
Married 2nd, Nancy F. Plummer on July 29, 1849

Henry B Huntoon
Birth:
Oct. 9, 1840
Salisbury
Merrimack County, New Hampshire
Death:
Jun. 18, 1909
Bristol
Grafton County, New Hampshire
Burial:
Lakeview Cemetery
Hampstead
Rockingham County, New Hampshire

He studied in the common schools and was converted in 1854. Licensed in 1883 and ordained in 1886 by the Wolfborough Quarterly Meeting. Besides his pastorates in that area he also served as a justice of the peace. Information from NH Vital Records at State Archives, Concord.

Rev Charles E. Hurd
Birth:
May 1, 1838
Death:
Jan. 27, 1911
Burial:
Pine Grove Cemetery
Gilmanton Ironworks
Belknap County, New Hampshire

His ministry was in Vermont. Enlisted in the US Army, Company D 4th NH Volunteers on 09/13/1861. Discharged 8/23/1865 Vermont and New Hampshire. Spouse: Anna A. Drake Hurd (1843 - 1908), Children: Eugene Carlton Hurd (1866 - 1868), Charles Austin Hurd (1871 - 1909).

Father, into thy hands I commend my spirit."
Luke 23:46

Elias Hutchins
Birth:
Jun. 5, 1801
New Portland,
Somerset County, Maine
Death:
Sep. 11, 1859
Dover,
Strafford County, New
Hampshire
Burial:
Pine Hill Cemetery, Dover,
Strafford County, New
Hampshire
Plot: Sect. 4, Lot 91

He was baptized by his uncle, Rev. Samuel Hutchins, in 1818, and joined the church. He felt called to preach and on 8 Jan 1823, he was licensed at the age of eighteen. He purchased a horse and saddle and entered upon an itinerant ministry for two years in the Farmington and Edgecomb districts.

He was ordained a minister at Wilton Feb. 1, 1824.

He set out as an evangelist in Ohio and Indiana for two years, principally in Marion, Clark, and Warren Counties, Ohio, and in Dearborn and Switzerland Counties, Indiana. The winter of 1829 he spent among Free Will Baptists in North Carolina, where many slaves flocked to hear him preach.

He returned to New England in 1831 in New Hampshire and Maine. In Oct. 1833, he became pastor in N. Providence, Rhode Island, until 1838, when he went to Lowell, Mass.

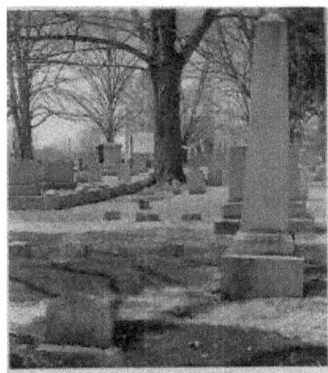

He entered a pastorate of five years at New Market, N. H. He was elected Corresponding Sec'y of Foreign Mission Society, an office he held until his death.

In May 1845, he accepted a call to Washington St. church in Dover, New Hampshire, and for a time was editor of the "Myrtle" and the "Gospel Rill" books used in Sunday School for children.

Dec. 26, 1846, he married Mrs. Marilla Marks, the widow of Rev. David Marks. He was 58 years at the time of his death. He died as he lived, a sweet, loving example of Christian trust. The heathen and the slave found a firm friend in him.

He represented Ohio in the

Second Gen. Conference, and was a member of the committee on an itinerant ministry. He served the General Conference in 1835, and 1850, on the committee on correspondence.

In 1842 he was president of the Home Mission Society, and in 1848-52 of the Education Society; in 1840-41 of the Sunday-School Union. He was a trustee 11 years, and corporator twenty-four years for the Printing Establishment.

Lorenzo Dow Jeffers

Birth:
Mar., 1821
East Haverhill
Grafton County
New Hampshire
Death:
Sep. 6, 1893
Grafton County
New Hampshire
Burial:
Number 6 Cemetery
East Haverhill
Grafton County
New Hampshire

He was converted to the age of 21; began to preach in 1846; and was ordained in 1854. He pastored a number of churches in the area where he was converted and ordained. He labored as an itinerant preacher and had revivals in his work. He was clerk of the Wentworth quarterly Meeting for a number of years.

Reuben Varney Jenness

Birth:
May 5, 1836
Strafford County, New Hampshire
Death:
Jun. 25, 1861
Dover
Strafford County, New Hampshire
Burial:
Pine Hill Cemetery
Dover
Strafford County, New Hampshire

Rev. Reuben V. Jenness, was the son of Nathaniel (1796-1882) and Lydia (Varney) JENNESS.He was converted at age fifteen, and baptized by his teacher, Rev. O.B. Cheney, joining the church in West Lebanon. He afterwards transferred his membership to Washington St. church, Dover, where his parents resided, and remained a devoted member for ten years. Feeling called to preach, he prepared for college principally at South Berwick, Maine, under the tuition of Dr. Grey. He entered Darmouth a year in advance, and graduated with high honors in 1859.He was married to Miss Emily C. Smith, of E. Randolph, VT, July 29, 1862, and was ordained Sept. 10, 1862, as pastor of the Pine Street Church in Manchester, not long before his failing health caused him "to go home to die." (i.e. Dover).He was a member of the FWB Foreign Mission Board, and especially excelled as a writer. He and had a bright future ahead of him, when he died at age 27 years.

He was a medical doctor, minister, and early church reformer. He was married 1804 to Damaris Prior, b. 6 Dec 1768 in Canaan, Conn., dau. of Clothier and Anna (Bramble) Prior.

Abner Jones
Birth:
Apr. 28, 1772
Worcester County,
Massachusetts
Death:
May 29, 1841
Burial:
Winter Street Burial Ground
Exeter,Rockingham County,
New Hampshire

We all have the same body, the same human flesh, and therefore we will all die.

Francis Kenerson
Birth:
Dec. 25, 1828
Albany, New Hampshire
Death:
Jan. 13, 1858
New Hampshire
Burial:
Chickville CemeteryCenter
Ossipee
Carroll County,
New Hampshire

He was 14 months old when his father died. At the age of nine, his mother moved with him to Great Falls. At 13 he returned to near the place of his birth to live with Joseph Bennett of Tamworth. At this time under, Rev. James Emery, experienced religion at age 14. Three years later he went to Hingham, Massachusetts to learn the trade of Carpenter. In the summer of 1851 he preached in Tamworth and vicinity till early in 1852 when he accepted a call to the Second Eaton church. Later he pastored a number of churches in the area. However, in November, 1857, his health failed and he preached his last sermon on November 29, at Tamworth in the very church where he preached his first sermon. Add age 29 years and 19 days.

Spencer Kenison
Birth:
1806
Death:
Mar. 10, 1884
Bartlett
Carroll County,
New Hampshire
Burial:
Garland Ridge Cemetery
Bartlett
Carroll County,
New Hampshire

Rev. Spencer Kenison, died in Bartlett, his native town,

at age 75 years. He early married Miss Judith Hazelton, daughter of Rev. Samuel Hazelton, of Jackson, afterwards of Bethel, ME. He cleared a farm and made himself a comfortable home. At the age of twenty-seven, he was baptized by Elder John Pinkham, and with his wife united with the church in Bartlett. From this time he was the leader of the church, and for many years successfully ministered to them as a licensed preacher. A lady visitor having offered $200 toward the erection of a meeting house, he and his neighbors took their oxen, and went to the woods, cut the timber, and soon had a neat chapel built.In 1864 he was ordained, and continued the acceptable pastor of the church fourteen years. The last six years he was unable to work. He suffered severely before death came to his relief.

"I see Heaven open and Jesus on the right hand of God

Thomas Keniston
Birth:
Dec. 9, 1819
Woodbury, Burma
Death:
Dec. 25, 1901
New Hampton
Belknap County,
New Hampshire
Burial:
New Hampton Village
Cemetery
New Hampton
Belknap County,
New Hampshire

He studied one year at New Hampton and was converted in his 21st year. He was licensed in February, 1842 and ordained the next year by the Lisbon Quarterly Meeting at Bethlehem. He labored for a number of years in Maine and New Hampshire where he baptized more than 1400 people.

We Are Made For A New Life And A New Body And A New Existence With The Lord.

Rev Clarion Hazen Kimball
Birth:
Oct. 11, 1844
Hopkinton
Merrimack County
New Hampshire
Death:
Nov. 8, 1901
New York
New York County
New York
Burial:
Contoocook Village Cemetery
Contoocook
Merrimack County
New Hampshire
Civil War: Company E, 1st U.S. Sharps Shooters (Berdan's) & Company G, 18th New Hampshire Infantry

Clarion Hazen Kimball was the son of Hazen Kimball and Mary Ann Baker. He was a 17-year-old resident of Hopkinton, New Hampshire, when he enlisted as a private August 27, 1862, and was mustered into Company E, 1st U.S. Sharps Shooters. He was wounded in action at Locust Grove, Virginia, November 27, 1863. Private Kimball was promoted to corporal March 1, 1864. Corporal Kimball was mustered out October 16, 1864, to accept a commission as a 1st Lieutenant and was commissioned into Company G, 18th New Hampshire Infantry February 13, 1865. He was promoted to Captain and mustered out the same day, July 29, 1865. After the war he married Lucy A. Challen at Sangamon, Illinois, October 9, 1866, and became a minister. He lived for a time in Holyoke, Massachusetts. Clarion filed for a Civil War veteran's pension in Ohio February 19, 1892, and received application No. 1,092,811 and certificate No. 984,486. He later moved to New York City, where he died and Lucy filed for a widow's pension December 2, 1901.

He attended Bates College in 1867 and Morgan Park,(Ill) Theological Seminary, class of 1869. Licensed in 1867 Weare, NH and ordained in 1872 in Evansville, Wisconsin. He left the Free Baptist and became a Baptist.

Samuel Knowles
Birth:
1777
New Hampshire, USA
Death:
Nov. 15, 1850
Ossipee, Carroll County
New Hampshire
Burial:
Fall Cemetery
Ossipee
Carroll County,
New Hampshire

About 1830 he joined the Free Baptists and was ordained to their ministry. In 1832 he became a pastor at Sandwich, New Hampshire. After a year and a half he moved to Eaton. In 1843 he went to Ossipee and continued to preach until a few months before his death of palsy.

He, That Has Learned To Pray, As He Ought, Possesses The *Secret* Of A Holy Life.

Elder Abner Leonard
Birth:
Nov. 4, 1777
Death:
Oct. 7, 1831
Hinsdale
Cheshire County
New Hampshire
Burial:
Oak Lawn Cemetery
Cheshire County
New Hampshire

A ministry connected to Dover NH Quarterly meeting, for about 10 years before his death.

Lincoln Lewis

Birth:
1799
Waterville, Maine
Death:
Apr. 21, 1858
Upper Gilmanton,
New Hampshire
Burial:
Sleeper Burial Ground
Gilmanton Ironworks
Belknap County,
New Hampshire

Rev. Lincoln Lewis was born to Thomas and Sarah (unk) LEWIS. He was ordained to the gospel ministry by the Free Will Baptist in 1822. He was married to Ruth P. (unknown m/n). He in 1824, was directed by the Lord in a vision to take a tour westward. He then passed through Parsonfield and was advised to go to Vermont, where Rev. Jonathan Woodman was laboring in great revival. On his way, through Franconia Notch, he says: "I turned aside into Ellsworth to spend a night with Elder Blake." He was overcome by a burden for that place, but the church there was divided, a separate meeting had been established, so he passed over the mountains. At Lisbon "I was kept awake most of the night by what seemed to me a voice saying, 'Ellsworth!--Ellsworth!' He returned the next day and discovered the church had met and prayed and were not surprised by his return. He then remained in the town a month; the church became united and enlarged; sinners were converted, and the same season a meeting-house was erected.

The Montville Quarterly Meeting sent Bro. Lewis with Rev. J. Farwell, in June, 1825, through the Exeter Q.M., and into "the Piscataquis country," to visit the feeble churches and explore the northern region between the Kennebec and Penobscot rivers. The report was favorable and led soon to the incoming of other ministers and the strengthening of the churches.

The ministry of Rev. Lewis was confined to Maine and New Hampshire.

In April 1858, he was moving his residence at Upper Gilmanton, NH. He went for a second load of goods and was taken ill. Recovering somewhat, he completed the removal, but sank into a serious illness that night and expired in the morning in his 60th year.

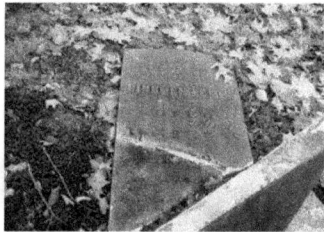

Nathan Chase Lothrop

Birth:
Jun. 19, 1839
Norton
Bristol County, Massachusetts
Death:
Feb. 15, 1920
Bristol

Grafton County, New Hampshire
Burial:
Homeland Cemetery
Bristol
Grafton County,
New Hampshire
Plot: Sec. 20E Lot 7, Grave 7

Son of Solomon Lothrop and Fanny Chase. He was converted at the age of 17, after baptizing united with the church at Colton. He graduated from New Hampton institution in 1861 and from the theological school in 1864. He was ordained in the South Berwick, Maine, where pastored 18 months. Most of his pastorate was in the confines of the state of Maine. He married on November 16, 1865 to Sarah J Lovejoy of Laconia, New Hampshire.

Francis H Lyford
Birth:
September 19, 1820
Pittsfield, New Hampshire
Death:
1891
Burial:
Union Cemetery
Laconia
Belknap County,
New Hampshire
Plot: Section 392-E Grave 6

He was converted at the age of eight and studied at Pittsfield Academy, Clinton Grove Seminary, and the Friends Institution at Weare, New Hampshire. In 1859 he was licensed and in 1860 was ordained by the Strafford

Quarterly Meeting, Vermont. His pastorates were in East Randolph and Thetford, Vermont; West Lebanon, Maine, Hampton, Laconia, and Meredith Ctr., New Hampshire; Haverhill, Massachusetts; Littleton, New Hampshire, to name a few. He was the author of the history of his hometown. In 1845 he married Miss Eunice Pickering and 1852 Miss Catherine S. Cox.

Josiah Magoon
Birth:
Jun. 25, 1758
East Kingston
Rockingham County,
New Hampshire
Death:
Feb. 5, 1841
New Hampton
Belknap County,
New Hampshire
Burial:
Magoon Cemetery
New Hampton
Belknap County,
New Hampshire
Plot: 4

He served his country faithfully in its struggle for independence and was present at Newcastle, Winter Hill and Ticonderoga. He accepted the Lord Jesus in the spring of 1780 and was baptized, joining a Baptist church. After he resided at New Hampton, in 1800, a remarkable revival was conducted by Rev. Winthrop Young. He was ordained in 1804 and remained faithful for nearly 40 years. Under the lead of brother Magoon, the church had almost yearly additions. For 10 years from 1833, 120 united with the church by baptism. He made occasional visits to Maine and Vermont, but most of his preaching was done in and around New Hampshire. He died at the age of 82

Note: Some information from the Inventory of New Hampton's Rural Burial Grounds, provided by the Town Clerk

---

Rev Benjamin Small Manson
Birth:
Mar. 5, 1802
Limington
York County
Maine
Death:
Dec. 7, 1879
Raymond
Rockingham County
New Hampshire
Burial:
New Market
Newmarket
Rockingham County
New Hampshire

Rev. Benjamin Small Manson was the son of John and Sarah (Small) MANSON.
He married Elizabeth Burnham,

and after her demise, at age 66y he m. Elizabeth Hoyt, dau. of Alexander McClure.

Rev. Manson was a successful minister. He attended school at Effington. In 1825, after he had been preaching, he was ordained in at the Session of Parsonsfield Quarterly Meeting held at Hiram in August 1825.

He and his friend and former classmate, Rev. John Stevens, made a tour into Canada, a the request of Rev. John Buzzell. Money raised was seven dollars. They had a difficult time at first as the people thought they were 'frauds.' Finally, they recognized they were not like the other itinerant preachers they had encountered, and treated them kindly. They organized the McClure Church in Farnham, and stayed until winter, but he was in need of clothing for which he had no means of getting, he returned to Maine, with ten coppers in his pocket.

Rev. Jabez Fletcher, a successful minister in Maine was one of his converts.

He preached in Conway, NH, and engaged in teaching also.

John McClary
Birth:
1784
Epsom,
Merrimack County,
New Hampshire
Death:
Dec. 22, 1821
Epsom,
Merrimack County,

New Hampshire
Burial:
McClary Cemetery,
Epsom,
Merrimack County,
New Hampshire

He was killed almost instantly by the fall of a piece of timber from the frame of a shed under which he was standing. From his earliest youth he possessed a remarkable degree the affection of his friends, and the confidence of his fellow citizens. He was repeatedly elected a Representative from his native town in the Legislature of this State, and two years he was chosen a Senator, by the fourth district.

James McCutcheon
Birth:
Unknown
Death:
Sep. 2, 1855
Burial:
Old North Pembroke Cemetery
North Pembroke
Merrimack County,
New Hampshire

He was ordained in 1828 and his labors were in New Hampshire.

Asa Merrill
Birth:
Mar. 10, 1783
Stratham, N.H.
Death:
Nov. 13, 1860
Burial:

Congregational Cemetery
Stratham
Rockingham County,
New Hampshire

His conversion occurred 9, 1800 at the age of seventeen the Congregationalists and feeling call to the ministry he began study the pastor of his church. Through differing from his church he was baptized uniting with the Christian church. After preaching much in the southern part of the town he was ordained there May 9 1827. Rev Mark Fernald of Kittery, Me. preaching the sermon. He served this church till 1834 when he and the church united with the Free Baptists. During the eight following years he enjoyed frequent revivals and a number were baptized. In 1842 the church lost its visibility and he joined the Raymond church and preached there for several years. He afterwards removed his standing to the New Market church. To his first wife were born twelve children. Sarah P. is the wife of Rev. O. R. Bacheler missionary to India, another daughter married Rev JT Eaton a Methodist minister, a son Daniel P. Merrill graduated from Dartmouth College in 1836 and for many years taught in Mobile Ala, As a preacher Brother Merrill was practical spirltual and rich in experience. Four years before his death he was prostrated with paralysis.

Nathan Merrill
Birth:
Unknown
Death:
Aug. 28, 1836
Burial:
Highland Cemetery
Rumney
Grafton County, New
Hampshire

He was ordained in the church at Gray, Me. by Randall and Tingley Oct 2 1787. Stinchfield says,' Merrill ran well for a while. He has been useful to the church by occupying his proper gift which was of exhortation.' He was pastor of Gray and New Gloucester church. When Stinchfield attempted to preach in 1793 he found little to help him. Merrill encouraged the church in military display declaring that they might innocently engage in parades, which annoyed his ministerial brethren. The matter was brought before the YM for four years where it occasioned serious discord. Alienation finally ensued and Nathan Merrill ceased to co-operate with the people of his early choice.

Inscription:
"A soldier of the revolution"

Atwood B Meservey
Birth:
Sep. 30, 1831
Appleton,
Knox County, Maine
Death:
Feb. 21, 1901
Belknap County,
New Hampshire
Burial:
New Hampton Village Cemetery,
New Hampton, Belknap County,
New Hampshire,
Plot: 307

Mr. Merservey chose medicine as his profession and attended lectures at Bowdoin College. He decided to become a clergyman and came to New Hampton in 1855 to prepare for college. He graduated from the literary department there in 1857 and past three years in the study of theology, also attending for six months the Andover Theological Seminary; plus, lectures on physical geography and geology at Brown University. In 1861 he was ordained pastor of the Freewill Baptist Church at Meredith Village. In 1867 he became principal of the Seminary at Northwood, returning to New Hampton after a year, to become principal of that town's Seminary.

The school honored him by establishing the "Meservey Medal" in his name, which is still awarded to a person for outstanding contribution to the academic and social life of the school. Mr. Meservey received the degree of A.M. from Brown University and a Ph.D. from Bates College. Republican in politics he represented New Hampton in the State Legislature in 1867.

Nathan H Milton
Birth:
1811
Death:
1839
Dover, New Hampshire
Burial:
Trickey
Brookfield
Carroll County, New Hampshire

He was ordained for five years prior to his death and was able to preach the gospel until failed in health took his life.

Elder David Moody
Birth:
Dec. 3, 1804
Death:
Apr. 7, 1892
Burial:
Sutton Mills Cemetery
Sutton
Merrimack County
New Hampshire

Labored in New Hampshire, Vermont and Canada. He was a delegate to the first General Conference in 1827 at Tunbridge, Vt. He attended nearly thereafter and for 50 times to the Yearly Meeting.

Rev John Morse
Birth
Jun. 21, 1794
Otisfield
Oxford County, Maine
Death:
May 20, 1887
Whitefield
Coos County, New Hampshire
Burial:
Riverton Cemetery
Jefferson
Coos County, New Hampshire

Served in War of 1812.

The first ordained minister in Randolph, NH was John Morse. On March 18, 1816, he moved from Otisfield, Me., to Randolph, NH. He labored here a great many years.

In 1887 he was the oldest man living that was here when the town was Durand (Randolph, NH). He lived at Jefferson Mills some years, where he died in 1887, over ninety years of age.

Mr. Morse held meetings in Randolph and adjoining towns. In 1824 a Free Baptist church was organized in East Jefferson, and practically placed in his care.

It consisted of a dozen or more members, and was in active operation while Elder Morse lived in Randolph.

In those days the people were poor, and the work of the minister was a labor of love. Religious meetings were held in schoolhouses and private dwellings. Ministers received little pay in money for services. On one occasion Father Morse walked twenty miles to attend a funeral, and then walked home again. He received a "present" of a pair of "feetings." He would get up early Sunday morning, walk to East Jefferson, hold three meetings, and then in the evening walk back to Randolph so as to be ready for his work Monday morning.

For miles the road lay through the wild, unbroken forest. One bright moonlit night a wolf trotted out into the road before him and sat down. The old man said he "was a little startled at first, but he grasped his stick more firmly and walked on. The wolf eyed him a moment and then trotted off." The old elder said "The exercise was good for him," and, said the man of ninety years as he straightened up, "I am better for it now." In 1837 Elder Morse moved from Randolph, and probably there has been no regular minister settled there since.

-History of Coös County, New Hampshire by George Drew Merrill; Syracuse N.Y.: W.A. Fergusson & Co., 1888.

Timothy Morse
Birth:
1765
Newbury, Massachusetts
Death:
Oct. 30, 1832
Burial:
South Newbury Cemetery
South Newbury
Merrimack County,
New Hampshire

In 1815 he was chosen to represent his town, and for several years said in the state legislature, and preaching as occasions offered. At one time three other ministers of Free Will Baptists denomination had seats in the legislature and boarded at the same house. When the days the work was ended they held religious meetings and evenings to as many as would come. Later, he abandoned his legislative career and gave himself wholly to the work as an itinerant preacher. His first tour was to Windsor, Vermont, where he was blessed in the gathering of the church of 60 members in 1822. In October, he returned to Rhode Island and added 42 to the Pawtucket church. Remaining there with the Rehoboth Free Communion Baptist Church, which was organized in 1777, and through his influence he so the church added to the Rhode Island Quarterly Meeting in August, 1823. In the summer of 1824, he saw large numbers converted in Randolph, Vermont. In July, 1825 he had good additions to the church in Danville. He remained in the area of Lyndon, Sutton and then removed to Strafford, Vermont where he had more than 300 people converted. His itinerant preaching took him into many states and regions. In October, 1830, he was an active and influential member of the fourth General Conference which was held at Greenville, Rhode Island. He had also been a member of the first General Conference. There was power in his presence which nothing could resist. He felt the power of Christ, and during his ministry baptize over 500 people.

Inscription:
Elder Timothy Morse
died Oct 30, 1832, aged 67 years.
The gospel was his joy and song,
E'en to his last breath, The truth
he had proclaimed so long, Was
his support in death.

William Alson Nealy
Birth:
Nov. 3,
Bolton
Chittenden County, Vermont
Death:
Jan. 28, 1890

Bristol
Grafton County,
New Hampshire
Burial:
Homeland Cemetery
Bristol
Grafton County,
New Hampshire
Plot: Sec. 15W, Lot 10, Grave 7

Rev. Wm. A. Nealy, studied at Green Mountain Seminary, and ordained Dec. 22, 1872. Pastored in Vermont, NY, and R.I. In 1887, took pastorate of Bristol, NH. Son of John Nealy and Sarah Cooper. William was a pastor of the Free Baptist Church in Bristol, Grafton, New Hampshire 1888-1890.

Samuel S Nickerson
Birth:
Sep. 24, 1835
Albany, New York
Death:
Apr. 2, 1930
Burial:
Sunny Side Cemetery
Grafton County, New Hampshire

He graduated from New Hampton Literary Institution in 1859 and from the theological department in 1863. He was licensed to preach on May 26, 1863 and ordained in Providence, Rhode Island on October 13, 1864 under the direction of the executive board of home missions. He was for four years a missionary to the Freeman in North Carolina and Virginia, from October 1863 to October 1867. He arrived at Roanoke Island, South Carolina and later was the society's first missionary to bear the word of life to this suppressed race. He pastored a number of churches in Vermont and also later in New Hampshire.He served faithfully the Free Baptist denomination from 1873 to 1918.

Jacob W. Nichols
Birth:
Nov. 25, 1823
Death:
Nov. 16, 1863
Burial:
Davis Meeting House Cemetery
Carroll County,
New Hampshire

Ordained, Effingham, March 1858, and pastor, First Church there, 1858-60 ;there to other churches before going to Effingham, July1863 where dies.

John Norris

Birth:
June, 1804
Death:
Aug. 15, 1870
Burial:
Glenwood Cemetery
Littleton
Grafton County, New Hampshire

He was married in October 1825 to Polly Sleeper. He was converted in March, 1828 and baptized in May by the Rev. Nathaniel Bowles joining the church in his town. Began to preach in 1839 and was soon ordained. He served for many years in New Hampshire and Vermont. After the death of Polly he married Mrs Ruth Nurse in December, 1861. He was thrown from a wagon receiving fatal injuries from which he died.

Josiah Norris, Sr

Birth:
Jul., 1779
Orange County, Vermont
Death:
Jan. 12, 1862
New Hampshire
Burial:
Wentworth Village Cemetery
Wentworth
Grafton County, New Hampshire

The son of Samuel Norris 1734 to 1816 and Huldah Bartlett 1734 to 1780 grew up in Corinth Vermont and continued living there until after marriage. He married, Aug. 25, 1801, Polly Adams, who was born in Moultonboro', N. H., Jan. 5, 1787.

A Baptist minister he began when young, he continued his ministry a Freewill Baptist thru Vermont and New Hampshire. Went to Hanover New Hampshire in 1812. Went from Dorchester to Wentworth New Hampshire. A man who truly loved the Lord Jesus Christ and strong Christian.

Micajah Otis

Birth:
May 21, 1747
Barrington,Strafford County,
New Hampshire
Death:
May 20, 1821
Barrington, Strafford County,
New Hampshire
Burial:
Center
Strafford Cemetery,
Strafford, Strafford County,
New Hampshire

Otis was very instrumental in the development of the early northeastern Free Will Baptist Church, along with Elders John Buzzell, and other church fathers. He was dedicated to his church and its doctrine of Free Grace, Free Will, and Free

Salvation to all. He preached until he died at nearly 74 years of age. In 1776, Micajah signed the Pledge to Support the American Revolution at Barrington, N. H. He was ordained a Free Will Baptist clergyman, and was a very respected and effective minister.

Rev Cumins Paris
Birth:
Sep. 24, 1810
Turnbridge, Vermont
Death:
Jul. 4, 1898
Burial:
Pine Hill Cemetery
Wolfeboro
Carroll County
New Hampshire

His father went from home when he was two yrs old, and he lived in the family of Thomas Button till his 17th year, his mother meanwhile dying. He was converted at sixteen and baptized by Rev. Geo S. Hackett, uniting with the Turnbridge church. He was at that time unable to read. At the age of twenty-one he went with his brother to work in Lowell, MA.

Here kind friends aided him and he was soon teaching a class in Sunday-school. At the age of 27, under the encouragement of his pastor, Rev. Nathaniel Thurston, he entered Strafford Academy and studied five terms.

Returning to Lowell, he married Eliza Martin, and soon after moved to Parsonfield, Maine, and entered the first class formed in the denomination in theology.

After a year of study he accepted a call to Eaton, NH. In three years he setled at Alexandria for two years and Andover NH one year. He then moved to Wolfborough, where, at the ripe old age, he now resides. He has been an acceptable minister and a worthy example.

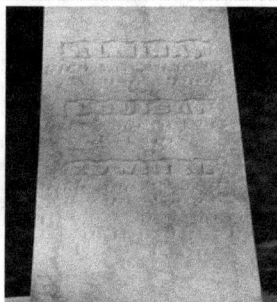

A. C. Peaslee
Birth:
May 29, 1832
Death:
Jul. 1, 1876
West Topsham
Orange County, Vermont
Burial:
Old South Sutton Cemetery
Sutton, Merrimack County,
New Hampshire

Rev. Arthue C. Peaslee, the son of Rev. Isaac and Hannah Peaslee, was born in Sutton, N.H. He was converted at the age of thirty-three, and soon after, he attended school at New Hampton, NH with the ministry in view. He was ordained at Newfield, ME, May 5, 1868, where there had been a revival under his labors. In the fall of 1874, he attended the Vermont Yearly Meeting at West Topsham. He with others, remained and held a series of meetings which resulted in his being chosen pastor. The work prospered under his labors. He held seven pastorates, in nearly all of which there was revival interest.

Isaac Peaslee
Birth:
Jun. 9, 1795
Death:
May 11, 1884
Sutton
Merrimack County,
New Hampshire
Burial:
Old South Sutton Cemetery
Sutton
Merrimack County,
New Hampshire

He was an active Christian for more than seventy years. He was deacon for several years in the Sutton Church, and on Feb. 15, 1832, he was ordained a Freewill Baptist minister and entered upon his ministerial labors, which were mostly in the Weare Quarterly Meeting (District). He baptized nearly one hundred in his own town.
Inscription:
Rev. ISAAC PEASLEE
DIED
May 11, 1884AE 89 yrs.

Elder Dudley Pettingill
Birth:
Mar. 21, 1786
Weare
Hillsborough County
New Hampshire
Death:
Apr. 29, 1850
Thornton
Grafton County
New Hampshire
Burial:
Wildcat Cemetery
Thornton
Grafton County, New Hampshire

Rev. Dudley Pettengill, of Thornton, N.H., died, aged 63 years. He spent much time as itinerant preacher in the Middle and Western States. His labors were blessed at Sandwich, Meredith, New Hampton, and Thornton, in his own state. He visited and preached to all the churches in the Lisbon and Sandwich Quarterly Meetings.

Revivals attended his labors. He twice represented Sandwich in the Legislature of the state. Son of Dudley S. & Mary (Heath) Pettingill and the husband of Hannah Boynton.

Charles L. Pinkham
Birth:
Nov. 18, 1841
New Durham
Strafford County, New Hampshire
Death:
Dec. 22, 1903
Burial:
Riverside Cemetery
Alton
Belknap County, New Hampshire

He studied at New Hampton and at Bates Theological School. He was converted in 1854. Licensed in 1874, and was ordained a Freewill Baptist minister, Oct 17, 1879, by Rev's E. Tuttle, J.C. Osgood, E.W. Ricker, G.M. Park and C.A. Bickford. He preached at Greene, ME, while in school (Bates) and received into the church forty. He is settled at Northwood, NH, where he baptized ninety-five and received into the church 127. He married Mary M. Muray Dec. 7, 1885. He has been several years treasurer of the New Hampshire Home Missionary Society. C.O. G. 7th REG. NH VOLS.

Daniel Pinkham
Birth:
Jan. 7, 1799
New Hampshire
Death:
Jun. 25, 1855
Lancaster
Coos County
New Hampshire
Burial:
Wilder Cemetery
Lancaster
Coos County, New Hampshire

His name is enrolled in list of Freewill Bapt. ministers, in NH, and it gives the dates as here posted. "He was born in Madbury, NH, and labored in the ministry in NH, where he died.

Rev George H Pinkham

Birth:
Aug. 21, 1821
Jackson
Carroll County, New Hampshire
Death:
May 6, 1886
Lewiston
Androscoggin County, Maine
Burial:
Pine Street Cemetery
Whitefield
Coos County, New Hampshire
Plot: Section J, Lot 74

Rev. George H. Pinkham, son of Deacon Rufus and Mary Pinkham, was born at Jackson, NH, Aug. 21, 1821, and died suddenly at Lewiston, ME, May 6, 1886.

He studied in neighboring academies and completed his preparatory studies at Lancaster. He became a teacher and ever after maintained a connection with school interests. In youth he sought Christ and united with the church at Jackson. He studied in the Biblical School at Whitestown, N.Y., graduating in 1849, and returned to Jackson, immediately beginning to preach. He was ordained at Tamworth Iron Works, Oct. 20, 1850, and remained at Jackson till 1853.

On October 12, 1851, he married Miss Susan E. Meserve of Jackson. He was pastor at Laconia two years, at Shelburne three yrs, and from 1858 at Whitefield 18 yrs, where a church edifice was built and many were added to the church. After a few months at Andover,

he preached at Franconia two yrs, and at Meredith Centre 3 yrs. While at these places he taught fifty terms of school.

He moved to Lewiston to educate his children [Bates] preaching in the vicinity. He was superintendent of public schools thirty yrs. Three times he was county commissioner of schools in Coos County. He did much for popular education.

Rev Stephen Jefferson Pitman

Birth:
May 10, 1807
Meredith
Belknap County
New Hampshire
Death:
Jul. 31, 1876
Concord
Merrimack County
New Hampshire
Burial:
Blossom Hill Cemetery
Concord
Merrimack County
New Hampshire
Plot: Section: No. Addition,
Lot 27, Grave 1

He became a Christian in April 18, 1824, when seventeen years of age, and was the first person baptized by Rev D.[avid] Moody. May 25, 1830, at the age of twenty-two, he was ordained, and at once made a tour to Ohio, where he preached one year with success.

He was married in november 1833, to Olive B. French, and with his wife, and in company with rev's Dudley Pettengill and Gordon F. Smith, made another tour to Ohio and Indiana. After two years' absence he returned to Meredith.

He taught school several terms. He labored faithfully as long as health permitted and led hundreds to the Saviour. He was a good scholar, a sympathetic and winning preacher, and modest, upright and true.

He was town clerk nineteen years. The last ten years of his life he resided in Concord. The last five years he was a great sufferer from an injury which finally caused his death

Inscription:
Rev. Stephen J. Pitman
Died
July 31, 1876
Aged 68
Olive B. His Wife
Died
May 31, 1909
Aged 96

He who has gone, so we but cherish his memory,

David Marks Place
Birth:
Feb. 4, 1831
Strafford County,
New Hampshire
Death:
May 13, 1900
Strafford County,
New Hampshire

Son of Rev. Enoch Hayes Place. Served in Co. C, 324 Reg. Mass. Volunteers (Civil War).

In God Is My Salvation And My Glory: The Rock Of My Strength, And My Refuge Is In God. (Psalm 62:7)

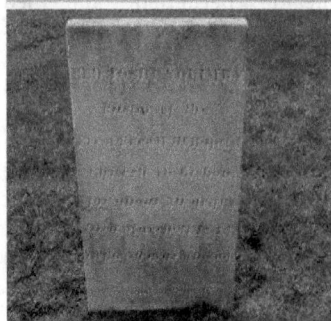

Enoch Hayes Place
Birth:
Jul. 13, 1786
New Hampshire
Death:
Mar. 23, 1865
Strafford, Strafford County,
New Hampshire
Burial:
Center Strafford Cemetery,
Strafford, Strafford County,
New Hampshire, Plot: 83

Elder Place was a very active and respected minister in the northeastern Free Will Baptist movement, and rode horseback, or in a carriage, to attend far away meetings, where he was in demand as a speaker. He kept detailed records in journals which were transcribed by William E. Wentworth, entitled "Journals of Enoch Hayes Place, 1810-1865." These volumes were published by New Hampshire Society of Genealogists in Concord, New Hampshire in 1998. Church records and books note that he always had sound words and wise counsel. His work as a pastor or preacher was of an inestimable value to his church.

Joshua Quimby
Birth:
Nov. 5, 1766
Rockingham County,
New Hampshire
Death:
Mar. 31, 1844
Grafton County,
New Hampshire
Burial:
Sunny Side Cemetery,
Grafton County,
New Hampshire

He began to preach in 1792. He was ordained at Lisbon in 1800. He was at first a Baptist, and in

1811 he became a Free Baptist and was for more than thirty years pastor of that church on Sugar Hill and his pure Christian character and exemplary life carried an influence that can hardly be estimated. During his long ministry he doubtless officiated at more funerals and united more people in marriage than any other clergyman in town or who ever lived in town." (History of Lisbon, ME., by Guy S. Rix.) Others helping in this church were Rev. Josiah Quimby, Moses Aldrich, Timothy Tyler and Jonathan Bowles. They erected the first church building in 1829 which served until 1884 when a new one was erected. Records state it would seat 300-400 and valued at $3,500. From this small beginning, the Lisbon Quarterly meeting has arisen, numbering now about 1200 members. Rev. Quimby was a man of good judgment, and a Christian of sincerity and honesty. He was one of the most faithful and capable men of his day in church labors and difficulties. He travelled to sit on committees and councils. Many old church records mention his ministerial labors, such as "Rev. Joshua Quimby here (Whitestown Free Will Baptist) in 1816-17, forming a Religious Society and several persons were baptized." (Rev. Benaiah Bean, an associate, was the first resident minister of Whitestown. He traveled all over the North Country, preaching his faith, and organizing churches.

Moses A. Quimby
Birth:
Oct. 5, 1821
Lyndon,
Caledonia County, Vermont
Death:
Dec. 7, 1895
Pittsfield,
Merrimack County,
New Hampshire
Burial:
Floral Park Cemetery,
Pittsfield,
Merrimack County,
New Hampshire

He was a grandson of the Rev. Daniel Quimby. He received his early education at the Lyndon Academy and at Geauga Seminary, Ohio and took the three years course for the ministry at Whitestown, New York.

In January, 1842 he received license to preach and on December 3, 1845 he was ordained by reference Daniel Quimby, Jonathan Woodman and others.

He had the care of 10 different

churches and his pastorates have averaged nearly 4 years. He closed the fourth pastorate with the Epsom church where he had been pastor for 10 years.

He baptized 160 converts. He was a member of two General Conferences and several years on the Home Mission Board. He built the new FWB Meetinghouse in Epson, N. H., 1854, which in 2007, has been moved into town and is being preserved for historical purposes.

Rev Daniel I Quint
Birth:
1836
Death:
1898
Eaton Center, New Hampshire
Burial:
Conway Village Cemetery
Conway
Carroll County, New Hampshire
Plot: Section B Block 3

He graduated from New Hampton Institution in 1869. His ministry was in New Hampshire, Vermont, and Maine.

Goram Parsons Ramsey
Birth:
Jan. 16, 1813
New Hampton,
Belknap County,New Hampshire
Death:
Aug. 23, 1876
Dover, Strafford County,
New Hampshire
Burial:
Pine Hill Cemetery,
Dover,

Strafford County,
New Hampshire,
Plot: Sect 4, Lot 91

We Are Made For A New Life And A New Body And A New Existence With The Lord.

At age seventeen he was converted and baptized by Rev. E. Fisk. Soon after, he attended school at Parsonsfield Seminary, a foundation he built upon to the end of his active ministry. He was ordained at Falmouth, Maine in Nov. 1839, and in June, 1840, settled in Epsom, New Hampshire. He spent one year at Hillsdale, Michigan, in charge of the Boarding Hall, and Mrs. Ramsey was lady principal. His pastorates always were fruitful, and under his ministry, churches obtained solidity, spirituality and efficiency. He was active in his denomination's Anti-Slavery

Committee, of which he served as Recording Secretary from 1843-44.He died in New Berwick about a year and a half after his last pastorate. Rev. O.T. Moulton conducted his funeral service. Rev's Hosea Quinby, his teacher, and Silas Curtis, who married him, assisted.

Vienna G. *Morrell* Ramsey
Birth:
Jan. 8, 1817
North Berwick
York ,County, Maine
Death:
Jan. 16, 1905
Dover, Strafford County
New Hampshire
Burial:
Pine Hill Cemetery
Dover, Strafford County
New Hampshire,
Plot: Sect. 4, Lot 91

At fourteen she taught school, and then went to Parsonsfield Seminary. She also studied at New Market Academy and Philadelphia Collegiate Institute. She married Rev. Goram P. Ramsey, a Free Will Baptist minister, in Aug. 1840. She was converted at age nineteen and soon became a contributor to the "Morning Star" and the Boston "Saturday Evening Post," and took a prize from the latter Aug. 5, 1840. She was a faithful helper to him in his several pastorates. When he served Hillsdale College in Michigan., she became the first lady principal there. She was deeply interested in foreign missions, and was very active in promoting the interests of the FWB Woman's Missionary Society. In 1851, she was elected as its president, serving several years. Before this, she was its corresponding secretary for three years. The Society often called upon her to deliver public addresses. Though she sacrificed her literary aspirations to home and parish work, her pen was not idle.

James Rand
Birth:
Sep. 15, 1815
York County, Maine
Death:
Dec. 24, 1888

Dover
Strafford County, New
Hampshire
Burial:
Pine Hill Cemetery
Dover
Strafford County, New
Hampshire
Plot: Section S-6 Lot 137 Grave 1

His father was John H. Rand, who was for more than 50 years a deacon of John Buzzell's church. He was converted at age 14 and baptized on January 18, 1830 by Rev. Elias Libby. He attended Parsonfield Seminary so he could teach. He was licensed from the Parsonlield quarterly meeting on September 11, 1833 and on September 25, 1840 was ordained by Rev. John Buzzell, B. S. Manson and others. He married on December 26, 1839 Miss Dorothy Fernald and they had four children. He pastored many churches in Maine and then in New Hampshire. Because he received meager offerings for his preaching he had to teach school and to engage in farming along with his work as a minister. He was for several years Pres. of the Home Mission Society and at one time member of its executive board. He also was a member of the Foreign Mission Board and was for 12 years its president. There were more than 16 ministers of the Free Will denomination present at his funeral.

Benjamin Odger Randall
Birth:
Feb. 7, 1749
Newcastle,
Rockingham County,
New Hampshire
Death:
Oct. 22, 1808
Burial::
Randall Cemetery,
Strafford County,
New Hampshire

He was the son of a sea captain. From age nine he followed his father at sea until age 18, when he tired of it, and at his request, his father put him as an apprentice to learn the art of sail making, which he followed until age 21. He served in the Revolutionary War as assistant commissary officer in the New Hampshire militia. He re-enlisted Sept. 10, 1776, and became a Sgt. in the company of Capt. John Calf., Col. Pierce Long's Regiment, New Hampshire Militia. A fellow officer, Joshiah Magoon, said that "He was accustomed to visit the sick and administer to them the consolations of religion; indeed doing largely the duties of a chaplain.

Thus many a desponding heart was cheered and made strong by his efforts."Upon hearing the Rev. George Whitefield, one of England's great preachers who came to America to preach, following his religious convictions, broke with his traditional religion of predestination and in 1780, founded the First Free Will Baptist Church of New Durham, New Hampshire, from which spread that church's beginnings in the northeast United States. His preaching was effective and he went near and far to preach, establish churches, and propagate the gospel. It was largely because of the exposures of the severe northeastern winters that his health failed and after 30 years of selfless service, died from lung disease, age 59 years, 7 mos. 27 days. The churches in that area erected a monument and slabs over his grave. His will was made 4 June 1808; a codicil was added 1 Oct; the will is on record at the county office.(taken from the book, "The Life of Elder Benjamin Randall, pub. 1827, Limerick. MA. By Eld. John Buzzell, a comtempary, who read Randall's notes and also had personal knowledge.) He was a great man who stood by his convictions and 'the Book.' His work, like the proverbial grain of mustard seed, grew to spread in all directions. He is remembered in books written about him and in many other ways after all these years. The large monument was erected a few years after his death by a grateful

church to this great leader. Inscription: West side of tall monument reads"Benjamin Randall died October 22, 1808, 59 years, 8 months and 15 days. Founder of the Free Will Baptists.

Benjamin Walton Randall
Birth:
May 4, 1776
New Durham
Strafford County, New Hampshire
Death:
Sep. 24, 1843
New Durham
Strafford County, New Hampshire
Burial:
Randall Cemetery
New Durham
Strafford County, New Hampshire
He followed his father on the homestead. Parents: Benjamin Odger Randall (1749 -

1808) Joanna Oram Randall (1748 - 1826) Spouse: Sarah Titcomb Parsons Randall (1774 - 1860) Children: Josiah Parsons Randall (1801 - 1808)* Sarah Sewell Randall (1803 - 1805)

Sarah Titcomb Parsons Randall
Birth:
1774
Maine
Death:
Nov. 8, 1860
New Durham
Strafford County, New Hampshire
Burial:
Randall Cemetery
New Durham
Strafford County,New Hampshire

For several years prior to her marriage Sarah, historically known as Sally Parson, traveled on horseback doing missionary work and was a early evangelist with Benjamin Randall. Sarah's father threw her out of the house for being a despised Baptist, but finally relented and invited her home just before her marriage to Benjamin W. Randall, the son of the founder of the Free Will Baptist of the north. Her spouse was Benjamin Walton Randall. and their children were Josiah Parsons Randall (1801- 08) Sarah Sewell Randall (1803 - 1805).

Rev Thomas F. Reynolds
Birth:
Jan., 1813
Death:
Aug. 27, 1864
Burial:
Chester Village Cemetery
Chester
Rockingham County
New Hampshire

His name/DOB/DOD, appears in Free Bapt. conference minutes as a minister having died in 1864, Chester, NH.

Caleb H. Richardson
Birth:
February 17, 1787
Death:
Apr. 25, 1868
Canaan, New York
Burial:
Wells Cemetery, Canaan

Grafton County, New Hampshire
He preached 35 years in Wilmot, Danbury, Grafton and vicinity. He took The Morning Star for over 40 years.

George Washington Russell
Birth:
Jun. 11, 1802
Woodstock
Grafton County, New Hampshire
Death:
Aug. 10, 1886
North Woodstock
Grafton County, New Hampshire
Burial:
Parker Cemetery
Grafton County, New Hampshire

He became a Christian when about 18 years of age and soon began to preach. He was ordained at Thornton Gore. He helped to form the Woodstock church, of which he continued a member until his death. The church edifice was built by him and in 1851.He was the son of Joseph and Mary (Robbins)

Russell. He married 1st, Margery W. Pinkham. She died and he married Sally Mills.

Alvan Sargent
Birth:
1814
union, Maine
Death:
1890
Burial:
Church Place Cemetery
Wilmot
Merrimack County
New Hampshire
He read theology and homiletics in Lowell, Maine. In 1844 and in 1845 he received license to preach. He was ordained in 1847 by the Weare Quarterly Meeting, in New Hampshire. He mainly pastored churches in New Hampshire. He baptized 203 converts, married 287 couples and attended 414 funerals. He was a Quarterly Meeting Clerk, a member of the General Conference and of the Home Mission Board. He served one term in the legislature. He was married in 1836 to Nancy Hayward who died and in 1880, then he married Miss Sarah Greely.

Seth Sawyer
Birth:
1808
Alton, New Hampshire
Death:
1892
Burial:
Riverside Cemetery
Alton
Belknap County,
New Hampshire

He was converted in 1831 and ordained in 1857. His labors were mostly confined to supplying churches where they had no settled pastor. He labored at Guilford village, new Durham, Middletown, Wakefield, East Alton, and Alton. He baptized among his converts a granddaughter of Rev. Benjamin Randall.

John Langdon Sinclair
Birth:
Jul. 10, 1809
Meredith,
Belknap County,
New Hampshire
Death:
Aug. 16, 1888
Burial:
Blossom Hill Cemetery,
Concord,
Merrimack County,
New Hampshire

He studied in the common school and at New Hampton he listened to the preaching of many of the fathers and before his twenty first year he was baptized by Rev B.S. Manson. In 1832 he was licensed. In 1833 he supplied the church in Lowell, Mass. and in May 1834 probably went to Dover, New Hampshire. On June 30 1835 he was ordained by Fisk Dana Hill and Pinkham and settled at Lynn, Mass. For nearly thirty years he was a member of the board of corporators of the Printing Establishment retained there for his business ability. He was twice president of the Home Mission Society.

He was President, Recording Secretary and Corresponding Secretary of the Sunday School Union. He was President of the Anti-Slavery Society. He was a strong and bold advocate of the right by prudence and economy he gathered in order that he might bestow upon the benevolent work of the denomination. From the time says Dr Brackett more than forty years ago when he as a pastor was laboring to build a church in Manchester and living on a meager salary gave the first hundred dollars of savings to our struggling Biblical School on to the day of his death he was a regular and liberal giver to all our benevolent causes. Many a poor student at New Hampton or elsewhere has received a regular donation from term to term to enable him to go on with his studies. Among the larger gifts already executed are $10,000 to

Storer College. $1,000 to the Sinclair Orphanage in India. $1,000 to Hillsdale College. $1,000 to the Concord church and $500 to the Lake Village parsonage. No man in our denomination minister or layman with so small an income has given so much money to benevolent work.

Rev Hiram S Sleeper
Birth:
Jan. 11, 1811
New Sharon
Franklin County
Maine
Death:
Aug. 11, 1867
Meredith Center
Belknap County
New Hampshire
Burial:
Highland Cemetery
Belmont
Belknap County
New Hampshire
Plot: 6

Rev. Hiram S. Sleeper's father frequently conducted the social meetings of the church, and at age twenty, Hiram was converted and baptized by Rev. Samuel Hawthorn, uniting with the Freewill Baptist church. For several years he was engaged in teaching. In 1835 he married Miss Cordelia French. After hesitation, he began preaching in his native place and received license from the Farmington Quarterly Meeting in 1839. His itinerant labors for the next three years were blessed. In October 1842, his wife died.

In December he was ordained by his Q.M. In May 1845, he married Miss M. A. Dyer, and entered on his first pastorate with the Georgetown church. After supplying the Augusta church for six months, in May 1847, he entered upon two yrars' pastorate at Gardiner. He was then called to Monhegan, an island destitute of religious privileges fifteen miles from the mainland. Here in less than a year one-fifth of the inhabitants were converted. In 1850 he began a four years' pastorate at Phippeburgh. After spending fifteen years in preaching he entered the Biblical School at New Hampton (NH) but he was called away, before the first year's study was completed by the church in Upper Gilmanton. Here he entered in Novemter 1855, upon a successful pastorate of five years. He spent two years at Bristol, four yrs at Loudon, and then began his last pastorate, at Meredith Centre where his health failed. After weary months of suffering he passed away, and was buried, according to arrangements made years before, by the request of his loving parish, at Upper Gilmanton.

As a preacher he ws earnest and fearless. He was a friend and supporter of all the benevolent enterprises of his denomination, and took deep interest in his country's welfare. He was delegate to General Conference.

How precious is the dust of a believer!

Rev Alpheus D Smith
Birth:
Aug. 25, 1813
Lebanon
Grafton County
New Hampshire
Death:
Feb. 9, 1886
Canterbury
Merrimack County
New Hampshire
Burial:
Union Cemetery
Laconia
Belknap County
New Hampshire
Plot: Lot 169-1

His father, Dr. Alpheus Smith, was a surgeon's mate in the War of 1812, and died after a few month's service, November, 1813. His mother was Mehitable (Foster) Smith. Dr. Smith was born in R.I., educated at Providence and practiced medicine awhile in that state. At the time of his death the subject of this sketch was two months old. When three or four yrs old, his mother moved to Hartford, VT. At fourteen he was "bound out" until he became of age. He made the most of his winter school privileges.

He became a Christian when seventeen years of age, was baptized at Norwich, VT, May 12, 1830, by Rev. H.N. Plumb, and united with the church in Hartford. On Nov. 5, 1834, he preached his first sermon in the dwelling-house of Reuben Paine. He then spent several weeks with Rev. Nathaniel Bowles, traveling and preaching among the churches of the Vermont Yearly Meeting (Freewill Baptist). Here he formed a taste for itinerating, which continued during his life. At the advice of Mr. Bowles, he visited a neighborhood in W. Corinth, VT, where about 25 were converted. During the next few months he travelled in 13 towns in VT as far north at Lyndon. In May 1834, he was licensed at the Strafford Quarterly Meeting (QM). Rev. J. Woodman being chairman of the examining committee. In the spring of 1836, in company with Ezekiel True, he attended Parsonfield Seminary. These two students preached nearly every Sunday from six to ten miles away. After the summer school he went to the town of Stowe, in northern VT, accompanied by Brother True. A revival followed with forty or fifty conversions. He then went to Corinth, much exhausted and afflicted with a severe cold which resulted in typhoid fever.

He was ordained at a session of the Corinth Q.M. June 22, 1837, held at that church.

In July he became pastor of the Dover church, NH.

He was married to Miss Emily B. TRUE, sister of Rev. Ezekiel True. In the autumn while engaged in extra meetings at New Market, he was taken with severe bleeding of the lungs. In the spring he returned to Corinth, VT and the following winter built him a house and remained there several years. He soon recovered so as to preach regular.

His wife Emily, died Oct 18, 1872, and later he married the widow of Charles Clough, Mary E. (Osgood) Clough.

Show thy vacant tomb, and let, As of old, the angels sit, Whispering, by its open door: "Fear not! He hath gone before!"

Rev. I. D. Stewart, D. D.

Rev Isaac Dalton Stewart
Birth:
Dec. 23, 1817
Warner
Merrimack County
New Hampshire
Death:
Jun. 7, 1887
Dover, Strafford County
New Hampshire
Burial:
Henniker Cemetery
Henniker, Merrimack County
New Hampshire

Isaac Dalton Stewart, D.D., was born the second child, to John and Hannah (Dalton) and the eldest son of their six children. His father's ancestry was Scotch, and several members of the family came to this country between 1725-1760. His mother was a descendant of Philemon Dalton, who came from England in 1635 and settled in Mass. His home was on a farm of 200 acres among the hills of Warner, NH, and commanded a wide prospect extending into more than twenty towns.

Isaac D. attended the district school of 25 scholars before he was five years old.

In Sept. 1834, when nearly seventeen years, he fully decided to live "with reference to God's claims." His mother had been fatally injured by being thrown from a wagon, and her death, with attendant circumstances, her prayers and instructions vividly brought to mind by this event were powerful motives in his conversion. During the next eight yrs he mostly taught school or studied in preparation for his life work. He was in Hopkinton Academy, at time of his conversion, and after this in Ohio about two years from 1836, engaged in teaching. While there he chose the profession of law, then returned to NH pursued his studies in the academy at Henniker until the spring of 1840, when he turned his attention to the ministry. He was convinced of his call to the ministry and 1841, entered the Biblical School at Parsonfield, ME, under instruction of Rev. Moses M. Smart. He then attended New Hampton Theological School, and studied under the Baptists. In the spring of 1842, he was principal of Henniker Academy, having as pupils, Edna Dean Proctor, and James W. Patterson, afterward US Senator. In June he attended for first time a session of the NH Yearly Meeting and from that time for forty-five years till the session that began on the day of his death he was absent but twice.

He began to supply the church at Meredith Village church and became pastor, receiving $140 per annum salary. Her he baptized 25 after a revival.

He was ordained to the ministry in the Free Will Baptists, Feb. 2, 1843; Rev. E. Fisk preached the sermon, and Dr. Simeon Dana, and Rev's Thomas Perkins and Samuel Thompson assisted the services. Soon after, Feb. 8, 1843 he married Miss Elizabeth G. Rice of Henniker.

April 1844, he began an eight-year pastorate at Laconia, NH where his only child, a daughter, Frances M. was born. He pastored many other places and into Ohio for his health, but returned, and became teacher of mathematics in New Hampton Institution.

In Nov. 1865, he accepted a call to Boston, and in April 1867, he became pastor of the noted Washington Street church in Dover, NH.

He made strenuous exertions on behalf of Storer College in VA due to a crisis that had arisen there. The Washington church sold their meeting house to the FWB Printing Establishment in Jan. 1868, he gave his time and strength to building a large brick church which they since occupied. Large spiritual prosperity attended his labors as pastor of this church. But in July 1873, he became agent of the Printing Establishment, having already been a member of its board of corporators fourteen years, and carefully managed the affairs of it.

Rev. Stewart was clerk of the YM seven years, and several times its moderator. He was delegate to three or more General Conferences before 1868, after which he was standing clerk of the Gen. Conf. until his death. He was rec. Sec'y of the Home Mission Society 3 yrs and on its Exec. Committee for several years, and held similar positions in the Education Society, and was fourteen yrs secretary of the Anniversary Convention.

He filled extended terms as trustee of Bates College, Storer College, and Hillsdale College (MI). Assisted by Rev. Silas Curtis, he prepared for publication the first volume of the *"Minutes of the General Conference.*

He wrote valuable chapters for the *"Centennial Record."* The *"Ministers' Manual,"* pub. by the Printing Estab., is his work.

A most valuable contribution to his Free Will Baptist denomination was his *"History of the Free Will Baptists," Vol 1,* pub. 1862, at Dover, NH. Preface: "In 1853 the Printing Establishment appointed a committee to collect materials for a history, and after five years' effort, the collection, consisting of books, records, papers, and reports from ministers, churches, Quarterly and Yearly Meetings, was placed in the hands of Rev. I.D. Stewart, to prepare the work for publication."

In his bio, "Bro. Stewart was distinguished for strict integrity, self-sacrificing devotion, efficiency, promptness and thoroughness; but to those who knew him as pastor and associate these traits became doubly impressive and influential through his uniform gentleness and unaffected kindness of heart.

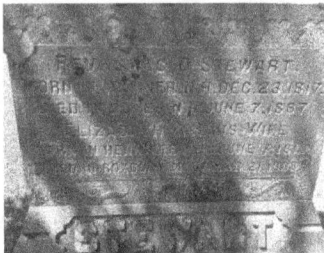

Elizabeth G. Rice Stewart
Birth:
Jun. 7, 1819
Henniker
Merrimack County
New Hampshire
Death:
Mar. 21, 1908
Massachusetts
Burial:
Henniker Cemetery
Henniker
Merrimack County
New Hampshire

Elizabeth G. Rice was mar. to Rev. Dr. I.D. Stewart, Feb. 8, 1843.

She was mother of one child, Frances M., b. Laconia, NH. She no doubt led an interesting life married to her husband who moved many times during his teaching, preaching assign-ments.Spouse:
Isaac Dalton Stewart (1817 - 1887)

Levi Streeter
Birth:
Apr. 10, 1806
Lisbon, New Hampshire
Death:
Jul. 22, 1886
North Lisbon, New Hampshire
Burial:
Glenwood Cemetery
Littleton
Grafton County, New Hampshire

He was a member of the Littleton church. He was born within the bounds of the Lisbon Quarterly Meeting.
He was licensed in 1826 and ordained 1881. His ministry was in New Hampshire.
He was a Christian over 40 years and 35 of those who use as an ordained minister.

Hiram Stevens

Birth:
December 12, 1806
New Chester, New Hampshire
Death:
Jun. 6, 1880
Meredith village,
New Hampshire
Burial:
Meredith Village Cemetery
Meredith
Belknap County, New
Hampshire

He began to hold meetings when he was about 15 and soon went to New York and for most of the time until 1827 preached with success in the various adjoining towns in the area. In April, 1825 he was licensed by the Ballston Christian church. He returned to New Hampshire in 1827 and in the following spring began to preach in Lowell as a Free Baptists. In June he was received as a licensed preacher by the New Hampshire Yearly Meeting at Strafford and in August of the next year he joined the New Durham Quarterly Meeting. He was ordained at Canterbury on January 20, 1830. He gathered a church at Lowell. He preached as an evangelist in different towns with much success. At Meredith Village there were many added to the church. After this he was at Farmington and Dover. He in 1852 he started the Belvedere mission in that part of the area called Centreville. He ultimately returned to Meredith Village where he spent his last years.

Edwin Byron Stiles

Birth:
January 16, 1860
Albany, Vermont
Death:
1917
New Hampshire
Burial:
Woodstock Cemetery
Woodstock
Grafton County, New Hampshire

He graduated from Bates College in 1885 and from Andover theological Seminary in 1888. He was licensed to preach in 1886 and ordained on February 15, 1888 by the Massachusetts Association. On June 25 he married miss Idaho in. Tucker a college classmate and after it became settled that the foreign mission field was to be his home. They sailed in November as missionaries to India.

Ada Henrietta Tucker Stiles

Birth:
1864
New Hampshire
Death:

1927
New Hampshire
Burial:
Woodstock Cemetery
Woodstock
Grafton County, New Hampshire

The wife of Rev. Edwin Byron Stiles. They married in Lowell, Massachusetts on June 25, 1888. She served as a missionary to India with her husband Edwin.

Rev William Swain
Birth:
May 13, 1788
Brentwood
Rockingham County
New Hampshire
Death:
Sep. 21, 1865
Burial:
Knowlton-Edgerly Cemetery
Chichester
Merrimack County
New Hampshire

William Swain, married Miss Sally Drake, Nov. 22, 1810, and in 1816 moved to Pittsfield, where

he became connected with the Free Baptists. He was ordained June 7, 1827, and next year he moved to Chichester where he raised up a church of which he remained the beloved pastor nearly forty years till his death. It was said by one who knew him, "If the New Testament should be lost to the world, from the chambers of his own retentive memory he could have replaced it. He was strong in faith and an example to to his flock. Rev. E. Tuttle attended his funeral.

Rev Levi B. Tasker
Birth:
Mar. 21, 1814
Strafford County
New Hampshire
Death:
Aug. 29, 1875
New Hampshire
Burial:
Baptist Burial Ground
Center Sandwich
Carroll County
New Hampshire

Rev. Tasker entered Strafford Academy at the opening in 1834, and continued four years. He had saved $300 by working at the shoemakers' trade, which he now used for his education. In 1837 he was converted. The prayers in his behalf when he became a Christian included the petition that he might be called into the ministry. For seven years he fought his convictions, and the remembrance of these prayers made the conflict more distressing. Unable to study, he left school and returned to his trade. As a layman, he was very active in the church in Northwood, which he joined at his conversion. He served as clerk and superintendent of the Sunday school. While a student he sent out the first call for a county temperance society and was active in its organization. He was excluded from his church becaused he opposed its withdrawal from the Rockingham Quarterly Meeting (QM). in hostility to the strong anti-slavery stand which the QM had taken but he was afterward restored.

In 1845 he yielded to his convictions, was licensed and was soon after ordained. He itinerated for a few years, and then settled in Sandwich in 1848. In that field he spent thirteen years out of the next twenty-six. Three times he went to other fields and as often returned. He once went to his native town and resuscitated the church at Bow Lake. Eight or nine years before his death he settled at Lyndon, VT and did valuable work there and in Wheelock Q.M.

The Lyndon Institution was greatly indebted to him at its establishment. He was clerk of the Sandwich Q.M. and of the New Hampshire Yearly Meeting (YM). many years. He was corporator of the Printing Establishment seven years and a member of its executive board, also of the executive boards of the Education and Home Mission Societies, of the latter about twenty years clerk. He was an excellent preacher, a good pastor, a wise counselor, and a worthy citizen. He had taken charge of the church in Sutton, VT, but after several months his failing health led him back to Sandwich, where he retained a pleasant home.

Rev Ezekiel True
Birth:
Jun. 5, 1811
Corinth Center
Orange County
Vermont
Death:
Feb. 18, 1883
Rochester
Strafford County
New Hampshire
Burial:
Rochester Cemetery
Rochester
Strafford County
New Hampshire

Rev. Ezekiel True was born Corinth, VT, June 5, 1814. He was fond of books in youth and became a Christian at fourteen, being baptized and received to church membership two years later. He began to preach at the age of twenty-one and was ordained at a session of the Corinth, VT Quarterly Meeting (QM) in 1837. In Jan. 1838, he began his first pastorate in Portsmouth, NH. which continued about 3 years and 100

were converted. He afterward held pastorates in Wells,ME; Ashland,NH; So Berwick,ME; Pittsfield,NH; Gilford,NH; Farmington, NH; Saco, ME; and Rochester,NH.

At the time of his death, which occurred suddenly, he was preaching at Walnut Grove, near Rochester. All his pastorates were marked by faithful service and gratifying results. He served as City Missionary during part of his stay in Portsmouth, and was a member of the school committee in most of the towns in which he lived.

He was the founder of the Rochester church, and the edifice erected soon after his death was named in honor of him, the "True Memorial Church."

His active intellect, fervor and power as a preacher, warmth of sympathy and congenial manners, made for him hosts of friends wherrever he lived.

Job C. Tyler
Birth:
unknown
Death:
Sep. 1, 1879
Canaan,
New Hampshire
Burial:
Wells Cemetery
Canaan
Grafton County,
New Hampshire

He was ordained in 1833 and preached constantly in the towns of Canaan, Orange, Grafton, and Hanover, until by old age. He was a main instrument of revivals in other places especially in East Andover and for years he preached in his own dwelling house. He died at 80yrs. 6mos.

Bartholomew Van Dame
Birth:
Jun. 21, 1807
Netherlands
Death:
Apr. 3, 1872
Nottingham,
Rockingham County,
New Hampshire
Burial:
Epping Central Cemetery,
Epping,, Rockingham County,
New Hampshire

He came over with Capt John C. Long of Portsmouth, New Hampshire in 1819 and came to Epping with Josiah Clark Feb 14, 1822 and served his time with Ensign John Dow from Feb 10, 1824 to June 21, 1828. He suffered many accidents, one that permanently maimed his right arm. In his sixteenth year with John Dow. He began to read, and thirsting for knowledge, he had in Epping acquired a good education. He studied under Dr. Timothy Hilliard, who deeply impressed him and with whom he went on lecture tours. After three terms with Dr. Hilliard he taught three months in Epping, having forty pupils. Again he entered the school of Dr. Hilliard, sometimes acting as his assistant while practicing the most rigid economy. In 1830, he entered New Hampton Institution. He studied mathematics of which he was fond. On Aug. 14, 1830, he was baptized in Epping by Rev. Israel Chesley of Durham. He prepared and published 500 copies of a small hymn-book, partly original. He studied Latin with, Dr. Hilliard, and he taught for three years to gather funds and uniting meanwhile with the Greenfield FWB church under Pastor Rev. John Kimball, where his membership remained until his death. He studied Greek under John D. Philbrick, afterward superintendent of the Boston public schools, and read the classics. He entered Strafford Academy in 1835, having Prof. John Fullonton as his classmate in Latin and Greek. He entered the Congregational Theological Seminary at Gilmanton Center soon after his graduation at Strafford. After teaching in various places in Maine and New Hampshire in 1837, he came to Epsom, New Hampshire to supply the vacant pulpit in connection with his teaching, and having a revival he held seventy meetings. Here, April 10, 1838, he was ordained by Arthur Caverno, John Kimball, and Daniel P. Cilley. During forty years, he taught thirty years in all. He was ever a promoter of education. He came and went visiting Washington and the South, looking on statesmen, while thinking and studying about the magnitude of the offense of slavery under his own keen observation. He went to gatherings, sacred, secular, and patriotic, delivering speeches abounding with information, and rendered interesting and fascinating by the quaint individuality of the man. He could hold an audience's attention for hours.

He left a manuscript of 10,000 closely written pages composed since 1834, among them a hymn-book, dictionary, chemistry, arithmetic, geometry, grammar, and lectures on anti-slavery and temperance.

Having willed to several churches and to the benevolent enterprises of his denomination his personal effects, he wrote in his epitaph: "This world I leave without a debt behind,"

Rev William H. Waldron
Birth:
1817
Farmington
Strafford County, New Hampshire
Death
Jan. 6, 1894
Burial:
Waldron F01-5B1
Farmington, Strafford County, New Hampshire

Studied at Parsonfield Seminary in Maine and began to preach, 1842. Ordained Jan. 26,

1848. Pastored in Mass., Maine, Rhode Island, New York and New Hampshire.

Inscription:
Hus. of Mary S. Waldron
& Sarah Clough

Granville C Waterman
Birth:
May 4, 1835
Booth Bay, Maine
Death:
1927
Burial:
Union Cemetery
Laconia, Belknap County,
New Hampshire
Plot: Section 87, Grave 6

He was a son of the Rev. Dexter Waterman. He was converted when 16 years of age and received his education at Litchfield Liberal Institute and Bowdoin College. He received license to preach in 1863 and was ordained on March 23, 1869 by Rev.'s D. Jackson, H. Perry, D. M. Stuart, George H. Ball and A. Aldrich. He held pastorates in New York. New Hampshire and baptized about 60 converts. For some years he was principal at Pike Seminary, New York. He held important positions on the denominational boards. From 1881 to 1886 he was editor of the Sunday school quarterly's and for years has been prominent in Sunday school work. On April 28, 1861 he was married to Miss Julia Mansfield and after her death on December 4, 1873 he married Marietta

Stewart. He had several years as a successful professor in Whitestown Seminary and has been active in literary and missionary work.Note: Interred 25 Apr

Rev Elijah Watson
Birth:
Sep. 2, 1777
Nottingham
Rockingham County
New Hampshire
Death:
Nov. 2, 1837
Burial:
Old North Church Cemetery
East Andover
Merrimack County
New Hampshire

Son of Nathan Watson and Ruth Hinkson. m1 Miriam Sawyer on March 9, 1798, m2 Rhoda Felch

on Sept 28, 1817, m3 Betsey Goss in 1854. Died aged 80 years 2 months

Source:
- History of the Town of Andover, New Hampshire: Genealogies By John Robie Eastman (1910)

Rev Horace Webber
Birth:
Apr. 19, 1807
Lyman
Grafton County, New Hampshire
Death:
Feb. 21, 1872
Ossipee
Carroll County, New Hampshire
Burial:
The Stevens-Burleigh Site
Ossipee
Carroll County, New Hampshire

Horace Webber was a Freewill Baptist minister throughout the state of New Hampshire. He baptized more than 600.

Nathaniel Marshall Webster
Birth:
Unknown
Death:
1827
Burial:
Baptist Burial Ground
Center Sandwich
Carroll County
New Hampshire

Rev. Nathaniel Webster, of Tamworth, N.H., was ordained in 1801, a Freewill Baptist minister, and for many years did good work in his itinerant ministry in Maine and New Hampshire. In 1804, he visited Richmond, N. H., in company with Timothy Morse, and having baptized thirty or more converts, gathered and organized a church. In 1809, he organized a church at Wells, ME.

Rev Dearborn Wedgwood
Birth:
Sep. 29, 1810
Death:
Oct. 7, 1876
Farmington
Strafford County
New Hampshire
Burial:
Pine Grove Cemetery
Farmington
Strafford County
New Hampshire

Ordained in 1844. His wife and seven children survived him. She was bn 1814, and d. in 1887, age 73y, at Boston, MA, but have not located her grave. Parents were Samuel and Betsey Deland. If found, please link to her spouse.

Abel Wheeler

Birth:
Unknown
Death:
Mar. 13, 1870
Burial:
Center Haverhill Cemetery
North Haverhill, Grafton County,
New Hampshire

When about twenty-six years of age he became a Christian. About twelve years afterwards he moved to Haverhill and was one of the original members of the Freewill Baptist church there. He was licensed to preach by the church, and soon after was ordained at Lisbon Quarterly Meeting in 1832. He preached Christ faithfully in several towns until obligated by failing health to retire from the work. He was much respected for his honesty as a man and his consistency as a Christian.He was married to Lipah Wakefield, 23 Oct. 1814, at Newport, NH. In census there is child in 1850 NH census, Lonia M. Wheeler, b. abt 1836.

Frederick L Wiley

Birth:
March 16, 1836
Maryland, New York
Death:
1926
Burial:
Union Cemetery
Laconia
Belknap County, New
Hampshire
Plot: Section 505, Grave 1

He received his preparatory education at Whitestown Seminary, New York and graduated from the theological school at New Hampton, New Hampshire in 1868. In 1865 he received license to preach and September 8, 1868 he was ordained by Rev's. J. Mariner, L. B. Tasker, and others. He was married in 1862 Miss Lena L. Smith who died in 1863. In 1868 he was again married to Miss Rebecca Weeks. He held pastorates at Sheffield and Sutton in Vermont; Bath, Maine; Concord, Whitefield and Gilford, New Hampshire. He received 250 people into churches, 127 by baptism. He was a member of the General Conference of 1877. He has for several years been editor of The Messenger. He also wrote *The Life and Influence of Benjamin Randall;* and *A History Of Free Will Baptists.*
Note: Interred 14 Apr 1926

Otis F. Willis

Birth:
1810
Hanover, New Hampshire
Death:
May 8, 1865
Franconia, New Hampshire
Burial:
Willow Cemetery
Franconia
Grafton County, New Hampshire

He was converted in March, 1830 and was baptized by Rev. David Cross. He began to hold meetings, traveling mostly in Vermont and New Hampshire and had several revivals. In 1832, he was licensed by the Strafford Vermont Quarterly Meeting. The same year he moved to Lyndon, Vermont to preach a part of the time at Daniel Quimby's church. In 1834, he was ordained at the request of the church in settled as pastor. In 1835 he entered on a six years pastorate with the church and Sugar Hill, New Hampshire where revivals were enjoyed. In 1841, he moved to Potsdam, New York and in the company of Rev. M. Cole labored in an extensive revival where a church was organized at West Potsdam where he pastored for two years. In 1849, he returned to Sugar Hill. He began to practice medicine in 1838. The ministry was down neglected for this calling, for the rest of his life. He preached but occasionally and on funeral occasions. He was often heard to regret that he had not followed the work of the ministry.

Though policy teacheth us not to trust our enemies, yet piety teacheth us to love them.

Ephraim Winslow
Birth:
May 6, 1805
Nottingham
Rockingham County
New Hampshire
Death:
Jan. 28, 1872
Pittsfield
Merrimack County, New Hampshire
Burial:
Quaker Cemetery
Pittsfield, Merrimack County
New Hampshire
He was ordained in Nottingham, 1846 and pastored it 1845-57. He went to South Candia, gathered a congregation and had a successful work. They went to Northwood, and later to Barnstead where he died.
Marriages: Mary Tucker - 24 MAY 1824. Sally Greene - 18 MAR 1827 in Pittsfield, NH.

Christ Has Led the Way

Rev Thomas Wyatt
Birth:
Sep. 5, 1818
Campton
Grafton County, New Hampshire
Death:
Oct. 24, 1895
Bristol
Grafton County, New Hampshire
Burial:
Blair Cemetery
Campton
Grafton County, New Hampshire

Son of Thomas Wyatt and Martha P Wilson. Married twice: 1. 4 Mar 1836 to Sarah Ann (Clark) Sawyer.
To thier union was born 6 children: George C Wyatt, Ellen A Wyatt, Nathaniel E Wyatt, Martha L Wyatt, Sarah Evangeline Wyatt, and Horace F Wyatt. 2. 14 Dec 1876 New Hampton, Belknap, New Hampshire to Mary Noyes (Hammond) Johnson. No children born of their union. Thomas was a farmer and Freewill Baptist Clergyman.
Thomas had resided in Campton, Grafton, New Hampshire; Thornton Gore, Grafton, New

Hampshire; Rumney, Grafton, New Hampshire; Bridgewater, Grafton, New Hampshire; and from 1887 in Bristol, Grafton, New Hampshire.

Winthrop Young
Birth:
1753
Barrington, Strafford County, New Hampshire
Death:
Jan. 6, 1832
Canterbury,
Merrimack County,
New Hampshire
Burial: Hackleboro,
Canterbury,
Merrimack County,
New Hampshire

Rev. Young became a school teacher, and after having lived in other locations, moved to Canterbury. Here he was chosen captain of the militia, and his tall, fine figure and courteous manners won him esteem and renown. In August, 1793, Benjamin Randall, visited the town and baptized a number. Finally, becoming deeply interested and zealous, Brother Young was ordained on June 28, 1796, by a council from the Yearly Meeting consisting of Whitney, Buzzell, Randall, Boody and others. He then entered upon a useful pastorate of thirty-five years. In 1798 he baptized thirty in Canterbury. In 1800, a remarkable interest sprang up chiefly through his labors at New Hampton. A church of sixty-four members was organized there by him on Jan. 6th, and for eight months, the glorious work continued, till 114 had been baptized and added to the church, "all or chiefly by our dear and precious brother, Elder Winthrop Young" as Elder Randall, who was present at the last baptism, makes the record. Possessing worldly means, he was benevolent and humble. He was of strong mind and large heart. His deep voice presented petitions in public prayer in such a way that Randall was heard to say, "We have no man among us that can pray like Brother Young." In 1822 at the age of nearly seventy, he was still active, baptizing a number at Northfield. In 1829, Rev. John Harrison was chosen as assistant pastor at Canterbury. Rev. Young died in the 80th year of his age.

Rev Zebina Young
Birth:
Dec. 15, 1795
New Hampshire
Death:
Dec. 24, 1874
New Hampshire
Burial:
Elmwood Cemetery
Franconia
Grafton County, New Hampshire

He was licensed to preach at Lisbon, 1829 and ordained there Dec. 29, 1831. His pastorates were in New Hampshire, Vermont and Canada.

New Jersey

Rev David Sidney Frost
Birth:
Jul. 14, 1813
Glover
Orleans County
Vermont
Death:
Dec. 30, 1902
Burial:
Washington Cemetery
Washington
Warren County
New Jersey

Attended schools at Lyndon and Brownington VT and Meriden NH; became a Free Will Baptist minister and held pastorates in ten different places in New Hampshire and Vermont; agent of Green Mountain Seminary six years; principal of Holderness Seminary two years; superintending school committee in New Hampshire and Vermont thirty years; member of Board of Foreign and Home Missionary Society; chaplain in military service three years; preached at East Andover. Ordained minister June 25, 1840. Sec'y of Education Society. Frank B. Frost, was son and worked for RR in Washington, NJ.

He was town clerk four years and justice of the peace an equal time. In his active life he was especially prominent in temperance and anti-slavery work. In 1843 he cast the only anti-slavery vote in town; in 1854 he was nominated for senator in district number 6 by a coalition of Democrats, Free Soilers and Whigs.

During the latter years of his life, Rev Frost suffered the loss of hearing and as a consequence, retired from ministry.

Source:- History of the Town of Andover, New Hampshire: Narrative By John Robie Eastman - Life and times in Hopkinton, N.H. By Charles Chase Lord

Father, into thy hands I commend my spirit."

Luke 23:46

NEW MEXICO

Rev W.W. Winters
Birth:
1910
Death:
1971
Burial:
Sunset Memorial Park
Albuquerque
Bernalillo County
New Mexico, USA
Plot: Sec 19, lot 4

He married Rev.Ola Mae Coker 19 Nov. 1932, Tillman Co. OK. --Okla. marriage records.

Inscription:
Reverend

He Is The Beginning And The End

Index

Amburgey	John R.	Georgia	168
Amerson	W. L.	Georgia	169
Ames	Moses	Maine	333
Ammons	H. A.	Georgia	169
Andrews	Otis	Maine	334
Anthony	Leonard Short	Georgia	170
Ard	Allen Bruce	Georgia	170
Arnold	John Calvin	Georgia	171
Arnold	Floyd	Missouri	574
Asberry	A. L.	Illinois	240
Ashby	D. W.	Illinois	240
Ashcraft	Ozra	Arkansas	25
Ashcraft	Richard	Illinois	240
Ashley	James	Michigan	485
Atwell	Johnny	Arkansas	25
Atwood	Brian	Alabama	10
Atwood	Hezekiah	Maine	334
Augir	Franklin page	Michigan	486
Avery	Austin	New Hampshire	646
Ayer	Aaron	Maine	335
Babb	J. Franklin	New Hampshire	646
Babcock	William S.	New Hampshire	647
Bacheler	Henry M.	New Hampshire	647
Badger	William	Massachusetts	476
Bagwill	J.H.	Illinois	241
Bailey	James M.	Maine	335
Bailey	John	Maine	336
Baker	Oscar E.	Iowa	283
Baker, Jr	Matthew	Illinois	241
Baldwin	E.	Arkansas	25
Baldwin	Jeremiah	Michigan	487
Ball	John C.	Massachusetts	475
Banghart	Andrew	Canada	138

Banks	John J.	Maine	337
Barard	George	Michigan	488
Bard	Nathaniel	Maine	336
Barker	James	Missouri	575
Barker	Lewis P.	Missouri	575
Barksdale	William J.	Georgia	170
Barnard	Laura Belle	Georgia	171
Barnes	John Nelson	Georgia	171
Barrett	Garland A.	Missouri	576
Bartlett	Willard	Canada	138
Bartlett	Favel	Maine	337
Bastow	William L.	Kansas	305
Batchelder	Tappan	Iowa	284
Batchelder	Otis Robinson	New Hampshire	648
Batchelor	John Lewis	Georgia	172
Batchelor	Johnny Ralph	Georgia	172
Batchelter	John	Maine	338
Bates	Isaac	Maine	338
Bates	David	Missouri	576
Bathrick	Stephen	Illinois	241
Batson	John D.	Minnesota	551
Baxley	Gerald	Georgia	172
Baxter	George	Michigan	488
Bayless	Joseph	Kansas	304
Beach	L. R.	Georgia	173
Bean	Selden	Maine	339
Bean	Charles	Maine	339
Bean	George Winthrop	Maine	339
Bean	Leroy	Maine	340
Bean	Benaiah	New Hampshire	649
Bean	Silas	New Hampshire	649
Beatty	Harry Howard	Missouri	577
Bedell	Isaiah M.	Massachusetts	475

Beebe	Hugh	New Hampshire	650
Beers	Ed C.	Georgia	173
Bell	Ralph J.	Georgia	174
Bennet	Archibald	Michigan	488
Benson	Herman Dean	Arkansas	26
Bequette	Lue	Missouri	578
Berreman	William Henry	Idaho	237
Best	Andrew	Arkansas	28
Bickford	Lewis P.	New Hampshire	650
Bignal	James	Michigan	489
Bingham	Manuel Eugene	Missouri	578
Bishop	Blaine David	California	114
Bixby	Loren	Illinois	242
Bixby	Ruby Knapp	Iowa	284
Bixby	Newell	Iowa	284
Blackwelder	Isaac Joshua	Florida	157
Blair	Roger Lee	Kentucky	317
Blake	Charles	Maine	340
Blake	Edwin	Maine	340
Blake	Israel	New Hampshire	650
Blanchard	George P.	Michigan	490
blanden	Thomas H	Illinois	242
Blanks	J. W.	Arkansas	26
Blanton	David W.	Georgia	174
Blanton	Isaac J.	Georgia	174
Blevins	Bobby	Kentucky	317
Boatright	David Louis	Georgia	174
Bodine	William	Illinois	242
Bolles	Simeon	New Hampshire	651
Bonar	William	Illinois	243
Bonar	William	Indiana	271
Bond	Walter	Alabama	10
Bone	Zachariah Taylor	Georgia	175

Boody	Joseph	New Hampshire	651
Boody, Jr.	Joseph	New Hampshire	652
Bowden	Stephen	Maine	340
Bowen	Seaborn	Georgia	175
Bowen	Thomas J.	Georgia	175
Bowling	Sterling	Arkansas	27
Boyd	James	Maine	342
Boyd	David	Maine	341
Boyd	David	Maine	341
Boydton	Lucius Darwin	Michigan	490
Boyer	Alder	Canada	139
Boyle	Francis	California	114
Boynton	Aldophus Eugene	Maine	342
Brackett	Nancy Cram	Maine	334
Brackett	Levi	Maine	344
Brackett	David	Maine	343
Braddy	Joe Burney	Arkansas	27
Bradeen	Allen	Maine	344
Bradeen	Frank	Maine	345
Bradford	Roscoe	Maine	345
Bradley	Barney B.	Georgia	176
Bradley	Richard A.	Illinois	243
Bradley	William	Illinois	244
Bradley	George	Michigan	491
Branch	Samuel S.	Illinois	245
Branham	Steve	Kentucky	317
Brashear	Thomas	Arkansas	27
Brasher	Miles Evans	Missouri	578
Braswell	David Rowan	Georgia	176
Bratcher	Benjamin F.	Georgia	176
Braughton	A.	Arkansas	28
Breshears	Nathan J.	Missouri	578
Brewer	Harvey	Massachusetts	477

Bridges	Henry Elmer	Georgia	176
Bridges	Oscar C.	Georgia	177
Bridges	Otis	Maine	346
Brock	Hezekiah	New Hampshire	651
Brock	Hezekiah	New Hampshire	651
Brodnax	James Edward	Georgia	177
Brooks	Nahum	New Hampshire	653
Brown	J. A.	Alabama	10
Brown	Henry P.	Arkansas	29
Brown	James F.	Arkansas	29
Brown	Bobby Lee	California	115
Brown	Gerald E.	Georgia	178
Brown	Henry	Illinois	246
Brown	Ebenezer	Maine	346
Brown	Jonathan	Maine	347
Brown	Albion	Maine	346
Brown	David D.	Michigan	491
Brown	Benjamin F.	Missouri	579
Brown	Amos	New Hampshire	654
Bryan	Claude R.	Missouri	580
Bryant	James Earl	Georgia	178
Bryant	Obed	Illinois	246
Bryant	George	Maine	347
Bugg	Harvey B.	Arkansas	30
Bullard	J. H.	Arkansas	30
Bullock	Almira Wescott	Maine	349
Bullock	Jeremiah	Maine	349
Bullock	Wescott	Maine	349
Bullock	George	Missouri	580
Burbank	Porter	Maine	348
Burch	Tommy Lynn	Alabama	10
Burgess	Chester	California	115
Burkholder	Julie Phillips	Michigan	494

Burnett	William R.	Arkansas	31
Burnett	Robert L.	Georgia	179
Burney	James Eli	Missouri	580
Burnham	Asa	Maine	350
Burns	William	Michigan	492
Burr	William	New Hampshire	655
Burris, Jr	George W.	Arkansas	31
Burton	William	Illinois	246
Butler	Oliver	Maine	351
Butler	John J.	Michigan	493
Buzzell	John	Maine	351
Buzzell	Aaron	New Hampshire	656
Buzzell	Hezekiah D.	New Hampshire	656
Buzzell	Alvah	New Hampshire	657
Calley	David	New Hampshire	657
Callison	William Halsey	California	115
Campbell	Clarence Elijah	Arkansas	32
Campbell	Glynn	Arkansas	33
Campbell	Clyde C.	Arkansas	32
Campbell	Byford Lee	Illinois	247
Campbell	Cyrus	Maine	352
Campbell	Cecil	Missouri	581
Cantrell	Charles	California	115
Capps	Willie K.	Arkansas	33
Carnahan	John M.	Missouri	581
Carner	Jacob Newton	Missouri	581
Carpenter	Elijah	Missouri	582
Carr	T. P.	Georgia	179
Carroll	William N.	Georgia	179
Carter	James C.	Arkansas	33
Carter	William Pleas	Arkansas	34
Carter	J. C. Hubert	Georgia	179
Carter	T. M.	Georgia	180

Carveno	Arthur	New Hampshire	659
Cason	Martin Franlin	Georgia	180
Castle	Scott	Kentucky	318
Cate	Carter E.	New Hampshire	658
Catrett	Henry L.	Georgia	181
Caverly	John	New Hampshire	658
Cavin	C . Z.	Kentucky	318
Chadbourne	Joseph	Maine	353
Chadwick	Edward	Maine	353
Chambless	L. J.	Georgia	181
Champlin	David E.	Iowa	285
Chandler	Hubbard	Maine	355
Chaney	S. Freeman	Maine	354
Chase	Albert H.	Connecticut	149
Chase	Lyman	Illinois	247
Chase	George Colby	Maine	356
Chase	Uriah	Maine	357
Cheney	Oren Burbank	Maine	354
Cheshire	Edward S.	Georgia	181
Chew	Enoch Thomas	Arkansas	34
Childers	Claude B.	Illinois	248
Christian	Earl	Arkansas	34
Christian	Peter	Illinois	248
Chronister	Jimmy Lee	Arkansas	35
Churchhill	Roger	Maine	357
Cilley	Ruth	Michigan	495
Cilley	Daniel Plummer	New Hampshire	661
Clark	Oscar T.	Illinois	249
Clark	Aaron	Maine	357
Clark	John	Maine	358
Clark	Dudley E.	Michigan	495
Clark	Peter	New Hampshire	662
Clay	David	California	116

Clay	Jonathan	Maine	359
Cleaver	Mike	Missouri	582
Clements	Tisdale	Maine	359
Cleveland	Edward	Maine	360
Clift	Marion Francis	Missouri	582
Coats	Romanzo	Idaho	238
Coats	David	Iowa	285
Cobb	Jackson Malone	Alabama	11
Cobb	Almira Wescott	Maine	360
Cobb	William	Maine	360
Coburn	Greenleaf H.	Maine	361
Coffin	Stephen	New Hampshire	662
Coffman	Arthur Edward	Arkansas	35
Coffman	Joseph Dempsey	Arkansas	35
Coffman	Lawnie	Arkansas	36
Colby	George	Maine	361
Colby	Joshua	Maine	362
Cole	Samuel	New Hampshire	664
Cole	Solomon	New Hampshire	665
Cole, Sr	Clefford	New Hampshire	663
Cole,Jr	Clefford	New Hampshire	663
Colegrove	William	Connecticut	150
Coleman	W. C.	Georgia	182
Collett	Caleb	Indiana	272
Collins	George W.	Georgia	182
Colliver	Lawrence	Kentucky	318
Coltrin	Cyrus	Iowa	286
Comer	Fred E.	Missouri	583
Condit	William E.B.	California	116
Conley	Harvey Burns	Kentucky	318
Conley	John Elliott	Kentucky	319
Conley	Joe	Kentucky	319
Cook	John	Maine	363

Cook	Gideon	Maine	363
Cook	Elijah	Michigan	495
Coombs	Lavina Carr	Maine	364
Cooper	Freeman	Maine	364
Cooper	Archie	Missouri	583
Copas	W. H.	Missouri	584
Copp	Roger	Maine	364
Copp	Ellen Gross	Michigan	496
Copp	John Scott	Michigan	497
Corey	A. P.	Minnesota	552
Corrales	Osmondo	California	117
Corson	Charles	New Hampshire	665
Cotton	Thomas	New Hampshire	666
Couillard	Jacob	Maine	362
Coursey	C. C.	Georgia	182
Cowell	David	Maine	365
Cox	John	Indiana	272
Cox	Simon	Maine	366
Cox	Authur Elmes	New Hampshire	666
Craddock	Charles B.	Alabama	11
Crafton	John Francis	Arkansas	36
Crase	Henry Clay	Missouri	585
Cravens	Grover C.	Missouri	585
Crawley	William Robert	Georgia	182
Creech	Tunis Michael	Alabama	12
Creech	R. Paul	Georgia	182
Crews	William Elvin	Missouri	585
Crockett	Charles	Maine	366
Crook	Madison Lamarr	Georgia	183
Crosby	James	Mississippi	564
Cross	Gene Autry	Georgia	183
Cross	Jesse	New Hampshire	666
Crossland	Emery	Arkansas	37

Crouch	John M.	Arkansas	37
Crowell	William D.	Canada	139
Crumb	Luther R.	California	118
Culley	John	Missouri	585
Curnett	William C.	Arkansas	37
Curtis	Alonzo	Nebraska	634
Curtis	Silas	New Hampshire	667
Dalton	William H.	California	119
Dalton	Effie Leona	California	119
Dame	Charles Dwight	Illinois	249
Daniel	Joshua Edward	Georgia	183
Daniels	Scott	Kentucky	320
Darling	James Harvey	Michigan	498
Darling II	Thomas J.	Indiana	273
Davis	Carl	Arkansas	39
Davis	Wilda	Kentucky	320
Davis	Jarius Eaton	Michigan	498
Davis	Eliphaz	Missouri	587
Davis	Samuel W.	Missouri	588
Davis	Winford C.	Missouri	588
Davis	Henry	Missouri	587
Davis	Kinsman	Nebraska	633
Davis	Jacob Burnham	New Hampshire	668
Davis	John	New Hampshire	669
Dawson	Willie	Georgia	183
Day	Tommy Sewell	Arkansas	38
Day	Willard C.	Arkansas	39
Day	Jack	Missouri	586
Dazey	John	Florida	156
Dees	Tracy	Illinois	250
Dees	Christian B.	Missouri	589
Dell	G. Thomas	Georgia	184
Denton	Preston C.	Arkansas	40

DePuy	Wellington	Michigan	499
DeWitt	A. W.	Nebraska	634
DeWitt	William	Nebraska	634
Dick	William	Connecticut	150
Dickey	Alice	Missouri	589
Dickey	Robert	New Hampshire	669
Dickinson	Egbert Oakley	Michigan	499
Dills	John B.	Kentucky	321
Dipboye	Glenn G.	Arkansas	40
Dodd	Sylvia	Georgia	185
Dodd	Damon C.	Georgia	184
Dodge	Milo William	Kansas	306
Doggett	Oris	Arkansas	41
Doggett	Ralph	Arkansas	41
Donaldson	Andrew	Iowa	286
Dore	TRUE	Maine	367
Doss	Orbin Hurst	California	119
Dotson	Claude A.	Missouri	589
Douglass	George	Maine	367
Dowell	William D.	Missouri	590
Doyle	Jefferson Davis	Arkansas	42
Doyle	Henry	Arkansas	41
Doyle	Edward John	Michigan	500
Drake	E. Allen	Georgia	186
Drake	W. A.	Georgia	186
Drew	Isaac W.	Iowa	288
Driggers	William S.	Georgia	186
Driver	William	Missouri	590
Duckworth	Earl B.	Georgia	186
Dudley	Edward	Iowa	288
Dunaway	Israel Bunyan	California	120
Dunlap	Harold Keith	Georgia	187
Dunn	James M.	Georgia	187

Dunn	Cyene Emery	Michigan	500
Dunn	Ransom	Michigan	501
Dunn	Francis Wayland	Michigan	502
Dupree	J. H.	Georgia	187
Durfee	Gilbert	Michigan	503
Durgin	Lucy Marilla	Minnesota	552
Durgin	Frank Llewellyn	Minnesota	551
Duvall	Adrian	Arkansas	42
Dyer	Joseph	Maine	368
Dyer	Daniel	Maine	368
Dyer	Samuel B.	New Hampshire	670
Eaggleston	Abner C	Michigan	503
Eastabrook	Caleb	Massachusetts	477
Eastman	Andrew J.	New Hampshire	671
Eaton	Ebenezer G.	Maine	369
Eaton	Ebenezer	Maine	370
Eddins	Benjamin	Alabama	12
Edgar	William Henry	Nebraska	635
Edwards	James Thomas	Georgia	188
Edwards	Eunice	Missouri	591
Elderidge	Clyde	Kentucky	321
Elkins	Daniel	New Hampshire	672
Elliot	George Columbus	Alabama	13
Elms	Ernest H.	Arkansas	43
Emanuel	Adolphus	Georgia	188
Emanuel	John M.	Georgia	188
Embry	George Troup	Georgia	188
Emerson	William H.	Georgia	189
Etheridge	Charles B.	Georgia	189
Etheridge	Grady C.	Georgia	189
Everson	Alton	Georgia	189
Ewer	Daniel	Michigan	504
Fadley	William B.	Missouri	591

Faircloth	Howard Dewitt	Georgia	190
Fairfield	Micaiah	Michigan	504
Farnam	Everett	Arkansas	43
Farnham	John	maine	371
Farwell	Josiah	Maine	371
Fasion	Kenneth	Georgia	190
Fast	John	Kansas	306
Felt	L. D.	Iowa	288
Felt	Marcus	Iowa	289
Fenner	Louisa	Connecticut	151
Ferguson	Aristide	California	120
Ferguson	Tom C.	Missouri	591
Fernald	Ebernezer N.	Maine	371
Fernald	Ebenezer	New Hampshire	672
Ferris	Jesse Calvin	Michigan	504
Fields	O. L.	Alabama	13
Fields	Jerry William	Missouri	593
Fifield	William Penson	Michigan	505
Files	Allen	Maine	372
Findley	Charles	Missouri	593
Finley	Hoyt Duard	Georgia	191
Fisher	Bennie	Arkansas	44
Fisk	Ebenezer	Michigan	505
Flanders	Thomas	Maine	373
Flanders	Timothy	New Hampshire	673
Fletcher	Jabez	Maine	373
Fletcher	Jonathan	New Hampshire	673
Florence	Virgil	Colorado	146
Flota	Howard	Illinois	250
Floyd	Drew	Georgia	191
Fondren	William	Mississippi	564
Ford	Henry Mead	Michigan	506
Ford	William Henry	Missouri	593

Ford Sr	Richard E.	Arkansas	44
Forrest	Charlie	Arkansas	45
Fort	Joseph O.	Georgia	191
Foss	Joseph	Maine	374
Foster	Charles	Maine	375
Foster	John	Minnesota	552
Fowler	Ralph	Arkansas	45
Fowler	Herschel Greeley	Georgia	192
Fowler	Spencer	Michigan	506
Foy	William	Maine	376
Franklin	Warren	Missouri	593
Frederick	Joe Sephus	Alabama	13
Frees, Jr	Retire D.	Michigan	507
French	Herbert Winfield	Kentucky	321
Frost	Charles	Maine	377
Frost	Harold	Maine	376
Frost	Robert	Maine	378
Frost	David Sidney	New Jersey	735
Fuller	Jarius	Maine	378
Fuller	Willard	Massachusetts	478
Fullonton	John	Maine	379
Gaines	Thomas	Missouri	594
Gallison	William F.	Maine	379
Gammon	Danville	Maine	379
Gann	Milton	Alabama	14
Gardenhire	Parry Thomas	Missouri	595
Garland	David	New Hampshire	675
Garner	Harold	Arkansas	46
Garrision	Cecil Oliver	Arkansas	45
Garvin	John	Arkansas	47
Gates	Jesse Franklin	Arkansas	46
Gates	Newton Preston	Michigan	508
Gearing	Levi	Missouri	595

Gentry	Earl W	Arkansas	47
George	Nathaniel	New Hampshire	674
Gerry	Benjamin	maine	379
Getchell	Mark	Maine	380
Getchell	William	Maine	380
Gibson	Stephen	Massachusetts	478
Gibson	Luther D.	Mississippi	565
Giddens	Harveu	Georgia	192
Giddens	Murray Elvin	Georgia	192
Giddens	Teedom M.	Georgia	192
Gidney	Harry	Maine	381
Gifford	Henry	Iowa	289
Gilbert	Chester A.	Georgia	192
Gile	Orison	Maine	381
Gile	Orison Levi	New Hampshire	675
Gilkey	Phillip	Maine	382
Gill	Benjamin Terrell	Georgia	193
Gill	Walter D.	Georgia	193
Gilliland	John	Arkansas	59
Gilliland	James Charles	Illinois	250
Gilman	Edmund	New Hampshire	675
Given	Lincoln	Maine	384
Given	Arthur	Maine	382
Gleason	Abel	Iowa	290
Glidden	Cleveland	Maine	384
Glover	John David	Arkansas	48
Glovier	Alba	Michigan	508
Goble	Jacob	Canada	140
Goff	Ken	Missouri	595
Goodrich	Bernard	Maine	385
Goodwin	Joseph	Maine	385
Goolsby	Richard M.	Georgia	193
Gordon	George Alexander	Illinois	251

Gordon	Henry Smith	Illinois	251
Gore	Ellis	Alabama	14
Gosline	James	Canada	140
Goss	Kyle	Arkansas	48
Gowell	William	Maine	386
Grant	John	Maine	387
Granville	Joseph	New Hampshire	675
Graves	Horace	California	121
Graves	Josiah	Connecticut	152
Graves	Lucien Chase	Massachusetts	479
Gray	William H.	Georgia	193
Gray	Andrew	Maine	387
Green	Benjamin Franklin	Georgia	194
Green	Doctor Evan	Georgia	194
Green	Ross H.	Missouri	596
Greene	Ted	Kentucky	322
Greenway	Virgil R.	Missouri	596
Greenwood	Herman A.	Arkansas	48
Grider	Leo	Illinois	252
Griffin	Benjamin J.	Georgia	195
Griffiths	Silas	Connecticut	152
Grimsby	William Thomas	Georgia	195
Grimsley	E. C.	Georgia	195
Grinnell	Thomas	Michigan	509
Gross	Stephen	Maine	387
Guinn	William M.	Arkansas	49
Guthrie	Don	Arkansas	49
Guyton	Whitaker	Alabama	14
Hackett	Moulton	New Hampshire	675
Hadden	Claude H.	Georgia	196
Hager	Charles Wesley	Arkansas	50
Haggett	S. M.	Maine	388
Hale	Joseph	Kansas	307

Halford	Archibald	Missouri	597
Hall	Ed	Arkansas	50
Hall	Faber	Arkansas	51
Hallack	John W	Michigan	509
Halsted	David	Iowa	290
Ham	Ezra	New Hampshire	677
Hames	Claudie	California	121
Handyside	John	Missouri	596
Hanna	Arlene	Illinois	253
Hanna	Louis Barrett	Illinois	253
Hanna	Marie	India	270
Hanscom	Pelatiah	New Hampshire	678
Hansley	Aquilla	Florida	158
Hanson	Turner	Maine	389
Hanson	Moses	New Hampshire	677
Harding	Ephraim	Maine	389
Harding	Elisha	Michigan	510
Hargrave	Opie	Arkansas	51
Harley	Floyd	Illinois	253
Harman	Lot	Maine	390
Harmon	Velon Eugene	Arkansas	52
Harper	Joseph	New Hampshire	678
Harrell	C. W.	Georgia	196
Harrell	Kelly C.	Georgia	196
Harrelson	Hosea	Arkansas	53
Harriman	David	New Hampshire	679
Harrington	James	Arkansas	53
Harrington	John	New Hampshire	680
Harris	Mark Metcher	Arkansas	52
Harris	James G.	Georgia	196
Hart	Henry	Arkansas	54
Hart	Ephriam	Maine	390
Hartley	John R.	Arkansas	54

Harvery	Erastus	Iowa	290
Harvey	C. J.	Georgia	197
Harvey	Ewin	Kansas	308
Haskell	George	Maine	392
Hassell	George W.	Arkansas	55
Hatfield	Lyle	Michigan	510
Hathaway	Asa	Maine	392
Hathaway	Leonard	Maine	393
Hathorn	Samuel	Maine	391
Hayden	Wilson warren	Maine	393
Hayden	Wentworth	Minnesota	552
Hayes	Francis little	District of Columbia	156
Hayes	R. Staten	Georgia	197
Hayes	James A.	Kentucky	322
Hayes	Benjamin F.	Maine	394
Hayes	Jesse	Maine	395
Heard	Chester	Canada	141
Heath	Josiah Lorenzo	Minnesota	553
Heath	Jesse	Mississippi	565
Henderson	Harvey Lee	Florida	160
Henderson	Benjamin F.	Missouri	597
Henderson	George W.	Missouri	598
Henderson	James Monroe	Missouri	598
Hendrix	Claude	Arkansas	55
Hensley	G. W.	Missouri	598
Hershey	Evelyn	Illinois	253
Hewes	Julius Perry	Michigan	511
Hicks	James Walter	Illinois	254
Hicks	Clifford Leon	Illinois	254
Higgins	Joseph	Maine	395
Higgins	Josiah	New Hampshire	680
High	Carl Leo	Arkansas	55
Hill	Edward	Arkansas	56

Hill	Joel	Georgia	197
Hill	Albert	Maine	396
Hill	William C.	Missouri	599
Hill	Samuel	New Hampshire	682
Hill	John	New Hampshire	681
Hill	trueworthy	New Hampshire	682
Hillis	Bessie Widener	Georgia	197
Hills	Marilla Turner	New Hampshire	683
Hiltibidal	Ellamae Harrelson	illinois	255
Hiltibidal	Opal	Illinois	256
Hiltibidal	John	Illinois	255
Hiltibidal	John J.	Illinois	255
Hilton	Charles	Minnesota	553
Hinckley	James	maine	397
Hinckley	Jonathan Niles	Michigan	511
Hinnant	Richard	Louisiana	329
Hix	Orrin	Iowa	292
Hobbs	Henry	Maine	397
Hobbs	Abiel W.	New Hampshire	684
Hobson	Andrew	Maine	398
Hobson	Pelathiah M.	Maine	399
Hodges	Elmer	Missouri	599
Hoffman	Truman	Missouri	600
Hogbin	Alfred C.	California	122
Holcomb	James	Missouri	599
Holder	David Monroe	Arkansas	57
Holiman	Elmer	Arkansas	56
Holland	Terrell	Arkansas	57
Hollis	Daniel G. W.	Alabama	15
Hollis	Martin Luther	Mississippi	566
Holloman	James Monroe	Arkansas	57
Holmes	Robert W.	Georgia	197
Holmes	W. H.	Georgia	198

Holmes	Daniel	Illinois	256
Holmes	Hiram	New Hampshire	684
Holmes	John C.	New Hampshire	685
Holroyd	Charles	Iowa	292
Holt	John Robert	Arkansas	58
Holton	George Sharrod	Georgia	198
Hoover	Arlie	Kansas	308
Hopkins	George	Illinois	257
Horne	Benjamin Franklin	Georgia	198
Horton	George	Massachusetts	479
Hoskinson	Andrew	Illinois	257
Houghton	Alphonso	Maine	399
Housley	James	Missouri	599
Houston	Carlton Robert	Georgia	199
Hovey	Samuel	Minnesota	554
Howard	Eugene	Alabama	16
Howard	Francis	Maine	400
Howard	Richard	Maine	401
Howard	George	Michigan	513
Howe	James	Maine	402
Howe	George Wilson	Massachusetts	480
Howes	Edward	Michigan	513
Hubbard	George	Illinois	257
Huckaba	Gaylord	Arkansas	58
Huckins	Thomas	Michigan	513
Huddleston	Truman	California	123
Hudguns	King David	Missouri	599
Hudson, Jr.	Francis Marion	Arkansas	58
Huffman	George H.	Missouri	600
Huggens	Earcel	Arkansas	59
Huggins	Orville	Illinois	258
Hughes	William Bonnie	Alabama	16
Huling	Ansell H	California	123

Hull	John Jay	California	124
Hull	John	Maine	403
Hulsey	Thomas Russell	Alabama	17
Hunt	Oscar	Arkansas	59
Hunt	Elihu	Missouri	600
Huntley	Leland	New Hampshire	685
Huntoon	Henry	New Hampshire	685
Hurd	Charles E.	New Hampshire	686
Hutchins	Leonard	Maine	404
Hutchins	Samuel	Maine	403
Hutchins	Elias	New Hampshire	686
Hutchinson	Asa	Maine	404
Hutchison	Joseph	Maine	405
Hutchison	Ebenezer	Maine	404
Hutchison	Joseph	Maine	406
Hyatt	Marie	Missouri	601
Ingram	John	Canada	141
Inman	David marks	Kansas	309
Irvin	Dennis Oliver	Georgia	199
Irvin	Paul H.	Georgia	199
Irvin	Von Deron	Georgia	200
Isbell	William Sherman	Arkansas	60
James	John Pierce	Georgia	200
Jaques	Benjamin	Maine	406
Jaquith	Phineus	Minnesota	554
Jeffers	Lorenzo	New Hampshire	687
Jeffrey	Jesse	California	124
Jeffreys	Opal	Missouri	601
Jeffreys	Lloyd	Missouri	601
Jenkins	John H.	Georgia	201
Jenkins	Enoch	Iowa	292
Jenne	Alonzo	Michigan	513
Jenness	Rubin V.	New Hampshire	688

Jobe	William Rufus	Arkansas	60
Johns	Edward	California	125
Johns	Henry	Missouri	601
Johnson	Joseph H.	Arkansas	61
Johnson	Keith	Arkansas	62
Johnson	M. P.	Arkansas	62
Johnson	Clyde	Arkansas	60
Johnson	Jennie	Canada	142
Johnson	Linton C.	Georgia	202
Johnson	David	Kansas	310
Jones	Dallas Jack	Alabama	17
Jones	Paul	Arkansas	62
Jones	G. W.	Georgia	201
Jones	Spurgeon	Georgia	201
Jones	Willis Marshall	Illinois	258
Jones	Ichabod	Indiana	273
Jones	M. H.	Indiana	273
Jones	Daniel Wyatt	Mississippi	569
Jones	Norlin	Mississippi	569
Jones	Bill	Missouri	602
Jones	Abner	New Hampshire	688
Jordan	John	Maine	406
Joslin	David A.	Arkansas	63
Joslin	Joel Arthur	Arkansas	64
Julian	Samuel	Michigan	514
Kalar	Anson	Michigan	515
Keene	Columbus	Maine	407
Keith	Ruth	Minnesota	565
Keith	Ruth	Minnesota	555
Kellam	Charles Rice	Arkansas	64
Kelly	Benjamin Franklin	California	126
Kelly	Hughie J.	Georgia	203
Kelton	Darwin Eugene	Arkansas	65

Kenerson	Francis	New Hampshire	689
Kenison	Spencer	New Hampshire	690
Keniston	Thomas	New Hampshire	691
Kennan	Ralph	Florida	160
Kennan	Ida M.	Michigan	515
Kennan	Ada M.	Michigan	551
Kennedy	Ernest McKinley	Arkansas	66
Kennedy	Paul	California	125
Kenny	Moses R.	Michigan	516
Kenny	Moses Rice	Minnesota	537
Kern	Arthur W.	Illinois	259
Kesner	James	Arkansas	66
Ketcham	Samuel	Michigan	516
Ketteman	Columbus Jackson	Illinois	259
Keyes	Samuel	Kansas	310
Kicenki	Arthur A.	Missouri	603
Killingsworth	John A.	Mississippi	570
Kimball	Clarion Hazen	New Hampshire	691
Kinder	Chester	Arkansas	67
King	Dimus Newton	Arkansas	67
Kingsbury	Elijah	Michigan	516
Kingsbury	Leonard	Michigan	517
Kinney	William	Maine	408
Kirkland	Zane T.	Arkansas	68
Kirkland	Charles	Maine	408
Kitchens	Charles C.	Arkansas	69
Knapp	George Washington	Nebraska	635
Knight	Arnold	Michigan	517
Knighton	Hiram Leroy	Georgia	203
Knowles	Samuel	New Hampshire	692
Knowlton	Ebenezer	Maine	409
Knowlton	Zina	Maine	411
Knowlton	Ebenezer, sr.	Maine	408

Koch	John	Missouri	603
Koch	Levi	Missouri	603
Lafferty Jr	Ollie	Michigan	524
Lamb	Elliot Sawyer	Maine	411
Lamb	George	Maine	412
Lamb	John	Maine	412
Lane	Samuel	Arkansas	69
Lane	William B.	Georgia	203
Laney	Greenville	Georgia	204
Lang	Larkin	Massachusetts	480
Langley	Miles R.	Arkansas	69
Lansing	Peter Alexander	Nebraska	635
Lash	John	Michigan	518
Latham	W. R.	Alabama	18
Latimer	George	Kansas	311
Lawhorn	Simeon Roy	Georgia	204
Lawhorn	William Randolph	Georgia	204
Lawless	Winston Benton	California	126
Lawrence	Richard	District of Columbia	155
Leach	Zachariah	Maine	413
Leatherbury	Glennda	Africa	9
Leavenworth	J. B.	Michigan	518
Leavitt	Benjamin	Indiana	273
Ledbetter	Willis Jackson (Jack)	Kansas	311
Lee	George Cullen	Mississippi	570
Lee, Jr.	Robert	Arkansas	70
Leonard	Abner	New Hampshire	693
LeRoux	Julius Arthur	Missouri	604
Lesher	John	Iowa	293
Letsinger	Raymond	California	127
Lewis	Herman A.	Arkansas	70
Lewis	Geraldine	Illinois	259
Lewis	Samuel	Maine	414

Lewis	Daniel	Maine	413
Lewis	Stephen	Maine	414
Lewis	Edward Dodds	Michigan	519
Lewis	Sylvester Bowman	Missouri	604
Lewis	Lincoln	New Hampshire	693
Libby	Almon	Maine	415
Libby	David	Maine	415
Libby	James	Maine	415
Lick	Absalon S.	Missouri	603
Lightsey	Ralph	Georgia	205
Lightsey	Tom Joseph	Georgia	205
Limbocker	Henry S.	Kansas	312
Lincoln	Claude	Missouri	605
Lisle	Bruce V.	Georgia	205
Little	James D.	Georgia	206
Little	S. N.	Georgia	206
Locke	Ward	Maine	416
Locklear	Rick	Michigan	520
Long	Theron W.	Georgia	206
Long	John David	Missouri	605
Loomis	Amaziah	Iowa	293
Lord	David	Michigan	520
Lothrop	Nathan	New Hampshire	694
Lovering	James B.	Georgia	207
Lovett	James Silas	Arkansas	71
Lovett	L.O.	Georgia	207
Lowe	Russell	Missouri	605
Loyless	J. W.	Georgia	207
Lumpkin	Henry Lewis	Georgia	208
Lumpkin	Johnnie B.	Georgia	208
Lumpkin	William Robert	Georgia	208
Lunsford	John T.	Georgia	209
Luther	Israel	Indiana	274

Lybarger	Curtis Lee	Arkansas	71
Lyford	Francis	New Hampshire	694
Lynch	George	Arkansas	72
Maddox	Walter B.	Arkansas	72
Magoon	Josiah	New Hampshire	695
Malone	Wallace	Illinois	260
Malvern	Lewis	Massachusetts	481
Maness	Bennie	Arkansas	72
Mann	Cora Ann	Missouri	606
Mann	Charles Earl	Missouri	607
Mann	Thomas J.	Missouri	607
Manning	Levi B.	Georgia	209
Manning	John S.	Michigan	521
Manson	Benjamin small	New Hampshire	695
Mantooth	Thomas	Arkansas	73
Marchant	Dock	Arkansas	73
Marcum	Samuel H.	Missouri	607
Mariner	Jason	Maine	416
Marks	Ives	Indiana	274
Marks	William	Nebraska	636
Marler Jr	Luke	Missouri	608
Marshall	Albert Josiah	Minnesota	553
Marston	James	Iowa	293
Martin	C.C.	Georgia	209
Martin	Robert	Louisiana	330
Marvel	John	Illinois	260
Massey	Newton Elmore	Georgia	210
Massey	Robert M.	Georgia	210
Matchett	Franklin Ray	Arkansas	74
Matney	Elias	Missouri	608
Matthews	Woodrow	Alabama	18
Mauck	Joseph William	Michigan	521
Mawhorter	Thomas J.	Indiana	275

Mayhall	Trellis L.	Alabama	19
Mayhew	Archie	California	127
Maynard	John H.	Michigan	522
Mayo	Elihue Roy	Alabama	19
Mayo	George	Mississippi	571
McAlister	Doice Lee	California	127
McAlister	J. L.	California	128
McBride	Leon	Illinois	261
McCall	James F.	Missouri	608
McCellan	Elbert	Arkansas	74
McCellan	James Samuel	Arkansas	75
McClain	George W.	California	128
McClain	Peter	Georgia	213
McClanahan	William	Missouri	609
McClary	John	New Hampshire	696
McClintock	Billy Gene	Missouri	609
McClintock	Evans Boyd	Missouri	609
McCorvey	Solomon Oscar	Georgia	211
McCuin	Robert Henry	Arkansas	76
McCullers	Jordan	Georgia	210
McCullough	Thomas	Michigan	525
McCullough	Patty	Michigan	526
McCutcheon	James	New Hampshire	696
McDanal	Frank Seeley	Georgia	211
McDaniel	John D.	Georgia	211
McDaniel	Walter Ballenger	Georgia	211
McDonald	Warren Arthur	Georgia	212
McFadden	Richard B.	Georgia	212
McFarland	Moses	Maine	417
McGee	Peter	Alabama	19
McGee	W. H.	Alabama	20
McGee	Wilton R.	Indiana	276
McGray	Asa	Canada	143

McKee	William Franklin	Arkansas	76
McKindsley	Elbridge L.	Maine	417
McKinney	Robert	Maryland	474
McKown	John D.	Missouri	610
McKown	William Henry	Missouri	610
McLendon	Seab A.	Georgia	213
McLeod	Joseph	Canada	143
McMillan	Clarence	Georgia	213
McMillan	George	Illinois	261
McMillan	John W.	Illinois	262
McMillian	Spartan	Arkansas	77
McMinn	Thomas	Illinois	262
McMinn	John B.	Michigan	526
Meade	Jesse	Kentucky	323
Mears	George Ziegler	Maine	418
Meigan	John	Michigan	524
Mellette	Thomas B.	Georgia	213
Merrill	Asa	New Hampshire	696
Merrill	Nathan	New Hampshire	697
Meservey	Atwood B.	New Hampshire	698
Millard	William F.	Missouri	611
Miller	John	Maine	418
Miller	George	Missouri	611
Miller	James F.	Missouri	611
Million	George W.	Arkansas	77
Million	R. F.	Arkansas	78
Mills	Henry	Georgia	214
Mills	Michael	Indiana	276
Mills	Charles Blunt	Michigan	523
Milton	Nathan H.	New Hampshire	698
Miner	Jared H.	Indiana	277
Minton	George W.	Illinois	263
Mishler	William J.	Illinois	263

Mock	Cecil C.	Georgia	214
Modlin	Samuel E.	Illinois	264
Molloy	Daniel	Arkansas	78
Montgomery	Steve	Arkansas	78
Montgomery	H. S.	Georgia	214
Moody	David	Maine	419
Moody	Samuel A. J.	Michigan	527
Moody	Brantley	Missouri	612
Moody	David	New Hampshire	699
Mooneyham	Joe	California	129
Mooneyham	Walter Stanley	California	130
Moore	Roy M.	Arkansas	79
Moore	Donald	Georgia	214
Moore	Tommy	Kentucky	323
Moore	John W.	Missouri	612
Morrill	Benjamin L.	Iowa	294
Morrill	Samuel Plummer	Maine	419
Morris	Schooley	Illinois	264
Morrison	Jewel	Arkansas	79
Morrow	John	Nebraska	637
Morse	Horace Washington	Kansas	312
Morse	John	New Hampshire	699
Morse	Timothy	New Hampshire	700
Moses	Theodore	Minnesota	556
Moulton	Areil	Canada	144
Moulton	Thomas	Iowa	294
Moulton	Levi	Maine	420
Moulton	Franklin	Minnesota	557
Mowry	John Russell	Iowa	294
Mowry	Junia Smith	Iowa	295
Mugg	Marcus	Michigan	527
Mullins	Earlist	Kentucky	323
Murray	Glenn	Missouri	613

Musgrove	George N.	California	131
Musgrove	Isaac Frank	Georgia	215
Myers	Seaborn Franklin	Georgia	215
Myers	A. A.	Michigan	528
Nance	Luther	Alabama	20
Nason	James	Maine	421
Nealy	William	New Hampshire	701
Newbold	Joshua G.	Iowa	296
Newell	Francis	Kansas	313
Nichols	Jacob W.	New Hampshire	702
Nickerson	Joseph	Maine	421
Nickerson	Samuel	New Hampshire	701
Niswonger	Jesse	Missouri	614
Noble	Joseph N.	Maine	422
Noble	John N.	Missouri	614
Noggle	A. A.	Arkansas	80
Norris	John	New Hampshire	702
Norris	Josiah	New Hampshire	702
Northrup	William A.	Kansas	313
Norton	Lemuel	Maine	422
Norton	Erastus	Michigan	528
Norton	William R.	Michigan	529
Norwood	James H.	Mississippi	571
Noyes	Eli	Indiana	277
Noyes	Chandler	Maine	422
Odell	Nathaniel	Iowa	297
O'Donnell	Herman	Alabama	20
O'Neal	E. J.	Arkansas	80
Orser	George	Canada	144
Otis	Micajah	New Hampshire	703
Overstocker	Jacob	Illinois	265
Owens	Benjamin M.	Missouri	614
Page	Ezekiel Gilman	Maine	423

Page	John	Maine	424
Paine	William	Maine	425
Palmer	Ottis Ray	Alabama	20
Palmer	Bernice	Arkansas	81
Palmer	Lonnie	Arkansas	81
Palmer	Asahel	Iowa	297
Parcher	George	Maine	425
Paris	Cumins	New Hampshire	703
Park	William T.	Georgia	215
Park	Thomas	Maine	425
Parker	Benjamin P.	Maine	426
Parker	Lowell	Massachusetts	481
Parker	Benjamin	Michigan	529
Parkman	William H.	Georgia	216
Parkyn	Joseph	Nebraska	637
Parmelee	Linus S.	Michigan	529
Parrish	Neal H.	Georgia	216
Parsons	William C.	Indiana	278
Partain	John	Arkansas	82
Partridge	Thomas	Minnesota	557
Patch	Orrin D.	Illinois	265
Patrick	James Monroe	Arkansas	82
Patrick	Raymond	Arkansas	83
Patterson	Alfred	Maine	426
Pauley	Henry Clay	Arkansas	83
Payne	L. D.	Arkansas	84
Payne	Kelvin	Illinois	265
Pease	Albert	Maine	423
Peaslee	A. C.	New Hampshire	704
Peaslee	Isaac	New Hampshire	704
Pelt	Daniel F.	Florida	161
Pelt	Chester H.	Florida	162
Pelt	Michael	Michigan	530

Pembrook	Roy E.	California	131
Pennington	Charlie	Kentucky	324
Perkins	Seth	Maine	429
Perkins	Charles Sumner	Maine	427
Perkins	Gideon	Maine	428
Perren	John Mason	Arkansas	84
Perry	Oliver Hazard John	Georgia	216
Perry	Peter Wells	Illinois	266
Peters	August Jonathan	Georgia	217
Pettingill	John	Maine	430
Pettingill	Dudley	New Hampshire	705
Phillips	Bruce Erwin	Arkansas	84
Phillips	Nellie Maria	Michigan	532
Phillips	Ida Orissa	Michigan	533
Phillips	Mary R.	Michigan	533
Phillips	Jeremiah	Michigan	530
Phinney	Clement	Maine	430
Phinney	Joseph	Maine	430
Pickney	C. A.	Arkansas	85
Pickney	Edward Lewis	Arkansas	85
Pierce	James H.	Arkansas	85
Pike	John	Maine	431
Pinkham	John	Maine	431
Pinkham	Isaiah	Massachusetts	482
Pinkham	Charles L.	New Hampshire	705
Pinkham	Daniel	New Hampshire	706
Pinkham	George H.	New Hampshire	706
Pinkson	David W.	Arkansas	85
Pitman	Stephen	New Hampshire	707
Pittman	James L.	Georgia	217
Pitts	Roscoe	Georgia	217
Pitts	Orrin	Maine	432
Pixley	Benjamin Perry	Arkansas	86

Pixley	Gilbert J.	Arkansas	86
Pixley	Rupert	Arkansas	87
Place	David Marks	New Hampshire	708
Place	Enoch Hayes	New Hampshire	708
Platts	Mary Ann	Michigan	534
Platts	Richard Gilbert	Michigan	534
Plumber	George	Maine	433
Poole	Geneva	Brazil	112
Porter	W. R.	Arkansas	88
Posey	James Monroe	Georgia	217
Postlewaite	John	Missouri	615
Poston	James L.	Georgia	218
Potter	James W.	Georgia	218
Powell	William S.	Georgia	218
Powell	James Coy	Missouri	615
Pratt	Jesse E.	Arkansas	88
Pratt	Albert	Maine	433
Pratt	Benaiah	Maine	433
Pratt	Cyprian	Maine	433
Preble	Henry	Maine	434
Preble	Nehemiah	Maine	435
Prescott	Elijah H.	Maine	435
Presley	William L.	Georgia	218
Preston	Jay Francis	Kentucky	324
Prickett	Jacob B.	Illinois	266
Prickett	John	Indiana	279
Privett	Oliver W.	Kentucky	324
Prude	William	Mississippi	571
Pruitt, Jr.	Reuben E.	Arkansas	88
Purinton	Albert	Maine	435
Purinton	Charles	Maine	436
Purinton	Humphrey	Maine	436
Purinton	Nathaniel	Maine	437

Purvis	William Lester	Georgia	219
Queen	Willis	Arkansas	88
Quick	J. T.	Alabama	21
Quimby	Joshua	New Hampshire	709
Quimby	Moses A.	New Hampshire	710
Quinn	Calvin C.	Georgia	219
Quinnam	Constant	Maine	438
Quint	Daniel	New Hampshire	710
Rail	Thomas	Arkansas	89
Ramsey	Vienna	New Hampshire	711
Ramsey	Goram Parsons	New Hampshire	710
Rand	John Holmes	Maine	438
Rand	James	New Hampshire	712
Randall	Freedom	Michigan	535
Randall	Sarah Titcomb	New Hampshire	714
Randall	Benjamin O.	New Hampshire	713
Randall	Benjamin Walton	New Hampshire	714
Ranger	Walter Eugene	Maine	439
Ratteree	John L.	Missouri	616
Rauls	J. C.	Arkansas	89
Ray	James	Florida	162
Reding	John	Arkansas	90
Redlon	Ebenezer	Indiana	279
Reed	Appleton W.	Maine	439
Reed	Delavan	Michigan	535
Reel	John Lee	California	130
Reese	Henry Smith	Georgia	219
Reeve	James	Iowa	298
Reeves	William T.	Missouri	617
Reeves	Joseph H.	Nebraska	638
Reger	Luster	Nebraska	638
Reid	Samuel Nelson	Missouri	617
Rendel	John	Indiana	279

Rendleman	Andrew Jackson	Illinois	267
Rentz	C.D.	Georgia	220
Rentz	Charlie T.	Georgia	220
Rentz	Wilbur L	Georgia	220
Revelle	William Haye	Missouri	617
Reynolds	Chauney	Michigan	536
Reynolds	Thomas	New Hampshire	715
Rhodes	G. W.	Georgia	221
Rich	John M.	Florida	163
Rich	Arthur	Missouri	618
Richardson	James	Arkansas	90
Richardson	Tip	California	132
Richardson	Caleb H.	New Hampshire	715
Richmond	Clarissa	Connecticut	153
Rickerson	Charles W.	Georgia	221
Rines	John	Maine	440
Ring	Dewitt	Arkansas	91
Risner	William	Michigan	536
Ritter	George Edward	Illinois	267
Roam	Charles	California	133
Roberts	Henry Leroy	Georgia	222
Roberts	John H.	Massachusetts	482
Robertson	J. R.	Alabama	21
Robinson	Bill	Georgia	221
Robinson	Joseph	Maine	440
Robinson	J. C.	Michigan	537
Robinson	Nathan	Minnesota	558
Rogers	Harris Edgar	Georgia	222
Rogers	John Alvin	Maine	441
Roler	J. L.	California	133
Rolf	E. R.	Michigan	537
Rollins	Andrew	Maine	440
Rollins	John Byron	Missouri	618

Root	Edward	Nebraska	639
Rose	Varnum	Maine	441
Ross	Eugene F.	Georgia	222
Rowlett	Andrew	Arkansas	91
Rowlett	Daniel	California	133
Rowlett	Tom	California	134
Royster	Dee Roy	Missouri	619
Rozell	Albert	Arkansas	92
Russ	Chadwick Beauford	Kansas	313
Russell	C. L.	Minnesota	558
Russell	George Washington	New Hampshire	715
Sadler	Vester	Georgia	222
Safit	Othaniel	Arkansas	92
Salley	Ashmun	Maine	442
Salyer	William	Indiana	280
Sangster	Pete Allen	Georgia	223
Sapp	Leon L.	Georgia	223
Sargent	Nathaniel	Maine	442
Sargent	Alvan	New Hampshire	716
Satterfield	Robert	Arkansas	92
Sauls	J. W.	Georgia	223
Savage	Edward	Maine	443
Sawyer	Calvin	Canada	145
Sawyer	Green	Canada	146
Sawyer	Seth	New Hampshire	716
Scales	Ebenezer	Maine	444
Schebaum	John F.	Missouri	620
Scogin	Floyd	Arkansas	92
Scott	Thomas M.	Alabama	21
Scott	Benjamin Randle	Arkansas	34
Scott	Linza D.	Georgia	225
Scott	George Washington	Missouri	620
Scudder	James Leroy	Arkansas	94

Seals	Charles	Arkansas	95
Sebastion	Arch	Arkansas	93
Sellards	James W.	Missouri	621
Sellers	Farest W.	Georgia	226
Sellers	Willie A.	Georgia	226
Senters	Carl Lee	Kentucky	325
Sewell	Caleb	Illinois	268
Sharp	Levi N.	Minnesota	559
Shattuck	Charles	Michigan	538
Shaw	Samuel	Iowa	298
Shaw	Sargent	Maine	444
Shelton	Melvin	Arkansas	95
Shelton	Robert S.	Arkansas	96
Shepard	Moses	Maine	445
Shipley	H. D.	Arkansas	96
Shutes	Kenneth	Georgia	224
Silvernail	John	Michigan	538
Silvey	John	Missouri	621
Simpson	Elzie Elisha	Missouri	621
Sinclair	John L.	New Hampshire	716
Sisson	George W.	Nebraska	639
Sleeper	Hiram	New Hampshire	719
Slone	Joe	Kentucky	325
Small	William	Iowa	299
Small	Humphrey	Maine	446
Small	James	Maine	446
Smart	Wiley L.	Illinois	267
Smith	Loy	Arkansas	97
Smith	Sheldon	California	134
Smith	Charles	Kansas	314
Smith	Tilton E.	Michigan	539
Smith	Sheldon	Michigan	539
Smith	Andrew	Minnesota	560

Smith	Samuel	Nebraska	640
Smith	Alpheus	New Hampshire	719
Smutz	David	Iowa	300
Snow	Fred Albertis	Maine	446
Snow	Henry	Maine	447
Sparks	Lonnie	Michigan	540
Sparks	Paul M.	Michigan	541
Spooner	Thomas	Maine	447
Springfield	Thomas Woods	Alabama	22
Springfield	Thomas Alden	Alabama	22
Springfield	William James	Alabama	22
Spurlock	William	Illinois	268
St. Clair	Henry	Michigan	543
St. Claire	Eugene Louis	Georgia	224
Staab	J. J.	Alabama	23
Stafford	Warren Chase	Massachusetts	482
Stahl	Berne Ora	Arkansas	97
Standley	Richard Milo	Missouri	622
Stanford	Federal A.	Michigan	541
Stanley	Iris Lyndon	Mississippi	571
Starbird	Freelon	Maine	449
Stark	Jeremiah	Arkansas	97
Starnes	Fred B.	Arkansas	98
Starr	Norman	Michigan	541
Staten	Charles R.	Arkansas	98
Staten	Ralph Lee	Arkansas	98
Stephens	J. D.	Alabama	23
Stevens	Moses	Maine	448
Stevens	James	Maine	447
Stevens	John	Maine	448
Stevens	Theodore	Maine	448
Stevens	Hiram	New Hampshire	723
Stevenson	William S.	Maine	450

Steward	Justice H.	Iowa	299
Stewart	Isaac Dalton	New Hampshire	720
Stewart	Elizabeth	New Hampshire	722
Stiles	Ada Henrietta Tucker	New Hampshire	724
Stiles	Edwin Byron	New Hampshire	724
Stilson	Cyrus	Maine	451
Stinson	Joseph	Maine	450
Stinson	William C.	Maine	451
Stogsdill	William Preston	Missouri	622
Stoup	James R.	Georgia	226
Stout	Alvah	Maine	452
Stout, Jr.	James	Maine	452
Stovenour	Frederick	Indiana	280
Straight	Freeborn W.	Minnesota	561
Stratton	Isaac	Kentucky	325
Streeter	Levi	New Hampshire	723
Strickland	Thomas J.	Georgia	226
Sturgis	Nathaniel	Maine	452
Sullivan	Glover Cleveland	Georgia	226
Summerlin	Spencer	Iowa	300
Sutton	Samuel Thomas	Arkansas	98
Swaffer	John C.	Missouri	622
Swain	William	New Hampshire	724
Sweatt	John	Iowa	301
Sweetland	Virgil	Maine	453
Swett	David	Maine	453
Swett	Jesse	Maine	454
Swift	Josiah Spooner	Maine	454
Sylvester	Bradbury	Maine	455
Tally	John H.	Missouri	622
Tanner	Lowell	Arkansas	99
Tappan	Edmund M.	Massachusetts	482
Tarbox	Moses H.	Maine	455

Tasker	Friend D.	Maine	456
Tasker	Levi	New Hampshire	725
Taster	Ebenezer	Maine	456
Taylor	Andrew	Arkansas	99
Taylor	John	Georgia	227
Teague	Rayburn	Arkansas	100
Tedder	J. L.	Georgia	227
Tedford	Charles	Massachusetts	484
Terry	Grover V.	Missouri	623
Tharp	John W.	Arkansas	99
Thatcher	William	Nebraska	641
Thigpen	Jonathan Noel	Illinois	269
Thomas	Roy L.	Colorado	147
Thomas	Rue	Idaho	239
Thomas	Sophia	Maine	456
Thomas	John	Michigan	543
Thomas	Nelson	Michigan	544
Thomas	Roena	Missouri	623
Thompson	Paul Timothy	Arizona	24
Thompson	Roy Lathan	Arkansas	100
Thompson	James Alford	Georgia	227
Thompson	George W.	Kansas	314
Thompson	Thomas	Maine	456
Thompson	Lawrence D.	Missouri	623
Thorne	Benjamin	Maine	457
Thornebury	Lewis J.	Arkansas	100
Thorton	Allen L.	Georgia	227
Tice	Clarence	Arkansas	101
Tingley	Pelatiah	Maine	458
Tinsley	Thomas M.	Kentucky	326
Tobey	Zalmon	Connecticut	154
Tolman	Benjamin	Massachusetts	484
Tomlinson	A. J.	Georgia	228

Toothacker	Edward	Maine	459
Totman	Alpheus M.	Nebraska	642
Touchton	Moutrie H.	Georgia	228
Touchton	Thomas T.	Georgia	228
Tracy	Etta G.	Maine	460
Tracy	Christopher	Maine	459
Tracy	Olin Hobbs	Maine	460
Tracy	Jonathan	Maine	461
Treadwell	James	Arkansas	101
Tripp	Isaac	Maine	462
True	Charles	Kansas	315
True	Ezekiel	New Hampshire	726
Trustworthy	Joseph	Maine	462
Tucker	Wayne	Arkansas	102
Tucker	Morris	Arkansas	102
Tucker	David A.	Indiana	281
Tucker	William	Indiana	281
Turner	Elmer	Arkansas	103
Turner	Willie Gus	Georgia	228
Turner	Abel	Maine	463
Turner	Kenneth	Missouri	624
Turney	George	Arkansas	103
Turney	John	Arkansas	103
Tyler	Job C.	New Hampshire	727
Uhles	Emma Serena	Illinois	268
Ulmer	Matthias	Maine	463
Urury	James	Georgia	229
Ussery	Charence	Missouri	624
Vail	Michael	Alabama	23
Valentine	Robert T.	Iowa	302
Vance	Leon	Alabama	24
Vandivort	Herbert	Missouri	625
Vanhoose	Nathan	Kentucky	327

Vanhoose	Eliphas Preston	Kentucky	326
Vanhoose	Frew Stewart	Kentucky	326
Vanhoose	Millard	Kentucky	327
Vanhoose	Richard Scott	Kentucky	327
Varney	Lincoln	Kentucky	328
Vaughn	James	Arkansas	104
Vaughn	Henry W.	Indiana	282
Venable	Ruben B.	Arkansas	105
Venable	Joe	Arkansas	104
Vickers	Julian	Georgia	230
Vinson	Robert Newton	Arkansas	105
Von Dame	Bartholomew	New Hampshire	728
Wade	Edgar Jackson	Georgia	230
Wade	Frank W.	Georgia	230
Wages	George W.	Mississippi	572
Wakely	Sidney	Maine	464
Waldron	William H.	New Hampshire	729
Walker	Charles P.	Massachusetts	485
Wallace	John	Maine	464
Walrath	Joseph Harvey	Michigan	544
Waltman	John Alexander	California	134
Ward	George Douglas	Illinois	270
Ward	John T.	Michigan	545
Warner	Robert J.	Missouri	626
Warren	Hugh	Arkansas	106
Waterman	Dexter	Maine	465
Waterman	Ira	Missouri	626
Waterman	Lemuel	Missouri	627
Waterman	Granville C.	New Hampshire	729
Watkins	Ray	Arkansas	106
Watkins	Samuel	Georgia	230
Watson	Jerry Dale	California	135
Watson	Benjamin Blanton	Georgia	231

Watson	Guy	Louisiana	330
Watson	Elijah	New Hampshire	730
Weage	John J.	California	135
Webb	Reece G.	Arkansas	106
Webber	Horace	New Hampshire	730
Webster	Nathaniel	New Hampshire	731
Wedgewood	Dearborn	New Hampshire	731
Weeks	John R.	Georgia	231
Weeks	Samuel	Maine	465
Weir	Chester	Arkansas	107
Wellbaum	Mary Elizabeth	Missouri	627
Weston	Willie K.	Missouri	627
Weymouth	Nathaniel F.	Maine	466
Wheeler	Bill	Arkansas	107
Wheeler	John B.	Georgia	232
Wheeler	Thomas	Kentucky	328
Wheeler	Samuel	Maine	467
Wheeler	Austin	Minnesota	562
Wheeler	Willamette marks	Nebraska	643
Wheeler	Abel	New Hampshire	731
Whitaker	Abraham H.	Michigan	545
Whitcom	Samuel	Michigan	547
Whitcomb	Simeon Coffin	Maine	467
White	James E.	Arkansas	107
White	Stanton B.	Arkansas	108
White	Will S.	Arkansas	109
White	William Pleasant	Arkansas	109
White	Connie C.	Georgia	232
White	Joseph	Maine	468
White, II	Thomas	Maine	469
Whitley	James L.	Georgia	233
Whitley	L. B.	Georgia	233
Whitly	Isaac Jasper	Arkansas	109

Whitney	John	Maine	471
Whitney	William E.	Michigan	547
Whittemore	Joseph	Iowa	302
Wiggin	John	Maine	469
Wiley	Green Thomas	Georgia	233
Wiley	William T.	Georgia	233
Wiley	Frederick L.	New Hampshire	731
Wilkinson	Samuel Longstreet	Georgia	234
Willey	Mabel Alice	Florida	164
Willey, Sr.	Thomas	Florida	165
Williams	Daniel	Connecticut	154
Williams	E. C.	Georgia	234
Williams	Jules Legender	Kansas	315
Williams	Paul	Missouri	628
Williams	Marion Henry	Missouri	628
Williams	Alvin Dighton	Nebraska	643
Williamson	Charles Cecil	Florida	166
Williamson	Stephen	Maine	470
Willingham	Jerrell	Arkansas	110
Willis	Otis	New Hampshire	732
Willis, Sr.	Kennebrew	Georgia	235
Wilson	Ethel	Arkansas	111
Wilson	Chester Emmett	Arkansas	110
Wilson	Isaac J.	Arkansas	111
Wilson	Harvey J.	Georgia	235
Winch	Joseph	Indiana	282
Windham	A. G.	Georgia	232
Winham	Riley H.	Georgia	235
Winslow	Ezra	Maine	470
Winslow	Ephriam	New Hampshire	733
Winters	W. W.	New Mexico	736
Wire	Samuel	Michigan	548
Witham	Lewis	Maine	471

Wolfe	Delia Scriven	Nebraska	645
Wolfe	John H.	Nebraska	644
Wood	James	California	136
Wood	Jeremiah	Missouri	629
Wood	John	Missouri	630
Wood, Jr.	Joshua	Missouri	632
Woodief	Maynard Blair	Florida	166
Woodman	James M.	California	136
Woodman	Joseph	Michigan	549
Woodsum	William	Maine	472
Woodworth	Nathan	Florida	167
Woolery	Arvel Earl	California	137
Wooley	Edward	Indiana	282
Wormwood	Samuel	Maine	473
Wright	Dewel	Arkansas	112
Wright	William	Iowa	303
Wright	Randy	Mississippi	572
Wright	Merl	Missouri	632
Wyatt	Thomas	New Hampshire	733
Wylie	James	Kansas	315
Yancey	John	Missouri	631
Yandell	Joseph Elzie	California	137
Yarbough	Needham Graham	Georgia	235
York	William	Missouri	633
Young	Thomas Patrick	Georgia	236
Young	Winthrop	New Hampshire	734
Young	Zebina	New Hampshire	735
Zabriska	Amos C.	Iowa	303
Zinn	Ferrel C.	Missouri	633
TRUE	Charles	Iowa	301

www.ingramcontent.com/pod-product-compliance
Lightning Source LLC
Chambersburg PA
CBHW071946270326
41928CB00009B/1366